EXPLORING THE
PACIFIC COAST
San Diego to Seattle

CHAPTER LIST

3

Pt. Arguello

Pt. Conception

• Santa Barbara

Santa Barbara Channel

• Ventura

• Port Hueneme

Pt. Dume

San
Miguel I.

Santa
Rosa I.

Santa
Cruz I.

Anacapa
I.

*Santa Monica
Bay*

• Santa Monica
• Marina Del Rey

• LOS ANGELES
• Long Beach

1

Palos Verde Pt.

San Pedro Channel

• Newport

• Dana Point

2

Santa
Barbara I.

Santa
Catalina I.

San
Nicholas I.

Oceanside

Pacific Ocean

N
W E
S

San
Clemente I.

SAN
DIEGO •

*Gulf of
Santa Catalina*

Coastal Cruising and Harbor Hopping are all about Local Boating—Exploration at your own pace

EXPLORING THE

PACIFIC COAST

San Diego to Seattle

**DON DOUGLASS &
RÉANNE HEMINGWAY-DOUGLASS**

FOREWORD BY RODERICK FRAZIER NASH

CONTRIBUTIONS BY
KEVIN MONAHAN
MICHELLE GAYLORD, ANN KINNER
AND CAROLYN & BOB MEHAFFY

FineEdge.com

Important Legal Disclaimer

This book is designed to provide experienced skippers with planning information on the Pacific Coast covering the area from San Diego to Seattle. Every effort has been made, within limited resources, to make this book complete and accurate. There may well be mistakes, both typographical and in content. Routes and waypoints should be verified, checked and plotted before use. Therefore, this book should not be used for navigation and only as a general guide, not as the ultimate source of information on the areas covered. Much of what is presented in this book is local knowledge based upon personal observation and is subject to human error.

The authors, publisher, local and governmental authorities, make no warranties and assume no liability for errors or omissions, or for any loss or damage of any kind incurred from using this information.

Credits:
Chief Editor: Réanne Hemingway-Douglass
Production Manager: Mark J. Bunzel
Book design: Melanie Haage Design
Front cover photo courtesy of Nordic Tug Inc., Burlington, Washington
Back cover photos by Kent Morrow, Downeast Yachts; John Sanger; David J. Shuler
Diagrams & maps: Sue Athmann
Editorial Assistant: Elayne Wallis
All photos by Don Douglass and Réanne Hemingway-Douglass unless otherwise credited

Excerpts from the United States Coast Pilot, Volume 7, 2001 33rd Edition
published by U.S. Department of Commerce National Oceanic and Atmospheric Administration
(NOAA) and "Boating in Oregon Coastal Waters," 2001, published by the Oregon State Marine Board

Library of Congress Cataloging-in-Publication Data

Douglass, Don.
  Exploring the Pacific Coast : San Diego to Seattle : including proven cruising routes, details and GPS of every harbor and cove / by Don Douglass & Réanne Hemingway-Douglass with contributions from Kevin Monahan ... [et al] ; foreword by Roderick Frazier Nash.
    p.   cm.
  Includes index.
  ISBN 0-938665-71-5
    1. Pilot guides—Pacific Coast (U.S.)   I. Hemingway-Douglass, Réanne.   II. Monahan, Kevin, 1951– .   III. Title.
VK947.D68   2002
628.89'2979—dc21   2002024462

ISBN 0-938665-71-5

Address requests for permission to Fine Edge.com LLC
13589 Clayton Lane, Anacortes, WA 98221
www.FineEdge.com

Printed in the United States of America

CONTENTS

Acknowledgments

The authors would like to thank the many mariners and cruising experts who have helped hone our ideas for this comprehensive cruising guide.

Foremost, is Kevin Monahan, friend, fellow navigator, and crew member who put the concepts of *Proven Cruising Routes—Seattle to Ketchikan,* published in 1998, into routes for the Pacific Coast and helped us take this guidebook to a new level of information-presentation for safe navigation. We are especially indebted for his work on defining the Crabpot-Free Tow Lanes. Roderick Frazier Nash, fellow explorer and crewmember and Professor Emeritus, UCSB Santa Barbara provided the Foreword and many suggestions that helped crystallize our concepts. We would also like to thank Warren Miller, filmmaker, boater and mentor for his encouragement and thoughtful ideas.

Many local experts shared their personal experiences to add local knowledge to this book, including Delivery Captain Ann Kinner of San Diego, Charter Captain John Sanger of Santa Barbara, Charter Captain Brian Saunders of Dana Point, Charter Captain Ronn Sterro-Patterson of *Delphinis,* San Francisco, Bruce Evertz, M/V *Tapawingo* of Anacortes, well-known authors Carolyn and Bob Mehaffy, S/V *Carricklee* of San Francisco, and Bob Botley, Farallon Islands patrolman and *Baidarka* crew.

Michelle and Jerry Gaylord provided their expressive sidebars, and John and Midge Stapleton, of San Francisco, their cruising insights. We also thank Jeff Douthwaite, *Flamingo,* of Seattle, for sharing his unusual cruising experience.

Herb and Wendy Nickles, Deerfield, Massachusetts, crew on every boat we have owned over the past 30 years, have provided us with the Information Technology support which has been superior in every way and makes the development of an extensive body of work like this book possible.

Several photographers and artists contributed their work to help visualize the many beautiful locations along the Pacific Coast including David Shuler, crewmember and explorer; Robin Hill-Ward and Fred Gamble of Channel Crossings Press; Tom Dore of the National Park Service; and Margy Gates of SeaGate Gallery, Channel Islands.

We also want to thank our *Baidarka* shakedown crew for their support: son-in-law Jeff Mach, skipper of *Cosmos,* Juneau, Alaska, and grandson, Joshua Douglass, helmsman.

Many of the harbormasters and their staff along the coast are to be commended for their cooperation and patience in verifying the data in this book, along with a number of local and federal agencies. The USCG on-site personnel in many ports and harbors provided local knowledge; NOAA and the Oregon State Marine Board also contributed expert assistance. We would like to thank the Washington State Department of Ecology for use of its aerial photos and Tracy Mills of Vessel Traffic Services, Seattle for his expert guidance.

We should also give a special thanks to the many unnamed boaters who have shared their experiences and encouragement during our research.

This book would not have been possible without our home port crew who brought this publication together: Melanie Haage for overall design, Elayne Wallis and Paul Goethel for editorial assistance, Sue Athmann for graphics, and FineEdge.com General Manager, Mark Bunzel, for his insight and creativity on the routes and weather portions, as well as production management and overall support.

And last, but not least, a special thanks to Réanne Hemingway Douglass, who, in addition to co-author, is chief editor and should be credited with making this book readable and as accurate as possible. She turned our ideas, concepts and the many facts from a variety of sources into a book we think you, the reader, will find useful and enjoyable as you explore the Pacific Coast.

Foreword

IT'S *ALL* LOCAL BOATING

Dr. Roderick Frazier Nash

"It's all local boating," was my response recently to a boater who asked how I fared so well in strange waters when I brought my 26-foot Nordic Tug down the coast from San Francisco. Boaters are often comfortable in their home waters, I told him, but they tense up at the thought of venturing over the horizon, around the cape, or out on the weather coast. "It's too dangerous," they say. But the fact is, if a skipper acquires the local knowledge needed, he can follow a dream with confidence. The solution is to treat any cruise as a series of short passages, connecting one destination to another so the voyage becomes feasible.

Don Douglass and Réanne Hemingway-Douglass have addressed boating concerns like this for thirty years. By doing their own research they have made it their business to increase boaters' confidence. Their cruising guides take you "inside" the charts, translating an abstraction into the reality you see from the helm. Although full of facts, the primary value of their books is psychological. They instill, in even the novice boater, the confidence to leave the harbor, round the headland, circle the island, and perhaps end up thousands of miles from home base.

The first local boaters on the west coast of the United States were, of course, Native peoples. There is considerable evidence that boats—not the land bridge—were the first means of crossings from Siberia to Alaska and of continuing down the coast. The Northwestern tribes, with their canoes, kayaks and baidarkas, were excellent mariners. Their "cruising guides" took the form of oral tradition: "Turn just past the whale-shaped rock into the inlet from the which the sun rises." Directions got more sophisticated over time. The Spanish explorers of the west

coast were under strict orders to make maps and keep careful logs. Juan Rodríguez Cabrillo, and the lieutenants who continued after his death, fully understood their role as nautical pioneers. In their remarkable voyage of 1542-43, they identified and named Point Loma (and San Diego Bay), Santa Catalina Island, and the Santa Barbara Channel Islands and eventually sailed north to the California-Oregon border. You can still gain valuable basic information from their charts, but it might be a good idea not to try circumnavigating California—for two hundred years the Spaniards believed it was an island.

Sir Frances Drake's voyage of 1578 in the legendary *Golden Hind,* and additional explorations under the Spanish flag by Juan de Fuca (1590) and José Vizcaíno (1602-03), blazed further water trails up the west coast. But none of the early northbound navigators discovered the Golden Gate and San Francisco Bay. The reasons are not hard to discover. This is fog country and, at the distance old sailing ships kept off the rocky coast, it was easy to miss the relatively narrow Golden Gate. Out where they sailed—what the Douglasses call the "Bluewater Route" —they spotted the Farallon Islands, 23 miles offshore, but they missed the golden gateway to history.

In fact, San Francisco Bay was not identified until 1769 and then only by an overland expedition led by Gaspar de Portolá. Indeed, the Spanish were so much in the geographic dark that Portolá first thought he had found a vast inland lake! The first ocean-going boat to enter the Bay was Juan Manuel de Ayala's in 1774. The beautiful Ayala Cove on Angel Island in the North Bay is named in his honor.

Accurate nautical charting is not just a convenience for recreational boaters; it can affect

John Sanger

Rod Nash's Forevergreen *anchored in Coches Prietos*

the course of history! Think about this: Cabrillo's expedition might have given the Spanish a *three hundred year* head start in the settling of Central California. Had he located San Francisco Bay, the greatest natural harbor on the west coast of the New World, it is conceivable that when the first settlers arrived in the 19th century they would have found a well-established Spanish civilization, not easily overturned by a rabble of gold miners.

As it turned out, the failure to find the Bay resulted in one of history's greatest lost opportunities. But, in fairness, winds and currents should also be factored into the equation. Toss a log into the section of the Pacific Ocean that the Douglasses detail in this book and you will quickly learn why the early navigators had such a difficult time with North America's west coast. Everything goes south! Beating up "against the grain" from Cabo San Lucas to California and beyond to Cape Flattery—the

northwesternmost tip of Washington—is a lot more difficult than "rolling downhill." All the early ships struggled on the northbound passage. In fact, after Vizcaíno's 1603 voyage to the Cape Mendocino area, Spain essentially gave up on a sea route for establishing an empire in California. As late as the 1770s brave men like Anza, Serra, and Escalante were still trying to work out a difficult overland trail across the deserts to the Golden State and Spain's chance to consolidate its empire by sea slipped away. In the next two decades systematic knowledge of the west coast would come from the British (James Cook, George Vancouver) and the American discoverer of the Columbia River (Robert Gray).

The Douglasses are pioneers in combining local knowledge and state-of-the-art technology into user-friendly nautical cruising guides. With their help any skipper equipped with GPS (global positioning system) can custom-design a cruise and enjoy many welcome rest stops along the route. Using the remarkable capabilities of GPS—the greatest advance in navigation since the compass—the Douglasses describe the exact location of every named place of maritime significance on the west coast of the United States. *Added to their comprehensive cruising guides to Alaska and British Columbia, this book adds to one of the most significant charting efforts in maritime history.* With *Exploring the Pacific Coast* in your pilothouse, you are on your way to cruising like a professional. Remember, if you have the right tools and the local knowledge *all* cruising becomes local boating!

John Sanger

Peaceful spring day in Frys Harbor

Roderick Frazier Nash, Professor Emeritus of the University of California Santa Barbara, is the author of Wilderness and the American Mind, *a classic in wilderness literature. Rod and his wife, Honeydew, have cruised in Puget Sound, Alaska, Mexico, the Columbia River, and along the Pacific Coast on their Nordic Tug,* Forevergreen.

Introduction and How to Use This Book

I. Welcome to the West Coast!

From San Diego to Seattle, the Pacific Coast offers some of the most interesting cruising grounds and varied scenery in North America. Where else in the world can you find a coast that has the palm-tree-lined beaches and convenient marinas of urban Southern California; the raw, natural beauty of the Channel Islands National Park; the protected waters and estuaries of San Francisco Bay; the quaint fishing ports of Northern California; the rugged, bold headlands, the rivers, lagoons and sandbars of Oregon; the lush rain forests, Northwest Native villages and the protected waters of Puget Sound?

This book—a celebration of all the places to visit, moor, or anchor along this 1300-mile coast—encompasses all the local knowledge needed to locate, enter, and explore more than 500 places. Over the past 30 years and, in particular, the last three, we have visited essentially all these places by diesel trawler, sailboat, or tandem kayak. To help you understand how this local knowledge is presented, see Section II of this Introduction.

Bow watch approaching San Francisco's Golden Gate Bridge

In Section III you will find a discussion on how we documented three unique Proven Cruising Routes© for use along the Pacific Coast. The routes allow you to see how *Baidarka* entered and departed ports along the coast (Approach Diagrams) and the routes we tested between these ports (Route Diagrams). With this information, you can plan trips to and from any place along the Pacific Coast. Once you verify the suitability of the GPS waypoints we have used, you can connect the appropriate waypoints into a series of day-trips to create a voyage of any length. See Appendix A and B for suggested itineraries and ideas for creating your own routes and itineraries.

We encourage you to extend your horizons, to "push the envelope" and discover new cruising areas; the key to that goal is to plan an itinerary using the Proven Cruising Routes© as a base to build upon. For each place you wish to visit, study the Local Knowledge presented in this guidebook and add information you find in other resources. As a beginning, you might consider using the Inshore Routes, designed to make daylight passages and, in your planning, use good judgment and avoid itineraries that push your boat or crew to the limits. Our philosophy of coastal cruising is to do whatever is required to sleep soundly every night and, when we follow our own advice, we find that our voyages become simply *all Local Boating*.

You can set your sights high by planning a trip that takes you, in a single season, from the sunny shores near the Mexican borders to the cool forests of the Pacific Northwest. Or, you can go even further to the glaciers of Alaska. We hope this guidebook will kindle your desire for exploration and provide you with the tools and information that give you the confidence to extend your cruising experience to new horizons. The satisfaction of executing a successful voyage is your reward!

II. How to Use This Book (Local Knowledge)

Each chapter in this book covers a separate cruising area, usually proceeding from south to north. An **area map** is included at the beginning of each chapter to serve as a quick reference to locate channels, passages, and coves found within the text. **Place names** are shown in bold type. We have tried in all cases to use established or local names for the documented coves and bays. However, in the few cases where we could find no reference to a name on either charts or the U.S. *Coast Pilot*, we used a new name that seemed appropriate. The **Chart number** listed first is the largest scale available and the one we recommend using. **GPS coordinates** for **Position, Entrance** and **Anchor** are given with a horizontal datum of NAD83. **Text in indented italics** is excerpted as a convenience when available, from the U.S. *Coast Pilot.*

The **main body of the text** describes the local knowledge we have discovered by personal observation or in conjunction with sources we believe to be reliable and knowledgeable.

The last entry under each place-name gives specific **Anchor** information for the Anchor Site Waypoint identified at the heading, and/or on the detailed diagram for that site. If you find conditions different than those described, double-check your position on the chart and make your own judgment about suitability.

Anchoring Information

The last paragraph lists depth(s) at zero tide, followed by specific bottom material (sand, mud, clay, rocks, gravel, kelp etc.), and our estimate of the relative anchor holding power.

Anchor Diagrams

We have included detailed diagrams for some of the more popular coves and anchorages. The

Sample Layout Selection

Place name → *Largest scale chart listed first; distance from known place*

Catalina (Cat) Harbor
Charts 18757; 5.8 mi SE of West End
Entrance (outer): (CA248) 33°25.10'N, 118°30.59'W
Entrance (inner): 33°25.67'N, 118°30.52'W
Anchor: 33°25.81'N, 118°30.47'W
Anchor (inner): 33°25.94'N, 118°30.30'W

All GPS coordinates adjusted to NAD83

> *Catalina Harbor . . . affords excellent shelter for small vessels in all but S weather. . . . The harbor, a popular yacht anchorage, is funnel-shaped, open to the S, and easy of access. Small and bare Pin Rock, close inside the E head of the harbor, is 150 yards offshore and has deep water around it. The anchorage is in 4 to 5 fathoms, soft bottom, abreast Ballast Point. . . . The head of the harbor is shoal. The 3-fathom curve is marked by kelp, and vessels entering should give the shores a berth of 150 yards. The facilities on Ballast Point are leased by a yacht club. From the head of the harbor it is only about 0.3 mile overland to Two Harbors. (CP, 33rd Ed.)*

excerpts from Coast Pilot (always in italics)

Cat Harbor, (the local name for Catalina Harbor)—the well-protected harbor on the south side of Two Harbors and the Isthmus—lies northeast of Catalina Head, a high bluff that gives it excellent protection from northwest swells and chop; it can be somewhat exposed to southwest swells and weather. However, it is designated by the U.S. Coast Guard as a Year-round Safe Harbor.

Our own recorded local knowledge based on personal experience

Cat Harbor has 97 mooring buoys and anchorage for some 200 boats. When anchoring, it's a good idea to match your techniques with other boats, particularly when the harbor is crowded. To take up less anchoring space consider using both a bow and stern anchor. Please note that Santa Ana gales have been clocked at 70 knots here; a funnel effect enhances both north- and south-flowing winds, but the fetch is relatively small, and some boaters prefer to anchor here during such conditions, rather than along the island's cliffs where winds may be less fierce.

There are a dinghy dock and shoreside picnicking facilities; Cat Harbor is a half-mile walk to Two Harbors village. In summer shuttle service is available.

Anchor in 4 to 6 fathoms over sand with fair holding.

Anchor (inner basin) in 2 fathoms over sand and gravel; fair holding.

Describes depth(s), bottom material and holding power

diagrams show the approximate routes we took, the typical depths, and the places we anchored. Note that these diagrams are for guidance and not to scale; they do not include all known or unknown hazards. They should always be used with caution and with prior self-verification on the appropriate and up-to-date charts for that location.

Please Note: *A detailed diagram does not mean to imply that a site is suitable for your particular boat or circumstances. Whenever you are faced with critical judgments involving navigation or anchoring, you should be the sole judge of what is appropriate and assume full responsibility for using this book.*

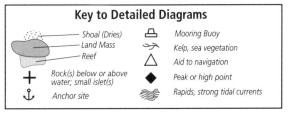

Key to Detailed Diagrams

- Shoal (Dries)
- Land Mass
- Reef
- Rock(s) below or above water; small islet(s)
- Anchor site
- Mooring Buoy
- Kelp, sea vegetation
- Aid to navigation
- Peak or high point
- Rapids, strong tidal currents

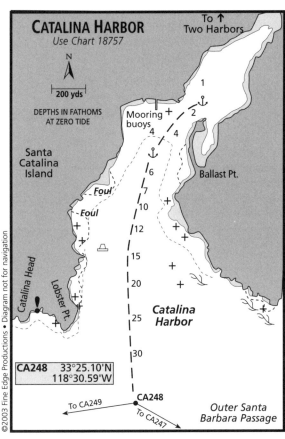

CATALINA HARBOR
Use Chart 18757

N

200 yds

DEPTHS IN FATHOMS AT ZERO TIDE

Santa Catalina Island

Mooring buoys

To ↑ Two Harbors

Ballast Pt.

Foul
Foul

Catalina Head

Lobster Pt.

Catalina Harbor

CA248   33°25.10'N
118°30.59'W

To CA249
CA248
To CA247

Outer Santa Barbara Passage

©2003 Fine Edge Productions • Diagram not for navigation

Definitions Used for Holding Power

Excellent—very good holding
Anchor digs in deeper as you pull on it—the preferred bottom in a blow, but a rare find—usually thick sticky mud or clay.

Good holding
Generally sufficient for overnight anchorage in fair weather—anchor digs in but may drag or pull out on strong pull; common in mud/sand combinations or hard sand.

Fair holding
Adequate for temporary anchorage in fair weather, but boat should not be left unattended. Bottom of light sand, gravel with some rocks, grass or kelp, or a thin layer of mud over a hard bottom. An anchor watch is desirable.

Poor holding
Can be used for a temporary stop in fair weather only. Bottom is typically rocky with a lot of grass or kelp, or a very thin later of mud and sand—insufficient to bury anchor properly; an anchor watch is recommended at all times.

Steep-to
Depth of water may decrease from 10 fathoms to 1/2 fathom in as little as one boat's length! (Approach at dead-slow recommended.) Use shore tie to minimize swinging and to keep anchor pulling uphill.

U.S. CHART TIDAL WATER SYMBOLS

Measurements Used in this Book
The spelling and use of place names follow—as closely as possible—local tradition and the lead of the *U.S. Coast Pilot.*

While our international neighbors on either side of the U.S. Pacific Coast have converted their charts into metric units, in this book we continue to use traditional English units of measurement such as of fathoms, nautical miles, yards, feet, degrees in Fahrenheit, etc. We urge both local and visiting navigators to double-check measurements units on each chart and to verify that echo sounder depth-settings and other instruments agree.

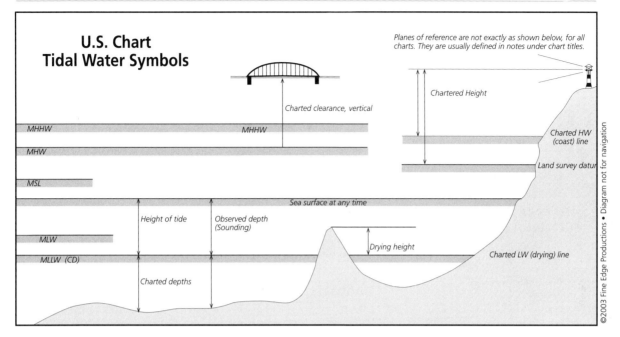

Unless otherwise noted, depths listed in the text or those shown on the diagrams are always given in fathoms, regardless of the measurement units on cited charts; depths are reduced to approximate zero tide. You should add the amount of tide listed in the corrected tide tables when you use these numbers. In U.S. waters, zero tide is the mean of the lower of low waters. In Canada, zero tide data is given as the lowest expected tide for the year. The depths shown on diagrams, or mentioned in the text, are typical of what we found and do not represent the exact minimums for any given area.

Bearings and courses, when given, are generally magnetic and identified as such. Courses are taken off the chart compass rose; they are approximate and are to be "made good." No allowances have been made for deviation, possible current or drift. When compass cardinal points are used (example NW or SE), these refer to true bearings and should be taken as approximate only.

Distances are expressed in nautical miles, and speed is expressed in knots unless otherwise stated. Scales on the diagrams are expressed in yards, and miles as noted and are approximate only. Time is given in four-digit 24-hour clock numbers, and all courses are given in three digits.

The Bibliography contains excellent references on general cruising books. If you are unsure of your cruising skills or the suitability of your vessel, we recommend that you consult with local experts —cruising instructors, yacht clubs, experienced Pacific Coast

USCG rescue boat checks Tillamook Bar

Bow watch approaching Coho Anchorage

sailors, commercial fishermen, the Coast Guard—and that you study many of the texts listed in the Bibliography.

When discussing local knowledge concerning routes, coves or anchoring, we make the assumption that you, as skipper, have the proper largest-scale chart available for the area you plan to visit, as well as the latest edition of the tide and current tables, the U.S. *Coast Pilot*, and that you are skilled in using them. We find that an investment in proper charts is the best insurance you can have. By knowing your own abilities and interests and by matching them to the unlimited cruising opportunities for exploring, you can enjoy the many options of a Pacific Coast trip.

III. How to Use this Book for Route Planning

In the text, and on diagrams, you will find reference to Bluewater Routes, Express Routes, and Inshore Routes. These are our names for traditional routes used for traveling up or down the coast. The three types of routes are based upon actual waypoints *Baidarka* used or modified to conform with current local knowledge. You may pick up and follow any one of these three suggested routes, departing from any place along the coast, as long as you make the transition from the harbor to the route by select-

ing the appropriate waypoints that are clear of hazards. The major harbor approach diagrams in the text will assist you in finding a good departure waypoint.

Route, Approach Entrance, Harbor and Cove Diagrams

The suggested Pacific Coast Routes, based upon the experience of *Baidarka*'s research, are found in the detailed diagrams in each chapter. The presentation of diagrams is based on the idea of coastal navigating from small scale (large area) charts to large scale (small area). This is illustrated in the adjacent composite layout of four detailed diagrams for the greater Los Angeles area.

The coastal routes are shown on the Los Angeles to Laguna Point Routes. The square box on this diagram covering the Los Angeles and Long Beach area indicates you can consult another diagram for that specific area. Look in the text for the diagram of Los Angeles Harbor/Long Beach Harbor Approaches. On that diagram you will find the approach waypoint latitude/longitudes listed and also another box indicating a further close-up diagram of the Los Angeles Harbor Entrance. This Entrance diagram shows the entrance waypoint positions and lists the latitude/longitudes. If you are interested in going to the California Yacht Marina or Watchorn Basin look in the text for the Los Angeles Harbor diagram. This Harbor diagram has details on the marina, fuel and pump out dock and anchoring positions. In each case the box on the area of interest indicates you need to search for the detailed diagram in the adjoining text.

This is the first nautical guidebook to feature detailed route information as well as comprehensive harbor data. While these diagrams are for reference planning only, and not for navigation, please send your comments and any errata by email to office@FineEdge.com. Whether

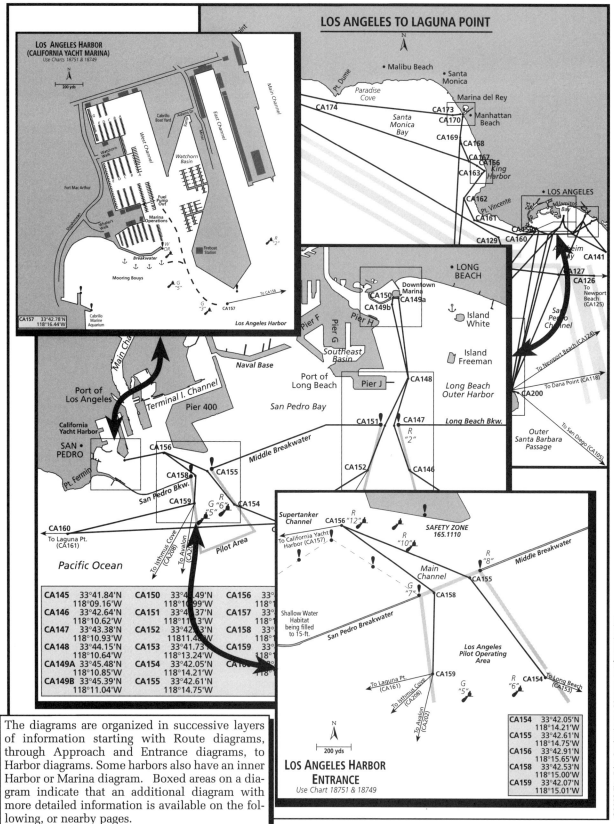

The diagrams are organized in successive layers of information starting with Route diagrams, through Approach and Entrance diagrams, to Harbor diagrams. Some harbors also have an inner Harbor or Marina diagram. Boxed areas on a diagram indicate that an additional diagram with more detailed information is available on the following, or nearby pages.

Baidarka passes inside Tillamook Rock

using NOAA charts, or our Route, Approach, or Harbor diagrams always make sure you are using the largest scale (smallest area) charts or diagrams for the detailed information you need. As a convenience, we list precise latitude/longitude for each waypoint shown on the diagram. It is up to each skipper to check and verify these waypoints before using them and make sure they are safe for his vessel, his experience, the weather and sea conditions. FineEdge.com diagrams are representational, are not to scale, and do not show all the navigation aids or hazards so must be used with caution and judgment. You must use the current NOAA chart listed on each diagram for navigation.

When joining a route assure yourself that your track is clear of hazards. Note that the increasing placement of large ocean weather

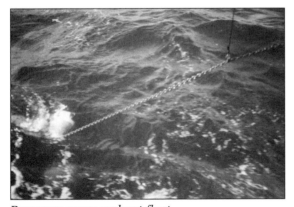

Paravane snags crabpot float

buoys and oil rigs along the coast requires careful attention to assure a fair passage. If you are using electronic charts to develop your routes, we highly recommend Kevin Monahan's *GPS Instant Navigation* (available from FineEdge.com) as a reference for selecting waypoints and compiling routes. You may also find the two FineEdge.com *Pacific Coast Route Planning Maps* (south and north portions) an aid in picking your route or to monitor your progress. Please see Appendix A and B for additional itinerary suggestions.

Bluewater Route

The Bluewater Route, which connects San Diego and San Francisco with Cape Flattery, the western entrance to the Strait of Juan de Fuca, follows a traditional north- south-direction remaining between 15 to 40 miles offshore—well outside the crabpot fishing limits and the tug towing routes—but inside the major tanker shipping routes.

The Bluewater Route is preferred by sailboats or larger powerboats wanting to make maximum speed to either San Francisco or Southern California during times of prevailing northwest winds or other favorable conditions. This route, which requires round-the-clock passage, is often used by solo sailors because there is usually less chance of traffic or an encounter with a crapbot float than the Express or Inshore routes. On a northbound voyage, in particular, the larger, faster yachts that don't mind going out 20 to 30 miles each day to join the route, seem to like this route for its simplicity.

The advantage of the Bluewater Route is that it is shorter and generally faster, requiring less attention to accurate steering, which can be important for sailors using wind vanes for steerage; it is also generally more efficient for a sailboat tacking to windward with long reaches. The disadvantages are sometimes greater offshore wind or weather (see Cape Mendocino sidebar), en route stops requiring more time, little visibility of coastal land-forms, and the difficulty of tucking into a harbor quickly when the weather takes a turn for the worse.

The Bluewater Route can be entered or exited anywhere along the coast by making an appropriate transition to the departure waypoint of the port(s) involved or to the adjacent Express or Inshore Route. For example, if San Francisco is not one of your scheduled stops, you can bypass it by navigating directly from Blue 3 to Blue 6 to avoid the traffic at the entrance channel. Please see the Blue Route diagrams for more detail on the route legs and waypoints.

Express Route

Our recommended Express Route is a popular trade-off for those who want a fast route but have several stops planned along the coast, or for those that want to remain fairly close to shore so they can seek a safe harbor if the weather changes. This route is used by many delivery skippers who require fuel stops and crew changes or who just want the option of a good rest every so often. We like the Express Route because it opens up the possibility of long coastal trips composed of mostly daylight passages with a minimal number of nights at sea. This route follows roughly the 20- to 40-fathom curve and averages 5 to 10 miles offshore.

Between San Francisco and Cape Flattery crabpot floats are a serious hazard to pleasure craft. The crabpots are identified by small floats attached to a small line; these floats with their lines are difficult to see in advance and therefore avoid. The lines are strong enough to foul a prop or completely stop the shaft from turning. They can also hang up passive or active stabilization fins, causing a pleasure boat to spin around in a circle.

Recently, the coastal fishermen and tug boat operators voluntarily reached an agreement to establish a lane where crabpots will not be set. The agreement will not only help reduce the number of pots fishermen lose each year but will help increase safety for pleasure craft. Our suggested Express Route follows the Crabpot-Free Tow Lane, thereby minimizing this serious and growing hazard. The lanes

average about 2 miles wide and, together with open fishing zones, are shown in color in our *Pacific Coast Route Planning Maps*. Please see Appendix A and B for the suggested Express Route Itineraries.

Inshore Route

Our recommended Inshore Route along the Pacific Coast is a harbor-hopping delight for boaters that like to keep one foot on the beach at all times. It allows smaller and under-powered vessels to avoid some of the typical afternoon chop by taking advantage of more settled seas inside reefs and islets, as well as lees and favorable currents found under major capes. It also minimizes rolling that occurs when you must follow a route at right angles to seas and wind from farther out in order to enter or exit a port. Using this route allows you to see and smell the land at all times and it opens up the possibility of making temporary rest stops in the tiny coves and lees found close to shore. It means that you can travel the full length of the coast with a bet-

Oil rigs and buoys near Coast Route

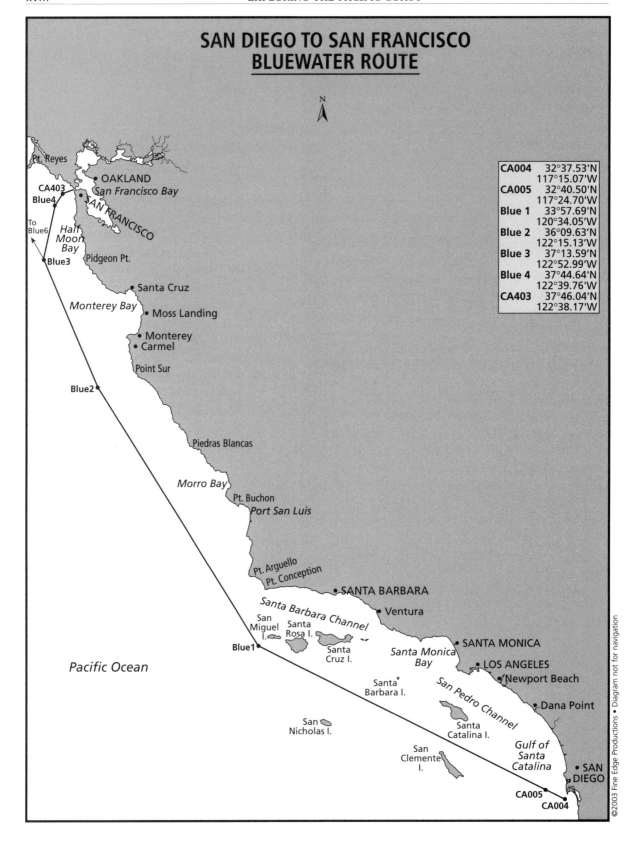

SAN DIEGO TO SAN FRANCISCO
BLUEWATER ROUTE

N

CA004	32°37.53'N
	117°15.07'W
CA005	32°40.50'N
	117°24.70'W
Blue 1	33°57.69'N
	120°34.05'W
Blue 2	36°09.63'N
	122°15.13'W
Blue 3	37°13.59'N
	122°52.99'W
Blue 4	37°44.64'N
	122°39.76'W
CA403	37°46.04'N
	122°38.17'W

Pt. Reyes

CA403
Blue4

OAKLAND
San Francisco Bay
SAN FRANCISCO

To Blue6

Half Moon Bay

Blue3   Pidgeon Pt.

Santa Cruz

Monterey Bay   Moss Landing

Monterey
Carmel

Point Sur

Blue2

Piedras Blancas

Morro Bay

Pt. Buchon
Port San Luis

Pt. Arguello
Pt. Conception

SANTA BARBARA

Santa Barbara Channel   Ventura

San Miguel I.   Santa Rosa I.
Blue1   *Santa Monica Bay*   SANTA MONICA

Santa Cruz I.   LOS ANGELES
                                             Newport Beach

Pacific Ocean

Santa Barbara I.   *San Pedro Channel*   Dana Point

San Nicholas I.   Santa Catalina I.

                                                      Gulf of Santa Catalina

San Clemente I.   SAN DIEGO

CA005
CA004

©2003 Fine Edge Productions • Diagram not for navigation

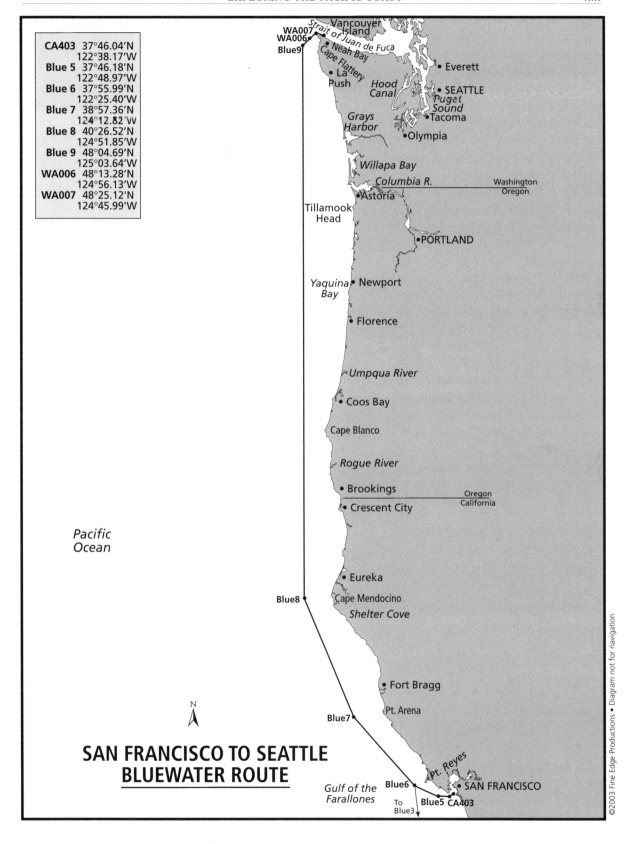

CA403 37°46.04'N
       122°38.17'W
Blue 5 37°46.18'N
        122°48.97'W
Blue 6 37°55.99'N
        122°25.40'W
Blue 7 38°57.36'N
        124°12.82'W
Blue 8 40°26.52'N
        124°51.85'W
Blue 9 48°04.69'N
        125°03.64'W
WA006 48°13.28'N
       124°56.13'W
WA007 48°25.12'N
       124°45.99'W

WA007
WA006
Blue9

Vancouver Island
Strait of Juan de Fuca
Neah Bay
Cape Flattery
La Push
Hood Canal
Grays Harbor
Everett
SEATTLE
Puget Sound
Tacoma
Olympia

Willapa Bay
Columbia R.
Washington
Oregon
Astoria
Tillamook Head

PORTLAND

Yaquina Bay
Newport

Florence

Umpqua River

Coos Bay

Cape Blanco

Rogue River

Brookings
Oregon
California
Crescent City

Pacific
Ocean

Eureka
Blue8
Cape Mendocino
Shelter Cove

Fort Bragg
Pt. Arena
Blue7

N

SAN FRANCISCO TO SEATTLE
BLUEWATER ROUTE

Pt. Reyes
SAN FRANCISCO
Gulf of the
Farallones
Blue6
To
Blue3
Blue5 CA403

©2003 Fine Edge Productions • Diagram not for navigation

ter chance of not having to spend a night at sea when strong head winds prevail. The advantage of moorage in a marina nearly every night, augmented with a few nights spent anchored in coves or open roadsteads, sits well with many first mates or crew who do not care for slogging to windward day and night. Harbor-hopping is generally easier on both a boat and its crew and is certainly more interesting and relaxing. The Inshore Route is potentially safer. You can stay close to the coast and quickly find temporary or overnight shelter. It does mean that you have to monitor weather closely and not leave a harbor until a front passes and good weather is reestablished.

The disadvantages to the Inshore Route are that it is circuitous, it takes more time and it requires superior helmsmanship. You must be a good navigator, know your precise position at all times, pay close attention to your charts and watch for visual signs of potential hazards. Avoiding the inshore obstacles of numerous rocks, reefs, islets, kelp beds, shoals, and crab-pot floats is a major challenge, but it is worth it. In short, the Inshore Route is much more interesting for those not in a hurry. Please see Appendix A for a sample itinerary using the Inshore Route.

Harbor-hopping Becomes Extended Cruising

Modern pocket trawlers, navigational technology, and expert local knowledge are leading the way to extended summer coastal cruises of a remarkable extent, and even to complete circumnavigations once thought difficult or impossible. Accurate positioning information, along with new-generation cruising guides, can turn a series of connected day trips into true coastal itineraries.

While the following account is far from harbor-hopping, it is an illustration of an extraordinary feat that can be accomplished by a pocket trawler. *Nordhavn*—a sister ship of our research vessel *Baidarka*—left Dana Point, 3 November 2001 and completed a circumnaviga-

Santa Cruz Harbor entrance warning

tion 19 June 2002, a first for a production boat of this size.

According to skipper Jim Leishman, *Nordhavn* traveled 26,000 nautical miles in 228 days for an average of 114 miles per day. During the seven-month voyage, they accumulated 3,900 engine hours and consumed 10,300 gallons of fuel. The vessel incurred no damage of any kind; the crew had to replace only the smaller engine alternator and make some repairs to their gyro-stabilized fins, but the manual paravanes worked fine and may yet prove to be a circumnavigator's best bet. The crew used the vessel's autopilot the entire voyage for steering along with electronic charting. They had an average of three crew members, with five crew changes en route.

While a globe-circling marathon of this magnitude will appeal to very few boaters, *Nordhavn*'s success does prove that the extended cruising horizon for a relatively small powerboat is much greater than ordinarily thought. While a circumnavigation requires crossing vast oceans and solving sophisticated logistical problems, the barriers to extended coastal cruising are being reduced every day and are limited only by one's imagination.

A well-found boat, crewed with a motivated and moderately experienced couple, can quite easily cruise from Southern California to Glacier Bay, Alaska, and return in one summer. A 4,600-nautical-mile trip such as this requires an average of 38 nautical miles a day for 120 days. Or, more practically, motoring to windward, *every other day*, for about 13 hours at 6 knots. This schedule is not difficult to maintain in the long days of a high-latitude summer. Throw in a few days here and there for weather-related layovers, and a skipper can complete an extended cruise in a four-month-summer and gain a sense of accomplishment and seldom-experienced freedom.

As an example of a reasonable harbor-hopping voyage, during *Baidarka*'s shakedown cruise in the year 2000, we motored from Dana Point, California, to Lituya Bay in the Gulf of Alaska, covering 2,500 nautical miles in

USCG Patrol departing La Push for bar check

48 days, and averaging 43 miles a day to windward. We took eight layover days and spent every night except one moored or anchored in port.

We found that, by leaving early each day, we could frequently move ahead a short distance to the next harbor when afternoon small-craft warnings were forecast. By following this schedule, we beat nearly all the larger delivery yachts that had to remain in port waiting for better weather for their longer runs. And by tying together a series of 40 fascinating day-trips, we had created a terrific extended cruise.

When we have completed our current research project on *Baidarka*—a comprehensive guidebook on the Gulf of Alaska—skippers will have the local knowledge they need to leave San Diego in April and day-cruise to Glacier Bay, Prince William Sound, Kenai Penninsula and Kodiak Island. Reversing the route, they could see California palm trees by October, all in a 6-knot boat, averaging 43 miles per day over the 6,500 nautical miles as a series of day-trips, securely anchored or moored every night.

With over 160,000 miles of bluewater cruising, from 60 degrees north to 56 degrees south, from the Gulf of Alaska to Cape Horn, Réanne and I find the most enjoyable cruising is the harbor-hopping possible along the west coast of

Mexico and the United States, British Columbia and Alaska. From the beautiful beaches of Mexico to the rain forests and glaciers of the Pacific Northwest you, too, can plan and enjoy your own extended cruise.

Other Strategies for West Coast Harbor-hopping

John and Midge Stapleton of the 38-foot M/V *Sundowner* have one of the best cruising strategies for the West Coast we know of. In the summer of 1982, they wanted to make a round-trip cruise from the Bay Area to the San Juan Islands with just two of them aboard, but they didn't want to spend a night at sea unless it was absolutely necessary. They knew they could be forced to if a harbor were closed by the wrong combination of wind, swell or tide.

At the time, John and Midge were living near Sacramento and had limited experience outside the protected waters of San Francisco Bay. In researching their route they found that existing written information was inadequate. So, they did a very practical and enterprising thing. They drove north via the coast route, visiting every potential stop along the way. They walked the breakwaters, watched local boats entering and exiting, talked to boaters and

Baidarka *running on a calm day*

found out where the transient floats were located. Then, they visualized themselves motoring into the harbor, heading for the marina and tying up. In just one week they did a masterful job of obtaining local knowledge to their own satisfaction for every major port along the coast. They learned many important things about crossing the shallow sandbars and, also, that they would not attempt to enter the more challenging ports of Rogue River or Depoe Bay.

So, armed with this valuable knowledge, they put together a plan to do the San Francisco to Anacortes trip, not as a single push to windward like a delivery skipper might, but to make the coast trip part of their vacation. Their boat is a single engine, basic trawler, without autopilot and with a maximum speed of 7 to 8 knots, and they planned to travel no more than 10 to 15 hours per day, spending every night tied up in port. They set a goal to do the entire trip in about 12 days, each way and, if the weather turned bad, they agreed to stay put until conditions stabilized; this happened less frequently than they anticipated.

Their 1982 summer trip went so well, they decided to do it again in 1987, in 1990, and again in 1993. The Stapletons have had their mid-sized trawler for 25 years and have visited upper British Columbia, as well as Alaska many times in their summer travels. They feel at home doing

it again and again. Theirs is a real success story and, as this book goes to press, John and Midge have returned from yet another Alaska trip to San Francisco Bay where John manages a West Marine store. In harbor-hopping northward, they like to stop in San Francisco, Bodega Bay, Fort Bragg, Eureka, Crescent City, Brookings, Coos Bay, Newport, Tillamook, Grays Harbor, Neah Bay and Anacortes.

For a different perspective, we have an acquaintance who has a lot of admiration for the fortitude of the classic fishermen of the Northwest. His burning desire was to experience the coast himself in a traditional, seafaring fashion. For a few thousand dollars, he bought a simple wooden 34-foot fishing boat that had been long retired in Seattle. With the barest of essentials, our friend filled the tank with gasoline and took off for a shakedown in lower B.C. His initial trip went fairly well on the Inside Passage's sheltered waters, so with his dog, he set out for California. Being short handed, like the Stapletons, he wisely decided that harbor-hopping was the way to go. For the details of his trip, please see Chapter 6: The Oregon Coast.

Michelle and Jerry Gaylord of M/V *Passing Thru* whose sidebars enliven our text, left Oxnard, California, in 1999 to cruise to the Northwest, Alaska and back. They tackled their northbound passage, harbor-hopping from Oxnard to Cape Flattery in 101 days. Their southbound trip, on the other hand, took a mere 15 days!

In both directions, they ran between 3 to 5 miles offshore, with the exception of the area of outside the Columbia River where they ventured out 8 miles. Pushing their way up the coast, they encountered the typical rolling seas and prevailing winds, but found that they soon became comfortable punching into those seas. Their only stretch of horrendously confused water lay off Cape Mendocino where their ride was frightfully uncomfortable. They say that they could have avoided that discomfort had they heeded the advice of local fishermen and tugboat captains, and tucked into Shelter Cove, making the passage around Cape Mendocino during the middle of the night. In all, they liked the Inside Passage so well that they spent nearly four years cruising before heading south again and, as we go to press, they are on their way down the coast of Mexico—intrepid and experienced cruisers!

We have included these true accounts to give you an idea of the different possibilities. There are no guarantees on the open ocean, but we suspect you will have an outstanding, memorable time. Of course, each boat, each crew is different; each has varying levels of experience, confidence and requirements for comfort. We suggest you set a date, prepare as best you can, being sure to carry all the local charts and armed with all the local knowledge available. Then, poke your bow outside the harbor and see how it goes.

IV. Prudent Coastal Navigation: Ideas for Remaining Safe at Sea

Safe operation of a vessel along the Pacific Coast requires both boat piloting skills and essential local knowledge when visiting new places. A prudent navigator considers several background factors when judging the quality and quantity of information he needs.

With a few exceptions, the harbors of the Pacific Coast, are located at the outlet of major creeks or rivers where sand tends to collect, causing shallow entrance bars. Even harbors without flowing rivers such as Ventura and Marina Del Rey have silting or shoaling problems as natural currents on the coast or storms rearrange nearby beach sand. Silting can be a problem also in Morro Bay and north of San Francisco in places such as Tomales Bay, Bodega Bay and Noyo River. Vessels harbor-hopping the Pacific Coast must have accurate information on entrance conditions to safely enter or exit these harbors under marginal conditions. It is wise to obtain accurate and timely information which

can be problematic at times; the information is best found by consulting the latest charts, and calling local authorities for current bar status. Generally the most favorable time to cross an entrance bar is during the last two hours of the flood current. Large-scale nautical charts corrected with the latest Notice to Mariners can provide the information you need. Many critical harbor entrances are monitored closely by local Coast Guard stations; a call on VHF Channel 16 will provide you with their latest observations. During strong winds or rough seas entrance bars are often closed to vessels of different sizes depending on conditions at the time.

A number of Pacific Coast harbors have undergone changes in the last five years. Some, like Marina del Rey, Brookings, and others have recently been dredged, while others, like Coquille River, Tillamook and Willapa have reconfigured entrance channels, range marks and/or buoys.

In some cases the U.S. *Coast Pilot*, paper charts and electronic charts differ on certain details of the above-listed navigational concerns. In general, charts (and guidebooks) become dated over time, as man-made or bottom-features change. All charts must be updated if you want to have the latest information at hand. Use the Route, Approach and Harbor diagrams in this book with a healthy dose of skepticism and apply prudent judgment. Chart dealers no longer make hand corrections to charts for you and we have found that you cannot depend on recently purchased paper or electronic charts having the most up-to-date corrections.

To assure that you have corrections, you can now check Notice to Mariners online by going to www.nima.mil or by visiting the FineEdge.com website and looking under links. Having the most current information is critical when you find yourself in limited visibility (fog) or during periods of stress due to weather or tight time constraints. In addition, you should be aware that government budget limitations have created a substantial time delay in dissemination of new Notice to Mariners. This holds true for U.S. as well as for Canadian waters.

To add to the challenge, aids to navigation, which are anchored, can move off location due to storms or collisions with barges, and lighted aids may become extinguished. Don't panic if a nav-aid is not where you thought it should be, is completely missing or is different in some way other than as charted. When this happens to you we suggest you use this as a red flag, slow down or stop, and double check your instruments and data sources to ascertain if it is safe to continue as planned. Occasionally, in over 60 years of combined cruising, we have run across every kind of problem possible with nav-aids. And every country has these problems.

Bear in mind that tide and current tables are projections based on mathematical formulas and do not include local weather effects. Don't be surprised to find actual local tide values that vary considerably from area predictions, with current speeds or even directions different than those predicted. Local weather and topography can make significant differences. Entering entrance bars requires particular attention. Slack current times rarely coincide with times of high or low water; the larger an inlet, lagoon, river or the more restricted a narrows is, the later slack currents will occur compared to local high or low water. In some lagoons or narrow passages, it is not uncommon for slack water to be delayed up to two hours or more after predicted time for high or low water outside.

If in doubt, and when possible, call the local experts, such as the local USCG station, harbormaster, or other authority, by VHF radio or cell phone for the most current information. The prudent mariner knows his precise position at all times when traveling in close quarters and does not depend on any single nav-aid or piece of equipment as the sole source of vital information. Cross-checking different information sources and equipment, and taking bearings with a hand-bearing compass or binoculars will provide the confidence you need to proceed.

Good paper charts marked with active routes, regular dead reckoning positions and occasional fixes are a good backup to the best of electronic navigation systems. We have been thankful more than once for these basic tools when our electronic navigation computers became overloaded, crashed, lost power or when an operator error created temporary problems.

Although today's coastal navigator lives in a full information environment there is still uncertainty and ambiguity. You need to seek information from a number of sources and make the best informed judgments possible; maintain skepticism when it comes to charts, the U.S. *Coast Pilot*, maps, diagrams, and guidebooks (yes even this one!). Cross check for credibility when possible; check websites for updates and errata before you leave or en route if possible; make local inquiries prior to entering or exiting entrance bars or intricate channels and passes.

When new to an area, it is a good idea to call local Coast Guard stations on VHF channels 16/22A, or local harbormasters, marina operators and port authorities for their current status on entrance conditions, status on moorage and anchorages available. In crowded places, or in limited visibility in tight quarters, make a Securité announcement on Channel 16, broadcasting your intentions and vessel name so that concerned traffic can call you back. (For updates or changes for Fine Edge publications please check www.FineEdge.com for the latest information.)

Remember this primary safety rule: Stop your vessel, or even drop anchor, to resolve any ambiguities found in your visual observations, your instruments, your charts, or any changes in the sound, and proceed only when it is safe.

Afternoon winds turn into gale force

Entrance Hazards

Starting at Brookings and harbors north, it is prudent to call the local USCG station before approaching. The harbor entrances are monitored by local USCG stations and bars are occasionally closed to vessels of different sizes depending on conditions at that time.

In general:
4' Seas—Advisory lights may be illuminated near the bar area (visible only from land)
4'-6' Seas—Rough bar conditions occasionally breaking—closed to sport fishing boats
6'-8' Seas—Rough bar conditions with breaking seas—closed to small boats, but may be open to larger craft
8' Seas and over—Dangerous bar conditions. Generally closed to all pleasure craft

Each port is effected by weather according to which way the entrance faces, how deep the entrance is, and how sheltered the coastline is. A prudent navigator never leaves port without having plans and charts for alternate harbors and coves in case conditions change making the destination difficult or impossible to reach safely. Along the coast, where entrance bars can be closed because of breaking waves, it is important to make sure the vessel is prepared to take a night at sea if it should become necessary.

Coos Bay and Newport are considered the harbors closed the least often by weather. Coquille and Tillamook are marginal in any fresh Northwest wind.

Crabpots

Crabpots are set by the tens of thousands along the Pacific Coast particularly north of San Francisco. They are a hazard to cruising boats as the floats can foul your prop or paravane stabilizers. Twin engine boats (without full keels) are particularly vulnerable. Only a sharp lookout and constant course corrections will avoid these ubiquitous hazards. They are generally found in the 10 to 30 fathom zone, but it is not unusual to find them as far out as 50 fathoms and several miles off shore.

At the first indication that you have, or are

Three-meter discus weather buoy

about to snag a float line—put your engine(s) in neutral. If you don't float free from the line, or cannot work the line free from the sides and stern of the boat, you may have to cut the line. Sometimes you can still work the line free from above after it is cut. Get your snorkel gear and sharpest knife out to dive under the boat and clear the line. It is critical you quickly place your engine in neutral when you snag a line. The longer your prop turns, the tighter the line grabs the shaft. A poly line on a turning shaft can quickly become a glob of molten plastic.

Crabpots are generally laid out on a string line, but not always, and some old floats are moss covered and almost invisible. One option is to stay 5 to 15 miles offshore, or use the Crabpot-Free Tow Zone used by tugs and barges, between San Francisco and the Straits of Juan de Fuca, indicated on the route diagrams and the FineEdge.com route planning maps.

And one final item: There is nothing more important in navigation than an alert watch. There is no electronic substitute for an awake, alert crew member, armed with a good pair of binoculars, who knows what to look for and what to do with the information observed. Standing orders should cover those things for the bow watch which must be brought to the attention of the skipper. Any information a watchman notices that represents a potential threat to the vessel should be given, *and acknowledged,* by the skipper/navigator whether or not he or she is busy or even asleep.

Baidarka never enters a narrow passage, a harbor, an anchorage, or a marina without one or more persons on bow watch, with standing orders of where and what to watch for. We have the watchman point continuously at an object of concern until the helmsman or navigator gives an acknowledgment. (We ask the watchman not to point in the direction he thinks the helmsman should turn, as that is the decision of the navigator.)

Baidarka's crew has been able to avoid almost all Pacific Coast charted and uncharted hazards from Cape Horn to the Gulf of Alaska by following this simple rule of maintaining a proper watch. There is absolutely NO substitute for open and alert eyeballs!

Waypoints and GPS

GPS is an excellent tool for navigating the Pacific Coast. Navigational aids become rare as you leave urban areas and commercial routes. Many inlets and channels can be confusing. GPS will help locate the proper entrances, detect cross-track errors, provide speed over the ground, and hence determine tidal currents.

Latitude and longitude for waypoints in this book—given to the nearest one-hundredth of a minute of latitude—are taken from the largest scale charts available and are referenced to NAD83 which, for practical purposes, are identical to the GPS default horizontal datum of WSG84. These latitude/longitudes are to be treated as approximate only and should be verified by each user. Many of the referenced charts are not accurate (nor can they be read accurately) to one-hundredth of a minute. We have approximated this last digit—which is about a boat's length—to provide as complete a picture as possible. With the removal of Selective Availability (SA), *Baidarka* has found both differential GPS and WASS GPS to be sta-

ble to within a boat's length, and very accurate. (See FineEdge.com's *GPS Instant Navigation* for a full discussion.)

Errata and Updates

When a new edition is published by FineEdge.com it contains all the known updates and supersedes the older edition which is no longer valid. Your comments, corrections or suggestions are welcomed. Please send them to office@FineEdge.com Errata and updates on current editions are posted when available on the publishers' website www.FineEdge.com

V. Weather Considerations

Key to a safe and comfortable passage along the Pacific Coast is knowledge of the weather. The U.S. National Oceanic and Atmospheric Administration (NOAA) and the National Weather Service (NWS) provide a number of comprehensive resources available to mariners along with up-to-date weather information.

Weather reports broadcast on VHF WX channels are invaluable for an update on the current state of the weather and the forecast. The recorded WX broadcasts have traditionally been used by boaters for a daily, or more frequent, update. The NOAA Weather Radio Network provides voice broadcasts of the local and coastal marine forecasts on a continuous cycle issued by the NWS every 3 to 6 hours, or amended as required, and broadcast continuously on Weather Channel 1 or 2. Local NWS Forecast offices located in San Diego, Los Angeles, San Francisco, Eureka, Medford, Portland and Seattle produce the forecasts for the Pacific Coast.

When one travels outside of their home waters, the locations used to describe a weather area are new and not easily comprehended as you hear the continuous broadcast. We have included diagrams for the Pacific Coast to illustrate the reporting area locations and the location of offshore weather buoys.

The additional services and resources from NOAA and NWS can present a deeper picture of the weather. In addition to VHF, extensive up-to-date weather data can now be obtained on the

A cozy cove in the Channel Islands

web, weatherfax and by telephone. While online resources are typically best for briefing before a trip when one can access weather data from an online connection on land, more and more vessels are being equipped with satellite connections for access to the internet and email. Marinas are now beginning to offer Internet connections for their customers. When you desire the most comprehensive report of the weather, an internet connection can provide you with access to all of the NOAA services including real-time NEXRAD Doppler Radar at www.nws.noaa.gov/om/marine/home.htm#dissemination.

Where possible, stop by the local NWS office. As an example, the Eureka weather office is only two blocks from the marina and it is open 24 hours per day, seven days per week. The staff provided the *Baidarka* crew with a personal weather briefing complete with time lapse video of the past few day's satellite shots and their fine-tuned forecasts for the route we had chosen. Let them know you appreciate their service and call them direct if you have a serious concern only they can address or assist with.

For those mariners considering the Express or Bluewater routes with access to cellular or satellite phone, you may want to consult the Dial-A-Buoy system. Along the Pacific Coast, NOAA maintains a network of weather reporting ocean buoys located between 15 and 40 miles off the coast, in addition to several buoys anchored about 300 miles offshore to report advancing weather. Buoy reports include wind direction, speed, gust, significant wave height, swell and wind-wave height and periods, air temperature, and sea level pressure. Some buoys report wave direction. To access Dial-A-Buoy, call 228.688.1948. Enter 1 and the 5 digit identifier for a buoy. The buoys and their locations are illustrated on the diagrams. The Dial-A-Buoy system can also read the latest NWS marine forecast for most station locations. If this option is available, the system will prompt you to press the # key after the buoy observation is read.

Semi-Annual Weather Patterns: Spring and Summer

The weather on the Pacific Coast follows a general semi-annual pattern. Changes are associated with the building up or breaking down of the North Pacific High Pressure Cell around the times of the spring and fall equinoxes.

Following the late winter storms, near March 21, the Pacific High begins to build about a thousand miles west of Vancouver Island. This more or less permanent high-pressure zone deflects most summer lows into the Gulf of Alaska where they either dissipate or take a varied path that affects coastal weather. We recommend waiting until the Pacific High is well entrenched—generally early to mid-May—before you head into northern waters.

During the summer months, in times of stable high pressure, the West Coast undergoes a daily pattern of diurnal micro-weather that is quite predictable. Nights are usually quite calm and quiet along the coast with fog or low clouds moving on shore. In the afternoon, moderate to strong northwest breezes pick up, dissipating the clouds and creating wind chop of several feet, until evening when conditions become calm again. During such periods, most weather

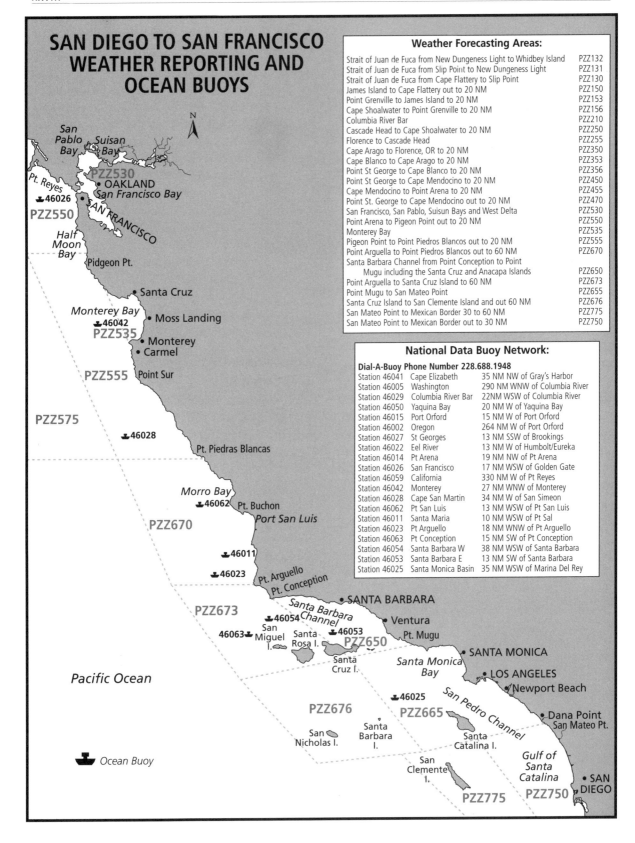

SAN DIEGO TO SAN FRANCISCO WEATHER REPORTING AND OCEAN BUOYS

N

San Pablo Bay
Suisan Bay
PZZ530
OAKLAND
San Francisco Bay
Pt. Reyes
⚓46026
SAN FRANCISCO
PZZ550
Half Moon Bay
Pidgeon Pt.
Santa Cruz
Monterey Bay
⚓46042
Moss Landing
PZZ535
Monterey
Carmel
PZZ555
Point Sur
PZZ575
⚓46028
Pt. Piedras Blancas
Morro Bay
⚓46062
Pt. Buchon
Port San Luis
PZZ670
⚓46011
⚓46023
Pt. Arguello
Pt. Conception
PZZ673
Santa Barbara Channel
⚓46054
SANTA BARBARA
46063⚓
San Miguel I.
Santa Rosa I.
⚓46053
Ventura
Pt. Mugu
PZZ650
Santa Cruz I.
Santa Monica Bay
SANTA MONICA
LOS ANGELES
Newport Beach
Pacific Ocean
⚓46025
PZZ676
PZZ665
San Pedro Channel
Santa Barbara I.
Santa Catalina I.
Dana Point
San Mateo Pt.
San Nicholas I.
Gulf of Santa Catalina
⚓ Ocean Buoy
San Clemente I.
PZZ775
PZZ750
SAN DIEGO

Weather Forecasting Areas:

Strait of Juan de Fuca from New Dungeness Light to Whidbey Island	PZZ132
Strait of Juan de Fuca from Slip Point to New Dungeness Light	PZZ131
Strait of Juan de Fuca from Cape Flattery to Slip Point	PZZ130
James Island to Cape Flattery out to 20 NM	PZZ150
Point Grenville to James Island to 20 NM	PZZ153
Cape Shoalwater to Point Grenville to 20 NM	PZZ156
Columbia River Bar	PZZ210
Cascade Head to Cape Shoalwater to 20 NM	PZZ250
Florence to Cascade Head	PZZ255
Cape Arago to Florence, OR to 20 NM	PZZ350
Cape Blanco to Cape Arago to 20 NM	PZZ353
Point St George to Cape Blanco to 20 NM	PZZ356
Point St George to Cape Mendocino to 20 NM	PZZ450
Cape Mendocino to Point Arena to 20 NM	PZZ455
Point St. George to Cape Mendocino out to 20 NM	PZZ470
San Francisco, San Pablo, Suisun Bays and West Delta	PZZ530
Point Arena to Pigeon Point out to 20 NM	PZZ550
Monterey Bay	PZZ535
Pigeon Point to Point Piedros Blancos out to 20 NM	PZZ555
Point Arguella to Point Piedros Blancos out to 60 NM	PZZ670
Santa Barbara Channel from Point Conception to Point Mugu including the Santa Cruz and Anacapa Islands	PZZ650
Point Arguella to Santa Cruz Island to 60 NM	PZZ673
Point Mugu to San Mateo Point	PZZ655
Santa Cruz Island to San Clemente Island and out 60 NM	PZZ676
San Mateo Point to Mexican Border 30 to 60 NM	PZZ775
San Mateo Point to Mexican Border out to 30 NM	PZZ750

National Data Buoy Network:

Dial-A-Buoy Phone Number 228.688.1948

Station 46041	Cape Elizabeth	35 NM NW of Gray's Harbor
Station 46005	Washington	290 NM WNW of Columbia River
Station 46029	Columbia River Bar	22NM WSW of Columbia River
Station 46050	Yaquina Bay	20 NM W of Yaquina Bay
Station 46015	Port Orford	15 NM W of Port Orford
Station 46002	Oregon	264 NM W of Port Orford
Station 46027	St Georges	13 NM SSW of Brookings
Station 46022	Eel River	13 NM W of Humbolt/Eureka
Station 46014	Pt Arena	19 NM NW of Pt Arena
Station 46026	San Francisco	17 NM WSW of Golden Gate
Station 46059	California	330 NM W of Pt Reyes
Station 46042	Monterey	27 NM WNW of Monterey
Station 46028	Cape San Martin	34 NM W of San Simeon
Station 46062	Pt San Luis	13 NM WSW of Pt San Luis
Station 46011	Santa Maria	10 NM WSW of Pt Sal
Station 46023	Pt Arguello	18 NM WNW of Pt Arguello
Station 46063	Pt Conception	15 NM SW of Pt Conception
Station 46054	Santa Barbara W	38 NM NW of Santa Barbara
Station 46053	Santa Barbara E	13 NM SW of Santa Barbara
Station 46025	Santa Monica Basin	35 NM WSW of Marina Del Rey

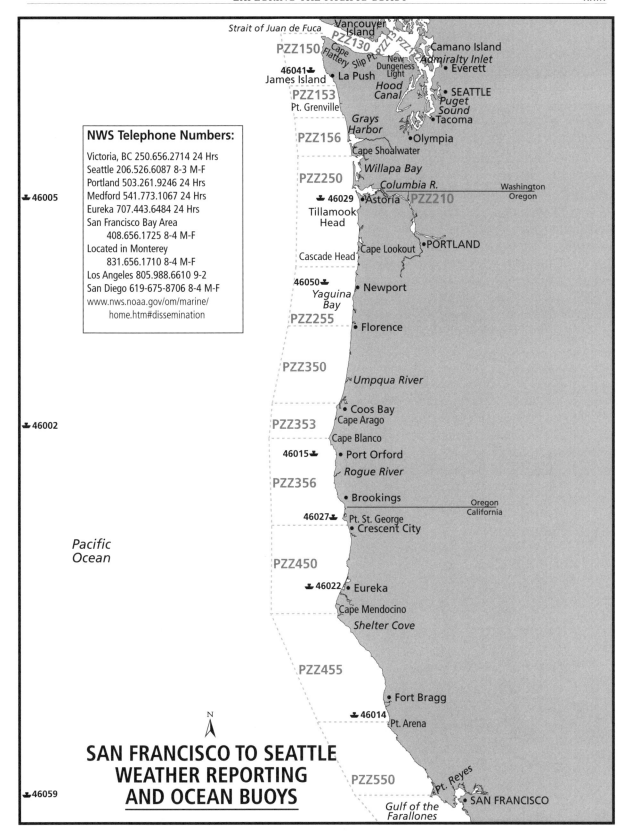

NWS Telephone Numbers:

Victoria, BC 250.656.2714 24 Hrs
Seattle 206.526.6087 8-3 M-F
Portland 503.261.9246 24 Hrs
Medford 541.773.1067 24 Hrs
Eureka 707.443.6484 24 Hrs
San Francisco Bay Area
    408.656.1725 8-4 M-F
Located in Monterey
    831.656.1710 8-4 M-F
Los Angeles 805.988.6610 9-2
San Diego 619-675-8706 8-4 M-F
www.nws.noaa.gov/om/marine/
    home.htm#dissemination

Strait of Juan de Fuca
Vancouver Island
PZZ130
PZZ150
Cape Flattery
Slip Pt.
New Dungeness Light
Camano Island
Admiralty Inlet
Everett
46041
James Island
La Push
Hood Canal
SEATTLE
Puget Sound
Tacoma
PZZ153
Pt. Grenville
Grays Harbor
Olympia
PZZ156
Cape Shoalwater
Willapa Bay
PZZ250
Columbia R.
Washington
Oregon
46029
Astoria
PZZ210
Tillamook Head
Cape Lookout
PORTLAND
Cascade Head
46050
Yaquina Bay
Newport
PZZ255
Florence
PZZ350
Umpqua River
46005
Coos Bay
Cape Arago
PZZ353
Cape Blanco
46015
Port Orford
Rogue River
PZZ356
Brookings
Oregon
California
46027
Pt. St. George
Crescent City
PZZ450
46002
Pacific Ocean
46022
Eureka
Cape Mendocino
Shelter Cove
PZZ455
Fort Bragg
46014
Pt. Arena
N
**SAN FRANCISCO TO SEATTLE
WEATHER REPORTING
AND OCEAN BUOYS**
PZZ550
Pt. Reyes
SAN FRANCISCO
Gulf of the Farallones
46059

stations report a high percentage of light to moderate winds with little or moderate precipitation—conditions that provide good cruising.

Although low-pressure fronts do manage to evade the Pacific High and hit the west coast, they usually occur at intervals of two to six weeks. These fronts, which are usually announced by a falling barometer, a change in both the direction and intensity of the wind, as well as by clouds and precipitation, normally last just a day or two and are well forecast. It is best to remain in a sheltered harbor or cove during the approach of unstable weather.

Although summer gales from the southeast are not unknown, they are not as intense as winter storms, and can still pack a dangerous wallop to small craft. More frequent is a common phenomenon of a low-pressure cell forming over the deserts and inland valleys of California, caused by thermal heating, which is felt all along the coast as strong summer northwesterlies. Although northwest gale-force winds of up to 40 knots do occur, strong winds of 20 to 30 knots are more common.

Take any summer storms or deep, low-pressure fronts seriously by noting barometric pressure and monitoring weather broadcasts

Sea lion at Monterey Marina

frequently. When you observe signs that a gale or storm from the southeast is developing, or if you hear a report of an impending gale or storm, head directly for a harbor or anchor site that offers protection from south or east winds. Take appropriate precautions for safety, such as maintaining sufficient swinging room and setting your anchor well. (It is always a good idea to take bearings on fixed objects to determine whether or not your anchor is dragging.)

In Southern California, when a stronger than average Pacific High is established, Northwest winds of 20 to 30 knots frequently occur off Point Conception and over the outer Channel Islands. The winds, with a duration of 12 to 18 hours, will produce wind waves of 10 to 16 feet. Coastal winds are usually light with this pattern; without a prior check of the weather, this situation can lead to unexpected and dangerously high seas.

The Santa Ana winds of Southern California, although quite localized, can cause dangerous seas particularly in Avalon Bay on Catalina Island. Avalon Harbor is exposed and unprotected to winds and seas from the East and Northeast, and the stronger Santa Ana winds can cause hazardous sea and surf in the harbor.

Semi-Annual Weather Patterns: Fall and Winter

Near the autumnal equinox (September 21), the Pacific High begins to collapse and the first major low-pressure fronts return, bringing foul weather and precipitation. Without the protection of a strong North Pacific High, about 10 low-pressure fronts per month affect the Northwest Coast; this occurs much less frequently south of Point Conception. During some of these storms, barometric pressure drops as low as 980 millibars, bringing hurricane force winds of 60 knots or more. In winter, prevailing winds are from the southeast, with heavy precipitation and high, dangerous seas. For this reason, offshore cruising along the Pacific Coast during the winter is usually not recommended; however we have heard of a number of skippers who have watched for the calms between fronts and have had successful trips.

In the southern areas of the Pacific Coast, well-developed cold fronts in the Fall through the Spring will produce strong and shifting winds. Winds preceding a front are usually from the south and southeast, and shifting into the northwest with the frontal passage. Wind speeds are generally in the 20 to 40 knot range with heavy and confused seas.

Barometric Pressure and Wind Velocities
Wind velocity tends to occur in direct proportion to the barometric pressure gradient—the rate of rise or fall of pressure. Falling barometric pressure that descends 1 millibar per hour usually means strong winds of 20 to 30 knots; a drop of 2 millibars per hour means gales of 35 to 45 knots; a drop of 3 millibars per hour brings storm-force winds of 50 to 60 knots. On the contrary, a rising barometer of 1 millibar per hour brings strong-to-gale-force winds of 25 to 40 knots.

By noting barometric pressure hourly in your ship's log, or by using a recording barometer, you can visualize this gradient of pressure and prepare for expected wind and sea conditions. During the prevailing summer northwesterlies, a steep pressure gradient lies parallel along the shore and you will find strong winds without noting a fall in the barometer, common with a low pressure front.

Wind Rotation
In the Northern Hemisphere, winds flow clockwise around a high-pressure cell and counterclockwise around a low-pressure cell. In other words, in the Northern Hemisphere, with the wind to your back, the low pressure is on your left, while the higher pressure is on your right. This simple test, and observation of the barometric pressure gradient, can give you an idea of the path of a storm cell and an idea of the strength and direction of upcoming winds. However, local topography can greatly affect the direction of the wind so, by studying the movement of clouds aloft, you can get a better idea of true wind direction and strength.

Wind Direction and Cloud Cover
Winds that arrive in advance of a low-pressure front generally blow from the south or southwest, then back (move counterclockwise) to the southeast as the front approaches. The strongest winds and highest seas usually occur just ahead of the low-pressure front. With the approaching front, clouds thicken and lower, taking on an ominous appearance; precipitation is heavy and may last for several hours. With the passage of a low-pressure front, the wind veers (moves clockwise), first to southwest, then to northwest. During the summer after the wind veers to its prevailing northwesterly direction, it may blow hard for a day or two, as if to send all the southern air back where it originated. We have experienced our lumpiest trips along the coast when we set out too soon after the barometer "bottomed out" and the wind veered to the west.

If high pressure over the interior of British Columbia sends strong outflow or arctic winds, with cold dry winds building from the northeast, along with a rising barometer, quickly seek shelter from downslope winds and seas. This is more common in the Northwest and is similar to the Santa Ana winds of Southern California, except that the high pressure is over Nevada or Utah. In addition, during times of strong runoff caused by heavy rainstorms or snowmelt, ebb currents tend to be quite strong and, in some cases, they completely override the direction of the flood on the surface of the water. It's a good idea to stay put during the periods when strong currents oppose the wind.

Micro-Climatic Conditions
Since wind forecasts usually cover a wide general area and are given for the strongest winds expected, local winds—influenced by the topography of an area—may vary significantly from the forecast. We frequently hear stories of boats that stay put far longer than they need to because of small craft warnings or high wind notices. Weather forecasts are conservative by nature. You won't hear one calling for a beautiful calm day; instead, it forecasts the worst weather expected to occur any time during that period.

Corner wind is the effect of increased wind speed when a wind blows past a headland, such as off Point Conception, Cape Mendocino, Point Reyes and the like. A corner wind is usually stronger than that experienced on either side of its land-mass.

Gap winds (or **funnel winds**) are caused by a funneling effect between islands—such as those occurring in Santa Barbara Channel, the Golden Gate, and at Cape Flattery. When gap winds blow against tidal currents, they can cause dangerous, steep, breaking waves.

Lee effect occurs along a steep shoreline where a turbulent and gusty offshore wind meets an opposing wind at the top of a cliff. Reversed eddies, along with onshore winds, may create confused, steep seas along the base of the cliffs.

During periods of moderate prevailing winds, **sea breezes** blow from sea toward land during the heat of the day (usually in the afternoon). The prevailing inflow and afternoon sea breeze can combine to reach 20 to 30 knots. Sea breezes may contribute to the prevalence of summer forecasts of moderately strong afternoon winds. These winds may intimidate a skipper new to the area who interprets them as winds that arrive in advance of a low-pressure front. Check forecasts and your barometer to verify whether they are prevailing afternoon sea breezes or a more serious change requiring you to seek alternative shelter.

Land breezes blow from land toward sea during the night and can be gusty, but—except for outflow winds—their velocity is usually less than that of a sea breeze. Both sea and land breezes die quickly, as does the chop they generate.

Anabatic winds, caused by rising warm air, are upslope winds that occur during the daytime near valleys and inlets.

Katabatic winds—downslope winds occurring at night (also known as **williwaws**)—are caused by falling cool air. These winds, which are usually stronger than upslope winds, often blast down a valley or gully below high ridges, giving you good reason to set your anchor well on an otherwise calm evening. Williwaws can reach frightening velocities when the sides of a fjord are steep and capped by ice or snow; they are usually of short (but intense) duration and they may affect just a small area. Since they are cyclonic in nature, the actual direction of a williwaw varies, and it can frequently be seen whipping up chop or foam wherever it hits the water. Williwaws require high mountains and are mostly found in the high latitudes.

Surge winds are strong winds generated occasionally in the summer during periods of high barometric readings (1010 to 1015 millibars). These winds disturb the stable weather of the Pacific Coast and can surprise a cruising boat. Caused by a lee trough which forms off the coast during a period of prolonged thermal heating of the interior land mass, this phenomenon causes prevailing light easterlies adjacent to the coast, but it can cause gale-force northwesterlies farther offshore. A more potentially dangerous condition called **stratus surge** occurs when a larger lee trough off northern California shoots north along the Oregon and Washington coasts, picking up speed as it surges, and bringing with it low clouds and fog. During a stratus surge, winds shift abruptly from light easterlies to southerlies of gale force or stronger; they can strike suddenly without much movement in the barometer, but they bring a sharp drop in air temperature. Local fishermen call these fog winds and, other than fog or low, dark stratus clouds from the south, there are no reliable signs of their approach. However, when such conditions do occur, they are usually forecast on the continuous weather broadcasts.

If you are in doubt about any weather forecast, or if you witness any unusual or rapid changes in prevailing conditions that could affect the safety of your boat, call the Coast Guard on Channel 16 at once and ask for a clarification or for their assistance, if you need it. They would rather give you the information you need for making a wise decision than risk a dangerous and costly rescue.

Marine Fog

Marine fog—formed when warm Pacific air moves over relatively colder seas—causes greatly reduced visibility in the Spring in the south west coast and late summer in the Northwest making navigation dangerous. At times the Pacific Coast visibility is reduced to zero. It can be highly localized or may cover a large region. Radio chatter can give you an idea how wide an area the fog covers. The *Coast Pilot* discusses the percentages of fog experienced by different areas. Cruising boats without radar often find they have to wait until the fog burns off before they can move on. Fog can be forecast quite well as the dewpoint approaches the temperature of the environment; local marine weather stations broadcast such conditions.

Marine fog frequently forms offshore, moves inland in early evening, remains all night, and then lifts or dissipates in the late morning. Many weather stations report the highest percentage of fog in their 7 a.m. observations, the least in their 4 p.m. observations. With the lengthened hours of daylight in summer, you can frequently get a late start after the fog lifts and still maintain your planned schedule.

During foggy periods, many sportfishing and commercial boats continue to fish, creating congestion and navigational hazards (or challenges!) for cruising boats, particularly near harbor entrances and across fishing grounds. It's a good idea when you approach congested

Breaking seas in afternoon near gale

areas to station an alert lookout on your bow and to listen carefully for foghorns, bells, or the sound of other propellers. Remain especially alert in shipping channels. Ferry boats and other commercial high-speed craft rarely slow down, and there's nothing quite so alarming as hearing the horn of a large ship as it bears down on your little vessel. Good radar reflectors and radar sets are critical in these situations, as is bridge-to-bridge contact on VHF. Also don't hesitate to monitor and/or call Vessel Traffic Services for a traffic report on the shipping lanes in your area.

Radiation fog, primarily a problem in harbors and inlets, forms over land during the early mornings on windless days and generally dissipates after the sun or wind comes up. During prolonged spells of radiation fog, winds are usually (but not necessarily) light, and the seas are nearly flat.

When fog moves offshore during the day, it is called sea fog. Formed when winds are moderate, **sea fog** moves back onshore in the evening, and may persist as winds become stronger, lasting just a day, or continuing without a break for several days at a time.

Rain

Rain—associated with the passage of a frontal system accompanied by low, dark clouds often lasting for several hours at a time—reduces visibility, although usually to a lesser extent than fog. Drizzle (fine precipitation) also occurs with the passage of a front. However, it sometimes persists between frontal systems. Rain showers cover a small area for short periods and fall from cumulus clouds, the heaviest usually occurring after a front has passed and cold northwesterly winds have set in.

Southern California can go for months at a time with little or no rain. However, the Northwest coast and the Inside Passage are located in a temperate rain forest zone with 5 times or more the average rainfall of the south. Rain is less pervasive in summer than in winter, however the need for foul weather gear increases sharply as you leave Southern California waters.

Sea Conditions

"Sea" is defined as that segment of a wave riding on top of the prevailing swell. Seas are caused by local winds while swells are caused by winds whose source lies outside the local region.

Forecasts sometime use the phrases "sea-state" or "combined wind-wave and swell height," which refer to the significant height of the combined wind-wave and swell. Significant wave height is the average height of the highest one-third of all waves present. Note that waves of half the forecast value can and do occur, while an individual wave in a period of three to four hours can occur that is double the forecast value. Values for sea-state are given in feet in U.S. waters and in meters in Canadian waters. Wave height is generally in direct proportion to the distance over which the wind has been blowing (the fetch), the wind speed, and the duration of time the wind has been blowing.

The ocean swells you encounter on long passages can be alarming if you've sailed only on inside waters. Shoaling water found off some bays and rivers like San Francisco can cause the background swell to reach 8 to 12 feet. However, the length of such swell is generally about 100 yards, and while the swells may appear large, they are usually not threatening. However, if a strong ebb current meets a moderate southwest or west wind, the seas heap up and are much closer together, causing an uncomfortable wet ride and can become a threat to small craft. It is best to avoid these conditions if possible or slow down considerably and move out of the fast-moving water.

Tides

In general, the farther north you go, or the farther removed you are from the open ocean, the greater the tidal range. The tidal range in Southern California is a few feet but in Glacier Bay, Alaska and heads of remote inlets, an extreme tidal range of well over 20 feet is not uncommon. As standard daily procedure, especially when anchoring, check tide tables and allow for changes in tide levels (as well as their associated currents)!

Steep Waves

A wave becomes steeper near shore, or when a current flows opposite to the direction of the wave. It is this steepness that presents the most danger for small craft.

All the major bays and rivers along the coast are subject to steep waves when ebb currents oppose the wind. (See our notes on *Baidarka* at Eureka.) We have seen three wind waves roughly double in height and steepen to the breaking point when the tide and current changed to ebb current of several knots; this condition is the primary reason for loss of boats off the entrance to the Columbia River.

A current flowing in the same direction as the wind has the opposite effect; swell height is diminished and the period lengthened, cutting the steepness dramatically. When the current is unfavorable, it's a good idea to hole up for a few hours, rather than stressing your boat and crew unnecessarily.

Narrows and Rapids

Uncomfortable or dangerous seas can also be found in tidal narrows and rapids and across channel or inlet bars. Rips are turbulent agitation of the water caused by the interaction of currents and wind waves. In shallow water, irregular bottom rips can create short, breaking waves. These conditions are common in the Northwest. Deception Pass, south of Anacortes, is a good place to observe this phenomena which occurs all the way up the Inside Passage. Overfalls are areas of turbulent water caused by currents setting over submerged ridges or shoals. A severe overfall can produce a sharp rise or fall in water level and may even create whirlpools. Short, closely spaced standing waves ("dancing waters") are also seen where currents meet. A small boat may be tossed from side to side in overfalls. Note the indications of rips and overfalls on the nautical chart and heed the warnings and instructions in the U.S. *Coast Pilot* or the Canadian *Sailing Directions*. The key is to plan your passage through critical narrows or rapids to occur at, or near, slack water to reduce the effect of overfalls and turbulent water.

Strategies for Coping with the Variables of Weather

If we haven't made you paranoid and wanting to stay home, here are a few tips that may allow you to keep moving up or down the coast with confidence:

1. Monitor weather broadcasts on VHF (or on continuous recordings by telephone) *before* you arrive in a critical area, and pay particular attention to the key area (automatic weather buoy) and the adjacent areas to give you an idea of the state and speed of any approaching front.

Pelican and seagulls guard San Luis pier

2. Monitor actual conditions at buoys or lighthouses and reporting stations to see if the forecast is indeed materializing. Since forecasts are given for the worst weather expected over a certain area during the period, you may frequently encounter lesser conditions on your actual route.

3. Track and record barometric pressure, wind direction and strength, cloud cover and sea conditions onboard your vessel and develop your own skills for monitoring and interpreting weather. Use every opportunity to check your findings against what is being reported and what you observe.

4. Maintain radio schedules with cruising boats that are ahead or behind you, and monitor their inter-boat transmissions on working channels to get a sense of the weather conditions over the horizon. Break in to ask for a report of local conditions from time to time if conditions are deteriorating.

5. Delay or advance your daily runs to arrive at critical passages, such as crossing the Columbia River Bar, when stable conditions are expected. We find that, under normal conditions, starting early in the day (near sunrise with due regard for favorable tidal currents) gives us an advantage before prevailing winds kick up. Be sure your boat is shipshape and secure prior to your departure.

6. Prepare alternative plans for anchorage in case the weather and seas exceed your expectations, and prepare for the possibility you may need to stay at sea overnight and don't be afraid to implement these changes.

7. In critical passages, talk with Coast Guard (via Channel 16 and working Channel 22A) about weather updates, and solicit their recommendations if you need to, particularly if unexpected changes occur.

8. We have found that cruise ships that pass several miles ahead of us are frequently happy to give us factual on-site reports that are useful.

9. Turn around and head back to a safe place anytime weather or boat conditions become marginal for any reason. A sudden warm and dry Santa Ana wind from the east along the coast near Ventura is a good example to make haste for a good lee.

Caroline Buchanan has written:

The power and the danger of a storm…
Carries a threat that makes you sorry to hear
        the rising wind…
Even tho' there is a beauty that fills you with
        awe….

If all else fails, slow down, take defensive measures, and experience the awesomeness of nature along the Pacific Coast.

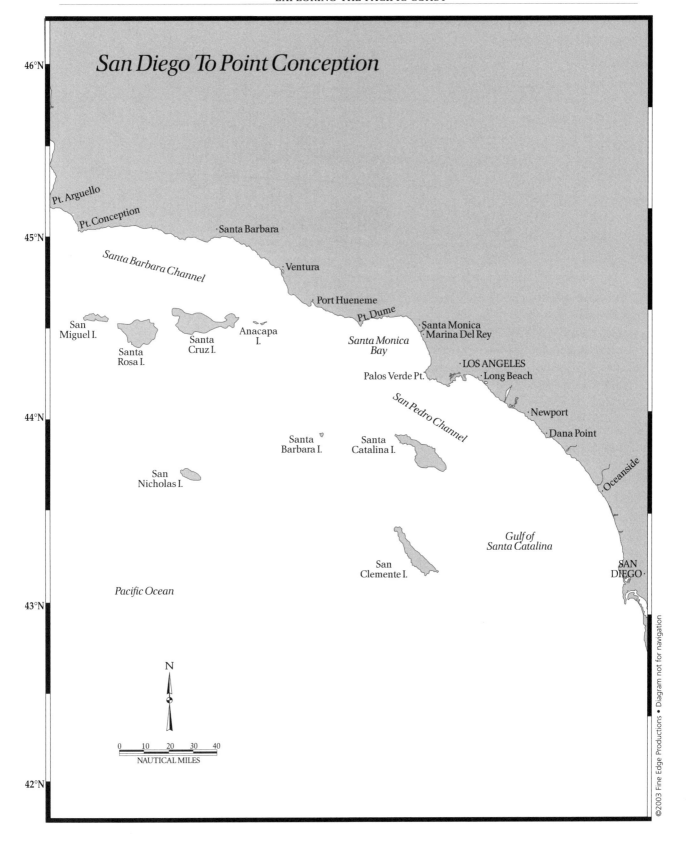

San Diego To Point Conception

1

Southern California Mainland Coast: San Diego Bay to Point Conception

Dramatic bluffs, white sand beaches, a moderate climate and largely sheltered waters make Southern California's unique 240-mile-long coastline some of the premier cruising waters in the country. The shape of the coast, curving east and south, is such that a sea breeze generally keeps winter temperatures more moderate than those inland, and summer temperatures lower. Notable exceptions to this pattern are outflow gale-force Santa Ana winds—common from October to March—and infrequent southeasterly storms that bring moisture to this otherwise arid climate. North of Santa Monica, sea fog frequently occurs in summer and fall; south of Santa Monica it occurs in fall and winter.

From San Diego to Oceanside the coast trends due north and begins a gentle northwest curve to Ventura, where it turns due west to Point Conception. This huge arc shelters much of Southern California from the prevailing northwest winds and swells prevalent the length of the coast between Point Conception and the Strait of Juan de Fuca.

South and east of Point Conception, a benign back eddy caused by the naturally arcing coastline, allows boats to sail here for years without experiencing more than an occasional gale such as the notorious downslope Santa Ana wind, or the tail end of a southeasterly playing itself out on its way north from Mexico. The limits of Southern California's cruising grounds are considered to lie between the northern border of Baja and Point Conception; it is within this area that seas diminish, causing boaters to remove their foul weather gear and reach for dark glasses and suntan oil.

Along the coast of Southern California, twelve developed harbors provide secure moorage, as well as extensive facilities and services for boaters: Oceanside, Dana Point, Newport Beach, Huntington Harbour, Alamitos Bay, Long Beach Harbor (Alamitos Bay), Los Angeles Harbor, King Harbor, Marina del Rey, Channel Islands Harbor, Ventura Harbor, and Santa Barbara. All are easily accessible to one another by a simple one- or two-day trip and all offer outstanding opportunities for rest, relaxation, exploration, or entertainment. This yachting paradise is protected on its south flank by the eight Channel Islands that lie from 10 to 40 miles offshore. San Clemente, Santa Catalina, Santa Barbara, and San Nicolas—grouped southwest of Los Angeles—break up the ubiquitous southwest swells originating from the tropical regions; while the northerly islands—Anacapa, Santa Cruz, Santa Rosa and San Miguel—shelter the Santa Barbara Channel. With the exception of Catalina, the Channel Islands retain, for the most part, their natural wilderness environment, lacking in development.

The four northerly islands, along with Santa Barbara Island, are included within the Channel Islands National Park and Marine Sanctuary and, along with Catalina Island, are major cruising destinations. Several of the islands are military reservations with restricted access, while others are privately owned or managed. (See Chapter 2 for details.)

Southern California yachting is a year-round activity. Spring and summer are full of shoreside entertainment, sailboat races, visits to the local islands, or departure time for the Hawaiian Islands. Fall and winter bring out boaters eager to sight whales on their migrating routes, as well as southbound "snowbirds" heading for Baja, the Marquesas or beyond.

For local navigation regulations, military restriction areas, climatologic, and meteorologi-

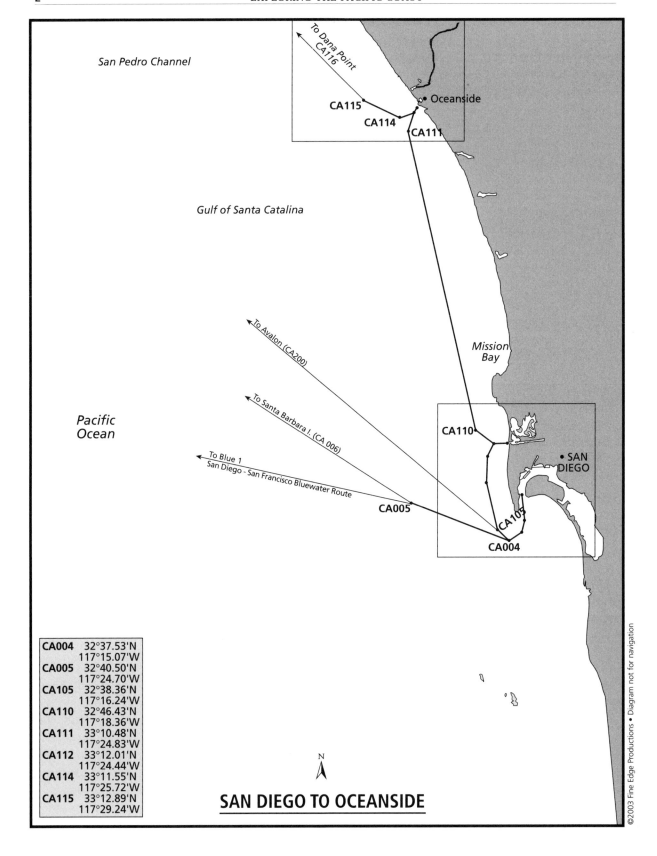

San Pedro Channel

Gulf of Santa Catalina

Pacific
Ocean

To Dana Point
CA116

CA115
CA114
CA111

• Oceanside

Mission
Bay

CA110

To Avalon (CA200)

To Santa Barbara I. (CA 006)

To Blue 1
San Diego - San Francisco Bluewater Route

• SAN
DIEGO

CA005

CA105
CA004

CA004	32°37.53'N
	117°15.07'W
CA005	32°40.50'N
	117°24.70'W
CA105	32°38.36'N
	117°16.24'W
CA110	32°46.43'N
	117°18.36'W
CA111	33°10.48'N
	117°24.83'W
CA112	33°12.01'N
	117°24.44'W
CA114	33°11.55'N
	117°25.72'W
CA115	33°12.89'N
	117°29.24'W

N

SAN DIEGO TO OCEANSIDE

cal information, please consult the current *Coast Pilot* and Notices to Mariners, available wherever nautical books and charts are sold. Or view and print out these publications at no cost by links provided on the Fine Edge website at www.FineEdge.com.

We have included our Proven Cruising Routes© for harbor approaches and entrances; these GPS waypoints can help you identify the main channels in otherwise confusing surroundings.

San Diego Bay

Charts 18773, 18765
Outer Entrance: (CA004) 32°37.53'N,
117°15.07'W
Inner Entrance: (CA001) 32°41.19'N,
117°13.85'W

The mild climate from San Diego to Point Arguello is controlled by the Pacific high-pressure system. This well-known phenomenon brings many northern boaters south for the winter or to outfit for a winter season in Mexico. Aided by the sea breeze, it brings winds from off the water, mainly S through N, that help keep coastal temperatures up in winter and down in summer. Coldest average temperatures range from the middle to upper fifties (12.8° to 15.0°C), while summertime readings are most often in the seventies (22° to 16°C). Occasionally a hot dry flow off the land in autumn causes temperatures to soar into the nineties (33° to 38°C), and a rare winter outbreak from the E can drop temperatures to below freezing (<0°C). Winter is the rainy season, although not much rain falls along these coasts. Strong winds and rough seas, while less frequent than farther N, can be a problem from the middle of fall through late spring. Strong pressure gradients, distant storms, and infrequent close storms account for most of the gales and seas of 12 feet (3.7 m) or more, particularly off Point Arguello and in the Santa Barbara Channel. Strong local winds (Santa

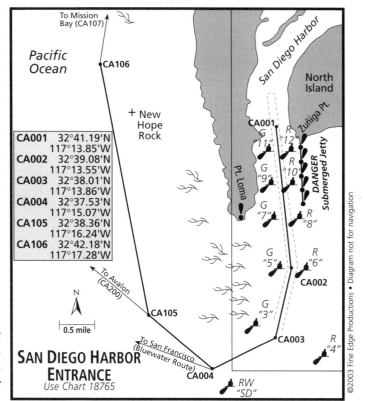

CA001	32°41.19'N
	117°13.85'W
CA002	32°39.08'N
	117°13.55'W
CA003	32°38.01'N
	117°13.86'W
CA004	32°37.53'N
	117°15.07'W
CA105	32°38.36'N
	117°16.24'W
CA106	32°42.18'N
	117°17.28'W

©2003 Fine Edge Productions • Diagram not for navigation

Aerial view: San Diego Bay Harbor

Ana) also generate gales along sections of this coast. Advection or sea fog, formed by warm moist air flowing over cool water, frequently confronts mariners in these waters. It is a persistent and widespread problem, particularly in the summer and fall N of Santa Monica, and in fall and winter S of Santa Monica. San Diego Bay, where California's maritime history began in 1542, is 10 miles northwest of the Mexican boundary. In September of that year, Juan Rodriguez Cabrillo, the Spanish explorer, sailed his frail bark into the bay. The bay is considered one of the finest natural harbors in the world, and affords excellent protection in any weather; it is free of excessive tidal current movements. A low, narrow sandspit, which

David J. Shuler

Approaching Pt. Loma from west with kelp patch in foreground

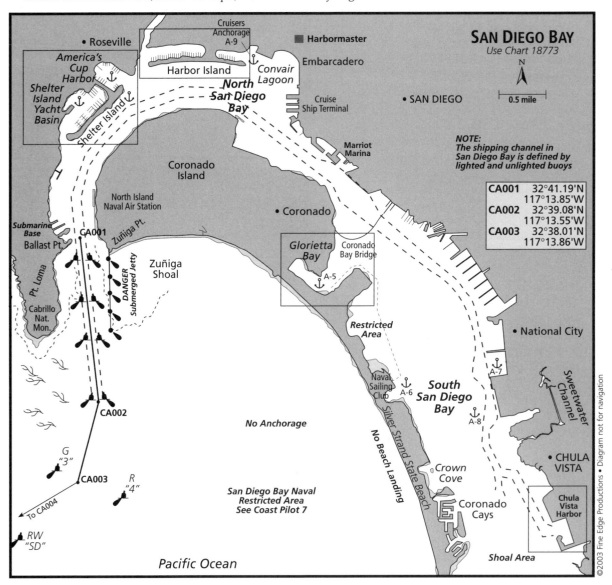

SAN DIEGO BAY
Use Chart 18773

N

0.5 mile

NOTE:
The shipping channel in San Diego Bay is defined by lighted and unlighted buoys

CA001	32°41.19'N	117°13.85'W
CA002	32°39.08'N	117°13.55'W
CA003	32°38.01'N	117°13.86'W

• Roseville

• Harbormaster

America's Cup Harbor

Cruisers Anchorage A-9

Embarcadero

Harbor Island

Convair Lagoon

Shelter Island Yacht Basin

North San Diego Bay

Shelter Island

• SAN DIEGO

Cruise Ship Terminal

Marriot Marina

Coronado Island

North Island Naval Air Station

• Coronado

Submarine Base
Ballast Pt.

CA001

Zuñiga Pt.

DANGER Submerged Jetty

Zuñiga Shoal

Pt. Loma

Glorietta Bay

Coronado Bay Bridge

A-5

Cabrillo Nat. Mon.

Restricted Area

• National City

Sweetwater Channel

CA002

Naval Sailing Club

A-6

South San Diego Bay

A-7

A-8

No Anchorage

G "3"

CA003

R "4"

Silver Strand State Beach

No Beach Landing

Crown Cove

• CHULA VISTA

Chula Vista Harbor

TO CA004

San Diego Bay Naval Restricted Area See Coast Pilot 7

Coronado Cays

RW "SD"

Pacific Ocean

Shoal Area

© 2003 Fine Edge Productions • Diagram not for navigation

expands to a width of 1.6 miles at North Island on its NW end, separates the bay from the ocean. Point Loma, on the W side of the entrance to San Diego Bay, is a ridged peninsula with heights of about 400'. The ridge is bare of trees except in the gullies and where planted around the houses near the summit, and is sparsely covered with grass, sagebrush and cactus. . . . At a distance the point usually has the appearance of an island.

Dangers. There are numerous wrecks and obstructions in the shallow area of SE San Diego Bay. Caution should be exercised when navigating outside the marked channels.

Quarantine, customs, immigration, and agriculture quarantine. Pleasure craft and yachts subject to such inspections can make arrangements through the harbor police at Shelter Island. Officials usually board documented vessels at their berths. Small commercial vessels and fishing boats are boarded at the Broadway Pier. Pleasure craft are boarded at the police berth at Shelter Island. (CP, 3rd Ed.)

San Diego skyline

Note: During times of heightened security, the Coast Guard maintains security zones around naval and other strategic facilities, and areas adjacent to cruise ships and associated vessels. Check Chart 18773 for numerous security and restricted zones along both shores and, basically, avoid all naval facilities. Generally, boaters must stay at least 100 yards away from naval vessels and reduce speed when transiting in close proximity to such vessels moving through the bay. Please contact authorities for current details.

Dense kelp forests extend along Point Loma from Mission Bay south in depths to 100 feet, extending to about 1.5 miles from shore. Southbound mariners are advised to stay well out of the kelp and, as indicated in our Proven Cruising Routes, to plot courses to the sea buoy ("SD") before turning into the entrance channel. The sea buoy is approximately three miles from the end of Point Loma. Stay generally west of longitude 117°17.5'W until you reach latitude 32°40.0'N. From this position, alter course either to the sea buoy (red/white striped "SD") or to buoy "3." At times kelp is scattered south and east of these lines, floating free on the surface. The actual kelp forest, however, stops just north of buoy "3"; if you proceed with a good lookout, you should be able to avoid any serious problems.

Note: Zuñiga Jetty, on the east side of the entrance channel to San Diego Bay, is partially submerged during all but the lowest tides; it appears as a series of rock "islands" in a straight line extending southward from Zuñiga Point. Each island is lighted with a white light. At no time should a boater attempt to pass between the lights when entering or exiting the bay. There have been serious accidents here over the years.

Once in the channel, follow the buoy line through the narrows at Ballast Point (32°41.2'N, 117°13.9'W); north of the point the channel begins to widen,

Pt. Loma with Coast Guard on patrol

allowing passage further outside the dredged channel. Immediately east of Ballast Point, a submerged jetty extends westward from North Island toward the entrance channel. The actual depth of the jetty is not noted, but it is the cause of numerous groundings by recreational vessels. The area, which has several small warning buoys, is adjacent to the Navy's degaussing range, which is marked by red-and-white striped poles.

Note: San Diego Bay is an area where numerous large naval vessels, car carriers, and cruise ships regularly transit the dredged channel. Recreational vessels are required by Rule 9 of the ColRegs to stay clear of these vessels and not to impede their passage. Rule 9 is heavily enforced, and all recreational vessels are on notice to comply. The penalties for non-compliance are substantial.

Vessels coming into the United States from foreign ports must check in with Customs at the Harbor Patrol dock on the southern tip of Shelter Island, just inside the Yacht Basin. Since the spring of 2001, Customs officials have been enforcing this requirement for vessels that have been in Mexican waters, even if they made no landfalls. If in doubt, check in with Customs.

San Diego has an active sport-fishing fleet. Most of the boats pick up their passengers at docks in America's Cup Harbor (known as the "Commercial Basin"). These boats, averaging 75 feet long, are usually running fast and tend to run the shortest line out of the bay, regardless of how many boats are out or what kind they are. At night they frequently keep their halogen deck lights on as they leave or enter the harbor, presenting a vision hazard to other boaters. Whenever possible, give them a wide berth.

The area between the A-4 mooring area (just east of the Coronado end of the bridge) and the barge moorings is relatively shallow. Avoid crossing under the bridge between columns 10 through 14 unless the tide is high or your draft is less than four feet.

The southern portion of San Diego Bay, south of the Coronado Bridge, tends to be quite shallow. As much as possible, stay within the marked channels, and watch your depths. This is particularly important when approaching Chula Vista. The channel buoys are not always obvious and the adjacent depths can be abruptly less than 3 feet.

When transiting under the bridge, be prepared for significant wind shifts. The bridge columns are all numbered and marked with controlling depths. Passage is safe between the columns north of column "14," as long as you anticipate the effects of wind shifts.

Immediately south of the bridge, on the west side of the dredged channel, a green buoy (Fl G 4s "1") frequently confuses boaters new to the area. It is the outermost buoy leading into the entrance channel for Glorietta Bay. If you are continuing into the south bay, keep this buoy to your right. If, however, you are entering Glorietta Bay, keep this buoy to your left. A shoal area roughly square in shape lies adjacent to the Glorietta Bay channel and extends to a line drawn between red buoy "26" and the pier extending eastward from the southeast corner of the Navy facility. This is another area to avoid except at maximum high tide or in a shallow-draft vessel.

Shelter Island Yacht Basin

Chart 18773; 2.6 mi N of Point Loma
Entrance (W of lower range mark FG light & vertical RW stripe daymarks): 32°42.74'N, 117°14.03'W
Anchor (La Playa Cove) Anch A-1: 32°42.93'N, 117°13.83'W (Fri-Mon morn only)
Harbor Patrol and Customs dock position: 32°42.53'N, 117°14.11'W

Marinas on Shelter Island

David J. Shuler

Shelter Island. . . includes the Shelter Island Yacht Basin on the S and the America's Cup Harbor on the N. Shelter Island is the most important small-boat area in San Diego Bay. The yacht basin has several large marinas and yacht clubs. It can accommodate more than 2,000 boats at its piers, floats, and moorings. The entrance channel has depths of 20 feet to inside the entrance, thence 15 feet to most of the facilities; the least depth is 9 feet. The entrance is marked by buoys and a light. The 353° lighted range marking the entrance to San Diego Bay also marks the approach to the entrance to Shelter Island Yacht Basin. The harbor police are at the Harbor Control Headquarters just inside the entrance to the yacht basin. The police dock is also the boarding station for the inspection of small craft by Customs, Public Health, Immigration and Agricultural quarantine personnel when such inspections are necessary. Harbor police boats, providing fire protection, law enforcement, and assistance to small boats in distress, operate from this facility on a 24-hour basis. Overnight berths for transient vessels are usually available at one of the marinas; if no such berth is available, temporary mooring or berthing may be made available through the harbor police. . . . In September 1988, several uncharted dangerous wrecks were reported about 0.4 mile SW of the entrance to the basin. (CP, 33rd Ed.)

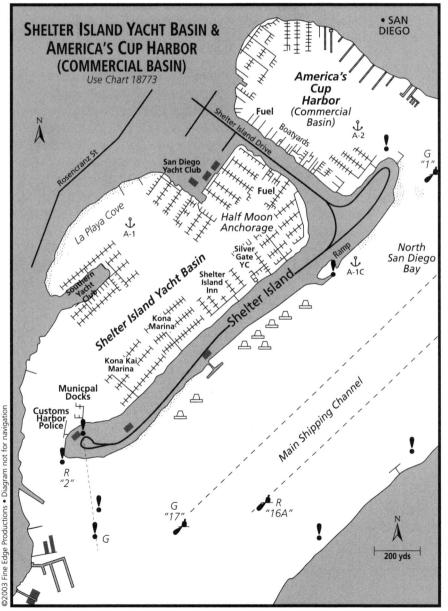

Shelter Island has the largest concentration of marine facilities and services in San Diego. Half a dozen boatyards line the north side of Shelter Island Drive (America's Cup Harbor), providing just about every kind of haul-out and yard work imaginable. The southern arm of the island (actually a peninsula) protects the Shelter Island Yacht Basin from the effects of traffic in the bay. The yacht basin is home to four yacht clubs and as many marinas. A fuel dock is located at the northeast end of the yacht basin; position: 32°43.20'N, 117°13.55W.

Both ends of Shelter Island have large shoal areas. Stay well clear of the marks and follow the entry channels into both the Yacht Basin and America's Cup Harbor. *Note:* Although the charts show a deeper channel close to the south end of Shelter Island through the shoal, its position is not exact. *Use extreme caution if you elect to try this channel.*

Anchor: La Playa Cove (A-1) is a popular weekend anchorage, available from 0900 on Friday until 0900 on Monday. The anchorage area is located midway between the San Diego Yacht Club (large brown club house on east) and the Southwestern Yacht Club. Contact the San Diego Mooring Office for information regarding anchoring and for permits. During holiday weekends, La Playa Anchorage fills rapidly and permits may not be available for late arrivals.

Launch Ramp: Shelter Island has the only launch ramp north of the Coronado Bridge and is about three miles from open sea. The ramp has 10 lanes and is open 24 hours a day. Use is free, and there is ample parking. From I-5 southbound, exit on Rosecrans. Turn left at Shelter Island Drive, then turn right at the traffic circle and look for the signs. From I-5 northbound, exit at Pacific Highway. Turn left at Barnett, then left again at Rosecrans and proceed as above.

⚓ **Gold Coast Anchorage** position: 32°43.20'N, 117°13.50'W; slips available occasionally, reservations required; tel: 619.225.0588 daily 0900 to 1700; website: www.fraseryachts.com

⚓ **Half Moon Anchorage** position: 32°43.05'N, 117°13.56'W; reservations required; tel: 619.225.0588

⚓ **Island Palms Marina** position: 32°42.91'N, 117°13.73'W; reservations required; tel: 619.223.0301; www.islandpalms.com

⚓ **Kona Kai Marina** position: 32°42.72'N, 117°13.96'W; reservations required; tel: 619.224.7547 daily 0830 to 1700

⚓ **Kona Marina** position: 32°42.80'N, 117°13.86'W; reservations required; tel: 619.224.7547 daily 0830 to 1700

⚓ **San Diego Yacht Club** position: 32°42.99'N, 117°13.76'W

⚓ **Southwestern Yacht Club** position: 32°42.87'N, 117°13.95'W

⚓ **Shelter Island Inn** position: 32°42.91'N, 117°13.73'W

America's Cup Harbor
(Commercial Basin)
Chart 18773; 1 mi NE of Hbr Patrol dock
Entrance: 32°43.17'N, 117°13.04'W
Anchorage (A-2): 32°43.27'N, 117°13.32'W

The America's Cup Harbor has accommodations for over 600 vessels and is the home port for many commercial fishing vessels. Its name derives from having hosted the race in 1995. Known locally as the Commercial Basin, this is the center for repairs and maintenance. Repair yards in the basin have marine railways that can handle craft up to 800 tons. Custom sails, canvas, fiberglass, electronic, and repairs for all types of small vessels and equipment can be obtained here. A fuel dock is located on the southwest side of the basin; position: 32°43.27'N, 117°13.57'W.

Shelter Cove Marina position: 32°43.21'N, 117°13.34'W

Anchorage can be found in Anchorage A-2, avoiding the numerous mooring buoys (32°43.27'N, 117°13.32'W).

Harbor Island West Basin
Charts 18773; 1.4 mi NE of Harbor Patrol dock
Entrance: 32°43.39'N, 117°12.86'W

Harbor Island West Basin has berthing and mooring accommodations for nearly 1,600 craft. A number of marinas, hotels, restaurants, and shops are along the shore of the basin. A light shows from atop a building near the W end of the island. (CP, 33rd Ed.)

Both Harbor Island and Shelter Island are man-made from material dredged out of the main channel and are actually joined to the mainland by wide causeways. Harbor Island is the newer of the two. The white light shown on the charts

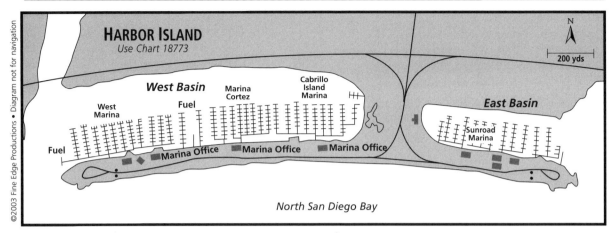

is actually located on top of a restaurant designed to look like a lighthouse, known as Tom Hamm's Light House. Both ends of Harbor Island are well marked, and there are no hazards. A fuel dock is located on the west end of Harbor Island.

⚓ **Cabrillo Island Marina** position: 32°43.65'N, 117°12.06'W; 455 slips 28 to 56 ft, reservations required; tel: 619.297.6222; website: www.cabrilloisle.com

⚓ **Harbor Island West Marina** position: 32°43.60'N, 117°12.71'W; 604 slips 25 to 60 ft, reservations required based on space availability; fuel dock on site; tel: 619.291.6440 daily 0830 to 1700

⚓ **Marina Cortez** position: 32°43.65'N, 117°12.33'W; no guest slips; tel: 619.291.5985

⚓ **Sheraton East Hotel and Marina;** no guest slips; tel: 619.692.2249

⚓ **Harbor Island East Basin** entrance: 32°43.45'N, 117°11.19'W

⚓ **Sunroad Resort Marina** position: 32°43.58'N, 117°11.30'W; 30 to 65 ft; end ties to 103 ft; reservations required based on space availability; tel: 619.574.0736 daily from 0800 to 1700; website: www.sdmarina.com

⚓ **Marriott Marina** entrance: 32°42.29'N, 117°10.00'W; 445 slips 25 to 83 ft with end ties to 130 feet; reservations required; swimming pool and Jacuzzi; tel: 619.291.8955; website: www.sdmarriottmarina@marriott.com

Cruisers' Anchorage (A-9 Anchorage)
Chart 18773; 3 mi NE of Harbor Patrol dock
Position: 32°43.47'N, 117°10.69'W

A-9 Anchorage, known locally as Cruisers Anchorage, is a small anchorage off the east end of Harbor Island, adjacent to the Coast Guard station. Contact the San Diego Mooring Office for permits. Maximum stay is three months. Holding is good over a somewhat muddy bottom. The anchorage is fully exposed to wakes

Star of India

and other effects of traffic on the bay. It is also close to the point at which aircraft departing Lindbergh Field make maximum noise, so it may not be a peaceful place to stay. Also, boats here tend to get dirty very quickly from the exhaust and aerosol jet fuels in the air.

The Laurel Street and Embarcadero moorings east of the Cruisers' Anchorage are rented to permanent tenants only. There are no transient moorings anywhere in the bay. All moorings are handled by the San Diego Mooring Office.

Tuna Harbor (1.1 mi SE of Harbor Isl)
Entrance: 32°42.55'N, 117°10.42'W

Tuna Harbor is closed to recreational boats and there are no shoreside facilities.

Glorietta Bay
Charts 18773; 1 mi SW of Coronado Bridge
Entrance, G buoy "1": 32°41.21'N, 117°09.23'W
Position: 32°40.82'N, 117°10.39'W
Anchor (A-5): 32°40.71'N, 117°10.13'W

Glorietta Bay, on the S side of Coronado and 6 miles from Ballast Point, is a small-craft harbor occupied by a yacht club and a small marina. The facilities include berths for over 215 yachts and small craft. A channel marked by lighted and unlighted buoys and a 232° lighted range leads from the main channel in San Diego Bay to the basin in Glorietta Bay. In February 1981, the reported centerline controlling depth in the channel was 13 feet, thence depths of 8 to 10 feet were reported in the basin except for lesser depths along the edges. A 5 mph speed limit is enforced in Glorietta Bay. Water, ice, and a launching ramp are available. (CP, 33rd Ed)

Boat Delivery—Next Time Tell Them the Plan!
by Ann Kinner

A couple of weeks ago I broke one of my own rules while delivering some new boaters and their first boat to their slip in San Diego. We arrived in the dark after a long cold, squally day. As we approached the marina, I made a quick request for dock lines and fenders to be deployed and moved to the fly bridge to bring the boat into the slip. As I focused on maneuvering into a crosswind slip with a downwind neighbor—one of those wonderful double slips we have in San Diego—the new owners started rigging the landing gear, she at the bow and he at the stern.

I brought the boat to the dock and, before I could tell them what to do next, she had stepped off the boat and was putting a strain on the bow line. He—still on board—tried his best but couldn't reach the dock cleat with the stern line. So, boats being cantankerous as they are on occasion, we started to pivot toward the downwind neighbor without any fenders rigged on either boat for cushioning.

I made a hasty trip down the ladder, grabbed the boat hook and gently pushed us away from the other boat and back toward the dock. By this time a helpful gentleman from another boat took charge of the stern line and secured us where we belonged.

The new owners were happy to be docked, to meet some neighbors, and to get shore power—and the heater—plugged in. I was relieved that nothing drastic had happened and I made a mental note to do a better job of prepping my crew next time I needed their cooperation.

Another delivery by Ann Kinner

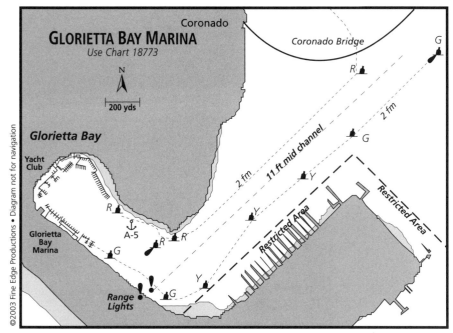

⚓ **Coronado Yacht Club** position: 32°40.88'N, 117°10.43'W; 150 slips for Yacht Club guests only

⚓ **Fiddler's Cove** position: 32°39.20'N, 117°08.85'W; (2.1 mi SE of Glorietta Bay). This small cove and marina is home to the San Diego Naval Sailing Club and open to military personnel only.

Anchor: No permit is required to anchor in Glorietta Bay in anchorage A-5. The anchorage is on the northeast side, near the golf course for a maximum of 72 hours. Depths are 15 feet over a muddy bottom with good holding.

Glorietta Bay, a popular weekend destination within the bay, is home to the Coronado Yacht Club. Downtown Coronado is within walking distance of the docks around the perimeter. One of the city's premier attractions, the Hotel Del Coronado, lies on the Silver Strand just north of Glorietta Bay.

When approaching Glorietta Bay from the Coronado Bridge, stay well within the marked entrance channel. The area immediately north of the first red buoy ("2") is shoal. The area immediately south of the Glorietta Bay entrance channel is shoal; stay within the channel marked by the green buoys.

There are no fuel docks south of the Coronado Bridge. Vessels needing fuel should make their stop before approaching the South Bay.

The southeastern shore, south of the entrance channel, is a Naval Restricted Area; pleasure vessels are not permitted to enter.

⚓ **Launch Ramp** 3 lane with concrete dock; free

⚓ **Glorietta Bay Marina** position: 32°40.75'N, 117°10.41'W; 125 slips 20 to 60 ft; fuel dock; reservations required; tel: 619.435.5203 between 0900 and 1700

Seals on buoy #5

Crown Cove (3.1 mi SE of Glorietta Bay)
Position: 32°38.22'N, 117°08.38'W

Crown Cove, a popular boat rendezvous and rafting area, has a shoreside park with facilities. The area immediately south of Crown Cove is shoal.

San Diego Naval Sailing Club
Chart 18773; 2.2 mi SE of Glorietta Bay
Position: 32°39.20'N, 117°08.85'W

San Diego Naval Sailing Club is located just south of the Naval Restricted Area along the west side of South Bay. Special Anchorage A-6 lies outside the naval floats. Check with San Diego Harbor Police about availability (tel: 619.686.6272).

Coronado Cays (0.5 mi SE of Crown Cove)
Entrance channel (buoy #1): 32°38.33'N, 117°07.99'W

⚓ **Loews Coronado Bay Resort** (Loews Crown Isle Marina) position: 32°37.83'N, 117°08.00'W

South Bay Anchorage A-8
(2.4 mi SE of Coronado Bridge)
Position: 32°39.17'N, 117°07.63'W

The nearest anchorage to Chula Vista is west of the 24th Street pier in National City, just north of Chula Vista. Known as the A-8 anchorage, it has been characterized by a variety of derelicts and has several submerged wrecks. During 2001 many unseaworthy derelicts were removed, and remaining vessels were required to pass safety inspections to remain in the area. The anchorage continues to be a subject of legal and

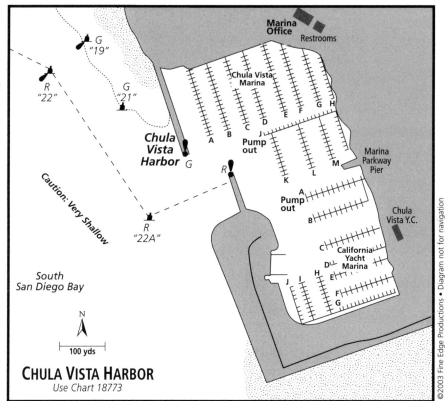

CHULA VISTA HARBOR
Use Chart 18773

©2003 Fine Edge Productions • Diagram not for navigation

safety challenges, and is probably a last-resort anchorage for most vessels. Avoid the 3-foot shoal north of the entrance to A-8 Anchorage (see Chart 18773). South of Anchorage A-8, the bay becomes progressively more shallow. Use extra care to avoid grounding.

Chula Vista Harbor
Chart 18773; 5.9 mi SE of Marriott Marina
Entrance: 32°37.39'N, 117°06.31'W

The entrance is protected by breakwaters marked at the outer ends by private lights. The entrance channel and basin channel are marked by private buoys, lights, and daybeacons. In 1994, the approach to the basin had reported depths of 18 feet with 15 to 18 feet reported alongside the piers. Berthing, electricity, water, ice, sewage pump-out, nautical supplies, and a launching ramp are available. (CP, 33rd Ed.)

Chula Vista Harbor is the southernmost small-boat basin in San Diego Bay and perhaps the most difficult to get to. The approach is through a narrow dredged channel close to the east side

Ready for cruising

⚓ **California Yacht Marina** position: 32°37.35'N, 117°06.17'W; reservations required two weeks in advance; tel: 619.422.2595 from 0900 to 1700 daily; website: www.slipscym chulavista.com

A row of pilings interspersed with caution buoys extends across the South Bay from red buoy "4" to the entrance channel to Coronado Cays. These pilings carry white lights and indicate the beginning of extreme shoal areas. Do not run south of this boundary except at maximum high tide, or in a very shallow vessel. Also, when transiting to Chula Vista, take caution to stay well within the marked channel, keeping to the red side as much as possible, and watching carefully for numerous jogs and turns. This area is particularly difficult to navigate at night because the lights are dim and fall in a plane with many background lights on land.

of the bay. Immediately west of the channel, the bay is extremely shallow. The entrance to the harbor is subject to shoaling, and the buoys do not always mark the safest area. Approach slowly with great caution. When crossing through the breakwater, stay to the left side as far as possible to avoid the shoals on the south side.

Launch Ramps: The Chula Vista Boat Ramp is at the "J" Street Marina Park. There is ample trailer parking, picnic facilities, and restrooms. Use of the ramp is free. From I-5 exit "J" Street and follow the signs. The ramp is on the south side of the harbor.

Another ramp in National City, just north of Chula Vista, launches into Sweetwater Channel. Exit I-5 at 24th Street to Pepper Park. The National City ramp is also free, with ample parking, restrooms, picnic facilities, trailer parking, and a fishing pier at the park.

⚓ **National City (Sweetwater Ch.) Launch Ramp** position: 32°38.97'N, 117°06.65'W

⚓ **Chula Vista Marina** position: 32°37.39'N, 117°06.31'W; 552 slips 24 to 54 ft, reservations recommended based on space availability; tel: 619.691.1860 daily 0830 to 1700; website: www.chulavistamarina.com

One of the most common grounding areas is immediately south of Sweetwater Channel. Unwary skippers who miss the warning marks and the lights (which are dim) run directly into one of the shallowest areas on the bay. Look for the large blue crane on the north side of Sweetwater Channel as a visual reference to the beginning of the hazard area. Once you are abeam the crane, look for the green buoy "41" (Fl G 4s) which marks the western corner of the shoal. If you are unable to identify the green buoy, then proceed as close to the red buoys and marks as feasible while remaining inside the channel. Be aware that there are several sharp turns in the channel and do not proceed if you are not certain of the marks.

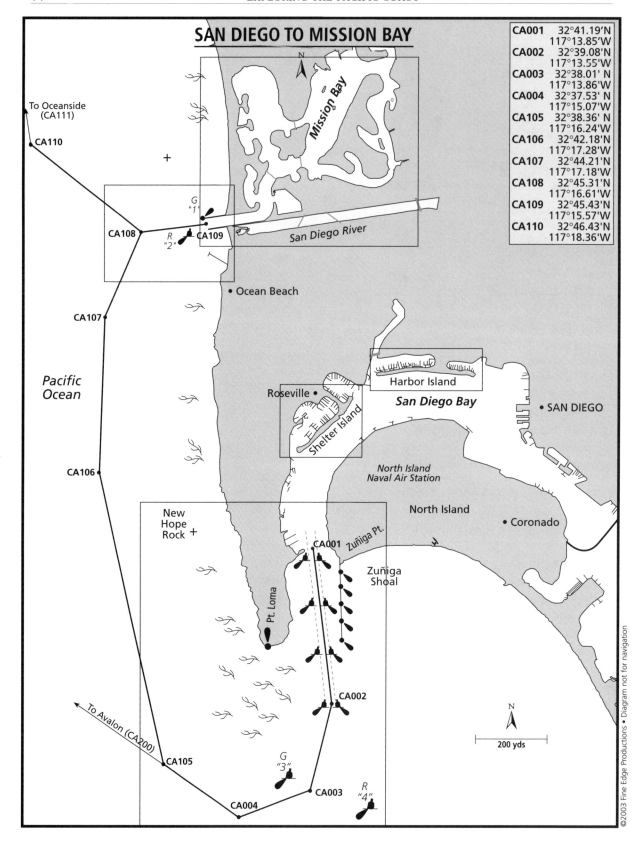

SAN DIEGO TO MISSION BAY

CA001	32°41.19'N 117°13.85'W
CA002	32°39.08'N 117°13.55'W
CA003	32°38.01' N 117°13.86'W
CA004	32°37.53' N 117°15.07'W
CA105	32°38.36' N 117°16.24'W
CA106	32°42.18'N 117°17.28'W
CA107	32°44.21'N 117°17.18'W
CA108	32°45.31'N 117°16.61'W
CA109	32°45.43'N 117°15.57'W
CA110	32°46.43'N 117°18.36'W

Mission Bay

To Oceanside (CA111)

CA110

G "1"

R "2"   CA109

CA108

San Diego River

• Ocean Beach

CA107

Pacific Ocean

Harbor Island

San Diego Bay

Roseville •

• SAN DIEGO

CA106

Shelter Island

North Island
Naval Air Station

New
Hope
Rock +

North Island

• Coronado

CA001   Zuñiga Pt.

Zuñiga
Shoal

Pt. Loma

CA002

To Avalon (CA200)

N

200 yds

CA105

G "3"

CA004

CA003

R "4"

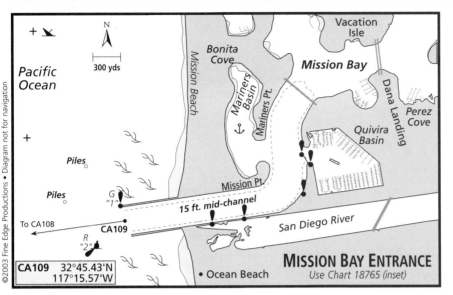

about 1 mile above the entrance. . . . It is reported that moderate to heavy swells from the W outside the entrance tend to break just inside the entrance along the S jetty. Under these conditions, the entrance is dangerous and should be made by staying in the left quarter of the channel (near the N jetty). With a rough sea outside, a heavy surge exists inside the bay, especially in Quivira Basin. Boats must be securely moored to prevent damage from this surge condition. A timber pile

Mission Bay

Chart 18765; 5.5 mi N of Point Loma
Outer Entrance: (CA108) 32°45.31'N, 117°16.61'W
Inner Entrance: (CA109) 32°45.43'N, 117°15.57'W
Anchor: 32°45.25'N, 117°14.90'W

Mission Bay . . . is a recreational small-craft harbor administered by the city of San Diego. The outer end of the S jetty is marked by a light. . . . A dredged channel leads from deep water in the Pacific Ocean to the highway bridge about 1.3 miles above the entrance. In February 1986, dangerous submerged rocks were reported in the entrance to Mission Bay in about 32°45'31"N, 117°15'29"W. Quivira Basin and Mariners Basin, on the E and W sides of the channel, respectively, are entered

Aerial view: Mission Bay

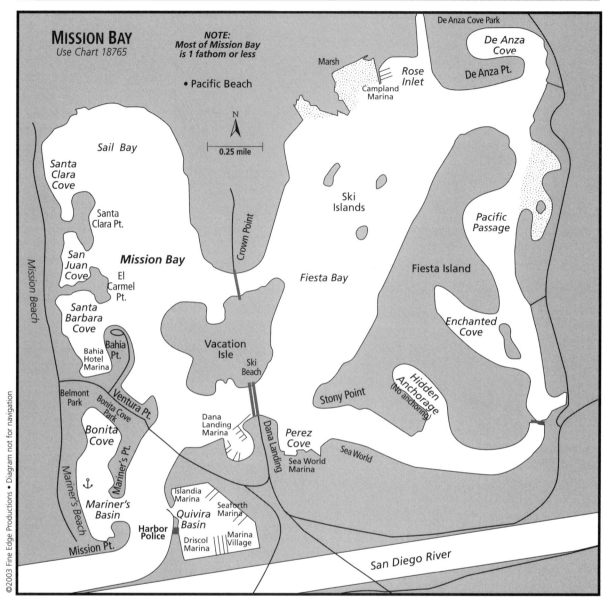

breakwater extends N from the S point of the entrance to Quivira Basin. The breakwater restricts over half of the entrance to the basin. Special anchorages are along the W side of Mission Bay in San Juan Cove, Santa Barbara Cove, Bonita Cove, Mariners Basin, and Quivira Basin. (CP, 33rd Ed.)

The Mission Bay Park headquarters and San Diego Lifeguard docks are located in Quivira Basin, south of the entrance. (The San Diego Lifeguards are available for assistance 24 hours a day and can be reached on VHF channel 16 or by calling 619.221.8800.)

When approaching Mission Bay from north or south, stay at least two miles off the coast to avoid the heavy kelp forests. Approach from due west of the entrance buoy, and stay to the left until you are in the lee of Point La Jolla and somewhat protected from the northwesterly swells. Look carefully for lobster pots, which are scattered on both sides of the entrance throughout the kelp.

The Coast Pilot understates the extent to which westerly swells affect the entrance to Mission Bay. A significant westerly swell, combined with an out-going tidal current, creates

Entrance to Mission Bay with swells running

hazardous breakers well into the channel. Check with the San Diego Lifeguards if you are approaching Mission Bay with a heavy following sea. During winter storms the entrance may be closed to navigation. Either anchor out until conditions improve or select another harbor as a destination.

At least once a year, some hapless boater puts his boat on the beach at the entrance to the concrete channel that lies immediately south of the entrance channel to Mission Bay. When approaching at night, be sure you have the proper lights in sight and that you are between the green jetty light and the red buoy light.

Important note: Although the chart indicates a flashing green light on a buoy and a flashing red light on the jetty, the actual configuration is a flashing green light on a tall tower at the end of the northern jetty. The flashing red light is on a buoy some distance west of the southern jetty. As of early November 2000, this discrepancy had not appeared in the Local Notices to Mariners for the region.

Fuel, pump-out services, bait, etc., are all available in Quivira Basin, which is opposite Mariners Basin off the main channel. There are no anchorages in Quivira Basin. Although the *Coast Pilot* discusses a "timber pile breakwater" on the Quivira Basin side of the entrance channel, this breakwater was replaced with a rip-rap stone breakwater several years ago, alleviating much of the surge within Quivira Basin. Dana Landing, approximately one quarter of a mile east of the Ventura Point Bridge on the south

side of the channel, also has a fuel dock.

Note: There is some discrepancy regarding the vertical clearances of the fixed bridges in Mission Bay. The Ventura Point Bridge is noted as having a 38-foot clearance at the center, which is consistent with local information. However, clearances for the Ingraham bridges, particularly the north bridge, may be less than those shown on the chart. One source shows the north bridge having a clearance of 35 feet, while another shows the bridge at only 29 feet. Boaters are advised to approach with caution, and, if there is any question, pass to the south of Vacation Isle when transiting into the Fiesta Bay area.

Beyond the highway bridges Mission Bay is primarily a haven for small sailboats (less than 18 feet) and a variety of powerboats and personal watercraft. Much of the bay is quite shallow, and there are few facilities for larger boats.

Seal haulout in Mission Bay

The entire area can be very congested during weekend hours.

Small boats can be launched within the bay at several locations; facilities are free.

Boat Launching Ramps:

⚓ **De Anza Cove** at the northwest corner of the bay

⚓ **South Shores Ramp**, immediately south of Hidden Anchorage is *not* an anchorage, and appears only on the most recent privately produced charts

⚓ **Dana Landing** between the bridges on the south side of the bay

⚓ **Ski Beach**, on the southeast side of Vacation Isle, north of the Ingraham Bridge

⚓ **Santa Clara Cove**, on the west side of the bay, primarily for very small boats

Marinas:

⚓ **Dana Inn Marina;** reservations required based on space availability; tel: 619.222.6440 at Dana Landing; website: www.danainn.com

⚓ **Sea World Marina;** reservations required based on space availability; tel: 619.226.3910 in Perez Cove

⚓ **Islandia Marina**; reservations required based on occasional space availability—call several days in advance; tel: 619.221.4858

⚓ **Seaforth Marina**; reservations required; tel: 619.224.6807

⚓ **Marina Village Marina**; call for space availability; tel: 619.224.3125

⚓ **Driscoll Mission Bay Marina;** reservations required based on space availability; tel: 619.221.8456; website: www.driscoll-boats.com

⚓ **Boat Yard:** Driscoll Marine operates the only boat yard in Mission Bay with haul-out facilities; tel: 619.223.5191

Place name positions:

⚓ **Quivira Basin** entrance: 32°45.76'N, 117°14.51'W

⚓ **De Anza Cove** (2800 East Mission Bay Drive, near the intersection of Clairemont Drive); entrance: 32°47.62'N, 117°12.65'W

⚓ **Dana Landing** (2590 Ingraham Street at Dana Landing Road, signalized intersection); position: 32°46.05'N, 117°14.16'W

⚓ **Perez Cove** position: 32°46.06'N, 117°13.81'W

⚓ **Fiesta Bay** position: 32°46.71'N, 117°13.66'W

⚓ **Hidden Anchorage** entrance: 32°46.08'N, 117°13.15'W

⚓ **Enchanted Cove** position: 32°46.58'N, 117°13.03'W

⚓ **Rose Inlet** entrance: 32°47.68'N, 117°13.24'W

⚓ **Sail Bay** entrance: 32°47.23'N, 117°14.79'W

⚓ **San Juan Cove** entrance: 32°46.84'N, 117°14.91'W

⚓ **Santa Barbara Cove** entrance: 32°46.61'N, 117°14.83'W

⚓ **Bonita Cove** position: 32°46.13'N, 117°14.88'W

⚓ **Mariners Basin** entrance: 32°45.77'N, 117°14.74'W

Anchor: Mariners Basin (Bonita Cove) is a comfortable anchorage to the west of the main channel into Mission Bay. Depths are two to three fathoms through the center of the basin. Avoid the east side, which gets quite shallow (less than one fathom) in the middle of the beach area. Holding is good.

Vessels may anchor temporarily during the day in San Juan Cove and Santa Barbara Cove, both of which are located north of Mariner's Basin, on the west side of Mission Bay.

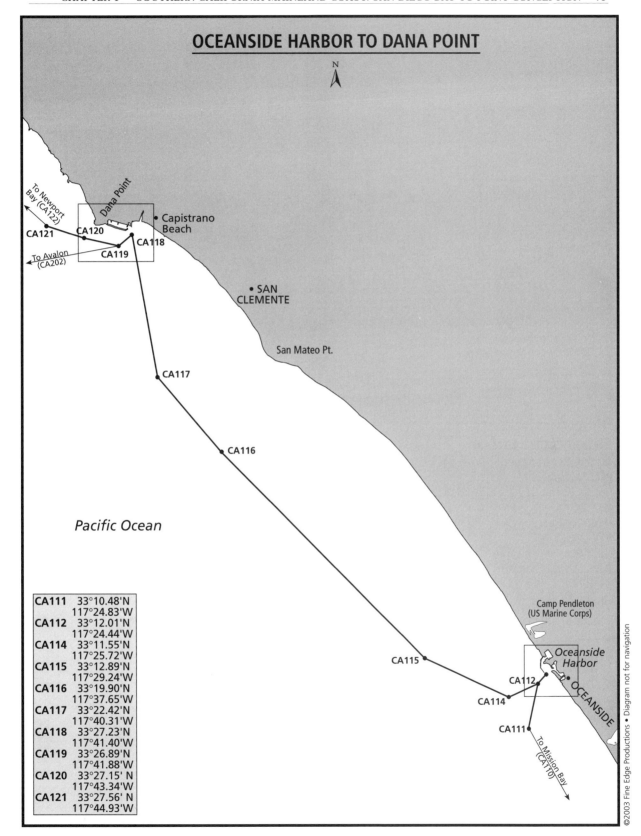

OCEANSIDE HARBOR TO DANA POINT

N

CA111	33°10.48'N
	117°24.83'W
CA112	33°12.01'N
	117°24.44'W
CA114	33°11.55'N
	117°25.72'W
CA115	33°12.89'N
	117°29.24'W
CA116	33°19.90'N
	117°37.65'W
CA117	33°22.42'N
	117°40.31'W
CA118	33°27.23'N
	117°41.40'W
CA119	33°26.89'N
	117°41.88'W
CA120	33°27.15' N
	117°43.34'W
CA121	33°27.56' N
	117°44.93'W

©2003 Fine Edge Productions • Diagram not for navigation

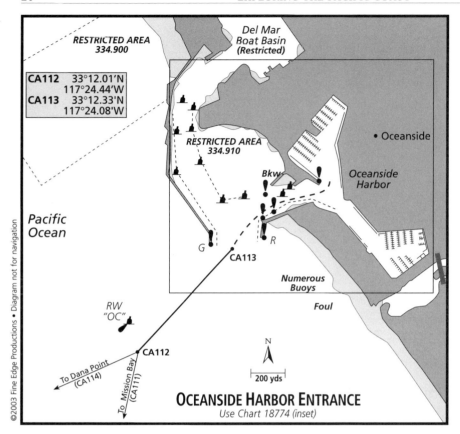

©2003 Fine Edge Productions • Diagram not for navigation

Map labels:

Del Mar Boat Basin (Restricted)

RESTRICTED AREA 334.900

| CA112 | 33°12.01'N 117°24.44'W |
| CA113 | 33°12.33'N 117°24.08'W |

RESTRICTED AREA 334.910

Pacific Ocean

Bkw

• Oceanside

Oceanside Harbor

G

R

CA113

Numerous Buoys

RW "OC"

CA112

Foul

N

To Dana Point (CA114)

To Mission Bay (CA111)

200 yds

OCEANSIDE HARBOR ENTRANCE
Use Chart 18774 (inset)

---

nal is at the S extension light. Inside the common entrance is a junction buoy separating the Oceanside Harbor entrance channel and the Del Mar Boat Basin entrance channel. About 300 yards NE of the junction buoy is an orange and white special purpose buoy with the words *"DANGER SUBMERGED JETTY."* The buoy gives warning to mariners of a submerged jetty close N of the Oceanside Harbor entrance channel.... A dredged channel leads from deep water through the entrance jetties, thence branches E to Oceanside harbor and N to Del Mar Boat

Oceanside Harbor

Charts 18774 (inset); 33.7 mi N of Point Loma
Outer Entrance: (CA112) 33°12.01'N, 117°24.44'W
Inner Entrance: (CA113) 33°12.33'N, 117°24.08'W
Del Mar Boat Basin (Camp Pendleton) restricted area entr: 33°12.74'N, 117°24.29'W

Oceanside Harbor . . . is a small-craft harbor administered by the City of Oceanside, Department of Harbor and Beaches. The harbor, which can accommodate about 800 small craft, shares a common entrance with Del Mar Boat Basin (Camp Pendleton Marine Corps Base) to the N. . . . The common entrance to Oceanside Harbor and Del Mar Boat Basin is between two jetties. The long W jetty is marked by a single light at the seaward end, and the short E jetty has a N and S extension; both extensions are marked at their ends by lights. A fog sig-

Aerial view: Oceanside Harbor

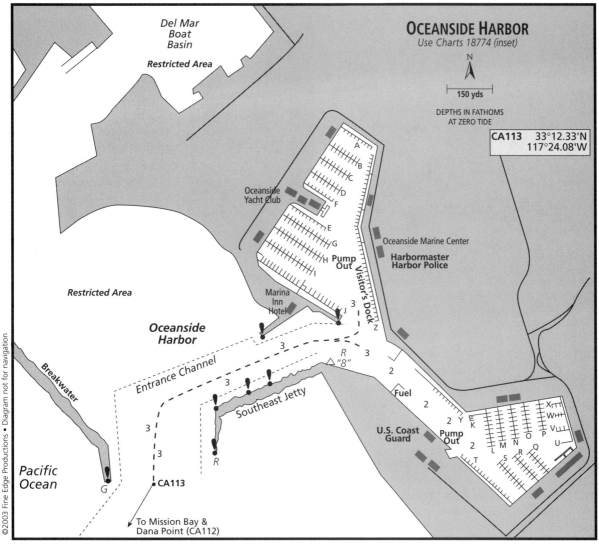

Basin. Strangers should not attempt the entrance at night in rough seas without assistance. The entrance channel is subject to severe wave action and shoaling, and buoys are frequently shifted with changing conditions. Mariners are requested to contact the harbor patrol on VHF-FM channel 16 before entering. (CP, 33rd Ed.)

Oceanside is a small haven that allows you to stroll along one of the longest wooden piers on the West Coast. You can also stretch your sea legs on the walking paths along the harbor's green belt. Harbor Police monitor Channel 16 and talk on 12. Their office is located in the white building on the east side as you enter the harbor. Tie up at the guest slips and walk to the office to check in. Amenities include showers, water and electricity, and restrooms. The pumpout station is located at the fuel dock as are ice, drinks, and various sundries. There are numerous shops and a variety of restaurants available.

The harbor entrance is subject to shoaling, and the buoys are moved frequently to reflect shifts in the navigable channel. During southerly storms (usually winter) the entrance may be closed because of unsafe conditions. Boats transiting the entrance must remain in the dredged channel, which may put them broadside to southerly swells, with very little maneuvering room as they make the turns into the harbor.

The prevailing wind and swell are from the northwest, which means a vessel transiting from the sea buoy will be in the trough for a lit-

David J. Shuler

Oceanside is a snug harbor

tle over a third of a mile. In a large swell, the best approach is from a more southerly direction, keeping to the left side of the entrance, until well inside the breakwater.

Vessels coming from the north (following seas) should chose a point about a third of the distance between the sea buoy and the outer jetty closer to the jetty, and turn close by the outer jetty into the entrance channel. There is no anchoring within the harbor.

Chart Corrections: In June 2000 the "Notice to Mariners" included a revised chartlet for the Oceanside Harbor inset to Chart 18774 that indicated the following changes:

The W jetty light has the same characteristics as previously but is now "1."

Kelp Is NOT Your Friend!
by Ann Kinner

Kelp challenges boaters around several Southern California harbors and causes a myriad of problems. It wraps securely around props and rudders. It gets sucked into the cooling water intakes of engines. It prevents anchors from reaching the bottom and also from being retrieved. It's a good thing not to get into, and yet unwary boaters regularly go into the kelp beds.

Kelp grows in depths of 60 to 90 feet, and the canopy can spread wide, so that the kelp "forest" appears to be dense even in depths of 125 feet or more. The best way to avoid getting tangled is to stay in depths of more than 150 feet, which in the vicinity of Point Loma means staying at least a mile and a half off shore. On the other hand, if you find yourself disabled and drifting into or through kelp, it may be better to drift until you find depths of 20 to 30 feet, and clear water, before setting your anchor.

I was called out one night to rescue a 30-foot sailboat off Mission Beach, in the La Jolla kelp beds. At the time the call came in, the boater had set two anchors and reported the on-scene conditions as "light winds, smooth seas." He gave his GPS position and I gave him a one-hour ETA and got underway. Swells were running up to two feet as I rounded SD "3" and were directly on my bow, slowing my progress. I hailed the boater and revised the ETA to add 20 to 30 minutes. When I was within 15 minutes of his reported position, I asked for an update. It had been just about an hour since the first call. His new position was almost exactly one mile southeast of his original position!

The good news was that I arrived on scene within minutes. The bad news: neither anchor had reached the bottom, and only one was retrievable. The cause of his distress: an overheated engine, probably because of a blocked cooling water intake from (can you guess?) kelp. Why had he spoken of "smooth seas?" Because the dense kelp tends to flatten any wind chop or swell, and the surface of the water appears glassy.

When I asked the boater how he happened to be in the kelp in the first place, he explained that he didn't know the area (he was en route from San Diego, where he'd just bought the boat, to San Pedro where he planned to moor it) and he figured that it would be safer to stay close to shore "in case something happened."

The E jetty light is now Fl R"2."

Two private Fl Y buoys just east of the Q R 26ft jetty light north of the E entrance jetty light have been removed. The chartlet still indicates that the southern side of the entrance channel is foul ground.

Chart 18758 shows the correct information for the lights.

Launch Ramp: The launch ramp (which is free) is located just south of the Coast Guard offices on the west side of the southern basin.

⚓ **Guest Slips:** The Oceanside Harbor District maintains about 50 guest slips in front of the Harbor Office on the east side of the harbor, opposite the entrance. Call the Harbor Police on Channel 16, or tie up in front of the Harbor Office when you arrive. Slips are rented first-come, first-served.

⚓ **Oceanside Small Craft Harbor**; no phone reservations, no credit cards; tel: 760.435.4000; website: www.ci.oceanside.ca.us

⚓ **Oceanside Harbor Master and Police** position: 33°12.61'N, 117°23.71'W

Beach Surfing under Sail
by DCD

One very foggy morning several decades ago—in the days before depth sounders and radar were affordable, and before GPS even existed—I was trying to find the entrance to Oceanside Harbor in our Columbia 29. The entrance is quite small along a flat coastline and I turned due east when our DR indicated it was time. I fell in behind a large sailboat that was on the same heading and was beginning to congratulate myself on my navigational skill when the sailboat crew suddenly started yelling. They executed a snappy 180-degree turn and I scrambled to get out of their way! We both suddenly realized we were in a shallow surf zone . . . but exactly where? Somewhat chagrinned we each dropped sails, started our auxiliary engine and slowly located the harbor entrance about a mile south.

These days, with much heavier traffic, with or without fog, it is a good idea—and much safer—to douse the sails outside the entrance and motor in.

⚓ **Oceanside launch ramp** position: 33°12.32'N, 117°23.57'W

⚓ **Oceanside transient slips** position: 33°12.52'N, 117°23.69'W

⚓ **Oceanside USCG facility** position: 33°12.34'N, 117°23.59'W

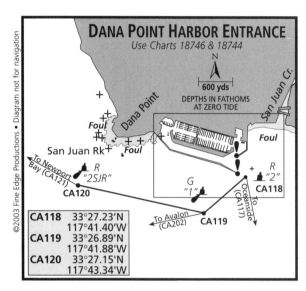

Dana Point Harbor
Charts 18746 (inset), 18774
Entrance: (CA118) 33°27.23'N, 117°41.40'W
Anchor (E harbor): 33°27.52'N, 117°41.44'W
Anchor (W harbor): 33°27.61'N, 117°42.37'W

Dana Point Harbor is a small-craft harbor in the lee of Dana Point. The harbor, administered by the Orange County Harbor, Beaches and Parks District, is entered from the E between two breakwaters each marked by a light on the seaward

Dana Point entrance

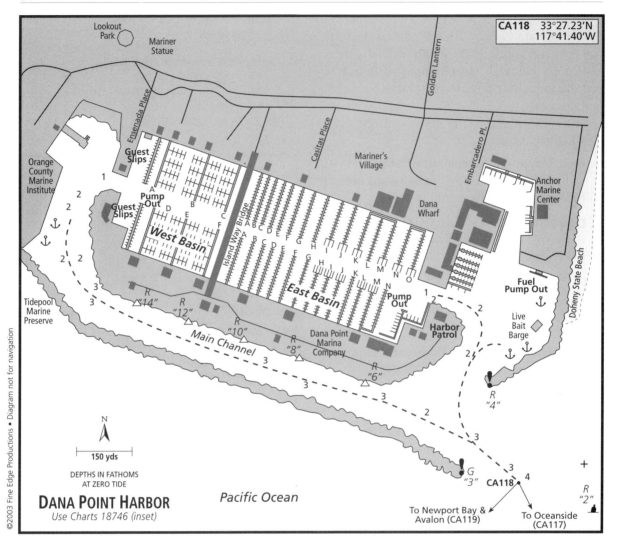

CA118   33°27.23'N
         117°41.40'W

Lookout Park
Mariner Statue

Ensenada Place

Guest Slips

Orange County Marine Institute

Pump Out

Guest Slips

West Basin

Island Way Bridge

Casitas Place

Mariner's Village

Golden Lantern

Embarcadero Pl.

Dana Wharf

Anchor Marine Center

Doheny State Beach

East Basin

Pump Out

Dana Point Marina Company

Harbor Patrol

Fuel Pump Out

Live Bait Barge

Tidepool Marine Preserve

Main Channel

R "14"
R "12"
R "10"
R "8"
R "6"
R "4"

G "3"
CA118
R "2"

©2003 Fine Edge Productions • Diagram not for navigation

N
150 yds
DEPTHS IN FATHOMS AT ZERO TIDE

DANA POINT HARBOR
Use Charts 18746 (inset)

Pacific Ocean

To Newport Bay & Avalon (CA119)

To Oceanside (CA117)

end. A fog signal and radio beacon are at the S light. A church with a giant cross is very visible on the hill above the harbor. A submerged sewer outfall line extends about 0.6 mile from shore, passing about 300 yards E of the S breakwater light. A rock, covered 7 1/2 feet and marked by a buoy, is about 300 yards NE of the S breakwater light. When entering the harbor care should be taken to remain clear of these dangers, especially during low stages of the tide and/or periods of heavy SE swell. Numerous uncharted private racing buoys are off the entrance to the harbor. In August 2000, the midchannel controlling depth was 11.5 feet in the entrance and in the channel that leads WNW to the W basin, except for severe shoaling on the W side starting from opposite Daybeacon 14 to near the W basin entrance. In August 2000, a midchannel controlling depth of 10.2 feet was in the

entrance to the E basin. The harbor is well protected from all sides. The harbor's E and W basins are separated by a fixed highway bridge with a 45-foot channel span and a clearance of 20 feet. . . .

David J. Shuler

Dana Point

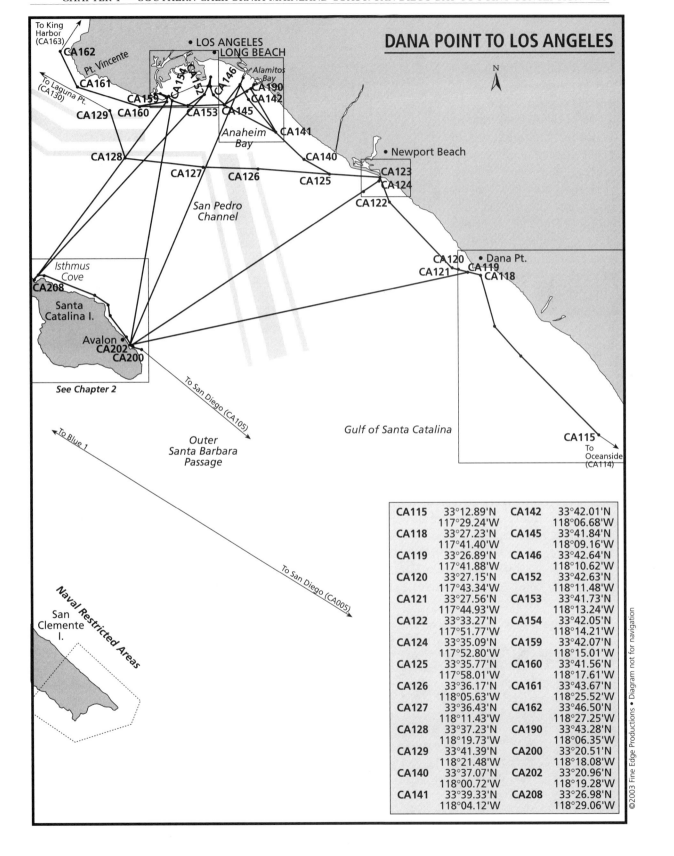

DANA POINT TO LOS ANGELES

CA115	33°12.89'N 117°29.24'W	CA142	33°42.01'N 118°06.68'W
CA118	33°27.23'N 117°41.40'W	CA145	33°41.84'N 118°09.16'W
CA119	33°26.89'N 117°41.88'W	CA146	33°42.64'N 118°10.62'W
CA120	33°27.15'N 117°43.34'W	CA152	33°42.63'N 118°11.48'W
CA121	33°27.56'N 117°44.93'W	CA153	33°41.73'N 118°13.24'W
CA122	33°33.27'N 117°51.77'W	CA154	33°42.05'N 118°14.21'W
CA124	33°35.09'N 117°52.80'W	CA159	33°42.07'N 118°15.01'W
CA125	33°35.77'N 117°58.01'W	CA160	33°41.56'N 118°17.61'W
CA126	33°36.17'N 118°05.63'W	CA161	33°43.67'N 118°25.52'W
CA127	33°36.43'N 118°11.43'W	CA162	33°46.50'N 118°27.25'W
CA128	33°37.23'N 118°19.73'W	CA190	33°43.28'N 118°06.35'W
CA129	33°41.39'N 118°21.48'W	CA200	33°20.51'N 118°18.08'W
CA140	33°37.07'N 118°00.72'W	CA202	33°20.96'N 118°19.28'W
CA141	33°39.33'N 118°04.12'W	CA208	33°26.98'N 118°29.06'W

A harbormaster assigns berths in the harbor. (CP, 33rd Ed.)

Aerial view: Dana Point Harbor

Dana Point Harbor houses two marinas that provide anchorage for more than 2,500 pleasure craft. Harbor facilities include ample guest slips, launch ramps, marine hardware stores, fuel dock, harbor cruises and a host of activities from windsurfing to certified dive charters. Restaurants and retail shops are sprinkled along the harbor and you can buy delicious hand-made chocolates, custom jewelry, designer perfumes, and casual clothing. Outdoor recreational offerings include a park, swimming beach, and fishing. Sport fishing excursions are available year-round and whale watching trips can be scheduled seasonally.

Named after Richard Dana (author of the classic, *Two Years Before the Mast*), Dana Point Harbor is also the home of the tallship *Pilgrim*—a full-sized replica of the vessel in which Dana sailed from Boston to California in 1834 as well as the Orange County Marine Institute.

Like many other Southern California harbors, Dana Point is plagued with heavy kelp

West-end anchorage in Dana Point

beds and mine fields of lobster pots immediately outside the harbor entrance. The safest approach is from a position about one mile out on a heading of due Magnetic North to the red buoy just east of the entrance (see Entrance Diagram). From there, the entrance is without hazards under most circumstances. Occasionally a southerly weather system may create swells that run into the outer channel, but they subside quickly inside the two jetties.

Guest slips are available at the west end of the harbor, on the westernmost dock at the north side of the channel. The larger slips are on the west side of the dock, the smaller slips, on the east side. Visitors must check in with the Harbor Patrol at the entrance to the east basin for slip assignments and to pay fees. Slips are available on a first-come, first-served basis. Reservations are not accepted. Vessels arriving after hours must still check in first and follow the instructions for selecting and paying for guest slips. A list of available slips will be posted on the office door. Cash and checks are accepted, and you must provide your boat's registration/documentation information.

Harbormaster dock, Dana Point

A word of caution: Dana Point slips are narrow relative to their length, and the lengths tend to be overstated. If possible, choose a guest slip that is larger than your boat, particularly if your boat is beamy or awkward to maneuver in tight quarters.

⚓ **Harbor Patrol Office** position: 33°27.47'N, 117°41.57'W (east basin, island side); Orange County Sheriff; tel: 949.248.2222

⚓ **Dana Point Marina Company**; reservations required; tel: 949.496.6137 from 0800 to 1700 Monday to Saturday; website: www.danapointmarina.com

Mariner statue throwing cowhides off bluff

Richard Dana statue

⚓ **Fuel Dock** position: 33°27.57'N, 117°41.42'W

⚓ **Launch Ramp**: position: 33°27.65'N, 117°41.53'W, located at the east end of the harbor; fees depend on the size of the boat;

Anchor in the West Basin, which offers good holding, but expect constant wind shifts during the afternoons. Prevailing winds in the anchorage are west to northwest and are most strongly influenced by the bluff and its small canyons. Once the afternoon wind subsides, the anchorage is generally very still. The area adjacent to the jetty is very shallow, so watch your depths carefully. The preferred anchorage is toward the north off the fishing pier. Holding is good over sand and mud.

The East Basin anchorage area is small, and traffic through the area makes for a bumpy ride. Boats are welcome in either anchorage for 72 hours but should not be left unattended for long periods.

Newport Bay

Chart 18754; 12.1 mi NW
of Dana Point
Entrance: (CA123)
33°35.29'N, 117°52.68'W
Anchor first position:
33°35.99'N, 117°52.86'W

Newport Bay, 64 miles NW of Point Loma is an extensive lagoon bordered on the seaward side by a 3-mile sand spit. The bay is an important yachting and sport fishing center and offers excellent anchorage for large yachts and small craft under all weather conditions. The city of Newport Beach embraces the districts of Newport and Balboa, on the sandspit, and Corona Del Mar, E of the entrance. . . . The entrance to Newport Bay is between jetties 275 yards apart with lights at their outer ends. A fog signal and a radio beacon are at the end of the W jetty. A lighted bell buoy is off the entrance. (CP, 33rd Ed.)

Aerial view: Newport Bay

Newport Bay, one of the most popular harbors in Southern California, has an easy approach that is generally free of hazards. The harbor

---

Late Night Arrival
by Ann Kinner

I arrived in Dana Point one evening at about 2130 and found the list of available slips posted on the door of the Harbor Patrol office. The slips were identified by length and number only, and there was no diagram showing their location on the dock. I filled out the paperwork, put my check in the envelope, dropped it through the door slot and headed for the West Basin.

The boat was a Baba 30, and based on the boats I could see, I made the heroic decision that my slip would be on the west side of the dock. However, the number sequence told me pretty fast that I was on the wrong side, so I turned the boat around and headed around the end into the next fairway. As I proceeded toward my chosen slip, the slips got shorter and narrower, and I discovered that my "30-foot" slip was more appropriate for a 25-foot boat, of much narrower beam than the Baba.

Fortunately, when I chose my slip from the list, I picked one that appeared to have two or three empty slips on each side, so there were no sterns hanging out, and, as luck would have it, no concrete columns to dodge.

It was now after 2200. I had been underway, single-handed, since 0730 in not-very-nice weather, and I was too tired to go back and pick another slip. I decided to give it my best shot and tuck in for the night. Conditions were about perfect: no wind, good lighting, no audience. I put fenders out on the starboard side only, lined the boat up, and eased her into the slip. In a matter of minutes, I had her tied up and closed and was off to sleep.

The next morning I took a good look at the slip and the boat. First, it was definitely the shortest 30-foot slip I had ever seen. The Baba overhung the slip by an easy five feet. Second, if the boat had been six inches wider, I wouldn't have been able to use any fenders at all!!

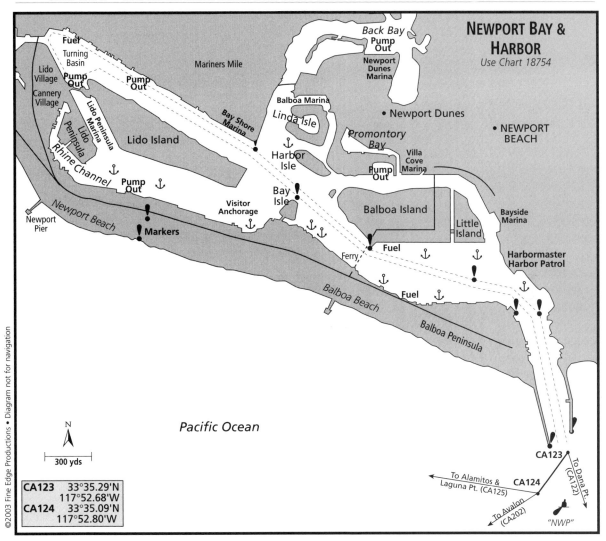

itself is protected in all weather conditions and is suitable for small boats and large yachts; it has 2,119 slips and 1,241 moorings.

When approaching in fog or limited visibility, use our Proven Cruising Routes© or set a course to the west of the entrance, and once you find the 20-fathom depth line, follow the line eastward to the sea buoy. This depth contour will be interrupted for a very short distance where depths fall away to 50 fathoms (due south of the Newport Pier) and then return to 20 fathoms within a space of half a mile.

Inside the bay, the channel runs between the permanent moorings and is generally well marked. Deep-draft vessels should pay close attention to depths, particularly in the area between Lido Isle and the Balboa Peninsula.

Ferries run between Balboa Island and the peninsula. During the busiest seasons, three ferries run in rotation, frequently with one at each landing, and one standing off waiting for its approach. Be sure to look for all three ferries before transiting this part of the channel. During off-peak times, there may be only two ferries operating. Each ferry carries only three or four cars, along with pedestrians and cyclists. The ferries are relatively small and may not be immediately visible if vessel traffic is heavy. The Balboa landing is adjacent to the Union fuel dock. The peninsula landing is within the "fun zone" area, close to the Balboa Pavilion and the ferris wheel.

Fuel is available at the ferry landing on Balboa Island, and at two fuel docks located at the Fun Zone, next to the Balboa Pavilion.

⚓ **Launch Ramp:** The launch ramp is located in the upper bay in the Newport Dunes marina complex. From I-405 exit on Jamboree Boulevard. Once across San Joaquin Hills Road, follow Jamboree down

Entrance to Newport Beach Harbor

the hill and look for the signs past the tennis club on the right.

⚓ **Newport Harbor Patrol office** (Orange County Sheriff) position: 33°36.17'N,

117°53.04'W; pumpout and slips; monitors Ch. 16; tel: 949.723.1002

⚓ **Lido Isle** position: 33°36.54'N, 117°54.54'W

New harbormaster facility at Newport

Marinas:

⚓ **California Recreation Company** (CRC), Bayside Drive; administers guest slips for several marinas; reservations required; tel: 949.723.7781 daily from 0800 to 1700

⚓ **Balboa Marina** (CRC) position: 33°36.92'N, 117°54.23'W; tel: 949.723.7781

⚓ **Bayshore Marina** (CRC) position: 33°36.77'N, 117°54.65'W; tel: 949.723.7781

⚓ **Bayside Marina** position: 33°36.39'N, 117°53.14'W; tel: 949.644.9330

⚓ **Lido Peninsula Marina** position: 33°36.83'N, 117°55.47'W; reservations required based on space availability; tel: 949.673.9330

Guest dock and Balboa Yacht Club

⚓ **Villa Cove Marina** (CRC) position: 33°37.21'N, 117°53.76'W; tel: 949.723.7781

⚓ **Newport Dunes Marina** position: 33°37.21'N, 117°53.76'W; must pass under 24-ft bridge at zero tide; reservations required; tel: 949.729.1100, after hours 949.729.3863; website: www.newportdunes.com

Anchor: The Corona Del Mar Bend anchorage is intended primarily for short-term or emergency use. It is subject to heavy swells during the winter months when the prevailing storms are from the south. The anchorage off Lido Isle is protected in nearly all weather and offers good

Newport moorings

Palm trees at Newport

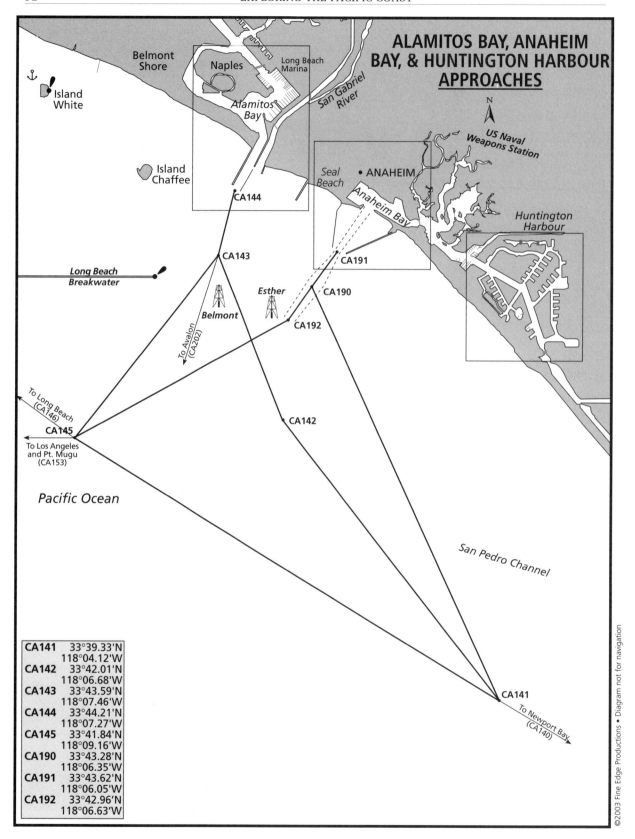

ALAMITOS BAY, ANAHEIM
BAY, & HUNTINGTON HARBOUR
APPROACHES

CA141	33°39.33'N
	118°04.12'W
CA142	33°42.01'N
	118°06.68'W
CA143	33°43.59'N
	118°07.46'W
CA144	33°44.21'N
	118°07.27'W
CA145	33°41.84'N
	118°09.16'W
CA190	33°43.28'N
	118°06.35'W
CA191	33°43.62'N
	118°06.05'W
CA192	33°42.96'N
	118°06.63'W

holding in a muddy bottom. During Santa Ana conditions when the winds are from the northeast, this anchorage may be a little rocky as the winds come directly down the channel from the upper bay, but holding is still good if you are properly set to the wind.

Note: Chart 18754 indicates numerous anchorages throughout the bay, but most are occupied by permanent moorings and have no spaces for transient vessels.

Anaheim Bay/Huntington Harbour

Chart 18749; 14 mi NW of Newport Bay
Outer Entrance: (CA192) 33°42.96'N, 118°06.63'W
Inner Entrance: (CA191) 33°43.62'N, 118°06.05'W

Anaheim Bay . . . is the site of the U.S. Naval Weapons Station. Jetties protect the entrance to the bay. Waters inside the jetties are within a restricted area, and an explosives anchorage has been established E of the channel. . . .

Huntington Harbour, a small-boat basin . . . is a private development, and, with the exception of two small marinas, consists of private docks adjacent to waterfront homes. The harbor is entered through the restricted waters of Anaheim Bay, and permission to pass must be obtained from the Commanding Officer, U.S. Naval Weapons

Balboa ferry

Station, Seal Beach, Calif. The Harbor Patrol office is adjacent to the boat launch ramp in the NW corner of the harbor. A repair yard can handle craft to 50 feet and 25 tons for engine and hull repairs. Gasoline, diesel fuel, and marine supplies are available in the harbor. Launching ramps are in the NW and SE corners of the harbor. (CP, 33rd Ed.)

Anaheim Bay is the entrance to Huntington Harbour. Since September 11, 2001, the Navy has imposed significant restrictions on boats going in and out of the bay. (Please see below.)

The Anaheim Bay National Wildlife Refuge, a vast natural area situated between the Naval Weapons Station and Sunset-Huntington Harbor, is home to numerous types of marine life and birds and is one of the most beautiful natural wildlife areas along the Pacific Coast.

Sunset Marina Park, adjacent to Huntington Harbour, features a 276-slip marina, a public boat launch ramp, restrooms, boat and trailer parking, boat repair yard, and public picnic areas. For guest slip and temporary anchorage information, contact the Harbor Patrol Office in Newport Beach at 562.673.1025. A full-service fuel dock is located at Mariners Point, where you can also buy groceries, bait, and tackle.

Huntington Harbour was built in the early 1960s as part of a large water-oriented residential community. It has become famous over the years for its annual Christmas boat parades and for the concurrent elaborate light displays on the houses along the channels. Spectators come from all over the area to watch the parades from

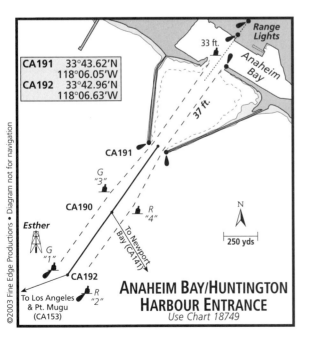

©2003 Fine Edge Productions • Diagram not for navigation

CA191 33°43.62'N 118°06.05'W
CA192 33°42.96'N 118°06.63'W

Range Lights

Anaheim Bay

33 ft.

37 ft.

CA191

CA190

Esther

G "3"

R "4"

G "1"

CA192

R "2"

To Newport Bay (CA141)

To Los Angeles & Pt. Mugu (CA153)

N

250 yds

ANAHEIM BAY/HUNTINGTON HARBOUR ENTRANCE
Use Chart 18749

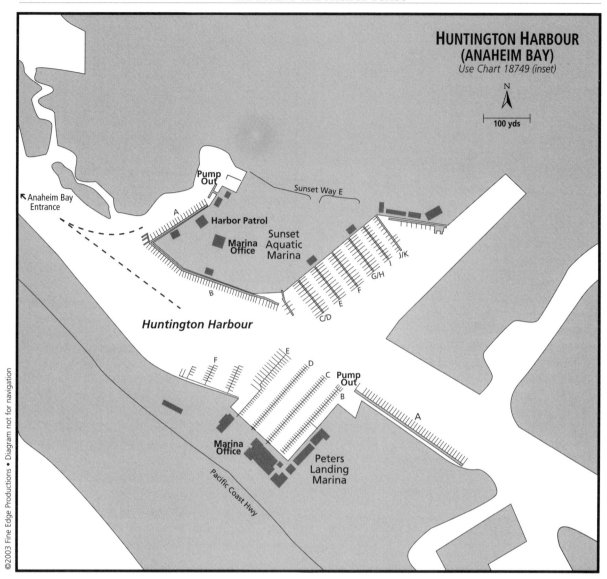

shore, and also to cruise the channels on non-parade evenings to see the spectacular shore-side displays.

Owned and controlled by the Seal Beach Naval Weapons Station, Anaheim Bay is used by the Navy to store and load explosives. Storage barges may be moored on both sides of the bay on unlighted moorings. The channel through the bay is clearly marked by range markers, lights and by channel buoys. Vessels transiting must stay within the marked channel.

Restrictions on speed and use of VHF radio through Anaheim Bay are posted on signs inside the bay. The Navy may restrict the hours during which vessels may pass through Anaheim Bay either entering or departing from Huntington Harbour. Check with local authorities for specific times and restrictions. Vessels must use auxiliary power when entering or exiting Huntington Harbor through Anaheim Bay. Personal watercraft must be tethered to another vessel.

Huntington Harbor is entered after passing through Anaheim Bay. However, the Pacific Coast Highway bridge restricts access to vessels able to clear 23 feet at low tide. Once past the bridge, stay within the marked channel which follows an S-curve through marshy areas. Outside the channel, the depths decrease rapidly, and much of the area is uncovered at low tide.

Guest slips may be available at two marinas that straddle the northern end of the harbor. Both require check-in during normal business hours and do not accept after-hours calls. There are no public docks or mooring facilities in Huntington Harbour, and the entire harbor is subject to usage restrictions.

Marinas:

⚓ **Peter's Landing Marina** (south side) tel: 562.840.1387; hours: 0900 to 1730 weekdays; 1000 to 1730 Saturday; 1100 to 1600 Sunday.

⚓ **Sunset Aquatic Marina** (north side) reservations advised; tel: 714.846.0179 daily 0800 to 1700

Launch Ramp: Adjacent to Sunset Aquatic Marina, at the north end of the harbor. From I-405 take Bolsa Chica west to Edinger Avenue, turn right and continue to the marina. Entry fee is paid through a machine at the gate. The ramp is available 24 hours a day. There are seven lanes leading from a paved parking lot and two loading docks. Entry fee includes one night of overnight use. Additional nights are payable at the office; tel: 562.592.2833.

During the boat parades and while the Christmas lights are on display, several commercial operators use the launch-ramp docks to pick up and discharge passengers, so the area can be very congested during these events.

Alamitos Bay (Long Beach Hbr)

Charts 18749, 18746; 15 mi NW of Newport Bay
Entrance (outer): (CA143) 33°43.59'N, 118°07.46'W
Entrance (inner): (CA144) 33°44.21'N, 118°07.27'W

Alamitos Bay . . . is the site of the Long Beach Marina, a small-craft harbor. . . . The harbor is entered from the S between two jetties each marked by a light on the seaward end. A fog signal is at the W jetty light. A nonanchorage area has been designated at the mouth of the entrance channel to Alamitos Bay. Berths in the Long Beach marina are limited to about 1,800 boats, but extensive parking and ramp-launching areas

Alamitos Bay Marina

are provided for trailer-drawn craft. Visiting yachts may obtain temporary berthing on a first-come first-served basis. All mooring is controlled by a harbormaster, who has an office on the E side of the entrance channel near the end of the point about 500 yards above the bend in the channel. (CP, 33rd Ed.)

Alamitos Bay is located at the east end of the Los Angeles-Long Beach harbor. Its entrance channel is to the northeast of the eastern end of

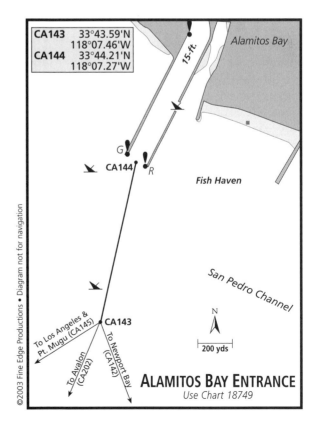

Aerial view: Alamitos Bay (Long Beach Harbor)

find themselves on the wrong side of the entrance and in hazardous waters.

Occasionally boaters will misidentify the entrance buoys, and find themselves entering Anaheim Bay which is 1.15 miles southeast of Alamitos Bay. Both bays have flashing green lights on the jetty with almost identical characteristics. However, the entrance to Anaheim Bay has a series of buoys marking the approach to the entrance, while Alamitos Bay does not.

Once inside the Alamitos Bay channel, stay to starboard of the centerline buoys when traveling in either direction. If a dredge is present in the channel, stay well away from the dredge barge and any marker buoys. The dredge hoses are submerged from the marker buoys. Speed throughout Alamitos Bay, including the

the Federal breakwater that defines Long Beach harbor.

The area immediately around the entrance to the harbor can be very rolly as swells wrap around the Federal breakwater and refract also around the Anaheim Bay jetties. Once inside the entrance, the swells quickly dissipate.

Immediately south of the Alamitos Bay jetties is the San Gabriel River. The river entrance shallows very quickly and the area around it is dotted with wrecks and rocky shoals. Do not attempt to enter Alamitos Bay until you have clearly identified both entrance jetties. This is another harbor where unwary boaters can quickly

Long Beach Yacht Club float

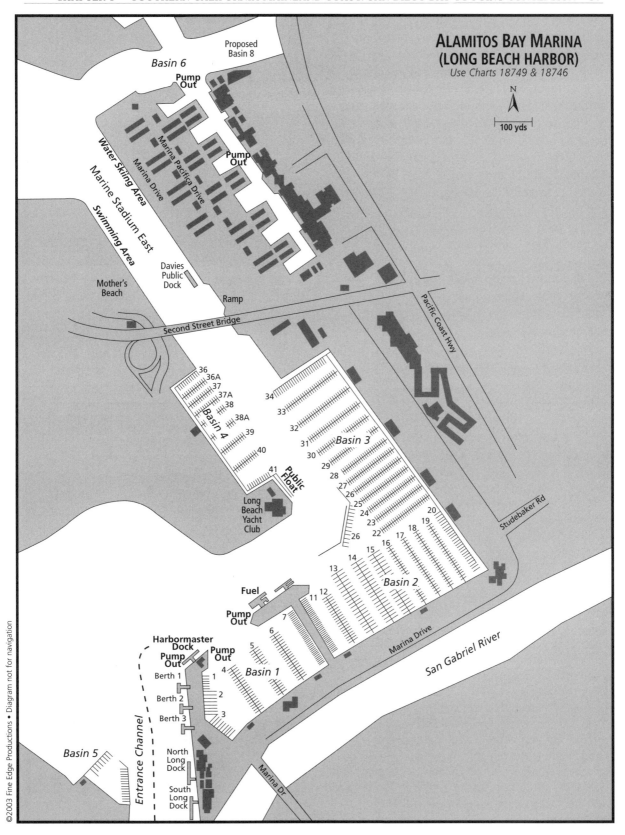

ALAMITOS BAY MARINA
(LONG BEACH HARBOR)
Use Charts 18749 & 18746

N

100 yds

Basin 6

Proposed Basin 8

Pump Out

Marina Pacifica Drive

Marina Drive

Pump Out

Water Skiing Area

Marine Stadium East

Swimming Area

Mother's Beach

Davies Public Dock

Ramp

Pacific Coast Hwy

Second Street Bridge

36
36A
37
37A
38
38A
39

34
33
32
31
30
29
28
27
26
25
24
23

Basin 4

40

41

Public Float

Basin 3

Long Beach Yacht Club

Studebaker Rd

20
19
18
17
16
15
14
13
12
11

22
21

26

Basin 2

Fuel

Pump Out

7
6
5
4

Harbormaster Dock

Pump Out

Pump Out

Basin 1

Marina Drive

San Gabriel River

Berth 1
Berth 2
Berth 3

1
2
3

Basin 5

Entrance Channel

North Long Dock

South Long Dock

Marina Dr

entrance channel, is 5 mph and strictly enforced by the Long Beach Marine Bureau patrol boats.

Alamitos Bay offers a fantastic choice of entertainment and activities. For a change of pace, the Gondola Getaway provides visitors with a real gondola ride. The boats are exact replicas of those in Venice and serve up wine, snacks and Italian songs. On Thursday nights during the summer, band concerts are held at Marine Stadium in Alamitos Bay. Boaters are welcome to enter the stadium after 1700 hours and anchor off the park area. This provides you with a great vantage point to see and hear the concerts. Be sure to stop in and visit the Aquarium of the Pacific. Boaters may park at the downtown guest docks and take the water taxi or walk to the aquarium. Boat shows are scheduled throughout the year and you may just be able to catch one while you're in port.

Marine Stadium is a long narrow area running between Naples Island and the mainland side of Alamitos Bay. The northern portion is restricted to small boats (less than 20 feet).

Launch Ramp: The northwest launch ramp has 8 lanes suitable for small boats. From the intersection of Pacific Coast Highway and Bellflower Boulevard, proceed south to Colorado Street, then west to Appian Way. Follow Appian Way southeast to the launch area. This is a residential area with narrow streets. If you have any concerns about your ability to make tight turns or if your trailer is wide, use the launch ramp adjacent to the Second Street Bridge.

Second Street Launch Ramp (position: 33°45.43'N, 118°06.98'W) is adjacent to the bridge at Second Street, just west of its intersection with Pacific Coast Highway. Second Street becomes Westminster Avenue east of Pacific Coast Highway. The ramp is commonly known as the Second Street ramp. Refer to an area highway map for the best approach routes. Several

Beware When Launching a Small Vessel!
by Ann Kinner

Because of its location in the middle of the Southern California population and its extremely good access from nearly all directions, the Second Street ramp is frequently a source of great entertainment as inexperienced boaters discover the wonders of trailer hitches, currents, and parking brakes under load. On some Sunday afternoons it resembles a set for the Keystone Cops.

Perhaps my favorite incident was the gentleman who, working solo, backed his boat off the trailer into the water, and then stepped nimbly off the boat into the water to go back to his truck. Realizing his mistake, he turned around and walked—fully clothed—back into the water to try to control his now-drifting boat. Fortunately some nearby boaters saw his dilemma and took hold of the boat so he could go back to his truck. I guess he hadn't thought the whole process through.

The dock adjacent to the launch ramp has plenty of room for short-term tie-ups. If you are launching without help, that's the place to get off your boat so you can walk in dry clothes back to your vehicle. Should be obvious, but . . .

GadZukes

freeways will bring you close to the launch area. From westbound Second Street, turn right at the entrance to the Marina Pacifica residential complex, then turn left onto the access road to the launch ramp and parking area. This is an extremely popular launch ramp because of its freeway access. On a busy weekend, launching or retrieving can require a long wait.

⚓ **Alamitos Bay Harbormaster's Dock and pumpout** position: 33°44.97'N, 118°06.95'W

⚓ **Fuel Dock** position: 33°45.05'N, 118°06.86'W

⚓ **Alamitos Bay Marina** (formerly Long Beach Marina) position: 33°45.21'N, 118°06.83'W; reservations recommended; tel: 562.570.4960; 0730 to 1900

Aerial view: Long Beach Harbor

Long Beach Harbor (San Pedro Bay)

Charts 18751, 18749; E end of San Pedro Bay Entrance (L.B. light): (CA151) 33°43.37'N, 118°11.13'W
Intermediate waypoint: (CA148) 33°44.15'N, 118°10.64'W
Marina (E entr inbound): (CA149a) 33°45.48'N, 118°10.85'W
Marina (W entr outbound): (CA149b) 33°45.39'N, 118°11.04'W
Anchor (Island White): 33°45.27'N, 118°09.63'W

Long Beach Harbor . . . includes the City of Long Beach and a portion of Terminal Island . . . . Long Beach and Los Angeles Harbors are connected by Cerritos Channel. The distance between the seaward entrance to the two harbors is about 4 miles. Long Beach Harbor, Middle Harbor, and Southeast Basin are protected by

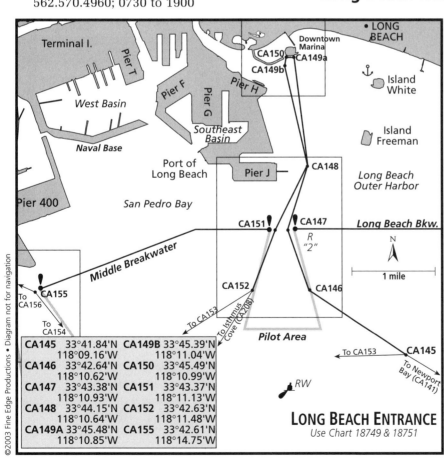

CA145	33°41.84'N 118°09.16'W	**CA149B**	33°45.39'N 118°11.04'W
CA146	33°42.64'N 118°10.62'W	**CA150**	33°45.49'N 118°10.99'W
CA147	33°43.38'N 118°10.93'W	**CA151**	33°43.37'N 118°11.13'W
CA148	33°44.15'N 118°10.64'W	**CA152**	33°42.63'N 118°11.48'W
CA149A	33°45.48'N 118°10.85'W	**CA155**	33°42.61'N 118°14.75'W

LONG BEACH ENTRANCE
Use Chart 18749 & 18751

©2003 Fine Edge Productions • Diagram not for navigation

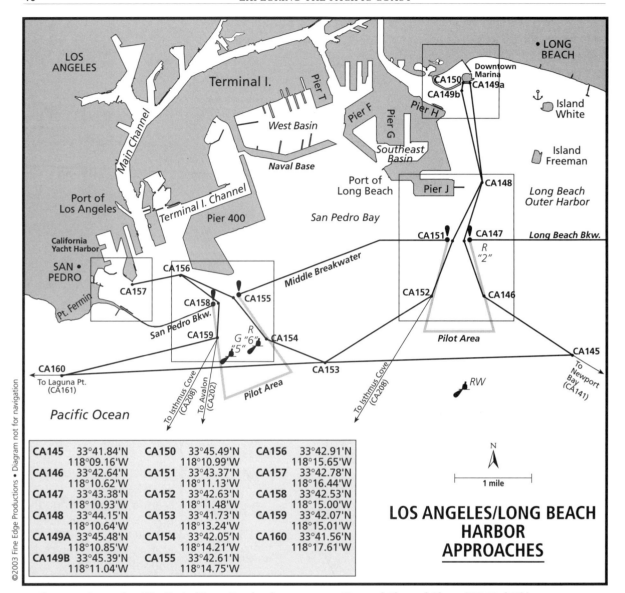

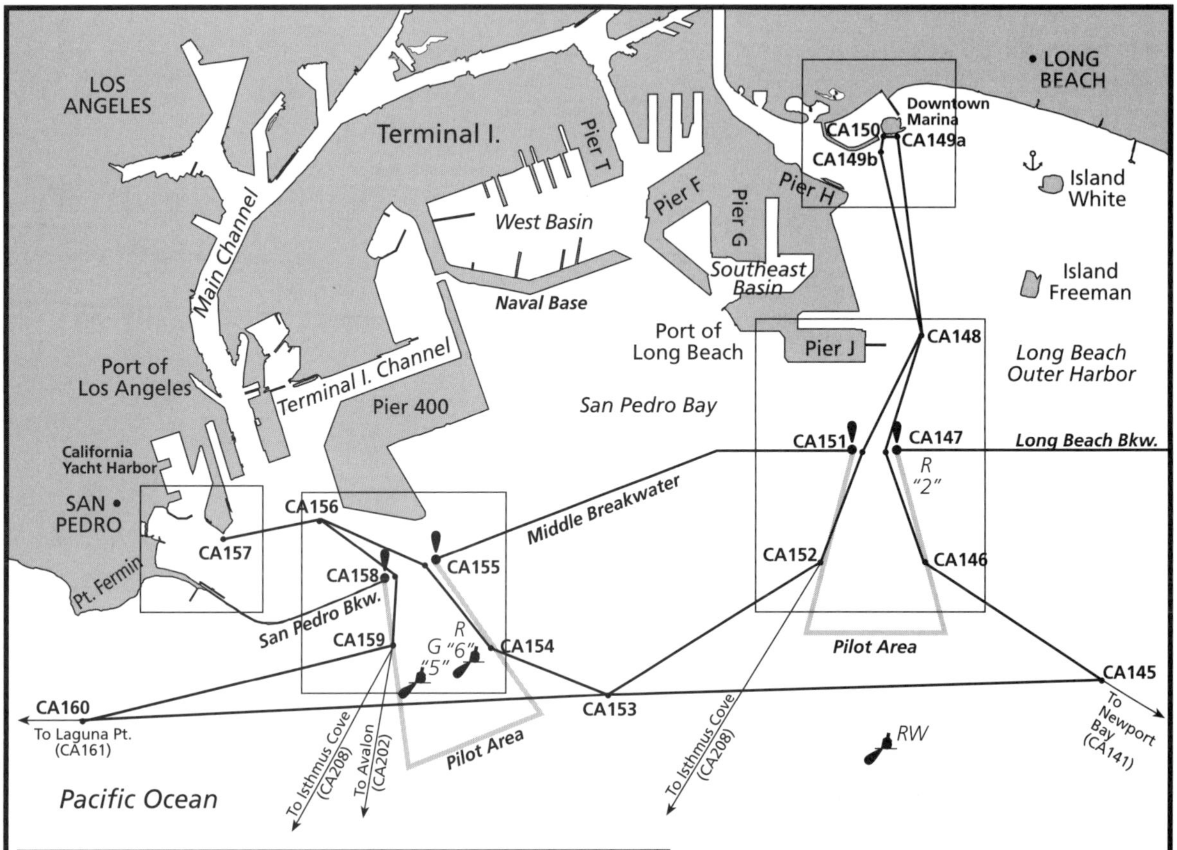
LOS ANGELES
Terminal I.
Pier T
Main Channel
West Basin
Naval Base
Pier F
Pier G
Pier H
Southeast Basin
Downtown Marina
CA150
CA149a
CA149b
• LONG BEACH
Island White
Island Freeman
Port of Los Angeles
Terminal I. Channel
Pier 400
Port of Long Beach
San Pedro Bay
Pier J
CA148
Long Beach Outer Harbor
California Yacht Harbor
SAN • PEDRO
CA151
CA147
R "2"
Long Beach Bkw.
CA156
Middle Breakwater
CA157
Pt. Fermin
CA158
CA155
CA152
CA146
San Pedro Bkw.
CA159
R
G "6"
"5"
CA154
Pilot Area
CA145
CA160
To Laguna Pt. (CA161)
CA153
To Isthmus Cove (CA208)
To Avalon (CA202)
Pilot Area
To Isthmus Cove (CA208)
RW
To Newport Bay (CA141)
Pacific Ocean
N
1 mile

©2003 Fine Edge Productions • Diagram not for navigation

CA145	33°41.84'N 118°09.16'W	**CA150**	33°45.49'N 118°10.99'W	**CA156**	33°42.91'N 118°15.65'W
CA146	33°42.64'N 118°10.62'W	**CA151**	33°43.37'N 118°11.13'W	**CA157**	33°42.78'N 118°16.44'W
CA147	33°43.38'N 118°10.93'W	**CA152**	33°42.63'N 118°11.48'W	**CA158**	33°42.53'N 118°15.00'W
CA148	33°44.15'N 118°10.64'W	**CA153**	33°41.73'N 118°13.24'W	**CA159**	33°42.07'N 118°15.01'W
CA149A	33°45.48'N 118°10.85'W	**CA154**	33°42.05'N 118°14.21'W	**CA160**	33°41.56'N 118°17.61'W
CA149B	33°45.39'N 118°11.04'W	**CA155**	33°42.61'N 118°14.75'W		

LOS ANGELES/LONG BEACH HARBOR APPROACHES

three curving moles. The Port of Long Beach, also one of the largest ports on the Pacific Coast, has the reputation of being America's most modern port. It has extensive foreign and domestic traffic with modern facilities for the largest vessels. The major small-craft facilities in Long Beach are Long Beach Marina in Alamitos Bay and the Downtown Marina on Queensway Bay, W of oil Island Grissom. Other facilities in Long Beach Harbor are just inside the entrances to both Channel Two and Channel Three, and in Cerritos Channel at the Heim lift bridge. All repair facilities, supplies, fuel, moorage, and related yacht requirements may be had in individual private marinas or from other establishments in the Middle Harbor. Several boatyards are in Channel Two and Channel Three. (CP, 33rd Ed.)

Long Beach outer harbor is part of the busy Los Angeles/Long Beach shipping port occupying the east side of San Pedro Bay. It includes Queensway Bay and Downtown Marina in its central part and Alamitos Bay at the extreme east end; it is a harbor of refuge. Commercial traffic is heavy and comes in all shapes and sizes, from slow cargo and tanker ships to fast-moving taxis and supply boats. Long Beach is also one of the departure points for passenger boats en route to Catalina Island. The protected harbor is used for sailboat racing, casual sailing,

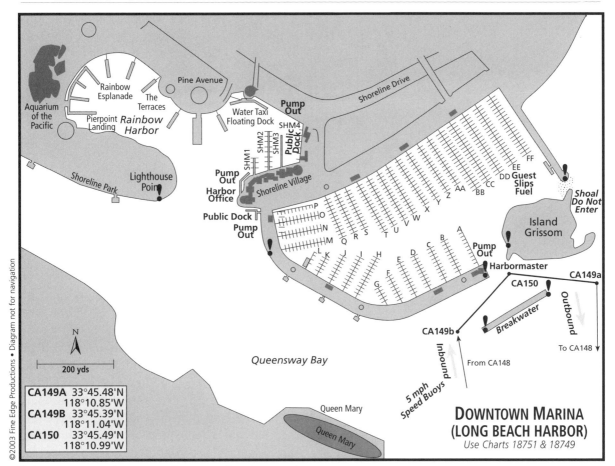

Aquarium of the Pacific

Rainbow Esplanade

Pine Avenue

The Terraces

Pierpoint Landing

Rainbow Harbor

Shoreline Park

Lighthouse Point

Shoreline Drive

Water Taxi Floating Dock

Pump Out

SHM4

SHM3

SHM2

SHM1

Public Dock

Pump Out

Harbor Office

Shoreline Village

Public Dock

Pump Out

P

O

N

M

L

K J I H E

Q R S T U V W X Y Z AA BB CC DD EE FF

Guest Slips Fuel

Shoal Do Not Enter

Island Grissom

Pump Out

A

B

C

D

E

F

G

Harbormaster

CA150

CA149a

Breakwater

Outbound

CA149b

Inbound

From CA148

To CA148

5 mph Speed Buoys

DOWNTOWN MARINA (LONG BEACH HARBOR)
Use Charts 18751 & 18749

N

200 yds

CA149A 33°45.48'N
       118°10.85'W
CA149B 33°45.39'N
       118°11.04'W
CA150 33°45.49'N
       118°10.99'W

Queensway Bay

Queen Mary

Queen Mary

©2003 Fine Edge Productions • Diagram not for navigation

fishing, personal watercraft, power boating, and just about every water-borne activity imaginable, including speedboat races.

A large white dome is a significant landmark to the downtown part of Long Beach Harbor. This dome formerly housed the Spruce Goose airplane, Howard Hughes' historic wooden aircraft. The Spruce Goose now makes its home in another city, but the dome remains and can be seen from well outside the harbor. Adjacent to the dome is the *Queen Mary*.

During daylight hours, the approaches to the Downtown Marina and Queensway Bay are relatively easy. The breakwater protects the harbor from nearly all swells, and the land mass buffers the harbor from the occasional northwesterly Santa Ana winds. Please obey a traffic separation scheme as noted on the entrance diagram. Note that inbound vessels keep to the west side of the marina breakwater and outbound vessels stay to the east.

Oil wells camouflaged as buildings

Downtown Shoreline Marina

The primary difficulty in entering Long Beach Harbor occurs at night, when the lighted aids to navigation are difficult to identify. All of the container piers, anchored ships, bridges, and buildings on shore are lighted. In addition, there are lighted oil islands, street traffic lights, lights on fishing piers and beach areas, which make it very difficult to identify the breakwater openings. The breakwater itself is low and may not be visible until you are quite close to it. One of the brightest lights in the harbor sits on top of the Port Authority Building. This light flashes once every 30 seconds, but it is so bright it is occasionally mistaken for Long Beach Light. Do not confuse the two: the Port Authority light is 147 feet high, and Long Beach Light is only 50 feet high, with a flash period of 5 seconds.

Vessels without radar are encouraged to approach slowly and to make sure of the lights before entering the harbor. If in doubt about what you can see, enter the harbor from the east end where the approach is wider—GPS is most useful. Look for the two lighted oil platforms just to the east of the breakwater and choose a route about midway between platform Belmont and the breakwater.

During part of the year a bait barge is moored just inside the breakwater's eastern end. The barge is usually well marked, although its exact position is not charted.

Passenger boats leave the Downtown Marina area on scheduled trips to Catalina Island. These boats generally follow a course close aboard the mooring buoys adjacent to Pier J, and then exit the harbor through the Long Beach entrance. These boats tend to move fast and frequently run close to recreational boats, so give them a wide berth.

Guest moorings are available year-round in this largest municipally run marina in the world. Visiting boaters may check in at the office or make advance reservations through the Marine Bureau at 562.570.3215. There are two fuel docks: one in Downtown Shoreline Marina and one in Alamitos Bay. These docks also have snacks and beverages, propane, and some maintenance services.

There is no shortage of restaurants in Long Beach harbor —from Mexican to fresh seafood

Queen Mary and Russian sub

fests, something is sure to appeal. Long Beach is also the home of the *Queen Mary,* which is open for self-guided shipwalk tours as well as behind-the-scenes guided tours. The harbormaster monitors VHF Channel 16.

Launch Ramp: Golden Shores launch ramp is northwest of the Queensway Bridge. There are 16 launch lanes. Immediately outside the launch area is a shoal area, on the eastern side. Watch your depths and move carefully between Golden Shores and Queensway Bay.

After heavy rains, the area adjacent to Golden Shores launch ramp is frequently filled with storm run-off including tree branches, trash, and miscellaneous other flotsam. Be extremely careful at such times not to get tangled in the debris. To reach Golden Shores launch area, take the Long Beach Freeway (I-710) south and exit right at Golden Shore Drive.

⚓ **Downtown Marina** position: 33°45.51'N, 118°11.03'W; 1,831 slips; reservations recommended; tel: 562.570.4950

⚓ **Harbormaster Office and pumpout dock** position: 33°45.51'N, 118°11.03'W

⚓ **Fuel dock** position: 33°45.66'N, 118°10.89'W

⚓ **Rainbow Harbor** position: 33°45.63'N, 118°11.57'W

⚓ **Anchor** (Island White): 33°45.23'N, 118°09.70'W

Fishing boat All Sons *finds* Queen Mary *to starboard*

Anchor (Island White): Three man-made islands form a triangle in the middle of Long Beach Harbor. The anchorage area is to the north of the northernmost island (Island White). Holding is good over 5 fathoms. The entire harbor may experience slow surges, but the anchorage is well protected and safe.

Los Angeles Harbor
(San Pedro Bay)
Charts 18751, 18749; W end of San Pedro Bay
Entrance outer (E bkw): (CA154) 33°42.05'N, 118°14.21'W
Entrance inner (E bkw): (CA155) 33°42.61'N, 118°14.75'W
Outer Entrance (W bkw): (CA159) 33°42.07'N, 118°15.01'W
Inner Entrance (W bkw): (CA158) 33°42.53'N, 118°15.00'W
Anchor (W Channel): 33°42.84'N, 118°16.77'W

Los Angeles Harbor . . . includes the districts of San Pedro, Wilmington, and a major portion of Terminal Island. It is a harbor of refuge. The Port of Los Angeles, one of the largest ports on the Pacific coast, has a history of leading the Pacific coast ports in terms of tonnage handled. It has extensive facilities to accommodate all types of traffic, and it is the only southern California port at which passenger vessels call regularly. Los Angeles Harbor has small-craft facilities on both sides of Cerritos Channel from the Heim lift bridge to East Basin, on the E side of East Basin, in Watchhorn Basin, and at the N end of West Channel. All the berths, fuel, supplies, and services required for small boats are available at the individual private marinas or may be obtained nearby. (CP, 33rd Ed.)

Los Angeles Harbor claims to be the busiest port in the U.S. Much of the harbor has been filled in with container piers, leaving relatively little open area for recreational boats. Commercial traffic moves constantly through the area from the approach off the San Pedro Breakwater into the various channels to the container and cargo piers. In addition, cruise ships transit from the northern end of the main channel to the breakwater opening on their way to the shipping lanes.

California Yacht Marina (formerly Cabrillo Marina) is the primary facility for recreational boats. The approach is west of the main channel and well marked, although at night the lights on shore can make it difficult to see the buoy and jetty lights. Proceed carefully until you are sure of the lights and the location of the inner breakwater that protects the marina.

Fuel is available at the Cabrillo Marine fuel dock at the marina. If the marina fuel dock is out of fuel (which happens occasionally), recreational vessels can find fuel at the commercial fuel dock on the west side of the main channel, across from the Coast Guard small-boat basin on Reservation Point.

Launch Ramp: The launch ramp is south of

LOS ANGELES HARBOR ENTRANCE
Use Chart 18751 & 18749

CA154	33°42.05'N 118°14.21'W
CA155	33°42.61'N 118°14.75'W
CA156	33°42.91'N 118°15.65'W
CA158	33°42.53'N 118°15.00'W
CA159	33°42.07'N 118°15.01'W

©2003 Fine Edge Productions • Diagram not for navigation

the California Yacht Marina at Cabrillo Beach. From the Harbor Freeway (I-110), exit to Gaffey Street. Drive south to 22nd Street. Turn east on 22nd Street, then south on Via Cabrillo Marina to the Y at Shoshonean Road, then south to the parking lot for the launch ramp.

⚓ **Los Angeles Harbor Fuel Dock and Pumpout**
position: 33°43.12'N, 118°16.76'W

⚓ **California Yacht Marina (formerly Cabrillo Marina)**
position: 32°37.35'N, 117°06.17'W; guest slips available; water & fuel; tel: 310.732.2252 daily from 0800 to 1700; website: www.cymcabrillo.com

Aerial view: Port of Los Angeles

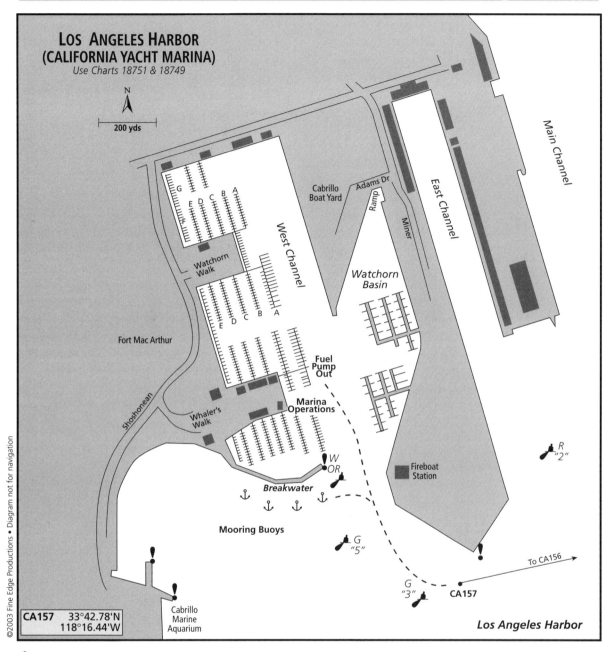

⚓ **Watchorn Basin** position: 33°43.13'N, 118°16.63'W

⚓ **Cabrillo Boat Yard** position: 33°43.39'N, 118°16.63'W

⚓ **Los Angeles Port Police** VHF Ch. 16; tel: 310.732.3500

⚓ **USCG** VHF Ch.16 and 22A; tel: 562.980.4444

⚓ **USCG Marine Safety Office;** tel: 562.980.4429

Anchor: Los Angeles Harbor is a harbor of refuge. The area immediately south of the California Yacht Marina breakwater is designated as a free anchorage. There are 14 mooring buoys available for vessels up to 50 feet long. Contact the Port Police at 310.732.3500 for mooring authorization.

The mooring area is subject to localized winds that sweep down the face of the San Pedro Peninsula and can be gusty and quite

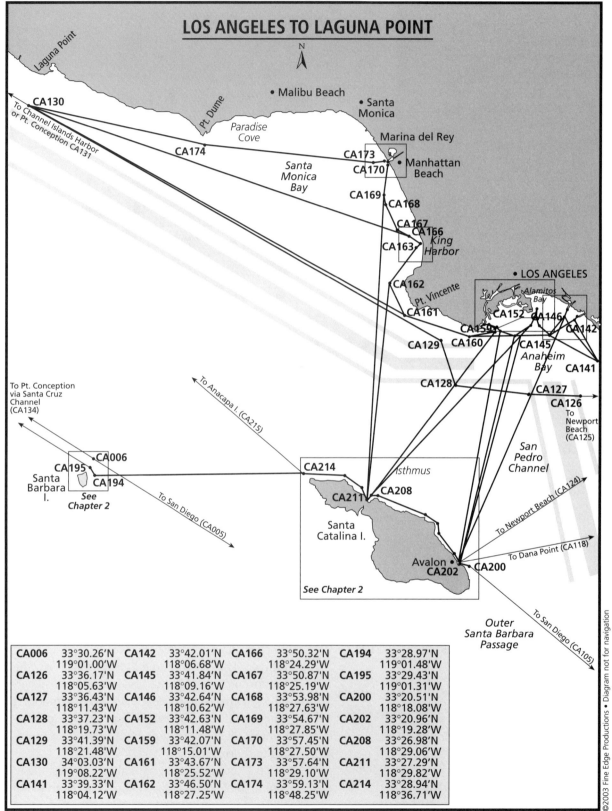

LOS ANGELES TO LAGUNA POINT

CA006	33°30.26'N 119°01.00'W	CA142	33°42.01'N 118°06.68'W	CA166	33°50.32'N 118°24.29'W	CA194	33°28.97'N 119°01.48'W
CA126	33°36.17'N 118°05.63'W	CA145	33°41.84'N 118°09.16'W	CA167	33°50.87'N 118°25.19'W	CA195	33°29.43'N 119°01.31'W
CA127	33°36.43'N 118°11.43'W	CA146	33°42.64'N 118°10.62'W	CA168	33°53.98'N 118°27.63'W	CA200	33°20.51'N 118°18.08'W
CA128	33°37.23'N 118°19.73'W	CA152	33°42.63'N 118°11.48'W	CA169	33°54.67'N 118°27.85'W	CA202	33°20.96'N 118°19.28'W
CA129	33°41.39'N 118°21.48'W	CA159	33°42.07'N 118°15.01'W	CA170	33°57.45'N 118°27.50'W	CA208	33°26.98'N 118°29.06'W
CA130	34°03.03'N 119°08.22'W	CA161	33°43.67'N 118°25.52'W	CA173	33°57.64'N 118°29.10'W	CA211	33°27.29'N 118°29.82'W
CA141	33°39.33'N 118°04.12'W	CA162	33°46.50'N 118°27.25'W	CA174	33°59.13'N 118°48.25'W	CA214	33°28.94'N 118°36.71'W

strong. These winds usually arise mid-day and subside late in the afternoon. The basin, known locally as Hurricane Gulch, is one of the windiest places in Southern California.

The Fish Harbor anchorages that can be reached from Terminal Island Channel are available to both recreational and commercial vessels. Fish Harbor is bordered by canneries and fish-processing plants.

Santa Monica Bay
Charts 18744; 18 mi NW of LA Hbr

From Flat Rock Point to Santa Monica the shore is comparatively low with a sand beach backed by a continuous city area to the inland mountains. The depths of Santa Monica Bay are comparatively shoal, the 10-fathom curve in general lying about 1 mile from shore, except at Redondo Beach where a deep submarine valley, Redondo Canyon, heads close to the shore. (CP, 33rd Ed.)

There are several submerged obstructions extending out toward 10 fathoms along the Santa Monica Coast. Extra caution is required anytime depths are 5 fathoms or less. (See the sidebar "Beware the Hyperion Pipeline!")

Lunada Bay
Charts 18744; 0.3 mi SE of Palos Verdes Pt
Position: 33°46.16'N, 118°25.55'W

Lunada Bay is a small bight. . . (CP, 33rd Ed.)

Lunada Bay is filled with rocks and mud and is too shallow for anything but a temporary stop.

Bluff Cove
Charts 18744; 1.7 mi NE of Palos Verdes Pt
Position: 33°47.59'N, 118°24.70'W

Bluff Cove is a shallow bight. . . . The beach is covered with boulders. . (CP, 33rd Ed.)

Bluff Cove is exposed and offers little protection.

David J. Shuler

Seals like the flat surface on buoys!

Docks at California Yacht Marina

California Yacht Marina at San Pedro

King Harbor . . . is a large small-craft harbor at Redondo Beach. The harbor is used mostly by pleasure craft and accommodates upwards of 1,400 boats. The entrance is between two lights at the ends of the breakwaters at the S end of the harbor. A fog signal is at the light on the E side of the entrance. A lighted bell buoy is 230 yards SSW of the S end of the W breakwater. . . . Sport fishing barges usually anchor 1 or 2 miles off-shore during the summer; caution is advised to avoid them. (CP, 33rd Ed.)

When approaching King Harbor from the north, stay outside 10 fathoms of depth. The area has numerous underwater hazards. On the south side of the entrance, the area is subject to shoaling. Watch for fishing barges moored off the harbor and give them a wide berth. Inside the harbor, there are still reports of uncharted wrecks sunk during the winter of 1988 when a storm severely damaged the breakwater.

From a position offshore, first go to the safe-water buoy (RW "RB" MoA Bell), southwest of the jetty, then set a course to the lighted green buoy just off the end of the breakwater; then, proceed into the channel.

Malaga Cove (Santa Monica Bay)
Charts 18744; 2.0 mi S of King Harbor
Position: 33°48.49'N, 118°23.91'W

Malaga Cove . . . is used occasionally by fishing boats with local knowledge, but it is open to the prevailing W winds. Boats enter through a break in the kelp and anchor inside in 6 to 7 fathoms, with the S point of the cove bearing 207°. (CP, 33rd Ed.)

Malaga Cove is useful only in calm conditions. King Harbor, two miles north, is a harbor of refuge providing superior anchorage.

King Harbor (Redondo Beach Harbor)
Chart 18744; 4.5 mi NE of Palos Verdes Pt
Entrance (outer): (CA164) 33°50.23'N, 118°23.86'W
Entrance (inner): (CA165) 33°50.45'N, 118°23.66'W
Anchor: 33°50.79'N, 118°24.01'W

Aerial view: King Harbor

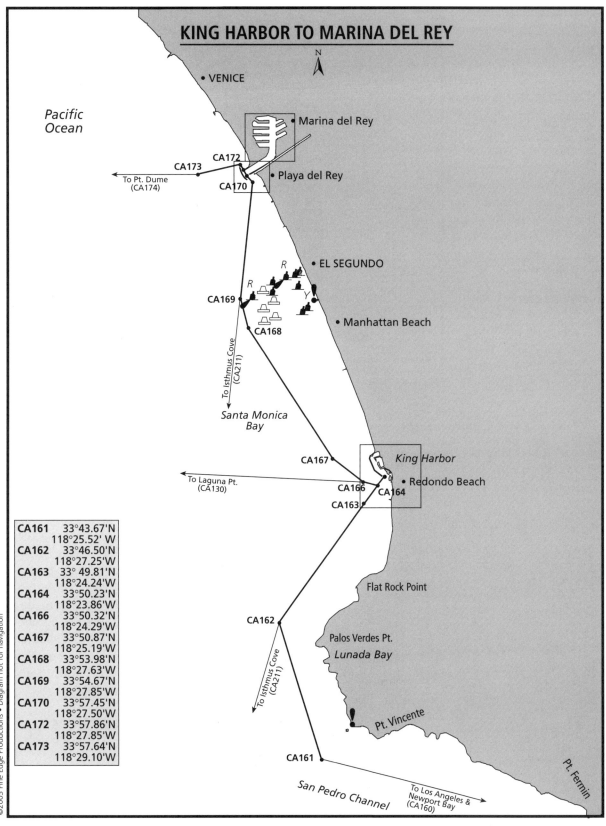

KING HARBOR TO MARINA DEL REY

N

Pacific Ocean

• VENICE

• Marina del Rey

CA173   CA172

To Pt. Dume (CA174)

CA170

• Playa del Rey

R

R   • EL SEGUNDO

CA169

Y

CA168

• Manhattan Beach

To Isthmus Cove (CA211)

Santa Monica Bay

CA167

King Harbor

To Laguna Pt. (CA130)

CA166   • Redondo Beach

CA164

CA163

Flat Rock Point

CA162

Palos Verdes Pt.

Lunada Bay

To Isthmus Cove (CA211)

Pt. Vincente

CA161

Pt. Fermin

San Pedro Channel

To Los Angeles & Newport Bay (CA160)

CA161	33°43.67'N
	118°25.52' W
CA162	33°46.50'N
	118°27.25'W
CA163	33° 49.81'N
	118°24.24'W
CA164	33°50.23'N
	118°23.86'W
CA166	33°50.32'N
	118°24.29'W
CA167	33°50.87'N
	118°25.19'W
CA168	33°53.98'N
	118°27.63'W
CA169	33°54.67'N
	118°27.85'W
CA170	33°57.45'N
	118°27.50'W
CA172	33°57.86'N
	118°27.85'W
CA173	33°57.64'N
	118°29.10'W

Launch facilities: Redondo Beach Marina (south of the main harbor) has both a hoist and a hand-launch area for small boats. There are no trailer launch ramps. Contact the marina for rates and instructions. The hand-launch area is adjacent to the Redondo Beach Marina parking lot, and can also be reached by taking Pacific Coast Highway to Catalina Avenue south to Portofino Way.

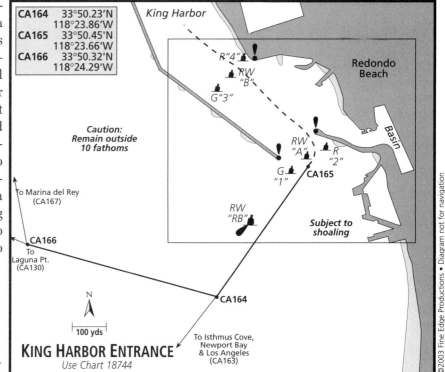

CA164	33°50.23'N 118°23.86'W
CA165	33°50.45'N 118°23.66'W
CA166	33°50.32'N 118°24.29'W

King Harbor

R"4"

RW "B"

G"3"

Redondo Beach

Basin

Caution: Remain outside 10 fathoms

RW "A"

R "2"

To Marina del Rey (CA167)

G "1"

CA165

CA166
To Laguna Pt. (CA130)

RW "RB"

Subject to shoaling

N

CA164

100 yds

KING HARBOR ENTRANCE
Use Chart 18744

To Isthmus Cove, Newport Bay & Los Angeles (CA163)

©2003 Fine Edge Productions • Diagram not for navigation

⚓ **King Harbor Harbormaster dock and pumpout** position: 33°50.80'N, 118°23.93'W; VHF Ch. 12; tel: 310.318.0632

⚓ **King Harbor Marina** position: 33°50.95'N, 118°23.96'W; tel: 310.376.6926

⚓ **Port Royal Marina** position: 33°50.85'N, 118°23.79'W; reservations required, openings based on space availability; fuel and water; tel: 310.376.0431; website: www.cymportroyal.com

⚓ **Portofino Marina** position: 33°50.80'N, 118°23.78'W; tel: 310.379.8481

⚓ **Redondo Beach Marina** position: 33°50.50'N, 118°23.51'W; reservations required; tel: 310.374.3481; website: www.rbmarina.com

Anchor: King Harbor is a harbor of refuge. All vessels must anchor bow and stern, along the west side of the main channel inside the breakwater. The preferred anchoring area is at the north end of the harbor, but watch for shoaling. Contact the Harbor Patrol for an anchoring permit; 3-day limit.

Hermosa Beach, Manhattan Beach
Charts 18744, 18740; both btw Redondo Beach & El Segundo

Entering King Harbor

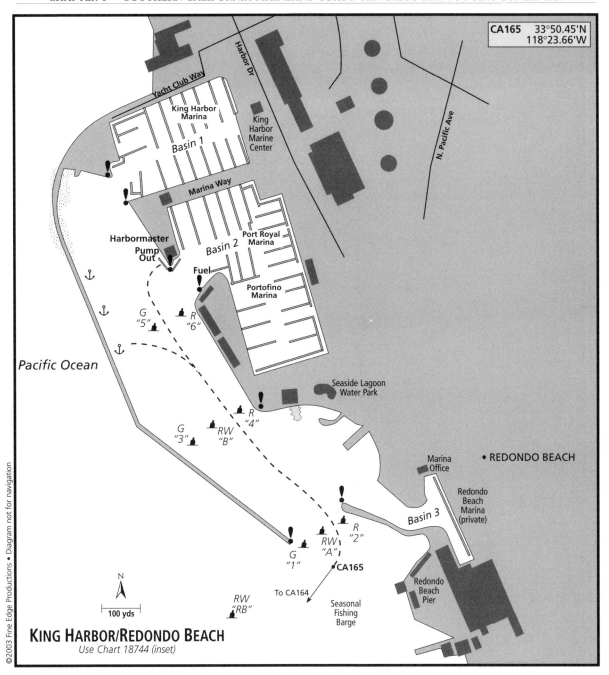

KING HARBOR/REDONDO BEACH
Use Chart 18744 (inset)

©2003 Fine Edge Productions • Diagram not for navigation

[Hermosa Beach and Manhattan Beach] *both have public fishing piers with fish havens covered 10 feet around their seaward ends. . . . Mariners should use caution when navigating over the sewer outfalls that extend seaward from El Segundo. The existence of the submerged sewer outfalls present a hazard to all types of craft.* (CP, 33rd Ed.)

Marina del Rey
(Santa Monica Bay)
Charts 18744, 18740; 7.6 mi NNW of Redondo Beach
Entrance (S) position: (CA170) 33°57.45'N, 118°27.50'W
Entrance (N) position: (CA172) 33°57.86'N, 118°27.85'W
Anchor: 33°58.93'N, 118°26.91'W

Marina del Rey . . . is a large manmade small-craft harbor . . . [with] a capacity for over 6,000 pleasure craft. A dredged entrance channel leads NE from the detached breakwater for about 0.7 mile, then the harbor channel continues N for about 0.6 mile to the N end of the harbor. There are two openings between the jetties and the detached breakwater. . . . A special anchorage is in the upper reach of the harbor channel. Anchoring is permitted only during storm, stress, or other emergency. . . . Guest berths are available. Transients should report to the harbormaster for berth assignment. (CP, 33rd Ed.)

Whales decorate a building in Redondo Beach

Slips at King Harbor in Redondo Beach

Marina del Rey Harbor is 1.2 miles northwest of Los Angeles International Airport. Vessels approaching in restricted visibility (smog or low fog) can use the planes departing from the airport as an intermediate target. Once you reach the 10-fathom curve, proceed with caution to the 5-fathom curve, then follow the 5-fathom curve to the south opening into Marina del Rey Harbor. In fog, don't confuse the Venice Pier foghorn with the Marina del Rey jetty foghorn which is approximately one mile northwest. Avoid the Hyperion Pipeline (see Sidebar).

The area around the Marina del Rey entrance jetties are subject to considerable shoaling and extends along the length of the northern jetty inside the channel. The main channel is dredged and all shoal areas are marked with buoys.

Note: The main entrance channel is divided by buoys that define traffic separation lanes for sail and power vessels. Power vessels must keep the buoys to port when entering or leaving the harbor. Sailing vessels are restricted to the center channel. Convention is for northbound vessels to use the north opening and for southbound vessels to use the south opening. However, in heavy weather vessels are advised to use the north opening, which is less affected by shoaling. Chart 18744, note F, reads Uncharted buoys, labeled "No Sail," mark the traffic separations lanes and entrance channel.

Guest moorings are available through the harbormaster. A transient dock is located on the north side of Basin H (next to the beautiful Burton Chace Park grounds). During busi-

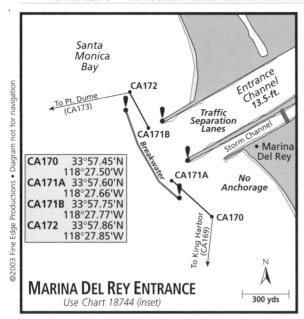

Santa Monica Bay

To Pt. Dume (CA173)

CA172

Entrance Channel 13.5-ft.

Traffic Separation Lanes

CA171B

Breakwater

Storm Channel

• Marina Del Rey

CA170	33°57.45'N 118°27.50'W
CA171A	33°57.60'N 118°27.66'W
CA171B	33°57.75'N 118°27.77'W
CA172	33°57.86'N 118°27.85'W

CA171A

No Anchorage

CA170

To King Harbor (CA169)

N

MARINA DEL REY ENTRANCE
Use Chart 18744 (inset)

300 yds

©2003 Fine Edge Productions • Diagram not for navigation

Marina del Rey transient dock looking northwest

Marina del Rey Visitors Center

ness hours (0600 to 2200), go to the Community Building in Burton Chace Park adjacent to the transient dock. After-hours arrivals must register in the morning. Pumpout stations are found at the fuel dock, at Burton Chace Park docks, and at launch ramp in Basin H. Burton Chace Park is a beautiful, landscaped area that offers a full range of activities including band concerts.

Launch Ramp: Small boats may be hand-launched from the beach in Basin D. Trailer boats may be launched from the ramp at the end of Basin H. The ramp is open 24 hours a day and has parking, restrooms, and wash-down facilities. From I-405, take the Marina Freeway (Route 90) west to Mindanao Way. Turn left on Mindanao and follow the signs to the launch ramp.

- ⚓ **MDR Launch Ramp** position: 33°58.64'N, 118°26.50'W
- ⚓ **MDR Fuel Dock** position: 33°58.30'N, 118°26.95'W
- ⚓ **MDR Boat Repair Facilities** position: 33°58.51'N, 118°26.76'W
- ⚓ **MDR USCG Base** position: 33°58.21'N, 118°26.79'W
- ⚓ **Marina del Rey Harbormaster** position: 33°58.23'N, 118°26.78'W; tel: 310.823.7762
- ⚓ **Marina Harbor Anchorage** position: 33°58.43'N, 118°26.96'W; no guest slips or transient dock; tel: 310.822.1659; daily from 0900 to 1800
- ⚓ **Burton Chace Park** position: 33°58.56'N, 118°26.77'W; call for space availability; tel: 310.305.9595; daily from 0800 to 1700

Aerial view: Marina del Rey

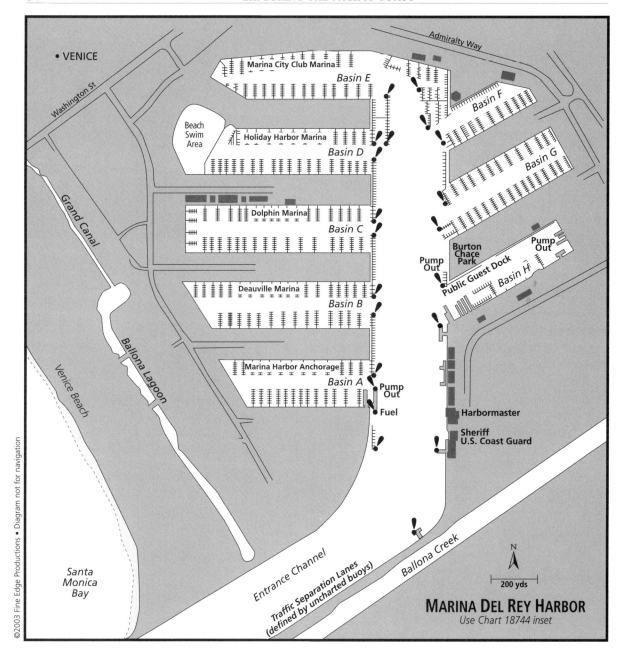

Marina Del Rey Harbor
Use Chart 18744 inset

⚓ **Deauville Marina** position: 33°58.59'N, 118°26.96'W; under reconstruction, reopening scheduled 2004 as Esprit

⚓ **Dolphin Marina** position: 33°58.75'N, 118°26.96'W; reservations required and based on space availability; tel: 310.578.0566; daily from 0900 to 1730

⚓ **Holiday Harbor Marina** position: 33°58.97'N, 118°27.18'W; prior reservations only; tel: 310.821.4582; from 0800 to 1600 Thursday to Monday only

⚓ **Marina City Club Marina** position: 33°58.99'N, 118°27.15'W; no guest slips or transient dock; tel: 310.822.1659; daily from 0800 to 1700

Anchor: Vessels may anchor in the northern portion of the main channel during storms or other emergencies only. Both bow and stern

Marina del Rey

anchors are required. Contact the harbormaster for permission to use the anchorage.

Santa Monica Pier
Charts 18740, 18744; 3.5 mi NW of Marina del Rey
Pleasure pier position: 34°00.41'N, 118°30.01'W

> *Santa Monica . . . has a large pleasure pier, but there is no water commerce. A private fog signal is on the outer end of the pier. A 0.3-mile-long breakwater, parallel to the beach and marked by private buoys, is off the outer end of the pier. A lighted bell buoy is about 550 yards S of the breakwater. . . . Mariners are advised to use extreme caution because of debris and hazardous conditions in the area.* (CP, 33rd Ed.)

The old breakwater northwest of the pier, largely submerged, is a sandtrap. The area inside the breakwater is more a hazard than the temporary anchorage it once was.

Kellers Shelter (Malibu)
Charts 18740, 18744; is 9 mi W of Sta Monica
Position: 34°02.02'N, 118°40.48'W

> *Kellers Shelter . . . is an open bight offering protection from N and W winds in 2 to 7 fathoms, sandy bottom. A reef marked by kelp extends a short distance offshore about 0.5 mile W of the anchorage. A fishing and pleasure pier, 700 feet long with 15 feet of water at its outer end, is on the W side of Kellers Shelter. . . . Private mooring buoys are maintained E of the pier for the use of sport fishing boats which leave for the nearby fishing grounds.* (CP, 33rd Ed.)

Temporary anchorage in fair weather can be found between the foul area off the beach and the private mooring buoys.

Transient dock with beautiful Burton Chace Park in background

Marina del Rey Visitors Center

Summer concert at Burton Chace Park

Marina del Rey's Mariner statue

Marina del Rey Visitors Center

Paradise Cove
Charts 18740, 18744; 1.6 mi NE of Point Dume
Position: 34°00.91'N, 118°46.93'W

Paradise Cove . . . affords protection similar to Kellers Shelter. The anchorage is abreast the fourth break or arroyo in the cliffs from Point Dume, and is immediately outside the kelp line, in 6 to 7 fathoms, sand bottom, with Point Dume bearing 240°. Kelp should be avoided because of possible dangers. A 300-foot sport fishing pier is on the NW side of Paradise Cove. A rescue vessel is moored in Paradise Cove. (CP, 33rd Ed.)

Paradise Cove offers temporary anchorage in fair weather as noted in *Coast Pilot.* Avoid patches of kelp.

Laguna Point / Point Mugu
Chart 18725; S of Channel Islands Hbr
Position (Laguna Pt): (CA130) 34°03.03'N, 119°08.22'W

A danger zone for Navy small-arms firing range extends about two miles offshore at Point Mugu. The U.S. Navy advises navigation interests and others that continuous guided-missile firing operations may take place in the Pacific Missile Range, Point

Beware the Hyperion Pipeline!

Skippers are advised that when approaching Marina del Rey Harbor, especially in fog, and hugging the coast, there are a number of obstructions that extend from both the Venice and El Segundo beaches. The Hyperion Pipeline, 2.5 miles south of the entrance to Marina del Rey, recently snagged a 28-ft sailboat with three persons aboard. Conditions at the time were partly cloudy, wind 12 knots and one to two foot seas. The skipper reported hitting the effluent pipeline in 32 feet of water, requiring a pumpout and tow to Marina del Rey. Damages were estimated at $10,000. Mariners are advised to stay seaward of the well-charted red buoy "12 ES" shown on Chart 18744 which marks the bitter end of the pipeline 0.8 mile from the beach on the south side of Los Angeles Airport. Buoy position is 33°55.08'N, 118°26.90'W.

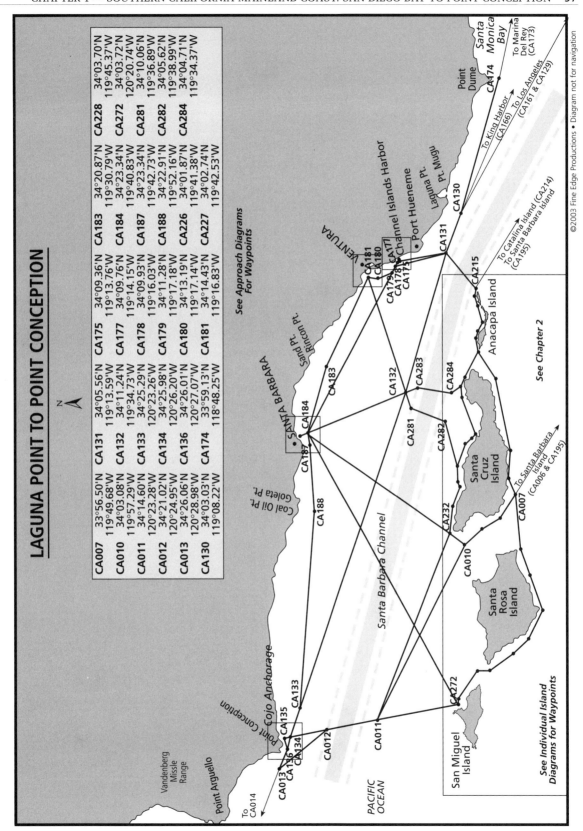

LAGUNA POINT TO POINT CONCEPTION

CA007	33°56.50'N 119°49.68'W	CA175	34°05.56'N 119°13.59'W
CA131	34°03.08'N 119°57.29'W	CA177	34°11.24'N 119°34.73'W
CA132	34°09.76'N 119°14.15'W		
CA133	34°14.60'N 120°23.28'W	CA178	34°09.93'N 119°16.03'W
CA134	34°21.02'N 120°24.95'W	CA179	34°25.29'N 120°23.26'W
CA136	34°26.06'N 120°28.98'W	CA180	34°25.98'N 120°26.20'W
CA174	34°03.03'N 119°08.22'W	CA181	34°11.28'N 119°17.18'W
CA130		CA226	34°13.19'N 120°27.07'W
		CA227	34°14.43'N 119°17.14'W

CA183	34°20.87'N 119°30.79'W	CA228	34°03.70'N 119°45.37'W
CA184	34°23.34'N 119°40.83'W	CA272	34°03.72'N 120°20.74'W
CA187	34°23.34'N 119°42.73'W	CA281	34°10.06'N 119°36.89'W
CA188	34°22.91'N 119°52.16'W	CA282	34°05.62'N 119°38.99'W
CA226	34°01.87'N 119°41.38'W	CA284	34°04.71'N 119°34.37'W
CA227	34°02.74'N 119°42.53'W		

See Approach Diagrams For Waypoints

See Individual Island Diagrams for Waypoints

©2003 Fine Edge Productions • Diagram not for navigation

Mugu, Calif., Sea Test Range, Monday through Sunday. The test area extends for 170 miles in a SW direction from Point Mugu and is up to 100 miles wide. . . . Mugu Canyon is a submarine valley with its head near Mugu Lagoon. The 50-fathom curve is about 0.5 mile offshore. (CP, 33rd Ed)

Point Mugu is the seaward termination of the Santa Monica Mountains. It is best to remain 3 miles offshore when transiting Point Mugu.

Port Hueneme
Chart 18725; 1.1 mi SE of Channel Island Hbr
Entrance (inner range): 34°08.60'N, 119°12.83'W
Entrance (outer range): 34°08.28'N, 119°13.11'W

Port Hueneme is an inland basin, about 1,300 feet long by 1,200 feet wide. . . . It is under the control of the U.S. Navy, Naval Construction Battalion Center. The SE part of the basin is owned by the Oxnard Harbor District and is operated as a deep-draft commercial terminal. The commercial terminal is used by cargo vessels; commercial and sport fishing craft; and oil company support vessels, which operate from here to offshore drilling rigs.

There is no anchorage area in the harbor basin because of space limitations. The recommended anchorage for deep-draft vessels is about 1.7 miles S of Port Hueneme Light. This location offers little protection in heavy weather. (CP, 33rd Ed.)

Port Hueneme (pronounced why-nee-me) is a restricted area. It is a military installation and container port. Pleasure craft may enter in emergencies with permission.

Channel Islands Harbor (Oxnard)
Chart 18725 (inset); 1.1 mi NW of Port Hueneme, 5.8 mi S of Ventura
Entrance (N bkwtr lt): (CA177) 34°09.76'N, 119°14.15'W
Entrance (midchannel): (CA175) 34°09.36'N, 119°13.76'W

Channel Islands Harbor . . . is a small-craft harbor. . . . used by pleasure and sport fishing vessels and has existing berthing facilities for over 2,400 boats. The entrance to Channel Islands Harbor is between two jetties protected by an offshore breakwater. Each end of the breakwater and both the seaward and inshore ends of both jetties are marked by lights. A fog signal is at the seaward end of the S jetty. The area SE of the entrance is subject to rapid and uncertain shoaling. Mariners should

exercise caution when approaching the harbor from the S, especially at night. (CP, 33rd Ed.)

Channel Islands Harbor calls itself the "gateway to the Channel Islands." From here it's 11 miles to Anacapa, 18 miles to Santa Cruz, and cruising distance to Santa Rosa, San Miguel, and Santa Barbara Islands. Necessities are within walking distance of the public dock and the 70 transient slips. The slips at the Peninsula Park guest dock and the East Bank guest dock have electricity, water, and shower and restroom facilities. The fuel dock, open seven days a week from 0700 to 1500, is north of the harbormaster's office on the east side of the main channel. The County of Ventura maintains pump-out stations at both guest docks.

You'll find a large grocery store and a chandlery within walking distance, as well as restaurants, dive shops, and specialty shops. You can rent boats or kayaks, take in the Maritime Museum, or visit a Farmers' Market every Sunday from 1000 to 1400. Channel Islands Harbor is home to 2,600 boats, four yacht clubs, nine marinas, and features year-round events both on and off the water. Miles of clean, sandy beaches near the harbor offer good surfing, although the area has a reputation for aggressive localism. Surf these waves at your own risk.

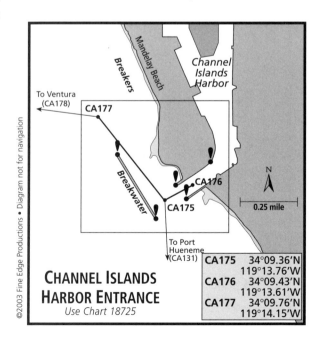

©2003 Fine Edge Productions • Diagram not for navigation

CHANNEL ISLANDS HARBOR ENTRANCE
Use Chart 18725

CA175	34°09.36'N 119°13.76'W
CA176	34°09.43'N 119°13.61'W
CA177	34°09.76'N 119°14.15'W

Aerial view: Channel Islands Harbor

Channel Islands Harbor jetties and breakwater

Don't miss Sea Gate Gallery, run by well-known local artist, potter, and ceramicist Margy Gates. Margy's gallery features nautical art—watercolors, note cards, pottery, candles—and many more gift items. Margy has crewed for the authors from the Sea of Cortez to Ventura, as well as on many excursions to the Channel Islands. Her paintings and sculptures are as authentic and salty as you will see anywhere.

The entrance to Channel Islands Harbor is protected by a 2,300-foot long detached rock breakwater. While you can enter or exit either end in fair conditions, the south end is closer to the harbor and is the preferred route. Like Ventura, the north entrance has a built-in sand-trap which catches sand from the Santa Clara River and fills from the beach outwards halfway or more to the breakwater. When the shoal exceeds a certain point, yellow flashing buoys mark the shoal area and you must pass between the yellow lights and the breakwater. We would recommend calling the Harbor Patrol for current conditions at the north entrance and be sure to watch your echo sounder so there are no

surprises. In either case, avoid the shoals and breakers by staying well off the beach along this coast. The charts do not always reflect the output of Santa Clara River. The large power station, with its tall smokestacks, at the north end of Mandalay Bay, is 3.2 miles north of Channel Islands—a good landmark for both Ventura and Channel Islands harbors.

There is no anchorage inside Channel Islands Harbor. For slip assistance, please call the Harbor Patrol. The Channel Islands Coast Guard Station is located south of the harbormaster's office.

- ⚓ **Harbor Patrol Office and Slip** position: 34°09.73'N, 119°13.38'W; tel: 805.382.3007
- ⚓ **USCG Base** position: 34°09.68'N, 119°13.37'W
- ⚓ **Bahia Cabrillo Marina** position: 34°09.75'N, 119°13.48'W; 805.985.0113
- ⚓ **Channel Islands Marina** position: 34°09.94'N, 119°13.56'W; tel: 805.985.7558
- ⚓ **Channel Landing and Dry Storage** position: 34°09.96'N, 119°13.39'W

⚓ **Peninsula Yacht Anchorage** position: 34°10.00'N, 119°13.49'W

⚓ **Channel Islands Boatyard** position: 34°10.10'N, 119°13.39'W

⚓ **Ch. Isls. Guest Dock** (W) position: 34°10.19'N, 119°13.64'W

⚓ **Vintage Marina** position: 34°10.21'N, 119°13.70'W; tel: 805.984.3366

⚓ **Anacapa Isle Marina** position: 34°10.27'N, 119°13.65'W; tel: 805.985.6035

⚓ **Ch. Isls. Small Boat Marine** position: 34°10.28'N, 119°13.41'W

⚓ **Ch. Isls. Launch Ramp** position: 34°10.34'N, 119°13.39'W

⚓ **Pacific Corinthian Marina** position: 34°10.43'N, 119°13.70'W; guest slips available seasonally, reservations required,

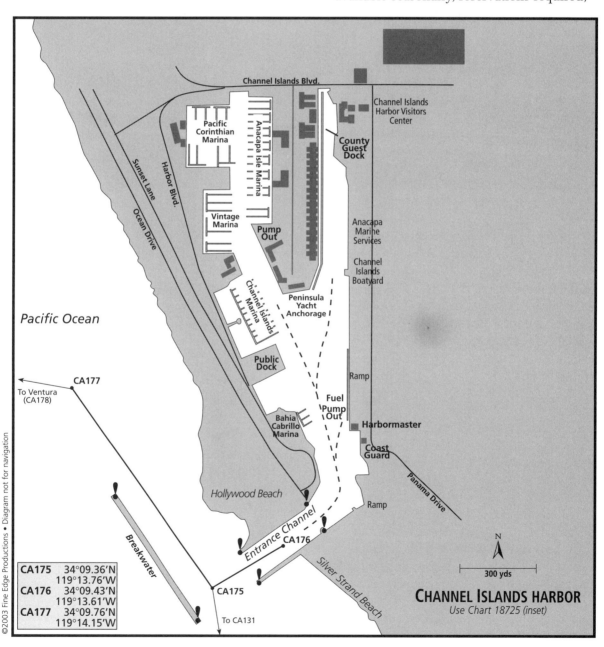

Bon Voyage party for the Gaylords' Passing Thru, *Channel Islands Harbor*

office open 24/7; tel: 805.984.2847; website: www.sailorschoice.com

⚓ **Ch. Isls. Guest Dock** (E) position: 34°10.46'N, 119°13.44'W

⚓ **Ch. Isls. Fisherman's Wharf** position: 34°10.50'N, 119°13.40'W

Ventura Harbor
Chart 18725; 5.8 mi NW of Channel Islands
Entrance (outer): (CA181) 34°14.43'N, 119°16.83'W
Entrance (inner): (CA182) 34°14.77'N, 119°16.30'W
Harbormaster office and slip position: 34°15.08'N, 119°16.03'W

Ventura Harbor . . . is a small-craft harbor used by pleasure craft and commercial fishing vessels. It has existing berthing facilities for about 1,500 boats. Commercial fish handling facilities are available in the harbor. (CP, 33rd Ed.)

Ventura Harbor is the home of the Channel Islands National Park and has upgraded its facilities over the years to become a first-rate yacht harbor.

The manmade harbor includes three marinas, two yacht clubs, several waterfront restaurants, repair facilities, and about 40 retail shops. The harbormaster's office is located on the point north of the entrance channel. Guest slips are handled by the three private marinas. Fuel is located at the south end of the harbor and by the six-lane launch ramp. The harbor also services a small commercial fishing fleet. There are chandleries and liquor stores within walking distance at the borders of the harbor; it's a mile and a quarter to the nearest major grocery store.

Sailboat entering main channel

Channel Islands National Park Headquarters and Visitor Center, with exhibits portraying the islands' history and native fauna and flora, is a recognizable landmark near the harbor entrance. The center distributes detailed maps and charts of all the trails and various points of interest. The beaches just south of the harbor host national surfing contests, and you'll also find a sheltered, shallow swimming beach. Ventura Harbor is home to what was once California's longest wooden pier. Locals consider Ventura one of the best kayaking and windsurfing spots in Southern California.

For fun and entertainment the harbor offers a lively year-round calendar of events starting with the Celebration of the Whale in January; President's Holiday Concerts and Shows in February; Seafest in June; 4th of July Celebration; California Beach Festival in September; and the Ventura Offshore Powerboat Grand Prix Festival (October). At any point throughout the year you're likely to encounter weekend concerts, regattas, and surfing events. Be sure to check out the Ventura Harbor Ceramic Mural Project at Ventura Harbor Village; sculpted from two tons

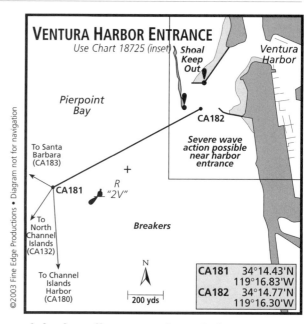

of clay by college art students, it depicts marine life found in the Santa Barbara Channel.

Like neighboring Santa Barbara, Ventura boasts a rich historical legacy. In 1782 Father Junipero Serra established Mission San Buenaventura, which can still be visited today at 225 E. Main St. Exhibits include Chumash Indian artifacts and various items from the mission's early days; the restored church is still used by an active congregation. The nearby Albinger Archaeological Museum displays artifacts spanning 3,500 years, all excavated from a single site next to San Buenaventura Mission. The Padre Serra Cross, erected in 1782 on what is now on Mission Hill in Grant Park, offers an impressive view of the area.

Frequent dredging and improvements in the design of the harbor entrance have made entering Ventura Harbor much safer. Enter or exit Ventura Harbor *only* via the main entrance, south of the breakwater, between the two jetties. The area behind the breakwater is designed as a sand trap and is subject to severe shoaling.

Aerial view: Ventura Harbor

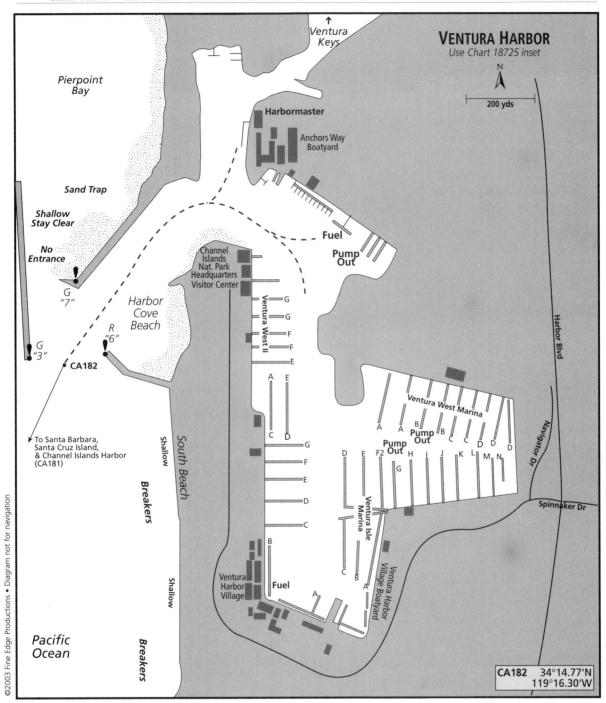

When approaching Ventura from the south, use waypoints CA179, CA180, CA181 to avoid the shoals and dangerous breakers off the Santa Clara River.

Entrance buoy "2VU" is located approximately 1/2 mile off the entrance. The prudent skipper always keeps this buoy to starboard when enter-ing. This keeps him or her away from the mouth of the Santa Clara River, 1/2 mile south of the entrance. As one of the largest naturally running rivers in Southern California, this river provides a tremendous amount of sand to the local beaches. Unfortunately this can create conditions of heavy surf far out to sea.

Note (from Chart 18725): *Mariners are cautioned that severe wave action may be encountered over the shoals either side of the marked entrance channel. Inbound and outbound boaters are advised by local interests to run a direct course from Ventura Marina entrance lighted whistle buoy "2V" to the breakwater entrance.*

⚓ **Ventura Harbormaster** monitors VHF 16 switch to Ch. 12; tel: 805.642.8618

⚓ **Ventura West Marina** position: 34°14.72'N, 119°15.62'W; reservations recommended; tel: 805.644.8266

⚓ **Ventura West Marina II** position: 34°14.82'N, 119°15.90'W

⚓ **Ventura Isle Marina** position: 34°14.60'N, 119°15.78'W; guest slips available, reserva-

Ventura entrance seen from Harbor Cove Beach

tions required, call on Channel 16; tel: 805.644.5858; website: www.venturaisle.com

⚓ **Ventura Yacht Club** floats position: 34°14.72'N, 119°15.89'W

⚓ **Launch Ramp and Fuel Dock** position: 34°14.97'N, 119°15.83'W

F/V Tradition *entering Ventura Harbor*

USA Avenger *on Ventura travel lift*

Larry Dudley's Yacht Sales floating office

⚓ **Ventura Harbor Village Boat Yard** position: 34°14.48'N, 119°15.72'W

⚓ **Channel Island National Park Service Visitors Center** position: 34°14.91'N, 119°15.97'W

⚓ **Ventura Keys** entrance: 34°15.15'N, 119°16.02'W

⚓ **Harbor Cove Beach** (kayak and canoe haulout beach) position: 34°14.84'N, 119°16.13'W

Enforcements
The speed limit in the harbor and entrance channel is 5 mph and strictly enforced; the same speed is enforced within 200 feet of all beaches frequented by bathers or within 100 feet of any bather. Pollution violations are enforced and anyone who suffers an accidental spill is required to contact the Harbor Patrol at once.

Launch Ramp use
The launch ramp has six lanes and about 180 parking spaces accessible 24 hours a day, and a parking fee applies at all times.

Swimming
Swimming is allowed only at Harbor Cove beach across from the National Park Service. Lifeguard services are provided at the beach during the summer. (It is illegal to swim any place else within Ventura Harbor.) The areas north and south of the harbor are posted as being hazardous for swimming. Rip currents and the jetties make it very dangerous to swim or even wade in either area.

Pierpont Bay
Chart 18725; 20.9 mi E Santa Barbara Hbr
Position (fishing pier): 34°16.28'N, 119°17.61'W

> *Ventura . . . has a 1,960-foot fishing pier with about 19 feet of water at the outer end, and about 18 feet at the inner end of a 250-foot loading face. Small craft may anchor anywhere in Pierpont Bay, but the anchorage is unprotected and is not recommended except for short day use. Boats may obtain moorage at Ventura Harbor. (CP, 33rd Ed.)*

Pierpont Bay is a bight east and south of the outlet of Ventura River. The city of Ventura lies to the north and east. A 2,000-foot-long pier extends southwest from shore. The point off the south side of Ventura River creates a good surfing beach. The bay, which is open to all weather and subject to swells most of the time, is useful only as a temporary stop in fair weather. Anchoring is advised only during daylight hours. Avoid the large oil buoys further out.

Anchor (temporary) in 4 fathoms over flat, somewhat packed, sand with fair holding.

Punta Gorda
Chart 18725, 12.6 mi E of Santa Barbara Hbr
Position: 34°20.92'N, 119°26.29'W

Punta Gorda is a major headland along the west-trending coastline west of Pierpont Bay. A small islet called Rincon Island is located at the end of an oil pipeline pier extending southwest from Punta Gorda. A number of oil rigs are hidden behind walls camouflaged as a south sea island. Small craft sometimes find temporary limited shelter between the lee of Rincon Island and the additional oil pier immediately east. The sand beach between the two piers attracts sunbathers during the summer. This is a fair weather site only and not recommended for overnight use.

Anchor (temporary) in 5 to 8 fathoms over mostly sand with kelp; avoid the submerged pipeline to the west of Rincon Island.

Rincon Point
Chart 18725; 10.6 mi E of Santa Barbara Hbr
Position: 34°22.41'N, 119°28.27'W

Rincon Point is a local surfer "hangout" because of the nice long break made as the westerly swells curve around the point. A temporary stop in fair weather can only be found east of the break with a good view of all the action. Not recommended for overnight use.

Fernald Point Cove
Chart: 18725; 3.4 mi E of Santa Barbara Hbr
Position: 34°25.12'N, 119°36.96'W

Fernald Point Cove is what local author Brian Fagen refers to as the bight behind Fernald Point at the foot of Montecito. He reports that this has been a favorite of local small craft looking for a short-term stop in fair weather. Except

---

In Memorium: Larry Dudley—A Sailor's Sailor
by DCD & RHD

Californian Larry Dudley bought his first boat in the 1930s at age 10, teaching himself to sail in Alamitos Bay. Within nine years he had skippered a three-month trip to Mexico. He loved all facets of boating, including racing, and in 1939 was the first to finish the TransPac Race to Hawaii.

By the time Larry was 24, he had earned the distinction as the youngest Chief Bosun's Mate in the U.S. Coast Guard in WWII. He participated in the Salerno landing in Italy and later worked his way through college by delivering boats through the Panama Canal.

In 1947 he was hired by Humphrey Bogart to serve as first mate and relief captain on Bogey's legendary 55-foot yawl, *Santana*—a position that spanned 10 years, until the actor's death. Larry also sailed with actor Sterling Hayden with whom he developed a life-long friendship.

Larry was proud of the fact that he never incurred any serious damage to any vessel under his command and never had an insurance claim. He felt at home on the water and was confident in his ability to deliver any reasonably seaworthy vessel in good order. He was a great advocate of matching the right person with the right boat. And indeed he did. One of his best matches was the sale of the *Swift of Ipswich* to the Los Angeles Maritime Institute to be used in a youth sailing program—a program he believed in and supported.

In 1980, Larry and his wife Ann Phillips opened Larry Dudley Yacht Sales on the dock at Ventura Harbor Village, which they ran together until the late 1990s.

Courtesy of Ann Dudley

Larry will be remembered for his professional integrity, his inspirational leadership, his willingness to lend a hand, to teach a newcomer needed skills, and to share a friendly yarn. It was our distinct pleasure to have him crew on our *Dauphin Amical* and to crew for him as well. Larry passed away at age 81 in August, 2001.

Sailing regatta east of Santa Barbara

for noise from Highway 101 and anchoring in view of someone's bay windows, the mountain backdrop and gentle rocking behind the off-lying kelp banks can be very soothing.

Along this entire coast you can find a curvilinear smooth-water route inside the kelp beds (if you are not in a hurry) by working your way

---

Fourth of July in Pierpont Bay
by DCD

For several years in a row on the Fourth of July we would anchor in Pierpont Bay, about 200 yards off the end of the Ventura Pier, and watch the fireworks display. We watched not only the colorful sanctioned displays but also the numerous unofficial and illegal displays set off by the crowds along the beach. One year we had our friend, the Ventura Chief of Police, on board. Seeing all the revelers breaking the law he said simply, "I hope not too many get hurt. There isn't a lot my men can do in these circumstances."

---

carefully along the shore. It is advisable to remain between 100 to 200 yards off the beach and avoid submerged rock piles along many headlands.

Anchor in 3 to 4 fathoms over sand and gravel with kelp.

Santa Barbara Harbor
Chart 18725 (inset); 29 mi NW of Pt Hueneme
Entrance (outer): (CA185) 34°24.32'N, 119°40.96'W
Entrance (inner): (CA186) 34°24.52'N, 119°41.23'W
Anchorage position (E of Stearns Wharf): 34°24.59'N, 119°40.47'W

> *Santa Barbara . . . is a resort city and popular yachting harbor. The harbor is used mostly by pleasure craft and fishing vessels. There are over 1,000 slips and 115 permanent moorings in the harbor.*
>
> *The harbor has a 500-yard breakwater extending NE from Point Castillo to an extensive sandbar which forms the S side of the harbor. A jetty extends across the sandbar about 400 yards N from the NE end of the breakwater. A light marks the connection between the breakwater and the jetty. The NE side of the harbor is formed by Stearns Wharf. A light is at the S end of the wharf. A groin, about 125 yards long and marked at its S end by a light, extends S from shore about 0.3 mile W of Stearns Wharf. At night, sometimes the lights are difficult to see against the background of city lights. A radio beacon and a fog signal are at the light on Stearns Wharf.*
>
> *A special anchorage area is in the basin behind the breakwater. Anchoring inside the harbor is usually prohibited by the harbormaster. Anchoring is prohibited within 300 feet E of Stearns Wharf and within 0.5 mile E of the wharf from December through March. Anchorage may be had inside the kelp, but large vessels should anchor outside of it in better holding ground. The harbormaster desires advance requests for permission to anchor.* (CP, 33rd Ed.)

The first thing you notice as you draw near the beautiful Santa Barbara area is the panoramic view of the Santa Ynez Mountains which embrace the city, and its long, white sandy beaches. There's so much to see and do here

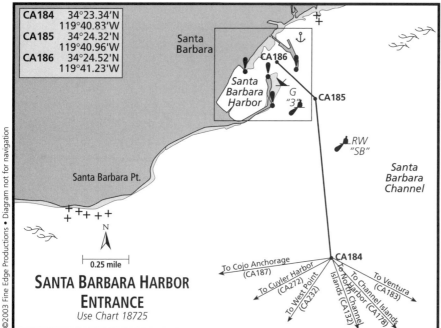

CA184	34°23.34'N 119°40.83'W
CA185	34°24.32'N 119°40.96'W
CA186	34°24.52'N 119°41.23'W

Santa Barbara

CA186

Santa Barbara Harbor

G "3"

CA185

RW "SB"

Santa Barbara Pt.

Santa Barbara Channel

N

0.25 mile

SANTA BARBARA HARBOR ENTRANCE
Use Chart 18725

To Cojo Anchorage (CA187)
To Cuyler Harbor (CA272)
To West Point (CA232)
To North Channel Islands (CA132)
To Channel Islands Harbor (CA178)
To Ventura (CA183)

CA184

©2003 Fine Edge Productions • Diagram not for navigation

that a quick pit stop is almost impossible. The harbor is convenient for provisioning, and it's another good takeoff point for the Channel Islands. To secure one of the approximately 100 guest slips, see at the Harbor Patrol at the west end of the harbor in front of the Chandlery building. You'll find the fuel dock at the end of the Navy Pier, and the launch ramp is located in the northwest corner of the harbor next to the breakwater that separates the marina from the main beach. Next to this at the end of the commercial dock is one of three pump stations; there's another at the head of the walkway to the outside docks (1A) by the restroom and shower facilities, and a third between docks O and R on the outside docks (1A). There are no moorings, but you can anchor outside the breakwater for free.

Restaurants and stores are within walking distance, and the waterfront is bordered by parks, walkways, and entertainment centers; downtown is a brief taxi or bus ride away. The harbor is home to Stearn's Wharf, California's oldest working wooden

wharf. Extending inland from the wharf is State Street, renowned for its shopping, nightlife, and access to several historic sites for which Santa Barbara is famous. Notable are the El Presidio State Historic Park on the site of the original presidio and the Santa Barbara Historical Museum, and especially Mission Santa Barbara, founded by the Spanish Franciscans on the Feast of Santa Barbara in 1786.

The waterfront along Santa Barbara offers the visitor plenty of sights and activities. Stearns Wharf, built in 1872, extends 0.5 mile into the Pacific. Plaques along the way detail the wharf's history, introduce the early explorers of the area, and describe the native sea life. The wharf also features a mix of fast food and fine restaurants, gift shops, and a

Aerial view: Santa Barbara Harbor

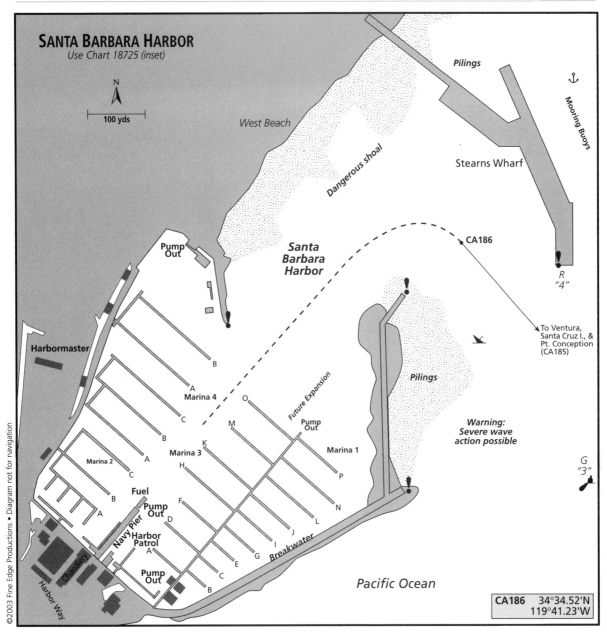

water taxi. The Sea Center, located at the spur of the wharf, houses aquariums, a touch tank, and a life-sized model of a California Gray Whale.

At this popular harbor you'll see world-class yachts amid commercial fishing boats and pleasure craft. You can also rent a fishing boat, sailboats, skates, rollerblades or bikes, go whale watching, or pick up marine supplies. Transient berths are available inside the harbor and there is a mooring buoy and anchorage area east

of Stearns Wharf, both of which are assigned by the Harbor Patrol (as noted above in *Coast Pilot*).

⚓ **Santa Barbara Harbor Patrol**; 100 guest slips, first-come, first-served basis; tel: 805.564.5530; website: www.ci.santa-barbara.ca.us

Anchor in 4 to 6 fathoms about 1/2 mile east of Stearns Wharf over packed sand; fair-to-good holding. Avoid numerous boats and private buoys.

Santa Barbarans are passionate about beach volleyball

Goleta Anchorage
Chart 18721; 7.5 mi W of Santa Barbara Hbr
Position: 34°26.27'N, 120°27.17'W

Goleta Anchorage is the local name for the lee found east of Goleta Point. From here you have a view of the beautiful buildings on the campus of UCSB. The coast between the campus and Atascadero Creek is a popular bathing and recreation area where catamarans, sailing dinghies, and kayaks are launched and landed

Harbor Patrol dock, Santa Barbara Harbor

Loading dock, Santa Barbara Harbor

on the beach. This is an open roadstead that offers no real shelter from serious wind or chop, but it is a great small-craft resource worth a visit. Check out the lagoon behind the sandspit formed by the convergence of Atascadero Creek and Golita Slough. It is easy to imagine that crews of small boats might have used this lagoon for shelter by dragging their craft over the shallow creek bar.

Goleta Beach County Park, on the spit, has parking, picnic tables, and restrooms. This is a great place to people watch and enjoy water sports. Because of the shallow, gradual beach, the surf tends to wash up in a series of small crests easily handled by watercraft and small children.

During stable conditions in summer the water is usually calm. Temporary anchorage can be found (weather permitting) west of the pier over a large shallow area, avoiding kelp patches. Overnight anchorage or anchoring in unstable weather is not advised.

Marine vaquero rides a seahorse in Santa Barbara Harbor

Anchor (temporary) in 2 to 3 fathoms at least 200 yards offshore over packed sand with fair holding.

Refugio
Chart 18721; 19.0 mi E of Govt Pt
Position: 34°27.51'N, 120°04.20'W

> *Refugio Beach . . . is a State Park for camping at the mouth of the canyon. A small bight here offers some protection for small boats in northwesterly winds in about 15 feet.* (CP, 33rd Ed.)

Refugio Beach, a lee found behind a small headland, was formerly the famous Spanish land grant Ortega Ranch, now El Capitan State Beach. The sandy beach is a good place from which to launch small watercraft, such as sea kayaks, for exploring this part of the coast. The park has a fully developed camping and picnicking area lined with palm trees, a boat launch ramp, and limited supplies.

A good temporary anchorage can be found in fair weather at the foot of Canada del Refugio, inside the kelp beds so typical of this coast. Because this is an open roadstead, offering no real shelter, overnight stays are not recommended. Occasional strong downslope winds occur from Refugio to Cojo Anchorage whenever there is a high-pressure system inland relative to the ocean and skippers need to have a plan to deal with these strong winds even though there is little fetch.

Anchor (temporary) in 2 to 3 fathoms over sand with fair holding.

Gaviota Landing
Chart 18721; 11.3 mi E Govt. Pt
Position: 34°28.10'N, 120°13.65'W

Gaviota Landing sits at the foot of Cañada de la Gaviota—a major pass through the Santa Rosa Hills and Santa Ynez Mountains. At this point, 26 miles west of Santa Barbara, Highway 101 turns sharply north and away from the coast toward Buellton. Good temporary anchorage can be found here tucked in at the foot of the sandy bluffs, and partially protected by the abundant offshore kelp patches. Overnight anchoring at Gaviota is not recommended. Sacate Anchorage, 4.5 miles west, is an alternative (see below), as well as Cojo Anchorage.

The land west of Refugio—in fact for the next 100 miles until north of the Vandenberg Missile Range—is, for the most part, primitive and wild without public facilities of any kind. This is where the real coast exploring begins; it is a coastline for serious passagemakers.

The authors, like other cruising boaters, have used Gaviota for years as a base camp for exploring the remote beaches, nooks and crannies, kelp forests, big surf, and big fish. Along this coast we have found the only sea lion rookery we know of on the mainland coast south of Point Arguello until well into Baja. As they say in Baja, *Abre ojos...* keep your eyes open!

Gaviota State Park has camping, picnicking and launching facilities; its 400-foot pier has an electric hoist for sportboats. Major supplies are a long way off so it pays to be self-sufficient here.

The open bight is shallow over a large flat area. The large kelp patches found along this coast grow thick in summer, sometimes requiring vessels to navigate following a circuitous route. Inside the kelp beds only low frequency swells are felt during stable weather. During the fall through winter and into spring, Canada de la Gaviota sometimes receives harsh downslope winds (junior versions of the Santa Ana winds). This type of wind, which funnels down the arroyos, can be avoided in many cases by moving away from its center.

We have kayaked close to shore in this area during such conditions and found paddling quite comfortable, with little fetch. When we wanted to rest we simply tied to the fronds of bull kelp for a while and enjoyed the clear air and bright sun brought on by these winds.

Anchor (temporary) in 3 to 4 fathoms about 200 yards off the beach over flat, packed sand with some stones and kelp; holding is fair-to-good, but be sure your anchor is well set, especially for downslope winds. Avoid underwater oil lines to the shore facility a mile east.

Sacate Anchorage
Chart 18721; 8.0 mi E Govt Pt
Anchor: 34°28.02'N, 120°17.64'W

Sacate Anchorage is tucked in behind one of the bigger headlands along this shore. Good protection in prevailing west to northwest winds can be found here, but like Cojo, it is open to the southeast. The water is a little deeper here than further east, so the fetch to shore is reduced in northerly winds. Avoid kelp patches and isolated submerged rocks near shore.

Some skippers consider Sacate a viable alternative to Cojo Anchorage and report that it can be smoother here when conditions pick up outside Pt. Conception and curve around into Cojo. We have found fewer downslope winds here than at either Gaviota or Refugio and, in general, there is less kelp here. The fishermen and intrepid surfers you find here, especially on weekends, know every inch of the beach and surf. Ask them for their local knowledge.

Anchor (temporary) in 3 to 4 fathoms over packed sand with stones and kelp patches; fair-

Avoid Santa Barbara Channel's offshore oil wells

to-good holding, but check the set to assure holding.

Santa Anita Anchorage
Chart 18721; 6.9 mi E of Govt. Pt
Position: 34°27.74'N, 120°18.87'W

Santa Anita is another small bight, useful as a temporary anchorage in fair weather a couple hundred yards offshore. There are submerged rocks near shore and thick kelp patches in late summer. Secate Anchorage offers more protection and is easier to enter.

Anchor (temporary) in 5 to 7 fathoms over sand, rock and kelp with fair holding. Avoid rocks and kelp patches.

Cojo Anchorage
Chart 18721; 0.6 mi NE of Govt. Pt
Entrance: (CA135) 34°26.64'N, 120°26.37'W
Anchor: 34°26.80'N, 120°26.59'W

Cojo Anchorage . . . affords protection off the mouth of the Cojo Valley from moderate W and NW winds. The suggested anchorage is opposite a culvert under the railroad tracks in 5 to 10 fath-

oms, hard sandy bottom. The cove 1.7 miles E of this anchorage known as Little (Old) Cojo, is foul and affords little protection. (CP, 33rd Ed.)

Cojo Anchorage has been either the last or first bastion of smooth water for sailors transiting Southern and Northern California since Richard Henry Dana wrote of the squareriggers plying the coast for the hides and tallow trade. Cojo is the first rest stop on a southbound voyage that gives respite from the strong afternoon northwesterly seas north of Point Conception, named early on the notorious "Cape Horn of California." On a northbound voyage, Cojo is strategically located for a quick rounding of Points Conception and Arguello.

Aerial view: Coho Anchorage

When northbound, lay a course line, first heading southeast passing the mooring buoys in order to avoid the kelp beds, then make a broad sweeping turn to the west, passing a half-mile or so south of Government Point. Using this route you can leave before dawn to minimize headwinds when heading (45 miles) to Port San Luis or to Morro Bay (60 miles).

Large kelp beds help reduce northwest swells that curl around Point Conception in brisk weather. Extreme surfers frequently anchor their small craft close to shore, waiting for the big surf to build along the beaches. Cojo is open to the south and southeast and can be uncomfortable when winds create chop from that direction.

Good shelter can be found in Cojo in a wild and scenic setting. Anchorage can be found inside the first large kelp bed east of Government Point, off the large railroad culvert. This keeps you inside the private oil company buoys and out of the comings and goings of their boats at all hours.

Little Cojo, 1.6 miles east of Cojo, is not recommended due to foul ground. Once, on a winter kayaking trip starting from the north side of Point Conception, we were almost capsized by a large breaking wave that heaped up and broke on an uncharted shoal area several hundred yards off Little Cojo. It gave us a real adrenalin

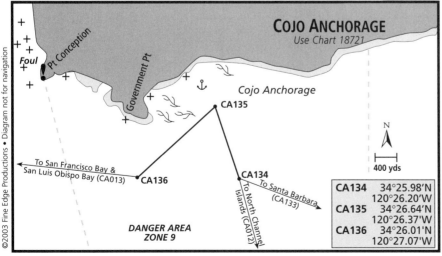

Ten seals bask on oil-boat mooring buoy at Coho Anchorage

taken for Point Conception. However, Point Conception, around the corner to the north-west, has a prominent light-house and foghorn that becomes visible as you leave Cojo. West of Government Point, the coast is rocky, with bold cliffs and acres of white water in unsettled conditions. This part of the coast at times can have uncomfortable turbu-lence and, unless you're in a kayak, we suggest remaining at least 0.5 mile offshore and 1.0 mile off Point Conception.

rush. These waves are an attraction for local summer surfers.

Anchor (temporary) in 4 to 6 fathoms over hard sand with stones and kelp; fair-to-good holding with a well-set anchor.

Government Point
Chart 18721; 1.0 mi SE of Point Conception
Position: 34°26.29'N, 120°27.17'W

Heading west from Santa Barbara, hugging the shoreline, Government Point can easily be mis-

Point Conception
Chart 18721; 38 mi W of Santa Barbara,
45 mi S of Port San Luis
Position (0.5 mi offshore): 34°26.49'N,
120°28.61'W

Point Conception . . . is a bold headland 220 feet high that marks an abrupt change in the trend of the coast. There is comparatively low land imme-diately behind it. At a distance from N or E, it usually looks like an island.

Point Conception has been called the Cape Horn of the Pacific because of the heavy NW

Our View of Point Conception
by Don and Réanne Douglass

In its comments about Point Conception, cited above, the official *Coast Pilot* notes that the point . . . *has been called the Cape Horn of the Pacific because of the heavy NW gales encountered off it during the passage through Santa Barbara Channel.* We sailed our heavy beamy ketch, *le Dauphin Amical,* around Point Conception, as well as our 40-foot trawler, *Baidarka,* in both a southerly and northerly direction several times, as well as south-bound once in our 2-person kayak. While Point Conception can be a challenge and should not be taken lightly, we exchange a chuckle every time we read this quotation. We can't help wondering if the authorities who coined the term have ever sailed beyond *this area,* much less to higher latitudes along the coasts of either

North or South America.

Northern California's Cape Mendocino is arguably as big or bigger a challenge than Point Conception, as are any number of capes in the Queen Charlottes, Solander Island off Vancouver Island, the west coast of Baranof Island, and capes Spencer and Fairweather in Southeast Alaska.

Having pitchpoled off Cape Horn in *le Dauphin Amical* and having later visited the memorial for the countless sailors who lost their lives in waters off the real Cape Horn (Isla de Hornos), we feel that "The Cape Horn of Southern California" would be more appropriate for Point Conception.

gales encountered off it during the passage through Santa Barbara Channel. A marked change of climatic and meteorological conditions is experienced off the point, the transition often being remarkably sudden and well defined. When the northwesterly winds are strong they blow down the canyons between Point Conception and Capitan and cause heavy offshore gusts. (CP, 33rd Ed.)

The rocky bluff of Point Conception is washed clean every half minute or so as low swells and some barely visible to the untrained eye, sweep up the smooth face as if they had the momentum to go all the way to the lighthouse, 133 feet above.

Baidarka *crew deploys double snubber as wind freshens in* Coho

We recommend rounding Point Conception by sea kayak if you really want to get the feel of the area. Tuck in close, just inside the thick pure white foam line caused by the back wave rushing back down the cliff towards the tropics it came from. The foghorn, blowing every 30 seconds, even on clear days, adds an eerie touch. You will see up close that Point Conception seems to draw swells from the southwest as well as the northwest, not evident in the rougher waters to the north, and you will be glad to get aboard your mothership and transit it the right way next time.

Rounding Point Conception, remain about a mile abeam, setting a course of about 305°T to clear Point Arguello.

Another View of Point Conception
by Michelle Gaylord

I got up at 3 a.m. today to batten down everything in preparation for our passage past Point Conception (aka: Cape Horn of the Pacific), and Point Arguello (aka: The Graveyard of Ships). I taped, glued, bungied, wrapped, stowed, and tied down literally everything that could possibly move on the boat.

We left Channel Islands Harbor and, about 15 minutes out of the breakwater, Jerry was unable to make the autopilot hold its course so we turned around and came back into port for repairs. We came back to the dock and, just as I was tying the last line, he leaned out the door and said, "OK, it's fixed. Untie us and let's go." It was simply a cable that had jiggled loose. So, we were off again, the autopilot working fine, and lunch preparations in process to be ready when we encountered those treacherous waters, because there's no way under those conditions I can open the refrigerator without everything falling onto the floor. As we approached Point Conception, I took one last look around the boat to be sure I hadn't missed nailing down any loose items. "OK, I'm ready now," I thought. "I know what button to push to give our lat/long to the Coast Guard if needed, I have the life jackets out and available for instant use, and I have our food and drink supply in a little ice chest in the pilot house so I won't have to crawl on my hands and knees to the galley."

Well, we passed Point Conception and the seas were calmer than they had been outside Channel Islands Harbor. Jerry said, "Just wait until we get closer to Point Arguello. All hell will break loose." So I kept waiting with anticipation and before I knew it we were going past Point Arguello, and the seas were a duck pond. Flat as glass, without a ripple!!!

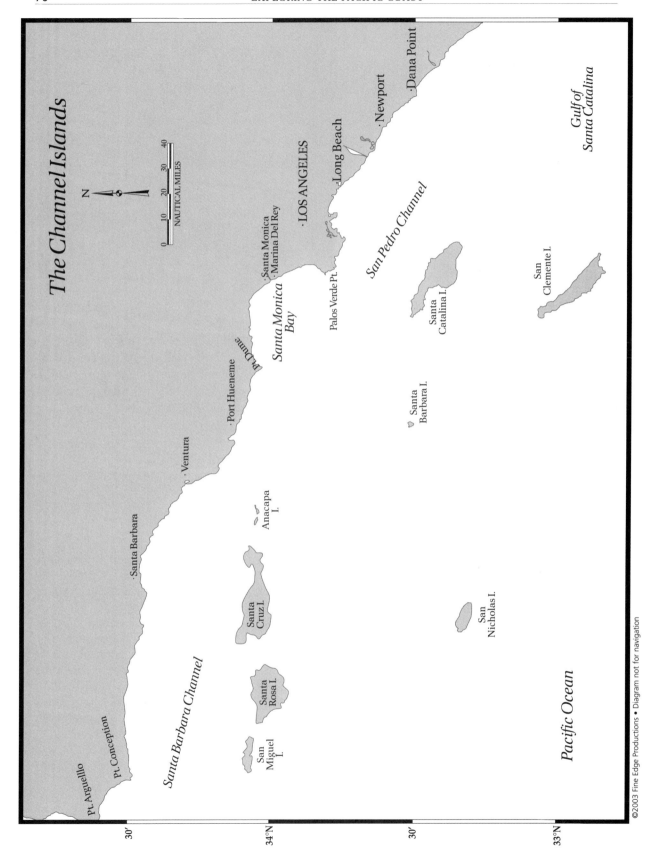

The Channel Islands

N

NAUTICAL MILES
0   10   20   30   40

Pt. Arguello

Pt. Conception

·Santa Barbara

·Ventura

·Port Hueneme

Pt. Dume

Santa Monica Bay

·Santa Monica
·Marina Del Rey

·LOS ANGELES

·Long Beach

·Newport

·Dana Point

Palos Verde Pt.

San Pedro Channel

Santa Barbara Channel

San Miguel I.

Santa Rosa I.

Santa Cruz I.

Anacapa I.

Santa Barbara I.

Santa Catalina I.

San Clemente I.

San Nicholas I.

Gulf of Santa Catalina

Pacific Ocean

30'

34°N

30'

33°N

2

Channel Islands

Southern California's Channel Islands, which number eight in all, extend for 130 miles in a northwesterly direction off the coast from San Diego to Point Conception. While the islands are close to the densely populated southern California coast, their isolation has left them relatively natural and undeveloped, offering boaters a quiet contrast to the hectic, congested life of the mainland.

For the most part, cruising the Channel Islands is a wilderness experience where adequate preparation and self-reliance are required. With the exception of Catalina Island, there are no slips, moorings, stores, restaurants or telephones; nor are there any harbors that guarantee safety in all storm conditions. Most of the anchor sites are small and suitable only in fair, stable weather and favorable seas—fortunately, conditions that occur frequently. Whatever the weather, however, skippers should always have a plan for seeking alternative shelter when conditions require a move to a more protected site; preparedness, awareness and vigilance are al-ways keys to safe and comfortable visits to the Channel Islands.

Adequate anchoring gear and skills are critical to cruising the Channel Islands. Anchoring is permitted in any site not officially restricted by regulations. Almost every sandy beach or shallow bight on these islands now has a local name; most offer some possibility for anchoring or mooring. Check carefully below for details on each island.

Because the more popular coves are crowded during the summer, attention to anchoring is imperative. A well-set anchor (usually both bow and stern anchors), properly buoyed to help prevent fouling and minimize swinging, and display of an anchor light, are not only good form, but insurance for a peaceful night's anchorage. Avalon and Two Harbors on Catalina Island have over 1000 mooring buoys that can be rented on an as-available basis. Buoys allocated to Park personnel, USCG emergency buoys, or those identified as privately owned should not be used.

The four southern Channel Islands —San Clemente, Santa Catalina, San Nicolas, and Santa Barbara, arranged in a trapezoid—are separated from the mainland by San Pedro Channel on the south and Outer Santa Barbara Passage on the north. The northern-most Channel Islands—San Miguel, Santa Rosa, Santa Cruz and Anacapa which run in a straight line nearly due east-west—are separated from the mainland by Santa Barbara Channel.

Catalina Island, a major tourist destination and the most developed of the Channel Islands, has airplane,

Cruise ship visits Avalon

cruise ship and water taxi service to

the mainland. The village of Avalon has full amenities, while Two Harbors (at the Isthmus) has some facilities. Both locations are popular rendezvous spots for visitors who arrive either on their own boats or by other transportation. Avalon and Two Harbors have the only fuel facilities in the Channel Islands.

Designated in 1980 as the Channel Islands National Park, the northernmost Channel Islands, plus Santa Barbara Island, and the waters surrounding them, form one of the most unusual of America's parks. These islands contain significant natural and cultural resources. There are 2,000 species of plants and animals within the Park of which145 species are unique to the islands and found nowhere else. The Park consists of 250,000 acres, half of which lie underwater and are a designated National Marine Sanctuary that extends from one to six nautical miles around the islands. Marine life consists of microscopic plankton, giant kelp forests with hundreds of resident sea creatures, pelagic birds, fish, and gray whales. Fishing regulations being considered at press time will increase no-fishing zones to encompass about 30% of Marine Sanctuary waters. For current regulations, contact Channel Islands National Park Headquarters and Visitors Center in Ventura (805.658.5700).

Point Bennett on San Miguel Island's westernmost point is reported to be the only place in the world where up to six species of pinnipeds can be found. During mating season, when thousands of seals, sea lions and elephant seals come to breed, the beaches and rocks ring with their barking and trumpeting. The Caliche "ghost" forests of San Miguel—lime castings of long-decayed trees—are remainders that this nearly treeless island was once forested.

Among the islands, archeological and cultural resources span a period of more than 10,000 years. The region was the ancestral home of the Chumash or "Island People," known for their fast, seaworthy canoes that impressed Cabrillo when he first encountered them in October 1542 west of Santa Barbara. Chumash cave paintings and rock art can be found in the

mountains immediately north of Santa Barbara Channel.

Cabrillo was the first European to land on the islands and, while wintering over on what he called San Lucas Island, he lost his life, reportedly from an accidental fall. His grave, thought to be on San Miguel or possibly Santa Rosa, has never been located. Subsequent explorers to the Channel Islands include Sebastián Vizcaíno and Gaspar de Portolá, as well as George Vancouver. In fact, it was Vancouver who first noted the names currently used for the islands on nautical charts.

Anacapa Island (actually three small islands) is the major breeding ground for the endangered California brown pelican; the island's name is the only one among the Channels Islands derived from a Native word (*Eneepah* meaning mirage or deception). Santa Cruz Island and Santa Rosa Island to its east are the two largest of the Channels Islands. For cruising boaters, these two islands hold the most attraction: Santa

Cruise ship unloads passengers at Avalon

Rosa for its sandy beaches and gentle hills; Santa Cruz for its myriad coves, canyons and sea caves. San Clemente and San Nicolas are military reservations; public use is not allowed without express permission. (See text under each island for contact information.) As we go to press, three companies have concessionaire status with the National Park Service and Nature Conservancy to lead tours to the Channel Islands (two by water; one by air). Please check the Appendix for these sources.

Compared to the mainland harbors, there is little immediate help on hand in the Channel Islands in case of emergency. When navigating these waters, you must take full responsibility for maintaining adequate margins of safety for both your boat and your crew.

Please check the Introduction for information on both Santa Ana winds and southeast storms that affect the northeastern or southeastern sides of the islands. If you are underway and uncertain about what to do when conditions change, always monitor weather radio broadcasts and call the USCG on VHF 22A.

Enhance your enjoyment and safety by studying the resources listed in the Bibliography. And remember to consult with local experts at yacht clubs, Power Squadrons, chandleries and government officials to determine your understanding and preparedness of this captivating offshore environment.

Approaches to the Channel Islands

From San Diego to Los Angeles Harbor the usual approach to the southern Channel Islands is directly from a coastal marina entrance buoy; pay attention to traffic separation schemes and maintain an alert lookout for hazards and traffic of any kind. From King Harbor or Marina del Rey, you can set a course directly for the north end of Catalina; to approach the northern Channel Islands, head directly for Anacapa then work your way west on either side of Santa Cruz. From harbors south of Palos Verdes Peninsula, it's convenient to head first to Catalina, next to Santa Barbara Island, then north to Anacapa or Smugglers Cove on Santa Cruz.

Cruise ship passengers disembark at Avalon

On a northbound voyage we prefer to continue west to San Miguel then north to Cojo Anchorage where we spend the night, leaving before dawn to round Points Conception and Arguello.

Crossing to the northern Channel Islands from a harbor on the north side of Santa Barbara Channel, use a direct course to the island of choice. Avoid oil rigs and for safety cross the traffic separation schemes at near right angles maintaining an alert lookout for hazards or heavy traffic. From Oxnard (Channel Islands Harbor) or Ventura in strong westerlies, first head west along the mainland coast avoiding oil rigs, then reach south to your cove of choice or cross to the east end of Anacapa Island following its south side and head west to Santa Cruz using the lee of Anacapa.

On a southbound voyage, when bound for a Santa Barbara Channel harbor, turn west at Point Conception. If you're heading south of Palos Verdes Peninsula, cross the separation scheme, pass between Santa Rosa and Santa Cruz Islands then head directly for San Pedro Channel.

On a direct route to San Diego, head for Little Santa Barbara Channel and pass west of Catalina Island on a direct line to Point Loma. You can remain overnight at Santa Barbara Island or Catalina Harbor, (known locally at "Cat" Harbor). See our recommended route-illustrations for details.

San Pedro Channel, which leads south of Santa Monica and San Pedro bays and north of

Catalina Island, is a busy ship channel requiring alert lookouts.

Outer Santa Barbara Passage is marked by Santa Barbara Island, the southwest shore of Catalina Island and the northeast shores of San Nicolas and San Clemente islands. This passage is the favorite of coastal cruisers who want a more direct and less crowded route.

Catalina Island forms the south side of San Pedro Channel and is central to all boat areas. It is 30 miles south of Marina del Rey; 21 miles south of Los Angeles Harbor; 26 miles southwest of Newport Beach; 32 miles west of Dana Point; 67 miles northwest of San Diego; 20 miles northeast of San Clemente Island; 21 miles east of Santa Barbara Island; and 49 miles south of Anacapa Island.

The Gulf of Catalina is a shelf of relatively shallow water bounded by San Pedro Bay on the north, Catalina and San Clemente Islands on the west, and San Diego on the south and east.

Note: Always navigate with the appropriate large-scale charts to avoid various banks, shoals, rocks, traffic separation schemes, military restricted areas and other hazards. In times of low visibility, be sure to slow down, maintain a sharp bow lookout, and monitor VHF Channel 16 for SECURITE announcements and Vessel Traffic Services channel for position reports of ships; listen carefully for small boats that may be blowing weak horns, whistles or banging pot and pans.

Baidarka *visits Avalon harbormaster office*

Santa Catalina Island
Charts 18757, 18746; 22 mi S of LA Hbr
Position (SE end): (CA242) 33°18.28'N, 118°17.87'W
Position (NW end): (CA214) 33°28.94'N, 118°36.71'W

Santa Catalina Island . . . is 18.5 miles long in a SE direction and has a greatest width of 7 miles. (CP, 33rd Ed.)

Catalina Island is 18 miles long, running in a northwest to southeast direction with a backbone ridge of rugged peaks that reach over 2,000 feet above a generally rocky shoreline. The high backbone ridge of the island looks like a sleeping dragon from afar but closer inspection shows a ridge eroded into many gullies where small sandy beaches lie at the foot. These many small beaches offer dozens of anchor or mooring sites around the island; each has a local name. Many of these coves have privately owned or managed facilities with

Avalon Wharf

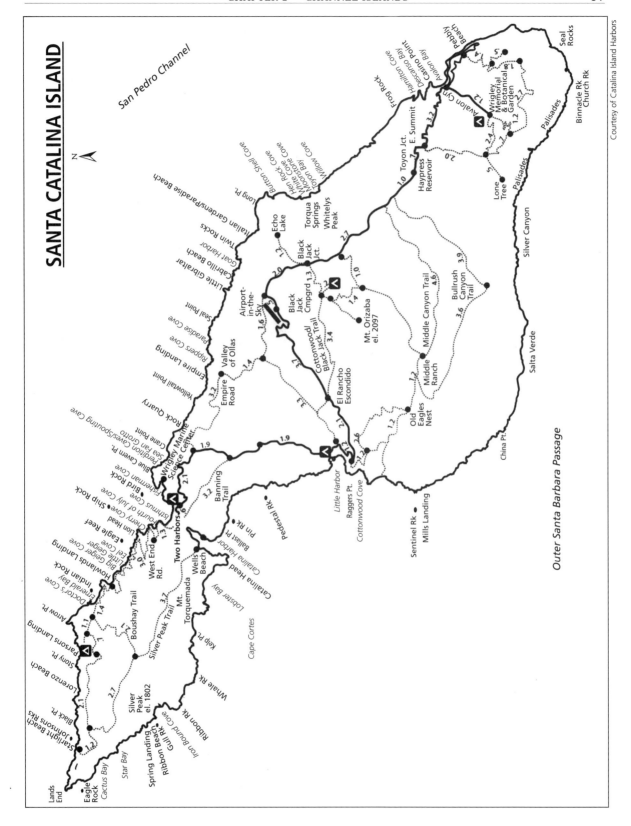

SANTA CATALINA ISLAND

San Pedro Channel

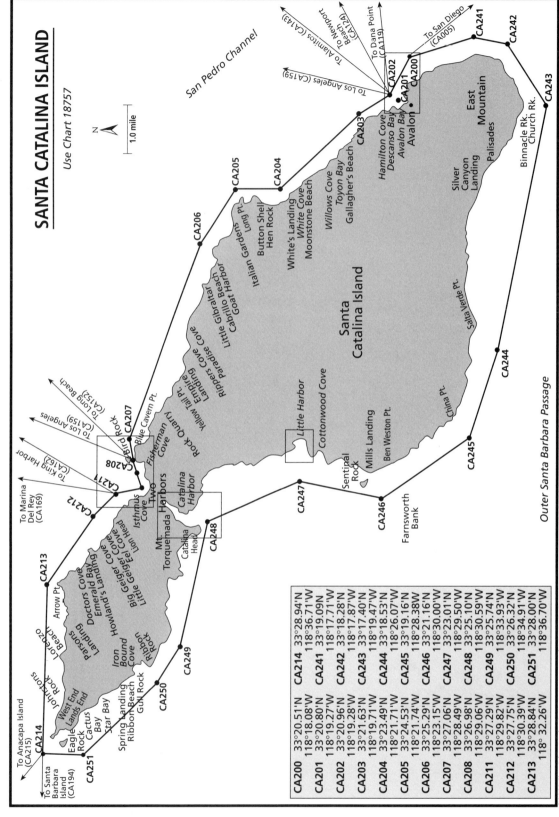

SANTA CATALINA ISLAND

Use Chart 18757

N

1.0 mile

San Pedro Channel

To Newport Beach (CA124)
To Alamitos (CA143)
To Dana Point (CA119)
To San Diego (CA005)
To Los Angeles (CA159)

CA241
CA242
CA243

CA202
CA201
CA200

Hamilton Cove
Descanso Bay
Avalon Bay
Avalon

East Mountain
Palisades

Silver Canyon Landing

Binnacle Rk.
Church Rk.

CA203

Willows Cove
Toyon Bay
Gallagher's Beach

White's Landing
White Cove
Moonstone Beach

Salta Verde Pt.

CA204

Long Pt.
Button Shell
Hen Rock

CA205

Italian Gardens

Little Gibraltar Beach
Cabrillo Beach
Goat Harbor

Paradise Cove
Ripper's Cove

CA206

Empire Landing Cove
Yellow Tail Pt.
Rock Quarry Cove

Santa Catalina Island

CA244

China Pt.

Little Harbor
Cottonwood Cove

Mills Landing
Ben Weston Pt.

Sentinal Rock

CA245

Blue Cavern Pt.
Bird Rock

To Long Beach (CA152)
To Los Angeles (CA159)
To King Harbor (CA162)
To Marina Del Rey (CA169)

CA207

Fisherman Cove

CA208
CA211
CA212

Two Harbors
Isthmus Cove

Catalina Harbor

Mt. Torquemada
Catalina Head

CA247
CA248

CA246

Farnsworth Bank

CA213

Arrow Pt.
Loretzo Beach

Doctors Cove
Emerald Bay
Parsons Landing

Iron Bound Cove
Howland's Cove
Geiger Cove
Big Geiger Cove
Little Geiger Cove
Eel Head
Lion Head
Ribbon Rock

Johnsons Rock

West End
Eagle Rock
Lands End

Cactus Bay
Star Bay

Spring Landing
Ribbon Beach
Gull Rock

CA249
CA250

CA251

To Anacapa Island (CA215)
To Santa Barbara Island (CA194)

CA214

Outer Santa Barbara Passage

CA200	33°20.51'N	CA214	33°28.94'N
	118°18.08'W		118°36.71'W
CA201	33°20.80'N	CA241	33°19.09N
	118°19.27'W		118°17.71'W
CA202	33°0.96'N	CA242	33°8.28'N
	118°19.28'W		118°17.87'W
CA203	33°21.63'N	CA243	33°7.40'N
	118°19.71'W		118°19.47'W
CA204	33°3.49'N	CA244	33°8.53'N
	118°21.71'W		118°26.07'W
CA205	33°24.53'N	CA245	33°19.16'N
	118°21.74'W		118°28.38W
CA206	33°5.29'N	CA246	33°21.16'N
	118°3.15'W		118°00.00'W
CA207	33°27.06'N	CA247	33°23.01'N
	118°28.49'W		118°29.50'W
CA208	33°26.98'N	CA248	33°25.10'N
	118°9.06'W		118°30.59'W
CA211	33°27.29'N	CA249	33°25.74'N
	118°29.82'W		118°33.93'W
CA212	33°27.75'N	CA250	33°26.32'N
	118°10.39'W		118°34.91'W
CA213	33°28.84'N	CA251	33°28.00'N
	118° 32.26'W		118°36.70'W

Harbor launch assigns mooring buoys

mooring buoys and are generally operated by yacht clubs or institutions such as scouting organizations. In some cases public use may not be permitted. All mooring buoys are private and most are available to the public on a first-come basis and require a daily usage fee. There are over 700 mooring buoys available in the Avalon and Two Harbors. There are no slips on Catalina Island. You may anchor in any cove that has no mooring buoys, or 100 yards outside the mooring-buoy areas; generally these anchor sites are more subject to afternoon chop and are in water 10 fathoms or deeper and may have gravel or rocky bottoms. Catalina is the most populated and most heavily visited of the Channel Islands and the only with one with facilities, fuel and supplies.

In the normally good weather found in the Gulf of Catalina, most of Catalina's mooring and anchor sites are pleasant in prevailing stable weather. All are basically open roadsteads exposed to seaward winds or swells. During the popular summer season you will find a thousand or more pleasure boats tied to tightly-spaced mooring buoys along the east shore. With the exception of local surge, passing wakes or some afternoon chop, the boats are secure and happy. Most moorings are comfortable in prevailing northwest weather or in light easterlies.

From time to time, all harbors and anchor sites on Catalina are exposed to gales; every few

years storm-force winds originate from a direction that make them untenable. While these conditions are infrequent, a boater maybe be required to seek shelter before dangerous conditions prevent taking defensive action. All coves and harbors are basically open roadsteads with none qualifying as storm refuges. A defensive plan should include returning to the mainland or moving to an alternative anchor location in the lee of the island before sea conditions deteriorate and make this impossible.

Sailors should monitor weather forecasts and have alternative plans if the weather deteriorates. Santa Ana winds (mostly November to March) from the east, and major gales or storms from the southeast (occasionally from fall to spring) may require seeking shelter on the lee side of the island; there is truly no bombproof harbor on Catalina in such conditions. A lee in Santa Ana winds can be found under the Palisades on the southwest corner of the island or in Cactus Bay near west end of the island. Moderate protection for a limited number of boats can be found behind the breakwaters in Avalon or in some coves protected from the north or northeast. Outside Avalon Harbor it is illegal to leave boats unattended at Catalina Island.

The island, largely owned and managed by the Santa Catalina Island Conservancy, is open to the public but usage other than day use requires a permit.

First visited by Europeans when Cabrillo landed in 1542, Catalina was named in the following century by Sebastián Vizacaíno. The indigenous Indian population succumbed to White man's diseases and the remaining survivors were evacuated to the mainland during the 18th century. The Mexican Governor gave Catalina as a land grant to sea captain Robbins in 1846 and it became part of the state of California in 1848. In 1850 the island was reportedly sold for $10,000. For many years the island was owned by the Wrigley Family and operated as a private sheep and cattle ranch. A buffalo herd once roamed the center part of the island, and planes landing at the airport had to watch for animals on the runway. During the 20th century Catalina became a prime tourist and cruising boat destination and, as the 21st century begins, its year-round economy still depends on tourism, private and public resorts, yacht club outstations, and private and transient moorings. Avalon Bay, on the southeast corner of the island, is Catalina's commercial hub.

Mooring area, Avalon Bay

Avalon Bay (Catalina Island)
Chart 18757; N shore of Catalina, 2.5 mi from SE end
Entrance: (CA202) 33°20.96'N, 118°19.28'W; 22 mi from LA Hbr

Avalon Bay . . . is entered between Casino Point, breakwater on the N and the breakwater extending from Cabrillo Peninsula, on the S. The breakwaters are marked by lights on their seaward ends.

The small bay has depths of 2 to 13 fathoms; a depth of 20 fathoms is immediately outside the points of the bay. The harbormaster reports that shelter is excellent in the harbor during SW weather and good during NW and SE weather if

the wind does not exceed 20 knots. The breakwater provides limited protection in the NW and SE ends of the harbor during NE Santa Ana winds that occasionally blow during the fall and winter.

The bay is extremely popular as a yacht haven and vacation resort during the summer. Yachting and fishboat supplies, limited engine and underwater repair facilities, and towing service are available at Avalon.

Yachts and other small craft moor to buoys in the bay; there are no alongside berths. The mooring buoys in the bay are either privately owned or owned by the City of Avalon and leased to private boatowners. The harbormaster, located on the pleasure pier, makes all temporary mooring assignments. A harbor boat will meet visiting yachts upon arrival and will escort them to a mooring if desired; a fee is collected for this service. Shoreboat and garbage collection services are available throughout the day. (CP, 33rd Ed.)

Avalon is an incorporated city with an attractive and famous palm tree-lined boardwalk filled with boutiques of all

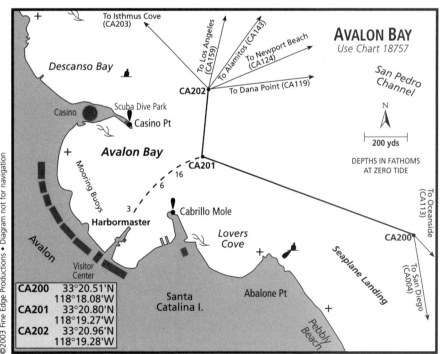

Cabrillo Mole, Avalon Bay

garbage as a fee per bag is charged to leave it ashore.) Weather lights and flag signals are shown on both the end of the Pleasure Pier and on Cabrillo Mole (Dock).

Mooring Procedures

Upon arrival, contact the Harbor Patrol on VHF Channel 9 and inform them of the cove where you wish to moor. The Patrol will meet you outside the mooring area, give you your assignment, and collect your fees. Each mooring has a mooring can, pick-up pole, and bow and stern lines with weights. The weights must be attached to your vessel.

Anchoring is allowed outside the breakwater, north of the Casino, 100 yards outside

kinds. Restaurants, resorts and full amenities are found nearby. Fuel and boat repairs are available; both air and sea services provide transportation to the mainland. Avalon is a strictly enforced No Discharge Harbor. If you plan to spend time ashore, you can choose from a variety of activities to keep you entertained, from tours of the island, the Wrigley Memorial and Botanical Garden, the Casino to kayaking, snorkeling, scuba diving and para-sailing.

Avalon Harbor is entered between Casino Point with its casino and palm trees conspicuous on the north and Cabrillo Breakwater and docks on the south. The Harbormaster's office, on the wharf at the south side of the bay, is accessible via a small, crowded float. The entire bay and harbor are lined with mooring buoys—just over 250 in all. Visiting boats are met by one or more of a fleet of small harbor motor launches that assign the mooring buoys based upon boat size, length of stay and availability. There are no slips in Avalon Harbor. Numerous water taxis create a busy, congested harbor, especially on weekends or during visits from off-lying cruise ships. The college kids who run these water boats take you to your mooring and assist you as required. No mooring assignments are given out over VHF and no reservations are taken. Daily shore and garbage pickup is available on short notice until late into the evening. (You may want to compact and store your

South end of Catalina Harbor

the mooring areas where depths run about 25 fathoms—convenient only for large vessels. Where to anchor is left to the discretion of each boater. Avalon Harbor Department office is located at the end of Pleasure Pier; they monitor VHF Channel 16; switch to Channel 12; tel: 310.510.0535.

There is no anchorage area inside Avalon Harbor (city limits or Descanso Bay); however, open roadstead anchoring is available, for large boats, 100 yards outside the mooring area in Descanso Bay, 0.5 mile north in 25 fathoms.

How to pick up a mooring

Each mooring consists of a mooring can, pick-up pole and two weights—bow and stern. Each weight is attached to lines which need to be attached to your vessel, bow and stern. See Figure 1. Follow this procedure:

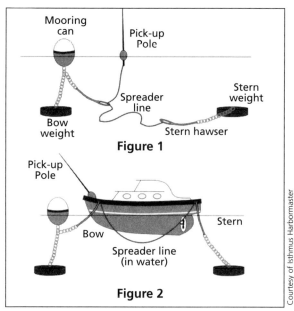

Catalina mooring procedures

Boutiques in Avalon

1) Pick up the pole and pull in the line until a large loop appears. Attach this loop (or hawser) to the bow cleat on your vessel.

2) Continue to pull up the smaller (spreader) line as you walk toward the stern of the boat. This spreader line should be pulled up until there is a fair amount of tension or until a loop on the stern hawser is reached.

3) Attach the spreader line or the loop to the stern cleat of the vessel. Your vessel will be secure if attached to the spreader line; it is not necessary to reach the loop. The proper stern line tension is essential.

4) Recheck bow and stern lines to be sure they are secured to each cleat.

5) Drop spreader line into the water. See Figure 2.

Lovers Cove/West Harbor

(Catalina Island)
Charts 18757; 0.5 mi SE of Avalon Hbr
Entrance: 33°20.66'N, 118°19.15'W

Lovers Cove is a glass-bottom boat reserve without moorings and closed to anchoring. It is open to snorkeling but not to scuba diving.

Descanso Bay (Cat. I.)
Charts 18757; 0.3 mi N of
Avalon Hbr
Entrance: 33°21.06'N,
118°19.56'W

*A small-craft anchorage is in
Descanso Bay. . . . In 1978, it
was reported that the holding
ground was poor, and that
heavy concentrations of kelp
made anchoring difficult.* (CP,
33rd Ed.)

Descanso Bay has 47 mooring
buoys. Check availability.

Anchorage for large boats
can be found 100 yards outside the buoys in about 25
fathoms over grey mud and
rocks with fair-to-good hold-

Avalon Pleasure Pier

ing. This can be a rolly anchorage. The large
buoy outside is for USCG use.

Hamilton Cove (Catalina Island)
Charts 18757; 0.5 mi N of Avalon Hbr
Position: 33°21.25'N, 118.19.75'W

Hamilton Cove has 52 mooring buoys backed
by large condos. Check availability.

Anchorage can be found in about 10 fathoms
over sand and mud with fair holding. Avoid the
foul area off the north end of the cove.

Gallagher's Beach (Catalina Island)
Charts 18757; 2.0 mi N of Avalon Hbr
Entrance: 33°22.30'N, 118°20.84'W

Gallagher's Beach, located directly below
Gallagher's Canyon, is the site of a Christian
Camp. Avoid private mooring buoys.

Fair **anchorage** for a few boats can be found in
about 10 fathoms.

Toyon Bay (Catalina Island)
Charts 18757; 2.3 mi N of Avalon Hbr
Entrance: 33°22.53'N, 118°21.10'W

Toyon Bay is located at the foot of attractive
Swains Canyon where you find large cottonwood, palm and eucalyptus trees. The nine

View of Casino

Catalina Island Visitors Bureau

Descanso Bay

mooring buoys here belong to Catalina Island Marine Institute camp on shore.

Fair **anchorage** can be found for half a dozen boats in about 12 to 15 fathoms over a mixed bottom.

Willows Cove (Catalina Island)
Charts 18757; 2.5 mi N of Avalon Hbr
Entrance: 33°22.70'N, 118°21.27'W

> *Willows Anchorage . . . can be used by small craft in NW weather and affords a good boat landing.* (CP, 33rd Ed.)

Willows Cove is a shallow bight, largely undeveloped, and the first place north of Avalon without mooring buoys.

Anchorage for a few boats can be found in fair weather in about 2 to 7 fathoms over sand with fair holding.

Moonstone Beach (Cat. I.)
Charts 18757; 3.0 mi N of Avalon Hbr
Entrance: 33°23.12'N, 118°21.61'W

Moonstone Beach shore, which is leased by Newport Harbor Yacht Club, has 39 mooring buoys.

Anchorage for a dozen boats can be found outside the buoys in about 10 fathoms.

Whites Cove (Cat. I.)
(Whites Landing)
Charts 18757; 3.5 mi N of Avalon Hbr
Entrance: 33°23.51'N, 118°22.00'W

> *White Cove . . . affords anchorage in 8 fathoms and provides almost the same protection as that found at Avalon. The beach in White Cove is known as Whites Landing.* (CP, 33rd Ed.)

Whites Cove is a fairly large bight with a long, sandy beach. Its shore is shared by the Los Angeles Girl Scout Camp and the Balboa Yacht Club. The cove has 17 mooring buoys.

Good **anchorage** in westerlies can be found for a dozen or more boats in 6 to 10 fathoms over sand with good holding. Avoid the pier area, on the south, and rocks off the north end of cove.

Hen Rock Cove (Catalina Island)
Charts 18757; 3.8 mi N of Avalon Hbr
Entrance: 33°23.81'N, 118°22.00'W

Hen Rock Cove, south of Hen Rock on the north side of White's Landing, has 25 mooring buoys

Baidarka avoiding water taxis

Kelpie on a mooring

and shore facilities leased to the Balboa Yacht Club.

Anchorage can be found for about 10 boats outside the buoys in about 12 fathoms over hard sand and rock with fair holding; check the set of your anchor well. This site affords good protection in westerly weather.

Button Shell/Camp Fox (Catalina I.)
Charts 18757; 4.2 mi N of Avalon Hbr
Entrance: 33°24.26'N, 118°21.98'W

Button Shell Beach is located immediately south of Long Point. Its facilities, including the pier, are leased to Glendale YMCA. Northbound this is the last anchorage (until the Isthmus)

that is protected from prevailing north and northwest weather. It has 7 mooring buoys.

Anchorage for about 10 boats can be found in 5 to 10 fathoms over sand with good holding. Good fishing and diving is found on the lee side of Long Point, and there are sea caves near the point.

Long Point (Catalina Island)
Charts 18757; 4.3 mi N of Avalon; 6.9 mi E of Isthmus
Position: 33°24.37'N. 118°21.95'W

Long Point marks a major change along Catalina's east shore. The coves and beaches south of here are fully developed and tend to offer fair to good protection in prevailing northwest winds. West of Long Point the coast trends west, is essentially undeveloped, and exposed to west and north winds. Although mornings along this coast are frequently calm, it can become choppy in the afternoon.

Italian Gardens (Catalina Island)
Charts 18757; 6.1 mi E of Isthmus
Entrance: 33°24.70'N, 118°22.73'W

Italian Gardens is the name for the bight and sand beach west of Long Point, marked by a small hand-lettered sign. Named after an Italian fisherman who dried his nets here, the bight has no mooring buoys and is undeveloped. A small dry canyon leads south from the beach. A large fiberglass derelict boat was beached on the north end of the sand in 2001. The water is unusually clear here and, because of its wild appearance, is a favorite place for *Baidarka*'s crew who like to relax, swim and snorkel.

Although exposed to heavy northwest weather, Italian Gardens receives

Summer campsite

Baidarka *anchored at Italian Gardens*

some protection from Twin Rocks on its north side. There is good diving around Twin Rocks.

Anchorage (temporary) can be found off the beach in about 5 fathoms over sand with some gravel and kelp; fair holding.

Goat Harbor (Catalina Island)
Charts 18757; 5.3 mi E of Isthmus
Entrance: 33°25.07'N, 118°23.71'W

Goat Harbor is a small picturesque anchorage less than a mile below the Catalina Airstrip that sits on a plateau to the west. It is undeveloped and has no mooring buoys. Although not really a harbor, Goat Harbor does offer some shelter in fair weather and perhaps in moderate southerlies.

Anchorage for about a half-dozen boats can be found just off the sand beach in 2 to 6 fathoms over sand; fair holding.

Cabrillo Beach (Catalina I.)
Chart 18757; 4.9 mi E of Isthmus
Position: 33°25.21'N, 118°24.16'W

Cabrillo Beach is located immediately south of Little Gibraltar. Its shore facilities are leased to the Long Beach Boy Scouts. There are no mooring buoys.

Anchorage for a half-dozen boats (from west-northwest weather) can be taken in 2 to 6 fathoms over sand with fair holding.

Little Gibraltar (Catalina Island)
Chart 18757; 4.7 mi E of Isthmus
Position: 33°25.34'N, 118°24.31'W

Little Gibralter, a prominent headland, lies just west of Cabrillo Beach and provides some protection from northwest wind and chop. Avoid the rock east of the point and a shoal farther south.

Rippers Cove (Catalina Island)
Chart 18757; 3.3 mi E of Isthmus
Entrance: 33°25.72'N, 118°25.99'W

Rippers Cove is an attractive undeveloped indentation under the Valley of Ollas, a major wash from the south. It has no mooring buoys.

Anchorage for about 10 boats can be found in 3 to 6 fathoms off the sandy beach over sand with fair-to-good holding. This is a fair-weather-anchorage and a good place to hike or camp. Avoid rocks off the points, both north and south of the cove, and beware of landing when a swell is running.

Empire Landing (Catalina Island)
Charts 18757; 2.8 mi E of Isthmus
Entrance: 33°25.79'N, 118°26.57'W

Empire Landing is a shallow bight with a size-able sand beach and shallow foreshore. It is exposed in most weather and landing can be

Sailboats at anchor

Thunderbird *anchored off Blue Cavern Point*

diving spot. Harbor Reef is a large dangerous area about 0.25 mile southwest of Bird Rock; the reef which is surrounded by kelp and rip tides is marked by five orange and white buoys. This is an area of very shallow depths, with several rocks that bare on low water. The reef can be safely passed on either its north or south side.

Big Fisherman Cove
(Isthmus-Catalina Island)
Chart 18757; 0.5 mi E of Isthmus
Entrance (Fisherman Cove): (CA209) 33°26.74'N, 118°29.25'W

Fisherman Cove . . . is small, but is said to be the only shelter against Santa Ana winds on the N shore of Santa Catalina Island. (CP, 33rd Ed.)

Big Fisherman Cove is leased by the U.S.C. Wrigley Marine Center (part of the Wrigley Institute for Environmental Studies). It is well protected from southeast weather and reported to be good in Santa Ana winds, but it is open to winds or chop from the north. Mooring, dock and ramp are for staff use only and anchoring is discouraged except in rough weather emergencies. The Science Center has a diver decompression chamber, (tel: 310.510.0811.)

difficult in surf. Shore facilities are leased to Connolly Pacific Company. Cattle once were loaded into boats from here for shipment to the mainland. Cement buttresses for the loading pier can still be seen. There are a few private buoys.

Anchorage (temporary) in fair weather for as many as two dozen boats can be found off the sandy beach between 3 and 5 fathoms over sand, shells, some rocks and kelp with fair-to-good holding.

Blue Cavern Point Bight (Catalina I.)
Chart 18757; 1.1 mi E of Isthmus
Position: 33°26.70'N, 118°28.50'W

Blue Cavern Point, a short dinghy or kayak ride from the Isthmus, is a popular place for fishing or diving. There are several caves in the bluffs on the south side, including a sizeable sea cave. A number of tiny sand beaches lie between the point and the rock quarry to the south. Fishing or diving boats anchor here close to the bluffs, but the bottom is rocky and holding is marginal; boats should not be left unattended.

Bird Rock and Harbor Reef (Cat. I.)
Chart 18757; 0.7 mi NE of Isthmus
Position (Bird Rock): 33°27.07'N, 118°29.23'W

Bird Rock, a highly visible white rock (due to bird guano), is a favorite kayaking, fishing and

Kayakers explore the caves up close

Little Fisherman Cove (Isthmus-Cat. I.)

Chart 18757; 0.3 mi E of Isthmus Cove
Entrance: 33°26.58'N, 118°29.52'W

Little Fisherman Cove is a small cove leased to King Harbor Yacht Club and Channel Cruising Club. Anchorage is allowed only outside the cove avoiding the mooring buoys and the rocks on the west side of cove.

Isthmus Cove

(Two Harbors-Cat. I.)
Chart 18757; 10.5 mi N of Avalon
Entrance (NE): (CA208) 33°26.98'N, 118°29.06'W
Entrance (NW): (CA211) 33°27.29'N, 118°29.82'W
Cove position: (CA210): 33°26.65'N, 118°29.72'W

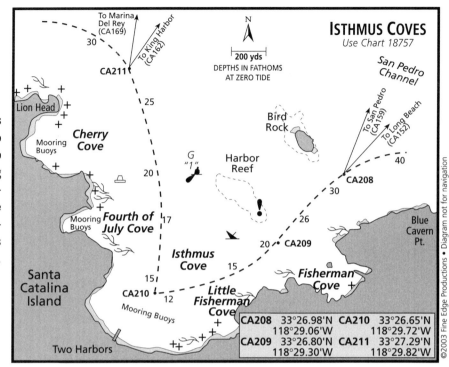

ISTHMUS COVES
Use Chart 18757

CA208	33°26.98'N 118°29.06'W	CA210	33°26.65'N 118°29.72'W
CA209	33°26.80'N 118°29.30'W	CA211	33°27.29'N 118°29.82'W

Isthmus Cove . . . affords shelter for small vessels in S weather, but is dangerous in NW weather. . . . The Catalina Cove and Camp Agency at Two Harbors at the head of the cove is the issuing agency for landing permits and leasing of mooring buoys for Santa Catalina Island (except Avalon). The approach to Isthmus Cove alongshore from the E is clear, but W of the entrance is Eagle Reef, covered 3 feet. The reef is marked by growing kelp and by a buoy about 100 yards to the E. In the approach from the N, Ship Rock, about

1 mile N of the cove, is the guide. The light is shown from a pole on the rock. From the channel the rock resembles a black haystack; the top is mostly white because of bird droppings. A reef extends about 120 yards S of Ship rock, ending in a rock that uncovers 3 feet. (CP, 33rd Ed.)

The village of Two Harbors at Isthmus Cove, a popular rendezvous spot for many boaters, is known for its variety of recreational activities. After Avalon it's the busiest cove on the island. Facilities for boaters include a dinghy dock (for dinghies less than 14 feet), picnic area, gas, diesel and water year-round at the fuel dock, showers and laundry a short distance from the Isthmus Pier. Provisions, marine hardware and fishing supplies and licenses can be found at Two Harbors General Store and there are several restaurants in the village.

Because all island trash (except Avalon) is shipped to the mainland, it must be separated—glass and metals in one bag, everything else in another. During summer, a trash pick-up boat serves all leeside coves, but the island appreciates it if you pack home your own trash. Showers, public restrooms, and laundry facilities are located a short distance from Isthmus Pier.

Scuba diving near the cliffs

David J. Shuler

Isthmus Cove/Two Harbors

There are 249 mooring buoys available on a first-come, first-served basis. Heave-to in the anchor-free fairway off the landing pier, call Harbor Patrol on VHF Channel 9 and they will meet you and assign you a buoy. It may be possible to side-tie to another boat but normal mooring fees apply. A 5-mile, no-wake speed limit must be observed both inside and outside the mooring and anchorage areas and boaters are asked not to run their generator between 2200 and 0700 hours. Both the Isthmus and adjacent coves are subject to passing wakes dur-ing the busy summer season.

Water taxi service is available anywhere in the greater Isthmus Cove and its adjacent coves by calling on VHF Channel 9; identify your position by cove name, buoy number or GPS position.

You are allowed to anchor at your own risk 100 yards off the mooring buoys in about 15 fathoms where there is room for over 100 boats, but be sure to stay clear of the fairway to the landing pier. Generally protected in stable weather, strong southwest winds can cross the Isthmus and rake the cove, even in fair weather; in northeast Santa Ana gales Isthmus Cove is exposed.

Boaters planning to visit the area for several days can choose from a variety of activities that includes scuba diving and snorkeling, Looking Glass Tours, Eco-Tours, fishing, kayak rentals and tours, and mountain bike rentals. Shoreside campgrounds for primitive and tent camping, in addition to cabin rentals, are available; reservations are advised during high season or on weekends. A limited number of boat-in sites are also

Catalina Island Visitors Bureau

Mooring buoys at Two Harbors

Bill of Rights *anchored in Isthmus Cove*

available by reservation only (tel: 310.510.1226 or fax: 310.510.3577). Two Harbors regularly schedules a number of monthly events around the calendar; for a list of these events write Two Harbors Enterprises, P.O. Box 2530, Avalon, CA 90704-2530 (tel: 310.510.0303).

⚓ **Two Harbors Harbor Department, Catalina Mooring Service,** tel: 310.510.2683 or 310.510.4253; website: www.catalina.com/twoharbors

⚓ **U.S. Coast Guard** monitors VHF Channel 16; tel: (Los Angeles) 562.980.4444

⚓ **Catalina Camping,** register by fax 310.510.7254 or on-line: www.scico.com/camping

Fourth of July Cove (Isthmus-Cat. I.)
Chart 18757; 0.35 mi N of Isthmus
Entrance: 33°26.83'N, 118°29.93'W

Fourth of July Cove and Cherry Cove . . . are popular day anchorages for yachts using the facilities at Two Harbors. There are a number of private moorings in both coves. The shore areas are leased. (CP, 33rd Ed.)

Fourth of July Cove and Cherry Cove are just northwest of Isthmus Cove. Fourth of July has 42 moorings and no anchorages; it is well protected from prevailing summer weather. The Fourth of July Yacht Club leases the facilities on shore. There are 42 mooring buoys, and anchoring inside the cove is not allowed. Don Douglass' family spent many summers anchored here prior to and after WWII and long before development and mooring buoys. (See sidebar.)

The Night the Lights Went Out
by DCD

In the early days, when I was a young boy, only a handful of boats anchored in the Isthmus or in Fourth of July cove. On a beautiful warm summer evening, my dad and mom, loaded their portable *Victrola*, their dance records, and my sister and me into the dinghy. We rowed from our boat *Carron*, anchored next to shore in Fourth of July Cove to the Isthmus Pier, and readied for an impromptu weekend hot dog and beer party to celebrate Independence Day.

Before long, with the party in full swing and well before the assembled boat crews had their fill of dancing at the end of the pier, the batteries of the *Victrola* went dead. What to do?

The adults could find just one light bulb hanging from two wires on a pole. Someone had a brilliant idea—pull out the AC cord from the *Victrola*, cut off the plug, strip back the wire, reach up to the bare white light bulb, unscrew the bulb and carefully twist the wires to make contact with the 110 volts in the socket.

Voilà! The dance music was back at full volume—for a while. As the old pier rocked and rolled, the wires shorted out, killing the power from the small generator at the Isthmus resort and cutting off all the lights and the cash register as well. The bar crowd emptied out with their free drinks and joined the pier party under the moonlight. Singing replaced the dance records . . . and so it went in the good old days.

Good day for snorkeling

Cherry Cove (Isthmus-Catalina Island)
Chart 18757; 0.6 mi N of Isthmus
Entrance: 33°27.08'N, 118°30.03'W

Cherry Cove is a large and popular summer "hangout," well protected by Lion's Head on its north side. The cove has a shallow bottom and a long, flat valley filled with Catalina Cherry trees. Its 99 mooring buoys tend to fill up early. This is a good diving spot, but watch for surge around Lions Head. Avoid the dangerous rocks that bare at low tide off the north end of cove. Check with Two Harbors Harbor Department about anchoring *outside* both Fourth of July and Cherry Coves. The water is 15 to 20 fathoms deep and you will want to avoid traffic.

Eel Cove (Catalina Island)
Chart 18757; 1.1 mi NW of Isthmus
Position: 33°27.39'N, 118°30.72'W

Eel Cove, a tiny cove that makes a good temporary lunch stop, is a favorite of beginning divers.

Baidarka at Emerald Bay

Little Geiger Cove (Catalina Island)
Chart 18757; 1.3 mi NW of Isthmus
Entrance: 33°27.47'N, 118°30.89'W

Little Geiger is a tiny cove leased to Offshore Cruising Club with a single mooring buoy. Anchoring is reported to be permitted only when the weather is good. It is close to Eagle Reef for good diving but Emerald Bay has more protection and swinging room.

Big Geiger Cove (Catalina Island)
Chart 18757; 1.4 mi NW of Isthmus
Position: 33°27.59'N, 118°31.02'W

Big Geiger Cove has no mooring and its shore is leased to the Blue Water Cruising Club. Anchorage for about 10 boats can be taken in fair weather. Shoreside facilities are for the Blue Water Cruising Club. It is near the good diving found at Eagle Reef.

Howland's Landing (Catalina Island)
Charts 18757; 1.7 mi NW of Isthmus
Entrance: 33°28.12'N, 118°31.84'W

Howland's Landing has 40 mooring buoys available; both Catalina Island Camp and L.A. Yacht Club have facilities on the private beach. No anchoring is permitted. Emerald Bay, close north, is preferred.

Emerald Bay (Catalina Island)
Chart 18757; 2.0 mi NW of Isthmus
Entrance (E): 33°28.01'N, 118°31.46'W
Entrance (N/Johnsons Landing): 33°28.19'N, 118°31.76'W

Emerald Bay is located in beautiful green waters behind Indian Rock and a reef that extends northwest. The water here is clear; depths are shallow and diving is excellent. This generally calm-water cove provides good shelter in summer weather. There are 100 moorings in the bay and anchorage for five to ten boats, although space is quite limited, with lots of through-traffic. Shore facilities are leased to Corsair Yacht Club and Great Western Boy Scouts. Johnsons Landing (position: 33°28.19'N, 118°31.76'W), the small beach at the north end of the cove, affords shelter from westerlies close to the beach. All boats maneuvering in Emerald Bay should stay clear of the area around Indian Rock and its outlying reefs.

Doctor's Cove (Catalina Island)
Chart 18757; 0.3 mi NW of Indian Rock
Position: 33°28.25'N, 118°31.87'W

Doctor's Cove is the local name for the small bight immediately northwest of Emerald Bay. Arrow Point, 0.6 mile northwest of Doctor's, is a good diving spot, known for its shellfish.

Arrow Point (Catalina Island)
Charts 18757; 3.0 mi NW of Isthmus Cove
Position: 33°28.67'N, 118°32.33'W

Strong currents flow at Arrow Point on spring tides or strong winds. West of here to West End you may frequently experience fresh winds and large swells.

Parsons Landing (Smugglers Den-Cat. I.)
Charts 18757; 3.4 mi NW of Isthmus
Entrance: 33°28.49'N, 118°33.13'W

Parsons Landing is exposed to fresh northwest winds and chop. There are no mooring buoys and anchoring is discouraged except in fair weather. There are several submerged rocks lying off the beach said to offer good camping. Keep a wary eye to windward—the local name for this site is Smugglers Den!

West End/Lands End (Catalina Island)
Chart 18757; 5.9 mi W of Isthmus; 16 mi NW of Avalon
Position: (CA214) 33°28.94'N, 118°36.71'W

West End of Catalina Island has a white flashing light that is visible for 16 miles. Current and swell are strong here. Use Cactus Bay, 1.0 mile southeast on the south shore, as a lee in Santa Ana wind conditions.

Cactus Bay (Catalina Island)
Chart 18757; 1.0 mi SE of West End
Entrance: 33°27.92'N, 118°35.84'W

Cactus Bay is considered by some boaters to be one of the better places to ride out a Santa Ana gale; the recommended site is about 0.5 mile south of Eagle Rock in about 5 fathoms. However, U.S. Coast Guard recommends Catalina Harbor.

Catalina Island Visitors Bureau

Cat Harbor, looking northeast across the Isthmus

Ironbound Cove (Catalina Island)
Charts 18757; 2.5 mi SE of West End
Entrance: 33°26.73'N, 118°34.56'W

Protection from Santa Ana gales is reported to be found north of Ribbon Rock in about 10 fathoms. However, U.S. Coast Guard recommends Catalina Harbor.

Lobster Bay (Catalina Island)
Charts 18757; 5.1 mi SE of West End
Entrance: 33°25.61'N, 118°31.42'W

Lobster Bay, below Mount Torquemada, can offer shelter from aggressive Santa Ana gales in 10 fathoms over a sandy bottom. However, U.S. Coast Guard recommends Catalina Harbor.

Catalina (Cat) Harbor (Catalina Island)
Charts 18757; 5.8 mi SE of West End
Outer Entrance: (CA248) 33°25.10'N, 118°30.59'W
Inner Entrance: 33°25.83'N, 118°30.44'W
Anchor: 33°25.93'N, 118°30.28'W

> *Catalina Harbor . . . affords excellent shelter for small vessels in all but S weather. . . . The harbor, a popular yacht anchorage, is funnel-shaped, open to the S, and easy of access. Small and bare Pin Rock, close inside the E head of the harbor, is 150 yards offshore and has deep water around it. The anchorage is in 4 to 5 fathoms, soft bottom, abreast Ballast Point. . . . The head of the harbor is shoal. The 3-fathom curve is marked by kelp, and vessels entering should give the shores a berth of 150 yards. The facilities on Ballast Point are leased by a yacht club. From the head of the harbor it is only about 0.3 mile overland to Two Harbors. (CP, 33rd Ed.)*

Cat Harbor—the local name for Catalina Harbor, the well-protected harbor on the south side of Two Harbors and the Isthmus—lies northeast of Catalina Head, a high bluff that gives it excellent protection from northwest swells and chop; it can be somewhat exposed to southwest swells and weather. However, it is designated by the U.S. Coast Guard as a Year-round Safe Harbor.

Cat Harbor has 97 mooring buoys and anchorage for some 200 boats. When anchoring, it's a good idea to match your techniques with

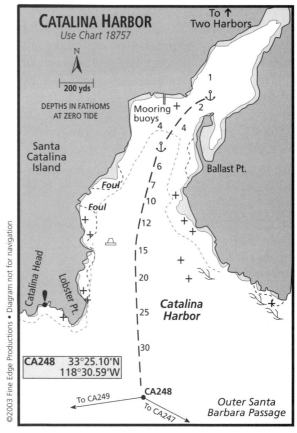

other boats, particularly when the harbor is crowded. To take up less anchoring space, consider using both a bow and stern anchor. Please note that Santa Ana gales have been clocked at 70 knots here; a funnel effect enhances both north- and south-flowing winds, but the fetch is relatively small, and some boaters prefer to anchor here during such conditions, rather than along the island's cliffs where winds may be less fierce.

Baidarka *gets underway*

Because of its isolation from the weekend crowds that favor the east side of the island, Cat Harbor has a bit more relaxed atmosphere and is more popular among the cruising crowd. When using the two anchor positions you must avoid the mooring buoys. There are a dinghy dock and shoreside picnicking facilities; Cat Harbor is a half-mile walk to Two Harbors village. In summer shuttle service is available.

Anchor in 4 to 6 fathoms over sand with fair holding.

Little Harbor/Shark Harbor (Catalina Island)
Charts 18757; 3.5 mi SE of Cat Hbr
Entrance: 33°22.99'N, 118°28.79'W
Anchor (inner basin): 33°23.13'N, 118°28.54'W

Little Harbor, also known as Shark Harbor, is tucked behind a reef and kelp beds that extend 200 yards from the north shore. This picturesque cove is a pleasant place to stay in stable weather. Larger boats can swing behind the reef in about 7 fathoms, while smaller craft can anchor inside the basin in about 2 fathoms. The inner basin offers a convenient landing place. Although there is reported to be room for one to two dozen boats to anchor here, in our opinion that's a bit tight. The bottom is hard sand with gravel with occasional rocks, requiring that you set your anchor well. The reef is submerged at

LITTLE HARBOR
Use Chart 18757

©2003 Fine Edge Productions • Diagram not for navigation

Little Shark
Little Harbor
Outer Santa Barbara Channel
Shark Harbor
Santa Catalina Island

DEPTHS IN FATHOMS AT ZERO TIDE
200 yds
N

high water and, while the kelp helps keep down the rolling, this can be a wild-looking place.

Shark Harbor, the local name for the tiny bight at the south end of Little Harbor, is open to northwest winds and swell; it is considered a rolly and marginal anchorage in anything but calm weather. Surf breaks heavily on the rocks along the south side of the bay, making landing difficult. In heavy westerlies, the surf and the rocks near shore make this a bad lee. Although hardly a harbor, this site does offer anchorage in fair weather for a few small craft.

Anchor (inner basin) in 1–2 fathoms over sand and gravel; marginal-to-fair holding.

Mills Landing (Catalina Island)
Charts 18757; 0.3 mi SE of Sentinel Rock
Entrance: 33°22.12'N, 118°29.19'W

Mills Landing, although somewhat sheltered by Sentinel Rock and the reef complex, is considered a temporary anchorage in fair weather only. It is exposed to all westerly swells and chop but it may be useful under east winds.

Silver Canyon Landing (Catalina Island)
Charts 18757; 3.8 mi NW of Church Rock
Entrance: 33°19.03'N, 118°23.47'W

Silver Canyon Landing offers some shelter from west winds with the best landing spot just east of the point behind Bulldog Rock. It is also considered a shelter from aggressive Santa Ana gales.

Anchor in about 5 to 10 fathoms over sand with some gravel and kelp with fair holding.

Palisades (Catalina Island)
Charts 18757; 3.1 mi NW of Church Rock
Position: 33°18.98'N, 118°22.53'W

Palisades is a long bight backed by striking bluffs 1,000 feet high. It is considered a good fishing and diving area and a good lee in Santa Ana gales. While partially sheltered from northwest winds and chop it is exposed to southwest weather and swells.

Anchor close to shore outside the kelp line in about 7 fathoms over sand and gravel; fair-to-good holding.

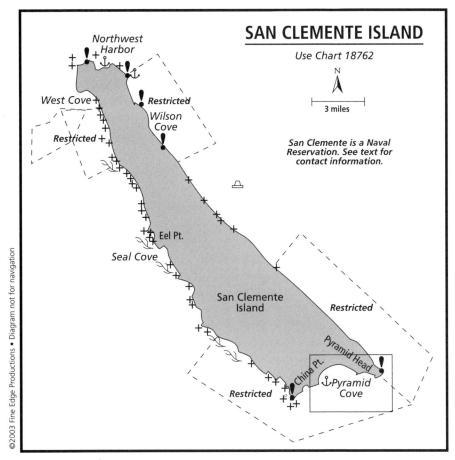

U.S. Naval Reservation and is closed to the public. Vessels including yachts and fishing craft are warned that the vicinity of the island may be dangerous at any time because of naval activities, including gunfire, bombing, and rocket fire . . . [See text below.]

. . . There are many places where vessels might anchor safely in the lee of the island during the NE storms, known as the Santa Anas. . . .

West Cove, on the NW side of San Clemente Island, 1.5 miles SE of Castle Rock, offers some shelter from Santa Ana winds; holding ground is good. A safety zone, naval restricted area, and a danger zone extend off the W coast of San Clemente Island from West Cove. (CP, 33rd Ed.)

San Clemente Island
Chart 18762; 18 mi S of Catalina
Position (Pyramid Head): 32°48.99'N, 118°20.98'W

San Clemente Island . . . is 18 miles long in a NW direction and 4 miles wide at its widest part, and reaches an elevation of 1,965 feet. The island is a

The southernmost of the eight Channel Islands lying 55 nautical miles south of Long Beach, San Clemente has been owned by the U.S. Navy since 1934. Its waters are used to support research and training for ships and aircraft in the Pacific fleet.

Pyramid Cove—First Anchor Site
by DCD

Pyramid Cove holds a fond place in our memory —it was the first anchor site of our planned circumnavigation of the Southern Hemisphere in the 1970s. We left Los Angeles Harbor October 12, 1974, our William Garden ketch—*le Dauphin Amical*—loaded with tons of gear and provisions and four teenage sons.

We were all exhausted from the last minute good-byes and hectic send-off early that morning. After a long day's sail, we needed to stow last-minute gifts and personal items that had been stacked in the way all over the

boat and were happy to drop anchor in the open road-stead just outside the kelp line. (At that time, there were no military operations being conducted around San Clemente Island.) We stowed the last-minute items, made the boat shipshape, and the six of us flopped into our berths at 0200. Four hours later we raised anchor and headed south to Turtle Bay, our first Mexican land-fall, on what became a very different itinerary than we had originally anticipated. [For full details read *Cape Horn: One Man's Dream, One Woman's Nightmare*.]

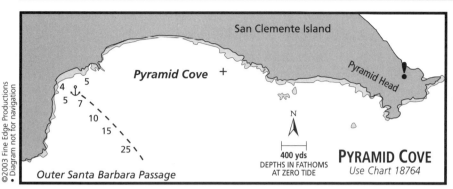

©2003 Fine Edge Productions
• Diagram not for navigation

San Clemente Island

Pyramid Cove   +

Pyramid Head

4   5
5   7
10
15
25

Outer Santa Barbara Passage

N

400 yds
DEPTHS IN FATHOMS
AT ZERO TIDE

PYRAMID COVE
Use Chart 18764

Although the waters surrounding the island are rich fishing grounds, they lie within or are adjacent to Security, Danger, and Restricted Areas. At press time, we have been notified by Naval operations authorities that, although Military operations occur regularly, the waters around San Clemente are not restricted at this time. The authorities recommend that cruising boats remain on the east side of the island since operations are usually carried out on the west side; they also recommend weekends when operations are not in process. Daily information on restrictions, schedules of operations, security announcements, etc. can be obtained on the website: www.scisland.org.

During times of heightened security, it is important that boaters in the area contact the Operations Center at 619.545.9464.

Pyramid Cove (San Clemente Island)
Chart 18762; 32 mi S of Avalon
Entrance: 32°48.62'N, 118°23.08'W
Anchor: 32°49.09'N, 118°23.93'W

Pyramid Cove . . . is used as a naval shore bombardment area and included in a danger zone. . . . The cove, closed to the public, offers protected anchorage in 10 fathoms or more in NW weather to authorized vessels and vessels in distress. Vessels should not enter the kelp as there are indications of other dangers in addition to those already charted. Some swell makes into the cove most of the time. Authorized landing on the beach is usually not difficult, but can be extremely hazardous because of unexploded ordnance. . . . (CP, 33rd Ed.)

Pyramid Cove, a deep bight at the south end of San Clemente Island, is located in or adjacent to a designated Danger Area. *Authorized* private

vessels or vessels in distress can anchor in Pyramid Cove which offers good protection from prevailing northwest winds but is completely open to all south weather. (Please see previous entry.) Information on restrictions, schedules of operations, security announcements, etc. can be obtained on the website: www.sciland.org.

Wilson Cove
(San Clemente Island)
Chart 18762; NE shore, 15.5 mi NW of
Pyramid Head
Anchor: 33°01.35'N, 118°33.79'W

Wilson Cove . . . is a fair anchorage in the prevailing W weather, but is uncomfortable at times as the swells make around the point from the NW. A strong wind usually blows down off the hills in the afternoon. A restricted anchorage area and a naval restricted area are in the vicinity of the cove. . . .

Wilson Cove should be approached from the NE to avoid the numerous buoys N and S of the cove. The buildings on the hill overlooking Wilson Cove are prominent from the SE. The best anchor-

John Sanger

Grebe *approaches Santa Barbara Island under sail*

age for small craft is in the lee of the kelp making off from a point nearly a mile NW of the pier. (CP, 33rd Ed.)

Wilson Cove, the main landing facility for San Clemente Naval Operations, encompasses a 200-yard pier, float, buoys and official buildings. Authorized private vessels or vessels in distress may be able to anchor in Wilson Cove. (Please see comments under San Clemente Island above.) Information on restrictions, schedules of operations, security announcements, etc. can be obtained on the website: www.scisland.org.

Northwest Harbor (San Clemente Island)
Chart 18762; NW shore, 22.7 mi SW of Avalon
Entrance: 33°02.13'N, 118°35.17'W
Anchor: 33°01.98'N, 118°35.36'W

Northwest Harbor . . . affords shelter in S weather and is a comfortable anchorage in the prevailing W weather, as the large beds of kelp and the low islet to the N of the anchorage afford protection. It is open N and is unsafe in heavy NW weather. (CP, 33rd Ed.)

Northwest Harbor at the northwest end of San Clemente Island offers good shelter for southerly gales and fair shelter from prevailing northwest winds. It lies within or adjacent to designated restricted areas. Authorized private vessels or vessels in distress may be able to anchor in Northwest Harbor. For current status check the website: www.scisland.org

West Cove (San Clemente Island)
Charts 18762; 1.5 mi S of NW Harbor
Entrance: 33°00.71'N, 118°35.89'W

West Cove . . . offers some shelter from Santa Ana winds; holding ground is good. A safety zone, naval restricted area, and a danger zone extend off the W coast of San Clemente Island from West Cove. . . . (CP, 33rd Ed.)

Seal Cove (San Clemente Island)
Charts 18762; W shore
Entrance: 32°54.02'N, 118°32.02'W

Seal Cove . . . affords a boat landing and indifferent anchorage for small craft in NW weather. (CP, 33rd Ed.)

Santa Barbara Island in sight!

Seal Cove, midway up the west coast of San Clemente Island, may be in, or adjacent to, a restricted area. Authorized private vessels, or vessels in distress, may be able to anchor in Seal Cove. The small beach at the head of the cove is reported to afford landing. For current status check the website: www.scisland.org

Santa Barbara Island
Chart 18756; 23.5 mi W of Catalina Isl
Anchor (0.3 mi S of Sta Barb light): 33°28.93'N, 119°01.68'W

Santa Barbara Island . . . is 1.5 miles long in a N direction and has a greatest width of 1 mile. . . . A general anchorage area extends 2 miles off the E coast of Santa Barbara Island. . . . For yachtsmen desiring to go ashore, an anchorage reported to give fair protection for small craft in the prevailing W weather is in the small cove about 700 yards W of Santa Barbara Island Light. (If the water is too deep or too rough to anchor off the cove, anchor inside, but maintain an anchor watch.) Swinging room on a single anchor is restricted in the cove. The cove affords no landing beach; yachtsmen can debark from a dinghy onto rock steps in the side of the cliff. Large vessels can anchor within the 30-fathom curve with hard gray sand bottom. (CP, 33rd Ed.)

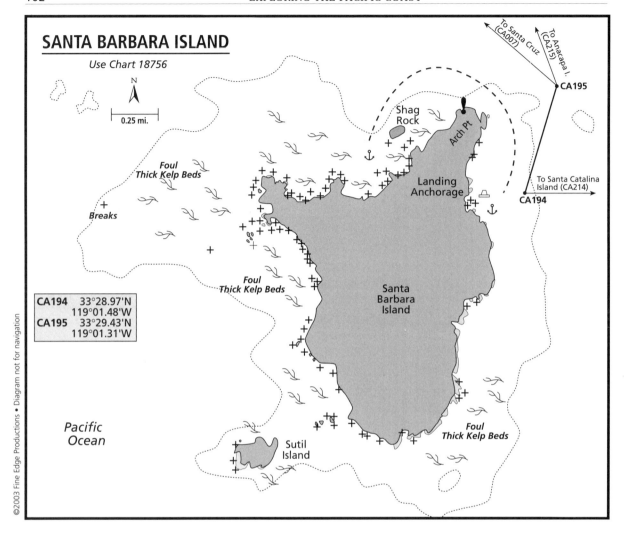

Santa Barbara Island, the smallest of the Channel Islands with just 639 acres, has a diversity of habitats, a few narrow rocky beaches, six canyons, and a badlands area. Formed by underwater volcanic activity, it is roughly triangular in outline. It emerges from the ocean as a giant twin-peaked mesa bordered by steep cliffs; the north (562 ft.) and south peaks (635 ft.) are connected by this mesa. Sutil Island, 0.4 mile off the southwest side of the island, is 300-feet high. (*Sutil* was a schooner belonging to the Spanish expedition of the West Coast under Galiano in the 1790s.) Like Anacapa, Santa Barbara Island is a major nesting area for thousands of sea birds.

Over five miles of winding trails fan out to major viewing areas from the Ranger Station and Visitors Center located on the mesa above Landing Anchorage. A booklet detailing a self-

Baidarka shares Santa Barbara Island anchorage with commercial dive boat

Santa Barbara Island landing and trail to ranger station

guiding nature trail is available near the station. The shrub-covered island has neither water nor trees, but it is resplendent in spring when the wildflowers bloom. A visitor contact station/ museum features exhibits, dioramas and murals of the island's natural and cultural resources. Facilities are limited to the museum/visitor center, primitive campground and picnic area.

The island is surrounded by large kelp beds and submerged rocks. Caution should be used when approaching from any direction. A 10-fathom line extends about a quarter-mile from the island's east shore.

Anchorage can be taken off Landing Anchorage at the northeast corner of the island, 0.3 mile south of Santa Barbara light. Landing Anchorage, itself, is tiny with inadequate swinging room, and most visiting boaters simply drop their hook in the lee of the island at an appropriate depth and swinging room. This site is a true open roadstead and useful only in fair-weather; however, in stable weather the surrounding kelp beds are quite effective in reducing roll. A steep trail leads up to the ridge; if you go ashore be careful getting in or out of your dinghy because of the surge. Sea lions have adopted the wharf so you need to be careful.

Santa Barbara Island is unsafe in southeast gales or Santa Ana winds. Although *Coast Pilot* mentions a cove 700 yards *west* of the light as an anchor site, we would not consider the area west of Shag Rock for anything but possible shelter from southeasterlies when absolutely necessary. (*Editor's Note:* The mention of the cove *west* of the light is an error in *Coast Pilot*; they may mean *south* on the east side.) This particular cove is poorly charted, choked with kelp and may contain uncharted rocks.

Much of the west side of the entire island is choked with kelp with an uneven bottom, suggesting uncharted rocks. The 10-fathom curve extends over a mile from the west shore and, while it is great fun to explore by dinghy in good weather, it can be dangerous when a swell is running.

The odors from seal and sea lion rookeries and the nesting birds and the cacophony of sounds lend an especially primitive feeling to Santa Barbara Island. We have cruised here on and off for many decades and yet we found it unchanged when we anchored here overnight in our new *Baidarka* in June 2000. Santa Ana winds are rare here but westerlies blow off the island almost every evening.

Distances to Santa Barbara Island are as follows:

    21 miles west of Santa Catalina Island
    33 mi south-southwest of Point Dume
    35 miles southeast of Anacapa Island
    40 miles southwest of Marina del Rey

Shag Rock Temporary Anchorage
(Santa Barbara Island)
Charts 18756; 0.5 mi SW of Arch Pt
Anchor: 33°29.11'N, 119°02.31'W

Temporary anchorage in southeast winds can be found southwest of Shag Rock over sand, rock and kelp.

San Nicolas Island
Chart 18755; 25 mi SW of Santa Barbara Isl
Position (Dutch Harbor): 33°12.96'N, 119°29.28'W

San Nicolas Island, the outermost of the group off southern California, is 53 miles off the nearest point of the mainland, 43 miles WNW of San Clement Island, and 24 miles SW of Santa Barbara Island. The island is a military reservation and off limits to the public.

A naval restricted area extends 3 miles from the shoreline around the island. . . . The island is

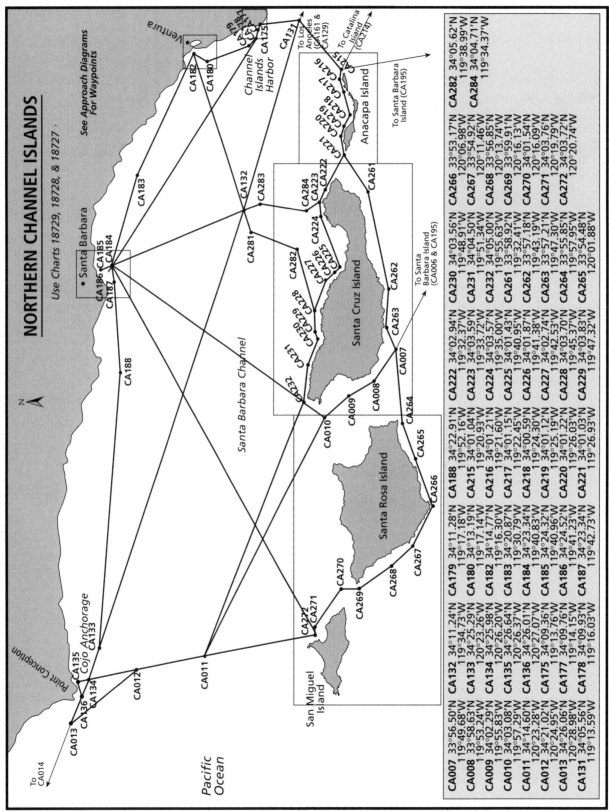

NORTHERN CHANNEL ISLANDS

Use Charts 18729, 18728, & 18727

See Approach Diagrams For Waypoints

CA007	33°56.50'N	19°49.68'W
CA008	33°58.63'N	19°53.24'W
CA009	34°02.29'N	19°55.83'W
CA010	34°03.08'N	19°57.29'W
CA011	34°14.60'N	20°23.28'W
CA012	34°21.02'N	20°24.95'W
CA013	34°26.06'N	20°28.98'W
CA131	34°05.56'N	19°13.59'W

CA132	34°11.24'N	19°34.73'W
CA133	33°58.63'N	20°23.26'W
CA134	34°25.98'N	20°26.20'W
CA135	34°26.64'N	20°26.37'W
CA136	34°26.01'N	20°27.07'W
CA175	34°09.36'N	19°13.76'W
CA177	34°09.76'N	19°14.15'W
CA178	34°09.93'N	19°16.03'W

CA179	34°11.28'N	19°17.18'W
CA180	34°13.19'N	19°17.14'W
CA182	34°14.77'N	19°16.30'W
CA183	34°20.87'N	19°30.79'W
CA184	34°23.34'N	19°40.83'W
CA185	34°24.32'N	19°40.96'W
CA186	34°24.52'N	19°41.23'W
CA187	34°23.34'N	19°42.73'W
CA188	34°22.91'N	19°52.16'W

CA215	34°01.04'N	19°20.93'W
CA216	34°01.21'N	19°21.60'W
CA217	34°01.15'N	19°22.45'W
CA218	34°00.59'N	19°24.30'W
CA219	34°01.12'N	19°25.19'W
CA220	34°01.22'N	19°26.03'W
CA221	34°01.03'N	19°26.93'W
CA222	34°02.94'N	19°32.37'W
CA223	34°03.59'N	19°33.72'W

CA224	34°03.57'N	19°35.00'W
CA225	34°01.43'N	19°40.95'W
CA226	34°01.87'N	19°41.38'W
CA227	34°02.74'N	19°42.53'W
CA228	34°03.70'N	19°45.37'W
CA229	34°03.83'N	19°47.32'W
CA230	34°03.56'N	19°48.91'W
CA231	34°04.50'N	19°51.34'W
CA232	33°56.85'N	20°13.74'W

CA261	33°58.92'N	20°16.13'W
CA262	33°57.18'N	20°16.09'W
CA263	33°57.21'N	20°19.79'W
CA264	33°55.85'N	19°57.95'W
CA265	33°54.48'N	120°01.88'W
CA266	33°53.17'N	120°06.98'W
CA267	33°54.92'N	120°11.46'W
CA268	33°56.85'N	120°13.74'W

CA269	33°59.91'N	34°01.54'N
CA270	34°01.54'N	20°16.09'W
CA271	34°03.76'N	120°19.79'W
CA272	34°03.72'N	120°20.74'W
CA282	34°05.62'N	119°38.99'W
CA284	34°04.71'N	119°34.37'W

To CA014

To Los Angeles (CA161 & CA129)

To Catalina Island (CA274)

To Santa Barbara Island (CA195)

To Santa Barbara Island (CA006 & CA195)

Ventura

Channel Islands Harbor

Santa Barbara

Point Conception

Cojo Anchorage

Santa Barbara Channel

Anacapa Island

Santa Cruz Island

Santa Rosa Island

San Miguel Island

Pacific Ocean

N

practically surrounded by kelp. . . . In thick weather great caution must be exercised in approaching from W and vessels should in no case pass inside the kelp. No dangers are known to exist outside the kelp.

. . . Upon approval by naval authorities, indifferent anchorage may be had on the S side of the 0.6-mile-long sandspit on the E end of the island. Small craft anchor in 8 fathoms, hard sand bottom, near the inshore edge of the kelp. Larger vessels anchor farther offshore in 10 to 17 fathoms, hard sand bottom. The anchorage is often uncomfortable because the island tends to split the W seas and they break with equal force on both sides and meet off the end of the spit in a maelstrom of breakers. . . . In a blow, local fishermen usually leave this anchorage, preferring the one at Santa Barbara Island. A landing can usually be made at the E end on the S side of the island during the summer without difficulty. (CP, 33rd Ed.)

San Nicolas Island is 8 miles long, has a 900-foot-high ridge with many antennas. Like San Clemente Island, San Nicolas is owned by the Navy and is closed to the public. The island is largely surrounded by kelp beds. 15-foot-high Begg Rock lies 8.0 miles northwest and is marked with a whistle buoy.

Dutch Harbor, an open roadstead on the

John Sanger

Anacapa Island

south side of San Nicolas Island, offers limited shelter in northerly or easterly weather only. Temporary anchorage is reported under the lee of the 0.6 mile-long, dangerous sandspit off the southeast corner of the island. This island is a military reservation, and Dutch Harbor lies within a restricted anchorage. See *Coast Pilot* and Notice to Mariners restricting public access.

The Lone Woman of San Nicolas
by RHD

Authors' Note: The story of the Lone Woman of San Nicolas was pieced together from several narratives published by the University of California in their Archaeological Survey No. 55. The following sidebar is a summary in our own words of John Nidever's account.

In the first third of the 1800s, Spanish missionaries began to press into service coastal Native peoples and, as their needs increased, they ordered that Island Natives be brought to the mainland. In 1835 a schooner called at San Nicolas Island to evacuate its Native residents. A young mother, thinking that her infant had already been taken aboard, discovered to her horror that the child was missing. She asked the captain to wait for her while she searched for the child. A storm had come up, putting the boat in danger, and the captain refused to wait. According to oral accounts, she leapt from the boat and

swam ashore to search for her child. When she returned, the boat was nowhere in sight. For eighteen years boats came and went, fishing or hunting for sea otters. Stories were told about the woman who'd been left on the island, but no one believed she could still be alive. In 1853, after several years of visiting San Nicolas and, suspecting that someone lived on the island, John Nidever, a sea otter hunter, discovered the lone woman and took her back to his home in Santa Barbara. She seemed happy to be reunited with other humans, particularly children, but could communicate with others only through gestures; none of the mainland Native speakers could understand her dialect. Sadly, the woman perished after just six weeks on the mainland.

The adolescent novel, *Island of the Blue Dolphins* by Scott Odell, is a fictionalized version of this woman's life.

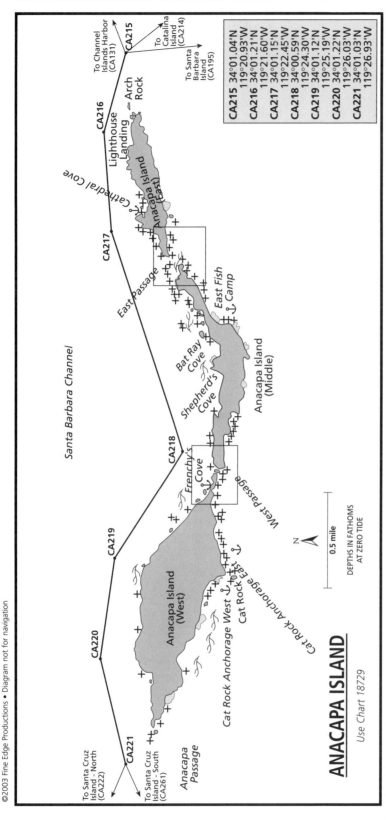

To Channel Islands Harbor (CA131)
CA215
To Catalina Island (CA214)
To Santa Barbara Island (CA195)

CA215	34°01.04'N
	119°20.93'W
CA216	34°01.21'N
	119°21.60'W
CA217	34°01.15'N
	119°22.45'W
CA218	34°00.59'N
	119°24.30'W
CA219	34°01.12'N
	119°25.19'W
CA220	34°01.22'N
	119°26.03'W
CA221	34°01.03'N
	119°26.93'W

Arch Rock
CA216
Lighthouse Landing
Cathedral Cove
Anacapa Island (East)
CA217
East Passage
East Fish Camp
Bat Ray Cove
Anacapa Island (Middle)
Shepherd's Cove
CA218
Frenchy's Cove
West Passage
Santa Barbara Channel
CA219
Anacapa Island (West)
Cat Rock Anchorage East
Cat Rock Anchorage West
CA220
N
0.5 mile
DEPTHS IN FATHOMS AT ZERO TIDE
CA221
To Santa Cruz Island - North (CA222)
To Santa Cruz Island - South (CA261)
Anacapa Passage

ANACAPA ISLAND
Use Chart 18729

©2003 Fine Edge Productions • Diagram not for navigation

Anacapa Island

Charts 18729; 14 mi from Ventura
Position: (CA215) 34°01.04'N, 119°20.93'W

Anacapa Island . . . consists of three islands separated by two very narrow openings that cannot be used as passages. The E opening is filled with rocks and is bare. The W opening is only 50 feet wide and is blocked by sand. Anacapa Island Light . . . 277 feet above the water, is shown from a 55-foot white cylindrical tower on the E end of the island. A fog signal is at the light.

The best anchorage in SE storms is on the N side about 0.2 mile N of the center of the middle island in depths of 9 to 12 fathoms. In NW weather the best anchorage is 0.3 mile S of the E opening in depths of 8 to 12 fathoms. However, it is best for larger vessels to lie at Smugglers Cove, on the E side of Santa Cruz Island, where the bottom is not so steep-to. Small boats anchor in 5 to 7 fathoms in East Fish Camp, a bight about 0.4 mile SW of the E opening. About the only protection from northeasters is to anchor as close as possible in the bight immediately W of Cat Rock, on the S side of the W island. (CP, 33rd Ed.)

Anacapa Island, the easternmost of the northern group of Channel Islands, is 11 miles southwest of Point Hueneme. The only one of the Channel Islands to retain a Spanish adaptation of its Chumash name—*Eneepah* (meaning island of deception or mirage), Anacapa has pristine tidepools, the largest breeding colony of the endangered California brown pelican, and Arch Rock, the spectacular natural bridge and trademark of the Channel Islands National Park. With approximately one-square-mile

Dinghy hoist at Landing Cove, Anacapa Island

Dive boat off east end of Anacapa Island

total land area, Anacapa is actually composed of three small islands; its sides are steep and landing can be a challenge. Ocean waves have eroded the perimeter of the islands, carving steep sea cliffs that tower above the water, exposing the volcanic origins in air pockets, lava tubes, and sea caves. Landings on the west island are permitted only at Frenchy's Cove; although it is by far the most sheltered anchorage, we recommend it *only* in calm conditions.

East Anacapa Island has hiking trails, a visitor center, lighthouse exhibits, and a primitive campground and picnic area. Scuba diving, snorkeling, bird watching, fishing, and marine mammal observation are the highlights of a visit. No water is available.

Anacapa's west island is home to the largest breeding colony of the endangered California brown pelican. Other sea birds that come here to nest include western gulls and several species of cormorants. The island's rocky shores provide resting and breeding areas for California sea lions and harbor seals. During summer, Park Rangers dive into the Landing Cove on East Anacapa with a video camera. Visitors can see, through the eye of a video camera, what the diver is witnessing. The video is beamed to monitors on the dock, as well as to the mainland Visitors Center. Springtime brings colorful flowers, including the brilliant yellow tree sunflower, or giant Coreopsis, a plant found only on the Channel Islands and in a few isolated areas on the mainland. Visit the museum on the island, which houses the original crystal and brass Fresnel lens from the lighthouse.

Bald Eagles Poised for Momentous Return to Channel Islands

In the summer of 2002—50 years after Bald Eagles were decimated by DDT pesticide contamination—a dozen chicks are being reintroduced in the Channel Islands. As part of a five-year study, a dozen Bald Eagle chicks will be released each year on the islands to determine whether they can survive here; the four islands included in the study are Anacapa, Santa Cruz, Santa Rosa and San Miguel.

The study is part of a 145 million dollar settlement against the pesticide manufacturer that dumped 1800 tons of pesticide along the coast between 1947 and 1971. This settlement is the second largest of its kind after the Exxon Valdez oil spill in Alaska.

While presently quite common in British Columbia and Alaska, the Bald Eagle came close to extinction in the continental United States after 1973. Its numbers have now increased to about 5,000 breeding pair nationwide.

Arch Rock, Anacapa Island

Looking west up Anacapa from lens room in the lighthouse

Arch Rock (Anacapa Island)
Charts 18729; 0.2 mi NE of Anacapa lt
Position: 34°01.07'N, 119°21.35'W

Arch Rock, on East Island, is the trademark of Anacapa Island and the Channel Islands National Park. The 50-foot natural bridge at the east end of Anacapa can be seen from miles around, including from Highway 101 in Ventura on a clear day. This beautiful arch is just one of the examples of the erosion that has occurred over the eons to these volcanic islands.

Lighthouse Landing (Anacapa Island)
Chart 18729; 0.3 mi W of Arch Rock
Position: 34°01.01'N, 119°21.70'W

Landing Cove, on the northeast end of the easternmost island is the access point to Anacapa's Ranger Station and small museum, the old lighthouse and the trails and camping area. Landing Cove is little more than a crevice in the solid rock cliffs and anchoring is marginal; the site is exposed, choppy, with a rocky bottom and poor holding. We do not recommend anchoring here; consider anchoring in Cathedral Cove in fair weather and take your dinghy from there or drop off your crew and return to your boat.

The landing platform built into the cliff has steel ladders leading vertically up from the water. Surge conditions make landing here difficult and you must haul your dinghy up behind you for safety using the 300-lb. davit.

The 154 stairs lead up to the trails where there is a beautiful view over the flat open terrain. In the spring, the island turns golden when the giant Coreopsis blooms. There is excellent diving here, with the best underwater visibility along the coast.

The large steel mooring buoys at Landing Cove are for water taxis and the Ranger patrol boat. We stayed overnight on one of these buoy years ago and banged into it all night, causing a rather sleepless night.

Cathedral Cove (Anacapa Island)
Chart 18729; 0.4 mi W of Lighthouse Landing
Position: 34°00.93'N, 119°22.20'W

Cathedral Cove is a small indentation on the north side of East Island, 0.5 mile west of Landing Cove. Anchorage, with moderate protection from westerlies in fair weather, can be found in this scenic place. However, it is exposed to the full blast of Santa Ana winds. We have spent many nights anchored here but consider it a temporary site only and would never leave the boat without someone aboard and in VHF radio contact with the shore party. Take care to avoid the numerous rocks and kelp patches. There are sea caves, a sea lion colony and a tiny stone beach here. Cathedral Cave, a large multi-room sea cave just west of the anchorage, is exciting to explore with a snorkel and lights. Respect all wildlife and remember disturbance or collection of anything is unlawful.

Water tank inside "chapel" building, east Anacapa

Anchor in about 4 to 5 fathoms over a sand and rocky bottom; fair holding if anchor is well set.

Bat Ray Cove (Anacapa Island)
Chart 18729; 0.8 mi E of Frenchy's
Position: 34°00.41'N, 119°23.45'W

Bat Ray Cove, an open roadstead, is useful as a temporary stop in calm westerly weather and is reported to be the best shelter at Anacapa from southeast gales. Drop your lunch hook and leave someone responsible onboard to allow the rest of the crew to view beautiful kelp forests in the adjacent shoals to the north or to visit the intriguing sea caves in the vicinity. Bat Ray Cove becomes untenable when Windy Lane starts to howl.

Anchorage can be taken outside the cove in about 9 fathoms over sand, rock and kelp; marginal-to-fair holding.

Shepherd's Cove (Anacapa Island)
Chart 18729; 0.6 mi E of Frenchy's
Position: 34°00.38'N, 119°23.72'W

Shepherd's Cove, a temporary anchorage in fair weather, makes a good lunch stop and a great place to snorkel to the sea caves a short distance to the east but surge can be strong. It becomes marginal when Windy Lane picks up in the afternoon. Anchor off the grove of eucalyptus trees and the tiny beach. (We have anchored here in 3 to 4 fathoms over a mixed bottom with marginal-to-fair holding.)

A trail leads to an old shepherd's cabin site on the east side of the cove.

Indian Water Cave (Anacapa Island)
Chart 18729; 0.3 mi NW of Frenchy's
Position: 34°00.55'N, 119°24.71'W

Indian Water Cave is a spectacular cave, 35 feet high with a saltwater entrance only. The fresh water dripping from the walls of the cave is said to have been a source of water for the Chumash.

Frenchy's Cove (Anacapa Island)
Chart 18729; 2.5 mi W of Arch Rock
Entrance (CA218) 34°00.59'N, 119°24.30'W
Anchor: 34°00.44'N, 119°24.42'W

Frenchy's Cove, the most popular and best all-around anchorage on Anacapa, is an open bight with limited swinging room for a number of boats. Fair shelter can be found in moderate westerlies because of the lee of West Island and in southerlies because of the lee of Middle

Frenchy's Cove, Anacapa Island

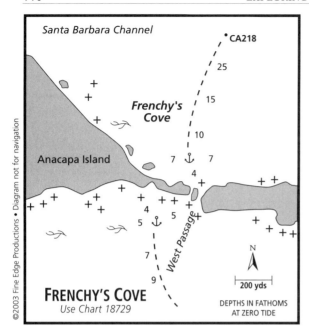

Boat headed into Frenchy's, Santa Cruz

ther west is the Indian Water Cave. The dripping fresh water inside the cave was said to be a source of water for the Chumash. From January 1 to October 3 no one is allowed northwest of Frenchy's from shore to the 120-foot depth contour (20 fathoms) because of nesting pelicans.

Anchor in 3 to 6 fathoms over packed sand with stone and some kelp; fair-to-good holding. (Depths depend on how close to the landing beach you want to be. Use adequate scope.)

East Passage (Anacapa Island)
Chart 18729; 1.1 mi SW of Arch Rock
Position (S side): 34°00.66'N, 119°22.63'W

East Passage is a foul area with just a "window" to the conditions on the opposite side of Anacapa. Avoid numerous submerged rocks and kelp. Sea lions haul out on sandy beaches just to the east.

East Fish Camp (Anacapa Island)
Chart 18729; 0.4 mi SW of East Passage
Position: 34°00.43'N, 119°23.05'W

East Fish Camp, on the south side of Middle Island 0.4 mile west of West Isthmus, is used largely by fishing boats that work the south area. The site provides good shelter from west to

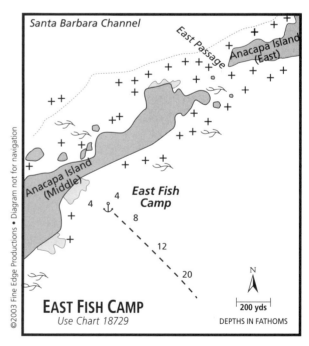

Island. However, it is fully exposed to blasts from Santa Ana winds. The cove is located on the north side of the Isthmus between Middle and West Island but you can also find anchorage on the south side of the Isthmus if need be but it is exposed to southerly swells. West Island, home to the largest group of California brown pelicans, is a research area and closed to the public. The sandspit between Middle and West Islands is an excellent picnic spot and features a good walking beach. Landing is fairly easy on either side of the spit at low tide unless swells are running. Don't miss exploring Frenchy's Cave by dinghy—a short ride west; a little fur-

northwest winds. Although the site is not good in northwest winds over 30 knots, it is the best at Anacapa. However, it is subject to southerly swell and is open to the blasts of Santa Ana winds.

Anchor in 3 to 5 fathoms over sand and rocky kelp; poor-to-fair holding. Avoid kelp patches.

West Passage (Anacapa Island)
Chart 18729; S side of Frenchy's
Position: 34°00.30'N, 119°24.48'W

West Passage is useful as a temporary anchorage in fair weather only. Avoid submerged rocks and kelp patches in the area.

Cat Rock Anchorages (Anacapa Island)
Chart 18729; 3.4 mi W of Arch Rock
Position (east): 34°00.25'N, 119°25.25'W
Position (west): 34°00.31'N, 119°25.42'W

Cat Rock Anchorages, located on either side of Cat Rock on the south side of West Island, are rather exposed and infrequently used except under certain specific wind conditions. The east side of Cat Rock can provide a defensive

A Margy Gates painting, Seagate Gallery, Channel Islands Harbor, Oxnard

position when Windy Lane is blowing along the north side of Anacapa; the west side of Cat Rock is the only defensive anchorage on Anacapa in northeast winds. In our opinion, Cat Rock is useful only in moderately strong winds. We would head to Santa Cruz Island, either Smugglers Cove or Yellow Banks in northwest winds, or to Potato Harbor in northeast or southeast gale-to-storm-force winds. There are interesting tide pools and marine life in and around the rocks and shoals of Cat Rock.

Anchor under the lee of Cat Rock with due attention to depths, kelp beds and submerged rocks. Depths around Cat Rock are reported to be on the order of 4 fathoms over a sand and rock bottom with poor-to-fair holding unless your anchor is well set.

Santa Cruz Island
Charts 18729, 18728; 4 mi W of Anacapa
Position (San Pedro Pt): 34°02.05'N, 119°31.19'W

Santa Cruz Island, 17 miles WSW of Point Hueneme . . . The E part of the land attains an elevation of about 1,800 feet. The E part is very irregular [and] barren . . . the W part [under the Nature Conservancy] has a few trees, is well covered with grass, and has several springs. The shores are high, steep, and rugged, with deep water close inshore, and there is considerably less kelp than around the other islands. The reefs, extending a mile offshore on the S coast at Gull Island, are the only outlying dangers. San Pedro Point is the E extremity of the island. (CP, 33rd Ed.) [Editor's note: The 33rd Edition of *Coast Pilot* information regarding the Administration of Santa Cruz is outdated. For current information, please contact the Channel Islands National Park Service at 805.658-5730.]

Santa Cruz Island, the largest of the Channel Islands, is co-owned by the National Park Service and The Nature Conservancy. The Nature Conservancy owns the western 75% and a landing permit is required. The eastern 25% of the island, up to and including Prisoner's Pier, is National Park property where no permit is required. Santa Cruz Island is the most diverse of the islands within the National Park. Its 77 miles of craggy coastline feature

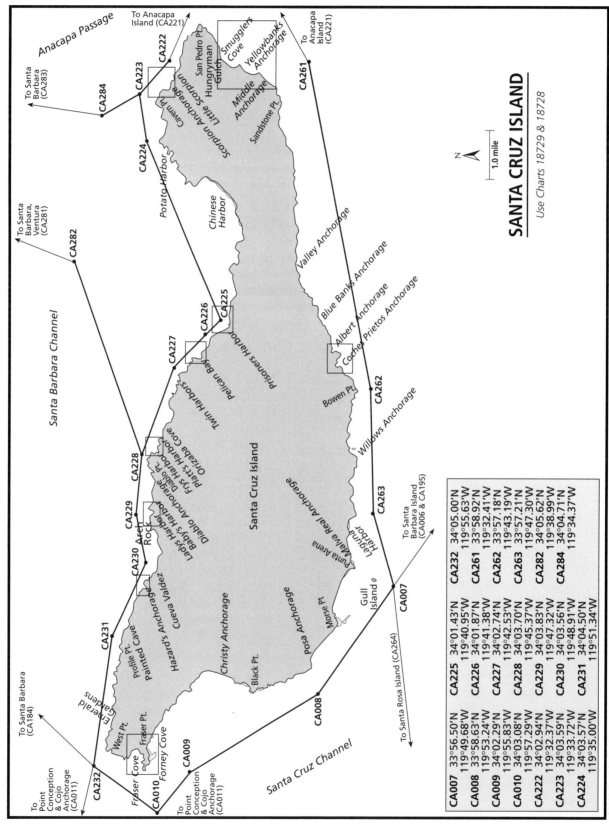

SANTA CRUZ ISLAND
Use Charts 18729 & 18728

N
1.0 mile

CA007	33°56.50'N		CA225	34°01.43'N	
	119°49.68'W			119°40.95'W	
CA008	33°58.63'N		CA226	34°01.87'N	
	119°53.24'W			119°41.38'W	
CA009	34°02.29'N		CA227	34°02.74'N	
	119°55.83'W			119°42.53'W	
CA010	34°03.08'N		CA228	34°03.70'N	
	119°57.29'W			119°45.37'W	
CA222	34°02.94'N		CA229	34°03.83'N	
	119°32.37'W			119°47.32'W	
CA223	34°03.59'N		CA230	34°03.56'N	
	119°33.72'W			119°48.91'W	
CA224	34°03.57'N		CA231	34°04.50'N	
	119°35.00'W			119°51.34'W	
CA232	34°05.00'N		CA261	33°58.92'N	
	119°55.63'W			119°32.41'W	
CA262	33°57.18'N		CA263	33°57.21'N	
	119°43.19'W			119°47.30'W	
CA282	34°05.62'N		CA284	34°04.71'N	
	119°38.99'W			119°34.37'W	

©2003 Fine Edge Productions • Diagram not for navigation

Little Scorpion, Santa Cruz Island

steep cliffs, huge sea caves, intimate coves and sandy beaches. Picacho Diablo at 2,434 ft. is the tallest peak on the Channel Islands and some of the largest and deepest sea caves in the world can be found on the north coast of Santa Cruz Island. The ceiling in the largest—Painted Cave—rises to over 120 feet; in the spring a picturesque waterfall covers its entrance.

Civilization has left its mark on Santa Cruz Island. Prior to the arrival of the Spaniards, the island was home to the Chumash Indians for 6,000 years or more. Speculation is that when Juan Rodriguez Cabrillo arrived in 1542, nearly 2,000 Chumash lived on the island in a dozen villages. The Chumash designed and built large

planked canoes called *tomols* to travel to the mainland; they were unique to the west coast of North America.

If you choose to spend some time on land, a year-round campground is operated by the National Park Service at Scorpion Ranch at the east end of the island. Many hiking trails and roads traverse the island and offer spectacular views. Camping reservations are required and can be made at 800.365.2267. No camping is allowed on the Nature Conservancy property.

NORTH SIDE OF SANTA CRUZ ISLAND, EAST TO WEST

Little Scorpion (Santa Cruz Island)
Charts 18729, 18728; 1.5 mi NW of San Pedro Pt
Position: 34°02.77'N, 119°32.73'W

Little Scorpion is a favorite scenic anchorage in the lee of two white stained rocks immediately east of Scorpion Anchorage. The largest rock (north) is 78 feet high, covered with guano, and should be given a clearance of about 100 yards because of thick kelp beds. Good shelter from prevailing northwest winds will be found here but it is open to the fury of northeast Santa Ana winds or to southeast gales.

Little Scorpion has arguably more protection and more room for boats than Scorpion and, in general, its bottom is less rocky. Smugglers Cove and the anchorages to the south of San Pedro Point are alternatives on busy weekends.

This is a good diving area and a popular place for exploring by dingy or kayak. Bull kelp forests, cliffs, tide pools, caves, rocks and submerged shoals add to the interest.

Anchor in 4 to 6 fathoms over sand and gravel with good holding.

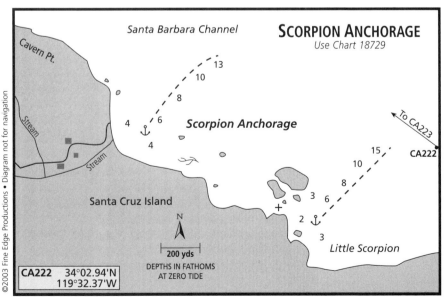

Scorpion Anchorage, Santa Cruz Island

Potato Harbor, Santa Cruz Island

Scorpion Anchorage (Santa Cruz Island)
Charts 18729, 18728;
1.8 miles NW of San Pedro Pt
Position: 34°02.97'N, 119°33.31'W

> . . . *a small-boat landing in Scorpion Anchorage*
> . . . *consists of a cribbed area with a float and*
> *gangway at the end of the roadway.* (CP, 33rd Ed.)

Scorpion Anchorage, the landing point for the eastern section of Santa Cruz Island, has a pier and a landing beach. Dinghies should not be left tied to the pier but should be landed on the beach and pulled above high-tide line. Anchorage can be found on either side of the pier, but the area to the southeast is generally preferred. Avoid small rocks and kelp beds. A large slab of the cliff northwest of the pier collapsed in the late seventies and left a lot of rock debris close to shore. This is the main landing area suggested by the National Park Service. Information, restrooms, and fresh water are available at the campground.

Anchor in 3 to 6 fathoms over a mixed bottom of mostly sand with fair-to-good holding.

Potato Harbor (Santa Cruz Island)
Charts 18729, 18728; 3.8 mi W of San Pedro Pt
Entrance: 34°02.94'N, 119°35.62'W
Anchor: 34°02.87'N, 119°35.47'W

Potato Harbor is a small indentation 1.8 miles due west of Scorpion Anchorage, which becomes invaluable when looking for good protection from northeast Santa Ana gales or southeast storms. Under prevailing weather it is open to westerly swells and chop and is quite uncomfortable. This coast has some unusual volcanic rock formations and is worth exploring.

Potato Harbor cuts deep into the surrounding cliffs, and gales from both the northeast and southeast literally blow over the top of you. The authors were blown out of Smugglers 25 years ago and found excellent protection here in a major southeast winter storm. Along with a small commercial fishing boat we anchored here for three days while the weather howled overhead.

The bottom may foul your anchor. In the course of the three-day storm we twisted round and round. When we finally were able to leave, it took us over an hour to retrieve our anchor,

Santa Cruz Island: Channel Islands Partnership
courtesy National Park Service

The Nature Conservancy property on Santa Cruz Island was purchased from Dr. Covey Stanton during the 1980s. The Nature Conservancy bought the western 90% and the National Park Service purchased the remaining 10% owned by the Gherini family. Soon after the completion of the Park Service purchase the Nature Conservancy gave, outright, the land leading up to a line stretching across from Prisoner's to Blue Banks. The Park Service and Nature Conservancy are working together as partners to speed the ecological recovery of the entire island which was degraded from years of grazing and the occupation of feral pigs.

unwinding the rode from rocks or whatever lies on the bottom. Swinging room is limited in Potato Harbor so, if other boats have beaten you here, consider Chinese Harbor as an alternative—it has much more swinging room.

Anchor in 2 to 4 fathoms over a mixed bottom with good holding if well set. (There appear to be some sizeable rocks or crevices on the bottom, which can foul your anchor.)

Chinese Harbor (Santa Cruz Island)
Charts 18729, 18728; 4.5 mi W of San Pedro Pt
Position: 34°01.57'N, 119°36.70'W

Chinese Harbor . . . affords anchorage in the kelp in 5 to 6 fathoms. The NE part of the harbor is an excellent anchorage in SE to SW weather in 9 to 10 fathoms. This harbor affords the best shelter on the island from NE winds. (CP, 33rd Ed.)

Chinese Harbor is not a good anchorage in westerlies when Windy Lane blows swell and chop directly on shore. In such conditions, the long sandy beach becomes a lee shore and is much too rough for dinghy landings. However, Chinese Harbor offers good protection in northeast Santa

Ana winds, and very good shelter in southeast winter storms and southwest gales; the long open beach provides an excellent lee with easy access and lots of swinging room for many boats.

In northeast winds we tuck in close south of Coche Point in 3 to 5 fathoms over sand and shell bottom with good holding. In southeast winds we move a little more to the south and put our storm anchor on the beach in 2 fathoms sand with good holding. In southwest gales, we move farther south but stay north of kelp patches that hide a rocky bottom.

Anchor in about 4 to 6 fathoms, sand and gravel with fair-to-good holding.

Prisoners Harbor (Santa Cruz Island)
Charts 18729, 18728; 8 mi W of San Pedro Pt
Anchor: 34°01.31'N, 119°41.15'W
Pier: 34°01.25'N, 119°41.07'W

Prisoners Harbor . . . affords shelter from all winds except from NE to W. Some protection from NW weather is afforded by the kelp, but a heavy swell rolls in. In NE weather the anchorage is unprotected and dangerous. A wharf with 16 feet at its face is in the harbor. . . . The best anchorage

---

Potato Harbor Episode
by John Sanger

We eased toward the crystalline waters lapping the inner beach of Potato Harbor. My wife Randi and I were near the end of a week-long spring sailing trip to the Channel Islands with six high-school students aboard our new 40-foot cutter *Grebe*. We were with two other boats also out of Santa Barbara. It was a calm morning and we were sightseeing under power along the northeast coast of Santa Cruz Island.

I knew the students gazing overboard would get a kick out of watching as the bottom grew ever shallower. Just before our keel touched the sand I shifted the idling engine into reverse. As the folding propeller began to spin there was a *clunk*; the prop shaft, released by a loosened set screw, had pulled out of the transmission coupling and lay suspended in the packing gland and external bronze strut. With no power, we continued into the beach and gently grounded. The tide was falling; we had to act fast or we'd be directly exposed to seas and swell from prevailing afternoon westerlies.

We threw a line to one of the other sailboats, but its 28 horsepower proved useless. A small high-speed power boater watching our plight handed us the bitter end of his anchor line pulling left, then right and straight to no avail. In desperation we rowed a big Danforth out about 100 feet and dropped it in 25 feet. Back on board, we sent all six students out to the end of our boom, now swinging 90° overboard, heeling the boat to port. I took a strain on the anchor line astern on our two-speed jib winch until water squeezed out of each strand in droplets. After a minute a weak swell lifted our beached boat ever so slightly and we made six inches astern. Another half crank; soon we moved again. Within four minutes we had pulled free of the beach and only one of our "heeled" students had fallen off the boom—or perhaps opted for a swim.

Within the hour the shaft was re-attached, the set-screw secured. Upon our return to Santa Barbara, set-screw and coupling bolt heads were drilled and each securely wired.

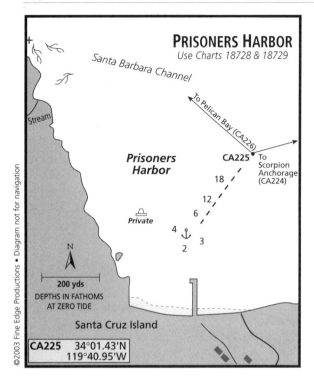

is in 12 to 15 fathoms, sandy bottom, abreast a white rock on the W shore of the bight, and the outer end of the wharf in range with the buildings at the inner end. (CP, 33rd Ed.)

Prisoners Harbor, Santa Cruz Island's major landing spot, offers good diving, great sunrises, and excellent fishing.

The National Park Service recently rebuilt the wharf at Prisoners and, as we go to press, is

Anchoring west of the pier at Prisoners

Tucked in close to the beach, Prisoners

considering a campground. As with any pier within Channel Islands National Park, because concessionaire boats tie to the dock, you are asked not to tie your dinghy to the pier or a piling. Please unload your passengers and return to your boat, or haul your dinghy up on the dock. The west side of the pier is almost always calm for allowing dinghy landings. You can land your dinghy on shore but swells may make this a wet experience. (Depths decrease rapidly inshore of the head of the pier.)

Prisoners Harbor is fully exposed to the northeast and is marginal in southeast winds. Unless the weather is calm, westerly swells tend to curl in from the north, making this anchorage uncomfortable. The best shelter from westerlies lies west of the pier in a partial lee close to the bluffs. (Pelican Bay provides somewhat better shelter from northwest winds and chop.)

A trail—actually a dirt road—leads south to primitive Del Norte Campground, a third of the way from Prisoners to Scorpion; facilities at the pack-in campground include only a

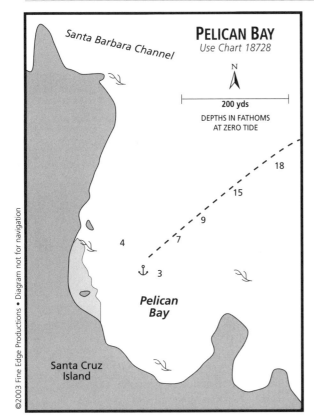

PELICAN BAY
Use Chart 18728

N

200 yds
DEPTHS IN FATHOMS
AT ZERO TIDE

18
15
9
7
4
3
⚓

Pelican
Bay

Santa Cruz
Island

Santa Barbara Channel

©2003 Fine Edge Productions • Diagram not for navigation

Pelican with Prisoners in the background

John Sanger

pit toilet—there is no water available. The five-mile hike to the campground involves a 700-foot elevation gain. You must be fully self-sufficient and carry enough water for the length of time you plan to camp. To make reservations phone 800.365.CAMP (800.365.2267).

Note: West of Prisoners, permits are required to go ashore on Nature Conservancy land. However, to protect its great beauty, *no one* is

admitted to the Central Valley. There is a very serious fence designed to keep people from trekking through the valley. To request a landing permit, contact the Nature Conservancy in Santa Barbara at 805.962.9111.

Anchor (NW of pier) in 2 to 3 fathoms over a hard sand with eel grass; fair holding. Check your anchor set to assure penetration. Larger vessels may want to anchor further north in 10 fathoms mud bottom for more swinging room.

A Different Perspective of Prisoners
by Tom Dore

Prisoners Harbor provides pretty good shelter from northwesterlies, and the average Santa Ana wind peters out just before Prisoners. This is actually a "sleeper" spot that is under-used but very effective shelter in up to moderate conditions from any direction. I ran a boat to Prisoners several times a week, year-round for four years and saw conditions here intolerable only twice. Granted, I was only there during the daytime and never experienced uncomfortable nights. Nevertheless, Prisoners is beautiful and one of my favorite spots on Santa Cruz. Besides, it's easy to exit if the weather does turn bad.

John Sanger

Pelican Bay through the trees

Pelican Bay framed by the cliff

Pelican Bay (Santa Cruz Island)
Charts 18729, 18728; 1 mi WNW of Prisoners
Entrance: 34°02.11'N, 119°42.08'W
Anchor: 34°02.00'N, 119°42.13'W

> *Pelican Bay . . . is used as a yacht anchorage during the summer. In NW weather small boats anchor close to the cliff that forms the W shore of the bay.* (CP, 33rd Ed.)

Pelican Bay has been a popular hangout for boaters since decades ago when Hollywood

Anchorages west of Pelican

Looking down on Pelican Bay

movie stars hosted exciting shoreside parties. (See Bogart sidebar.) The bay is small but many boats cram in here using both a bow and stern anchor. Good shelter from northwest winds is found close to the high bluffs on the west side of the bay but small swells tend to enter on the beam and rock boats to some extent.

This is no place to be caught in a northeast Santa Ana wind or in a major southeast gale. One or two small boats can get some shelter in moderate southeast winds tucked in close to

John Sanger

Arch rock at Twin Harbors, Santa Cruz

Twin Harbors are two tiny and picturesque inlets that lie side by side. Each one is isolated from the other; the easternmost inlet provides good shelter for one or two smaller boats but with limited swinging room. This is a picturesque place with bold bluffs on either side and small, secluded beaches at their head. An arch rock—a small version of Anacapa's famous arch—sits off the separation point. We have seen boats webbed in at the deep end of the east inlet, secured with multiple shore ties on both the west and east inlets. While a webbed boat looks secure for most summer weather, it is not safe to say that strategy would work for Santa Ana winds or southeast storms in the winter. If the surge isn't excessive, it may work, but there's little time for a reaction if any tie were to give way. The western inlet is less sheltered and scenic but it is used as an overflow area in calm weather. Check out both "harbors." This is a sample of the stunning and varied topography that makes Santa Cruz "Queen of

the southeast shore behind the point but all others should clear out for Chinese Harbor or points well down wind. *Note:* Landing permits are required to go ashore.

Anchor in 4 to 9 fathoms, with due regard to other boaters, over a mostly sand bottom with fair-to-good holding.

Twin Harbors (Santa Cruz Island)
Charts 18729, 18728; 0.9 mi NW of Pelican Bay
Entrance (E): 34°02.62'N, 119°42.89'W
Entrance (W): 34°02.66'N, 119°43.01'W

Pelican Cove and Hollywood

In its prime, Pelican Cove was a watering hole for the rich and famous. It was also the place where Humphrey Bogart first learned about the novel, *African Queen.*

We heard the story from our friends Larry and Ann Dudley who were crewing aboard our William Garden ketch, *Le Dauphin Amical,* in the 1980s as we were on our way home from wintering in the Sea of Cortez.

In 1947, Bogey hired Larry to serve as his first mate on board his beautiful 55-foot yawl, *Santana.* One night as they were anchored in Pelican Cove, awaiting Lauren (Betty) Bacall's impending arrival, Bogey was having trouble sleeping. He came into Larry's cabin and asked him if

he had any reading material that would help put him to sleep. Larry had just finished the novel *The African Queen* earlier that day and tossed it to Bogey, suggesting that he might enjoy the crazy plot.

As Larry told it, Bogey was hooked. He didn't fall asleep at all, but finished the book in the wee hours of the morning, instead. He identified with the main character and immediately had Larry call his agent on their ship-to-shore radio to have him to purchase the rights to the manuscript. He wanted to play the main character and eventually talked the studio into producing what became an all-time classic film, *The African Queen.* The rest is history.

John Sanger

Nature Conservancy trail near Pelican

Orizaba Cove
(Santa Cruz Island)
Charts 18729, 18728; 1.2
mi NW of Pelican Bay
Position: 34°02.75'N,
119°43.31'W

Orizaba Cove is the local name for a picturesque anchorage, 0.35 mile west of Twin Harbors. Shelter can be found in the lee of Pelican Rock and a flat cove tucked in close to shore. Pelican Rock, the leading mark, is easily identified by its wedge-shape with the high end towards shore and guano stains on the rock. High rounded bluffs with many scat-

the Channel Islands." *Note:* Landing permits are required to go ashore.

Anchor in either harbor in about 3 fathoms over sand and gravel with fair holding. Shore ties may be used for additional safety and to limit swinging room, but take possible surge loads into proper account.

tered trees surround the cove. This was a popular Indian camp as identified by middens and it is a truly beautiful spot; there is good hiking on the rather open and rounded terrain. (See note below.) Shelter from summer prevailing westerly afternoon chop is fairly good, and it is a pleasant anchorage in fair weather. (We use a

John Sanger

Orizaba Cove seen from the cliff

John Sanger

Orizaba Cove with Pelican Rock in the background

Orizaba Cove, tied with breast line to shore

Platt's Harbor (Santa Cruz Island)
Charts 18729, 18728; 1.0 mi W of Twin Harbors
Position: 34°02.94'N, 119°44.15'W

Platt's Anchorage, 0.9 mile east of Frys Harbor, is a wide bight chock with islets, rocks and kelp patches at its eastern end. This is a popular diving spot and is used by commercial fishing boats. Fresh water can be found up the canyon. Some lee effect is noticed from Diablo Point; kelp patches and fair anchorage can be found off the little cove and sandy beach in the southwest corner when weather is stable or calm. There is insufficient shelter in gales or when strong westerlies start blowing; have an alternative plan ready. *Note:* Landing permits are required to go ashore.

Anchor in 5 to 7 fathoms over a mixed bottom of sand patches, gravel or stones with fair holding.

Frys Harbor (Santa Cruz Island)
Charts 18729, 18728; 0.4 mi SE of Diablo Pt
Position: 34°03.28'N, 119°45.22'W

Frys Harbor is another stretch of the word "harbor." It does not have the size or shelter expected from a "harbor;" we would call it a cove. In spite of this and its notorious reputation for a major boating disaster (see below), it is still quite popular. Although some writers have counted at least 35 boats anchored here, we find those numbers difficult to believe. The inner cove itself is far smaller than a football field and, just outside, depths drop very quickly to over 100 feet.

Frys Harbor provides stable shelter in fair summer weather for smaller boats that tuck inside the cove proper (mostly anchored with two anchors); larger and commercial vessels must anchor outside in much deeper water. Those that anchor outside will find it rolly, partially caused by the downstream turbulence found off Diablo Point.

Much of the Santa Barbara breakwater stones came from a quarry located directly above the beach. The loading platform and parts of old track can still be found on the east shore and some of the bottom off that side is surely foul.

single anchor here.) There is no protection from north to southeast winds, including Santa Anas or whenever significant swells are running. Avoid the kelp patches surrounding Pelican Rock or the rock pile inshore of the rock. *Note:* Landing permits are required to go ashore.

Anchor in 3 to 5 fathoms over sand patches between a gravel and rocky bottom with some kelp; holding is fair-to-good if anchor is well set.

Rock formations at Platt's harbor

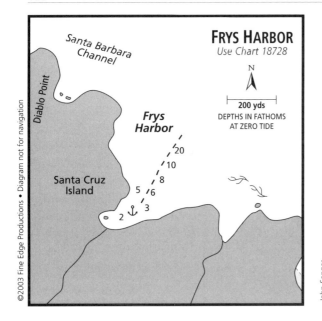

Grebe *at anchor in Frys Harbor*

Frys offers no protection in Santa Ana winds and must be vacated in anything more than moderate north or northeast winds. We can remember visiting here 25 years ago just a week after a major Santa Ana windstorm and seeing hulls of almost a dozen boats that washed ashore—all beyond salvage. This storm created one of the biggest boat losses in the Channel Island's history. Inter-boat collisions and lines that fouled props, as everyone tried to evacuate at the same time in the dark, caused much of the loss. We can imagine the desperation in this small cove where most of the vessels ended up on the tiny lee shore.

One phenomenon that occurs with regularity after nightfall in Frys are strong, gusty downslope winds that can last several hours. This may have to do with the fact that Diablo Peak (the highest spot on Santa Cruz at 2,434 feet) is just two miles southwest. One reason we won't anchor inside Frys Harbor (unless we're the sole boat) is the pandemonium we have witnessed too many times. When boats start moving in response to a brisk 180-degree wind shift, each skipper starts accusing the other of causing his boat to drag out of position. The small inner cove is simply too small for what is recommended. Consider Diablo Anchorage, 0.6 mile due west, as a viable alternative.

We anchored our new research vessel here in early June and found that between the downslope gusts, the swells curling around Diablo

Frys Harbor from hilltop

Frys Harbor—using bow and stern ties

Relaxing at Frys Harbor

Head, and the marginal holding, we did not get much sleep.

This part of the Santa Cruz coast is increasingly steep and rocky, and exploring by dinghy or kayak close to the rock faces yields fascinating experiences. Be sure not to disturb the seals, sea lions and nesting birds while in kayaks and dinghies. (The Marine Mammal Protection Act of 1972 requires that people keep 300 feet away from seals, sea lions, whales and dolphins.) The lava rock itself is worth close inspection; on a calm, quiet morning you can find caves of all sizes, tiny blowholes, and crevices full of noisy frogs, crustations and shellfish. In the 1980s we published an audio tape based upon our early

morning visits to the north shore of Santa Cruz and Anacapa islands that included the sounds of the water swooshing in and out of the sea caves and the bellowing of sea lions in their rookeries. There is a large cave 200 yards west of Frys, but the granddaddy of all is the Painted Cave, 5.6 miles due west.

In stable weather, anchorage can be found in what is called locally the Grotto, a small, well-shaped cove to the east. The bottom at this more scenic site is also rocky with marginal holding. *Note:* Landing permits are required to go ashore.

Anchor in Frys in 3 fathoms, inside the inner cove over mostly sand with some stones or rocks; fair holding (check your set well and have an evacuation plan); or anchor outside in 12 to 16 fathoms over what we found to be a pretty rocky bottom with poor-to-fair holding.

Diablo Anchorage (Santa Cruz Island)
Charts 18729, 18728; 0.3 mi SW of Diablo Pt
Position: 34°03.45'N, 119°45.89'W

Diablo Anchorage, 0.4 mile southwest of Diablo Point, is another scenic cove offering good anchorage in moderate stable weather. High steep cliffs surround the cove and a picturesque steep canyon features nice, gushing waterfalls in the spring. The anchor area is larger than Frys and in many ways we enjoy it more. It is more exposed to westerly swells but is less exposed to winds or chop with an easterly com-

Peaceful spring day in Frys Harbor

Frys Harbor Beach

As we recall, nighttime downslope winds are not as severe as in Frys since this is more of a box canyon.

Diablo Anchorage is a good diving place and there are a number of rocks, caves and kelp beds in the vicinity to explore. *Note:* Landing permits are required to go ashore.

Anchor in 3 to 4 fathoms over a mostly sand bottom with fair to good holding.

Little Lady's Harbor (Baby's)
(Santa Cruz Island)
Charts 18729, 18728; 1.5 mi W of Diablo Pt
Entrance (E): 34°03.41'N, 119°47.23'W

ponent. The two large entrance rocks and their adjacent kelp do a good job on knocking down afternoon chop. While we do not know how secure this would be in any easterly gales, it could be relatively good in southeast conditions being shielded to some extent by Diablo Point.

Lady's Harbor, similar to Twin Harbors, 3.7 miles east, has two inlet. Little Lady's, also known as Baby's, is the eastern finger of Lady's Harbor. It is a charming place; one that you hope to have to yourself and you frequently

Anchored along Santa Cruz's volcanic north coast

Warm pool at Diablo Anchorage

John Sanger

Grebe's favorite hidden cove

can, if you avoid cruising in high season. Little Lady's is longer and narrower than Lady's with more protection. However, its narrow width, with several uncharted rocks along its sides, offers little turning room with swinging room severely limited, of course. Be careful of turbulence and uncharted rocks in the narrow inner entrance. Lady's Harbor, immediately west of Baby's, has more swinging room although it, too, is somewhat restricted.

For all its natural beauty and charm Little Lady's is not a place for novices, but in calm weather it is idyllic. When set and secure, with stern or side ties in your womb-like sleepy hollow, you feel like you own the world. When a

strong westerly swell is running during Windy Lane conditions, Little Lady's develops an uncomfortable surge, and foam across the opening makes for dangerous conditions unless you are well set. We once saw a vessel that had used shore ties successfully to both port and starboard (as well as a strong stern tie to the beach) so that it was webbed in and quite secure for almost anything short of a gale—but it must have required several hours of planning and execution. When webbed like this, no other vessel—other than a dinghy or kayak—can pass you to reach the beach area. In calm weather, a second anchor as a minimum is required because of the nighttime downslope winds. Arch Rock, 0.4 mile west, is another beautiful arch surrounded with kelp beds and calling for exploration by dingy or kayak. On shore above Baby's there is a lovely tight canyon choked with trees a short distance upstream. *Note:* Landing permits are required to go ashore.

Anchor in 2 to 3 fathoms over a sand patch near shore; watch for and avoid submerged rocks on either side that have fallen from the high cliffs. Lady's Harbor, immediately west of Baby's, will accommodate larger boats but it is a little less sheltered.

Lady's Harbor (Santa Cruz Island)
Charts 18729, 18728; just W of Baby's
Entrance (W): 34°03.40'N, 119°47.28'W

Lady's Harbor, a small inlet west of Little Lady's, provides fair anchorage in stable weather for a few boats. Anchor off an attractive beach and beautiful steep canyon choked with oak trees and a lovely freshwater stream with many nice pools in the wet season. This is a lovely place to spend some time, particularly if you happen to be alone.

Lady's Harbor is considered a fair weather anchorage. It is exposed

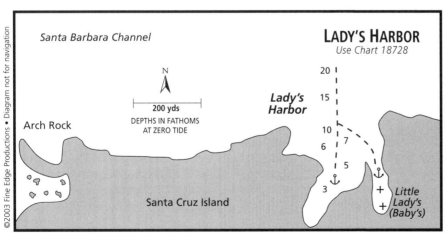

©2003 Fine Edge Productions • Diagram not for navigation

Santa Barbara Channel

LADY'S HARBOR
Use Chart 18728

N

200 yds
DEPTHS IN FATHOMS
AT ZERO TIDE

Arch Rock

Lady's Harbor

Santa Cruz Island

Little Lady's (Baby's)

Grebe *at anchor in Lady's Harbor*

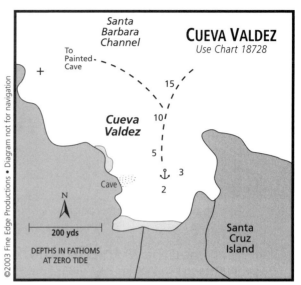

Santa Barbara Channel

CUEVA VALDEZ
Use Chart 18728

To Painted Cave

15

Cueva Valdez

10

5

Cave

3

2

N

200 yds

DEPTHS IN FATHOMS
AT ZERO TIDE

Santa Cruz Island

©2003 Fine Edge Productions • Diagram not for navigation

in anything more than a moderate easterly but may provide fairly good shelter in southerly weather. It is a great base camp from which to explore the fascinating shoreline along this part of the coast by dinghy or kayak. *Note:* Landing permits are required to go ashore.

Anchor in 2 to 3 fathoms off the beach over sand; fair to good holding.

Arch rock west of Lady's

Cueva Valdez (Santa Cruz Island)
Charts 18729, 18728; 3.1 mi W of Diablo Pt, 2.4 mi E of Profile Pt
Entrance: 34°03.30'N, 119°49.07'W
Anchor: 34°03.18'N, 119°49.06'W

Cueva Valdez is a great destination in itself and is used as a base camp for excursions to Painted Cave. Cueva Valdez is a unique cave with a rare triple entrance. (We have seen only one other such cave, and that is on San Miguel Island.) In the vicinity you can find some pioneer rock paintings, a beautiful canyon, many superb pools for freshwater bathing, and middens. There is a small waterfall hidden on the east end of the beach where we have spent endless hours recording frog "serenades."

Other than an uncharted shoal (rock) off the entrance to the cave and a rock pile to its west, we find the approach and access quite easy and the anchorage with adequate turning and swinging room. We always anchor a little east of the giant cave. Ashore you can take a classic boat photo from inside the cave looking out. Around the edges of the bay you will find more stones or rocks and eelgrass or kelp. On southeast gales you can find emergency shelter below the cliff on the northeast side of the bay. We have taken a strong Santa Ana here and feel this is one of the better survival places along the north coast of Santa Cruz Island. However in storm-force Santa Anas (somewhat rare) we

North coast of Santa Cruz Island

would recommend Fraser Cove in the lee of the north side of Fraser Point, 5.4 miles due west.

Cueva Valdez is crowded on holiday weekends, so use such times for going further afloat—perhaps to Santa Rosa or San Miguel islands or to the more remote south-facing anchorages on Santa Cruz.

When large swells run in strong westerlies, Cueva Valdez experiences rollers that make the anchorage uncomfortable, requiring lots of scope, or, in rare cases, the necessity to run your engine.

In our personal experience, the only place that makes a better anchorage is off the east end of Santa Cruz Island in Smugglers. For some boaters, the west end of Forneys can offer shelter in the lee of the reef from where you can watch spray and foam crashing over the rocks . . . provided you let out a ton of scope. *Note:* Landing permits are required to go ashore; to request a permit, phone The Nature Conservancy in Santa Barbara: 805.962.9111.

Anchor in 3 to 4 fathoms over sand near the beach with good holding. (Holding is poor or fair in stony areas where the weeds grow.) Outside the 10-fathom curve that extends west from the east point, seas get choppy.

Hazard's Anchorage (Santa Cruz Island)
Charts 18729, 18728; 0.7 mi NW of Cueva Valdez
Position: 34°03.63'N, 119°49.72'W

Hazards Anchorage, which has a pleasant sand beach with easy access, provides reasonable anchorage in calm and fair weather with good swinging room. Because it is more exposed to

Calm anchorage, north shore, Santa Cruz

A Lost Magnum of Champagne
by DCD

Was it a set of rollers or was it the wake of a passing tanker that toppled our unopened magnum of champagne? We had set it on the pilothouse roof of our William Garden ketch in anticipated celebration of our last night out on one of our Pacific Adventure charter cruises. The bottle rolled over, bounced off the deck and headed for the deep six. Herb Nickles (FineEdge.com's current webmaster) and I both dove in the water hoping to retrieve it. Too late. Our expensive champagne disappeared and we had to resort to cheap Cucamonga red. We wonder if anyone has ever found our bottle in the last 25 years.

westerlies than Cueva Valdez and becomes rolly sooner in the afternoon, it is less frequently used. It is also exposed in anything more than light-to-moderate easterlies.

Hazards is a quiet place to explore and the closest anchorage, to Painted Cave, 1.9 miles northwest. In good weather only, you can take a high-speed dinghy ride to Painted Cave in a short time.

Anchorage can be taken in four fathoms over sand and gravel with fair-to-good holding. However, we would not recommend leaving a boat here without someone on board and in VHF contact with the skipper. *Note:* Landing permits are required to go ashore. To request a permit contact The Nature Conservancy in Santa Barbara: 805.962.9111.

Profile Point (Santa Cruz Island)
Charts 18729, 18728; 2.5 mi W of Cueva Valdez
Position: 34°04.36'N, 119°51.71'W

Profile Point has a distinctive face-profile when viewed from the west or east; it marks the entrance to Painted Cave within the next cove to the west.

Painted Cave (Santa Cruz Island)
Charts 18729, 18728; 3 mi E of West Point,
NW side of Santa Cruz
Position: 34°04.25'N, 119°51.88'W

> *Painted Cave . . . is a large cave into which dinghies may be rowed for a considerable distance. The entrance is over 150 feet high. The inner end of the first chamber, 600 feet from the entrance, has depths of more than 2 fathoms.* (CP, 33rd Ed.)

Painted Cave is one of the biggest and most remarkable sea caves in the world. It is some 600 feet long in a north/south direction and composed of a series four "rooms." The first room is big enough to hold a good-sized boat. The cave gets progressively smaller until you are in complete darkness at the bitter end of the third room where it turns west for another 150 feet to the fourth room. Water drips continuously down the rocky sides of the cave in a musical pattern. At the very end, sea lions haul out on a small beach; their barking reverberates throughout the cave.

The cave walls are covered with beautiful

Kayaker entering Painted Cave

lichens, and small mosses and ferns that vary from greens and blues to yellows and reds. The natural symphony of echoing bird calls, tiny blow holes, dripping fresh water and the guttural sounds of the sea lions at the haul out beach are captivating.

When we had our sailboat charter business, Painted Cave was by far the most popular feature of an island trip. To experience this magnificent cave, circle well outside and take your tender in (weather permitting and *without* engine).

In order to reach the farthest dark reaches of the cave the water must be flat calm on the outside. Otherwise, a pulsating surge that develops inside the cave creates standing waves that build to dangerous proportions. On occasions we experienced a standing wave at the end of the second room, so large we almost crashed into the 20-foot-high ceiling. (See the adjoining map and sidebar from our *Exploring California's Channel Island* guidebook published by Fine Edge Productions in 1986.)

The entrance bight west of Profile Point is too exposed, too deep and its bottom too hard and rocky for anchoring. You must have someone circle your mother ship outside, or visit the cave by tender from a safe anchorage in fair weather. Only once in our experience did we find it calm enough to anchor outside when the marginal bottom was of little concern. It is a good idea for a cave party to remain in VHF contact with the mother ship for safety reasons both inside and out. It is exciting and interesting to visit what we call the Grotto and the inner cave at the end. Time flies very quickly inside this cave! Be sure everyone wears a life jacket; remain alert, use good judgment, and take good flashlights if you are headed into the darkness. The sights and sounds will amaze even the most blasé salts.

Magical Painted Cave *from Exploring California's Channel Islands: an artist's view*
by Margy Gates

Rowing into Painted Cave on a quiet day can be a magical experience. Sheer walls plunge into emerald water, deep, deep down and finally out of sight. Inside the entrance, the cave arches more than 100 feet above the water's surface. High pitched screeches of the oyster catchers echo throughout the chamber and droplets of fresh water fall from the ceiling. Brightly colored lichen blanket the volcanic walls. If the California Sea Lions are at home in the far black reaches of their inner sanctum, you may begin to hear their barking.

Light begins to fade as one moves through the second cavern, then finally, 600 feet deep into the mountain at the farthest reaches of the third chamber, the watery passage turns sharply into a realm of total darkness. Small waves break on a pebble beach somewhere ahead, resonating in the rocky chamber; their backwash sloshes against the cave walls. Big rocks, a favorite sea lion perch, almost block the passage, and further on, the cave roof slopes to the beach where the sea lions haul out.

The dinghy moves back and forth, rising and falling with the surge. Droplets fall from the ceiling, ping, pong, plot, in the penetrating coolness. In the many subtle sounds there is a great silence. This is a primeval and awesome place.

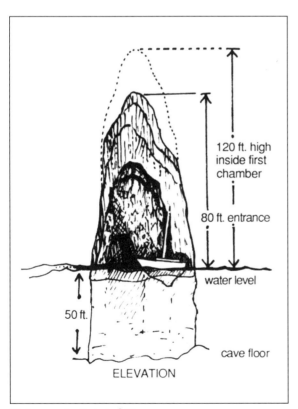

Entrance to Painted Cave

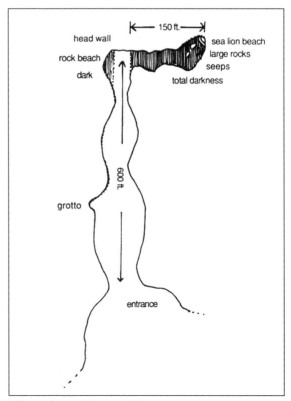

Floor plan of Painted Cave

Anchoring along Emerald Gardens coast

Painted Cave is big enough to enter carefully (in flat calm weather only) with a sizeable sailboat or trawler. On more than one occasion during the 1970s, we took our William Garden Porpoise totally inside the first room. Once a large well-known sloop-rigged yacht, with a very tall mast, entered the cave and dislodged a heavy rock from the roof. The rock crashed through their deck, nearly wiping out a crew member. Another time, in our dinghy, we rescued a family in a sportfishing boat whose outboard engine had quit. We rowed the boat out to our sailboat, then towed it to Cueva Valdez where the Coast Guard met us and took the mother and children back to Santa Barbara. In retrospect, these things seem like stunts today and oddly out of place in the 21st century.

Authors' comments: Bear in mind that 25 years ago there were many fewer cruising boats and no Park Status. We rarely shared the cave or an anchorage with another boat. These days, with more intense use and enlightened concern for conservation, boating ethics require that users enter the cave in relays and without using a motor. Motors disturb the nesting sea birds and sea mammals that live and breed here and the noise destroys the natural ambience for other floating visitors. It would be a shame to foul the wonderful quietness and delicate sounds of a living cave or create engine fumes in this truly remarkable pristine place.

Emerald Gardens (Santa Cruz Island)
Chart: 18729; 1.1 mi W of Painted Cave
Position: 34°04.52'N, 119°53.27'W

The north shore of the west end of Santa Cruz Island is a most intriguing place to explore. The volcanic cliffs look positively ancient and menacing but they hold some provocative secrets.

Painted Cave—Stop, Look, and Listen
by John Sanger

Windy Lane was brisk, and the usual restless chop bounced off the entrance walls as I maneuvered the 33-foot cutter *Grebe* under power in front of Santa Cruz Island's fabled Painted Cave. Three crew members put over the *Avon* and climbed in, eager to explore this wonder, whose opening rose higher than our masthead. Counseled and armed with PFDs and a flashlight, they rowed slowly down the 100 yards or so of narrowing corridor leading to the cave's inner chamber. Soon they were lost in the mist with only an occasional blink of their light visible; finally even that disappeared from sight.

Suddenly a swell swept around the western wall, rolling into the entrance. Then another. By the time the third swell came, the first appeared to be building and cresting as it approached the narrowest part of the corridor. *Grebe* danced in the refraction and, as the waters gradually quieted again, we peered into the thickened mist. A minute went by. What if the dinghy had been overturned in the blackness of the inner chamber? We had no way to reach them. Then the flash of a light and the unmistakable boil of each blade appeared as the *Avon* emerged from the blackness and returned with redoubled vigor.

That was our last entry into the cave for the day and we had not to delayed our entrance long enough to detect the presence of the intermittent ground swell. We were grateful to have all *Grebe*'s crew members safely back aboard!

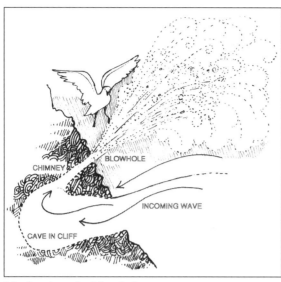

Mechanics of a blowhole

Starting 1 mile west of Painted Cave, an area known locally as Emerald Gardens contains three caves of historic and prehistoric interest. The bights along here are exposed and offer lit- tle shelter. (See illustrations in *Exploring California's Channel Island.*)

Temporary anchorage in calm weather (good for lunch stops) can be found along the shallow bights of Emerald Gardens. The bottom is mixed stone and rocks, so holding is poor. *Note:* Landing permits are required to go ashore.

West Point (Santa Cruz Island)
Charts 18729, 18728; 20.0 mi W of San Pedro Pt
Position: 34°04.78'N, 119°55.41'W
Position: (CA232) 34°05.00'N, 119°55.63'W

West Point is a meeting place of currents and, during gales, there are standing waves for half a mile or more westward. The area of turbulence in heavy westerlies can be **dangerous** and deserves giving this place a wide **berth** and hav- ing every moveable thing onboard well tied down. Frazer Cove and Forney Cove just south of West Point provide good shelter under cer- tain conditions.

Tom Dore

Looking south from Fraser Point with Forney Cove behind the reef

SOUTH SHORE OF SANTA CRUZ ISLAND, EAST TO WEST

Hungryman's Gulch (Santa Cruz Island)
Charts 18729, 18728; 0.5 mi SW of San Pedro Pt
Position: 34°01.68'N, 119°31.57'W

Hungryman's Gulch, a tiny bight 0.8 mile northeast of Smugglers Cove, offers good anchorage in westerly weather for one or two small boats that can tuck in close to shore. Avoid off-lying kelp patches and submerged rocks close to shore. There is a tiny gravel beach at the bottom of a small arroyo. On the north side is a large bird-nesting cliff in the sunny lee of San Pedro Point. *Note:* Landing permits are required to go ashore.

Anchor in about 3 fathoms over mostly sand; fair-to-good holding.

Smugglers Cove (Santa Cruz Island)
Charts 18729, 18728; 1.2 miles SW of San Pedro Point
Entrance: 34°01.18'N, 119°32.13'W
Anchor: 34°01.23'N, 119°32.40'W

> *Smugglers Cove . . . affords shelter in NW weather in 5 fathoms, sandy bottom.* (CP, 33rd Ed.)

Smugglers Cove, 1.2 miles southwest of San Pedro Point, offers very good anchorage for a large number of boats in fair weather, prevailing westerlies and in northwest gales. In south-

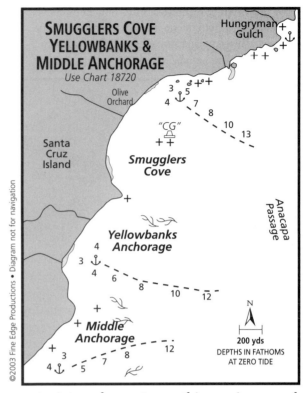

east winter gales or storms, this area is exposed to the brunt of northeast Santa Ana winds. Downslope winds in the summer can be almost violent here in the evenings or after dark; at such times, anchor or move a little south to Yellow Banks or Middle Anchorage to escape this effect. In fall to spring, when Smugglers Cove becomes a lee shore during the season of easterlies, have a plan to head either for Potato or Chinese Harbor or seek a lee at the west end of the island.

Smugglers Cove takes its name from the fact that it was the preferred hideout for sailing ships that wanted to avoid Customs; anchored here the vessels could not be seen from the mainland shore.

There is easy access in day or night. The area inside the 10-fathom curve will hold dozens of large boats with lots of swinging room and it's a good place to practice sailing on and off the anchor. The

Anchored at Smugglers

Setting sail from Smugglers

bottom is mostly sand with some mud.

There is a nice beach here, an old ranch adobe and olive tree and eucalyptus groves on the otherwise dry grassy hills. In stable weather, we find Smugglers to be a pleasant and warm anchorage at all times of the year; it is reported to have more sunny days than any other anchorage in the Channel Islands National Park. Its Chumash name which translates to "Hole in the Sky" is an indication that the Natives knew the secret to Smugglers' weather long ago.

Anchor in 3 to 6 fathoms over sand with mud, some stones and kelp; generally good holding.

Memories of Smugglers Cove
by DCD

We have seen several small boats drag out to sea from Smugglers Cove in gusty downslope winds at night—an occurrence due, probably, to inadequate anchor gear or improper use. A good set under pull with good scope is all it takes. (Those who believe marine catalogue copy that an aluminum Danforth-type anchor a child can lift will hold anything more than a dinghy are in for unpleasant surprises anchoring anywhere outside San Diego or San Francisco bays.)

Once, a boat closer to shore than we were started dragging and continued slowly down onto our anchor which held us both for the rest of the night.

Another time, during a winter storm we got caught here in a morning blow. Our anchor was holding but the surf line moved out toward us as the tide dropped and the swell and chop grew. We got underway at dawn but our small diesel auxiliary was not strong enough to pull us off the lee shore. We had to tack back and forth with staysail and mizzen and full engine rpm until we could clear San Pedro Point and sail into Potato Harbor where we were stormbound for three days. (Since that time we always plot an escape route and note the safe heading, as soon as we anchor.)

Once, we were frightened when a large, black, unlighted trawler cruised the anchorage stealthily, apparently to make a drug drop-off. And, on another occasion we heard the USCG setting up a sting operation using coded phrases on VHF; they were looking for an alleged murderer reported to be hiding on a boat somewhere in the islands.

Yellowbanks Anchorage
(Santa Cruz Island)
Charts 18729, 18728; 1.9 mi SW of San Pedro Pt
Position: 34°00.65'N, 119°32.69'W

Yellowbanks Anchorage, immediately south of Smugglers, is an open roadstead offering a chance to get away from the crowd or to find shelter from northwest gales or downslope winds behind the bluffs. It is fully exposed to northeast Santa Ana winds or southeast storms. Although this anchorage can be warm and pleasant in winter, be sure to have an evacuation plan on any sign of easterly winds (e.g. to Potato or Chinese Harbors, or the lee at the west end of Santa Cruz).

Head in for the yellow bluffs, directly below the high peaks to the west. Avoid the shoal off the point that separates Yellowbanks from Smugglers as well as a drying rock off the south side the bay. Large bull kelp patches grow a quarter-mile offshore in the late summer at either end of the anchorage. This kelp keeps afternoon chop down but allows a low rolling swell to enter; setting a second anchor to keep your bow into the swell will make life more comfortable.

Anchorage can be taken in 3 to 5 fathoms over sand and gravel with fair-to-good holding.

Great White Shark at Yellowbanks
by DCD

Late in the fall when Yellow Banks was almost empty we woke up one morning to see a small commercial fishing boat anchored nearby. Its excited crew was rushing about the stern. Suspended from the vessel's boom was a Great White Shark at least 15 feet in length with its tail folded under. This monster was a first for them as well as for us, probably an El Nino traveler at the north end of its territory. The crews were attempting to separate the jaws—a pretty bloody procedure. With its huge, sharp teeth exposed, it was an amazing and frightening sight.

We had been snorkeling in the Anacapa kelp beds the previous day and we each felt a little squeamish thinking that such a big killing machine had been lurking in these waters. *(The Park Service calls the west end of San Miguel "shark park.")*

John Sanger

Reaching on a double-reefed main

Middle Anchorage (Santa Cruz Island)
Charts 18729, 18728; 2.5 mi SW of San Pedro Pt
Position: 34°00.03'N, 119°32.91'W

Middle Anchorage, on the south side of Yellowbanks, is less frequently used because of extensive kelp banks that extend a mile or more, a rocky bottom, and submerged rocks outside the 1-fathom curve. This makes a good temporary lunch stop while you go for a swim or snorkel; there is no need to drop the hook just drop the sails or turn off the engine.

Anchorage can be taken in a sand patch in 4 to 7 fathoms avoiding the kelp; holding is dependent on the set of your anchor.

Valley Anchorage (Santa Cruz Island)
Charts 18729, 18728; 4.9 mi W of Sandstone Pt
Position: 33°59.03'N, 119°39.67'W

Valley Anchorage, 5.6 miles west of Middle Anchorage, offers some anchorage tucked in close to shore; however, the buildings, facilities and extensive submerged hydrophonic cables and mooring buoys associated with the underwater acoustical range are not a particularly attractive background. This place was very active during the Cold War. Among the studies done here were some to determine limits of detection and identification of propeller signa-

Where did the wind go?

tures. One winter, all craft were forbidden to visit the south side of these islands for some time when calibrations were going on.

Temporary anchorage can be found in about 0.5 mile east outside the cable area in 5 to 7 fathoms over sand and shells.

Blue Banks Anchorage (Santa Cruz Island)
Charts 18729, 18728; 5.5 mi W of Sandstone Pt
Position: 33°58.74'N, 119°40.32'W

Blue Banks Anchorage, 0.6 mile west of Valley Anchorage, gets its name from the color of its submerged blue-green cliffs. It is a favorite diving spot and since the small bay is largely filled with kelp and shallow reefs little shelter is found here. Blue Banks is popular as a temporary stop in fair weather for diving or snorkeling. This marks the National Park Service property line on the south side of Santa Cruz Island. *Note:* Landing permits are required to go ashore.

Anchorage can be taken outside in about 5 to 7 fathoms over a mixed bottom.

Rod Nash's Forevergreen *anchored in Coches Prietos*

Good day for a spinnaker

John Sanger

Alberts Anchorage (Santa Cruz Island)
Chart 18729; 6.9 mi W of Sandstone Pt
Position: 33°58.17'N, 119°41.90'W

Alberts Anchorage, 0.4 mile east of Coches Prietos, offers good shelter in northwest winds but it is fully exposed to southeast winds or swells or to Santa Ana winds. Several boats can find room to anchor in this scenic place; however, there are shoals and rocky patches, so be sure to set your anchor well before leaving your boat. The tide pools and small reefs along the shore are fun to explore, but *remember:* Landing permits are required to go ashore.

Alberts Anchorage, an alternative to busy Coches Prietos, is popular in the summer. We have found it also a nice warm place in the winter in fair weather. To the east it has a fine view of Anacapa with the sun casting long shadows along the high bluffs on the west side of the bay. Southeast swells have a way of setting into the cove making it uncomfortable at times. Landing is straightforward unless a southeast swell or chop is running. The short steep canyon, with springs in the winter, is filled with small oaks and is a delight to hike or climb. This part of the coast is where the black boars lived and jawbones with curved tusks were there for the picking several decades ago. At press time, all the sheep had been removed from the island and removal of pigs had just begun.

Anchor in 4 to 6 fathoms avoiding the rocky/reef patches over sand with fair holding. Anchors can drag with SE swell during the winter so be sure a shore party monitors a VHF handheld in case you need to move. *Note:* Landing permits are required to go ashore.

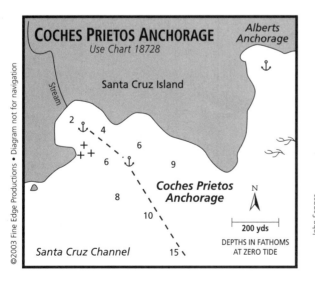

©2003 Fine Edge Productions • Diagram not for navigation

COCHES PRIETOS ANCHORAGE
Use Chart 18728

Alberts Anchorage

Santa Cruz Island

Stream

Coches Prietos Anchorage

N

200 yds

DEPTHS IN FATHOMS
AT ZERO TIDE

Santa Cruz Channel

John Sanger

Randi Sanger gazing at Grebe *from shore, Coches Prietos*

Coches Prietos Anchorage

(Santa Cruz Island)
Charts 18729, 18728; 7.3 mi W of Sandstone Pt
Position: 33°58.05'N, 119°42.34'W

Coches Prietos Anchorage, 1.0 mile northeast of Bowen Point, is the most popular anchorage on the south side of Santa Cruz Island. It has a wide sandy beach at the head of a small curving cove, not unlike a classic Baja hideaway. It is said to have been a major Chumash canoe haulout village site and it's easy to imagine what a good campsite it would have made while they foraged the coast. Its Spanish name means Black Pig or Boar which roamed the south facing ridges.

Coches Prietos offers very good shelter in west to north gales and is a warm place during fair weather in the winter. A good-sized stream descends the canyon into the ocean during the rainy season. It is fully exposed to southeast storms and to some extent to Santa Ana winds.

On entering, avoid the rocks on the east

Good Seamanship

by DCD

One of the best examples of seamanship I ever witnessed occurred in Coches Prietos one Friday night well after dark in the middle of winter. We dropped our CQR in the center of the beach behind the reef not expecting to see another vessel, certainly not that night. Several hours after total darkness, with a moon rising to the east, a beautiful, sleek racing sailboat flying the burgee of Santa Barbara Yacht Club came charging effortlessly in behind the reef under sail alone. Passing smartly behind us, it turned parallel to the beach.

Without so much as a flashlight the crew accurately dropped a stern anchor a few yards off the beach, headed up into the gentle south wind, and dropped the mainsail while paying out the stern rode. Just shy of the reef, the crew dropped the bow anchor without an audible comment and started paying out the bow line while the stern crew pulled in half the stern rode.

Within two minutes these experts had entered and made full-fast a beautiful yacht, without resorting to lights, engine or shouts. Réanne and I had just witnessed the precision of a well-executed drill team or perhaps a prima donna ballerina and it took our breath away.

---

entrance point and the reef extending a good way across from the inner west entrance point. Smaller boats, and those that know this site well, anchor behind the kelp-marked reef (mostly with bow and stern anchors) while larger boats swing on a single anchor outside. *Note:* Landing permits are required to go ashore.

Anchorage can be taken behind the reef in 2 to 3 fathoms over sand with fair-to-good holding, or in 5 to 7 fathoms outside the reef.

Willows Anchorage

(Santa Cruz Island)
Charts 18729, 18728; 3.6 miles E of Gull Isl
Entrance: 33°57.48'N, 119°45.30'W
Anchor: 33°57.71'N, 119°45.26'W

> *Willows Anchorage . . . can be used by small craft in NW weather and affords a good boat landing.* (CP 33rd Ed.)

Willows Anchorage, 2.5 miles west of Coches Prietos, is a lovely cove offering good shelter in north to west winds or gales. Large pinnacle-shaped rocks define the eastern side of the cove, creating almost a breakwater with the surrounding kelp and rock piles. When Windy Lane is howling you can get strong downslope winds here; the canyon has a large, flat water-shed that acts as a funnel. Make sure you have adequate scope for these conditions.

Willows Anchorage has a small sandy beach and is a good place to stretch your legs. Landing is mostly calm except when prevailing southeast swells pick up. We have found Willows satisfactory in moderate easterly winds, but would guess it becomes marginal in northeast Santa Ana gales. It is vulnerable in strong southwest winds, as well, so keep one eye to the south.

A tiny canyon and beach east of the pinnacle rocks provides overflow anchoring but with a little more exposure to easterly winds and chop. *Note:* Landing permits are required to go ashore.

Anchor in 3 to 5 fathoms over sand and gravel with some rocks and kelp; fair-to-good holding.

Laguna Harbor (Santa Cruz Island)
Charts 18729, 18728; 1.7 mi NE of Gull Isl
Position: 33°57.66'N, 119°47.63'W

Laguna Harbor, 1.9 miles west of Willows, is another open bight posing as a "harbor." It has a wide sandy beach backed by a large north-trending canyon. In fair weather this can be a temporary anchorage. It is completely exposed to the southwest and to any chop entering from Santa Cruz Channel. It does not benefit from the large kelp beds that shelter the next two anchor sites west, and it is seldom used. *Note:* Landing permits are required to go ashore.

Anchorage can be taken in 5 to 7 fathoms over sand with fair holding.

Malva Real Anchorage (Santa Cruz I.)
Charts 18729, 18728; 0.85 mi NE of Gull Isl
Position: 33°57.55'N, 119°48.71'W

Malva Real Anchorage, 1.0 mile west of Laguna, is the lee behind Punta Arena (Sandy Point) due south of a high inland peak. The surroundings are low flat sandstone that extends all the way out to Gull Island on its south side. This area is full of shoals and thick kelp patches as far as 0.25 mile south of Gull Island light. While it offers fair shelter in north and northwest winds, southerly swells can enter and make it uncomfortable. Although we have passed inside Gull Island many times for a close look, it is slow-going through the bull kelp forests and usually faster to take the longer route passing well outside Gull. This is a wonderful place for diving and exploring and is frequently used by commercial fishermen. *Note:* Landing permits are required to go ashore.

Anchorage can be taken in 5 to 6 fathoms over sand, gravel and rock with kelp; fair holding only; be sure you don't foul your anchor.

Gull Island (Santa Cruz Island)
Charts 18729, 18728; S side Santa Cruz
Position: (0.5 mi NNE of CA007) 33°56.50'N, 119°49.68'W

Gull Island, 65 feet high and about 0.2 mile in extent, is the largest and outermost of a group of

Beating to windward

small rocky islets. The area around Gull Island is surrounded by thick kelp beds including, at times, the passage between Gull Island and Punta Arena. It is unlawful to board offshore rocks. *Note:* Landing permits are required to go ashore.

Morse Point Anchorage
(Santa Cruz Island)
Charts 18729, 18728; 1.3 mi NW of Gull Isl
Entrance: 33°57.47'N, 119°50.28'W
Anchor: 33°57.97'N, 119°50.54'W

Morse Point Anchorage, 1.4 miles northwest of Malva Real, is at the north end of a long flat beach backed by low rounded hills. It is very dry and, like Malva Real, has an entirely different feel from the north side of the island. Anchor in the eastern lee of Morse Point avoiding kelp patches and a rock pile near shore. It may seem like you are more exposed than you really are because of all the openness.

Approach Morse Point only from the east, avoiding the dangerous shoals and thick kelp patches that extend 0.6 mile southeast from Morse Point. *Note:* Landing permits are required to go ashore.

Anchor in about 6 fathoms over sand with good swinging room; fair-to-good holding.

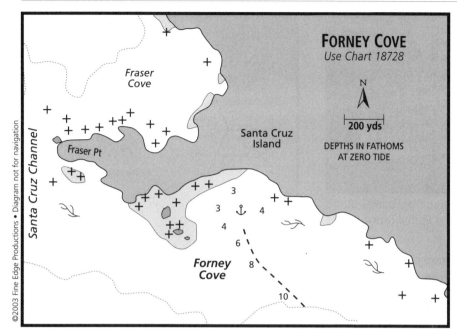

Caution: Posa Anchorage (spelled Pozo or Poso in some sources) is poorly charted. It has several kelp-covered reefs or shoals off the nearby point that sometimes break unexpectedly. We would not proceed closer than the 5-fathom curve without sounding ahead first. Note: Landing permits are required to go ashore.

Anchorage can be taken in 6 fathoms over a mixed bottom of unknown holding.

Posa Anchorage (Santa Cruz Island)
Charts 18729, 18728; 2.7 mi NW of Gull Isl
Position: 33°58.59'N, 119°52.09'W

Posa Anchorage, 1.6 miles northwest, is an open roadstead and useful as a temporary anchorage in fair weather only. Exposed to near-constant offshore swells from the southwest, it gets hit with chop coming down Santa Cruz Channel.

Christy Anchorage (Santa Cruz Island)
Charts 18729, 18728; 2.7 mi SE of Forney Cove
Anchor: 34°01.50'N, 119°52.81'W

Christy Anchorage, 5.2 miles northwest of Gull Island, is an open roadstead useful in calm weather or in strong Santa Ana winds. The leading mark for the anchorage is the center of the long low canyon with building on either side of the watercourse. The long beach is open to swells and the surf can be hazardous.

Note: Landing permits are required to go ashore.

Anchor in 3 to 7 fathoms over hard sand; good holding only if your anchor is well set.

Forney Cove
(Santa Cruz Island)
Chart 18728; 0.6 mi E of Fraser Pt
Entrance: 34°03.08'N, 119°55.07'W
Anchor: 34°03.35'N, 119°55.12'W

Sailboat at anchor behind reef at Forney's

John Sanger

Lunch in the cockpit at Forney's

Forney Cove . . . affords shelter in N weather in 7 to 8 fathoms. The surf is heavy on the beach, but the rocky islet W and the reef connecting it with the shore lessen the swell at the anchorage. (CP,33rd Ed.)

Forney Cove (known locally as Forney's), 1.6 miles south of West Point under the lee of Fraser Point, is one of the most beautiful anchorages on Santa Cruz. It is tucked in behind several islets and a kelp-covered reef with grand, wide-open views in all directions. Some find Forney's desolate and remote; we find it refreshing and stimulating. We have spent many a chilly winter weekend here entirely alone and enjoyed it immensely. This is a great place to dive (summer of course!), to hike or to dream a bit. Don't miss exploring the near shore by dinghy or kayak—it's a marvelous experience. Landing requires careful timing to avoid getting wet.

When a strong westerly blows into Forney's Cove, we feel snug close in behind the islets and reef. Lots of spray blows horizontally, but if we are well anchored, the boat feathers into the wind like a bird, and the swells at high-water lack sizeable punch and flow right on by. We have also spent weekends here under moderate Santa Ana conditions and found it quite com-

fortable. We move to the east side of the cove to maximize our swinging room. We haven't seen much swell or chop from northeast winds here and have sometimes used our engine in idle to take strain off the anchor and hold us in place. We would also consider moving around Fraser Point to Fraser Cove if a storm-force Santa Ana were expected. *Note:* Landing permits are required to go ashore.

Anchor close in to the reef in 3 fathoms or further east in 5 fathoms in firm sand; good holding if well set.

Fraser Cove (Santa Cruz Island)
Chart 18728; 0.5 mi NW of Forney Cove
Position: 34°03.83'N, 119°55.33'W

Fraser Cove, between Fraser Point and West Point, is a rocky, noisy cove except in dead-calm conditions. In years past it yielded fine abalone and lobsters. In prevailing westerly weather it is a dangerous, foam-covered lee shore. However, in storm-force Santa Anas we would sound our way as close to the beach as possible, set our storm anchor, let out lots of scope and watch the proceedings. We would also drop a working hook off the stern just in case the current reversed itself and we swung around before the echo sounder alarm went off.

Both Fraser Point and West End Point have turbulent waters and, when westerly gales blow, the surface turns nasty with standing square waves that have steep fronts. Avoid the area of turbulence off both of these points, staying outside the white water and foam. This can be dangerous to small craft. *Note:* Landing permits are required to go ashore.

Santa Rosa Island
Charts 18728, 18727; 25 mi SW of Santa Barbara; 6.5 mi SW of Forney Cove

Santa Rosa Island . . . is 15 miles long in a W direction and has a greatest width of nearly 10 miles. . . . There are no harbors, but anchorage may be made in Bechers Bay and Johnsons Lee. There are several good boat landings. (CP, 33rd Ed.)

In the past, cruising boaters have largely neglected Santa Rosa Island due to its lack of

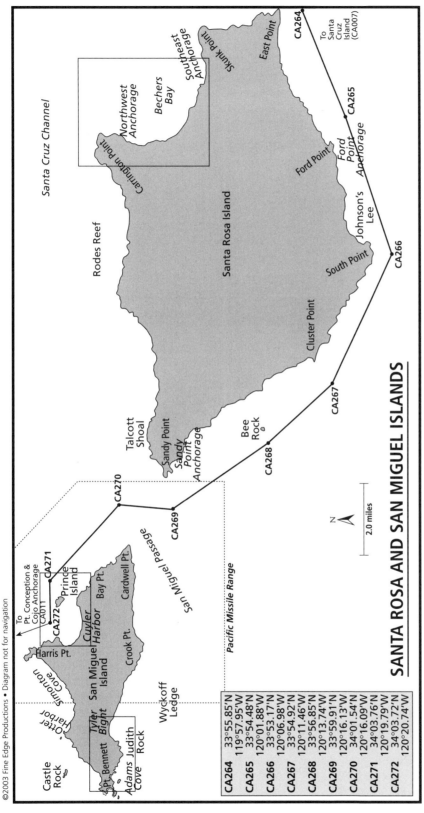

SANTA ROSA AND SAN MIGUEL ISLANDS

CA264	33°55.85'N	119°57.95'W
CA265	33°54.48'N	120°01.88'W
CA266	33°53.17'N	120°06.98'W
CA267	33°54.92'N	120°11.46'W
CA268	33°56.85'N	120°13.74'W
CA269	33°59.91'N	120°16.13'W
CA270	34°01.54'N	120°16.09'W
CA271	34°03.76'N	120°19.79'W
CA272	34°03.72'N	120°20.74'W

©2003 Fine Edge Productions • Diagram not for navigation

well-sheltered or scenic anchorages. But Santa Rosa has some unusual qualities. It is the second largest of the Channel Islands and it has some fine sandy beaches, high sand dunes, rocky inter-tidal areas, steep canyons, vast grasslands, rare plants and archeological finds that date back to the Pleistocene era.

In Arlington Canyon, alone, the 100-foot deep arroyo has yielded strata dating back 9,200 years, human bones from 10,000 years, fire areas to 12,000 years, nine caves and recent Canaliño burials to 620 years ago. Cañada Verde inside Rodes Reef has five native villages and three Dune Dweller cemeteries 3,000 years old. Cañada Tecolote, inside Talcott Shoal, has 16,000-year-old tree stumps with village sites dating as current as Cabrillo's time. The south coast canyons have yielded several dwarf mammoth skeletons. In 1994, the world's most complete skeleton of a pygmy mammoth— a dwarf species related to the Columbian mammoths— was excavated on Santa Rosa. Archeological and paleontological sites are abundant, and discoveries continue.

This is a special place to keep your eyes open and appreciate the delicate balance of life that has survived in such a small concentrated area. Remember that distributing or taking any artifact is strictly prohibited. Recent Park status and patrolling by Park personnel are helping conserve this unique place for everyone to enjoy. We have been thrilled just trying to imagine what life was like over the millennia and excited by what we've been privileged to see. You can feel the spirits of the past. You can try to describe your feeling as you walk the beach: is it sacred, haunted, calling out, lonely, desperate, or serene? This is your National Park—as such, it will never change or be developed.

Bring a kayak and your snorkel—this is a place to do it. A permit is not required for beach day-use; a reservation is required for overnight camping. Camping on the south beaches from East Point to South Point is open June 1 through Sept. 15; from South Point all the way around and down to Carrington it is open from Sept. 15 through Dec. 31. For beach camping reservations, call 805.658.5711.

Bechers Bay (Santa Rosa Island)
Charts 18728, 18727; NE side of Sta Rosa
Position: 34°00.34'N, 120°02.10'W

Bechers Bay, a broad semicircular bight . . . , is 4.5 miles wide between Skunk and Carrington Points and 1.5 miles in depth. Southeast Anchorage, 1.3 miles W of Skunk Point, affords protection in SE weather in about 6 fathoms, sandy bottom. Northwest Anchorage, in the W part of the bight and 1.5 miles S from Carrington Point, affords fair shelter in NW weather. (CP, 33rd Ed.)

Bechers Bay, 7.0 miles southwest of Forney's Cove, is the best-sheltered anchorage on Santa Rosa Island and, in many ways, better than Smugglers Cove.

Bechers is a large bight, well protected from northwest to southwest weather; it is also useful in moderate easterlies. There is a large shallow sandy bottom with easy access and mostly calm water. While northwest gales fly across the low flats south of Carrington Point, the surface of the bay is quite calm making it a great place to practice dinghy sailing. Imagine 3-mile-long tacks in 10 fathoms or less. We did our high-performance test sailing of *Le Dauphin Amical's* rigging here when a northwest gale was blowing in Windy Lane. We repeatedly put the rail under, sailing close-hauled back and forth across the bay. The lifeline stanchions, half under water, had flying rooster tails. This is also the best place we know of to practice sailing on and off the anchor or to hone other anchor or tacking skills.

Bechers Bay is open and exposed to points from northeast to southeast. In gales or storms it must be vacated to a more sheltered lee on Santa Cruz's west end or a lee fur-

BECHERS BAY
Use Chart 18728

200 yds

DEPTHS IN FATHOMS AT ZERO TIDE

Carrington Pt.

Coati Pt.
Corral Pt.

Santa Cruz Channel

Northwest Anchorage

Bechers Bay

Southeast Anchorage

Santa Rosa Island

©2003 Fine Edge Productions • Diagram not for navigation

ther west toward San Miguel. Swells from the east are not common; however, north or northwest swells sometime curl around Carrington Point. We broached our sailing dinghy here several times trying to land in two-foot swells or more.

Shelter from moderate southeast winds can be found in Southeast Anchorage. However, this is not adequate in a southeast storm. You can find brisk winds and strong current in Santa Cruz Channel as Windy Lane splits north of Carrington Point with one segment heading southeast down the channel.

Santa Cruz Channel is on the primary California Gray Whale migration route to and from Alaska and the secondary route for Humpback Whales. Sei and Blue Whales generally pass on the south side of Santa Rosa Island.

Ranger contact is made in Bechers, the main entrance to Santa Rosa Island. The steel pier, some 150 yards long, and a nearby private mooring buoy are used by the Park Ranger. The Ranger Station lies a short way inland.

Northwest Anchorage (Santa Rosa Island)
Charts 18728, 18727; NW corner of Becher's Bay
Anchor: 34°00.88'N, 120°02.81'W

We usually anchor 0.3 mile north of the pier in Northwest Anchorage to be close to the shore action.

Baidarka Cove

Anchor (Northwest Anchorage) in 3 fathoms over a packed sandy bottom with fair-to-good holding.

Southeast Anchorage (Santa Rosa Island)
Charts 18728, 18727; SE corner of Becher's Bay
Anchor: 33°58.91'N, 120°00.61'W

We like to anchor 2.4 miles southeast of the pier in Southeast Anchorage for more solitude or shelter from southerlies.

Anchor (Southeast Anchorage) in 3 to 4 fathoms sand with some sea grass with fair holding.

Baidarka Cove (Santa Rosa Island)
Chart 18728; 1.5 mi S of Skunk Pt
Position: 33°57.43'N, 119°58.52'W

What we call Baidarka Cove is a small bight between Skunk and East Points, south of the Rancho Viejo site, that makes a good temporary anchorage or lunch stop. The attractive sandy beach is nice for walking and, just behind, is a small brackish lagoon frequented by birds and small animals. There are sand dunes and game trails here. This is one of our favorite places to find solitude and observe nature. In a wet year, the flats are a riot of colors with fields of lupine, poppies, and thistles.

Although Baidarka Cove offers fair shelter in northwest winds, it is fully exposed in northeast or southeast gales; it is also subject to downslope westerly winds. Landing is generally easy in fair weather but it would be difficult-to-dangerous if a southeast swell were running. This area is not well charted so beware of isolated rocks, some marked by kelp. For safety, it's a good idea to leave someone on board in communication with the shore party.

As you head south for East Point from Baidarka, there are numerous submerged and drying rocks; shoals and kelp patches extend a third of a mile from shore. Give Skunk Point a wide berth where there can be strong currents; avoid the sand spit that extends seaward and breaks in bad weather. The sand dunes southwest of the Skunk Point reach almost 300 feet in height. This is excellent sea kayak country but it is also a nesting area for Snowy Plover and the beach is off limits during nesting season. This is a coast of environmental concern, so please check with Channel Islands National Park for regulations about going ashore (tel: 805-658-5730).

Anchor in 3 fathoms over hard sand and some sea grass; fair-to-good holding if well set.

Skunk Point (Santa Rosa Island)
Charts 18728, 18727; 2.5 miles N of East Point

> *Skunk Point . . . is formed of drifts of sand; it is difficult to see on dark nights. There are sand beaches W and S, and the sand dunes behind the point are as much as 300 feet high. Care should be taken to avoid the sandspit off the point where the sea breaks heavily in bad weather. The current is sometimes strong in the vicinity of the point.* (CP, 33rd Ed.)

Eagle Rock Anchorage
(Santa Rosa Island)
Charts 18728, 18727; 1.9 mi W of East Pt
Position: 33°56.32'N, 120°00.30'W

Eagle Rock Anchorage, 1.9 miles west of East Point, provides fair anchorage at the foot of the bluff on the north side of Eagle Rock. Although quite secure in northwest winds, it is open to all southerly weather. Fishermen find shelter here in prevailing westerlies or in moderate Santa Ana winds. *Caution:* The anchorage is not well charted.

Anchorage can be taken in 3 to 5 fathoms over mostly sand with fair holding. Avoid kelp patches that may hide rocks.

Ford Point Anchorage (Santa Rosa Island)
Charts 18728, 18727; 4.3 mi SW of East Pt
Position: 33°55.02'N, 120°02.79'W

Ford Point Anchorage, 2.5 miles southwest of Eagle Rock, is located in a small bight on the north side of Ford Point. This is a fair-weather anchorage with some swell, used primarily by fishermen who want to remain close to their grounds. The steep canyons to the north are the ancestral home of the pygmy mammoths.

While useful in northwest winds, Ford Point Anchorage is fully exposed to storms from the southwest to the southeast, and partially exposed to stronger Santa Ana winds.

Anchorage can be taken inside the bight in 2 to 3 fathoms over sand and stones with fair holding, avoiding rocks and shoals along shore.

Johnson's Lee (Santa Rosa Island)
Charts 18728, 18727; 7.3 mi SW of East Pt
Position: 33°54.02'N, 126°06.27'W

> *Johnsons Lee, an open roadstead . . . affords fair shelter from W and NW winds, but is dangerous in S weather.* (CP, 33rd Ed.)

Johnson's Lee, 2.9 miles southwest of Ford Point, is in the large bight ending at the bottom of the high bluffs on South Point. It provides fair anchorage in stable north and northwest winds tucked in behind the kelp. Don't be surprised by downslope winds at night.

We don't agree with those who say this is the best anchorage on the island. We feel much more comfortable in Southeast Anchorage which has interesting sandy beaches. Johnson's

John Sanger

SS Chickasaw *on Santa Rosa still in one piece, September 1976*

Strong westerlies blowing in Windy Lane

Lee is fully exposed to any weather from the south and is a long way to another lee if adverse winds kick up. The old military barracks that housed an Air Force radar station until 1963 are now used by the Park Service. The south end of Santa Rosa is bone-dry, like Baja, and mostly void of vegetation. An old steel pier once located here is gone, but some of the pilings are still laying bent over on the sea floor where the pier was. Most buildings were removed in the 1990s and the land re-vegetated. One or two buildings have been repaired and remain as a research station.

Anchor in 4 to 5 fathoms over sand and stones with kelp; fair holding. On entering, avoid the USCG mooring buoy and the rocky areas near shore.

S.S. Chickasaw (Santa Rosa Island)
Charts 18728, 18727; 1 mi NW of South Pt
Position: 33°53.92'N, 120°07.91'W

In 1963 the freighter S.S. *Chickasaw* ran aground here during a rainsquall. For years this wreck lay intact on her lines, taking a pounding from southwest swell, and looking strangely as if she were southbound under full steam. Twenty years later, she broke in two and, by 1986 her bow and stern sections had separated

by fifty feet. Later she broke up completely. (See the drawing in *Exploring California's Channel Islands,* pgs. 44-45, of the two sections as they were in the 1980s.)

Sandy Point Anchorage
(Santa Rosa Island)
Charts 18728, 18727; 0.3 mi SE of Sandy Pt
Position: 33°59.85'N, 120°14.99'W

> [The] *anchorage . . . affords shelter from N and NW winds to small vessels, but local knowledge is necessary to avoid outlying rocks.* (CP, 33rd Ed.)

Sandy Point Anchorage, 9.2 miles northwest of South Point at the extreme west end of Santa Rosa Island, is reported to offer marginal shelter for small craft with local knowledge. Some reports indicate that this place may provide useful shelter in Santa Ana winds. Viewed through binoculars, this bold and rocky point looks like it should be given a wide berth.

Some references indicate that the tiny cove immediately southeast of Sandy Point offers

Cabrillo Monument, San Miguel Island

protection from north and northwest winds; other references indicate that the second cove just south of a short, stubby peninsula is the site of the anchorage. Both anchorages are quite shallow (1 to 2 fathoms) with a rocky, kelp-infested bottom and both are exposed to swells from the west or southwest. Enter only with local knowledge or by reconnoitering first by dinghy. Swinging room here is severely limited.

Talcott Shoal (Santa Rosa Island)
Charts 18728, 18727; 1.5 mi NNE of Sandy Pt
Position: 34°01.05'N, 120°14.57'W

Talcott Shoal, covered 1 3/4 fathoms, is on the edge of the kelp. . . . Depths surrounding the shoal range from 4 to 12 fathoms. The shoal breaks only in heavy weather. In calm weather there is little indication of the shoal as the kelp is light and there is little lumping of the water. A detached kelp patch is 1 mile N of the shoal. (CP, 33rd Ed.)

Talcott Shoal and the entire north coast of Santa Rosa have thick kelp beds that extend a mile or two from shore. This is a good place for shallow-draft boats, especially sea kayaks. This area was the ancestral home of the Chumash and Canaliño Indians; its sizeable shoals and kelp beds provided abalone, mussels, crustaceans, as well as fish and sea mammals, for their vibrant culture.

Contact Channel Islands Park personnel for information on the exciting discoveries of archeology and paleontology on Santa Rosa; tel: 805.658.5730.

Rodes Reef (Santa Rosa Island)
Charts 18728, 18727; 3.8 mi W of Carrington Pt
Position: 34°02.18'N, 120°07.04'W

Rodes Reef breaks on westerly swells. The area to its south and east is full of kelp beds and, like Talcott Shoal, was a popular area among the Chumash.

San Miguel Island
Chart 18727; 41.8 mi SW of Santa Barbara

San Miguel Island . . . is the most dangerous [island] to approach. . . . San Miguel Island, although a military reservation, is administered on a day to day basis by the National Park Service. Cuyler Harbor is the only place landing is allowed. (CP, 33rd Ed.)

San Miguel Island, the most remote of the islands within the Channel Islands National Park, is perhaps the most unique. The western-most tip of the island at Point Bennett is reported to be the only place in the world where up to five different species of pinnipeds can be found; in winter, as many as 20,000 seals and sea lions can been seen here. The island's unusual Caliche "forests"—lime castings of long-decayed trees—are ghostly remainders that this nearly treeless island was once forested.

Due to its position in the open ocean, San Miguel is subject to high winds and heavy fog, and this abundance of moisture brings forth a spectacular show of wildflowers in the spring. The island has a primitive campground, miles of beaches and a long hiking trail that traverses the island from Cuyler Harbor to Point Bennett. Bird watching is excellent on San Miguel.

More than 500 relatively undisturbed archeological sites, some dating back as far as 11,000 years, exist on San Miguel. Juan Rodriguez Cabrillo, European discoverer of California, is believed to have died at Cuyler Harbor in 1543 and, in 1937, a monument was erected here to commemorate his exploration. No permit is needed to go ashore and hike up-canyon to Cabrillo Monument, but past the Monument, all hiking requires a Ranger escort.

Although regulations indicate that anchorage can be taken in almost all of the coves of the Channel Islands, Cuyler Harbor is the only place you may go ashore at San Miguel. When you anchor in any cove on the south side of San Miguel, you must anchor outside a certain proscribed depth contour. The public can use the Cuyler Harbor beach and campground but all other hiking requires a Ranger escort. Contact Channel Islands National Park Visitor Center in Ventura (805.658.5730) for current regulations; to make reservations, phone 800.365.CAMP (800.365.2267).

The trail leading across San Miguel Island to Point Bennett from Cuyler Harbor is 16 miles round-trip. To take the guided tour you need to

Entrance into Cuyler Harbor looking from Hare Rock to Prince Island

be in good physical condition, wearing comfortable hiking boots or walking shoes. (We do not recommend boat shoes, sandals, or boat boots!) Be sure to take a quart of water and snacks. It's a long walk, but definitely worth doing. Camping is allowed above Cuyler Harbor, north of the Ranger Station.

Approach: Because San Miguel Island is surrounded by a number of isolated rocks, shoals and kelp patches it is particularly dangerous to approach in foul weather from the west or north without first identifying Wilson and Richardson Rocks and the off-lying hazards. From the east, the easiest approach to San Miguel Island in prevailing summer northwesterlies is to take advantage of the lee provided by the Channel Islands. After leaving South Point on Santa Rosa, follow the route indicated through San Miguel Passage, being careful to pass well east of Cardwell Point (position 34°01.19'N, 120°17.36'W).

Cardwell Point is the meeting place of southwest ground swells from the tropics and northwest swells that create amazing and frightening overfalls with breaking waves that extend more than a mile offshore. These waves, which heap up with a fast-paced west-to-east break, are quite an impressive sight. In such conditions, the mile or so east of Cardwell Point has the most dangerous summer waters we know of south of Nakwakto Rapids in British Columbia.

Because of San Miguel's exposure to the open ocean, we recommend visiting only in conditions of fair-weather.

Cuyler Harbor

(Santa Miguel Island)
Chart 18727; N shore of
San Miguel Isl, SW of
Prince Isl
Anchor: 34°03.27'N,
120°21.46'W

*Cuyler Harbor is a bight
1.2 miles long and 0.6*

CUYLER HARBOR
Use Chart 18727 (inset)

N

400 yds

DEPTHS IN FATHOMS
AT ZERO TIDE

Nifty Rk.

Santa Barbara Channel

To Cojo (CA011)

To Santa Barbara (CA184)

To
Santa
Cruz
Island
(CA007)

Hare Rk.

CA272   CA271

San Miguel Island

Bat Rk.

Kid Rk.

Prince
Island

10

8

Cuyler Harbor

7

Middle Rk.

Awash at
3/4 tide

Can Rk.

6

7

6

5

Clover
Rk.

Awash at
LW

Landing

Judge Rk.

| CA271 | 34°03.76'N 120°19.79'W |
| CA272 | 34°03.72'N 120°20.74'W |

©2003 Fine Edge Productions • Diagram not for navigation

Tom Dore

mile wide. . . . The anchorage is in the W part of the harbor; the E part is foul. Good shelter may be had in S weather, but the holding ground is poor. In strong NW weather the heavy swells that sweep around the N shore and into the harbor make the anchorage dangerous. The harbor is not safe in rare N or E winds. (CP, 33rd Ed.)

North side of San Miguel Island looking at Prince Island and the Santa Rosa coast

Cuyler Harbor is one of the most hauntingly beautiful harbors along the 1000-mile coast covered in this book; we would rank it with La Push on the coast of Washington. In the past, Cuyler was a favorite of explorers, sealers, whalers, and fishermen; now it is becoming popular among cruising boaters.

Cuyler is as close to a *true* harbor as any found in the Channel Islands. It is well protected in westerly through south winds. Northwest winds do not directly enter the harbor except over the flats south of Harris Point. However, northwest swells driven by gales off Point Conception do curl around and make the harbor quite rolly on occasion. The jury is out regarding anchoring here in northeast gales and southeast storms; as far as we can tell, Santa Ana gales tend to dissipate to a large degree before they reach Cuyler, and we are sure that small boats could find an adequate lee directly under the 200-foot cliffs on the west side of Prince Island with adequate swinging room. Prince Island is over a quarter-mile long and surrounded by kelp beds. If Prince Island does not provide enough shelter, the sandy beach at Simonton Cove, 2 miles northwest (just southwest of Harris Point),

Excellent lunch stop north of Cuyler

Sea lion hauled out on Sea Ranger *swim step*

should provide relief in 50- to 60-knot winds if necessary. Park personnel have reported that east and north winds of force are rare at San Miguel and that when Santa Anas register 60 to 70 knots at Oxnard and Point Mugu, east winds at San Miguel frequently attain no more than 2 knots, with conditions beautiful.

Enter the harbor from the north, passing midway between Middle Rock and Bat Rock, and find anchorage in the west to northwest section, tucked up against the westernmost shore. Be aware of hazards in the vicinity of Cuyler, Bat Rock Middle, Can, Clover, Judge and Gull Rocks. The southern and eastern parts of the harbor are choked with kelp. GPS and electronic charting make entering Cuyler easy, but an echo sounder and alert bow watch are critical, as well. The southeast section of the harbor is full of kelp patches with a number of charted— as well as uncharted—isolated rocks. You can find a path through the kelp, but it's safer to go around this section.

A full-on southeast storm would be a challenge in Cuyler Harbor; however shoals and large kelp beds that cover the southeast side of the harbor would help knock down serious breaking waves. One strategy to ride out a storm is to motor slowly into the wind at anchor with several

hundred feet of rode out. We feel that the heavy-weather options here in Cuyler Harbor are better than at other sites in the Channel Islands.

It is important, when traveling between this part of the coast and the Strait of Juan de Fuca, to have serious ground tackle. Although many open roadsteads along the Pacific Coast provide protection from northwest or southeast gales, it is critical to carry good anchor gear, along with the knowledge of deploying and maintaining it. Most studies of boats lost in the Channel Islands, as well as in Mexico and the South Pacific, have to do with inadequate ground tackle or failure to use it correctly. Dragging anchor or chafing anchor lines can be prevented; we strongly recommend Earl Hinz' *Complete Book of Anchoring.*

The best anchor site in Cuyler is at the far west side of the bight. An attractive sand beach surrounds Cuyler Harbor and, although landing can be made anywhere along the beach, it is generally best to go ashore in the northwest corner, just south of the shoal south of Bat Rock, where ground swells that curl around Harris Point tend to dissipate. From this spot, it's safer to walk south to the trail than to try to make a landing elsewhere and risk a dunking.

Anchor in 3 to 5 fathoms over hard packed sand; good holding with a well-set anchor. If you plan to leave your boat to take the shore tour, be sure

Elephant seal comes over to the boat

to set your anchor well, with adequate scope to accommodate a brisk changeable wind.

Tyler Bight (Santa Miguel Island)
Chart 18727; S shore of San Miguel, 1.8 mi E of Point Bennett
Position: 34°01.80'N, 120°24.86'W

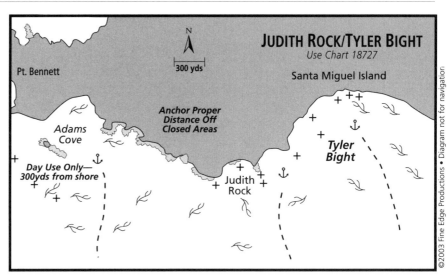

Tyler Bight . . . affords shelter for small craft in NW weather. Anchor in 7 fathoms, sand bottom, at the NW part of the bight under the high bluff, with Judith Rock, at the W entrance of the bight, bearing 265°, 500 yards distant; kelp extends S and E of the point. In moderate NW weather, the winds may attain velocities up to 45 knots 0.5 mile offshore; the sea in the bight, however, is quite smooth. (CP, 33rd Ed.)

Note: To protect the elephant seals and sea lion rookeries located in Tyler Bight, current regulations do not allow anchoring within 300 yards of shore. Contact the local Ranger or Park headquarters in Ventura at 805.658.5730 for the latest information. Navigation in this area should be attempted only with local knowledge and great care.

Chart 18727 indicates a small anchor site at Tyler Bight, 1.8 miles east of Point Bennett at the foot of a small canyon and immediately east of a dangerous rocky reef that extends 0.25 mile directly from shore. This was considered the usual anchorage for small fishing boats in 2 to 3 fathoms over sand patches and a gravel and stony bottom; it is well protected from northwest winds that can howl across the land here. The approach is through large kelp patches containing hidden hazards, so proceed slowly with an alert bow watch.

Note that the anchor directions given by range and bearing in the *Coast Pilot* for Tyler Bight were in error for several years and were subsequently dropped from the 32nd Edition published in 2000. *Caution:* Cruising guides for

this area have several inconsistencies regarding range, bearings, and location on their diagrams.

Judith Rock Cove (Santa Miguel Island)
Chart 18727; 0.4 mi SW of Tyler Bight
Position: 34°01.54'N, 120°25.18'W

The small cove we refer to as Judith Rock Cove is just east of Judith Rock and its associated rock pile off a small beach. The area is unsounded and poorly charted. Rocks and foul ground are found on the east side of the cove off the point.

Night at Judith Rock from
Exploring California's Channel Islands: an artist's view
by Margy Gates

On a dark night in the lee of Judith Rock with the wind screaming through the rigging, I went out on deck for an anchor check and was stunned to see the water filled with bioluminescence.

Three-dimensional patterns of loops and figure-eights drew themselves in the black water. I realized it was sea lions playing and diving and that they were covered with lighted bubbles that defined their movements. They were not just dancing with each other but with the hull of our boat as well. They may have been telling us that our anchor was dragging because the next morning we were far out into the kelp. But, at the moment, I was too enchanted to notice.

John Sanger

Otter Harbor on a calm, warm day

The bottom is marginal but, when we were preparing our book, *Exploring California's Channel Islands,* we anchored here overnight and had a wonderful view of the cavorting sea lions immediately to our west (shown in the

---

Opposing Seas Cause Big Rips
by DCD

Under certain conditions, a distant offshore tropical storm sends long, low swells to the Channel Islands. At the same time, a series of local swells caused by prolonged northwesterlies meet the southerly swells in the shoals off Cardwell Point and create pandemonium. These two wave patterns, one from the north, the other from the south, come together in the shallow water at slightly different angles and heap up into opposing walls of water that crash just offshore. The breaking water moves rapidly east for a mile at high speed before finally dying off. When this condition occurs, heave-to from a safe distance, take out your binoculars, and watch the show. The only other place we have witnessed such a dramatic display of wave interaction is off the Fernando de Narohna Islands, along the coast of Brazil where the North and South Atlantic currents meet.

---

drawing on page 55). The area east of Judith Rock Cove is foul and should not be approached closely until you are east of the long rocky reef that defines Tyler Bight, as shown on Chart 18727.

Judith Rock Cove is fully exposed to the south and can be used only as a temporary anchorage in fair weather. Holding is poor and vessels should not be left unattended here. Contact the local Ranger or Park headquarters in Ventura at 805.658-5730 for the latest anchoring regulations.

Anchor (temporary) in about 5 fathoms over a sandy patch with gravel and rocks and kelp; holding is poor to fair with an anchor watch advised.

Adams Cove Rookery (Santa Miguel Island)
Chart 18727; 1.3 mi W of Tyler Bight
Position: 34°01.63'N, 120°26.33'W

Adams Cove, under the lee of Point Bennett, is home to a spectacular annual pinniped rendezvous. Overnight anchoring is not allowed. A large sandy beach and foreshore are the major landing and haul-out spots for thousands of pinnipeds that come to breed here. This is a noisy area and quite foul-smelling in downwind conditions. The giant elephant seals are an amazing sight, best viewed from afar with binoculars (preferably from a spotter's blind ashore as part of the guided tour). The cove, which is choked with kelp and has a rocky 4-fathom bottom with underlying hazards, should be entered only in an emergency.

Again, remember that current regulations do not allow anchoring within 300 yards of shore. Contact the local Ranger or Park headquarters in Ventura at 805.658-5730 for latest restrictions.

Otter Harbor (Santa Miguel Island)
Chart 18727; 1.3 mi E of Castle Rock
Position: 34°03.38'N, 120°24.59'W

Otter Harbor, a small bight at the southwest end of the long sweeping beach that defines Simonton Cove, has limited protection from

Tom Dore

Simonton Cove, San Miguel Island, looking west

springs in the bluffs just above high water. (CP, 33rd Ed.)

Simonton Cove has a 2-mile-long beach reaching from Otter Harbor to Harris Point. Most of the time the surf pounds heavily here and landing is difficult, if not impossible—the area is considered a 1-mile surf zone in prevailing north-westerlies. Simonton Cove should provide a good lee in rare easterly storms tucked in close to the sand beach after east winds have knocked down the westerly swells and chop. You would need to make a fast retreat as the post-storm front passes and the wind returns with a vengeance from the northwest!

Anchor, as an easterly storm defense, a half-mile due south of Harris Point in about 4 fathoms over a hard sandy bottom with maximum scope; avoid kelp patches to minimize fouling anchor.

the southwest. The area is best explored by small craft or kayak in stable, calm weather; the small beach may be a good kayak haul-out spot, but if you plan to land, check first with the Ranger or Park Service 805.658.5730 for current regulations. There are springs behind the beach north of a normally dry lakebed. We find the name Otter Harbor first appearing in our field notes taken over 25 years ago, possibly it was first mentioned by the ranger who guided us on our hike from Cuyler Harbor to Point Bennett. We have not anchored here.

Simonton Cove

Chart 18727; 0.5 mi SW of Harris Pt
Position: 34°04.14'N, 120°22.36'W

Simonton Cove . . . is a very shallow bight 2.4 miles long and 0.6 mile wide. This cove has considerable kelp and a few covered rocks. There are several freshwater

Tom Dore

Cardwell Point sandspit on a calm morning

Cardwell Point (Santa Miguel Island)
Chart 18727; E extremity of San Miguel
Position (1.0 mi E of Cardwell Pt): 34°01.28'N,
120°16.80'W

Cardwell Point . . . terminates in a low sandy point extending 0.5 mile E of a cliff 40 feet high. A dangerous reef extends 0.4 mile E of the point, and foul ground extends 0.8 mile NNW. . . . During prevailing weather, breakers off this point are caused by the meeting of the seas. (CP, 33rd Ed.)

Chart 18727 has a notation "Breaks" off the east end of San Miguel, a subtle way of describing a magnificent show of force that nature occasionally puts on here. We have witnessed breaking waves that extend a mile or more east of Cardwell Point and consider this one of the more dangerous areas of any in the Channel Islands.

Point Bennett (Santa Miguel Island)
Chart 18727; W point of San Miguel
Position (0.9 mi SW of Pt Bennett): 34°01.19'N,
120°27.36'W

Point Bennett . . . is a long, narrow, jagged bluff, 74 feet high, rising rapidly to 337 feet. High sand dunes extend from the point for 2 miles. There are two rocky islets S of and close under the

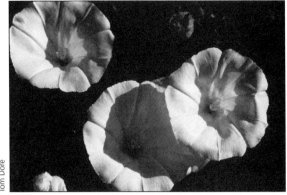

Island morning glory, endemic to the islands

point, and foul ground extends about 0.5 mile W and 1 mile N of the point but inside the limit of the kelp.

Caution. Navigation in this area should not be attempted without local knowledge. (CP, 33rd Ed.)

Point Bennett marks the west end of San Miguel Island and has extensive foul ground best avoided by passing well north of both Castle Rock and Westcott Shoal. Otter Harbor and Simonton Cove, open to the full fury of northwest gales, are protected with thick bull kelp and can be safely approached only in calm or easterly conditions.

Pinnipeds ("fin-footed ones")

All seals and sea lions are pinnipeds. Channel Islands National Park has the distinction of being the only area in the world where five species of pinnipeds are found. Four species breed on San Miguel where, during mating season, beaches and rocks ring out day and night with the sounds of their barking and trumpeting.

Despite his 16-foot length and great weight (6,600 lbs!), the Northern Elephant Seal can move surprisingly quickly when angered. A powerful swimmer, he feeds normally at depths of 600 feet or more on shark, skate, ratfish and squid. Elephant seal pups weight 80 pounds at birth and gain 200 more their first month. Smaller than the males, females average 12 feet in length. Almost extinct at the end of the 19th Century, they now flourish on San Miguel Island. Their name derives from the floppy, bulbous proboscis that magnifies their trum-

peting during breeding season.

Harbor seals have large eyes and are often quite fat and very shy. Their silver coats are spotted with dark gray or brown.

California Sea Lions range in color from gray and tan to almost black. Roughly 6 feet long and over 300 pounds, it is the female sea lion that performs the "trained seal" acts in the circus. Males have three times the bulk of the females. The earflap and the jointing on the back flipper not only allows the sea lion to "walk" on land, but also to scratch an itch under his chin.

Male elephant seals double-migrate from San Miguel Island to Alaska, arriving in the south in January to mate, heading back to Alaska for food before returning to San Miguel in June to molt. Their annual 16,000 mile-migration is more than that of any other mammal.

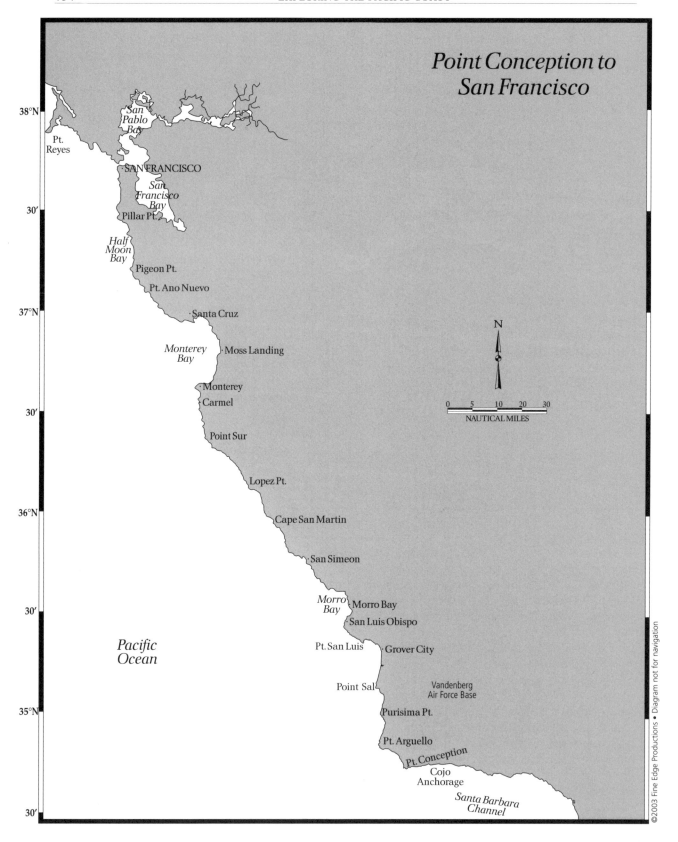

Point Conception to San Francisco

38°N

Pt. Reyes

San Pablo Bay

SAN FRANCISCO

San Francisco Bay

30′

Pillar Pt.

Half Moon Bay

Pigeon Pt.

Pt. Ano Nuevo

37°N

Santa Cruz

Monterey Bay

Moss Landing

Monterey

Carmel

30′

Point Sur

Lopez Pt.

36°N

Cape San Martin

San Simeon

Morro Bay

Morro Bay

30′

San Luis Obispo

Pacific Ocean

Pt. San Luis

Grover City

Point Sal

Vandenberg Air Force Base

35°N

Purisima Pt.

Pt. Arguello

Pt. Conception

Cojo Anchorage

30′

Santa Barbara Channel

N

0   5   10   20   30

NAUTICAL MILES

©2003 Fine Edge Productions • Diagram not for navigation

3

Central California Coast: Point Conception to the Golden Gate

Introduction

In many ways, the Central Coast of California between Point Conception and the Golden Gate is the most feared of all California coastal waters, but it needn't be so. We hope the information in this chapter helps make these waters seem less fearsome and allows more boaters to travel this beautiful coast safely and with less trepidation by combining a series of fun day-trips into a substantial voyage.

Northbound boaters leaving the warm lee of the Southern California coastline from Cojo Anchorage for the 35-mile trip into San Luis Harbor, frequently encounter a stiff beat to windward as they round points Conception and Arguello—both of which share the reputation for some of the most challenging waters between San Diego and San Francisco.

This sudden transition, with its complement of low clouds, swells, and chilling wind, has given the area its label, "the Cape Horn of California." While this term developed during square-rigger days, modern electronics, diesel engines, and sailboats that can point to windward, make passages up and down the coast easier these days. Be aware that, for all the equipment available in the 21st century, this area still lags in VHF Channel 16 radio reception; cell phone coverage is spotty, and there is a paucity of safe anchorages and little documented information. However, for boaters looking for a place to drop an anchor, there are a surprising number of coves and anchorages along this coast that can be used in stable weather.

Electronic navigation, with its continuous data of exact location, opens up possibilities for boaters that like to keep "one foot on the beach" by catching the lees and back-eddies of capes and headlands (what we call the inshore route). Many good temporary lunch or rest stops exist close-in that allow respite from the concentration required by skirting the shore. Always be aware, however, that some of these sites, which we call "temporary" anchor sites are marginal and may not be suitable for remaining overnight; their use would require a vigilant anchor watch. In stormy weather, it's best to remain outside the 20- to 30-fathom curve and head for the nearest harbor.

The weather usually changes dramatically north of Point Conception and Point Arguello: cool, damp and foggy in the summer, mild and wet in the winter. Foul weather gear feels good

An early start is best around Point Conception

along this coast. Summer afternoons often bring clear and pleasant weather, dominated by the semi-permanent Pacific high-pressure system. In winter, the high pressure weakens, and southeast storms or frontal systems move through the area about every 7 to 10 days. During rare winters the frontal systems back up, causing prolonged periods of strong winds along the coast.

During summer, a clockwise flow of wind around the North Pacific high-pressure system creates prevailing northwest winds along the coast. These winds are enhanced by the formation of thermal lows over the land to the southeast—especially true over California's Central Valley or the desert near Las Vegas—and it is common to hear small-craft or gale warnings for afternoon winds of 20 to 30 knots along the coast and the headlands; although these winds ease after sunset, they can remain gusty until midnight.

In early morning hours, dry offshore winds crossing the cool water create low marine clouds and sea fog that tend to burn off during the day near shore. Fog reduces visibility as frequently as 15 days a month during August and September. From fall to spring, when a high-pressure system builds over the Great Basin relative to a low pressure off the coast, strong-to-very-strong northeast Santa Ana winds blow down the canyons and into coastal basins. By monitoring VHF weather forecasts you can determine when it might be safe to move up or down the coast. In fair weather the best general advice is to leave at first light each day and be safely tucked into an anchorage when afternoon wind-driven chop begins to build. When frontal activity passes through, you can stay put.

North of Point Mugu, the atmosphere at the marinas becomes more relaxed, and regulations less stringent. Port San Luis—the first port north of Point Conception, and conveniently close to San Luis Obispo—is undergoing expansion and renovation, with plans for new upscale facilities. Morro Bay, the next harbor north of Port San Luis and our favorite of those along the Central Coast, was our homeport when we left to circumnavigate the Southern Hemisphere in our sailboat, *Le Dauphin Amical*.

In good weather, San Simeon offers fine shelter off a remote sandy beach lined with pungent eucalyptus trees. Although temporary anchor sites can be found off the coast between San Simeon and Monterey, this is the most isolated stretch of the Central Coast with the spottiest radio reception. Monterey, itself, is a vibrant and picturesque city worth a stop of several days. Many visiting boaters like to rent a car to tour the Monterey Peninsula, taking the 17-Mile Drive through Pebble Beach to Carmel and south along Highway 1 to Big Sur. Moss Landing, Santa Cruz, and Pillar Point Harbor in Half Moon Bay are the last convenient stops before the dramatic entry to San Francisco Bay and the Golden Gate Bridge. (Cojo Anchorage and Point Conception are covered in Chapter 1.)

Rogue Wave Sinks NOAA Research Vessel *Ballena*
by RHD

On 4 November 2000, a beautiful fall day in Santa Barbara, Don was in a meeting with Rod Nash and John Sanger when they received word that the 56-foot NOAA Research Vessel *Ballena*—primary research ship for the Channel Islands Marine Sanctuary—had foundered and sunk near Point Arguello, 45 miles to the west.

According to later reports from the three crew members, the vessel had been taking a series of soundings in 30 feet of water about 400 yards offshore. Continuous rounded swells were running about 8 feet high when the seas suddenly heaped up and a 15-foot monster capsized the boat filling it so fast with water that it sank within minutes.

All three crew were able to swim out of the vessel and get into the life raft, but as they pulled for shore, the two oars broke. At that point they abandoned the life raft and ended up swimming for a small beach along the rocky shore. From there, they scrambled up the rocks, fashioned sandals out of their life preservers and walked about a mile before they were able to flag down a bus on the Vandenberg Missile Base. We'd like to hear the "Rest of the Story" . . . !

POINT CONCEPTION TO GOLDEN GATE

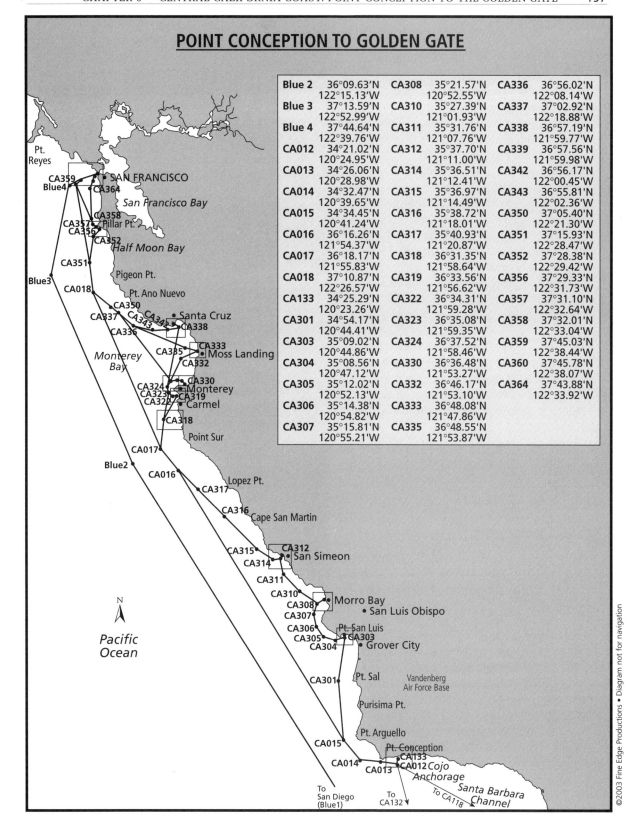

Blue 2	36°09.63'N 122°15.13'W	CA308	35°21.57'N 120°52.55'W	CA336	36°56.02'N 122°08.14'W
Blue 3	37°13.59'N 122°52.99'W	CA310	35°27.39'N 121°01.93'W	CA337	37°02.92'N 122°18.88'W
Blue 4	37°44.64'N 122°39.76'W	CA311	35°31.76'N 121°07.76'W	CA338	36°57.19'N 121°59.77'W
CA012	34°21.02'N 120°24.95'W	CA312	35°37.70'N 121°11.00'W	CA339	36°57.56'N 121°59.98'W
CA013	34°26.06'N 120°28.98'W	CA314	35°36.51'N 121°12.41'W	CA342	36°56.17'N 122°00.45'W
CA014	34°32.47'N 120°39.65'W	CA315	35°36.97'N 121°14.49'W	CA343	36°55.81'N 122°02.36'W
CA015	34°34.45'N 120°41.24'W	CA316	35°38.72'N 121°18.01'W	CA350	37°05.40'N 122°21.30'W
CA016	36°16.26'N 121°54.37'W	CA317	35°40.93'N 121°20.87'W	CA351	37°15.93'N 122°28.47'W
CA017	36°18.17'N 121°55.83'W	CA318	36°31.35'N 121°58.64'W	CA352	37°28.38'N 122°29.42'W
CA018	37°10.87'N 122°26.57'W	CA319	36°33.56'N 121°56.62'W	CA356	37°29.33'N 122°31.73'W
CA133	34°25.29'N 120°23.26'W	CA322	36°34.31'N 121°59.28'W	CA357	37°31.10'N 122°32.64'W
CA301	34°54.17'N 120°44.41'W	CA323	36°35.08'N 121°59.35'W	CA358	37°32.01'N 122°33.04'W
CA303	35°09.02'N 120°44.86'W	CA324	36°37.52'N 121°58.46'W	CA359	37°45.03'N 122°38.44'W
CA304	35°08.56'N 120°47.12'W	CA330	36°36.48'N 121°53.27'W	CA360	37°45.78'N 122°38.07'W
CA305	35°12.02'N 120°52.13'W	CA332	36°46.17'N 121°53.10'W	CA364	37°43.88'N 122°33.92'W
CA306	35°14.38'N 120°54.82'W	CA333	36°48.08'N 121°47.86'W		
CA307	35°15.81'N 120°55.21'W	CA335	36°48.55'N 121°53.87'W		

Pt. Reyes

CA359
Blue4
CA364
• SAN FRANCISCO

San Francisco Bay

CA358
CA357 Pillar Pt.
CA356
CA352
Half Moon Bay

CA351

Blue3

CA018
Pigeon Pt.

Pt. Ano Nuevo

CA350
CA337
CA343 CA342 • Santa Cruz
CA336
CA338

Monterey Bay

CA335
CA333
• Moss Landing
CA332

CA330
CA324 • Monterey
CA323 CA319
CA322 • Carmel

CA318

Point Sur

CA017

Blue2

CA016
Lopez Pt.

CA317

CA316
Cape San Martin

CA315
CA312
CA314 • San Simeon

CA311

CA310
Morro Bay
CA308
CA307 • San Luis Obispo
CA306
CA305 Pt. San Luis
CA304 CA303
• Grover City

CA301
• Pt. Sal   Vandenberg
Air Force Base

Purisima Pt.

N

Pacific Ocean

Pt. Arguello

CA015
Pt. Conception
CA133
CA014 CA012 *Cojo Anchorage*
CA013
Santa Barbara Channel

To San Diego (Blue1)
To CA132
To CA118

Point Arguello

Chart 18721; 11.8 mi NW of Pt Conception
Position: 34°34.63'N, 120°39.63'W; (CA015)
34°34.45', 120°41.24'W

Danger zones extend offshore from Point Conception to Point Sal. . . .

Point Arguello is a narrow, jagged, rocky projection, extending about 800 yards W of the general trend of the coast. An outlying rock is about 200 yards seaward. The extremity of the point overhangs the water's edge, and about 200 yards inshore the point is nearly divided by gullies on the N and S sides.

Off Point Arguello, sea fog becomes a persistent and frequent navigational hazard. The cool California Current is responsible for a sudden increase in fog frequencies. These fogs are often thick, and Point Arguello is considered by many mariners to be one of the most dangerous areas along the coast. From June through October, visibilities drop below 0.5 mile (0.9 km) on about 12 to 20 days per month; July and August are the worst months. During August the fog signal is operating more than 30 percent of the time, compared to 17 percent at nearby Point Conception. (CP, 33rd Ed.)

For several miles north of Point Arguello the giant missile gantries of the Vandenburg Air Force Missile Range are visible landmarks in clear weather. (The base is closed to the public.) We generally pass two miles west before heading north to Point Sal and into Port San Luis.

The rock outcropping of Point Pedernales (flint in Spanish) can be seen 1.7 miles north of Point Arguello. About 500 yards offshore a partially submerged rock, known as Destroyer Rock, which has a longitude *east* of Point Arguello, was the site of an embarrassing tragedy for the U.S. Navy. In foggy weather, and navigating by dead reckoning, a squadron of seven southbound Navy destroyers turned east, believing they were south of Point Conception. (See Sidebar.)

Point Sal

Chart 18700; 19.5 mi N of Point Arguello.
Position: 34°54.16'N, 120°41.31'W
Anchor: 34°53.78'N, 120°39.51'W

Point Sal . . . is a bold dark headland marked by stretches of yellow sandstone. From the NW the headland looks like a low conical hill with two higher conical hills immediately behind it. It rises gradually to a ridge, 1,640 feet high, 3 miles to the E. From the S the hills are not so well defined. . . . Breakers and reefs extend nearly 600 yards S and W from Point Sal and 200 yards SW of Lion Rock.

Anchorage under Point Sal affords some protection from NW winds in 7 to 9 fathoms, sandy bottom, but is subject to swells. Shoal water extends nearly 0.5 mile W from the SE point of the anchorage. The best anchorage is in 7 fathoms 500 yards 123° from Lion Rock and with the northern end of the rock just open of the extremity of Point Sal. (CP, 33rd Ed.)

Point Arguello—Site of the U.S. Navy's Worst Peacetime Disaster
by DCD

On September 8, 1923, fourteen of the Navy's best, 314-foot-long high-tech destroyers were returning to San Diego from maneuvers on the Washington coast. As they approached Santa Barbara Channel, the lead destroyer determined by dead reckoning that its position was south of Point Arguello and 12 miles offshore. Heavy fog closed in as the fleet turned east to 095° in single file at 20 knots, with only 150 yards of separation.

A young second lieutenant navigator told both the Fleet Commodore and the Captain of the Flagship Delphy that the new Point Arguello Radio Direction Finding station indicated the ship's position was still

north of the point. The two officers in charge of the squadron dismissed this new technology, as well as the suggestion to slow down and take soundings and continued on at flank speed. At 2105 hours the *Delphy* plowed into the mainland coast, 1.7 miles north of Point Arguello. At 2-minute intervals, seven of the fourteen ships were completely destroyed.

Known in naval history as the Honda Incident, after the nearby Santa Fe Railroad site, this incident is significant because it repudiated the unwritten doctrine that destroyer captains must follow the leader wherever they go.

Pelicans and seagulls congregate on Pt. San Luis pier

site, avoid the shoal and rocks west to southwest of the point. North of Point Sal the coastline makes a wide sweeping curve and the white sand dunes and beaches of Pismo Beach become visible. As you approach the lee under Point San Luis, 16 miles to the northwest, seas become gentler.

Anchor (temporary) in 7 fathoms over sand with fair holding.

San Luis Obispo Bay
Charts 18704, 18703; 35 mi N of Point Arguello.
Entrance (off Whaler I Brkwtr): (CA303)
35°09.02'N, 120°44.86'W

San Luis Obispo Bay . . . is a broad bight that affords good shelter in N or W weather. S gales occur several times during the winter. The E shore is a narrow tableland that ends in cliffs 40 to 100 feet high to within 0.5 mile of San Luis Obispo Creek where a sand beach fronts Avila Beach. . . .

San Luis Obispo Bay may be entered from S by passing 100 yards W of the lighted gong buoy marking Souza Rock, thence a 000° course for about 2 miles until past Lansing Rock, and thence to anchorage or to the wharves. From N stay outside the lighted bell buoy marking Westdahl Rock and the lighted whistle buoy off Point San Luis breakwater, then head into the bay as previously mentioned. (CP, 33rd Ed.)

Point Sal, 29.7 miles north of Point Conception, provides temporary shelter from northwest winds for small craft that can tuck in close to shore. The lee is fully exposed to southerly winds and swells. When entering the anchor

San Luis Obispo Bay is the wide bight between Pismo Beach and Avila Beach to the northeast; Port San Luis, the seaport for San Luis Obispo,

---

Beware of Those Crabpot Floats
by RHD

With northwest gales predicted for the day, we raised *Baidarka's* anchor at 0300 to round the "three points"— Point Conception, Point Arguello and Point Sal—before daybreak. We wanted to get as far to windward as possible before the gales hit.

We headed out of Cojo Anchorage, following a route that cleared thick kelp patches, and rounded Point Conception into open, confused, rough seas. Just before first light, 1.5 miles west of Point Pedernales and in 20 fathoms, *Baidarka* jerked to a stop, turned suddenly to starboard and pointed straight for Destroyer Rock. Then she made another abrupt turn, pointing south before

Don could cut the power and kill the way.

We raced to the stern, suspecting the problem. Yes, our starboard paravane had snagged a crabpot float. We aimed our spotlight on the culprit, lifted the paravane aboard and sliced through the crabpot line. This was our first serious emergency drill and fortunately, we didn't incur any damage. However, we were discovering a drawback to our chosen inshore route that hadn't existed on our previous trips—numerous crabpot floats. We decided that, along this coast, we should always have a second pair of eyes glued to the binoculars and scanning the horizon.

Harford Pier looking south toward cruising mooring buoys

lies on its west side. The bay provides good shelter from northwest winds and the seas common in summer, but it is open to the south. Port San Luis creates a large lee effective for several miles toward Point Sal. While several hundred boats can be found moored here during the summer, boats are occasionally lost here during storms. The nearest storm shelters are in Morro Bay or Santa Barbara or hauled out on the hard.

Aerial view: Port San Luis

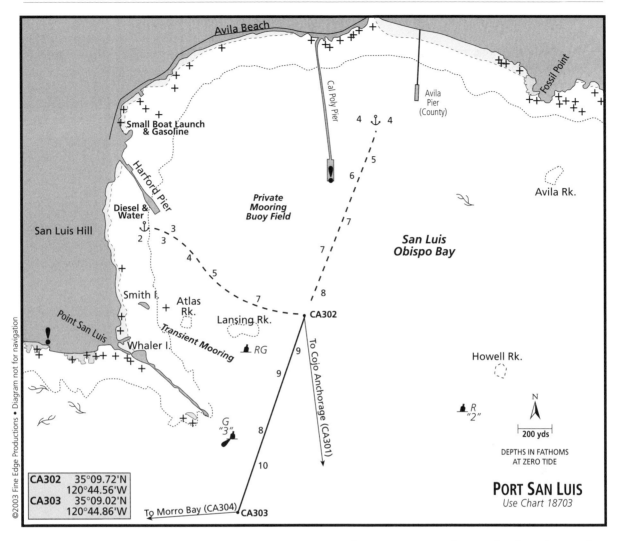

Port San Luis

Charts 18704; W shore of San Luis Bay
Position: (CA302) 35°09.72'N, 120°44.56'W
Anchor (SW of Harford Pier): 35°10.02'N, 120°45.29'W
Anchor (E of Cal Poly Pier): 35°10.49'N, 120°44.28'W
Harford Pier: 35°10.05'N, 120°45.19'W

Port San Luis . . . is primarily a base for commercial fishing boats, sport-fishing boats, and recreational craft. The general anchorage is inside a line extending SW from Fossil Point to the outer end of a breakwater which extends SE from Whaler Island. Mariners should contact the harbormaster's office for anchorage information. Special anchorages are E of County Wharf [Avila Pier] and in the W end of the harbor. . . [See anchoring information in text below.] All an-

chorages are exposed to weather from the S and SE which cause heavy swells. The general anchorage is inside a line extending SW from Fossil Point to the outer end of a breakwater

Port San Luis harbormaster's office

which extends SE from Whaler Island. Mariners should contact the harbormaster's office for anchorage information. Special anchorages are E of County wharf and in the W end of the harbor. The dangers off the entrance to San Luis Obispo Bay are buoyed; the east part of the bay has many rocks and heavy growths of kelp. Souza Rock, 2.1 miles southeast of San Luis Obispo Light, is covered 16 feet and rises abruptly from 19 fathoms. A 2,400-foot breakwater, extending SE from Point San Luis through Whalers Island to a ledge partly bare at low water, provides some protection to vessels at anchor or at the wharves. (CP, 33rd Ed.)

Port San Luis, known for its sportfishing, recreational boating and commercial fishing, sits in "the Central Coast's pocket of sunshine" so-called for its many fog-less days. As we go to press, Port San Luis is undergoing major development with numerous changes scheduled for Avila Beach. What was formerly the Unocal Pier off Avila has been purchased by Cal Poly University and is being developed into a major marine research and education center where students of all ages can study everything from meteorology to plankton. Future plans call for stationing submersibles to aid in teaching underwater biology.

When the "Front Street Enhancement Project" is complete, Avila Beach will have a new look with a pedestrian plaza and artistic stepped-seating as the main feature, a landscaped walkway along the beach, rebuilt pier, new restrooms and lifeguard station, and a new community park at the west end of town. Additional plans include a first-class boating area.

One of the harbor's current popular attractions is the Point San Luis Lighthouse, established in 1890, overlooking the west end of San Luis Obispo Bay. Getting to the lighthouse requires a moderate 2.5-mile hike over rolling terrain. Limited access to the historic lighthouse can be arranged every third Saturday by calling 805.546.4904.

Facilities in Port San Luis include a diesel fuel pump located at the west end of the Harford Pier, guest moorings (first-come, first-served), showers, marine supply store, bait and tackle, boat repair, fish markets and a 24-hour

Work dock and mooring buoys, Port San Luis

Port San Luis: The End of Avila Village
by Michelle Gaylord

We moved out onto a mooring right at the breakwater to have a view of the entire bay. Because it was too hard to get our bikes ashore via dinghy we decided to walk into Avila for lunch. It was quite a little hike; I estimated about 4 miles round-trip. (Jerry insisted it was 10, and that I was trying to walk him into a heart attack so I could put my newly learned CPR to use!) When we got into Avila, half the town had been torn down and construction crews were excavating the beach and waterfront. We had lunch at the "Old Customs House" and found out that UNOCAL was being forced to excavate the entire town of Avila to do environmental cleanup of crude oil. The restaurant where we ate, which has been there for 70 years, along with the other half of the town was to be demolished within a week. The cleanup was expected to last 18 months. So, the little town of Avila will be no more. We were told the San Luis Bay Inn would be spared, and there was talk of building a large resort town similar to Monterey Bay when all the cleanup is complete. We're happy we got there when we did, as Jerry would have been quite livid if he had walked all that way and found nothing to eat at the end of the trail!

Wind picks up off Pt. Buchon in the afternoon

restaurant. Gasoline and a small boat launch are located northeast of Harford Pier. The Harbor Patrol monitors VHF Channel 16; their office is across from the parking lot; tel: 805.595.5435

Transient vessels can arrange for mooring on several mooring buoys inside the breakwater at the far west side of the bay. A water taxi service is available for boaters who prefer not to take their dinghy ashore. (Call on Channel 16 and working Channel 12.) Harford Pier has a skiff tie-up for dinghies.

The recommended anchorage sites are between Cal Poly Pier and Avila Pier on the east side of the bay and the area west of Harford Pier, but it's best to check ahead with Harbor Patrol before you drop your hook. This bay is not storm-proof and boats have been damaged or lost under certain storm conditions. In 1998—an El Niño year—a front moved through with gusts of up to 70 knots and 10 to 15-foot seas; 13 moored boats were lost. There were no failures of mooring buoys, but many Samson posts gave way and lines chafed through. Be

prepared to haul out or head to Morro Bay or Santa Barbara if a major weather front is approaching.

⚓ **Port San Luis Harbor District;** tel: 805.595.5400; website: www.portsanluis.com

⚓ **Gasoline Dock** position: 35°10.30'N, 120°45.32'W

⚓ **Diesel Fuel (Harford Pier)** position: 35°10.08'N, 120°45.22'W

Anchor (west of Harford Pier) 4 fathoms packed sand and shells with fair holding.

Anchor (east of Cal Poly Pier) in 3 to 4 fathoms packed sand with gravel; fair holding.

Diablo Canyon and Point Buchon
Charts 18703, 18700; 5.8 mi NW of Point San Luis Light
Position (Boat Haven): (0.4 mi SW of Diablo Canyon Pwr Plt) 35°12.26'N, 120°51.41'W
Position (Pt. Buchon): (0.75 mi W) 35°15.27'N, 120°54.99'W

Diablo Canyon . . . is the site of a large nuclear power plant. The two concrete dome-shaped

Pelican guards his territory on Pt. San Luis Wharf

Old Port Inn, San Luis

structures and other large buildings are conspicuous from well offshore. Point Buchon ends in an overhanging cliff 40 feet high, with a low tableland behind that rises rapidly to a bare hill a mile to the E. There are a few detached rocks close under the cliffs. A lighted whistle buoy is 1 mile SW of the point and about 400 yards WSW of a rock covered 3 3/4 fathoms. (CP, 33rd Ed.)

In the waters off Point Buchon and Diablo Canyon, watch closely for small bobbing heads of sea otter that play in the kelp beds. They made a significant comeback along this section of coast; some can also be found inside Morro Bay. We have been told that the small bight at the bottom of Diablo Canyon is a legal safe-haven anchorage large enough for only one boat. No one is permitted on shore. Chart 18703 is too small a scale to be of much use. There are many off-lying rocks and kelp. There appears to be a tiny temporary anchor site south of a 111-foot islet about 0.4 mile southwest of Diablo Canyon Power Plant.

The coast north of Point Buchon forms a long bight called Estero Bay that ends at Point Estero, 13.5 miles north. The rocky coast with thick kelp beds gives way to a long sandy spit that forms Morro Bay. Estero Bay is a natural lee during prevailing northwest winds but is known for foggy weather.

Estero Bay
Chart 18703; N of Pt. Buchon, S of Pt. Estero
Entrance (buoy RW"MB"): 35°21.65'N,
120°52.51'W

> *The N part of Estero Bay is fringed with covered rocks and scattered kelp. Estero Bay is one of the foggiest areas along the Pacific Coast. The fog is most common in the mornings and evenings. (CP, 33rd Ed.)*

Estero Bay encompasses the area from south of Morro Bay to its northernmost point at Cayucos. Morro Rock is a prominent landmark along this coast whose south flank marks the entrance to Morro Bay—the best shelter along this section of the Central Coast. Partial shelter can be obtained at Cayucos at the northeast corner of Estero Bay.

Diablo Canyon nuclear power plant from afar

Morro Bay

Charts 18703, 18700; 6 mi N of
Point Buchon
Entrance (outer): (CA308)
35°21.57'N, 120°52.55'W
Entrance (inner): (CA309)
35°21.72'N, 120°52.10'W
City T pier: 35°22.23'N,
120°51.50'W
Anchor: 35°21.69'N, 120°51.23'W

Mooring buoys and anchorage area on west side of Morro Bay

Morro Bay . . . is a shallow lagoon separated from Estero Bay by a narrow strip of sand beach. The port facilities at the city of Morro Bay, a mile inside the entrance, are used by commercial fishing, sport-fishing, and recreational craft. Morro Rock, the tall cone-shaped mound on the N side of the entrance to Morro Bay, is the dominant landmark in this area. A breakwater, extending 600 yards S from the rock, is marked at its outer end by the Morro Bay West Breakwater Light. . . . Sections of the S end of the breakwater are reported to be frequently awash under heavy seas and high tides, but have never been observed completely submerged.

The entrance to Morro Bay is through a buoyed channel between the protective breakwaters. Due to continual shifting of the channel, the buoys are not charted as they are frequently shifted to mark the best water. Mariners are advised to use extreme caution when entering the bay and to contact the harbormaster or Coast Guard Group Monterey on VHF-FM channel 16 for current entrance and channel conditions. . . . Swells from North Pacific winter storms sometimes break across the entire entrance. Special anchorages are in Morro Bay, 1 and 2 miles above the entrance. . . . Extremely high waves created by the sandbars in the entrance to Morro Bay make dangerous navigation conditions. . . .

It is advisable to approach the entrance from the SW because of the currents and sea conditions. Sharp turns should be avoided in the vicinity of the breakwaters, especially in heavy weather. It is reported that currents in the N part of the bay, especially flood currents, have a tendency to set vessels toward the city T-pier. (CP, 33rd Ed.)

Aerial view: Morro Bay

Morro Bay—the most secure harbor between Santa Barbara and Monterey—has a

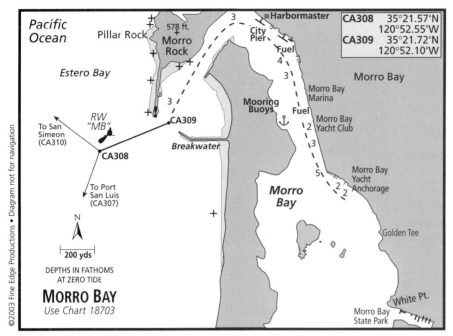

Pacific Ocean

Pillar Rock

578 ft.

Morro Rock

Estero Bay

RW "MB"

To San Simeon (CA310)

CA309

CA308

Breakwater

To Port San Luis (CA307)

N

200 yds

DEPTHS IN FATHOMS AT ZERO TIDE

MORRO BAY
Use Chart 18703

©2003 Fine Edge Productions • Diagram not for navigation

Harbormaster

City Pier

Fuel

Mooring Buoys

Fuel

Morro Bay

Morro Bay Marina

Morro Bay Yacht Club

Morro Bay Yacht Anchorage

Morro Bay

Golden Tee

White Pt.

Morro Bay State Park

| CA308 | 35°21.57'N 120°52.55'W |
| CA309 | 35°21.72'N 120°52.10'W |

reputation for warm, helpful hospitality, making it a favorite stop for both north- and southbound boaters. While the shape of the bay resembles that of a miniature San Diego Harbor, the similarity stops there, for it's here that boaters get the feel of the real Central Coast and realize they've left the big city with its big marinas far behind. Low-key Morro Bay is quiet and more natural than its Southern California "look-alike," and its lovely undeveloped sand dunes and wide beaches give boaters the feel of the "old" California Coast. Three PG&E power plant smokestacks, at the north end of the harbor, can be seen for miles from sea on a clear day.

On a northbound route, Morro Bay is the first of many harbors that has a shallow entrance bar. During foul weather these bars —which become dangerous in certain combinations of local current, wind, and offshore-generated swells—are infamous for maritime tragedies. A strong ebb against westerly swells can cause giant breaking waves at the entrance to Morro Bay. Spring tides create ebb currents to 4

knots or more and many divers have been lost due to turbulence in the channel waters. During such conditions, waves create hazardous boating conditions off the south end of the breakwater. Call the USCG on VHF 16 for a bar report before entering and use extreme caution in marginal conditions. The Coast Guard in Morro Bay maintains a 24-hour watch on VHF Channel 16. Phone numbers for search and rescue purposes are 805.772.2167 and 805.772.1294.

On February 16, 1983 a breaking rogue wave capsized the 45-foot *San Mateo* dumping its whale-watching passengers, 23 children and 9 adults, into the chilly waters and the breaking surf. Ask to see the photo sequence of the incident at the Harbor Patrol office—you will be amazed. The "rogue" wave occurred on an otherwise fairly calm winter day. The quick and skilled response by the Harbor Patrol and crew of the Coast Guard cutter *Cape Walsh* saved the entire group.

As boaters living in the Northwest who are used to marine weather and strong currents, we

Morro Rock and the smoke stacks are the leading marks for Morro Bay

find the salty local comments about Morro Bay interesting. You'll hear, "When the wind stops, the fog comes—after the fog comes the rain . . ." "You can't study the harbor entrance enough . . ." "You can't count waves . . ." "It's more dangerous at low tide . . ." or "You can't predict the big waves."

Our guess is that low-frequency swells, barely noticeable from far offshore, are focused by the shape of the shoreline and, sensing the shallow entrance, they heap up. In spring, ebbs can race out of Morro Bay causing the waves to triple in size and break with little warning. Any 8- to 9-foot swell has the potential to break. The most hazardous times seem to be October through March or April.

We have found that inside waters, too, can create havoc under strong ebbs and wind, generally during spring tides. (The authors encountered a serious winter rogue wave in Puget Sound caused by spring tide currents opposing a northeast gale. Read "Sneaky Rogue Waves in Rosario Strait?" in *Northwest Yachting*'s June 2001 issue).

Impressive 581-foot high Morro Rock is the leading mark for the harbor entrance. (The word *morro* in Spanish means rock and the redundancy of Morro Rock amuses our Spanish-speaking friends.) This volcanic for-

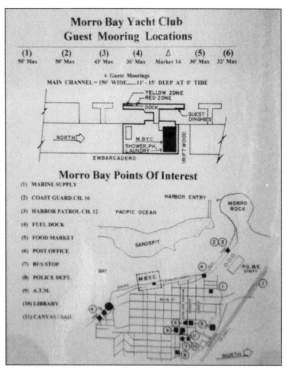

Morro Bay Yacht Club sign shows guest moorings

mation was first sighted and named by Portuguese explorer Juan Rodriguez Cabrillo in 1542. Since then the landmark has been used by sailors and fishermen to guide them through the sometimes-treacherous entrance and into the safety of the harbor. Birdwatchers can often be seen lying flat on the ground at the base of the vertical-sided Morro Rock, binoculars raised and pointed up at the peregrine falcons perched high atop the rock.

The harbor community offers a variety of services including transient moorage, fuel, boat maintenance and repair, food and lodging. If you're looking for seasonal fruits and veggies, Farmer's Markets are held every Thursday from 1500 to 1700 at Young's Giant Food. Nearby points of

Baidarka at Morro Bay Yacht Club float

Shakedown cruise of Le Dauphin Amical—*at her home port, Morro Bay, July, 1974*

social occasions. The nicely maintained facilities include showers, laundry and use of their lounge. One day a week the club hosts a potluck. Since on-dock accommodations are limited in Morro Bay, be prepared to raft, anchor or moor on the west side of the bay and dinghy across.

Twenty-five years ago when we set sail for the Great Southern Ocean and Cape Horn, we were members of this yacht club, and Morro Bay was the home-port of our 42-foot William Garden ketch, *le Dauphin Amical.* (See photo of *le Dauphin* on its shake-down cruise July 1975.)

Montaña De Oro State Park, south of Morro Bay, contains 8,000 acres of rugged coastline and lush habitat that supports thriving wildlife and plant communities. In Spanish, its name means "mountain of gold," so named for the proliferation of poppies, wild mustard, and the profusion of golden wildflowers that grace its hillsides in the spring. This is a wonderful place to take your folding bikes or rent a mountain bike to spend hours pedaling over the rolling hills. The park's shoreline is home to more than 100 species of migrating and native birds—a veritable birdwatcher's paradise. Its lovely surroundings, sand dunes and wide beaches are undeveloped and it is a favorite of boaters, hiker, surfers and campers alike.

interest include Hearst Castle, the Morro Bay Aquarium and Marine Rehabilitation Center, and the Morro Bay Natural History Museum. The town has many good restaurants, including an excellent Japanese restaurant; for breakfasts and lunch you can't beat the Coffee Pot Restaurant at the north end of the embarcadero. For provisioning, Dial-a-Ride service is available to the supermarket. Morro Bay State Park, south of White Point, has a launch ramp and a small craft float.

The USCG office is located at the north "T" Pier, 1279 Embarcadero. The harbor office at the city pier maintains radio watch on VHF Channel 16 from 0800 to 1700. Harbor Patrol operates radio-equipped patrol boats during these hours and is on call 24 hours a day.

Morro Bay Yacht club, which looks out across the sandy spit, is a delightful facility open to all cruising boats for a moderate daily cost on a reciprocal basis for yacht clubs. Accommodations are first-come, first-served, and the members welcome visiting boaters to their

Morro Bay Estuary—spread out over 2,720 acres at the south end of the bay—has three distinct areas managed by the city of Morro Bay, the Dept. of Fish and Game, and Morro Bay State Park. The estuary boasts more species of wildlife and waterfowl than any other bay in California. It has over 60 species of fish, more than 70 species of waterfowl and shore birds; the mudflats are home to numerous shellfish, including oysters, crabs, and clams.

Wildlife is well protected in this area. From

the first of June through September halibut can be plentiful in Morro Bay. This is a great place to explore by kayak. *Caution:* Boaters should check their tide books to ensure they do not become stranded on a mud flat at low tide.

⚓ **Harbormaster** position: 35°22.27'N, 120°51.50'W; **Harbor Patrol** tel: 805.772.6254

⚓ **Morro Bay Yacht Club** position: 35°21.69'N, 120°51.15'W; tel: 805.772.3981; website: www.mbyc.net

⚓ **Morro Bay Marina** position: 35°21.87'N, 120°51.21'W; tel: 805.772-8085

⚓ **Fuel (N)**: 35°22.12'N, 120°51.29'W

⚓ **Fuel (S)**: 35°21.82'N, 120°51.19'W

⚓ **Morro Bay Yacht Anchorage**: 35°21.37'N, 120°50.89'W

⚓ **Morro Bay State Park Marina** entr (small craft): 35°20.75'N, 120°50.64'W; tel: 805.772.8796

Cayucos
Charts 18703; 4.5 mi N of Morro Rock
Pier: 35°26.76'N, 120°54.46'W

Cayucos . . . has a fishing and pleasure pier; a depth of 12 feet is at the outer end. Anchorage with fair shelter from the N and NW may be had in 11 fathoms, sandy bottom, with the prominent white concrete tank on a hill W of Cayucos bearing 017°. (CP, 33rd Ed.)

Cayucos, tucked into the northeast corner of Estero Bay, can provide lovely temporary

---

Watching the Sea Otters
by Michelle Gaylord

The harbor here in Morro Bay is full of sea otters. Quite a current flows through this channel—into the harbor with the flood tide and out of the harbor on the ebb. This morning all the otters just floated on their backs taking a sunbath while cruising upstream. Then this afternoon, it must have been feeding time, because they were all floating back downstream, pounding shellfish on their tummies then leisurely eating their catch. It's quite a sight.

---

anchorage in fair weather. In northwest winds, you can anchor temporarily near the Cayucos pier, avoiding the rocks, kelp and shoals in the vicinity. Avoid Constantine Rock, 1.8 miles west, that breaks and is marked with a buoy.

Upon entering, avoid Mouse Rock, 0.4 mile in front of the pier, by keeping the green entrance buoy to port. The reefs and kelp beds along the coast from Cayucos to Point Estero are known for their excellent scuba diving opportunities. The reef surrounding Mouse Rock, which breaks in all but calm weather, is considered a very good diving area, too.

Cayucos has miles of sandy beaches, great for walks, swimming and surfing, as well as tide pools to explore, and a historic pier with free public fishing. Antique stores, gift shops and restaurants line the main street (Ocean Avenue) and the town is close to neighboring wineries. If you're in for winter cruising, you might try the Polar Bear dip at Cayucos on New Year's Day, but we'd prefer to watch it from shore at this time of the year!

Fishing fleet at Morro Bay

China Harbor

Chart 18700; 0.5 mi E of Pt. Estero
Position: 35°27.57'N, 120°59.58'W

China Harbor, the small bight immediately east of Point Estero, provides temporary shelter for small craft in fair weather only. It is exposed to any southerly weather and to swells curling around the point; it is also choked with kelp that may hide isolated rocks.

Anchorage (temporary) is reported in about 4 fathoms tucked behind the kelp beds.

San Simeon Bay

Chart 18700; 14 mi NW of Point Estero
Entrance (outer): (CA312) 35°37.70'N, 121°11.00'W
Entrance (inner): (CA313) 35°38.29'N, 121°11.31'W
Anchor: 35°38.47'N, 121°11.52'W

Aerial view: San Simeon Bay

San Simeon Bay . . . is formed by the shoreline curving sharply to the W, and on the W side by San Simeon Point, a low wooded projection extending SE. . . . . A lighted bell buoy, 0.4 mile SE of the point, marks the entrance to San Simeon

---

Heading Up Coast—San Simeon
by Michelle Gaylord

When we got up this morning at 0400, the weather didn't look conducive for leaving Morro Bay, so we went back to bed. After waking up again about 0700 we decided, "Oh, what the heck," and headed out for San Simeon Bay, which is only 23 miles from Morro Bay.

Are we glad we did! This is the most beautiful anchorage we have seen so far between here and San Diego—it far surpasses any anchorages in the Channel Islands. It is a huge, calm, sheltered bay with pine trees that grow all the way down to the water in the north end of the bay, and rolling green and yellow hills that drop off into steep cliffs in the south end of the bay. There are no moorings or docks, only anchoring, and we are the only boat here. We arrived about 1030 to overcast skies, but it has cleared now and we have a perfect view of Hearst

Castle high on the hill. I'm anxious to see if it is all lighted up at night. It looks like there is a campground ashore; a few buildings that probably once belonged to Hearst and serviced the Castle; and not much of anything else.

En route we encountered a huge gray whale that surfaced right next to the boat, lots of seals, and some sea otters all wrapped up in seaweed and kelp to keep warm so they could nap. The seas were a little rolly with 5 to 6 foot swells, but not bad. I figure that as long as I can make us something to eat without everything falling on the floor, then it's OK.

Tomorrow, regardless of weather reports, we will head out about 0400. If our coffee cups fall on the floor we'll turn around and come back. If it looks good out there, we'll make our 90-mile passage into Monterey Bay.

Bay. The bay offers good shelter in N weather, but is exposed to S gales in winter. The best anchorage is in the middle of the bight in 5 to 8 fathoms, hard sand bottom. A small ravine due W of the anchorage can be used to go ashore. (CP, 33rd Ed.)

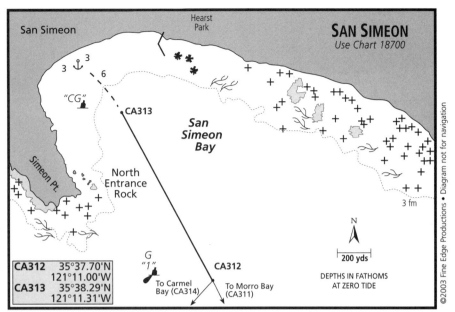

San Simeon Bay is the quintessential Central California scene with a long, wide, sandy beach, and eucalyptus trees splayed against a background of grassy plains that climb to foothills and then to tall, rugged peaks. This fine summer anchorage is strategically placed within an easy day's run north of Morro Bay, or a longer day's run from Port San Luis. Good shelter from west and northwest winds can be found at the west end of the beach. Although well protected from prevailing west and northwest winds, the anchorage is totally exposed to southwest weather—fortunately, conditions that are rare in summer.

As a precaution we would monitor VHF weather forecasts and return to Morro Bay if anything more than a moderate southeast front were expected. For protection in a storm, Morro Bay is the alternative to San Simeon Bay. However, plan to cross the Morro Bay bar *before* gales or storms become threatening. From San Simeon northward, moderate southeast winds generally provide a welcome push.

Sebastian's, the town's general store founded in 1852, is designated a historical landmark and worth a visit; the store carries groceries and a few purchases. This tiny settlement was once the hub of a thriving whaling village. The San Simeon Pier, built in 1878 by William Randolph Hearst's father and renovated in the years since

Entering San Simeon with pier to right

Good anchorage west of the pier

then, is still used by area commercial and sports fishermen. If you'd like to go ashore to stretch your legs, you might consider packing a picnic in your dinghy. Hearst Memorial State Park, above the pier, has restrooms and picnic facilities. And, while we don't advise leaving your vessel without someone aboard, if you spend several days anchored in San Simeon Bay, some of your crew might want to arrange taking the tour of Hearst Castle. The visitors center is within walking distance on the east side of Highway 1.

To anchor, we prefer to tuck in close to the beach, west of the pier where we have a good view of Hearst Castle high atop the hill, 2.5 miles east. Landings can be made on shore (the far west end has the least surf) or at a ladder on the pier. (There is no float, so watch your dinghy carefully.)

Anchor in 3 to 4 fathoms over packed sand; good holding.

Tucked in in the west corner near the landing beach

San Simeon has room for a dozen or more boats

Point Piedras Blancas
Chart 18700; 4.7 mi NW of San Simeon
Anchor: 35°39.87'N, 121°16.81'W

Point Piedras Blancas is a low rocky point projecting about 0.5 mile from the general trend of the coast . . . . Anchorage for a small vessel, with protection from NW winds, may be had under Point Piedras Blancas in 4 to 5 fathoms, sandy bottom, with the light about 0.2 mile bearing 280°. (CP, 33rd Ed.)

The beach at Piedras Blancas (white rocks) is home to the 110-foot tall Piedras Blancas Lighthouse. Built in 1874, it stands as a beacon to warn boaters and fishermen of the area's dangerous reefs and rocky shores.

Small craft can find moderate, temporary shelter from northwest winds under the lee of Point Piedras Blancas. However, with lovely

San Simeon pier, with Hearst Castle high on the hill above

San Simeon so close, most northbound boaters who find the beat north a little too much will head back south to San Simeon. The entire coast north of Cambria to the Farallon Islands, including the rugged Big Sur coast, lies within the Monterey Marine Sanctuary, where there are restrictions on fishing and other activities.

Anchor (temporary) in 4 fathoms sand (avoiding kelp patches) with fair holding.

La Cruz Rock
Chart 18700; 0.4 mi SE of Point Sierra Nevada; 3 mi NNW of Piedras Blancas Lt
Position: 35°42.47'N, 121°18.69'W

A sandy beach inshore from the rock is a fair landing place in heavy NW weather. This stretch of beach is fairly free of breakers in NW weather. There is a suitable anchorage for small boats E of the N limits of the rock in heavy NW or light S weather.

Point Sierra Nevada, a low conspicuous bluff, is named for the steamship SIERRA NEVADA, which stranded on the rock 400 yards NW of the point. About 1.8 miles N of Point Sierra Nevada is a group of isolated buildings inland from Breaker Point; the point is not prominent or easily identified. The highway along the coast is plainly visible from seaward. There is a suitable anchorage

for small boats E of the N limits of the rock in heavy NW or light S weather. (CP, 33rd Ed.)

La Cruz Rock looks like minimal shelter to us but we understand that in the right conditions it can provide good temporary anchorage and a possible landing. The area is basically uncharted and, with lurking hazards, caution is advised, maintaining careful and alert bow watches. Approach slowly in fair weather only.

Anchor (temporary) behind the 48-foot high La Cruz Rock and in the lee of kelp in about 4 fathoms over sand or gravel; unknown holding.

Rockland Landing
Chart 18700; 2.6 mi SE of Lopez Pt
Position: 36°00.19'N, 121°31.34'W

Rockland Landing, whose name appears on the chart but is not mentioned in *Coast Pilot*, lies in a tiny lee on the south side of Hare Creek. This appears to be the site where sailing ships or coastal steamers once picked up cattle from a shore rancho. The area is very poorly charted and should be approached only with great caution and expert local knowledge. Lopez Point, 1.5 miles northwest, is reported to offer anchorage.

Monterey Bay National Marine Sanctuary

The Monterey Bay National Marine Sanctuary, a vast haven for unique marine treasures that dwell off the coastline, stretches roughly from Cambria, at its southern boundary, north to the Gulf of the Farallones National Marine Sanctuary. Its waters, which include all of the beautiful Big Sur coast, extend seaward an average of 30 miles. The Sanctuary—which encompasses Pillar Point Harbor in Half Moon Bay, Monterey Harbor, Santa Cruz Harbor, and Moss Landing Harbor—is the largest area of protected coastal waters in the United States. Approximately 21 endangered and threatened animals spend all or part of their lives in the Sanctuary; at any given time you might catch a glimpse of gray whales, blue whales, Minke whales, fin whales, humpback whales, Pacific right whales, sperm whales, several species of porpoise and dolphin, sea otters, and many other marine creatures.

The deep waters within the Sanctuary are nutrient-rich, critical to the food web that feeds a diverse mix of organisms from microscopic plants to mighty blue whales. Upwellings—the mixing of these waters—occur on the West Coast during summer months and, as cold water rises to the surface, it contacts the warmer air, producing marine fog.

Recognized as one of the cleanest coastal areas in the world, the Sanctuary is truly a boater's paradise, providing recreational opportunities and scenic beauty for thousands of visitors each year. But make no mistake—this pristine environment is under constant threat from pollution related to boating. The price of continued enjoyment of this unspoiled marine sanctuary is *vigilance* against lapses in proper boating etiquette. Exercising common sense and courtesy will help preserve this wonderful sanctuary for generations to come.

Lopez Point

Chart 18700; 9.5 mi NW of Cape San Martin
Anchor: 36°00.76'N, 121°32.86'W

Lopez Point . . . is a narrow tableland, 100 feet high, projecting a short distance from the highland. . . .

An open anchorage affording some protection from NW weather may be had about 1 mile SE of Lopez Point in 10 fathoms, sandy bottom. Smaller vessels may obtain better shelter by anchoring inside the kelp bed in about 5 fathoms, sandy bottom, with Lopez Point bearing about 287°. A rock covered 1 3/4 fathoms is in the kelp beds 0.5 mile SE of Lopez Point. (CP, 33rd Ed.)

Lopez Point is reported to offer temporary anchorage under its lee as noted in the Coast Pilot. Once again, this is a poorly charted area with many off-lying rocks and kelp patches that hide potential hazards. Use caution when approaching. A shoal less than 2 fathoms extends about 0.4 mile south of the point; its kelp beds may offer the shelter mentioned above. Northwest swells curve around the point making for a rolly anchor site when winds howl.

Anchor (temporary) in 5 fathoms, inside the kelp beds, over sand, stones and kelp; poor-to-fair holding.

Baidarka approaching Pfeiffer Point

Pfeiffer Point (Wreck Beach)

Chart 18686; 17.5 mi NW of Lopez Pt; 6 mi SE of Pt Sur.
Entrance: 36°13.33'N, 121°47.96'W
Anchor: 36°13.86'N, 121°47.85'W

Pfeiffer Point . . . is 400 to 500 feet high; it is the seaward end of a long ridge 2,000 feet high, 1.5 miles NE of the point. . . . Anchorage, affording fair protection in N and NW weather, may be had for small vessels about 0.9 mile ESE of Pfeiffer Point and 500 yards offshore in 8 fathoms, sandy bottom, with chain sufficient to clear the kelp line. This anchorage is used extensively by local

---

How to Appreciate a Calm Day
by Michelle Gaylord

You must experience a rough sea in order to appreciate a calm one. Today is the day. We called up a weather report early this morning, and although it warned that conditions would be rough, we decided it couldn't be all that bad. We pulled anchor at San Simeon about 0430, hung a right, and headed north for Monterey. It was lumpy and rolly, but bearable. About 30 minutes out we ran through a massive patch of kelp—which we couldn't see because it was still dark—and did a number on the shafts and stabilizers. But, after going in forward then reverse; forward then reverse; forward then reverse (you get the idea) we broke it all loose. We made a pact not to venture into unfamiliar waters in the future until it is light enough to see where we are going.

About an hour out of the anchorage came the monster swells. They were running 10 to 12 feet, with a periodic 14- to 16-footer thrown in. Not at all fun, and

certainly not comfortable, but after literally being airborne, crashing down in the trough, hearing sounds like every seam in the boat being split open and then finding out we were still in one piece and hadn't splintered into toothpicks, we felt quite a sense of security in the stability of *Passing Thru* and just how much she can handle! There is some other good news; we aren't seasick. I am now sitting on the floor writing this, and every so often Jerry yells, "Look out, here comes a big one," so I stop typing and hold onto the computer!

I have found my "little corner" of the boat where it's the most comfortable in rough seas. I prop the beanbag chair up against the stairs leading to the fly bridge, pack in a few pillows and my San Diego lap blanket. Down here, if I fall out of the seat, I don't have far to go. And when I can't see those huge walls of water coming straight at me it doesn't seem to be so bad.

fishermen. Access by land is difficult as the road is poor. (CP, 33rd Ed.)

Temporary anchorage can be found behind and inside the off-lying kelp patches in the lee of Pfeiffer Point. With any swell this is a rolly anchor site, but it makes a good temporary stop in fair weather. It can give needed rest not far from the 20-fathom curve; *Baidarka's* crew found it refreshing. This is the southern boundary of the Sea Otter Refuge.

Some trailer boats are reportedly launched over a small steep dirt road. A few houses on shore and private buoys lie close off the launch ramp.

Anchor (temporary) in 4 to 6 fathoms sand with fair holding.

Point Sur

Chart 18686; 6.5 mi NW of Pfeiffer Pt
Position (0.75 mi W): 36°18.37'N, 121°55.07'W

Point Sur, 12 miles NW of Point Arguello and 96 miles SSE of San Francisco Bay entrance, is a black rocky butte 361 feet high with low sand dunes extending E from it for over 0.5 mile. The buildings of a U.S. Naval Facility for oceanographic research are about 0.5 mile E from the light. Sur Rock, 1.8 miles SSE form Point Sur Light and nearly 0.8 miles offshore, is awash. A

David J. Shuler

Fishing boat southbound off Pt. Sur Light

shoal covered 2 fathoms, 0.3 mile W of Point Sur, breaks heavily in all but very smooth weather.

Baidarka Mistaken for Poacher—June 14, 2000
by RHD

We certainly didn't expect to hear a voice on Channel 16. The stretch of coast we were following off Big Sur is so remote we couldn't even raise San Francisco Coast Guard for a weather report!

"Fishing vessel off La Cruz Rock, please respond on Channel 16. This is the Monterey Sanctuary Patrol." We looked aft and didn't see another boat. As a matter of fact, we hadn't seen another boat all day. The voice repeated the message. Don picked up the microphone and answered, "This is the vessel, *Baidarka*. We're the only boat off La Cruz Rock. Might you be calling us?"

"Are you the boat with your fishing poles out? This is a no-fishing zone. There's a serious penalty for fishing in this area."

"We're not fishing; we're a research vessel on our

way north to Alaska and we have our stabilizer poles out."

"Oh, what are you researching?"

Don explained what we do and that we were keeping one foot on the beach to research nooks and crannies where coastal cruising boats could duck in.

"Sounds really interesting, Captain. Let us know if we can be of any help, and come by our new office in Santa Cruz."

"Thanks, and keep up the good work," Don replied, scanning the high cliffs above with binocs. "No sign of the Sanctuary Patrol; they must have good telescopes." he said.

And so . . . *Baidarka* had survived another close encounter with anti-poacher authorities.

About 0.5 mile SW from Sur Rock is a shoal covered 4 1/2 fathoms that breaks in heavy weather. Extending 0.9 mile from Sur Rock toward Point Sur are many covered rocks that show breakers in moderately smooth weather. Foul ground lies between the rocks and the beach. These dangers are usually well marked by kelp, but it is a dangerous locality in thick or foggy weather, and vessels should stay in depths greater than 30 fathoms. (CP, 33rd Ed.)

Bixby Bridge and Castle Rock at Bixby Landing

Point Sur makes a large lee against prevailing northwest winds; however it is poorly charted and very dangerous due to the number of isolated rocks and thick kelp patches hiding submerged. Avoid the foul area north of Sur Rock—it is hazardous.

Although we find the area intriguing and it could offer some smooth water, its cruising potential remains a mystery until better charts or resources are available. A large foul area known as Sur Breakers extends over a mile offshore between the Big Sur River and Point Sur.

Bixby Landing
Chart 18686; 3.9 mi N of Point Sur
Position: 36°22.23'N, 121°54.31'W

Bixby Landing,... N of Point Sur, is identified by a prominent concrete arch bridge across Bixby Creek; the bridge shows well to the W, but is obscured to the N. Less prominent is another concrete arch bridge across Rocky Creek, which is just N of Bixby Creek. (CP, 33rd Ed.)

Bixby Landing is a tiny cove reported to offer temporary anchorage in fair weather under the lee of "Bixby Point," Castle Rocks, and the adjacent kelp beds off the old but photogenic Highway 1 arched bridge. This area is poorly charted, so be sure to maintain an alert bow watch inside the 15-fathom contour because of numerous rocks and foul areas. We have looked

into the spot only from offshore and would not recommend entering unless the weather is calm. Avoid a dangerous rock awash on low water, 0.19 mile southwest of Bixby Point. Like Point Sur, the cruising potential for Bixby Landing remains a mystery at this point.

Pinnacle Point (Point Lobos)
Chart 18686; 13.2 mi N of Point Sur
Position: 36°31.45'N, 121°57.89'W

Pinnacle Point, the outer tip of Point Lobos and the S point at the entrance to Carmel Bay, is an irregular, jagged, rocky point 100 feet high. Sea Lion Rocks are a group of rocks off the point. A rock, formerly known as Whalers Rock, is the farthest offshore of the group and is 0.5 mile SW of the point. The entire Point Lobos area is included in a State ecological reserve. Regulations prohibit landing anywhere within its boundaries. (CP, 33rd Ed.)

Many hazards exist inside the 30-fathom contour. Our waypoint CA318 (36°31.35'N, 121°58.64'W) is 1.1 mile west of Pinnacle Point.

Carmel Bay (Pebble Beach)
Chart 18686; Carmel Bay, between Pinnacle Point and Cypress Point
Position: 36°32.75'N, 121°57.35'W

Carmel Bay is a 2.8-mile-wide open bight between Pinnacle Point and Cypress Point. The

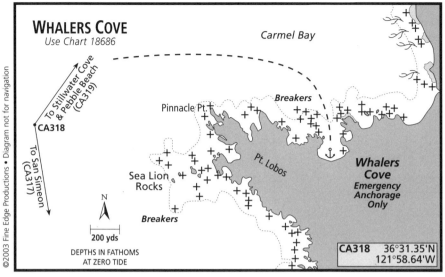

WHALERS COVE
Use Chart 18686

Carmel Bay

To Stillwater Cove & Pebble Beach (CA319)

CA318

To San Simeon (CA317)

Pinnacle Pt.

Breakers

Pt. Lobos

Sea Lion Rocks

Breakers

N

200 yds

DEPTHS IN FATHOMS
AT ZERO TIDE

Whalers Cove
Emergency Anchorage Only

| CA318 | 36°31.35'N |
| | 121°58.64'W |

©2003 Fine Edge Productions • Diagram not for navigation

Whalers Cove

(Carmel Bay)
Chart 18686; 0.8 mile ESE of Pinnacle (Carmel) Point
Entrance: 36°31.51'N, 121°56.40'W
Anchor: 36°31.21'N, 121°56.33'W

Whalers Cove, the bight on the N shore 0.8 mile ESE of Pinnacle Point, may be used as a harbor of refuge only. Kelp growth is quite heavy in the cove. In S weather, anchorage may be had in Whalers Cove in 3 to 4 fathoms, rock or gravel bottom, but there is a rock covered 1 3/4 fathoms near the middle of the cove. (CP, 33rd Ed.)

beach in front of the city of Carmel is low, but the sand on the S side of the bay is bare and mountainous, and the N side is hilly and heavily wooded.

Carmel Bay affords shelter in N and S weather to small craft having local knowledge. In N weather anchorage may be had in two coves on the N shore, Pebble Beach on the W and Stillwater Cove on the E. These are shallow kelp-filled bights, with rock and gravel bottom. Anchorage is in 1 to 3 fathoms, but local knowledge is necessary to avoid the dangers. (CP, 33rd Ed.)

Consider Carmel Bay for an overnight stop if you are beating north in the afternoon and seas begin to get choppy. We use Stillwater Cove if it's not too crowded. Here, you will have an excellent, if crowded, view of the celebrities and immaculate golf greens. If you want more swinging room, consider the area just south of Stillwater or in Rocky Pebble Beach. Whalers Cove offers good southerly shelter on an emergency basis. Avoid the charted rock "The Pinnacles" on the north side of Carmel Bay which breaks on moderate swells, as well as the rocks extending 0.5 mile west of Pinnacle Point on the south side of the bay.

Whalers Cove, in the south corner of scenic Carmel Bay, is available as a harbor of refuge only, with very good protection from southerly gales. Unless it's an emergency (i.e. a southerly gale) and it is dangerous to try for Monterey Bay, boaters should anchor in Pebble Beach or Stillwater Cove. Avoid the foul areas on both sides of the cove entrance partially marked by kelp.

Anchor close to shore in southerly gales in about 2 fathoms over sand; fair-to-good holding.

Approach to Stillwater Cove

Stillwater Cove

Chart 18686; 1 mi NW of the town of Carmel
Entrance: (CA319)
36°33.56'N, 121°56.62'W
Anchor: 36°33.77'N, 121°56.52'W

In N weather anchorage may be had in two coves on the N shore, Pebble Beach on the W and Stillwater Cove on the E. (CP, 33rd Ed.)

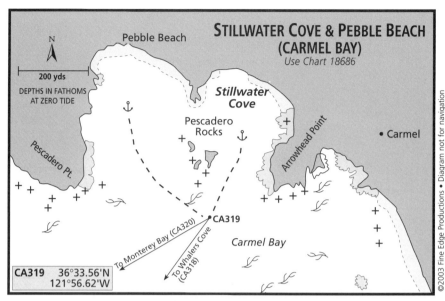

Stillwater Cove gives the opportunity to anchor just a few yards off Pebble Beach's scenic and impeccable golf course. The cove is quite small with limited swinging room. Enter slowly from the south, avoiding kelp patches that hide hazards off Arrowhead Point. In periods of poor visibility it is advisable to anchor south of Arrowhead Point. Avoid several private mooring buoys, and anchor just inside the entrance. Check the set of your anchor; the bottom is marginal. Stay clear of the foul areas north and south of Pescadero Rocks. A shore tender may be available.

Anchor in 2 to 4 fathoms over sand, rock and kelp with poor-to-fair holding; limited swinging room.

Pebble Beach

Chart 18686; 0.3 mi W of Stillwater Cove
Entrance (Pebble Beach): 36°33.66'N, 121°56.81'W
Anchor (Pebble Beach): 36°33.87'N, 121°56.91'W

Anchorage with good shelter from northwest winds is reported deep in the rocky cove of Pebble Beach. The narrow entrance requires avoiding several shoals and rocky areas marked by kelp during the summer season. Enter slowly with an alert bow watch, avoiding the shoals off Pescadero Rocks and Pescadero Point.

Anchor in about 2 fathoms over sand and stones; poor-to-fair holding. Avoid the private buoys and kelp beds.

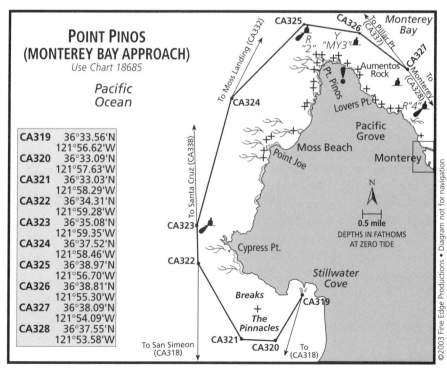

Monterey Harbor mooring buoy area

Monterey Bay

Chart 18685; between Point Pinos and Point Santa Cruz, is 20 miles wide.

Monterey Bay is a broad open bight 20 miles wide between Point Pinos and Point Santa Cruz. The shores decrease in height and boldness as Point Pinos is approached, while those of Monterey Bay are, as a rule, low and sandy. The valleys of Salinas and Pajaro Rivers, which empty into the E part of Monterey Bay, are marked depressions in the coastal mountain range and are prominent as such from a considerable distance seaward. From Point Santa Cruz the coast curves W and N for 23 miles to Pigeon Point, and then extends for 25 miles in a general NNW direction to Point San Pedro, the S headland of the Gulf of the Farallones. . . .

The shores are low with sand beaches backed by dunes or low sandy bluffs. Shelter from NW winds is afforded at Santa Cruz Harbor and Soquel Cove, off the N shore of the bay, and from SW winds at Monterey Harbor, off the S shore.

Sea fog is a problem on the bay from about July through September. It is worse over open waters and along the exposed E shore. Around Monterey Harbor in the S and Santa Cruz Harbor in the N, fog reduces visibility to less than 0.5 mile (0.9 km) on 4 to 8 days per month during the worst period. Close to shore, cloudiness begins to increase and descend in the evening by 2100 or 2200. The best conditions occur in the early afternoon, when visibilities are less than 3 miles (6 km) and cloud ceiling are (sic) less than 1,500 feet (458 m) only 10 to 20 percent of the time. Moss Landing is an exposed location, and fog signals operate about 25 percent of the time in August.

Gales are rare over Monterey Bay; extreme gusts have been reported at 40 to 50 knots from October through May.

Monterey Bay National Marine Sanctuary was established to protect and manage the conservation, ecological, recreational, research, educational, historical and esthetic resources and qualities of the coastal and ocean waters and submerged lands in and surrounding Monterey Bay.

The shores are low with sand beaches backed by dunes or low sandy bluffs. . . . The great mountain barriers N and S of Monterey Bay and the receding shoreline to the E offer a broad entrance to the cold foggy NW winds of the summer, and they drive over the bay and well into Salinas Valley to the S. (CP, 33rd Ed.)

Monterey Bay has been used for shelter since the old square-riggers made this their first stop on return voyages from the Philippines. The north end of Monterey Bay provides shelter from northwest swells and chop and the south end from southeast swells and chop.

Monterey Harbor

Chart 18685; 3 mi SE of Point Pinos
Outer Entrance (R"2") (CA 325) 36°38.97'N, 121°56.70'W
Inner Entrance (Breakwater lt): (CA 330) 36°36.48'N, 121°53.27'W
Inner Entrance (Hbr ent): (CA 331) 36°26.29'N, 121°53.48'W
Anchor (E of basin): 36°36.23'N, 121°53.27'W

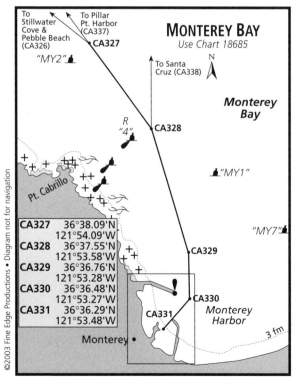

Monterey Harbor . . . is a compact resort harbor with some commercial activity and fishing. The harbor can accommodate over 800 vessels.

Depths of more than 20 feet are available in the outer harbor and entrance, and 10 to 16 feet in the small-boat basin. There are many sport-fishing landings, and the small-craft basin provides good shelter for over 500 boats. There are four public

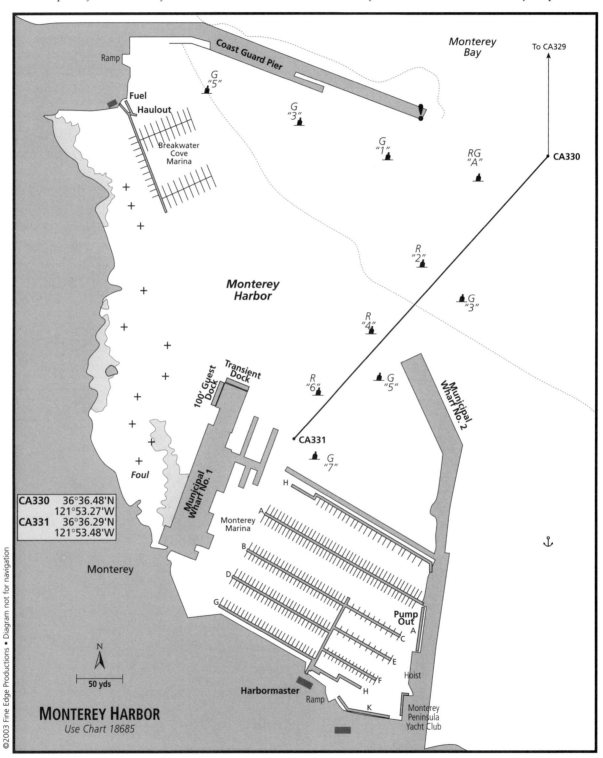

To CA329

Monterey Bay

Ramp

Coast Guard Pier

G "5"

G "3"

G "1"

RG "A"

CA330

Fuel

Haulout

Breakwater Cove Marina

R "2"

G "3"

Monterey Harbor

R "4"

R "6"

G "5"

Municipal Wharf No. 2

100' Guest Dock

Transient Dock

CA331

G "7"

Foul

H

A

| CA330 | 36°36.48'N 121°53.27'W |
| CA331 | 36°36.29'N 121°53.48'W |

Municipal Wharf No. 1

Monterey Marina

B

D

G

Monterey

Pump Out

A

C

E

F

Hoist

N

Harbormaster

H

K

Ramp

Monterey Peninsula Yacht Club

50 yds

MONTEREY HARBOR
Use Chart 18685

©2003 Fine Edge Productions • Diagram not for navigation

Monterey Harbor small boat basin

launch ramps and a 3-ton public hoist in the municipal marina. The boat yard, located just inside the breakwater has a 70-ton travel lift . . .

Two radio towers just inshore from the sand dunes at Marina, 6.5 miles NE form the breakwater, are conspicuous in the S part of Monterey Bay. Special anchorages are S and SE of the breakwater.

A very strong current is reported to exist at the small-boat basin entrance when swells run following winter storms. The current runs mainly from the breakwater towards Municipal Wharf no. 1; caution is advised. The speed limit in the harbor is 3 knots. (CP, 33rd Ed.)

Monterey Harbor and Municipal Marina are open 24 hours a day, seven days a week. The Municipal Marina is a full-service facility offering transient berths, bilge pump-out stations, block ice, fuel dock, marine supplies, laundry facilities, and propane. A 3-mph speed limit is observed in the harbor.

Breakwater Cove Marina operates a fuel dock seven days a week from 0800 to 1700. Monterey Municipal Marina does not take reservations and guest slips are available on a first-come, first-served basis. The harbormaster assigns slips when you are within VHF range (or at the launch ramp if you're trailering). All moor-

ings in the outer harbor are privately owned, so before tying up you'll need the owner's permission. However, there's an open anchorage east of Municipal Wharf No. 2 outside the mooring field, and you can dinghy in to the wharf. Stop by the Harbor Office for a map and directions to the many stores and three chandleries within walking distance of the marina.

Popular Fisherman's Wharf features fine restaurants, fish markets, art and gift shops, sportfishing and whale-watching concessions. The spectacular Monterey Bay Aquarium, located approximately one mile north of the Harbor Office, is easily accessible using the Recreation Trail from the head of Fisherman's Wharf. If you have time, this marvel showcases more than a hundred exhibits that recreate the bay's habitats—tide pools to the open ocean. The aquarium houses more than 300,000 aquatic creatures from sharks and octopus to starfish and jellyfish. Check out the "touch" pools for a real hands-on experience. Monterey's historic Cannery Row, originally the site of a sardine canning operation in the early 1900s, is now home to more than 75 upscale clothing stores, art galleries, restaurants and gift shops. (As a young student in the late 1950s, Réanne

Monterey Harbor boat launch

Fishing fleet at Monterey Harbor

Monterey Path of History that starts at the foot of Fisherman's Wharf with the Old Custom house.

⚓ **Breakwater Cove Marina**
tel: 408.373.7857

⚓ **Monterey Municipal Marina** tel: 831.646.3950

⚓ **Harbormaster** tel: 831.646.3950

Moss Landing
Chart 18685; E shore of the bay, is 12.5 mi NE of Point Pinos
Entrance (outer): (CA 333) 36°48.08'N, 121°47.86'W
Entrance (inner): (CA334) 36°48.53'N, 121°47.18'W
Position (transient slip): 36°48.09'N, 121°47.16'W

remembers Cannery Row when it was still in an "arrested state of decay." At that time it was still possible to get the feeling of Steinbeck's novel, *Cannery Row*.)

If you haven't had your fill of boating by this time, you can also rent paddle boats on nearby Lake El Estero. Be sure also to check out the

Moss Landing Harbor, . . . just N of the small town of Moss Landing, is a good harbor of refuge. The harbor is used by pleasure craft and a fishing fleet of about 300 boats. . . . The harbor has 500 berths. . . . The anchorage off Moss Landing Harbor is unprotected, but the holding ground is good.

The prevailing winds are NW, but there are a few SE winds and N gales during the winter. Mariners in the area should be aware of reported unique environmental conditions. Vessels have experienced sudden wind shifts during late morning to early afternoon hours. At this time the new wind begins to generate its own waves from the W and NW, dissipating existing swells, and creating a cross pattern of waves giving the

Watch out for sea lions on the Monterey dock

Moss Landing entrance markers

Aerial view: Moss Landing

The north slough (North Harbor) is home to Elkhorn Yacht Club, which usually has one or two slips for reciprocal yacht club members. Although its facilities are limited, you'll receive a warm welcome.

Transient berths are available in South Harbor. Facilities include: showers, laundry, pumpout station, launch ramps, several restaurants, fish market, antique shops, and kayak rentals. Hourly bus service is available to Salinas and Monterey. The west side of South Harbor houses a number of fish processing plants, the Monterey Bay Aquarium Research Institute (MBARI), and Phil's Fish Market and Eatery—the best place in the harbor for fresh fish. Kayak rentals or tours as well as whale watching can be arranged. Elkhorn Slough is a popular kayak and small-boating destination to view its myriad bird life. (See Appendix for kayak and whale-watching concessions.) A 5-mph speed limit is enforced in Elkhorn Slough. On our last visit we watched blue heron and egrets tiptoeing in the pickleweed along the edges of the slough—a marvelous sight!

sea a "choppy" or confused appearance. During the first few hours following the wind shift, the appearance of the sea surface may not provide a reliable indication of the wind speed. This condition has affected ship handling by setting deep-draft vessels. Occasionally, when there is a southeasterly wind during an ebb tide, slight breaking seas cross the harbor entrance. (CP, 33rd Ed.)

Moss Landing sits amid a low, sandy area in Monterey Bay whose Elkhorn Slough—an Ecological Reserve—is one of California's largest wetlands. Behind the sand dunes, shallow sloughs lead south, east and north. The south slough (South Harbor) is Moss Landing. The harbor, identifiable from seaward by two 500-foot power plant stacks, caters to all types of vessels—commercial fishing boats, Monterey trawlers, sailboats, and pleasure craft.

Transient dock at Moss Landing

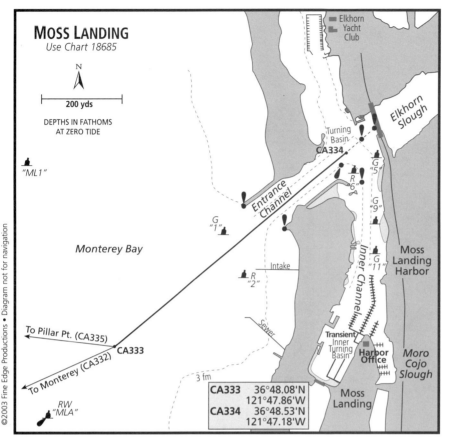

MOSS LANDING
Use Chart 18685

N

200 yds

DEPTHS IN FATHOMS
AT ZERO TIDE

"ML1"

Monterey Bay

Elkhorn Yacht Club

Turning Basin
CA334

Entrance Channel

Elkhorn Slough

G "5"

R "6"

G "9"

Moss Landing Harbor

G "1"

Intake

R "2"

Inner Channel

G "11"

Sewer

To Pillar Pt. (CA335)

CA333

To Monterey (CA332)

3 fm

Transient Inner Turning Basin

Harbor Office

Moro Cojo Slough

Moss Landing

RW "MLA"

CA333	36°48.08'N 121°47.86'W
CA334	36°48.53'N 121°47.18'W

©2003 Fine Edge Productions • Diagram not for navigation

The harbor entrance is open during all weather. When Santa Cruz is pounded by surf, the Moss Landing entrance is seldom, if ever, closed. No anchoring is permitted within Moss Landing harbor limits. All moorage is assigned by the harbormaster's office, which monitors VHF Channels 16 and 9. All vessels must check in before taking a berth. Call by VHF, or cell phone (831.633.2461) between 0600 and 1900 daily. (After hours, call VHF Channel 9.) The harbor personnel say they do not turn a vessel away and that there is rarely a need to raft.

Moss Landing floats

Moss Landing Harbor District

⚓ **Moss Landing Marina transient slip** pos: 36°48.09'N, 121°47.16'W; tel: 831.633.2461

⚓ **Elkhorn Yacht Club** pos: 36°48.76'N, 121°47.27'W

Soquel Cove
Chart 18685; E of Santa Cruz Harbor
Position: 36°58.14'N, 121°56.22'W

Fair shelter is afforded in NW weather, but the cove is open to S weather. The best anchorage is SE of the mouth of Soquel Creek in 5 to 6 fathoms, sandy bottom. (CP, 33rd Ed.)

Soquel Cove, at the north end of Monterey Bay, while really an open bight, is protected from prevailing northwesterlies by Soquel Point. In stable weather, anchoring here may offer a quieter, more calming experience than trying to find space in Santa Cruz Harbor.

Old ship and pier at Seacliff Beach

Seacliff Beach
Chart 18685; 0.5 mi W of Aptos Creek
Position: 36°58.14'N, 121°54.86'W

At Seacliff Beach . . . a concrete ship as been beached and filled with sand. The pleasure pier for sport fishing extends from ship to the shore. (CP, 33rd Ed.)

Seacliff is too exposed for anything but a temporary anchorage in calm weather.

Capitola
Chart 18685; NW side of Soquel Cove
Position (Capitola Wharf): 36°58.12'N, 121°57.19'W

A small fishing and pleasure wharf at Capitola . . . has 11 feet alongside the landing at the outer end. There are facilities to hoist out small boats. (CP, 33rd Ed.)

Capitola, located on the west side of Soquel Cove, is three miles east of Santa Cruz Harbor. Seasonal mooring buoys are available here from March to October.

Santa Cruz Harbor
(Municipal Pier)
Chart 18685 NW shore of the bay, btwn Pt Santa Cruz & Soquel Pt
Entrance (small-craft hbr): 36°57.11'N, 122°00.64'W
Anchor (E of Municipal Pier): 36°57.56'N, 122°00.90'W

Santa Cruz harbor…has a municipal pier and a small-craft harbor. . . . Good anchorage can be had anywhere off the pier in 5 fathoms, sand bottom. Santa Cruz Harbor provides good shelter in N weather, but in W weather a heavy swell is likely to sweep into the anchorage. In S weather there is no protection in the harbor; vessels must run for Monterey or Moss Landing Harbor or take refuge in Santa Cruz Municipal small-craft harbor. . . . (CP, 33rd Ed.)

Santa Cruz Harbor, the 1.7-mile-long bight located between Santa Cruz Point and Black Point has a large ocean pier that extends 0.4 mile in a southeastly direction from the main part of town. The Santa Cruz marinas are all located in Woods Lagoon, 0.8 mile east of the pier.

There is shelter from prevailing northwest winds on either side of the pier in Santa Cruz Harbor, but this area is fully exposed to souther-

Aerial view: Santa Cruz Harbor

Santa Cruz boat launch ramp

Marina floats in Santa Cruz Harbor

Santa Cruz Small Craft Harbor
(Woods Lagoon)
Chart 18685
Outer Entrance (SW Black Pt): (CA338)
36°57.19'N, 121°59.77'W
Inner Entrance (marina hbr): (CA340)
36°57.66'N, 122°00.09'W

ly weather. Anchorage can be found east of the Municipal Pier and northwest of the Coast Guard buoy. The wharf has a public dinghy dock. This outer area is the only anchoring site for the city of Santa Cruz; no anchoring is permitted inside the Small Craft Harbor.

Anchor (east of Municipal Pier) in 4 fathoms over packed sand and stone; poor-to-fair holding.

Santa Cruz Harbor tel: 831.475.6161; website: santacruzharbor.org

The Santa Cruz small-craft harbor is just E of Seabright and has slips and end-ties or about 1,200 small craft. . . . Transient vessels should report to the harbor office at the SE corner of the small-craft harbor, for berth assignments. The entrance to the small-craft harbor is protected by jetties; a light, fog signal, and radio beacon are at the end of the W jetty. The least clearance for the bridges between the north and south basins is 18 feet.

The Santa Cruz harbormaster advises that extensive shoaling occurs at the harbor entrance from November through May. Persons unfamiliar with the area should contact the harbormaster's office prior to entering the harbor; a radio guard on VHF-FM channel 16 is maintained 24 hours a day or telephone 831-475-6161 between 0830 and 1700 daily. The Santa Cruz harbormaster further recommends that mariners without local knowledge should not attempt to enter the harbor during periods of high ground swells. (CP, 33rd Ed.)

Santa Cruz Small Craft Harbor — a harbor of refuge for coastal mariners—encourages transient berthing on a space-available

Santa Cruz small craft harbor

Seabright

Twin
Lakes

**Santa
Cruz
Harbor**

CA340

CA339

Black Pt.

Pt. Santa Cruz

"CG"

Dumping
Ground

CA338

To Monterey
(CA328)

To Stillwater Cove &
Pebble Beach (CA323)

Monterey Bay

N

"SC2"

0.25 mi.

RW
"SC"

DEPTHS IN FATHOMS
AT ZERO TIDE

CA342

To Pillar Pt.
Harbor (CA343)

CA338	36°57.19'N
	121°59.77'W
CA339	36°57.56'N
	121°59.98'W
CA340	36°57.66'N
	122°00.09'W
CA342	36°56.17'N
	122°00.45'W

SANTA CRUZ HARBOR
Use Chart 18685

©2003 Fine Edge Productions • Diagram not for navigation

Santa Cruz Harbor entrance can be dangerous in strong south winds

weeks, though extensions may be granted with harbormaster approval. Most of the transient berths are end-ties at the end of the floats along the main channel and are subject to wake at all hours; rafting may be necessary and adequate fenders are required on either side of your vessel. Speed is limited to a no-wake 5 mph, and all traffic is required to keep to the right side of the channel when entering or exiting. A free water taxi conveniently connects the west and

basis. The entrance, which is exposed directly to southeast, has been plagued over the years with serious shoaling problems that cause its closure in times of high ground swells or under storm conditions. The Port District Commission keeps the harbor open year-round by dredging sand from the entrance, usually between November and April, with its own dredge; contact the dredge *Seabright* for passing instructions.

The Small Craft Harbor is located in nearly mile-long Woods Lagoon which is filled with wall-to-wall slips on both sides, accommodating 1,200 wet-berthed and 275 dry-stored vessels. There is no anchoring inside the harbor. Berthing must be arranged by calling the Harbor Patrol on Channel 16 and switching to Channel 9. Santa Cruz Harbor Patrol and Post District Telephone (831.475.6161) is just east of the fuel dock and launch ramp on your starboard side inside the entrance.

When entering, do not cut the corners; there is breaking shoal water with swells that run on both sides of the outer channel. Use Chart 18685, and keep the catamaran storage area and volleyballs courts well to starboard until inside the harbor, then turn north as illustrated in our diagram.

Guest berthing is permitted for up to two

Outrigger canoe on beach at entrance to Santa Cruz Harbor

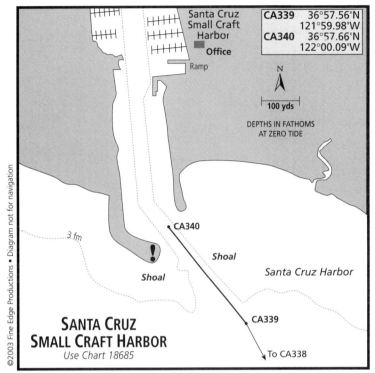

| CA339 | 36°57.56'N 121°59.98'W |
| CA340 | 36°57.66'N 122°00.09'W |

SANTA CRUZ SMALL CRAFT HARBOR
Use Chart 18685

east sides of the harbor.

Gate and restroom keys can be obtained with a $20 deposit; 110 volt, 20/30 amps, service is available with a $60 refundable deposit required. Parking is by permit only anywhere within the harbor grounds. An excellent public bus system with a stop near the harbor office is available; the schedule is available by calling 831.425.8600. The fuel dock is open from 0600 to 1630 daily with a pump-a-head located nearby. Santa Cruz is the last of the high-intensity

Red buoy #8, Point Año Nuevo

marina ports along the outside coast as you head north to Seattle or Vancouver.

The harbor is host to numerous special events throughout the year, from sailboat races to evening beach barbecues to a lighted boat parade in December. Fishing derbies are also big here. This harbor provides a full range of services to the visitor, including retail stores, restaurants, boat haul-out and repair, fuel dock, bait and tackle, sailing lessons, whale watching trips, and kayak rentals; the office of the Monterey Marine Sanctuary is located just within the Small Craft Harbor.

Point Año Nuevo
Chart 18680; 18 mi NW of Sta Cruz
Entrance: 37°05.54'N, 122°19.44'W
Anchor: 37°06.48'N, 122°19.19'W

Anchorage with protection from N and NW winds can be had in the bight S of the point. The kelp bed and reef, extending a little over 0.5 mile SE from the islet, break the force of the swell. (CP, 33rd Ed.)

The anchor site behind Año Nuevo Reef is a beautiful place to drop anchor temporarily for lunch or for a rest. South of Point Año Nuevo, a lee is formed by a low, flat island with abandoned buildings, a reef and several rocky areas. Large kelp patches give relief from the outside swells; however, the kelp may also hide isolated rocks. Proceed with caution; a large-scale chart for the area does not exist, so you're on your own here.

On shore, 4,000 acres of land are set aside as Año Nuevo State Reserve to protect the thousands of northern elephant seals that haul out on the beaches and rocks along this coastline. The dunes and beaches of the Reserve lie along the Pacific flyway, attracting over 200 species of birds during the course of a year. If you visit by land in the winter, you can make reservations for tours to watch the elephant seals giving birth, fighting or mating. (Check

South Island at Año Nuevo Reef

David J. Shuler

Pigeon Point Lighthouse

the website: www.anonuevo.org for further information.)

On Año Nuevo Island the ruins of the abandoned lighthouse are visible. Sea lions have appropriated the lighthouse as their own and, according to Reserve tour guides, some even manage to make it up the stairs to the second floor and into the bathtub!

We anchored here temporarily on our way south in *le Dauphin Amical* in the 1970s, before it was made a reserve. Although we have since visited Año Nuevo several times by land, it's always treat to view the rugged rocky coast and dunes by boat. When we stopped here in 2000 on *Baidarka*, we still found the place hauntingly beautiful.

Anchorage (temporary) can be taken in 5 to 7 fathoms over sand patches with rocks and kelp; poor-to-fair holding.

What a Ketch!
by RHD

In 1973, we purchased a crudely finished William Garden ketch in San Rafael, planning to sail her to Southern California to renovate and reinforce her for our voyage to Cape Horn. At that point, the boat resembled a small Navy tanker, gray and white and fitted with used iron and steel hardware. We left San Francisco Bay with three of our four sons as crew, along with our friend Al Ryan, who would spend a year rebuilding the boat. Al has an acerbic sense of humor, and it wasn't long after we'd crossed under the Golden Gate Bridge at the beginning of our southward journey that his tongue began to spout sarcasms about what "had to go," what was needed, what had to be redone, etc.—the list was long.

As the boat met the first Pacific swells she began to roll, sending us all scrambling for the minimal hand-holds previously installed—as yet, there were no lifelines along the deck.

It wasn't long before what Al referred to as "dinghy tackle" gave way. While we were running under sail off Año Nuevo, the wind changed suddenly and caught us unprepared. We jibed, and the main sheet blocks exploded under the impact load. We pulled into the lee of Año Nuevo, jury-rigged some blocks and limped the rest of the way into Monterey Bay where we spent the night beefing up the running tackle. But—as Al predicted, more surprises awaited us before we reached Southern California!!

Half Moon Bay

Chart 18682; 18 mi S of the entrance to
San Francisco
Outer entrance (G"3"): (CA353) 37°28.87'N,
122°28.90'W

Pillar Point . . . is the S extremity of a 2.5-mile low ridge. Several black rocks extend over 300 yards S of the point; from N these appear as three or four, but from S as only one. Half Moon Bay comprises the bight from Miramontes Point on the S to Pillar Point on the N. (CP, 33rd Ed.)

Half Moon Bay is just that—a lovely, sandy beach that curves west to Pillar Point on the north side of the bay. Pillar Point Harbor is the well-protected and popular marina north of the town of Half Moon Bay.

Pillar Point Harbor (Half Moon Bay)

Chart 18682; 39.9 mi NW of Santa Cruz
Entrance (outer): (CA352) 37°28.38'N,
122°29.42'W
Brkw entr: (CA355) 37°29.68'N, 122°29.02'W
Marina (W entr): 37°30.03'N, 122°29.10'W
Anchor: 37°29.96'N, 122°29.54'W

Pillar Point Harbor. . . is used by fishing vessels and pleasure craft. The harbor is well protected by breakwaters. The entrance, 200 yards wide, is between the E and W breakwaters. A light marks the end of the E breakwater, and a light and fog signal are on the end of the W breakwater. The entrance has a depth of about 20 feet with depths of 2 to 17 feet inside the harbor. Shoaling has been reported along N side of the breakwaters inside the harbor. The harbor provides good holding ground for anchored and moored vessels. The breakwaters and a detached breakwater, protect a marina on the N side of the harbor. The detached breakwater is marked by lights on the E and W ends and in the middle.

Caution is necessary in approaching Pillar Point Harbor because of the foul ground off the entrance. Rocks and reefs, marked by kelp and a lighted bell buoy, extend SE for over 1 mile from Pillar Point. Southeast Reef, extending from 1.5 to over 2 miles SE of Pillar Point, is covered 4 to 20 feet and has a pinnacle rock awash at extreme low water at the

Half Moon Bay Search and Rescue preparing for practice

SE end. Mariners are advised to exercise caution in the vicinity of Pillar Point in dense fog.

There are only private mooring floats so transients must anchor. The harbormaster should be consulted before tying alongside piers.

Aerial view: Pillar Point Harbor

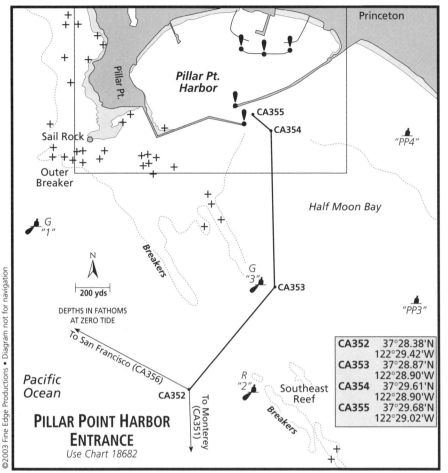

PILLAR POINT HARBOR
ENTRANCE
Use Chart 18682

CA352	37°28.38'N 122°29.42'W
CA353	37°28.87'N 122°28.90'W
CA354	37°29.61'N 122°28.90'W
CA355	37°29.68'N 122°29.02'W

©2003 Fine Edge Productions • Diagram not for navigation

ambience is one of a relaxed, broad-based marine center at peace with itself, enjoying the good life without stuffiness. The area is scenic, quiet and somewhat remote and rural—far removed from the bustle of the nearby city.

The Harbor, operated by San Mateo County, also provides search and rescue services to all boaters. The District has recently made improvements in the breakwaters, berthing, and launching facilities and upgraded its pollution prevention equipment. The marina area has all the conveniences you could want—a good pub, restaurant, public fishing pier, small chandlery, fresh fish market and a most helpful, professional and friendly staff. Transient dockage is available.

An L-shaped pier, 590 feet long with 13 feet alongside the 275-foot outer face, is on the N side of Pillar Point Harbor. Water, ice, and electricity are at the pier, and gasoline and diesel fuel are pumped at the landing. A skiff hoist is on the end of the pier.

The 660-foot pier W of the L-shaped pier has about 5 feet at the outer end. A surfaced launching ramp and parking area are near the inshore end of the E breakwater. (CP, 33rd Ed.)

We consider Pillar Point Harbor a great stop for coastal cruisers and *Baidarka* doesn't miss a chance to visit here. The

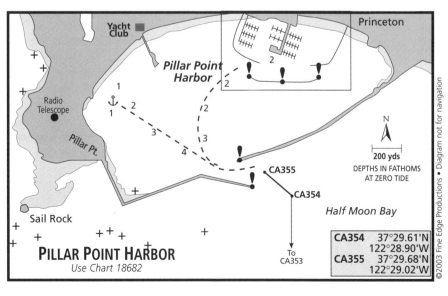

PILLAR POINT HARBOR
Use Chart 18682

| CA354 | 37°29.61'N 122°28.90'W |
| CA355 | 37°29.68'N 122°29.02'W |

©2003 Fine Edge Productions • Diagram not for navigation

Buoy G1 at dawn off Sail Rock at Pillar Point

Pillar Point Harbormaster's Office

Here you will find a good mix of small fishing vessels, salty commercial vessels of various types, live-a-boards, sportfishing boats, and coastal cruisers who stopped for a night and are staying for weeks, city boaters who will gladly do the commute, and beach bums who add to the local color.

You can anchor here if you want and the harbor officials will watch your boat for you. A dinghy dock is centrally located below the har-

SOS—Save our Sharks

The great white—the world's largest known predatory shark—is a creature surrounded by danger and mystery. Although popular books, movies, and magazines have spread the great white's notoriety far and wide, very little is actually known about this awe-inspiring animal. What factors influence its population? Where do these sharks come from, and where do they go when not congregating around seal colonies like Año Nuevo Island, 17 miles northwest of Santa Cruz, during the fall and winter? Where do they mate? How do young sharks survive as they grow to full maturity? Effective management and protection of great whites hinge on these basic questions.

The great white is protected not only within the Monterey Bay National Marine Sanctuary, but in all California waters. And since 1992, the Santa Cruz-based Pelagic Shark Research Foundation has worked to pursue the answers that will shed more light on the plight of these massive fish. The foundation, headquartered on Año Nuevo Island and its associated field station, is one of only two places in the western hemisphere conducting extensive research on great white sharks. A scant 22 miles north of Santa Cruz, this site is frequented by what

may be one of the most intact great white populations left in the world.

Using non-invasive methods, researchers working from a 22-foot research vessel and coordinating with the island field station via VHF radio have identified, photographed, and tagged 57 individual great white sharks at Año Nuevo Island. They average over 15 feet long and 3,000 pounds, with a few of these beefy locals approaching 20 feet and 5,000 pounds. They're mostly adult females, with very few sub-adults and no juveniles yet observed. Researchers hope DNA analysis will provide insight into the genetic relationship between these animals and great white populations elsewhere in the world. Observation of the sharks' natural social and predatory behavior—another key part of the study—can be conducted only in protected environments like the Monterey Bay National Marine Sanctuary.

Even with their protected status, observers have seen evidence that some great white sharks are still being hunted. This underscores the critical nature of the Año Nuevo research project, which seeks to better understand and appreciate great whites as apex predators and valuable components of the marine ecosystem.

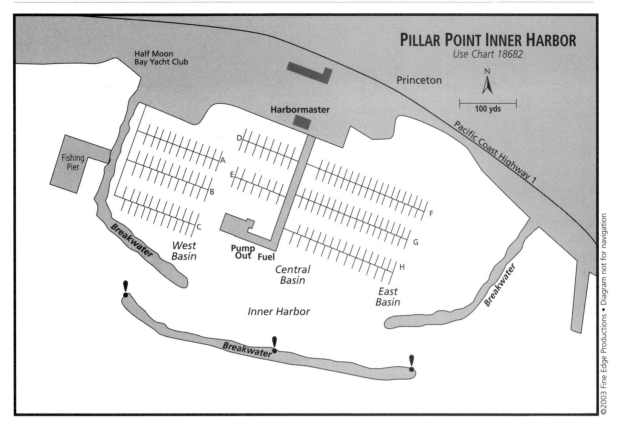

bormaster's office. Morro Bay Yacht Club, at the base of the old pier in the west end of the bay, has a Steinbeck atmosphere to it, as do the small firms clustered around the far west shore. Here you can find businesses that specialize in kayaking, day sailing, boat maintenance and storage, as well as local guide services. Walking through the nearby village of Princeton, or on the Coast Trail south along the shore of Half Moon Bay provides a good opportunity to stretch your sea legs.

All in all, Pillar Point Harbor is an excellent place for north or southbound boaters to take a break and visit the city by car without the hassle of dealing with the big city boating environment. It is also a

Trollers leaving outer breakwater at Pillar Point

Pillar Point Harbor—seriousness or humor . . . ?

Fresh fish market at Pillar Point

Sheriff's search and rescue team—Pillar Point

good place to prepare to enter San Francisco Bay or to let down and regroup when exiting. Its location, only 19 miles south of the Golden Gate, makes it an important safe harbor of refuge. Relatively easy to enter, Pillar Point gives excellent protection and should be used as an alternative to entering San Francisco during times of marginal bar conditions.

When entering Pillar Point Harbor avoid the foul area that extends south for 1.25 miles from radio telescope and radar towers on Pillar Point by staying south of both green gong buoys #1 and #3. If approaching from the south, stay east to avoid Southeast Reef, 2.1 miles southeast of Pillar Point, and marked by entrance green gong buoy #1S. Use Chart 18682 as a guide, and check your position carefully when entering in limited visibility; do not confuse the two different entrance buoys #1 and #1S.

⚓ **Pillar Point Harbor** tel: 415.726.5727

⚓ **Launch ramp** (E shore): 37°30.07'N, 122°28.58'W

⚓ **Fuel dock:** 37°30.08'N, 122°28.94'W

⚓ **Half Moon Bay Yacht Club** tel: 650.728.2120; website: hmbyc.org

Pillar Point fishing fleet

Half Moon Bay Yacht Club

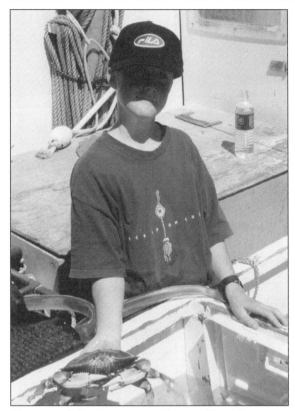

Young crab boat crewman shows off catch

Tide rips off Seal Rocks at Point Lobos (Cliff House)

bathers on warm sunny days. Although Shelter Cove is fully open and exposed to west and northwest winds and chop, you can find good temporary shelter from east gales and occasional east storm-force winds tucked in next to the beach. When entering from the south, avoid San Pedro Rock close west of the islet that forms the south side of the cove. Shelter Cove is exposed to the full brunt of prevailing northwest winds and chop.

Anchor (temporary) in about 5 fathoms over grey sand with good holding.

Shelter Cove, San Pedro Point and Rock
Chart: 18645; 7.3 mi N of Pillar Pt. Hbr, 10.9 mi S of Pt. Lobos
Entrance: 37°36.06'N, 122°31.66'W
Anchor: 37°35.82'N, 122°31.05'W

> *Point San Pedro is a dark, bold, rocky promontory, 640 feet high. A 200-yard long Municipal fishing pier is about 2.5 miles NW of Point San Pedro. San Pedro Rock and Point...are good radar targets. Shelter Cove, on the N side of Point San Pedro, provides shelter from the E storms with good holding ground in gray sand bottom. San Pedro Rock, close to the point and 100 feet high, also gives some protection in S weather. (CP, 33rd Ed.)*

Shelter Cove, immediately north of San Pedro Point, is the last indentation in the coastline until Point Lobos, 11 miles north, and this long stretch of sandy beach is full of

South Bay
Chart: 18649; 1.1 mi SW of Golden Gate Bridge
Position: 37°47.61'N, 122°29.30'W

> *The S shore of the Golden Gate extends in a gentle curve NE for 2 miles to Fort Point, forming a shallow bight called South Bay. The cliffs rise*

Mile Rocks and South Bay outside the Golden Gate

abruptly from narrow beaches, except near the middle of the bight where a valley terminates in a sand beach 0.3 mile long. Sailing craft are sometimes obliged to anchor here when becalmed, or when meeting an ebb current, to avoid drifting onto Mile Rocks, but the anchorage is uncomfortable and it is difficult to get underway from it.

South Bay is the bight off Baker Beach between Point Lobos and the Golden Gate Bridge. It can be fully used by under-powered boats to wait for slack water and it may offer shelter from southeast gales as well. It is exposed to west and northwest gales and the wake of the busy shipping lanes.

Anchor in 5 fathoms over a mud bottom with good holding.

Approach to the Golden Gate
Chart: 18649,18645; 216 mi N of Pt. Conception; 187 mi SE of Cape Mendocino

The entrance to San Francisco Bay is through the Gulf of the Farallons and the narrow Golden Gate.

The gulf extends from Point San Pedro on the S for 34 miles to Point Reyes on the N, and has a greatest width of 23 miles from Farallon Islands on the W to the mainland.

In clear weather many prominent features are available for use in making San Francisco Bay, but in thick weather the heavy traffic and the currents, variable in direction and velocity, render the approaches difficult and dangerous. Point San Pedro, Montara Mountain, Farallon Islands, Mount Tamalpais, and Point Reyes are prominent in clear weather and frequently can be seen when the land near the beach is shut in by low fog or haze. Radar navigation on the approach to San Francisco Bay is not difficult because of the numerous distinctive and high relief of targets available. Southeast Farallon Island, Point Reyes, Double Point, Bolinas Point, Duxbury Point, Rocky Point, Point Bonita, San Pedro Rock and Point, and Pillar Point are good radar targets. (CP, 33rd Ed.)

Entering San Francisco and sailing under the Golden Gate is about as dramatic a cruising experience as you can have. The beautiful bridge connecting two scenic points, the water smoothing out and the view of the city spreading before you is like a theater set.

Baidarka passes Mile Rocks with paravanes deployed

San Francisco and the Columbia River both have shallow bars that require careful navigation; both also have fast commercial traffic converging into restricted narrow channels that require a laid-back cruising boat to be sure its crew is on constant alert and watching in all directions.

If you have no previous experience in entering San Francisco Bay we recommend that northbound boats stay overnight in Pillar Point Harbor, 19 miles south, or that southbound boats remain in Bodega Bay, 40 miles north, to allow choosing good weather and an optimum time to cross the San Francisco Bar. Avoid entering the Golden Gate during times of strong ebb currents and strong westerly winds or swells; the entrance bar is very dangerous to small craft during such times. The San Francisco Bar is generally entered by pleasure craft from sea via the side of the main ship channel or, in good weather and sea conditions, via South Channel (northbound) or Bonita Channel (southbound).

Baidarka *approaching the Golden Gate Bridge*

Traffic Separation Scheme San Francisco

A Traffic Separation Scheme has been established off the entrance to San Francisco. The Scheme is composed basically of directed traffic areas each with one-way inbound and outbound traffic lanes separated by defined separation zones; a precautionary area; and a pilot boat cruising area. The Scheme is recommended for use by vessels approaching or departing San Francisco Bay, but is not necessarily intended for tugs, tows, or other small vessels which traditionally operate outside of the usual steamer lanes or close inshore. . . .

The precautionary area off the entrance to San Francisco Bay is inscribed by a circle with a radius of 6 miles centered on San Francisco Approach Lighted Horn Buoy. . . . Extreme caution must be exercised in navigating within the precautionary area inasmuch as both incoming and outgoing vessels use the area in making the transition between San Francisco Main Ship Channel and one of the established directed traffic areas as well as maneuvering to embark and disembark pilots. It is recommended that all vessels in the precautionary area guard VHF-FM channels 13 and 14. (CP, 33rd Ed.)

Although the traffic separation scheme in San Francisco applies only to ships of 1,600 gross tons and over, pleasure boaters should be aware of the location of the lanes to avoid causing problems for large ships that are required to stay in these designated lanes. Chart 18649 shows these lanes across the bar and through the Golden Gate; Chart 18645 shows the lanes inside and outside the Bay. Every year large vessels using the shipping lanes have near misses with pleasure boaters who misjudge the speed of the ships. Operators of pleasure craft should stay out of the designated shipping lanes as much as possible and keep a sharp lookout whenever they must enter those lanes. A complete and detailed description of the system is available at www.CO/VTSSFRAN@CGSMPT.COMDT.USCG.MIL.

Entrance to Golden Gate

Golden Gate, the passage between the ocean and San Francisco Bay, is 2 miles wide at the W end between Point Bonita and Pont Lobos, but the channel is reduced in width to 1.5 miles by Mile Rocks and to less than 0.7 mile by the Golden Gate Bridge pier. Depths in the passage vary from 108 feet to over 300 feet.

Point Lobos, the S entrance point to the Golden Gate, is high, rocky, and rounding with black rugged cliffs at its base. A large water tank is on the summit. Passage between Mile Rocks and Point Lobos should not be attempted because of the covered and visible rocks extending over 300 yards from shore and the rocks covered 6 and 14 feet S of Miles Rocks Light.

Golden Gate Bridge, crossing the Golden Gate from Fort Point to Lime Point, has a clearance of 225 feet at the center of the 4,028-foot-wide channel span between the 740-foot-high supporting towers; the least clearance is 211 feet at the S pier. The center of the span is marked by a fixed green light with three fixed white lights in a vertical line above it and by a private fog signal; a private light and fog signals are on the S pier. When approaching Golden Gate Bridge in the eastbound traffic lane in fog, channel Buoy 2 sometimes provides a radar image that indicates the location of the S pier of the bridge.

Golden Gate Coast Guard Station is about 0.4 mile NNE of the bridge at the entrance to Horseshoe Bay.

From S, some coasters and fishing vessels drawing not more than 15 feet use unmarked South Channel, parallel to and 0.7 mile off the peninsula shore. A reported obstruction, covered 25 feet, is near the S end of the channel about 3.5 miles 192° from Miles Rocks Light. From N, coasters and other vessels use buoyed Bonita Channel, between the E end of Potatopatch Shoal and the shore N of Point Bonita. The channel is narrowed to 0.2 mile by several rocky patches including Sears Rock, covered 19 feet, 1.2 miles NW of Point Bonita.

Vessels departing San Francisco Bay through Bonita Channel on the ebb current must use extreme caution when crossing the tide rip off Point Bonita. When the bow passes the rip the stern is thrown to port and, unless promptly met, the vessel will head straight for the rocks of the point. Vessels favoring Potatopatch Shoal too closely have reported a set toward it.

Strangers wishing to cross the bar in thick weather should either wait for clearing or take a pilot. Fog is prevalent in the Golden Gate; radar is a great aid here.

Winter winds, from about November through February, are variable. The procession of lows and highs brings frequent wind shifts and a great range of speeds. Calms occur from 15 to 40 percent of the time inside the bay and about 10 to 12 percent outside, while extreme winds of 50 knots with gusts of 68 knots (January 1951) have occurred in winter.

Wind speeds over the bay increase during the day...depending on exposure, winds blow at 3 to 10 knots from 2300 to 0900. During the morning hours they increase to 6 to 15 knots. By early afternoon they are blowing at 14 to 20 knots, and this usually lasts until early evening, when they begin to drop off to nighttime levels. This same diurnal variation exists over the Gulf of the Farallons, with speeds sometimes reaching 25 knots or so during the afternoon. (CP, 33rd Ed.)

Vessel Traffic Service San Francisco

Vessel Traffic Service San Francisco serves San Francisco Bay, its seaward approaches and its tributaries as far inland as Stockton and Sacramento . . . The purpose of the San Francisco Vessel Traffic Service (VTS) is to help facilitate the safe and efficient transit of vessels in San Francisco Bay in an effort to prevent accidents, associated loss of life, damage to property, and harm to the environment. VTS also fully supports Coast Guard and other public service missions through its unique communications and surveillance capabilities. The Vessel Traffic Center (VTC), located on Yerba Buena Island in San Francisco, is staffed 24 hours a day, seven days a week by Coast Guard personnel.

The VTS uses radar, closed-circuit television and VHF-FM radiotelephone to gather information, and uses VHF-FM radiotelephone to disseminate information. . . . The VTS maintains a continuous radiotelephone watch on VHF-FM channels 12, 13, 14, and 16. The VTS is also equipped to communicate on all VHF-FM radio telephone channels. The radio call sign is "San Francisco Vessel Traffic Service." (CP, 33rd Ed.)

Vessel Traffic Service (VTS) tracks incoming and outgoing ships in an attempt to prevent collisions. VTS monitors VHF channels 12, 13, 14, and 16 continuously. Recreational boaters are not required to check in with VTS, as are commercial ship captains; however, they can listen in on VHF Channel 12 at 15 and 45 minutes past each hour to determine if ship traffic is approaching their area.

Call VTS any time you feel uncomfortable near the traffic lanes or crossing them. They are happy to tell you what traffic is near your position, how fast they are traveling, and where they are headed.

San Francisco Bar
Chart 18649; extends 8.5 mi W of
Golden Gate Bridge

San Francisco Bar, a semicircular shoal with depths less than 36 feet, is formed by silt deposits carried to the ocean by the Sacramento and San Joaquin River systems. The bar extends from 3 miles S of Point Lobos to within 0.5 mile of Point Bonita off the southern coast of Marin Peninsula; the extreme outer part is about 5 miles WSW of San Francisco Bay entrance. . . . Potatopatch Shoal, the N part of the bar on Fourfathom Bank, has reported depths of less than 23 feet. The name is said to have originated from the fact that schooners from Bodega Bay frequently lost their deck load of potatoes while crossing the shoal. The S part of the bar has depths of 31 to 36 feet.

Very dangerous conditions develop over the bar whenever large swells, generated by storms far out at sea, reach the coast. A natural condition called shoaling causes the large swells to be amplified and increase in height when they move over the shallow water shoals. This piling up of the water over the shoals is worsened during times when the tidal current is flowing out (ebbing) through the Golden Gate. Outbound tidal current is strongest about 4 hours after high water at the Golden Gate Bridge and attains a velocity in excess of 6 knots at times. The incoming large swells are met by the outbound tidal current causing very rough and dangerous conditions over the bar. Steep waves to 20 or 25 feet have been reported in the area. Mariners should exercise extreme caution as the bar conditions may change considerably in a relatively short period of time.

The most dangerous part of the San Francisco Bar is considered to be Fourfathom Bank. Bonita Channel, between the shoal and the Marin coast, can also become very dangerous during large swell conditions. The safest part of the bar is the Main Ship Channel through the center of the bar. But even that area can be extremely dangerous when the tidal current is ebbing. (CP, 33rd Ed.)

Every boat entering the Bay must cross the San Francisco Bar. Ships crossing the bar must stay in the dredged channel marked by buoys 0.3 mile apart. Because of the deep water in this channel and the distance of the channel from

Sailboat turns into San Francisco Bay at Seal Rocks

Bob & Carol Mehaffy

Baidarka *underneath the Golden Gate Bridge at last!*

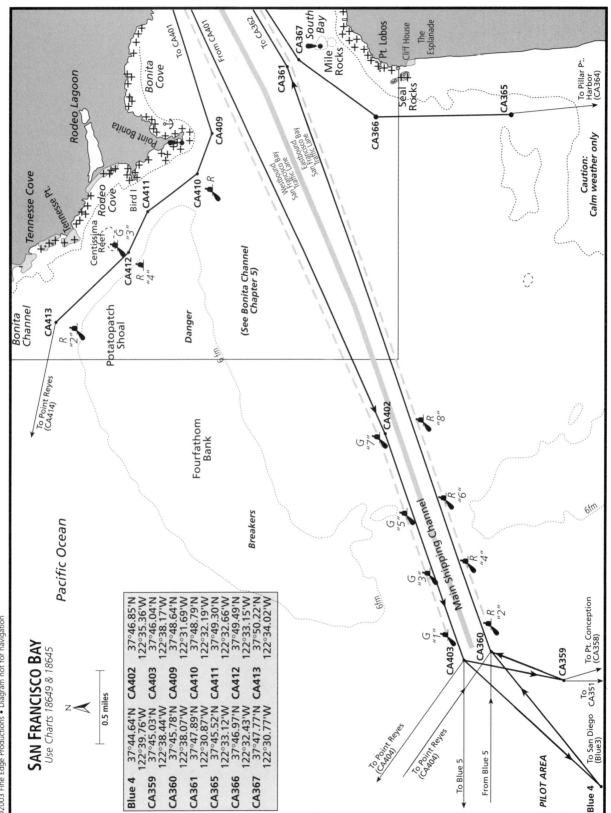

SAN FRANCISCO BAY
Use Charts 18649 & 18645

N

0.5 miles

Blue 4	37°44.64'N	CA402	37°46.85'N
	122°39.76'W		122°35.36'W
CA359	37°45.03'N	CA403	37°46.04'N
	122°38.44'W		122°38.17'W
CA360	37°45.78'N	CA409	37°48.64'N
	122°38.07'W		122°31.69'W
CA361	37°47.89'N	CA410	37°48.79'N
	122°30.87'W		122°32.19'W
CA365	37°45.52'N	CA411	37°49.30'N
	122°33.12'W		122°32.66'W
CA366	37°46.97'N	CA412	37°49.49'N
	122°32.43'W		122°33.15'W
CA367	37°47.77'N	CA413	37°50.22'N
	122°30.77'W		122°34.02'W

©2003 Fine Edge Productions • Diagram not for navigation

Point Bonita, to the north, and Seal Rocks, to the south, operators of pleasure boats often follow the ship channel when high winds are blowing and large seas are running—especially during strong ebb flows which can reach 6 knots. It is best not to enter or leave San Francisco during these conditions.

Looking southeast toward San Francisco from Marin Headlands

When approaching San Francisco from the south in calm weather, it is recommended that you stay at least 1 mile offshore until you see the Golden Gate Bridge. In heavy weather, however, stay at least 2 miles offshore, turning toward the Golden Gate only when you're in the ship channel. The inside passage close to Seal Rocks is subject to large, square waves that can wash completely over a small craft, rolling it in the surf. These conditions are exaggerated on strong ebb flows and turbulence from Mile and Seal Rocks. Every year boaters lose their boats, and sometimes their lives, because they approach the shore too closely near Seal Rocks. Note that *Baidarka* has comfortably used the south channel, which is 0.4 mile offshore, but only on a flood tide and only in near-calm conditions; trying this route against an ebb current would have been marginal.

If you approach the Golden Gate Bridge from the north, you must consider the infamous "Potato Patch." In normal conditions, local boaters pass over this large area—labeled on Chart 18649 as "Fourfathom Bank" and as "Potatopatch Shoal"—without concern. But in heavy weather conditions, they all use Bonita Channel (also clearly labeled on the chart) to skirt around the east side of the Potato Patch,

between the patch and the shoreline north of Point Bonita. Boaters departing from San Francisco should, of course, observe the same precautions as those entering.

Before entering or departing from San Francisco Bay, check the tide state. During a heavy ebb, the strong current colliding with the ocean swell outside the Golden Gate creates dangerously steep waves and confused seas, especially in the area of the Potato Patch. In such a heavy current, use the Bonita Channel, and expect to make a slow passage between Point Bonita and the Golden Gate. Although you might think a strong ebb current would be excellent for exiting the Bay, such is not necessarily the case. Though the passage through the Golden Gate would almost certainly be fast, the ride would be uncomfortable at best when you reached Point Bonita and encountered these steep, confused seas.

Boaters should also avoid departing the Bay when a strong flood current is flowing. For the typical pleasure boat, the combination of a strong flood and the prevailing northwest winds coming in under the Golden Gate Bridge make getting from the Bridge to Point Bonita in a reasonable length of time difficult at best.

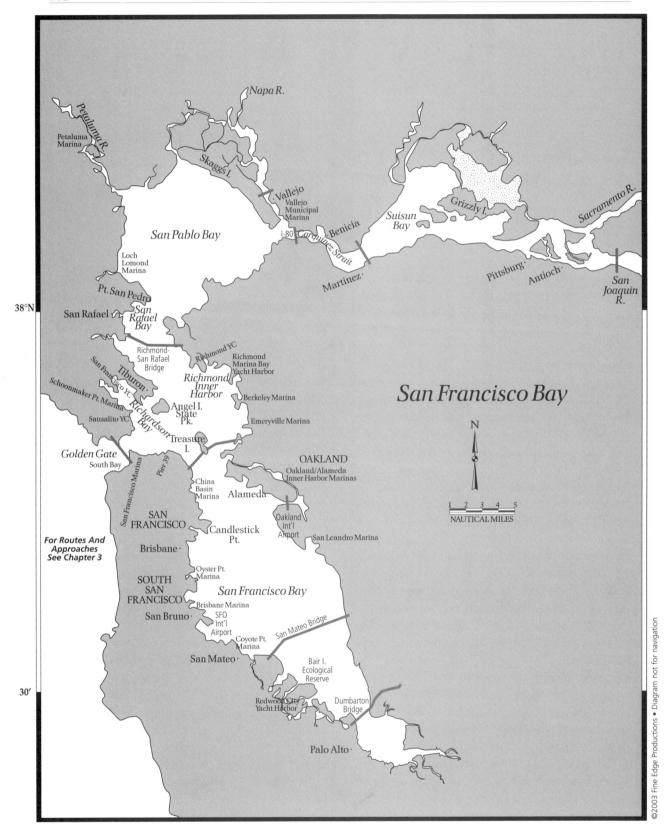

Napa R.

Petaluma R.

Petaluma Marina

Skaggs I.

Vallejo
Vallejo Municipal Marina

I-80   Carquinez Strait   Benicia

Grizzly I.

Sacramento R.

San Pablo Bay

Suisun Bay

Loch Lomond Marina

Martinez·

Pittsburg·   Antioch·

San Joaquin R.

Pt. San Pedro

38°N

San Rafael

San Rafael Bay

Richmond-San Rafael Bridge

Richmond YC

Richmond Marina Bay Yacht Harbor

San Francisco YC

Tiburon·

Richmond Inner Harbor

San Francisco Bay

Schoonmaker Pt. Marina

Richardson Bay

Berkeley Marina

Angel I. State Pk.

Sausalito YC

Emeryville Marina

N

Treasure I.

Golden Gate

South Bay

Pier 39

China Basin Marina

OAKLAND

Oakland/Alameda Inner Harbor Marinas

Alameda·

1   2   3   4   5
NAUTICAL MILES

San Francisco Marina

SAN FRANCISCO

Candlestick Pt.

Oakland Int'l Airport

San Leandro Marina

For Routes And Approaches See Chapter 3

Brisbane·

Oyster Pt. Marina

SOUTH SAN FRANCISCO

San Bruno·

Brisbane Marina

SFO Int'l Airport

San Francisco Bay

Coyote Pt. Marina

San Mateo Bridge

San Mateo·

Bair I. Ecological Reserve

30'

Redwood City Yacht Harbor

Dumbarton Bridge

Palo Alto·

4

San Francisco Bay

San Francisco and the Golden Gate

Although archeological evidence reveals human occupation of the Bay Area as early as 5,000 years ago, Europeans did not learn of this remarkable bay until 1769, when the Gaspar de Portolá expedition sighted it from a mountaintop near Montara. Earlier explorers of the California coastline, such as Sir Francis Drake in 1579 and Sebastián Cermeño in 1595, passed by the fog-shrouded entrance to San Francisco Bay, never realizing what treasures lay inside. Soon after Portolá's discovery, however, the Spanish established a fort, the Presidio, and Mission San Francisco de Asis, today called "Mission Dolores." After the signing of the Treaty of Guadalupe Hidalgo in 1848, California became a territory of the United States. Two years later, it became the 31st state.

Several years before California statehood, the potential of San Francisco Bay had been recognized. In 1835 Richard Henry Dana wrote in *Two Years Before the Mast*: "If California ever becomes a prosperous country, this bay will be the center of its prosperity."

While today Southern California harbors rival San Francisco Bay as the hub of California's prosperity, San Francisco is the major boating area between Los Angeles and Seattle. With an area of over 400 square miles and 276 miles of shoreline, it has over 50 marinas with thousands of slips, scores of anchorages, and a full range of service facilities.

Resident boaters can cruise here their entire lives without tiring of exploring the protected waters of the Bay proper. Some local boaters venture inland up the estuaries, popularly called "rivers"—the Petaluma, the Napa, and the Suisun. And when these boaters hunger for a little more adventure, they can head east for the even more protected, and warmer, waters of the Sacramento-San Joaquin Delta, with its more than 1,500 miles of navigable waterways.

In addition to the Bay, the estuaries, and the Sacramento-San Joaquin Delta, some of the destinations within a few hours' travel outside the Bay are also worth considering. Local boaters with two, three, or four days of vacation often make passages to nearby Drakes Bay or the Farallon Islands. (Please see Chapter 5 for Point Reyes and the Farallon Islands.)

The entrance into San Francisco Bay is through the Golden Gate, a 3-mile-long rupture in the Coastal Range. At the east end of the

Sailing on a broad reach into San Francisco just west of the Golden Gate Bridge

North tower of the Golden Gate Bridge

Golden Gate, the famed Golden Gate Bridge crosses the rupture at its narrowest part. Depths in the Golden Gate range from 50 feet where the ship channel crosses the bar to 300 feet directly under the Bridge. Although two-thirds of San Francisco Bay has depths of 18 feet or less, the submarine channel beneath the Bridge is kept deep by the tremendous volume of water that sweeps under the Bridge and out to sea. Approximately 40% of all the run-off water in California drains into the Pacific Ocean through the Golden Gate. (Please see the end of Chapter 3 for information on approaches to San Francisco, crossing the bar and related data.)

The Golden Gate Bridge, with its 746-foot towers, 4,600-foot span and bright orange paint, contrasts dramatically with the blue water and surrounding green or golden hills. Approaching the bridge by water gives boaters the premier photo shoot.

The bridge has a vertical clearance of 226 feet and a horizontal clearance of about 0.66 mile. Boaters entering or exiting the Bay should determine the tide and wind state before attempting to pass under the bridge, where tidal current commonly runs 5 knots, and where turbulence and heavy chop occur when a strong ebb opposes a westerly. When you go ashore, don't miss a chance to walk or bicycle across the bridge for a panoramic view of the city, Alacatraz Island, the Bay Bridge and its surroundings.

For additional information on Bay Area cruising possibilities, we recommend consulting Carolyn and Bob Mehaffy's book *Cruising Guide to San Francisco Bay* (published by Paradise Cay).

San Francisco Bay
Charts 18649, 18651, 18654, 18656
Entrance: (CA362) 37°48.94'N, 122°28.68'W

San Francisco Bay, the largest harbor on the Pacific coast of the United States . . . is more properly described as a series of connecting bays and harbors of which San Francisco Bay proper, San Pablo Bay, and Suisun Bay are the largest. Depths of 29 to 49 feet are available for deep-draft vessels to San Francisco, Oakland, Alameda, Richmond, and Redwood City in San Francisco Bay proper; to Stockton on the San Joaquin River; and to Sacramento through the lower Sacramento River and a deepwater channel. (CP, 33rd Ed.)

San Francisco Bay offers excellent shelter from the Pacific Ocean and, inside, you can find all the tourist and boating facilities you can imagine, as well as access to hundreds of miles of river and delta cruising. Passing under the Golden Gate Bridge, you leave behind the typical marine weather of cool temperatures, low clouds or fog and encounter warmer temperatures, more sun and better visibility as you continue east. In summer, when California's inland valleys are heated by the sun, a large, low-pressure thermal system often produces strong westerlies during the afternoon and evening that create significant chop within the Bay.

Because of the number of destinations, most local boaters divide San Francisco Bay into three logical sections:

⚓ **The Central Bay** is that portion bounded by the Golden Gate Bridge on the west, the San Francisco-Oakland Bay Bridge to the east, and the Richmond-San Rafael Bridge to the north. We cover this area in a clockwise direction starting on the north shore, visiting slower-paced Sausalito, around to Berkeley, back across Treasure Island and ending in the fast-paced and crowded San Francisco.

⚓ **The South Bay** includes the areas south of the San Francisco-Oakland Bay Bridge known as East Bay and, on the west, the Peninsula. Our coverage starts with the largest concentration of boats found in the entire bay, the Oakland-Alameda Estuary. From there we take you down to the bottom of the bay at Redwood City and back up the Peninsula via Candlestick Point to the south ramparts of the Bay Bridge.

⚓ **The North Bay** covers all the area north of the Richmond-San Rafael Bridge, including San Rafael Bay, San Pablo Bay, Suisun Bays and the Napa, Sacramento and San Joaquin Rivers which connect to Sacramento and Stockton.

The San Francisco skyline is a gleaming backdrop to the Golden Gate Bridge

Bob & Carol Mehaffy

THE CENTRAL BAY

Described clockwise starting just northeast of the Golden Gate Bridge's north tower and ending in San Francisco.

Horseshoe Bay
Charts 18650; 0.5 mi NE of Golden Gate Bridge
Entrance: 37°49.89'N, 122°28.55'W
Anchor (outside): 37°49.80'N, 122°28.62'W
Anchor (inside): 37°49.98'N, 122°28.56'W

Horseshoe Bay, a small bay about 500 yards northeast of the north tower of the Golden Gate Bridge, offers good protection from prevailing winds. However, as attractive as it may seem, it is small and offers limited swinging room. The Presidio Yacht Club small boat docks, around the east and southeast sides of Horseshoe Bay, and the Coast Guard docks, at the west, limit the anchorage area to two or three boats swinging to a single anchor.

Anchorage can be taken at least 200 feet from the Coast Guard facility. (Rescue boats frequently depart on emergency missions at all hours of the day and night.)

Hiking trails that begin at Horseshoe Bay will take you along the Marin Shoreline. You can also take a 1.5-mile walk into Sausalito for supplies and services. (No supplies or repair facilities are available closer.) Boaters anchored at Horseshoe Bay enjoy unparalleled views of the Golden Gate Bridge and the city of San Francisco.

Anchor (Horseshoe Bay) in 6 feet over soft mud; good holding with a well-set anchor. (Local boaters generally prefer to use a fluke-type anchor here.)

Richardson Bay
Chart 18653; 2 mi N of Golden Gate Bridge
Entrance (light "2"): 37°51.31'N, 122°28.15'W
Anchor: 37°51.68'N, 122°28.58'W

Strong westerlies make for good sailing inside the Bay

Richardson Bay . . . is shoal except for the S part fronting Sausalito. . . . Local authorities control the anchoring of vessels and the placement of mooring in Richardson Bay. Mariners should contact the Richardson Bay Regional Agency at (415) 289-4143 for specific information. Richardson Bay is a no discharge zone; it is illegal for vessels to discharge any form of waste into the bay. A channel leading NW through Richardson Bay to facilities

at Sausalito is marked by lights, daybeacons, and buoys. (CP, 33rd Ed.)

Richardson Bay, beginning 1.5 miles northeast of the Golden Gate Bridge, extends inland approximately 3 miles from the northwest side of the Bay. During the Gold Rush of the 1850s, dozens of clipper ships bringing people and supplies for the gold fields anchored in this spacious bay. Almost 100 years later World War II brought another kind of maritime importance to Richardson Bay with the building of Liberty ships along the western shoreline at Sausalito. After the war was over, these same facilities were used to build pleasure boats.

Although Richardson Bay once had enough depth to allow square-riggers with their deep draft hulls to be anchored safely, shoaling has reduced the depths in the majority of this bay to less than 6 feet. Vessels with more than 6-foot drafts will almost certainly go aground at low tide if they stray outside the channel.

Anchorage can be taken in Richardson Bay across from the Spinnaker Restaurant, located at the beginning of the row of marinas along the west shore of Richardson Bay.

Anchor in about 8 feet over mud; good holding. *Note:* This area offers little protection from the winds that kick up in the afternoon and evening hours.

A view of the Golden Gate from Horseshoe Bay

Sausalito

Chart 18653; 2.1 mi N of
Golden Gate Bridge
Entrance: 37°51.58'N,
122°28.71'W

Sausalito harbors some commercial fishing boats and many pleasure craft. Several boatbuilding and repair yards have marine ways, the largest of which can handle craft up to 350 tons. (See the small-craft facilities tabulation on chart 18652 for services and supplies available.) (CP, 33rd Ed.)

Located just north of the Golden Gate, Sausalito was named by the 18th century Spanish explorers for the

Horseshoe Bay with Richardson Bay and Sausalito to the left, Angel Island in the background

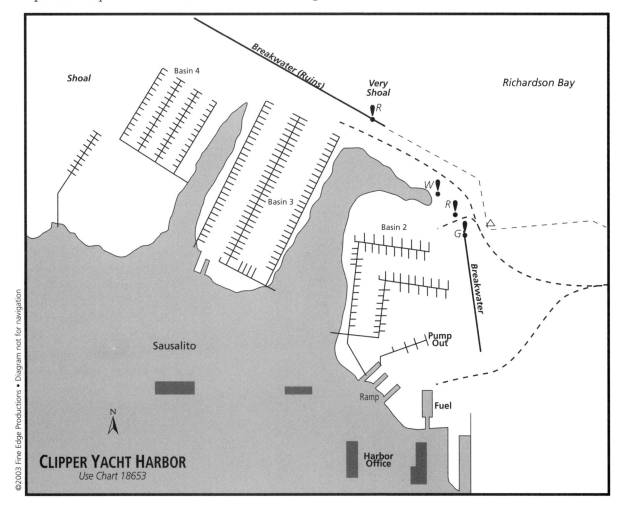

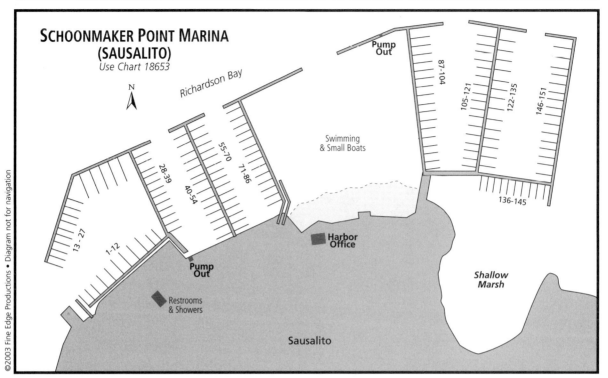

"little willow" trees along its banks. A small town of fewer than 10,000 people on the west side of Bay, it is the only development in Richardson Bay.

When approaching Sausalito, give the ferry landing a wide berth, for ferries arrive and depart regularly. You can anchor 200 yards west of the ferry landing in front of the Horizon Restaurant in 15-20 feet of water on a rock and sand bottom with good holding. Although this anchorage is often rolly because of the boat traffic, many boaters think the splendid views of both San Francisco and Sausalito more than compensate for the discomfort. If you wish to dine at the restaurant, get permission from the staff to leave your dinghy at the small dock below the restaurant (provided this dock is in place, of course).

Another anchorage area lies immediately east of the ferry terminal just offshore of the Sausalito Yacht Club. Identify this anchorage by the sign on the SYC building and the six or more mooring buoys in the cove. Although the Club grants visiting yacht club members permission to use the mooring buoys, the buoys are usually occupied by club members on weekends during the

Mooring buoys at Sausalito Yacht Club

Under full sail at Sausalito anchorage

Most boaters who visit Sausalito spend a few nights at one of the marinas. Although Sausalito's five marinas have over 1,000 slips, only two have guest slips. Schoonmaker Marina, approximately 0.5 mile northward of the Spinnaker Restaurant, generally reserves a few slips for visiting boats, as does Clipper Yacht Harbor, located about 0.75 mile farther northward into Richardson Bay.

Schoonmaker and Clipper are both within walking distance of the town of Sausalito. Schoonmaker is closer to markets, bookstores, and restaurants; Clipper is closer to West Marine. Both are close to marine repair facilities. And both marinas are near a "must-see" attraction for boaters: the Bay Model. Operated by the U.S. Corps of Engineers, the Bay Model is a one-acre scale model of the San Francisco Bay and Delta region. With the use of hydraulic pumps, the model simulates the ocean tides and Delta river-flows to demonstrate effects on the Bay that can't be determined mathematically.

summer months. These buoys are wonderfully secure and a pleasure to tie up to during the week. If you decide to anchor outside of the mooring buoys, you'll find good holding in rock and sand with depths of 15-20 feet. If you're a member of a yacht club, sign in with the club to tie your dinghy to the yacht club float.

If you're not a yacht club member and wish to anchor out and go ashore, you can usually leave your dinghy in either the Sausalito Yacht Harbor Marina or Pelican Marina. But do get permission or your dinghy may be padlocked to the dock when you return. Sausalito also has a launch ramp approximately 0.5 mile north of the Spinnaker Restaurant, with docks where you might get permission to leave your dinghy. Check with personnel in the nearby restaurants or boat brokerages. From all these locations, exploration of Sausalito is easy.

Sausalito has a good public launch ramp at Clipper Yacht Harbor, immediately adjacent to the fuel dock. Contact personnel at the Yacht Harbor office or the fuel dock for permission to use the ramp. A parking area for vehicles and trailers is close at hand.

Belvedere Cove

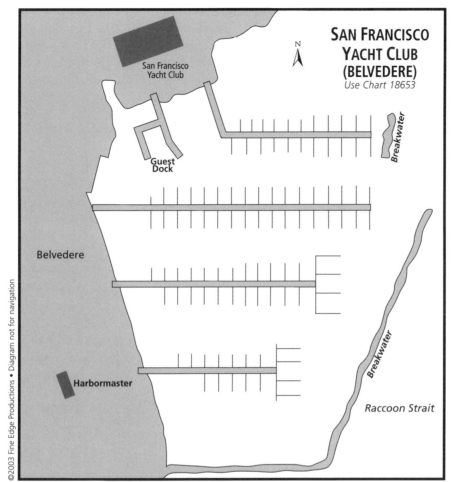

SAN FRANCISCO
YACHT CLUB
(BELVEDERE)
Use Chart 18653

⚓ **Schoonmaker Marina** position: 37°51.89'N, 122°29.34'W; tel: 415.331.5550

⚓ **Sausalito Yacht Club** position: 37°51.45'N, 122°28.63'W; tel: 415.332.7400 (wkends only)

⚓ **Sausalito Pt. Marina** position: 37°51.89'N, 122°29.34'W

⚓ **Sausalito Cruising Club** position: 37°51.76'N, 122°29.25'W; tel: 415.332.9922

Belvedere and Tiburon

(Belvedere Cove)
Chart 18653; 3.0 mi NE of Golden Gate Bridge Entrance (light "1"): 37°52.26'N, 122°27.26'W
Anchor (S): 37°52.03'N, 122°27.54'W

⚓ **Clipper Yacht Harbor** position: 37°52.29'N, 122°29.73'W; tel: 415.332.3500

⚓ **Kappas Harbor** position: 37°52.61'N, 122°30.14'W; tel: 415.332.5510 (no guest slips)

Belvedere Cove . . . is entered between Peninsula Point on the S and Point Tiburon on the N. Two private yacht clubs are in the cove. . . . (CP, 33rd Ed.)

The communities of Belvedere and Tiburon wrap around the shores of Belvedere Cove, east of Belvedere Point. Each of these communities has a long-established yacht club. At Belvedere is the San Francisco Yacht Club, and at Tiburon, the Corinthian Yacht Club. Each of these clubs provides some guest docking for members of other yacht clubs.

The San Francisco Yacht Club facility is in the extreme northwest corner of Belvedere Cove. As you enter, stay carefully in the channel, especially at low water. The guest dock is directly in front of the yacht club, immediately

San Francisco Yacht Club at Belvedere

west of the Travelift. Call ahead to check on slip availability.

The Corinthian Yacht Club, its entrance 200 yards east of the San Francisco Yacht Club channel, is housed in the large white structure on the point in the center of Belvedere Cove. The entrance to the club is on the east side of the yacht club. The yacht club has very limited space available for reciprocals and frequently turns visitors away because of space considerations.

Other than these two clubs, the Belvedere-Tiburon area has no slips, nor does it have launch ramps or a fuel dock.

Visiting boaters can anchor in Belvedere Cove near the point, or in front of the Corinthian Yacht Club. If you choose to anchor anywhere in this scenic cove, check your depth

Big Ebb at the Golden Gate
by Roderick Frazier Nash

A hand wave is usually a sign of friendship. But at sea it can spell "problem"—especially when it comes from someone frantically swimming in the middle of San Francisco Bay!

My wife Honeydew and I were making a familiar crossing in our Nordic Tug, *Forevergreen,* from the St. Francis Yacht Club to the lovely village of Tiburon about 4 nautical miles across the heart of the Bay. There was a brisk afternoon westerly blowing in through the Golden Gate, and it was opposing a strong ebb tide. The tables showed currents in the 5-knot range. The result, as mariners know, is "square waves"—very steep and close together. Weather bulletins talked of 6 feet at 6 seconds—very square!

No panic that day on our Nordic 26, but we were taking shots of saltwater over the cabin roof and there was lots of rocking and rolling. Unless we kept "a hand for the boat," we were going to launch into something hard!

And that's when we saw the group of sea kayakers—one in the water and several others waving for help. I'm almost ashamed to say our first reaction was to look around for another boat that might have come to the paddlers' assistance. But none was anywhere near, and the entire group was rapidly being carried toward the Golden Gate and the open ocean.

When we eased to within shouting distance, we learned that the kayaker was a beginner who'd been out of his boat for half an hour. He couldn't climb back in and he was cold and swallowing water with every wave. The group had no radio or cell phone.

Keeping my boat pointed somewhat into the sea, I called to the man to swim to my transom. "I can't," he responded. A look at his eyes showed he wasn't kidding—he was close to surrender. We estimated he had about 10 minutes.

Plan B was to use the engine to position him alongside the boat, but I was afraid of injuring him with the propeller. The viable option was to toss him a line. Honeydew had considerable experience with river (whitewater) throw bags, and she succeeded on the first attempt. I doubted he could hang on as we retrieved the line, but she talked him into it. Survival is a powerful incentive!

The stern was hobby-horsing violently, and the swim deck a battering ram from the perspective of someone in the water. I left the wheel (which, of course, was useless without a spinning prop) and, together with Honeydew, rolled the victim onto the swim deck. He was dead-weight and the problem—as in many man-overboard situations—was getting him on board. With effort, we dragged him over the transom and flopped him onto the aft deck like a tuna. I was back at the wheel when he vomited; Honeydew brought out some blankets to address his obvious hypothermia.

Still in their boats, the kayakers were moving toward the Marin mainland with difficulty. I followed them and, once inside Belvedere Point, the chop eased dramatically. Kids were even sailing dinghies around the cove! When we tied up at the San Francisco Yacht Club we learned the paddlers were enrolled in an East Bay kayak school. They were novices and had started out in the morning under good conditions. But later in the day, west of Angel Island, the nightmare began. They terminated their trip as soon as they landed at the yacht club, calling for vans to pick them up.

The companion of the man we rescued came down to the dock to thank us. So, eventually, did the leader. "Thanks," she said. "You saved our bacon." Then she told us that in exchange for our trouble her company would give us a complimentary instructional kayak trip on the Bay. We thanked her, of course, but privately we wondered if the course ever included interpretation of tides and current tables.

carefully as you choose a location; much of the cove has less than 6 feet at low water.

Restaurants and markets are within easy walking distance for boaters in Belvedere or Tiburon, but a car is necessary to get to a large chandlery.

⚓ **Corinthian Yacht Club** position: 37°52.32'N, 122°27.31'W; tel: 415.435.4771

⚓ **San Francisco Yacht Club** position: 37°52.32'N, 122°27.64'W; tel: 415.435.9133

Corinthian Yacht Club at Belvedere

Anchor (south) in about 1 fathom, mud bottom with fair-to-good holding; adequate swinging room for several boats.

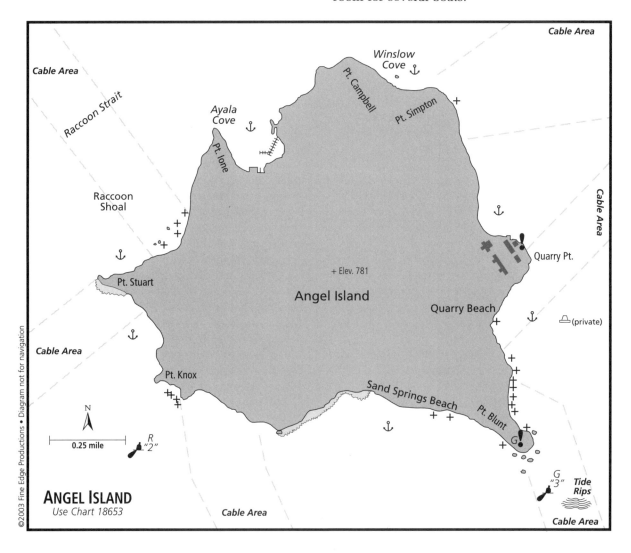

Bob & Carol Mehaffy

Mooring buoys in front of Corinthian Yacht Club

Angel Island
Charts 18653, 18649; 2.1 mi E of Sausalito
Sand Springs Beach anchor: 37°51.23'N,
122°25.65'W

Angel Island...is partially wooded and level on top. The irregular-shaped island is separated from the mainland by Raccoon Strait. Point Blunt, the SE extremity of Angel Island, terminates in a 60-foot-high knob, and is connected to the island by

Bob & Carol Mehaffy

Boats on a mooring at Ayala Cove, Angel Island

a low neck of land. . . . A shoal with visible and covered rocks extends SSE for 0.1 mile. Tide rips and swirls are heavy around the point, especially with a large falling tide. (CP, 33rd Ed.)

Angel Island is one of the most popular boating attractions in the San Francisco area, with its four major destinations for boaters. This island, a 750-acre California State Park, has extensive hiking trails, all offering unparalleled vistas of the Central Bay. Even more appealing for history buffs are the remains of old cavalry facilities at Camp Reynolds, which dates back to the Civil War era; the Immigration Station, from the late 1800s and early 1900s; Fort McDowell Induction Center, from the first 50 years of the 20th century; and the Nike Missile site, from the middle of the 20th century. A ferry runs between Angel and Tiburon islands.

Bob & Carol Mehaffy

Ayala Cove, Angel Island

Ayala Cove (Angel Island)
Charts 18653, 18649; 0.6 mi NE of
Point Stuart, indents the N side of
Angel Island
Entrance: 37°52.11'N, 122°26.19'W

Ayala Cove, indenting the N side of Angel Island, about 0.6 mile NE of Point Stuart, is reported to afford good anchorage in depths of 10 to 12 feet, mud bottom, and protection from S and W winds. Slips are available for day use only; mooring buoys are available for overnight stays. A pier at the State park facility in the cove is used by ferries and State park personnel. . . .

Raccoon Strait, nearly 0.5 mile wide, . . . is used by ferry boats and pleasure craft. The tidal currents in the strait have considerable velocity, and rips and swirls are heavy at times. . . .

The charted recreation area extending SW of Angel Island and including all of Raccoon Strait and Richardson Bay is intended primarily for use by recreation vessels. It should not be utilized by vessels 300 tons or more for through passage or for any other purpose, except in case of emergency or special circumstances. (CP, 33rd Ed.)

Tied fore and aft to mooring buoys, Ayala Cove

Ayala Cove, on the north shore of Angel Island facing Raccoon Strait and the town of Tiburon, contains docks with 47 slips for day use only. Boaters may use these slips on a first-come, first-served basis between 0800 and sunset for a reasonable fee. All boats on these docks must depart before sunset. The cove also contains a number of mooring buoys for both day and night use. Boaters tie to bow and stern buoys, facing north. Demand for these buoys far exceeds availability during summer months, especially on weekends.

Point Stuart
Chart 18653; W pt. of Angel Island
Anchor: 37°51.73'N, 122°26.69'W

A light is on Point Stuart, the W extremity, of Angel Island. (CP, 33rd Ed.)

Temporary anchorage in fair weather can be found on the north side of Point Stuart, south of the cable area. The current in Raccoon Strait can be strong with significant turbulence.

Anchor in 3 to 5 fathoms over a mixed bottom; fair holding with a well-set anchor (anchor watch advised).

Winslow Cove (Angel Island)
Charts 18653; 0.5 mi NE of Ayala Cove
Winslow Cove (China Cove) anchor: 37°52.28'N, 122°25.55'W

Winslow Cove (China Cove), located around Point Campbell immediately east of Ayala Cove,

has no docks or mooring buoys but has the same splendid views as Ayala. Ashore at Winslow are the remains of the Immigration Station building. A tour of these facilities gives a sobering look at early U.S. immigration practices.

Anchor in 20-30 feet over mud and clay; excellent holding. Since a strong tidal current runs through this anchorage, let out extra anchor rode.

Winslow Cove, Angel Island

East Garrison Anchorage

(Angel Island)
Chart 18653; 0.5 mi SE of Winslow Cove
East Garrison anchor: 37°51.87'N, 122°25.24'W

East Garrison Anchorage is situated below the remains of Fort McDowell, the world's largest military induction center during World Wars I and II. Most of the old buildings are boarded up, but you may land your dinghy on the beach nearby and go exploring. Don't tie to the dock where ferries regularly stop. The best anchorage at East Garrison is north of the dock in front of the old buildings of Fort McDowell. As at Winslow, set your anchor well, and let out extra rode to make sure your anchor holds when the strong current is flowing.

Anchor in 20-35 feet over mud and clay; excellent holding.

Quarry Beach Anchorage (Angel Island)

Chart 18653; 0.3 mi S of East Garrison
Quarry Beach anchor: 37°51.56'N, 122°25.09'W

Quarry Beach anchorage, on the southeast corner of Angel Island, around Quarry Point from East Garrison anchorage, is the largest of the island's anchorages. Though gusty winds often

East Garrison Anchorage, Angel Island

blow through this anchorage, the scenery at Quarry Beach encourages sailors to return again and again. Anchor in 15-30 feet of water on a mud and clay bottom with excellent holding. Land your dinghy anywhere on the beach at Quarry to explore the island. No fuel or supplies are available at Angel Island.

Sandsprings Beach Anchorage

(Angel Island)
Chart 18653; 0.6 mi SW of Quarry Beach
Anchor: 37°51.23'N, 122°25.65'W

Anchorage open to all southerly weather can be found 0.4 miles west of Blunt Point.

Anchor in 3-4 fathoms over mud and clay with excellent holding.

West Garrison Anchorage (Angel Island)

Chart 18653; 0.7 mi SW of Ayala Cove
Anchor: 37°51.49'N, 122°26.64'W

Anchorage can be found between Point Stuart and Point Knox, south of the charted cable area.

Anchor in 2 to 3 fathoms with fair holding.

Paradise Cove

Chart 18653; 1.5 mi N of Belvedere Cove
Anchor: 37°53.80'N, 122°27.34'W

Bluff Point, directly north of Ayala Cove and across Raccoon Strait, lies on the southeastern

Paradise Cove Pier

Bob & Carol Mehaffy

Paradise Cove Anchorage

extremity of Tiburon Peninsula. Northward 1.5 miles along the eastern shore of this peninsula is Paradise Cove, another popular anchorage among Bay Area boaters. You can identify the anchorage by the large T-shaped pier extending from the shore and by the green lawn of Paradise Park, on the slope behind the beach.

During WWII the present site of the park was a U.S. Navy base; the men stationed there set anti-submarine nets beneath the Golden Gate

Shipbuilding in WWII
by Carlyn Stark

In 1939 England was fighting for her life against the German war machine. U Boats were sinking her merchant ships far faster than she could replace them, and there was no other way to supply the embattled island with arms, raw materials and food. She turned to the U.S. and President Roosevelt for help.

The Maritime Commission wanted to establish shipyards on the west coast and Henry Kaiser won the bid to build the Liberty ships, described by the English as "great galumphing seagoing improvisations." They were easy to build, cheap to operate and maintain, and carried a huge load.

At the end of December, 1940 the first of 300,000 cubic yards of rock were dumped on a bog along the shores of Richmond, California to provide a firm foundation for what was to be one of four shipyards built in Richmond. On April 14, 1941, before the yard was half-built, the first keel was laid. Eventually 100,000 workers and their families swamped the Richmond area.

As the need for shipping grew, three more yards were built in the Portland-Vancouver area. Where traditionally riveting had been the mode of shipbuilding, all seven shipyards were designed to weld together huge sections of ship and move them, with immense cranes, to the ways where they were welded to the ship already in progress.

While traditional yards took at least three months to build a ship, the Kaiser yards, under the direction of Clay Bedford in California and Edgar Kaiser in Oregon-Washington, were turning them out in a month from keel-laying to launch.

Edgar Kaiser decided he could build one in ten days, and President Roosevelt and Clay Bedford attended the

Bob & Carol Mehaffy

Liberty Ship Jeremiah O'Brien

launching ten days after the keel was laid. The Richmond yards retaliated by building a ship in seven days, 14 hours and 23 minutes. She was complete with grease guns and oil rags in the engine room, and sharpened pencils on the bridge when she went down the ways. One worker asked why they hadn't put a prefabricated captain on the bridge.

After that major effort, twenty-three days from keel-laying to launching was the norm for the Liberties. In all, the Richmond yards built 747 ships and the Northern yard built 743. Without this immense contribution to wartime shipping, the outcome of the war might have been very different.

Carlyn Stark, granddaughter of Henry J. Kaiser, lives in Washington State overlooking Port Townsend Channel.

Bridge. Some of the large concrete blocks used to hold the nets in place remain along the beach by the pier. No fuel or provisions are available near Paradise Cove.

Paradise Cay, 1.6 miles north, is a marina and housing development catering to smaller boats.

Anchor in about 200 feet off the end of the T-pier at Paradise Cove in 10-15 feet over primarily clay; excellent holding. (Expect your anchor and rode to come up covered with gooey clay.)

Paradise Cay
Charts 18653, 18649; 1.5 mi NW of Paradise Cove

Paradise Cay, a filled real estate project, . . . has a small-boat harbor that accommodates about 200

boats. The harbor is on the N side of the project. (CP, 33rd Ed.)

Paradise Cay is a large housing development with a marina that caters to smaller shallow-draft vessels.

Richmond
Charts 18653; 4.4 mi N of Treasure Island
Richmond Yacht Hbr position: 37°55.42'N, 122°22.39'W
Richmond Marina Bay entrance "R18": 37°54.53'N, 122°21.63'W

Small-craft facilities. Some small-craft facilities are along Santa Fe Channel. A marina and yacht club are in Richmond Marina Bay, and a private yacht harbor is on the E side of Point Richmond. (CP, 33rd Ed.)

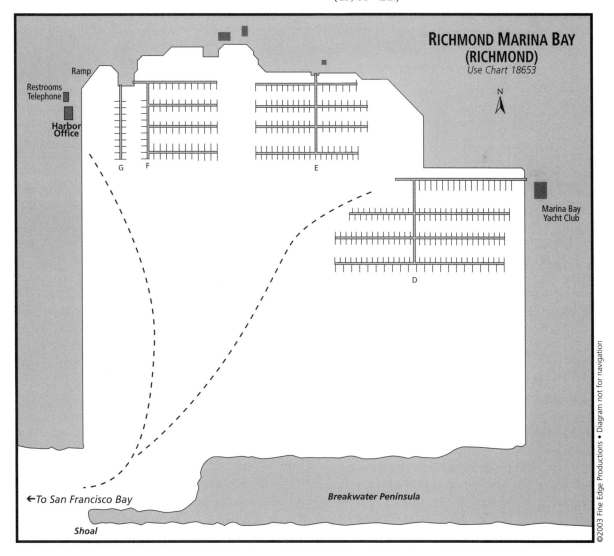

RICHMOND MARINA BAY
(RICHMOND)
Use Chart 18653

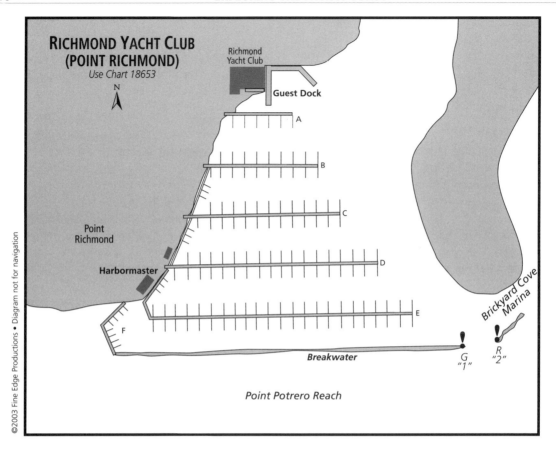

The large Richmond area accommodates about 1,000 boats and is home to three yacht clubs. Many Bay Area boaters choose the repair facilities in Richmond when they need to haul their boats or have work done on them.

To visit the Richmond area, use the Richmond Harbor Channel, entering 2.5 miles southeast of the east end of the Richmond-San Rafael Bridge. Richmond has a number of possible destinations for visiting boaters.

The Richmond Yacht Club and Brickyard Cove Marina share the first cove on the north side of the Richmond Channel. Buoy 7 marks the entrance into this cove. The Richmond Yacht Club is on the west side of the cove; Brickyard Cove Marina is on the east side. The Richmond Yacht Club provides guest berthing for boaters from other yacht clubs. As always, call ahead to check on slip availability. Brickyard Cove has no guest slips.

Richmond Marina Bay Yacht Harbor, the city's large marina, has 750 slips, some of

which are usually available for visiting boaters. Turn to the east into the Marina Bay channel immediately after passing Buoy 18. Check the tide before entering this marina; shoaling at the entrance frequently reduces the depth to less than 6 feet at low water. Marina Bay has an excellent launch ramp for those who trailer their boats. Marina Bay Yacht Club does not have docks designated for guest berthing. Visiting yacht club members do get a special rate, however, from the marina harbormaster.

Point San Pablo Yacht Club, located at the end of the Richmond Channel, across from the yacht repair facilities, accommodates members from other yacht clubs with notice of a day or so. The two buoys in the turning basin between the club and the repair facilities are private. Anchoring in the area is not recommended because of the boat and ship traffic.

A fuel dock and three chandleries in the Richmond area are in the basin near Point San Pablo Yacht Club as are the boat repair facilities of KKMI and Richmond Boat Works. West Marine, Whale Point, and KKMI chandleries are all easily accessible from the Point San Pablo Yacht Club, but are not so convenient for boaters docked at Marina Bay or Richmond Yacht Club.

⚓ **Richmond Marina Bay**
position: 37°54.54'N, 122°21.24'W; tel: 510.236.1013

⚓ **Marina Bay Yacht Club**
position: 37°54.75'N, 122°21.08'W; tel: 510.232.6292

courtesy of Berkeley Marina

The Berkeley Marina

⚓ **Pt. San Pablo YC**
position: 37°55.41'N, 122°22.55'W; tel: 510.620.9690

⚓ **Richmond YC**
entrance: 37°54.41'N, 122°22.98'W; tel: 510.237.2821

⚓ **Brickyard Cove**
position: 37°54.48'N, 122°22.90'W; no transient docks; tel: 510.236.1933

Berkeley Yacht Harbor

Charts 18653, 18649; 3.2 mi NE of Treasure Island
Entrance (outer): 37°50.86'N, 122°22.12'W
Entrance (inner): 37°51.99'N, 122°19.09'W

Berkeley Yacht Harbor . . . is protected at the entrance by two detached breakwaters. The S breakwater is marked by a light on the S end, a light at the center, and a light and fog

BERKELEY MARINA
Use Chart 18653

N

Breakwater

Haul Out

Fuel
Pump
Out

A B C D E

Hotel Vistors

Marina Blvd.

Breakwater

Berkeley
Yacht
Club

O

F

G

San Francisco Bay

M Guest Docks L

N

K J H

I

Pump
Out

Seawall Drive

Fishing Pier

University Ave.

South Sailing Basin

©2003 Fine Edge Productions • Diagram not for navigation

Art on the pilings, Emeryville Marina

Bob & Carol Mehaffy

signal at the N end. The N breakwater is marked
by a light on the NE and SW ends. The N side of
the entrance into the harbor is marked by a private light, and the S side by a private light and fog
signal. Berkeley Reef, awash, is 0.9 mile NW from
the inner harbor entrance; it is marked by a light.

*. . . Transients should report to the harbor-
master's office on the S side of the harbor.*
(CP, 33rd Ed.)

Popular Berkeley Marina, inside Berkeley Harbor, has accommodations for
nearly 1,000 boats from 16 to 110 feet. In
1999, extensive renovations to the marina were completed, and it now boasts
that it is the largest marina in the region. Guest slips are available on a first-
come, first-served basis; tie up at K dock
or the harbormaster's office for a slip
assignment. Facilities include showers, three pumpout stations, a chandlery and nearby restaurants; fuel and laundry
are nearby. Berkeley Yacht Club has limited
space available for reciprocal club members.

Berkeley Marine Center, next to Berkeley Marina, has no guest slips.

⚓ **Berkeley Marina
Harbormaster;** tel:
510.644.6376; VHF
16; website: www.ci.
berkeley.ca.us

⚓ **Berkeley Yacht Club;**
tel: 510.843.9292

Emeryville City Marina

Chart 18652; 2.8 mi E of
Treasure Island
Outer entrance "1":
37°50.60'N, 122°19.33'W
Inner entrance "8":
37°50.54'N, 122°18.63'W

*Two marinas are at Emery-
ville. . . . The enclosed
basin can accommodate
about 730 small craft.* (CP,
33rd Ed.)

Emeryville makes a good
destination because of its
location. On the east side
of Central Bay, Emery-
ville has good protection
from much of the wind

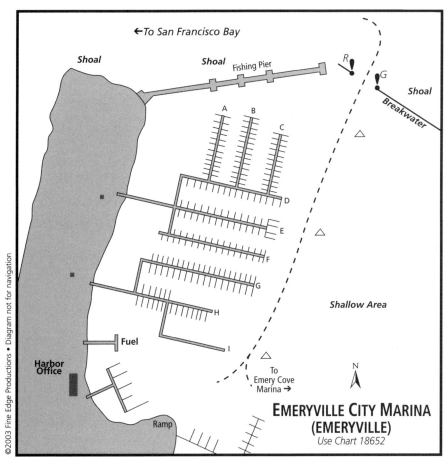

©2003 Fine Edge Productions • Diagram not for navigation

**EMERYVILLE CITY MARINA
(EMERYVILLE)**
Use Chart 18652

Emery Cove Marina

that can make other destinations on the Bay uncomfortable. In addition, Emeryville can generally provide slips for visiting boaters. The two marinas within the harbor are Emeryville City Marina and Emery Cove Yacht Harbor.

When entering Emeryville, stay in the channel, which has a dredged depth of 6 feet at low water. If your boat draws more water than that, plan to enter only at high tide. Don't turn into the marina until you've passed Buoy 6, for water depths south of the channel between buoys 4 and 6 are much less than 6 feet.

Emeryville Marina has a launch ramp and fuel dock; guest slips are on space availability; reservations required. Although Emery Cove Marina slips are privately owned (dockominium), about 15 guest slips are available. Facilities include showers and laundry and two pumpouts. Restaurants and a market are within easy walking distance. From Emeryville, boaters who want to see Bay Area sights can use public transportation.

⚓ **Emeryville City Marina** position: 37°50.45'N, 122°18.69'W; tel: 510.654.3716

⚓ **Emery Cove Yacht Harbor** position: 37°50.36'N, 122°18.72'W; tel: 510.428.0505

⚓ **Emeryville Harbormaster** tel: 510.428.0505

Treasure Isle Marina
Chart 18650; 2.2 mi E of Pier 39

Until 1997, manmade Treasure Island was under naval jurisdiction. Since then the City of San Francisco has taken over management of the island and has plans for total renovation and construction of new marina facilities. A new management company is now running the marina and new guest docks are now available.

⚓ **Treasure Island Marina** tel: 415.981.2416; website: www.treasure-isle.com

Clipper Cove
Chart 18650; btwn Treasure & Yerba Buena Isls
Entrance: 37°49.09'N, 122°21.64'W
Anchor: 37°48.84'N, 122°22.10'W

Treasure Island is a low filled area N of and connected by a causeway to Yerba Buena Island. Built originally for the San Francisco International Exposition of 1939-40, Treasure Island now belongs to the city of San Francisco. Some of the piers around the island have lights. A shoal covered 15 feet, is off the N end of the island. (CP, 33rd Ed.,)

Clipper Cove, between Treasure Island and Yerba Buena Island, lies almost directly below the northeast span of the Bay Bridge, nearly in the middle of the Central Bay. This cove was

Clipper Cove, Treasure Island

Bob & Carol Mehaffy

Clipper Cove Anchorage

named for the Pan American China Clipper sea-planes that flew in and out of here to the Hawaiian Islands between 1939 and 1946. Clipper Cove, Carol and Bob Mehaffy's favorite anchorage in San Francisco Bay, is large enough to provide excellent protection from prevailing winds for 50 anchored boats. They have anchored in Clipper when 30-knot winds were blowing from the northwest and felt little or no wave action. Most areas in the cove have a sticky clay bottom that holds anchors well but makes a mess of the foredeck when the anchor and rode come aboard.

Use caution when entering the cove to avoid the shallow water at the bar on the south two-thirds of the entrance. (Use entrance waypoint shown above.) Once inside, get as far west into the cove as possible for protection from the strong winds that often blow through the anchorage during the afternoon and evening hours.

Treasure Island Marina, in the extreme northwest corner of Clipper Cove, was original-ly reserved for retired and active-duty military but is now operated by a private company. At present, this small marina has no guest slips; however, the operator plans to renovate, reserv-ing some slips for visiting boaters.

A museum displaying nautical and miscella-neous artifacts from the building of the Bay Bridge was housed in one of the 1939–40 Golden Gate International Exposition buildings on Treasure Island. All the artifacts are current-ly in storage while the building is being reno-vated. Ask about the museum when you visit this location; this collection is worth your time. No fuel or supplies are available at the marina or nearby.

Anchor (Clipper Cove) in 8-20 feet over sticky mud with some soft spots; back down at least a full minute after dropping anchor. If your anchor drags, hoist and re-anchor in another location.

⚓ **Treasure Island Marina** position: 37°48.92'N, 122°22.18'W; tel: 415.981.2416 (open Wed-Sun)

⚓ **Harbormaster** tel: 415.274.0382; VHF Ch 16

Michelle Gaylord

Ghirardelli Square, Fisherman's Wharf

Point Rincon Anchorage (Bay Bridge Anchorage)
Chart 18650; 0.2 mi N of Bay Bridge
Position: 37°47.56'N, 122°23.35'W

The area along the sea wall, from where the Bay Bridge meets the city northwest to the Ferry Building, is available for public anchoring. There are no facilities, but it's a temporary stop just for viewing the bridge up close. Because of poor landing opportunities, street people, the wake of passing ferries, pilot boats and pleasure craft, it is little used by cruising boats. However, it is easy to spot in limited visibility or during night approach.

Anchor in 12 to 15 feet with reportedly good holding.

Pier 39 Marina at Fisherman's Wharf
Chart 18650; 1.5 mi W of Bay Bridge
Entrance (E brkwtr): 37°48.53'N, 122°24.44'W

Pier 39 Marina . . . is a boat harbor with 360 slips. . . . Limited space is available for transient vessels by appointment only. The harbormaster monitors VHF-FM channel 16 0830-1700 daily. (CP, 33rd Ed.)

Pier 39 is one of the top tourist attractions in San Francisco, drawing more than 10 million people each year. There is a harbor on the west side of Pier 39 but it is densely inhabited by sea lions. Do not enter unless you have permission from the harbormaster. Pier 39 Marina, on the east side of the pier, attempts to accommodate all visiting boaters, but with its slips in high demand, they advise calling up to a month in advance. If you arrive without first obtaining a slip, you may have difficulty maneuvering in the limited room, especially when strong winds are blowing and a current is running. Nearby facilities include a grocery store, laundromat, restaurants, showers, and shopping.

Pier 39 Marina is an ideal base of operations for boaters to enjoy the city of San Francisco. Hundreds of shops and tourist facilities are within walking distance. In addition, public transportation, ferries to Alcatraz, cable cars to the downtown area, and dozens of restaurants are found nearby.

Large signs facing the water identify Pier 39. Enter the marina on the east side of the harbor at the back of the breakwater. This marina has no

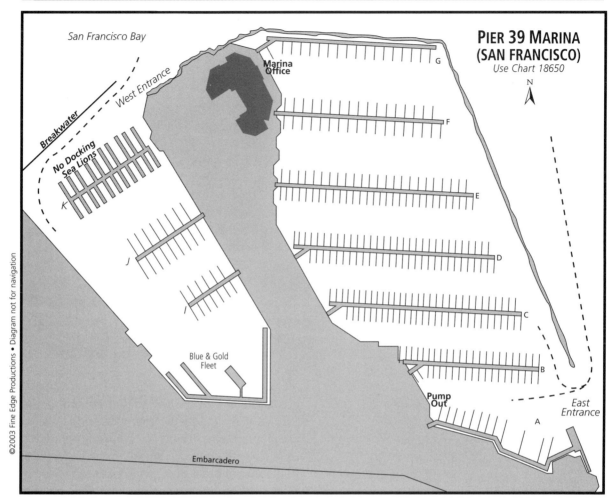

the back of the breakwater. This marina has no fuel dock, and few boat supplies or repair services are available nearby.

⚓ **Pier 39 Harbormaster**: tel: 415.705.5556 or VHF Channel 16

Aquatic Park
Chart 18650; 0.7 mi E of Municipal Yacht Harbor
Entrance: 37°48.65'N, 122°25.43'W

The basin is closed to power vessels, and other vessels must stay offshore away from buoys marking a swimming area. The speed limit is 3 knots. Depths of 9 to 16 feet are inside the basin. . . . . Permission to anchor for more than 24 hours must be obtained from the Aquatic Park Ranger Station. (CP, 33rd Ed.)

The San Francisco Maritime National Historic Park is located opposite Alcatraz Island on the city front. Because of the area's popularity with

Balaclutha *moored to pier at Aquatic Park anchorage*

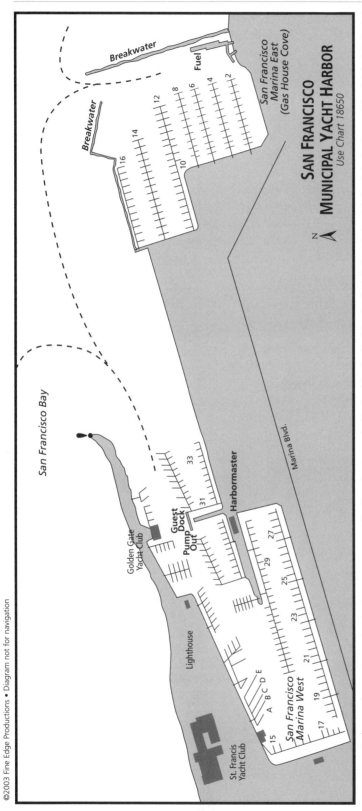

local swimming and rowers, the park is closed to power vessels and park regulations state that sailboats can enter the park only under sail to anchor. Check with the park ranger at 415.556.1238 for current regulations.

Aquatic Park is arguably the most dramatic site in San Francisco Bay, with views of the historic ships of the Maritime Museum, Ghirardelli Square, Alcatraz Island, and the Golden Gate Bridge. But don't plan on anchoring at Aquatic Park. This lovely anchorage is under the jurisdiction of the Park Service at the Maritime Museum, which has established rules forbidding boats to enter the Park under power because of the large number of year-round swimmers in the water. Given the wind and current, and the danger of collision with one of the historic ships at the Museum, few boaters choose to sail into and out of Aquatic Park. The handful of boats you may see at anchor inside the Park are used to teach sailing to the Sea Scouts.

San Francisco Municipal Yacht Harbor

Chart 18650; 1.8 mi E of the Golden Gate Bridge
Entrance (W basin): 37°48.53'N, 122°26.33'W
Entrance (E basin): 37°48.51'N, 122°25.97'W

Small-craft facilities. San Francisco Municipal Yacht Harbor, . . . with a W and E basin about 0.3 mile apart, has depths of 8 to 12 feet to the berths. A light near the end of a point marks the N side of the entrance to W basin; a prominent stone tower is 0.2 mile W of the light. The E basin is protected on the N by a breakwater extending E from the W shore, and on the E by a pier of Fort Mason. The seaward end of the breakwater is marked by a light. E basin is entered between the breakwater light and the pier. The harbor accommodates about 700 boats in the W and E basins. Guest berths are available; transients should report to the harbormaster's office on the S side of the W basin for berth assignment. (CP, 33rd Ed.)

San Francisco Municipal Yacht Harbor is the

San Francisco Marina West entrance

home of the famous St. Francis Yacht Club and San Francisco Marina West, as well as San Francisco Marina East, also known as Gas House Cove.

San Francisco Marina West
Charts 18650; 1.3 mi SW of Alcatraz Isl
Entrance: 37°48.53'N, 122°26.33'W
Transient dock and pumpout: 37°48.44'N, 122°26.54'W

The San Francisco waterfront, forming the southern boundary of Central San Francisco Bay, has one major destination for visiting boaters, the San Francisco Marina. The entrances to the two sections of this marina, West and East, are 600

San Francisco Bay
by Michelle Gaylord

As we entered San Francisco Bay, the skies were overcast and cloudy, which was a disappointment because I wanted our first pass underneath the Golden Gate to be perfect. Our first sighting of the harbor entrance and the bridge in the fog was really awesome. Just as we were about 1/4 of a mile from the bridge, the sun broke out. Wow. What a spectacular sight! Going under the Golden Gate Bridge and entering the San Francisco Bay was almost as thrilling as going through the Panama Canal. There was Alcatraz, big as day right inside the harbor entrance.

Just before Alcatraz, on the right, is St. Francis Yacht Club, which is so big it looks more like a small hotel than a yacht club. We continued on up the harbor, taking a mini cruise toward the Bay Bridge. Right there was the Palace of Fine Arts, Fisherman's Wharf, Coit Tower, Pier 39, and the unmistakable San Francisco skyline. I had never viewed the city from this perspective and was surprised to see all these famous landmarks so close together.

After our little cruise we filled up with fuel and headed back to the entrance of the harbor and the St. Francis Yacht Club. Our fee for the night was $45. It has no bathroom facilities, no showers, no 50-amp electrical service, a no-generator policy, and they are out in the boonies. We would have to take a taxi to get to any civilization at all. We did go up for lunch and I have to admit that the Club is pretty darn impressive; it's quite large, and has two stories. The view from the Club I'm sure is unsurpassed, and the interior is elegant. The food was excellent and wasn't unreasonably priced.

Alcatraz Island

We found Fisherman's Wharf greatly changed from our last visit 20 years ago. Tacky shops now line some of the streets and piers, and derelicts lie in the gutters. However, we ended up eating at a little hole-in-the-wall restaurant and had a great dinner.

We had trouble locating a slip in downtown San Francisco, Sausalito, or Tiburon; they ranged from $50 to $92.75 per night. I checked around Alameda Bay and found slips at Marina Village—right across the channel from Jack London Square—for $10 a night! It was fabulous—a huge, new, clean marina with 750 slips all filled with Bristol boats. The place is landscaped with lakes, water fountains, large grassy areas, duck ponds, and bike/jogging paths with fitness stops along the way. We dined at the Oakland Yacht Club, only 1/8 of a mile from our slip, and it was perfectly suitable.

Hyde Street cable car

yards apart. The harbormaster in West Marina manages both.

West Marina, the closer of the two to the Golden Gate Bridge, is slightly less than 2 miles inside the Bay. The entrance into the San Francisco Marina is about 500 yards east of a white cupola on the seawall. Another landmark you can use to locate the entrance is the Palace of Fine Arts, designed for the Panama Pacific Exposition of 1915. The huge cream-colored dome of this landmark is visible above the trees and houses south of the marina.

Observe the buoys closely, and proceed slowly when entering West Marina. Despite regular dredging, a sandbar forms repeatedly at the end of the spit protecting the harbor, leaving a channel over the bar less than 6 feet deep at low water.

West Marina has some guest berthing but before entering this marina with its limited space for maneuvering—call ahead. From the marina, you can walk to a supermarket but boat parts and services are sparse in the area.

Two major yacht clubs—St. Francis and Golden Gate—are located in San Francisco Marina West. Both clubs have a few slips for visitors from other yacht clubs, but demand is high, particularly during the busy summer months. The harbormaster's reporting guest dock is near the pump out station on your port hand.

⚓ **Saint Francis Yacht Club** position: 37°48.40'N, 122°26.73'W'; tel: 415.563.6363

⚓ **Golden Gate Yacht Club** position: 37°48.47'N, 122°26.51'W; tel: 415.346.2628; website: www.ggyc.com

⚓ **Harbormaster dock** position: 37°48.44'N, 122°26.54'W; tel: 415.292.2013

San Francisco Marina East (Gashouse Cove)
Chart 18650; 0.3 mi E of West Basin
Entrance: 37°48.51'N, 122°25.97'W

San Francisco Marina East, commonly called Gashouse Cove, is a 24-hour facility with limited guest space on space availability only. The best landmark to distinguish this marina is the busy fuel dock at the back of the

Palace of Fine Arts

Fuel dock at Gashouse Cove

⚓ **San Francisco Marina Harbormaster** position: 37°48.44'N, 122°26.54'W; tel: 415.292.2013

THE SOUTH BAY

The South Bay includes the area south of the Bay Bridge beginning in Oakland and moving counterclockwise across the bay and north up the Peninsula.

San Francisco-Oakland Bay Bridge

Chart 18650; San Francisco-Bay Bridge crosses the Bay from Rincon Point in San Francisco to Yerba Buena Island, and then to Oakland
Position (southbound): 37°47.60'N, 122°22.99'W
Position (northbound): 37°48.20'N, 122°22.35'W

entrance channel. A Safeway is available just south, as well as restaurants, laundromats and public transportation.

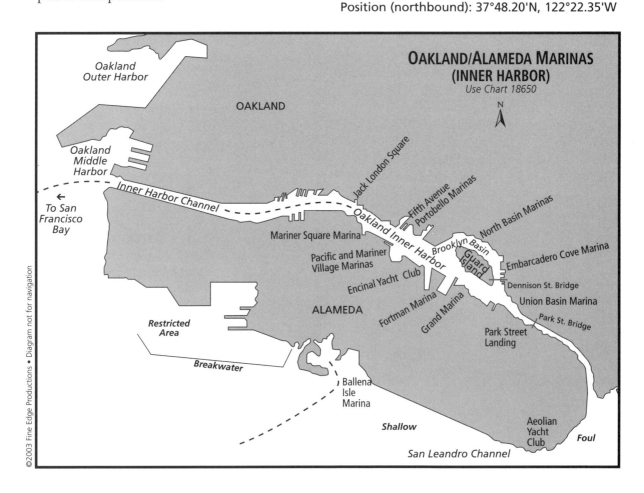

Serious yacht racing off St. Francis Yacht Club

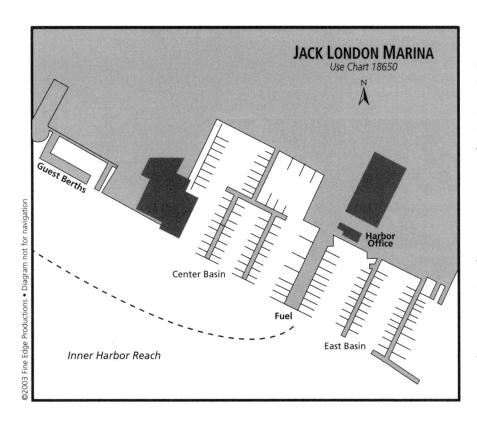

The San Francisco-Oakland Bay Bridge [is] said to be the eighth longest bridge in the world. Racons mark the main bridge spans. The recommended passage for southbound traffic is under the NE half of span A-B (midspan clearance 204 feet). Northbound traffic should use the SW half of span D-E (midspan clearance 204 feet). The midspan clearance of spans B-C and C-D are each 220 feet. These clearances are approximate; they may be reduced by several feet due to heavy traffic on the bridge and prolonged periods of ex-

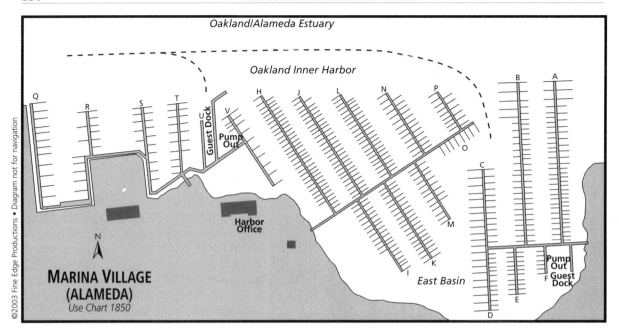

Oakland/Alameda Estuary

Oakland Inner Harbor

B A

Q

R S T U V H J L N P O

Guest Dock

Pump Out

C

M

Harbor Office

N

MARINA VILLAGE (ALAMEDA)
Use Chart 1850

I K

Pump Out
F Guest Dock

East Basin

E

D

©2003 Fine Edge Productions • Diagram not for navigation

tremely high temperature, and as much as 10 feet under extreme conditions. (CP, 33rd Ed.)

Once you pass under the San Francisco-Oakland Bay Bridge, you enter what is often referred to as the South Bay. Many visiting boaters go directly to the South Bay on the east shore of San Francisco Bay because it has the largest concentration of marinas, boat yards, chandleries, repair technicians, and yacht clubs in the Bay Area.

Oakland Inner Harbor (Oakland-Alameda Estuary)

Chart 18650, 0.75 mi SE of Yerba Buena Island
Entrance (Channel): 37°48.08'N, 122°20.53'W

Oakland Inner Harbor is that part of Inner Harbor Channel extending E from San Francisco Bay to Tidal Canal. It is adjacent to the most highly developed section of the city, bordering Oakland to the N and Alameda to the S.

Small-craft facilities. There are many small-craft facilities on both sides of the channel from Oakland Inner Harbor entrance to the airport at the S end of San Leandro Bay. . . . Mariners should exercise caution when transiting Oakland Inner Harbor to prevent wake damage to boats moored at marinas along the waterway. (CP, 33rd Ed.)

The entrance to the Oakland-Alameda Estuary, the hub of boating activity in the Bay, is 1.5 miles east of the center span of the Oakland-Bay Bridge. After entering the Estuary, you pass a 2.5-mile stretch of container ship and ship repair facilities before you begin to see the marinas

Container ship cranes, Oakland-Alameda

Bob & Carol Mehaffy

Ship facilities, Oakland

and small boat repair facilities. Chart 18650 is inadequate for locating facilities in Oakland Inner Harbor; the scale is too small to be of any help. For example, Jack London Square (which is not shown on the chart) is located on the north shore, west of the two Alameda transit tunnels and east of the old ferry pier.

Although many of the marinas and yacht clubs in the Estuary have guest berthing, you can save time and frustration by calling ahead before you get there. Jack London Square Marina, the first marina in the Estuary, is located on the port side immediately after you pass Scott's Seafood Restaurant. The marina office, officially the Port of Oakland Harbor Office, is behind the fuel dock. The marina has free guest berths for up to 4 hours for boaters who want to visit the square. If you enter the Estuary without making

prior arrangements for a slip it's a good idea, while you're fueling, to send a crewmember to the harbor office to request a slip.

The harbormaster at Jack London Square Marina also assigns guests to slips in North Basin I, North Basin II, Central Basin, and Union Point Basin, all positioned along the Oakland shore of the Estuary. Each of these marinas has location advantages. Jack London Square Marina is best if you want to visit FDR's presidential yacht, the *Potomac*; the relocated Jack London Klondike cabin; the numerous restaurants; or the wholesale produce market on Webster Street, where boaters can get bargain prices on the freshest produce.

You may prefer Central Basin Marina (Embarcadero Cove) to be closer to West Marine or Quinn's Lighthouse. This location also puts you closer to many other marine businesses.

On the Alameda side of the Estuary are six marinas, beginning almost directly across from Jack London Square Marina. Mariner Square Marina, the first, normally has no guest berthing. Marina Village Yacht Harbor, the second and largest, provides guest berthing but often can't accommodate all visitors wanting slips. Pacific Marina, the third, is the Oakland Yacht Club's marina and has guest slips for members of reciprocal yacht clubs. The Encinal Yacht Club also has facilities in Pacific Marina.

Svendsen's Boat Yard, Alameda

These first three marinas on the Alameda side of the Estuary are close enough to a market and restaurants for convenient walking. Unfortunately, major chandleries and repair facilities are far enough away to preclude walking.

Fortman Marina—also the home of Alameda Yacht Club—keeps some guest berths open, but in summer months this marina has difficulty meeting the demand. Grand Marina, after Fortman, easily identified by its name painted in large letters on the warehouse behind the boats, has some guest berths and is home to the Mariner boat yard. Alameda Marina, the last on the Alameda side of the Estuary, immediately after Grand Marina, is identified by the Svendsen's boat yard sign at the back of the marina. These latter three marinas on the Alameda side are all close to a major chandlery, two boat yards, and many other boat repair facilities.

In addition to Svendsen's boat yard and chandlery, marine suppliers and repair facilities in the area are too numerous to list. Whatever you need for your boat or whatever you want to have repaired, you can almost certainly find someone here to answer your call. On the Alameda side of the Estuary, the fuel dock is at Grand Marina.

Along the Estuary are numerous launch ramps for those who trailer their boats. The Estuary has no anchorage, but the large anchorage at Clipper Cove is only 5 miles from the marinas in the Estuary.

⚓ **Port of Oakland Harbormaster** tel: 510.272.4800

⚓ **Jack London Square Marina** position: 37°47.67'N, 122°16.83'W; tel: 1.800.675.DOCK

⚓ **Mariner's Square Marina** position: 37°47.34'N, 122°16.42'W

⚓ **Marina Village Harbormaster** tel: 510.521.0905; website: www.marinavillage-harbor.com

⚓ **North Basin Marina** position: 37°47.23'N, 122°15.19'W

⚓ **Fortman Marina Harbormaster** tel: 510.522.9080

⚓ **Grand Marina Harbormaster** tel: 510.865.1200

⚓ **Alameda Marina Harbormaster** tel: 510.521.1133 (no guest slips)

⚓ **Alameda Yacht Club** tel: 510.865.5668

⚓ **Central Basin** position: 37°46.98'N, 122°14.69'W

⚓ **Union Point Basin** position: 37°46.63'N, 122°14.61'W

⚓ **Aeolian Yacht Club** position: 37°44.97'N, 122°14.05'W

⚓ **Encinal Yacht Club** tel: 510.522.3272

⚓ **Oakland Yacht Club** tel: 510.522.6868

Ballena Bay Yacht Harbor
Chart 18650; 3.6 mi SE of Oakland Inner Hbr entr
Entrance Buoy R"2": 37°45.82'N, 122°16.93'W

Ballena Bay Yacht Harbor, a large small-craft harbor, is on the E side of an island along the S shore of Alameda. This harbor offers safe refuge in storms. A private light marks the entrance to the harbor. (CP, 33rd Ed.)

Ballena Bay Yacht Harbor, located 3.6 miles southeast of the entrance to the Oakland-Alameda Estuary, is the home of Ballena Isle Marina. It is the only Alameda marina entered directly from the South Bay. The facilities at Ballena Isle Marina are excellent, and the marina staff attempts to provide accommodations for all visiting boaters, although the demand often outstrips the available guest slips during summer months.

When you're still 2 miles from the marina, you'll be able to see the masts of boats and the breakwater. The harbor entrance is at the south end of the breakwater. Since the area south of the entrance channel is shoal, do not stray outside the channel. As you round the corner and proceed into the marina, you'll see the fuel dock at the north end of the harbor.

The guest docks, adjacent to the fuel dock, are typically full of brokerage boats at Ballena Isle, so you should have a slip assignment before entering the harbor. Call ahead on VHF

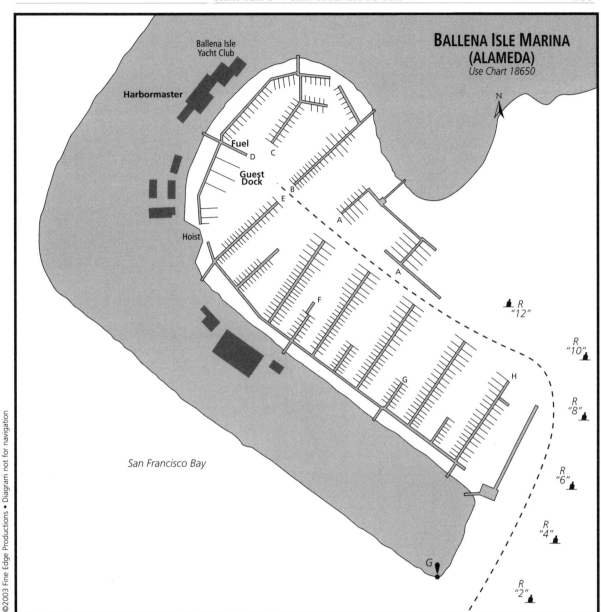

BALLENA ISLE MARINA
(ALAMEDA)
Use Chart 18650

16 to ask about a guest slip if you haven't previously reserved a slip.

Ballena Isle Marina has some facilities for cruising boaters. Adjacent to the harbor office is a small chandlery with limited supplies. Brokerage offices and a boat charter service are also in the area. Of more interest, perhaps, for most visitors are the restaurants.

For boaters needing supplies or repairs, Ballena Isle Marina presents a location problem. All major chandleries and repair facilities are located in the Estuary, some 2 miles or more distant. Public transportation, while available, doesn't provide convenient connections for those needing to get to the Estuary. Most visiting boaters find they need to rent a car or take a taxi to get boat parts or to provision before continuing their cruise.

Ballena Bay has no anchorage area. Although the area immediately south of the entrance channel appears to be a potential anchorage area, it is shoal. The Ballena Bay Yacht Club has no guest berths for visiting boaters.

⚓ **Ballena Isle Harbormaster** tel:
 1.800.675.SLIP or VHF 16

⚓ **Ballena Bay Yacht Club** tel: 1.510.523.2292

San Leandro Marina

Chart 18651; 6.4 mi SE of Ballena Bay off S end
Oakland Airport
San Leandro Marina (outer) entr lt. "1":
37°40.25'N, 122°13.37'W
San Leandro Marina (inner) entr: 37°41.66'N,
122°11.57'W
San Leandro Marina pos: 37°41.83'N,
122°11.54'W

San Leandro Marina, located almost exactly 10 miles SE of the Bay Bridge, is entered through a 2-mile long channel from the South Bay. When approaching the entrance, enter the channel only after identifying the #1 and #2 channel markers. Although the channel has a minimum depth of 7 feet in most places, the water outside the markers is less than 2 feet at low water.

The marina at San Leandro has 450 slips behind an excellent breakwater. With modern facilities and an accommodating marina staff, San Leandro makes a good destination for cruisers wanting to explore the South Bay area. Visiting boaters are limited to a 2-day stay aboard although they may leave their boats in the marina and travel inland if the marina has guest slips.

Like some other marinas, however, San Leandro Marina has limited repair and supply facilities nearby. Unfortunately, visiting boaters will need to rent a car or use public transportation to visit a large chandlery. Good bus service is available between the marina and the town of San Leandro, some 4 miles distant.

There are no anchorage areas near the San Leandro Marina, so all boaters wanting to visit the area should contact the harbormaster or one of the yacht clubs prior to arrival. Both yacht clubs have limited guest slips, but both have excellent clubhouse facilities.

Services of interest to visiting boaters include a fuel dock and restaurants at the marina, and a bank, supermarket, and post office within one mile of the marina.

⚓ **San Leando Harbormaster** tel: 800.559.7245

⚓ **Spinnaker Yacht Club** pos: 37°41.81'N, 122°11.50'W; tel: 510.351.7905

⚓ **San Leandro Yacht Club** tel: 510.351.3102

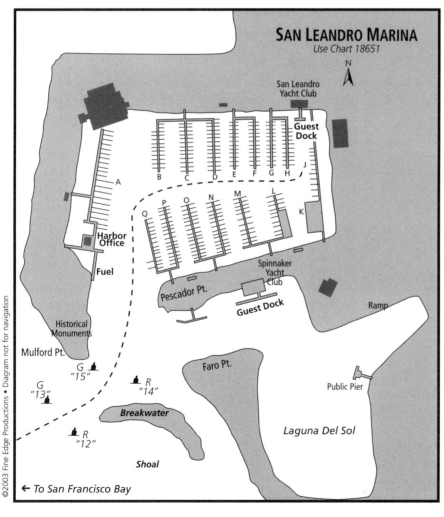

SAN LEANDRO MARINA
Use Chart 18651

©2003 Fine Edge Productions • Diagram not for navigation

Redwood City
Chart 18652; 6.2 mi SE of Coyote Pt.
Entrance (outer) light "2": 37°33.17'N,
122°11.74'W
Westpoint Slough (entr to anchorages):
37°31.19'N, 122°12.32'W
Westpoint Slough anchor: 37°31.08'N,
122°12.25'W
Downtown position: 37°29.78'N, 122°13.20'W

Redwood City Municipal Marina, just S of the port, can accommodate about 225 small craft. Other small-craft facilities are SW of the Municipal Marina. (CP, 33rd Ed.)

The Redwood City area has three major marinas. Boaters cruising to this destination will go under the San Mateo Bridge and follow a southwest course, staying in the ship channel. The channel into Redwood City exits to the starboard of the ship channel, 3.1 miles beyond the bridge.

Like other South Bay destinations, Redwood City has a dredged channel into the marinas—in this case a 3.25-mile channel. Unlike other South Bay areas, the channel at Redwood City has depths of 40 feet or more, enough for the cargo ships that visit the harbor, so visitors do not have to worry about going aground as long as they stay in the channel.

Visiting boaters will proceed past the piers where ships are often loading or unloading to the first of the marinas, the Redwood City Yacht Harbor, which is off the port side of the channel. This municipal marina usually has guest berths available for visiting boaters.

The Sequoia Yacht Club, located in the marina, keeps a guest berth open for use by visiting yacht club members.

The Redwood City Yacht Harbor has two restaurants, but it has no other services for visiting boaters. Boaters who need boating supplies or repair facilities may have to go by rental car or taxi. The harbor has no fuel dock; in fact, none of the marinas in Redwood City has a fuel dock. The nearest fuel dock is at Coyote Point.

The second major marina at Redwood City is Pete's Harbor. The slips at Pete's are normally full, so you should call ahead if you want to

visit. Pete's Harbor is the site of a popular restaurant.

The third major marina at Redwood City, the new Bair Island Marina, has concrete docks that will accommodate boats to 60 feet.

Pete's Harbor and Bair Island Marina are within walking distance of restaurants, a marine and RV supply house, a dive shop, a canvas shop, and movie theaters. A 3-mile trail along the levee around Bair Island provides a remarkable opportunity to view many species of shorebirds.

⚓ **Redwood City Yacht Harbor** position: 37°30.20'N, 122°12.87'W; tel: 650.306.4150 or VHF 16

⚓ **Peninsula Marina** position: 37°29.81'N, 122°13.22'W

⚓ **Bair Island Marina** tel: 650.701.1382

⚓ **Pete's Harbor** position: 37°30.05'N, 122°13.27'W; tel: 650.366.0922

⚓ **Sequoia Yacht Club** tel: 650.361.9472

Coyote Point Marina (San Mateo)
Charts 18651, 18652; 2.3 mi SE of SFO Intl Airport
Entrance (outer) light "1": 37°35.61'N,
122°18.76'W
Entrance (inner): 37°35.44'N, 122°18.92'W

Coyote Point is covered by a heavy growth of trees and is raised as an island. It is the most prominent point on the S bay. . . . The entrance channel, marked by a private lighted range and two private lights, had a reported controlling depth of 9 feet in 1994. . . . Transients should report to the harbormaster's office on the NW side of the harbor for berth assignment; guest berths are usually available. A harbor patrol boat is maintained. (CP, 33rd Ed.)

Coyote Point Marina sits at the base of steep bluffs that rise to a hill creating the appearance of an island along an otherwise flat coastline of the Peninsula. The entire point, preserved years ago as part of the San Mateo County Recreation Area, is covered with California live oak trees making its location one of the loveliest in the South Bay Area.

The marina has over 500 slips, some of which are available for visiting boats; reservations are required several days in advance; electricity, gas and diesel are available. Coyote Point Yacht club, at the south end of the marina, has guest dock for reciprocal yacht club members. Attractions include a swimming beach and park north of the marina, Coyote Point Museum for Environmental Education, and a golf course. Groceries and marine products are available in San Mateo or Burlingame, a good two-mile-bike ride from the marina.

⚓ **Harbormaster** position: 37°35.31'N, 122°19.08'W; tel: 650.573.2594; website: www.coyote-pointmarina.org

⚓ **Guest dock,** office, fuel dock, & pumpout position: 37°35.44'N, 122°19.08'W

⚓ **Coyote Point Yacht Club** position: 37°35.24'N, 122°18.94'W; tel: 650.347.6730

Oyster Point Marina (South San Francisco)

Chart 18652
Entrance (outer) lt "1": 37°39.85'N, 122°22.14'W
Entrance (inner): 37°39.85'N, 122°22.42'W

Oyster Point, a low filled area, is the site of a small-boat harbor accommodating about 570 boats. Depths of about 6 feet are in the harbor. The entrance channels E and NE of the harbor are marked by private lights. . . .

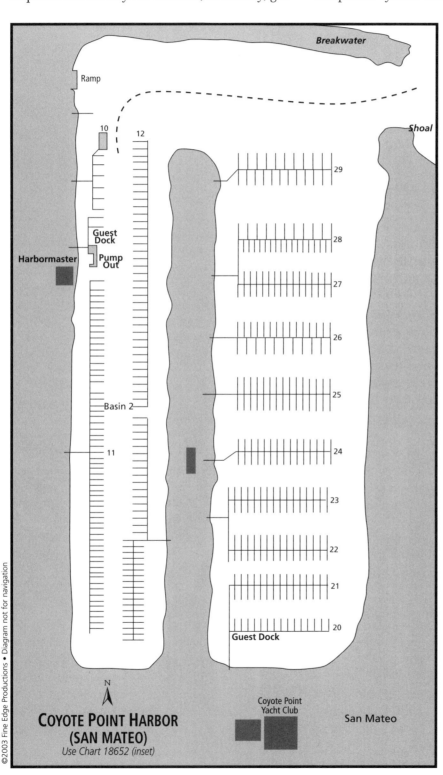

COYOTE POINT HARBOR (SAN MATEO)
Use Chart 18652 (inset)

©2003 Fine Edge Productions • Diagram not for navigation

Franklin Delano Roosevelt's Potomac *sails on San Francisco Bay*

Transients should report to the harbormaster's office for berth assignment. (CP, 33rd Ed.)

Oyster Point Marina has over 500 slips with space for a few guest boats; call ahead for availability. There is also a concrete fishing pier visitors can use. The Oyster Point Marina Harbormaster can be reached over VHF 16 or by telephone as listed below. Facilities include laundromat, boat and maintenance repair, fuel, pump-out station, and showers. Provisions and a restaurant are within walking distance.

Oyster Point Yacht Club has guest berths for reciprocal yacht club members. Call well in advance for space availability.

⚓ **Oyster Point Marina Harbormaster** tel: 650.952.0808; website: www.smharbor.com

⚓ **Oyster Point Yacht Club** tel: 650.873.5166 (weekends)

Oyster Cove Marina

Charts 18651, 18652; 0.8 mi NE of San Bruno Pt
Entrance (inner) "13": 37°40.07'N, 122°23.21'W

Boaters visiting Oyster Cove Marina will proceed 3 miles south after passing the Hunters

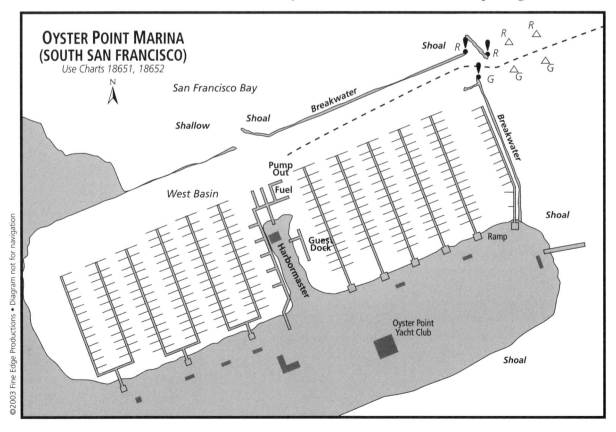

Point Naval Shipyard facilities. A mile-long channel leads from the South Bay into the Brisbane and Oyster Cove marinas. Brisbane Marina exits to the starboard 0.50 mile from the beginning of the channel. Oyster Cove Marina exits to the port side 1.0 mile from the beginning of the channel. Since the water outside this channel is shallow, do not stray outside the markers.

Oyster Cove Marina has 235 slips and welcomes visiting boaters. Although no fuel is available at the marina, nearby Oyster Point Marina does have fuel. The area has no haul-out facility, and boat repair facilities are limited. A West Marine store and restaurants are located about 2-1/2 miles from the marina, making a rental car or taxi essential for most visiting boaters.

⚓ **Oyster Cove Harbormaster** tel: 650.952.5540 or VHF 16

Brisbane Marina at Sierra Point

Charts 18651, 18652; 2.7 mi S of Hunters Pt
Entrance (outer) "1": 37°40.62'N, 122°22.73
Entrance (inner) "6": 37°40.21'N, 122°22.67'W

One of the largest marinas in the area, Brisbane Marina has 570 slips. The harbormaster attempts to keep some slips open for visiting boaters but recommends calling ahead to check on slip availability. The Sierra Point Yacht Club, located in the marina, has no guest slips.

Boaters are cautioned to stay carefully inside the channel markers since the water on either side of the channel is shallow. Facilities

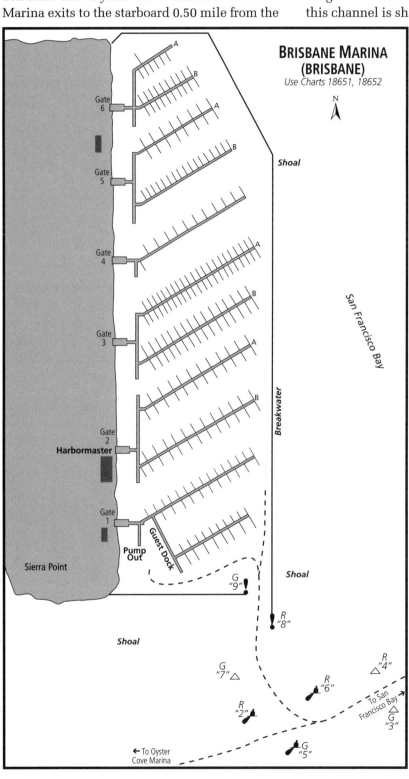

BRISBANE MARINA
(BRISBANE)
Use Charts 18651, 18652

at Brisbane are limited. A restaurant is located at the marina, but marina repair facilities and a chandlery are not within comfortable walking distance.

⚓ **Brisbane Marina Harbormaster** tel: 650.583.6975 or VHF 16

⚓ **Sierra Point Yacht Club tel:** 650.952.0651

Candlestick Park
Chart 18651; 4.7 mi N of SFO Airport
Anchor: 37°42.40'N, 122°22.77'W

If you're a sports fan, on occasion you can join like-minded mariners at anchor, off the ballpark in a nautical "tailgate" party. You can hear the sounds of the fans in the stadium while watching the game on television close-up.

Anchor in about 1 fathom over mud; good holding. Avoid the shoal water further west.

Hunters Point
Chart 18651; 1.4 mi E of Candlestick Park
Position: 37°43.29'N, 122°21.31'W

> . . . *a Naval restricted area is offshore of Hunters Point.* (CP, 33rd, Ed.)

The complex at Hunters Point is a major landmark for taking bearings in the South Bay.

Central Basin Anchorage (SFO)
Chart 18650; 1.5 mi S of Bay Bridge
Entrance: 37°45.98'N, 122°22.82'W
Anchor: 37°45.97N, 122°23.05'W

> *Central Basin . . . has depths of 10 to 24 feet. Limited berthing facilities are on the W shore of the basin. Gasoline, water, covered and open storage, and some small-boat supplies are available. There are a surfaced boat ramp and a portable lift; hull and engine repairs can be made.* (CP, 33rd Ed.)

Approximately 1 mile south of South Beach Harbor Marina, Central Basin provides an opportunity to anchor out along the San Francisco City shoreline. This anchorage has good protection from prevailing winds, but the scenery is less than exciting. The old pier immediately to the north is in the process of falling into the Bay, and the commercial shipyards immediately south of the anchorage are noisy and dirty. Ships being brought into or taken out of this large facility by tugs often need much of the anchorage area for maneuvering. For this

South Beach Harbor, China Cove anchorage

Bob & Carol Mehaffy

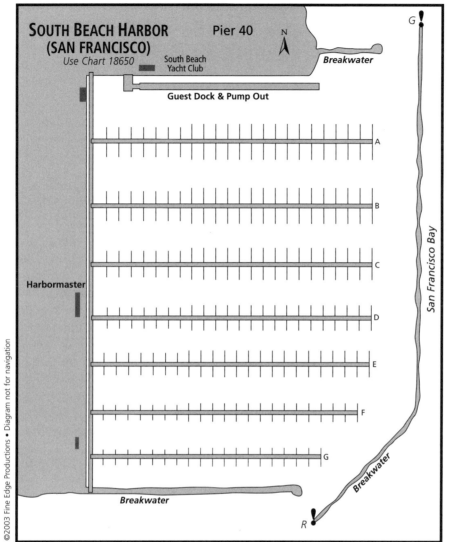

SOUTH BEACH HARBOR (SAN FRANCISCO)
Use Chart 18650
Pier 40
South Beach Yacht Club
Breakwater
Guest Dock & Pump Out
Harbormaster
San Francisco Bay
Breakwater
Breakwater
©2003 Fine Edge Productions • Diagram not for navigation

South Beach Harbor . . . is a marina with 700 slips. . . . Berths are assigned by the harbormaster; VHF-FM channel 16 is monitored 24 hours a day or telephone (415) 495-4911. (CP, 33rd Ed.)

Boaters can enter South Beach Harbor through either end of the breakwater and tie up at the guest dock at the northeast end of the marina or in one of its vacant slips. This harbor is protected from the wind and waves by the nearby shipping terminal warehouses. From here you can take public transportation into the city or walk to some of the City's fine nearby restaurants.

South Beach Harbor, 0.5 mile southeast of the city end of the Bay Bridge, keeps a few slips open for visiting boaters. This marina is a favorite of visiting boaters because it's protected from

reason, few boaters feel comfortable leaving their boats unattended here.

Ashore at Central Basin is the San Francisco Boat Works. Small craft can arrange for haulouts at this facility. Two nearby restaurants serve lunches and dinners. Boaters dropping anchor at Central Basin can leave their dinghies at the docks behind the Mission Rock Resort if they want to go ashore for lunch or dinner.

Anchor in 20 feet of water over a soft mud bottom.

South Beach Harbor (SFO)

Chart 18650; 0.55 mi S of Bay Bridge
Entrance (S): 37°46.70'N, 122°23.12'W
Entrance (N): 37°46.93'N, 122°23.07'W

the wind and surge that plague many of the other marinas in the city, and it gives easy access to San Francisco restaurants and public transportation. From South Beach, you can take public transportation to Fisherman's Wharf, where you can catch the ferry to Alcatraz Island or take one of the legendary San Francisco cable cars to downtown. You can go aboard the last surviving Liberty ship, the *Jeremiah O'Brien,* berthed near South Beach, for a memorable tour.

When approaching South Beach Harbor, you'll see hundreds of sailboat masts behind the breakwater. You can use either the north or the south entrance, but enter slowly and watch for exiting boats.

⚓ **South Beach Harbormaster** tel: 415.495.4911

⚓ **South Beach Yacht Club** tel: 415.495.2295

⚓ **Mariposa Hunters Point Yacht Club** tel: 415.495.9344

⚓ **Bay View Boat Club** tel: 415.495.9500; guest slips available; website: www.bvbc.org

THE NORTH BAY

The Richmond-San Rafael Bridge makes an arbitrary dividing line between the Central Bay and the North Bay. Whereas the Central Bay has cities in virtually every direction you look— along with constant boat and ship traffic—the North Bay is quiet. Many boaters who keep their boats in the Central Bay go to the North Bay for a peaceful escape.

As you pass under the Richmond-San Rafael Bridge, you cross San Pablo Strait and turn eastward. Past the Brothers Islands, San Pablo Bay opens up. For a much faster trip, time your passage to go with the tide rather than fight against it. From San Pablo you have access to Carquinez Strait, Suisun Bay, or the Delta.

Point San Pablo
Charts 18653, 18649; 5.6 mi N of Angel Island

A small-boat basin used by commercial and sport fishermen is 0.5 mile SE from Point San Pablo.

A private yacht basin is 1 mile SE from Point San Pablo. A channel leading to the basin has reported depths of about 2 feet. (CP, 33rd Ed.)

San Pablo Bay
Chart 18654; N of Pt San Pablo & Richmond

San Pablo Bay is nearly circular, 10 miles long in a NE direction, with a greatest width of 8 miles. . . . There is considerable traffic through the bay. . . . Mariners are advised that winds in San Pablo Bay may be particularly strong and must be taken into consideration. . . . (CP, 33rd Ed.)

San Pablo Bay is quite shallow, and Chart 18654 is in *feet,* not fathoms. To enter both San Rafael Creek and Petaluma River you must stay inside the well-marked, dredged channels.

San Rafael Creek
Charts 18653, 18649; 6.7 mi NW of Angel Island
Entrance (outer) "17": 37°57.45'N, 122°27.43'W
Yacht Harbor position: 37°58.03'N, 122°30.80'W

San Rafael Creek . . . is used by many small craft basing at the city of San Rafael. A dredged channel leads across the flats in San Rafael Bay into San Rafael Creek to a turning basin about 1.1 miles above the mouth, thence for another 0.2 mile above the turning basin. In June-August 1999, the controlling depth in the entrance channel was 3 1/2 feet (5 1/2 feet at midchannel) to the mouth of the creek; thence in December 1997, the midchannel controlling depth was less than 1 foot from the mouth of the creek to the turning basin about 400 feet below the Grand Avenue Bridge. The controlling depth was 2 feet within the limits of the turning basin. . . .

The municipal yacht harbor is on the S side of San Rafael Creek, about 400 yards E of the turning basin, and there are numerous small-craft facilities elsewhere along the creek. (CP, 33rd Ed.)

San Rafael Creek, inside San Rafael Bay, is the first possible moorage north of the Richmond-San Rafael Bridge. While *Coast Pilot* information may discourage boats with draft of more than 2 feet from entering the creek, if you pay careful attention to the condition of shoaling in the channel and the proper tide level, with a deeper draft boats you should have no problem. The entrance channel, shown on Charts 18653 and 18649, is marked with porthand markers only. Boaters should enter at G"17" and remain within the channel the entire way. Minimum depth in the channel—which is subject to shoaling—is 5 1/2 feet. There is no anchoring within San Rafael Creek.

Loch Lomond Marina, on the north side of the entrance channel, is the first of three San Rafael marinas and the easiest to enter. The marked marina channel turns north off the San Rafael Channel, 1.35 miles from G"17," and marina personnel tell us that they keep the channel dredged to 7 feet. Loch Lomond is a full-service marina with fuel, pump out, groceries and snack shop. Transient slips are on a space-available basis; the marina suggests that you call ahead for a slip.

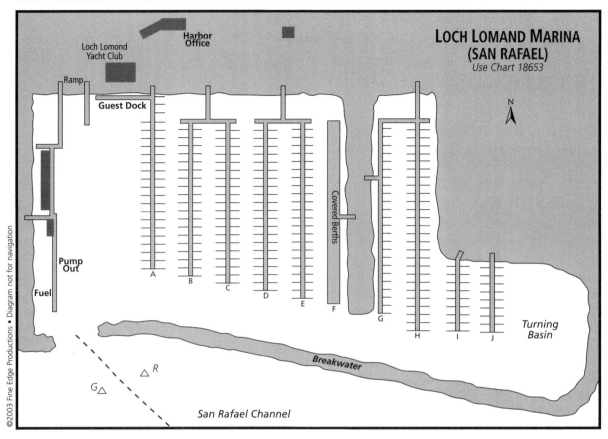

Marin Yacht Club, located within the first basin (on the north) where the channel meets San Rafael Creek, has guest slips available for reciprocal club members. Lowries Yacht Harbor, about a half-mile further in and also on the north side of the creek, has some guest berths (no fuel); call ahead for availability. San Rafael city center is 2 miles from Lowries, the closest marina.

For entertainment you may want to tour the Marin County Civic Center, which was Frank Lloyd Wright's last project, or take a self-guided walking tour through downtown San Rafael which includes a visit to the replica of Mission San Rafael Arcangel. For a little workout, if you carry a bicycle on board, you can follow San Pedro Point Road east to the point, then north through China Camp State Park.

⚓ **Loch Lomond Marina** entrance: 37°58.28'N, 122°29.02'W; tel: 415.454.7228; website: www.lochlomondmarina.com

⚓ **Marin Yacht Club** entrance: 37°58.20'N, 122°29.96'W; tel: 415.453.9366

⚓ **Lowrie's Yacht Harbor** entrance: 37°57.99'N, 122°30.47'W; tel: 415.454.7595

⚓ **San Rafael Yacht Harbor** tel: 415.456.1600

⚓ **San Rafael Yacht Club** position: 37°58.15'N, 122°31.06'W; tel: 415.459.9828

McNears Beach & China Camp Anchorage
Chart 18654; 7.8 mi N of Angel Island
McNears Beach anchor: 37°59.72'N, 122°27.05'W
China Camp anchor: 38°00.09'N, 122°27.46'W

McNears, or China Camp, appeals to boaters wanting a quiet anchorage close to the Central Bay. (These two anchorages are so close to one another that most people don't distinguish between them.) In addition to the quiet, McNears and China Camp have less fog than

Bob & Carol Mehaffy

China Camp anchorage

Surprise Find on San Rafael Creek
by DCD & RHD

It was an unlikely place to find a 42-foot William Garden Porpoise ketch, but there she was tied to a float a few feet from Highway 101—a salty-looking ship surrounded by land. *Liddy Mae* was her name, and she sat abandoned by her builder in San Rafael, a "For Sale" sign on the port side of her bow.

The story of *Liddy Mae*'s abandonment came in pieces as we talked to the broker. Her owner had left Seattle to begin a world cruise. The sailboat was unfinished, but her owner planned to finish her as he, his wife and son sailed down the coast. Their voyage began inauspiciously. As she was leaving Juan de Fuca Strait in the middle of the night, a Russian fishing trawler hit *Liddie Mae*. She went home to make repairs, and set out again.

Following a rough pounding off Cape Mendocino, the crew pulled in to San Francisco Bay. Giving up their thought of a world cruise, they turned the boat around and headed back for Seattle. Rounding Cape Mendocino for the second time, they took another pounding and returned to San Francisco. Enough! They "parked" the boat in San Rafael where they couldn't see the open ocean and hopped a bus to Seattle and terra firma.

Liddie Mae had a good sturdy hull and when we took her out for a sea trial—a quick day sail out of the Golden Gate toward the Farallons and back—we decided she was the boat for us. We plunked down our down payment and a month later motored out of San Rafael, navigating the back channels without a VHF or echo sounder—our keel of 5 1/2 feet draft. We committed to rebuilding and outfitting her for the Great Southern Ocean and quickly changed her name to *le Dauphin Amical*. We became hooked on a life of small boat exploration, which hasn't diminished in 160,000 miles of cruising!

other Bay Area locations, and the winds are typically light.

As you pass under the central span of the Richmond-San Rafael Bridge, set a course north to head directly for the Sisters Islands, approximately 2 miles away. Pass on either side of the low-lying, barren Sisters, though you may wish to avoid the passage between Point San Pedro and the Sisters, since tugs with barges occasionally frequent this area.

Exploring the estuary near China Camp by dinghy

On the approach to McNears Beach Anchorage, the area between the Sisters and the pier at McNears has depths generally less than 10 feet at low water. Passing the pier, stay at least 200 yards offshore to avoid the shallow water.

The favorite anchorage area at McNears is 400 yards north of the pier and 200 yards from the beach. The current here is frequently strong enough to hold anchored boats beam-on to the wind. While this position is not dangerous, it can be a little unsettling until you've become accustomed to it. You can take your dinghy ashore and enjoy the park or get treats at the small snack shop open during the summer.

China Camp Anchorage, about 1 mile north of McNears, is also shallow. And, like McNears, the bottom at China Camp is hard clay. Go ashore at China Camp, leaving your dinghy on the beach beside the foot of the old pier, and visit the small museum chronicling the lives of the Chinese families who lived here in the late 1800s. These residents harvested the once plentiful grass shrimp in San Pablo Bay. Another reason to go ashore at China Camp is to take the extensive hike along the shoreline north of the museum. This trail wanders through the oaks and brush, where deer and quail are commonplace.

McNears and China Camp are isolated. Other than the snack bar at McNears and a small restaurant at China Camp, both open only on weekends and only during the summer. The nearest services are in the Loch Lomond area, 1.5 miles from McNears.

Anchor (McNears) in 8-10 feet at low water on a clay bottom with good holding.

Anchor (China Camp), about 200 yards from shore and 100 yards south of the old pier, in 8-10 feet at low water over hard clay with good holding.

Petaluma River

Chart 18652; 15.0 mi N of Angel Island
Entrance (outer) "3": 38°02.76'N, 122°25.54'W
Entrance (outer) R"6": 38°04.24'N, 122°25.65'W
Entrance (inner) R"20": 38°06.63'N, 122°29.32'W
Petaluma Turning Basin: 38°14.12'N, 122°38.27'W

Petaluma River enters San Pablo Bay on the NW side. . . . A marked dredged channel leads through San Pablo Bay to the entrance of the Petaluma River. In August 2000 the controlling depths were 3.2 feet (6.4 feet at midchannel) to the mouth of the river; thence in 1996 5.5 feet at mid channel to a fixed bridge, about 11 miles above the mouth, thence 8 feet at midchannel to

McNear Canal and to a turning basin at Petaluma, with depths of 7 to 10 feet (lesser along the edges) in the basin. (CP, 33rd Ed.)

A cruise up the Petaluma River to the town of Petaluma can provide a great challenge for the navigator. The mid-channel water depths are slightly less than 6 feet in places, and the bottom of the San Pablo Bay often bares at low water outside the channel markers. Boaters should make this passage on a flood tide to enable them to float off if they go aground and

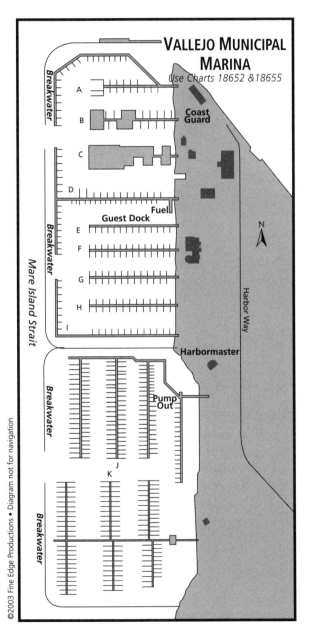

then proceed slowly as they transit the channel through San Pablo Bay.

A railroad bridge crosses the river some 5 miles from the entrance to the Petaluma River Channel. Unless a train is nearby, the bridge stands open, and boaters can proceed through carefully. Note that a current flows briskly through on strong ebb and flood tides; take this current into account when passing through the bridge. The fixed bridge (Highway 37), just north of the railroad bridge, has a 70-foot vertical clearance.

The Petaluma Marina, on the starboard side of the channel, 11 miles north of the Highway 37 bridge, usually has guest slips, but visiting boaters should call ahead since demand is heavy for slips during spring and summer months. Visiting boaters often leave their boats in Petaluma Marina and take their tenders to the town of Petaluma, slightly more than 1 mile farther up the channel.

Those boaters wishing to take their boats into the turning basin in the center of Petaluma must call the Petaluma Visitors Program office at least 4 hours (preferably 24 hours) before their arrival to have the D Street Bridge raised. Once inside, they can dock at the city pier to port if space is available or drop anchor in the turning basin if room is available. Be forewarned that the turning basin becomes crowded at times, so plan to be flexible.

Petaluma has a haul-out facility and limited marine supplies. Restaurants, shops, and historic buildings abound in this attractive small town.

⚓ **Petaluma Marina Harbormaster** tel: 707.778.4489

⚓ **Petaluma Visitors Program** tel: 707.769.0429

⚓ **Petaluma Yacht Club** tel: 707.765.9725

⚓ **Port Sonoma Marina** position: 38°06.93'N, 122°30.14'W

⚓ **Petaluma Marina** position: 38°13.70'N, 122°36.78'W

Vallejo

Charts 18652, 18655; 12.8 mi NE of Richmond
Vallejo Municipal Marina (S entr): 38°06.52'N, 122°16.27'W
Vallejo Municipal Marina (N entr): 38°06.61'N, 122°16.34'W

The Vallejo Marina, S of the Vallejo-Mare Island Causeway on the E side of Mare Island Strait, has accommodations for about 500 boats. Other small-craft facilities are also on the E side of the strait. . . . (CP, 33rd Ed.)

Boaters visiting San Francisco Bay with time to spare often enjoy venturing east beyond San Pablo Bay for a few days. Vallejo Marina, in Mare Island Strait, and Benicia Marina, in Carquinez Strait, are two easy half-day sails from the Central Bay, as well as good intermediate stops for boaters heading up into the Sacramento-San Joaquin Delta. To avoid turning either passage into an all-day ordeal, however, boaters should time their voyages —whether going to or returning from these destinations—to go *with* the tide.

Vallejo Municipal Marina has about 800 slips, and the harbormaster can accommodate nearly all visiting boaters. This marina is on the east side of Mare Island Strait, 2.6 miles north of Carquinez Strait, which joins the strait a mile west of the Carquinez Bridge. A new Coast Guard station has recently been relocated on the marina site.

Vallejo Municipal Marina has a full-service boat yard and a fuel dock. A large launch ramp is located one mile south of the marina. It offers berths up to 105 feet long and end ties for even larger boats, with guest slips available, gated docks, and night security. Fuel docks, pump-out facilities and a laundromat are available, and there's a mile-long waterfront promenade with two restaurants. There are no grocery stores within walking distance. The marina office is open seven days a week.

When you approach Vallejo Marina, you pass the Vallejo Yacht Club 200 yards south of the marina. Although the club has guest docks, do not attempt to enter the club basin at low water; many boats have gone aground on the bar at the

entrance, which has less than 4 feet of water at low tide. The marina, recognizable by its blue-roof buildings, is a safer place for visiting boaters.

⚓ **Vallejo Municipal Marina** tel: 707.648.4370; website: www.ci.vallejo.ca.us/marina.html

⚓ **Vallejo Yacht Club** entrance: reservations required; tel: 707.643.1254

Napa River

Charts 18652, 18654; continuation of Mare Isl Strt above Naval shipyard
Entrance: 38°07.29'N, 122°16.83'W

Napa River . . . is used by barges and pleasure boats. . . . A dredged channel leads from the Vallejo-Mare Island Causeway Bridge to a turning basin at Jacks Bend, thence to the head of navigation at the 3rd Street Bridge in Napa, 13 miles above the causeway bridge. In April 1999, the midchannel controlling depth was 8 feet from the Vallejo-Mare Island Causeway Bridge to Horseshoe Bend. . . .

A small-craft basin is on the W side of Napa River opposite Bull Island, 8 miles above the Vallejo-Mare Island Causeway, and several other small-craft facilities are elsewhere on the river. (CP, 33rd Ed.)

A Napa River cruise is the perfect way to enjoy peace and quiet as you make a transition from busy San Francisco Bay to the warm vineyards in the rolling hills of Napa Valley. The river is navigable for 13 miles, passing a number of bridges—some swing, others draw.

Navigating Napa River requires local knowledge. In addition to studying Chart 18652, we recommend consulting Carolyn and Bob Mehaffy's book *Cruising Guide to San Francisco Bay.* Napa Valley Marina is 7.0 miles northwest of Vallejo Marina. It has guest slips available; reservations are required. Provisions are available on site. Napa Valley Yacht Club is 0.25 mile north of the Maxwell Lift Bridge (Imola) and 4.1 miles northeast of Napa Valley Marina. Prior arrangements with the Yacht Club and the bridge operator are necessary. Arrangements to open Maxwell Bridge require 72 hours advance notice.

⚓ **Napa Valley Marina** position: 38°13.22'N, 122°18.65'W; tel: 707.252.8011

⚓ **Napa Valley Yacht Club** position: 38°17.12'N, 122°17.16'W; tel: 707.224.3030; website: www.nvyc.com

⚓ **Maxwell Bridge operators (CalTrans)** tel: 707.253.4919 (must call 72 hrs in advance prior to transit)

Carquinez Strait
Chart 18656; 11.6 mi NE of Richmond

Six-mile-long Carquinez Strait connects San Pablo and Suisun Bays. For the first 3.5 miles it is a little less than 0.5 mile wide, and then widens to about 1 mile. It is deep throughout with the exception of a small stretch of flats on the N shore, and a small shoal area in the bight on the S shore near the E end.

. . . In October 1991, tidal currents in Carquinez Strait were reported to deviate significantly from official predictions published by the National Ocean Service. Mariners should exercise caution and discretion in the use of published tidal current predictions. (CP, 33rd Ed.)

Elliot Cove
Chart 18656; 0.55 mi E of Carquinez Bridge
Entrance: 38°03.94'N, 122°12.83'W

A marina is on the S shore just W of the highway bridges, and a small-boat basin is in Elliot Cove on the N side of the strait opposite Crockett. (CP, 33rd Ed.)

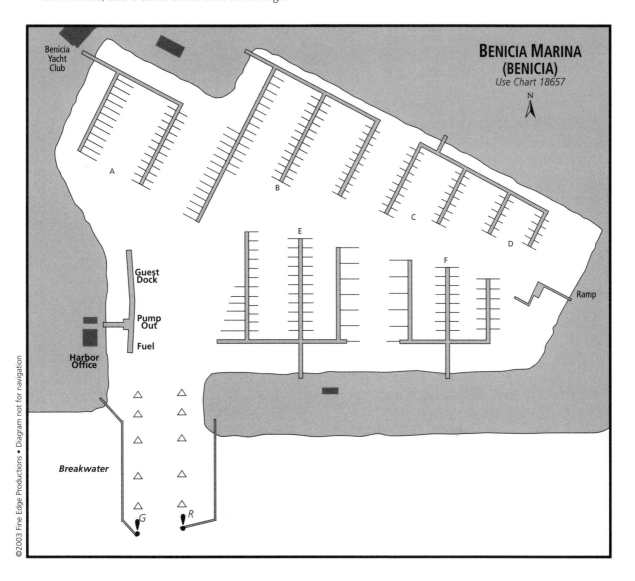

BENICIA MARINA (BENICIA) Use Chart 18657

©2003 Fine Edge Productions • Diagram not for navigation

Historic California State Capitol, Benicia

Glen Cove Marina
Chart 18655; 0.85 mi E of Carquinez Bridge
Position: 38°03.87'N, 122°12.52'W

Located in Elliot Bay, on the north shore of Carquinez Strait, Glen Cove Marina is a small marina where some boaters stop while en route to the Delta. The harbormaster typically keeps a few slips open for visiting boaters, but he advises visitors to make advance reservations because demand often exceeds slip availability.

Plan to arrive at Glen Cove at high water on slack tide, for shoaling frequently reduces the depth at the entrance to less than 6 feet at low water. In addition, the current at the entrance during strong ebb and flood tides can cause serious problems for unwary boaters.

Glen Cove has no fuel dock. Restaurants, supermarkets, and marine supply businesses are located 2 miles or more from the marina.

⚓ **Glen Cove Harbormaster** tel: 707.552.3236

Benicia Marina
Chart 18657; N shore at the E end of Carquinez Strait
Entrance: 38°02.53'N, 122°09.45'W

A marina, protected by breakwaters, is at Benicia.
(CP, 33rd Ed.)

Benicia Marina—a popular destination for Bay Area boaters that has been voted several times as the best marina in Northern California—basks in warmer weather than most Central Bay marinas.

The entrance to the marina is on the left side of Carquinez Strait, 3.5 miles east of the Carquinez Bridge. This marina, like so many in the area, has a continuing problem with shoaling at the entrance. Call the marina to check depths before entering at low water. The marina attempts to keep the entrance dredged to 7 feet, but shoaling occasionally reduces that depth considerably.

The popularity of the marina sometimes

makes getting a slip impossible on some summer weekends. Call ahead (tel: 707.745.2628) before you set a course for Benicia. The marina has a fuel dock and a launch ramp.

The lovely town of Benicia—named after Vallejo's wife—is within walking distance of the marina. The city, which served as California's state capital from 1853 to 1854 has preserved and restored the capitol building as Benicia Capitol Historic Park. The town features an old-fashioned farmer's market on Thursday nights during six months of the year where you can enjoy artisans, Dixieland jazz, and local foods.

Martinez Marina
Chart 18657; 4.5 mi SE of Carquinez Bridge
Entrance: 38°01.67'N, 122°08.30'W

There are three wharves extending out to deep water at Martinez . . . A small-boat harbor, protected by breakwaters, is on the E side of the pier. . . . In 1994, shoaling to a depth of about 4 feet was reported at the entrance to the marina. (CP, 33rd Ed.)

The Martinez Marina accommodates visiting boaters with two guest docks to the right as you enter the marina. Slips are available for boats up to 45 feet on a first-come, first-served basis. A fuel dock, pump-out station, launch ramp and haulout are located near the office at the southwest corner of the marina. Most provisions are within walking distance, and boaters who arrive after hours should tie up at the fuel dock until morning.

⚓ **Martinez Marina** tel: 925.313.0942; monitors VHF 16

Suisun Bay
Chart 18656; 5.3 mi E of Carquinez Bridge
West Entrance: 38°02.81'N, 122°06.98'W

Suisun Bay is a broad shallow body of water with marshy shores and filled with numerous marshy islands, many of which have been reclaimed and are now under cultivation. It is practically the delta of the Sacramento and San Joaquin Rivers which empty into the E part of the bay. Two narrow winding channels lead to the mouths of the rivers. They are marked by lights.

Several small-craft facilities are at Suisun City. . . . (CP, 33rd Ed.)

Suisun City
Charts 18652, 18655; 13.0 mi NE of Benicia

A dredged channel leads from Suisun Bay into the entrance to the slough. In 1990, the controlling depth was 6 1/2 feet. The entrance channel is marked by lights. Above the dredged channel the channel has a controlling depth of 8 feet to Suisun City, 12 miles above the entrance. The mean range of tide is about 4 feet. (CP, 33rd Ed.)

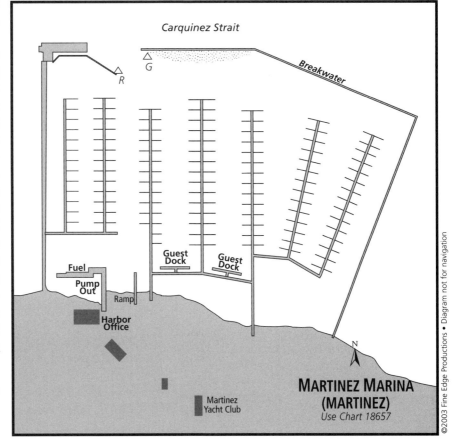

Sacramento-San Joaquin River Delta
Charts 18662, 18664

The 1,000-mile-long Sacramento-San Joaquin River Delta is a labyrinth of fresh-water systems composed primarily of fertile agricultural islands that sit below sea level, protected by a stout system of levees. This waterway, which is fed by five major rivers, including the Sacramento and the San Joaquin, offers over 100 marinas and waterside resorts, plenty of campgrounds, and waterside restaurants, grocery stores, bait and tackle shops, and over 50 boat launching facilities. Most marinas and waterside resorts that offer public facilities have guest docks; with only a handful of exceptions, there is no charge to use the dock for a few hours while you visit the marina facilities. There are almost no restrictions on anchoring out, although it would be unwise to anchor in the middle of a narrow channel or heavily used waterway. The only buoy-tie anchorages we know about in the Delta are next to Tinsley Island and they are private. A Danforth-type anchor seems to be most successful in the Delta.

Water depths in much of the Delta are controlled by tidal action. This condition extends to above Sacramento on the Sacramento River, and to above Mossdale on the San Joaquin River. The variation between high and low tides can be as much as 8 feet, but typically is 4 to 6 feet. While occasional droughts here have almost no negative effect on water recreation, floods can be devastating; during heavy flood times it's a good idea to stay away until things settle back down. Owners of vessels over six feet in height need to be aware of the bridges along their intended cruising routes; some open, some don't. Clearances vary with the tides. You can find most necessary information, including hours of operation for drawbridges, on the Delta maps or charts, or in a free bridge booklet available from the U.S. Coast Guard in Alameda.

Pittsburg Municipal Marina
Chart 18659; 13.0 mi E of Benicia
Harbor entrance: 38°02.45'N, 121°53.13'W
Small craft basin entr: 38°02.18'N, 121°52.91'W

Pittsburg, on the S side of New York Slough 12 miles E of Suisun Point bridges, is a manufacturing city with several deepwater berths. (CP, 33rd Ed.)

Located between the Sacramento and San Joaquin Rivers, Pittsburg is a post-industrial town in the process of re-inventing itself as a tourist attraction. The municipal marina here features two basins, each with its own entrance, but the east basin is closed until approximately mid-2003 for dredging and remodeling. You'll find guest slips usually available at the west basin, except during summertime when it's a good idea to call ahead for reservations. Full provisions and a fuel dock with gas and diesel are available on site, and there's a post office within walking distance.

Established in 1830, Pittsburg was first named New York of the Pacific, and later New York Landing. When coal was discovered in the nearby hills in 1903, the town was renamed Back Diamond, which was finally changed to Pittsburg in 1911.

⚓ **Pittsburg Municipal Marina** tel: 925.439.4958

Antioch Municipal Marina
Chart 18656; 16.0 mi E of Benicia
Marina entrance: 38°01.29'N, 121°49.29'W

Several small-craft facilities are at Pittsburg and Antioch. (CP, 33rd Ed.)

The relatively new Municipal Marina at Antioch is well protected and a popular stopping point for boaters on their way to and from the Delta. We found an average water depth in the marina of about 8 feet. The 305 concrete berths range from 24 to 70 feet, providing even floatation and clean, smooth dock surfaces. Unrented slips are usually available to visiting boaters; call ahead to inquire about availability and to make reservations. A fuel dock at the marina's entrance dispenses gas and diesel from 0830 to 1630 daily and also houses a free pump-out station, which is open 24 hours. If you're going ashore you'll find an excellent restaurant onsite and a sprawling wetlands preserve nearby with abundant bird-watching opportunities.

⚓ **Antioch Municipal Marina** tel: 925.779-6957; website: www.ci.antioch.ca.us

San Joaquin River
Charts 18661, 18659; 18.2 mi E of Vallejo
Stockton deepwater channel: 38°01.25'N, 121°48.66'W

San Joaquin River rises in the Sierra Nevada, flows 275 miles in a W direction, and enters Suisun Bay through New York Slough. The wind-ing river is navigable for deep-draft vessels to Stockton. The water is generally fresh at Antioch. The mean range of tide is about 3 feet from the entrance to Stockton. Major floods in the river valley may occur from November to April, caused by intense general storms of several days' duration. At the mouth of the river an ordinary flood will cause a rise of 8 feet and an extreme flood a rise of 10 feet in the river level. (CP, 33rd Ed.)

Waterfront Yacht Harbor (Stockton)
Charts 18663, 18661; 28.4 mi E of Pittsburg
Yacht Harbor position: 37°57.22'N, 121°17.86'W

Stockton, the county seat of San Joaquin County, is . . . on the SE corner of the broad delta formed by the confluence of the San Joaquin and Sacramento Rivers. . . .

In late autumn and early winter, clear still nights give rise to the formation of dense fogs, which normally settle in during the night and burn off sometime during the day. . . .

Small-craft facilities. Several small-craft facilities are at Stockton or nearby. (See the small-craft facilities tabulation on chart 18661 for services and supplies available.)

From its junction with Stockton Channel, the river has a controlling depth of about 3 feet for 70 miles to Hills Ferry, and is used only by small pleasure craft, fishermen, and an occasional small barge. The only facilities available are those dispensing gasoline, lubricants, and water at a few points. (CP, 33rd Ed)

Located in an area that was once used commercially for shipping and grain hauling, the Water Front Yacht Harbor is

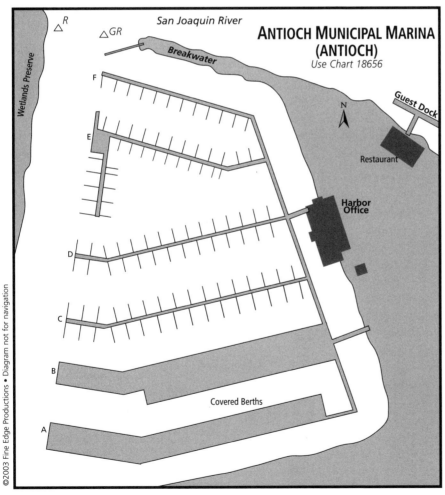

ANTIOCH MUNICIPAL MARINA (ANTIOCH)
Use Chart 18656

part of a restoration project that was completed in 1982. The marina, which features 175 covered and open berths, has an average depth of 15 feet. Guest berthing is available for a maximum of three days. The pump-out station and fuel dock with gas and diesel are at the end of the guest dock to the right as you enter; hours are 0830 to 1630 daily. The marina features four restaurants and a laundry facilities onsite, and a grocery store and post office are within walking distance.

⚓ **Waterfront Yacht Harbor** tel: 209.943.1848

Sacramento River
Charts 18661, 18662, 18664; W entr: 20.5 mi E of Vallejo
Entrance deep-water channel: 38°03.81'N, 121°51.15'W

The Sacramento River rises in the Trinity Mountains in N central California, flows S for 325 miles, and enters Suisun Bay on the N side of Sherman Island. Deep-draft vessels follow the lower Sacramento River to Cache Slough, 1.5 miles above Rio Vista Bridge, thence through a deepwater ship channel to Sacramento, a distance of 37 miles above the mouth of the river. Barges and other small craft also use Sacramento River all the way to Sacramento, a distance of 50 miles. Above Sacramento, small craft go to Colusa, 125 miles above the mouth, but there is no regular navigation above this point. (CP, 33rd Ed.)

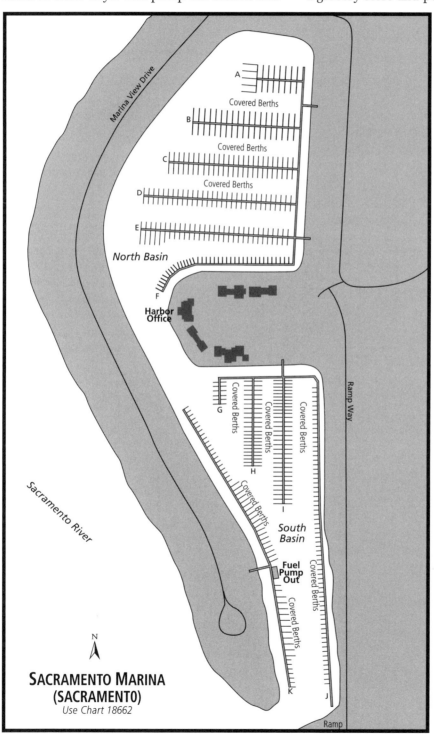

SACRAMENTO MARINA
(SACRAMENTO)
Use Chart 18662

Hiking the Headlands near Golden Gate Bridge

showers are also available. A free launch ramp is at the marina's entrance.

The marina is a quick 2 miles from the historic attractions of Old Town Sacramento, with easy freeway access to either I-5 or I-80. Other marinas in the area include the River Bank Marina and the River View Marina, both upriver from the Sacramento Marina.

⚓ **Sacramento Marina** tel: 916.264.5712; website: www.sacramenities.com /marina

Sacramento

Chart 18662; 36.6 mi NE of Pittsburg
Sacramento (Hwy 80 Bridge): 38°34.28'N, 121°30.95'W
Entrance at American River: 38°35.83'N, 121°30.51'W

Sacramento, the State capital, is the head of navigation for most of the shipping on the river, and is a distribution and transportation center in California and parts of Nevada and Oregon. The Port of Sacramento, at the head of the deep-water channel, is an important point for the interchange of cargo between rail, highway, and water transportation. (CP, 33rd Ed.)

Sacramento Marina

Chart 18662
Entrance: 38°33.65'N, 121°31.01'W

For boaters who make their way up the Sacramento River to the California State Capital, the Sacramento Marina offers 553 covered and open berths, with guest-slip accommodations (when available) for up to 15 days. The year-round fuel dock pumps mid-octane gasoline only (Sacramento Marina advertises the lowest gas prices in the area), with pump out, restrooms and telephone facilities nearby. Limited groceries and marine supplies and

A great wind for sailing on San Francisco Bay

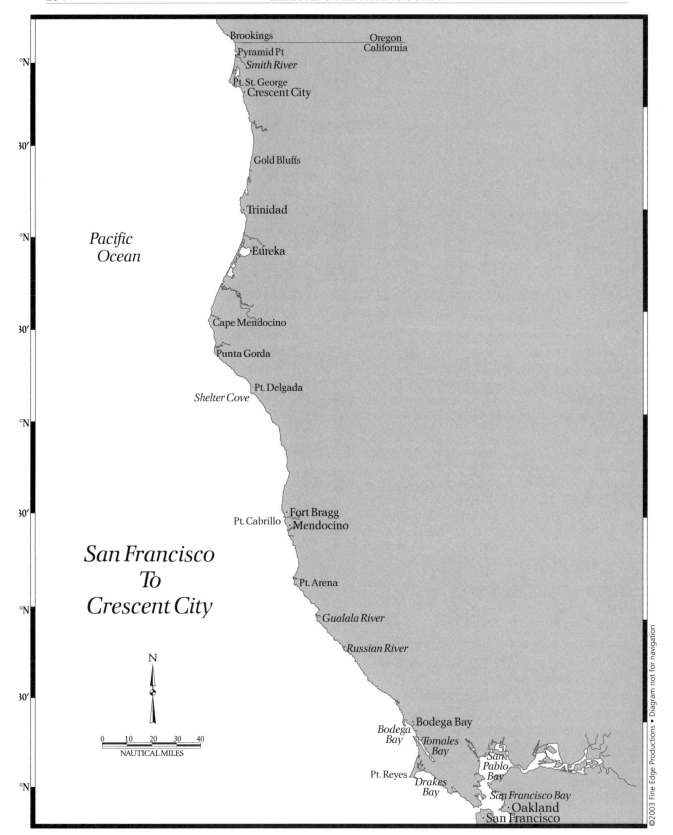

Brookings
Pyramid Pt
Smith River
Pt. St. George
Crescent City

Oregon
California

Gold Bluffs

Trinidad

*Pacific
Ocean*

Eureka

Cape Mendocino

Punta Gorda

Pt. Delgada
Shelter Cove

Fort Bragg
Pt. Cabrillo · Mendocino

*San Francisco
To
Crescent City*

Pt. Arena

Gualala River

Russian River

N

0   10   20   30   40
NAUTICAL MILES

Bodega Bay
*Bodega
Bay*   *Tomales
Bay*
*San
Pablo
Bay*
Pt. Reyes
*Drakes
Bay*   *San Francisco Bay*
· Oakland
San Francisco

°N
30'
°N
30'
°N
30'
°N
30'
°N

©2003 Fine Edge Productions • Diagram not for navigation

5

Northern California
San Francisco to Crescent City

Introduction

Northern California has some of the most rugged and isolated coastline along the entire Pacific Coast north of Mexico. The shoreline varies from cliffs, undulated hills, and mountainous terrain with gulches that dissect the coast.

Many off-lying rocks—some of which have arches—add to the scenic qualities while others lie undetected below the surface or announced only by surf that heaps up in unexpected places. Just inland from the Sonoma coast are vineyards that produce fine wines; farther north in Mendocino, Humboldt and Del Norte counties lie forests of giant redwoods broken by rivers whose shores offer warm, quiet recreation.

Eureka is the only major town of any size affording a choice of facilities and air connections. Fort Bragg, a small, scenic community on the Noyo River, and Crescent City—the most northerly harbor inside the California border—have good shelter but limited facilities. Drakes Bay and Bodega Bay offer good shelter and are popular cruising stops. Shelter Cove and Trinidad Harbor are convenient, but temporary open roadsteads along the route. If you plan to "hug the shore" to minimize exposure to wind and swells and to play the back eddies off headlands and points, you can find a lee from northwest wind and chop in a number of small

bights that provide a temporary rest. However, any time you navigate in waters inside the 30-fathom contour you must be particularly careful to watch for off-lying rocks and reefs that can occur up to a mile offshore.

With the exception of one stretch where the chart has a scale of 1:20,000, the coast north of San Francisco is poorly charted. Most of the charts are drawn to a scale of 1:200,000—almost useless for close-in work. An alert bow watch and a slow approach are absolute requirements any time you enter poorly sounded coastal waters. Crab-trap floats become an increasing hazard as you move northward, especially near Crescent City; following our "Express Route" can minimize this problem.

Cape Mendocino and nearby Point Gordo represent major challenges to coastal skippers, requiring careful planning and navigation. Cape Mendocino, with its bold headland and outlying reefs, is the most westerly point

Northbound, heading out under the Golden Gate

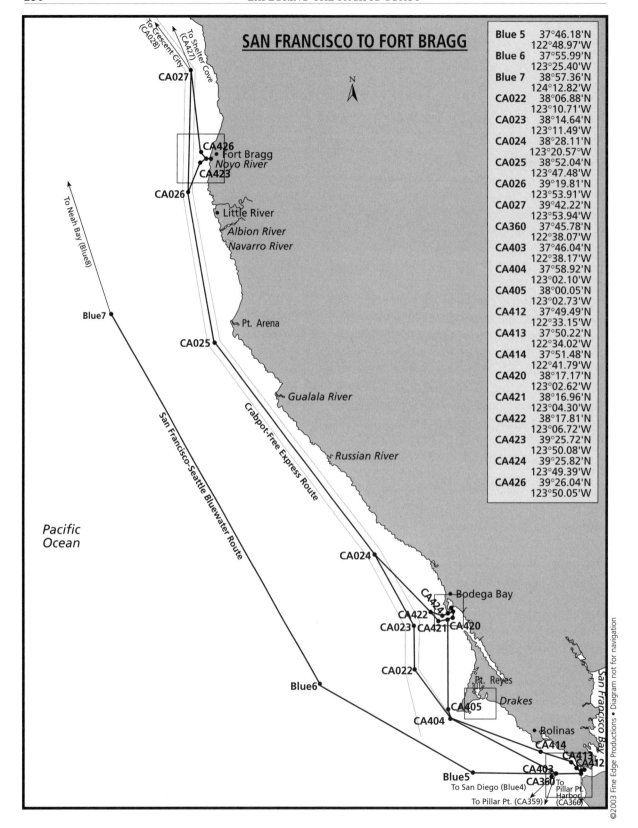

SAN FRANCISCO TO FORT BRAGG

Blue 5	37°46.18'N 122°48.97'W
Blue 6	37°55.99'N 123°25.40'W
Blue 7	38°57.36'N 124°12.82'W
CA022	38°06.88'N 123°10.71'W
CA023	38°14.64'N 123°11.49'W
CA024	38°28.11'N 123°20.57'W
CA025	38°52.04'N 123°47.48'W
CA026	39°19.81'N 123°53.91'W
CA027	39°42.22'N 123°53.94'W
CA360	37°45.78'N 122°38.07'W
CA403	37°46.04'N 122°38.17'W
CA404	37°58.92'N 123°02.10'W
CA405	38°00.05'N 123°02.73'W
CA412	37°49.49'N 122°33.15'W
CA413	37°50.22'N 122°34.02'W
CA414	37°51.48'N 122°41.79'W
CA420	38°17.17'N 123°02.62'W
CA421	38°16.96'N 123°04.30'W
CA422	38°17.81'N 123°06.72'W
CA423	39°25.72'N 123°50.08'W
CA424	39°25.82'N 123°49.39'W
CA426	39°26.04'N 123°50.05'W

Golden Gate tower on a foggy day

between the Mexican border and Grays Harbor in Washington; it has a reputation for changeable weather, strong winds, fog, and confused rough seas. Gales occur along this coastline between 5% and 10% of the time during the summer. Fog is heaviest in and around Humboldt Bay, Point Reyes and Point Arena. While northwest winds are most prevalent in the summer, moderate south winds do occur occasionally which can help make a passage relatively fast and easy. Above all, on a trip either north- or southbound along the coast, do not rush. The more time you can spend, the more enjoyable your passage will be.

A successful passage of California's North Coast requires a careful reading of the weather, then moving only when conditions are favorable. The major NOAA weather facility, located on Woodley Island in Eureka, is helpful in giv-ing mariners a personal weather briefing. You can call them by telephone at any time for a recent update. If you visit their facility, they will show you computer models of weather patterns and explain how to interpret the close bunching of isobars that indicate northwest gales.

Point Bonita
Charts 18645, 18649; 2.4 mi W of N entr to Golden Gate
Position: (CA409) 37°48.64'N, 122°31.69'W

Point Bonita . . . is a sharp black cliff 100 feet high, increasing to 300 feet on its seaward face, 0.3 mile N. From NW it shows as three heads. (CP, 33rd Ed.)

Majestically guarding the north side of the entrance to the Golden Gate, Point Bonita marks the spot where protected waters and the open ocean meet. The light on Bonita, 126 feet above the water, spreads the welcome mat for mariners entering San Francisco Bay. Boaters entering after a long passage can begin to relax

Point Bonita Light

Bob & Carol Mehaffy

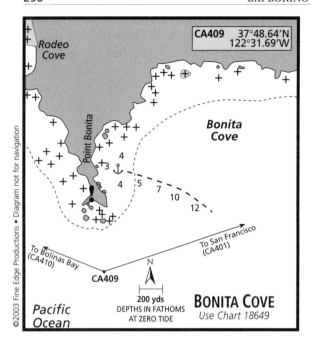

Bonita Cove
Chart 18645; 2.3 mi W of Golden Gate Bridge
Entrance: 37°48.90'N, 122°31.12'W
Anchor: 37°49.08'N, 122°31.61'W

Bonita Cove . . . is occasionally used as an anchorage by small vessels. The anchorage is close under Point Bonita in about 36 feet. (CP, 33rd Ed.)

Bonita Cove, under the lee of Point Bonita, is the first anchorage available to boaters entering or leaving the Golden Gate. It is also the first place to find a lee when leaving San Francisco via Bonita Channel. You can stop here to make adjustments or await better conditions but, because it is somewhat exposed to chop, wake, and current, it is used as a temporary anchorage only.

Bonita Cove is just slightly more than two miles west of the Golden Gate Bridge and San Francisco Bay's myriad anchorages and marinas east of the Bridge, therefore few boaters choose to stop here. Occasionally, large fishing boats do anchor in Bonita Cove for a few hours to allow crew members to rest before going back out to sea. We anchored here only once and found the motion a little too lively for comfort. Not only did the waves wrap around Point Bonita, but also the changing current kept our boat changing direction.

Perhaps this anchorage is best for boaters who are coming up the coastline midday, beating into a northwest wind and swell and looking for temporary shelter. Drakes Bay, 24 miles northwest, provides better shelter and is closer to the coastal rhumb line.

Anchorage can be found southeast of the radar tower, avoiding rocks and kelp extending out from the cliffs.

Anchor in 5 fathoms over mixed sand; avoid the rocks and kelp off Point Bonita.

after passing Point Bonita. Conversely, when outbound traffic passes Bonita, all questions about what the seas will be like are quickly answered. Bonita Cove, immediately east of the point, is useful as a temporary anchor site.

When entering or exiting the Golden Gate, you can pass fairly close to Point Bonita, but beware of the rocks awash directly south of the lighthouse about 200 yards from shore.

Point Bonita with Bonita Cove to starboard

Vessel Assist towing a broken-down ketch, Bonita Channel in foggy weather

Bonita Channel

Chart 18649; NE side of Potatopatch Shoal
Entrance (E): (CA410) 37°48.79'N, 122°32.19'W
Entrance (W): (CA413) 37°50.22'N, 122°34.02'W

The most dangerous part of San Francisco Bar is considered to be Fourfathom Bank. Bonita Channel, between the shoal and the Marin coast, can also be very dangerous during large swell conditions. The safest part of the bar is the Main Ship Channel through the center of the bar. But even that area can be extremely dangerous when the tidal current is ebbing.

From S, some coasters and fishing vessels not drawing more than 15 feet use unmarked South Channel, parallel to and 0.7 mile off the peninsula shore. A reported obstruction, covered 25 feet, is near the S end of the channel about 3.5 miles 192° from Mile Rocks Light.

From N, coasters and other vessels use buoyed Bonita Channel, between the E end of Potatopatch Shoal and the shore N of Point Bonita. The channel is narrowed to 0.2 mile by several rocky patches including Sears Rock, covered 19 feet, 1.2 miles NW of Point Bonita.

Caution. Vessels departing San Francisco Bay

through Bonita Channel on the ebb current must use extreme caution when crossing the tide rip off Point Bonita. When the bow passes the rip the stern is thrown to port and, unless promptly met, the vessel will head straight for the rocks off the point. Vessels favoring Potatopatch Shoal too closely have reported a set toward it. . . .

Strangers wishing to cross the bar in thick weather should either wait for clearing or take a pilot. Fog is prevalent in the Golden Gate; radar is a great aid here. (CP, 33rd Ed.)

During fair weather, Bonita Channel is used by many small craft and commercial fishing boats headed into and out of San Francisco. While Bonita Channel is sometimes used in marginal weather, it can be very rough and nasty on spring ebbs when strong westerlies are blowing. The channel, which skirts along the north side of Potato Patch—a rough and sometimes dangerous patch of water 4 fathoms deep—has an average depth of 9 fathoms.

Avoid Centissima Reef and Sears Rock to starboard midway through the channel; Sears Rock is marked by buoy G"3." Rodeo Cove lies behind Centissima Reef. Be particularly careful when

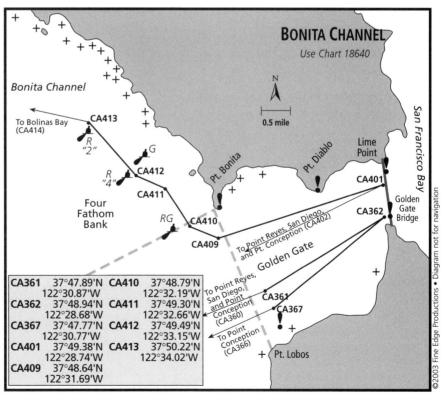

CA361	37°47.89'N 122°30.87'W	CA410	37°48.79'N 122°32.19'W
CA362	37°48.94'N 122°28.68'W	CA411	37°49.30'N 122°32.66'W
CA367	37°47.77'N 122°30.77'W	CA412	37°49.49'N 122°33.15'W
CA401	37°49.38'N 122°28.74'W	CA413	37°50.22'N 122°34.02'W
CA409	37°48.64'N 122°31.69'W		

running Bonita Channel in poor visibility; the channel is narrow and often filled with commercial traffic heading through at high speed — not a pleasant situation. In rough weather, some outbound fishing vessels pass east of Centissima Reef (Sears Rock) to avoid incoming traffic.

Rodeo Cove

Chart 18649; 0.45 mi E of Sears Rock
Position: 37°49.75'N, 122°32.41'W

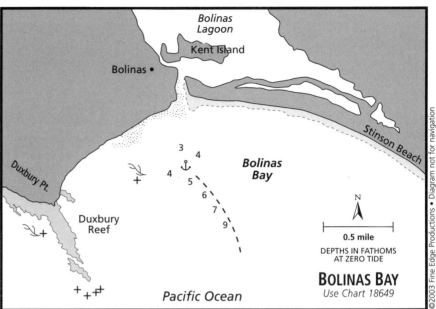

©2003 Fine Edge Productions • Diagram not for navigation

BOLINAS BAY
Use Chart 18649
DEPTHS IN FATHOMS AT ZERO TIDE
0.5 mile

Rodeo Cove, located east of Centissima Reef near the middle of Bonita Channel, is exposed to westerly chop and numerous wakes. Temporary shelter from occasionally strong east winds can be found close to shore off the sandy beach in front of Rodeo Lagoon. Tuck in north of Bird Island where fair protection is provided by Point Bonita. Rodeo Cove is open to westerlies and only partially protected by the kelp beds around Sears Rock. Take care to avoid the kelp beds.

Anchor in about 5 fathoms over sand and rock; poor-to-fair holding.

More on the Great White Shark: Attack in Bolinas Bay

Lee Fontan of Bolinas was surfing with a dozen other surfers on May 31, 2002 when he was attacked and critically wounded by a great white shark about 300 yards offshore. Fortunately, he was able to fight off the shark which inflicted an 8-inch laceration on his left leg and another on his upper back. An average great white is about 16 feet long, weighs 1.5 tons, and has four rows of teeth. There have been about 100 shark attacks in California waters since 1920 when records first were kept.

Bolinas Bay

Charts 18649, 18645; E of Duxbury Point
Entrance: 37°52.85'N, 122°40.28'W
Anchor: 37°53.80'N, 122°40.88'W

Bolinas Bay . . . is an open bight 3.5 miles wide. . . . The bay affords shelter in NW weather in 24 to 36 feet, sandy bottom. Care must be taken to avoid Duxbury Reef and the dangers extending up to 0.7 mile E of it. Bolinas Lagoon is separated from the bay by a narrow strip of sandy beach that is cut by a narrow shifting channel. The lagoon is shoal and entered only by small boats with local knowledge. The entrance has a depth of less than 3 feet. (CP, 33rd Ed.)

Bolinas Bay, 8 miles north of the entrance to San Francisco Bay, offers temporary anchorage in fair weather. Local and visiting boaters rarely use this anchorage, however, because it is so close to the excellent anchorages at Drakes Bay, 15 miles northwest, and San Francisco Bay, 11 miles southeast. Because of shallow water that extends 200 yards and luxuriant kelp beds, you probably won't be able to anchor close enough to shore to gain much protection from Duxbury Point and Reef. Although we haven't anchored here, other sailors have told us that the swell makes the anchorage uncomfortable.

The only place we've seen boats anchored at Bolinas Bay is to the east of the town of Bolinas, just west of the entrance to Bolinas Lagoon avoiding the submerged 2-foot rock due east of Duxbury Point.

Once a wharf town for schooner traffic across the Golden Gate, today Bolinas and its environs are popular with birders, surfers, and sunbathers. While it toyed with becoming a resort town, the counter-culture discovered the town in the 1970s and turned it into a bohemian community. It used to be that to keep tourists away, townspeople disposed of Highway 1 turnoff signs. Nevertheless, this town is worth a visit. It has a cafe, bed and breakfast and a wonderful bakery. There is a small, well-curated museum and a gallery that exhibits photos from the past. Bolinas is also near the site of Audubon Canyon Ranch, where visitors can get a peek at the nests of great blue herons, great egrets, and snowy egrets. The preserve is open mid-March through mid-July and the overlooks are open limited hours Saturdays, Sundays, and holidays. The Ranch also has exhibits of coastal nature and Native American Indian artifacts.

Mount Tamalpais—at the north end of Marin Peninsula—rises to an elevation of 2,571 feet, 3 miles east of Bolinas Bay, and can be seen in clear weather for over 60 miles.

Anchor in 3 to 4 fathoms over a sandy bottom with some gravel and rocks; fair-to-good holding.

Duxbury Reef
Chart 18649; extends 1.2 mi SE of Duxbury Pt
Position (buoy "IDR"): 37°51.70'N, 122°41.60'W

Warning. It was reported that in heavy weather strong N currents resulting from prolonged S winds may exist in the area from Duxbury Reef to Golden Gate. (CP, 33rd Ed.)

Duxbury Reef extends a mile southward from Duxbury Point, forming the western side of Bolinas Bay. White water breaks on most of this reef only when large seas are running. Although a buoy marked "DR" warns of Duxbury Reef, boaters—especially those who like to work their way north by following the coastline—can easily stray too close. Do not succumb to the temptation to cut inside the "DR" buoy.

Point Reyes
Chart 18647; 17 mi NW of Bolinas Bay;
18 mi N of Farallon Lt
Position (1.0 mi W): (CA405) 38°00.05'N, 123°02.73'W

Point Reyes . . . is a bold, dark, rocky headland 612 feet high at the W and higher extremity of a ridge running in an E direction for 3 miles. . . . (CP, 33rd Ed.)

Point Reyes, 28 miles northwest of the Golden Gate and the first major point north of San Francisco, is easily recognized by its majestic headland that extends 10 miles west of the general trend of the coast. And from a distance, the tip of Point Reyes appears to be an island. Point Reyes Light (flashing 5 seconds), at the west tip of the point, 265 feet above the water, is visible for 24 miles in clear weather. As you approach Point Reyes, northwest swells become evident, winds increase dangerously offshore, especially in the afternoon, and big rollers sweep close to the point by early evening.

Bob & Carol Mehaffy

Lighthouse on Point Reyes

When prevailing strong winds blow, boaters northbound from San Francisco usually stop overnight in Drakes Bay to time their passage around Point Reyes for shortly after dawn. Then they generally set their course for at least a mile offshore before turning due north to Bodega Bay.

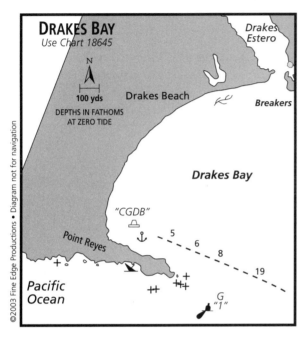

On a northbound route with a 15-knot south wind, *Baidarka* noticed that as we approached the eastern side of Point Reyes, swells picked up to about 15 feet and the wind increased to 25 to 30 knots. We passed Point Reyes in lumpy seas, rather close-in, following the 15- to 20-fathom curve. A short distance north of the point the wind decreased to a moderate 10- to 15-knot southerly, and we had a good smooth ride into Bodega Bay. This phenomenon is an example of a "corner" wind that occurs near a major protruding headland.

North of Point Reyes the coast is low and sandy with sand dunes extending 10 miles north.

Drakes Bay

Chart 18647; 2.5 mi NE of Pt Reyes Lt
Entrance: 37°59.35'N, 122°56.60'W
Anchor: 37°59.95'N, 122°58.46'W

Drakes Bay [was] named after English explorer Sir Francis Drake, who anchored here in 1579. . . . This curving shoreline forms Drakes Bay, which affords good anchorage in depths of 4 to 6 fathoms, sandy bottom, in heavy NW weather.

Drakes Bay is used extensively in heavy NW

Drakes Bay anchorage

weather and many fishing vessels operate from here during the season. A fish wharf is about midway along the inner side of the peninsula. (CP, 33rd Ed.)

Drakes Bay offers almost perfect protection from prevailing northwest winds and from occasional strong north winds. Our sailing friends, Caroline and Bob Mehaffy, report having spent comfortable, almost motionless days and nights at anchor here as well as times when the anemometer registered 40 knots and the bay was full of white caps. However, if east or southeast winds of more than moderate strength are blowing—a rare occurrence in summer—don't anchor here.

From November through April, you can watch migrating gray whales pass near shore on their way from the Gulf of Alaska to the warmer waters of Baja California. Remote Drakes Bay is a quiet respite from the busy San Francisco Bay waters. The shore and hills around Drakes Bay are part of Point Reyes National Seashore. Facilities at the Kenneth C. Patrick Visitor Center (three miles northeast of the pier) include restrooms, showers, and phone. A snack bar is open seasonally.

Named after explorer Sir Francis Drake—who some believe spent five weeks in the protection of this bay repairing his ship—Drakes Bay, like Port Orford in Oregon, is one of the best natural lees between San Francisco and Cape Flattery.

On a recent southbound passage, the Mehaffys were rounding Point Reyes with all sails aloft, slowly sailing along in 8-10 knots. As they came abeam of the point, the winds coming over the transom increased to 40 knots within a few minutes. They had a wild ride for 20 minutes or so while they shortened sail. Had they been northbound, they would have been unable to make any headway and would have been forced to turn back.

When approaching from the south, use the Point Reyes headland for a landmark. Once you're about 5 miles south of Reyes, look for the G"1" buoy off the east end of Drakes peninsula. When you see it, alter course and head directly for the buoy, then enter the protected anchorage to the east of the peninsula.

The best anchorage in Drakes Bay is off the westernmost of the two piers in the southwest corner of the bay south of the Coast Guard buoy. *Caution:* Kelp and sea grass thrive in Drakes Bay, so set your anchor well enough to hold in 40-knot winds.

To explore the shore, you can land your dinghy on the rocky beach next to the fish buyer's warehouse on the southwest side of the anchorage. Another possibility is to land on the beach to the north side of the bay, but pay attention to the swell to avoid a wet landing.

Ashore at Drakes Bay, the trails along the windswept, grassy headlands present opportunities to watch songbirds, sea birds, seals, sea lions, dolphins, and whales. From the beach at the north side of the bay, you can enjoy a 2- or 3-mile hike on the soft sand. Alongside that beach is the Kenneth C. Patrick Visitor Center, with exhibits of the wildlife in the Point Reyes National Seashore, and of the Coast Miwoks who once inhabited this area. Sailboats from San Francisco sometimes take a departure from Drakes Bay when doing a loop trip to the Farallon Islands.

Anchor in 2 to 3 fathoms over sand and sea grass; fair-to-good holding with a well-set anchor.

Bob & Carol Mehaffy

Anchored at Drakes Bay on a windy day

Approaching the Farallons from the east

Gulf of the Farallons National Marine Sanctuary
Charts 18645, 18640; extends from Farallon Is to Bodega Head

The Gulf of the Farallons National Marine Sanctuary has been established to protect and preserve the marine birds and mammals, their habitats, and other natural resources in the waters surrounding the Farallon Islands and Point Reyes, and to ensure the continued availability of the area as a research and recreational resource. . . . The sanctuary includes Bodega Bay but not Bodega Harbor. Recreational use of the area is encouraged. (CP, 33rd Ed.)

The Gulf of the Farallons National Marine Sanctuary includes the waters off Bodega Head and Point Reyes and the waters surrounding the Farallon Islands. The U.S. Fish and Wildlife Service prohibits unauthorized landings on the Farallons in order to protect the 200,000 birds that nest and mate there. These islands are a major nesting area for Western gulls, cormorants, puff-

ins, murres, Cassin's auklets, and ashy storm petrels. If visitors were to walk around the island, they could easily crush the nests of birds in burrows, killing the adults and chicks. Even those birds that have nests on the rocky slopes are frightened by humans and leave their nests, allowing the gregarious Western gulls to invade and eat the eggs or chicks of the absent parents.

In addition to the birds on the islands, hundreds of harbor seals, sea lions, and elephant seals inhabit the beaches and rocks along the shoreline. Because these mammals are easily disturbed, and human intrusion could result in the death of the newborn, the U.S. Fish and Wildlife Service has established a 300-foot restricted area along the entire shoreline of the islands. Great white sharks and turtles are also common in the waters surrounding the Farallons.

The only human inhabitants on these islands are the half-dozen marine biologists who study the wildlife of the islands and the surrounding

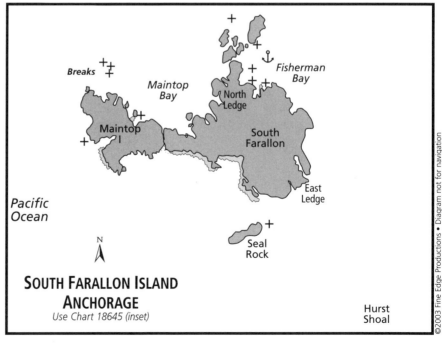

waters. If you decide to visit the Farallons, you can contact the biologists on VHF 16 with questions about the wildlife and activity there. They are proud of the work they do and will happily explain what is happening on and around these remote islands.

Farallon Islands

Charts 18645, 18640; 23 mi W of SF Bay entr
Position N. Farallon Is (3.8 mi NW of Mid Farallon Is): 37°46.03' N, 123°05.76'W
Position Mid. Farallon Is (6 mi NW of SE Farallon Is): 37°04.71'N, 123°01.82'W

Farallon Islands . . . are rocky islets extending NW for 7 miles. Southeast Farallon, the largest of the group, actually consists of two islands separated by a narrow impassable gorge. The larger E island is pyramidal in shape . . . a small-boat landing is on the S side. Farallon Light . . . 358 feet above the

Biologists at work, Farallon Islands

The Fall and Rise of the Farallon Common Murres
by Bob Botley

The Southeast Farallon Island has been the southernmost breeding ground of the common murre for centuries. This incredible black pelagic bird evolved to swim far under water in search of food. Its body is heavy, its wings small and its feet are located as rudders far back on the body. As a consequence, it is very awkward on land and unable to take off from flat land surfaces. To gain speed for flight it needs great distances at sea, where it spends its entire life except during the nesting season. In selecting a place to lay eggs, the murre chooses a rocky ledge on a steep cliff above the water and, to achieve flying speed it dives off the ledge. Because of its awkwardness on land it quickly takes flight when disturbed by land animals. When this happens, gulls fly in to take their eggs and tiny chicks.

For most of its existence Southeast Farallon Island had no land creatures to disturb it. That all changed following the discovery of gold in California. San Francisco became the major point of entry for both the 49ers and the businesses that developed to meet their needs. The population grew more rapidly than the availability of many foods, including eggs.

Unfortunately, the murre egg tastes enough like chicken eggs to be a desirable substitute, and this oddity almost led to the destruction of their southern breeding grounds. Enterprising groups went to the Island during breeding season and harvested the eggs which brought $1.00 a piece—an enormous price in those days. Soon, many groups were competing to harvest the eggs in what came to be known as the "egg wars" that resulted in several poachers' deaths. To stop the fighting, San Francisco incorporated Southeast Island into the city limits, but local police were ineffective in ending the "wars."

It was not until farmers started raising chickens in Petaluma, providing fresh eggs to the area, that the harvesting stopped. In the meantime, the common murre population dropped from 110,000 birds to 10,000 and remained that low for a century.

About the same time, the Coast Guard installed a manned lighthouse on the island allowing caretakers and their families to live year there year around. About 1968, groups from Point Reyes bird observatory were allowed to do research on the island. One of their goals was to discover why the population of murres had not increased after the harvesting ended. The answer was simple. When members of the Coast Guard and their families inadvertently walked near the breeding areas the adult murres flew away and the gulls took the eggs. Without realizing what they were doing, they had kept the population growth at near zero.

Once the discovery was made, the rookeries were declared off-limits and the population regained its original numbers.

Note: Bob Botley was a founding member of the Farallon Patrol and served for many years as its coordinator. The Farallon Patrol was formed in the early 1970s to provide transportation to the Southeast Island for research personnel. Bob and his wife, Annamae, helped crew on *Baidarka* in our original explorations of Southeast Alaska and Vancouver Island's west coast.

water, is shown from a 41-foot white conical tower on the highest peak of the island. Dwellings are on the lowland on the S side of the island. (CP, 33rd Ed.)

Located 27 miles west of San Francisco's Golden Gate Bridge, the Farallons are a good diversion for boats heading south along the coast. The 20-mile trip from Point Reyes to the islands is a pleasant downwind run in prevailing conditions, followed by an often-thrilling broad reach into San Francisco Bay. However, boaters leaving San Francisco Bay to head northward will more likely want to skip the Farallon Islands, instead passing close to Duxbury Reef and probably tucking in behind Point Reyes for a good night's rest in the excellent anchorage at Drakes Bay.

The low-lying Farallon Islands are a National Wildlife Refuge and Marine Sanctuary with a 300-foot restricted boundary, except for Fisherman Bay where you may anchor. *Note:* Landing is forbidden by U.S. Fish and Wildlife Service regulations. This sanctuary is home to a dozen species of birds, including the world's largest nesting popula-

Sea lions congregate in the Farallon Islands

tion of ashy storm petrels and a sizeable population of western gulls. Migratory birds have a feast here in one of California's richest fisheries. A lighthouse, built in 1855 by the Coast Guard, is not automated and can be seen atop the 365-foot peak of South Farallon island. For nearly 100 years, the lighthouse keepers and their families occupied the two wooden houses still visible at the foot of the peak.

Even though the light on the summit of Southeast Farallon Island is high above sea level, due to fog and haze the island is typically invisible until you're within 5 miles of it. For this reason, radar and GPS are useful in making this passage. Southeast Farallon makes a clear target for radar, often showing up at a distance of 10 miles.

Fisherman Bay

(Southeast Farallon Island)
Chart 18645; 0.2 mi N of
Farallon Lt
Anchor (SE Farallon Isl):
37°42.12'N, 123°00.08'W

Fisherman Bay, just N of

North Cove, Southeast Farallon Island

Farallon Light, is somewhat protected by several rocky islets on the W side and affords anchorage in 8 fathoms in the outer part. Boats can be landed on a small sand beach on the largest islet. (CP, 33rd Ed.)

Fisherman Bay, on the north side of Southeast Farallon Island, is the only reasonable anchorage around these islands and is not an ideal anchorage. Even though the large rocks on the northwest side of the anchorage provide some protection from prevailing northwest winds and waves, the waves wrap around these rocks and create an uncomfortable motion. The Mehaffys have anchored here a few times but have never been completely comfortable. In relatively calm seas, however, you can anchor in Fisherman Bay for a short time to have lunch and observe the wildlife.

The buoy is exposed to the wind and waves. East Landing has a crane used to transfer personnel and supplies to shore.

Anchor in 6 to 8 fathoms over rock and sand; set your hook carefully.

Sea lions feeling frisky, Farallon Islands

Bob & Carol Mehaffy

Tomales Bay (Bodega Bay)
Chart 18643; 15 mi N of Pt. Reyes
Entrance Buoy R"2": 38°15.20'N, 123°00.05'W
Entrance Bar: 38°14.39'N, 122°59.25'W

Tomales Bay . . . extends SE for 12 miles with an average width of 0.5 mile. The channel with depths of 3 to over 10 feet is marked by buoys and daybeacons for about 4 miles to deeper water inside the bay. The shoals and channels within the bay are subject to continual change, local knowledge is advised. . . .

The entrance bar is dangerous and should not be attempted by strangers. A 6-knot current may be encountered on a spring tide at the entrance to the bay. The shallow area on the entrance bar frequently becomes rough, and it is reported that the sudden appearance of breakers in a calm sea is common. Because such waves appear with little warning, they are called "sneaker waves." These waves occur primarily during the ebb tide, but the entire bar area can become rough owing to strong afternoon winds. Boatmen should plan to leave the area before the tide turns or be prepared to remain outside until the rough water subsides, or to go to another harbor such as Bodega. . . .

A small-craft facility on the bay can

Bob & Carol Mehaffy

Baby sea lion checks out the photographer

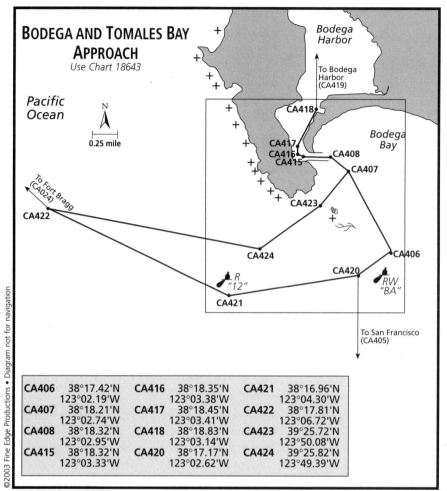

BODEGA AND TOMALES BAY APPROACH
Use Chart 18643

Pacific Ocean

0.25 mile

CA406	38°17.42'N 123°02.19'W	CA416	38°18.35'N 123°03.38'W	CA421	38°16.96'N 123°04.30'W
CA407	38°18.21'N 123°02.74'W	CA417	38°18.45'N 123°03.41'W	CA422	38°17.81'N 123°06.72'W
CA408	38°18.32'N 123°02.95'W	CA418	38°18.83'N 123°03.14'W	CA423	39°25.72'N 123°50.08'W
CA415	38°18.32'N 123°03.33'W	CA420	38°17.17'N 123°02.62'W	CA424	39°25.82'N 123°49.39'W

©2003 Fine Edge Productions • Diagram not for navigation

make hull and engine repairs and is equipped with a travel lift and a crane, each capable of handling craft up to 15 tons. . . . (CP, 33rd Ed.)

Tomales Bay is a scenic, quiet bay seldom visited by cruising boats due to the reputation of its hazardous entrance bar and shifting shoals inside. Bodega Bay, 5 miles northwest, is easier to enter and has more convenient facilities.

Entering Tomales Bay is particularly dangerous when strong ebb currents meet a northwest swell. Do not attempt to enter without Chart 18643. The narrow fairway is lined by extensive mud flats and it's easy to go aground here.

Although the bay is popular among commercial and sportfishing vessels for its abundant clams, oysters, and mussels, it is not recommended for deep-draft cruising vessels without local knowledge. Facilities for small boats are available inside the bay.

Bodega Bay
Chart 18643; 19 mi N of Pt Reyes
Position: 38°16.08'N, 123°00.67'W

Bodega Bay, a broad opening between Tomales Point and Bodega Head, affords shelter from NW weather at its N end, but is dangerous in S or W weather. . . .

Danger. In good weather small boats having local knowledge sometimes use the passage between Bodega Head and Bodega Rock. The passage is unsafe whenever breakers from heavy ground swells reduce the width of the passage. Large breaking waves can occur inside the 30-foot depth contour line NW and SW of Bodega Rock. The safest part of the passage between Bodega Head and Bodega Rock is along the deeper part of the passage. When the width of the passage is reduced by breakers, mariners entering Bodega

---

San Francisco to Bodega Bay
by Michelle Gaylord

July 10: We had relatively calm seas all the way to Bodega Bay from San Francisco, but the weather was overcast so couldn't see much of the shoreline. The mile-long channel into the harbor has been dredged and is well marked with buoys. We stayed at Spud Point Marina, not terribly picturesque, but the facilities were certainly adequate, and it's well protected from the weather. There were about 12 transient boats in the harbor with home ports from all over the west coast. We met one couple with a similar itinerary to ours, so we will touch base with them from time to time. I must say that people doing serious cruising whom we have met are some of the most interesting and engrossing people. We did our usual biking, walking, and exploring, and stayed here for two nights.

Bay should pass S of Bodega Harbor Approach Lighted Buoy BA. (CP, 33rd Ed.)

Bodega Bay is a 5-mile-long bight that curves northward from Tomales Point to Bodega Head. Bodega Harbor, which has excellent shelter, lies 3 miles northeast of Bodega Head at the head of a narrow channel.

Named for Bodega y Quadra, the Spanish explorer whose name figures in much of the history of the Northwest, the area profits from a mild climate, lovely hills, a rugged, rocky coastline, and sand dunes. Just north is Sonoma County's lovely Russian River.

Baidarka's logbook records that we saw a spouting whale surrounded by six dolphins, a pod of grey whales, and a school of dolphins as we approached the entrance to Bodega Harbor.

In fair weather you can take a shortcut through the slot between Bodega Rocks and the peninsula. However, watch for crabpot floats and don't be surprised to find them (black in color!) out to nearly the 40-fathom curve.

Bodega Harbor

Chart 18643; N part of Bodega Bay
Entrance: (CA420) 38°17.17'N, 123°02.62'W
Breakwater entr: (CA408) 38°18.32'N, 123°02.95'W
Position: (Spud Point Marina) 38°19.85'N, 123°03.38'W

Bodega Harbor . . . is an important commercial fishing base and, in season, an active sports fishing and recreation harbor. During salmon season more than 500 fishing craft either anchor just outside in the shelter of the N part of the bay or dock at the numerous marinas inside the harbor.

A federal project provides for a 12-foot channel, protected by entrance jetties, which leads from Bodega Bay to facilities along the N and NE sides of the harbor at the town of Bodega Bay. The channel has a turning basin just inside the entrance, at the N end of the harbor, and along the NE side of the harbor. . . . The channel is marked by buoys, daybeacons, and lights; lighted ranges also mark the channel from the entrance to the turning basin at the N end of the harbor.

The marina at Spud Point on the W side of the harbor has the largest lift in the area, which can handle boats up to 20 tons. (CP, 33rd Ed.)

Bodega Harbor—frequently called just Bodega Bay—sits at the foot of a bluff below the town center, 3 miles from the channel entrance. The inner harbor offers excellent shelter and quiet seclusion with a rustic feel. It is a convenient stop-over for many coastal cruisers, including delivery skippers who make it here in one day from Pillar Point Harbor, or from points farther south. The town has three marinas: Spud Point Marina, the first marina to the left as you enter the harbor, caters to cruising vessels of all sizes; Mason's Marina, north of Spud Point, serves mostly commercial fishing vessels; Porto Bodega, to the northeast below the townsite, handles small sportfishing and trailerable boats up to a maximum of 40 feet. There is a launch ramp on site.

Aerial view: Bodega Bay

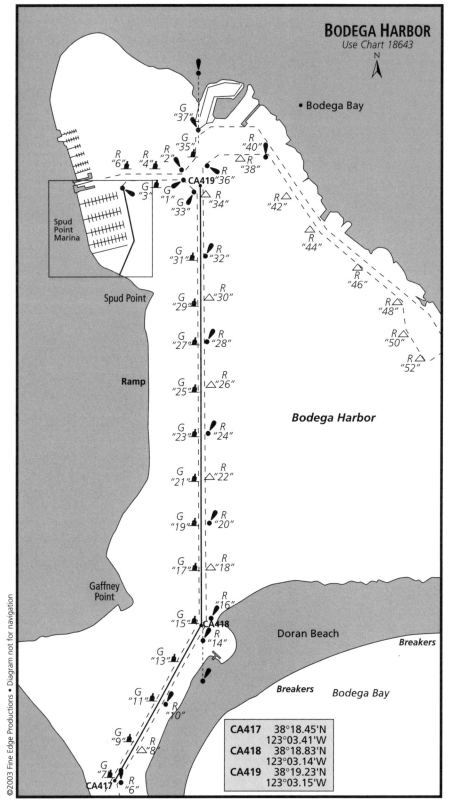

BODEGA HARBOR
Use Chart 18643
N

• Bodega Bay

Spud Point Marina

Spud Point

Ramp

Gaffney Point

Doran Beach

Breakers

Bodega Harbor

Breakers   *Bodega Bay*

CA417	38°18.45'N 123°03.41'W
CA418	38°18.83'N 123°03.14'W
CA419	38°19.23'N 123°03.15'W

©2003 Fine Edge Productions • Diagram not for navigation

Bodega Harbor is entered between twin breakwaters at the south side of Doran Beach. A narrow dredged channel leads west for about 350 yards, then north for nearly a mile and a half to the inner harbor. The USCG station is located a half-mile from the breakwaters. Follow the Range Marks "A" through the breakwaters, then turn northeast, following the channel markers R"2" to R"34" on your starboard hand ("red right returning") to the marina areas at the north end of the harbor. Begin your turn west into Spud Point Marina *only* after you have passed portside flashing G"33." The dredged channel carries about 12 feet at zero tide, but use care because the bay shoals rapidly outside the channel. We have found Bodega Harbor relatively easy to enter and exit in serious fog using radar and preset courses.

The mild climate and variety of habitats at Bodega Bay make it a good place for observing diverse shorebirds and waterfowl. We've seen white pelicans feeding on the adjacent mud flats, watched snowy egrets stalking their prey along the channel and, just outside the harbor, spotted more than 50 yellow-billed birds lifting their wings and ducking their heads to bottom fish in the shallow ponds. Inside the harbor, hundreds of ravens call raucously while a covey of quail scamper quickly across the road above the marina.

The historic and archaeological value of Bodega Bay and its harbor area are preserved as a National and State Historical landmark. The town claims to be the busiest fishing port between Ft. Bragg and San Francisco, and side-benefits of this industry include some of the best seafood restaurants along the coast. The town has long been a tourist destination for Bay Area residents but, as the "world" has learned about the beauty of Highway 1, lodges and inns have sprung up in the area. If you have a way to get to the Russian River, north of Bodega Bay, you can find sun, swim in comfortable water and rent a kayak.

Spud Point Marina has guest slips and general facilities, including a fuel dock, restrooms, electricity, dock carts, water, laundry, ice, showers, and pump out. We find it to be one of the quietest marinas on the entire coast. At night when northwesterlies are blowing, you can hear the surf crashing on the beach outside. No vehicle or industrial sounds spoil the quiet and, when the wind stops, you're aware of your pulse throbbing in your ears. Bodega Bay is a great place to unwind from the fast pace of nearby San Francisco.

⚓ **Spud Point Marina** entrance: 38°19.85'N, 123°03.38'W; tel: 707.875.3535

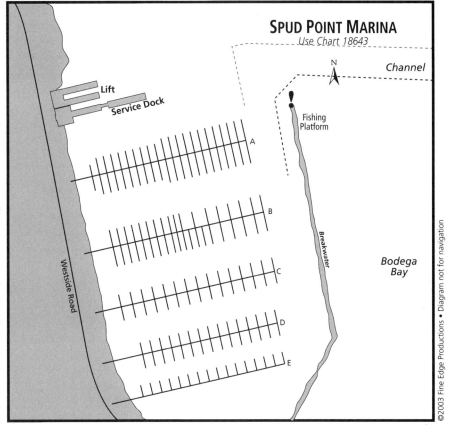

⚓ **Mason's Marina** position: 38°19.90'N, 123°03.48'W; tel: 707.875.3811

⚓ **Porto Bodega Marina** position: 38°19.96'N, 123°03.17'W; tel: 707.875.2354

Bodega Head to Point Arena
Chart 18640

The coast from Bodega Head for 52 miles to Point Arena trends in a general NW direction. There are some dangers, but they do not extend over a mile offshore, and in thick weather the 30-fathom curve may be followed with safety. . . . (CP, 33rd Ed.)

Every country explored by the Spanish has at least one Point Arena (Sandy Point); some have dozens. Between Bodega Head and California's Point Arena there are at least eight possible temporary anchor sites. All of these sites are small bights with a lee created by an adjacent rocky or sandy point. Although they are exposed in some manner, all have been used traditionally for temporary shelter in prevailing summer northwesterly weather.

Many of the small anchor sites along the coast were used to load lumber or other local products onto sailing ships. Fort Ross was built to help supply badly needed vegetables for the Russian colonists of Sitka over a thousand miles to the north, as well as to supply coastal sea otter hunters! In some of these rocky coves and bays you can still find evidence of the cables or loading platforms once used in transferring goods to and from shore.

Most of these coves are still poorly charted and require great caution when entering. A skipper must be ready to clear any of these sites when wind or wave conditions increase or change direction and become threatening.

About 0.25 mile north of Sail Rock there is a lovely grassy hill. Breaking surf over Saunders Reef creates a surfers' paradise. Beware of Arena Rock, a mile offshore; it is marked by breakers even in moderate swells.

Duncans Landing
Chart 18640; 5.9 mi N of Bodega Head
Position: 38°23.55'N, 123°05.59'W

Duncans Landing . . . is a fair small-boat landing in NW weather. (CP, 33rd Ed.)

Duncans Landing is the first of a number of small bights in the lee of points that provides some shelter in prevailing northwest weather. Like the rest of the entire coast, it is poorly charted and unsounded, requiring great caution when approaching. Temporary anchorage can be found in about 5 fathoms over a sandy bottom.

Russian River (Jenner)
Chart 18640; 9.7 mi N of Bodega Head
Entrance: 38°26.37'N, 123°08.04'W

The spit making out from the S point of Russian River has been partially reinforced by a short rock jetty, but the mouth of the river is closed by a shallow bar. . . . Many summer resorts are on the shores of Russian River; at the settlement of Jenner there is a landing. Gasoline and water can be obtained nearby. (CP, 33rd Ed.)

The Russian River outlet is very poorly charted and its entrance bar silts up every summer. The

area northeast of Mile Rocks, however, appears to offer temporary anchorage in fair weather. Anchorage may be found in about 6 fathoms over a sand and rocky bottom behind the rocks and kelp patches that extend southward a mile from the point north of the outlet of the Russian River. This area, too, is poorly charted, so use caution if you choose to explore it. Along this section there are many interesting indentations at the foot of gulches and steep, wooded ridges that invite exploration.

Fort Ross Cove
Chart 18640; 15.5 mi N of Bodega Head; 33 mi N of Point Reyes
Position: 38°30.59'N, 123°14.82'W

Fort Ross Cove . . . affords good shelter in NW weather. The holding ground is poor, and the anchorage is constricted by a rock that uncovers in the middle of the cove and a rock about 50 yards N of it that is covered 14 feet. The cove is divided into two bights, the W one being slightly the larger. The anchorage is suitable for small vessels only, and if used by strangers should be entered with caution. (CP, 33rd Ed.)

It is hard to believe that Russian sailing ships, built by hand in the Far East, would sail down from Sitka, Alaska to Fort Ross in a desperate bid to set up a supply chain of fresh produce, more agreeable to the Russian diet than the seafood enjoyed by the Tlingit of Southeast Alaska.

The small bight below an unnamed point appears to offer good shelter in prevailing summer weather, but avoid the rocks noted above in *Coast Pilot*. The bottom is rocky with marginal holding.

When approaching from the south, avoid Sunken Reef, 1.2 miles southeast of Fort Ross reef, marked by bell buoy "R14."

Gerstle Cove
Chart 18640; 7.4 mi N of bell buoy "R14"
Position: 38°33.84'N, 123°19.82'W

Gerstle Cove, the small cove in the lee of Salt Point, appears to offer some temporary shelter in fair weather but it is not mentioned in the

Coast Pilot and we can find no local knowledge about it. It is poorly charted, like this entire coast (no large-scale charts), so feel your way in carefully.

Salt Point
Chart 18640; 4 mi N of Fort Ross Cove
Position: 38°33.89'N, 123°19.99'W

> *Salt Point . . . is 35 feet high, very rocky, and bare of trees; it is bordered by outlying rocks for 200 yards. The 30-fathom curve is less than 0.5 mile off this point. (CP, 33rd Ed.)*

Fisk Mill Cove
Chart 18640; 2.5 mi N of Salt Point
Position: 38°35.70'N, 123°21.26'W

> *Fisk Mill Cove . . . affords fair shelter for small vessels in NW weather. The bottom is rocky, but there are no hidden dangers. (CP, 33rd Ed.)*

Fisk Mill Cove, a small bight in the lee of Horseshoe Point one mile to the north, appears to offer some shelter from prevailing northwest winds if you tuck in close to the beach.

Fisherman Bay
Chart 18640; 26.5 mi NW of Bodega Head
Position: 38°38.89'N, 123°24.39'W

> *Fisherman Bay . . . is a fair shelter for small craft in NW weather. There are two covered rocks marked by kelp 350 yards off the S point of the bay. There is a general store at the village of Stewarts Point on the N side of the bay. (CP, 33rd Ed.)*

Fisherman Bay is a tiny indentation on the south side of the village of Stewarts Point. The site has very limited swinging room, with off-lying rocks. The area is uncharted and must be approached with great caution.

Bourns Landing
Chart 18640; 1.5 mi NW of Gualala River
Entrance: 38°46.88'N, 123°33.56'W

> *The anchorage here is exposed and can be used only in the sum-*

mer. Local knowledge is necessary because the approaches have several covered rocks. Lumber from the Gualala mills was formerly shipped from here. (CP, 33rd Ed.)

Bourns Landing is an uncharted area north of Robinson Reef. Both the exit of Gualala River and Bourns Landing may offer temporary anchorage in fair weather, but no local knowledge is available.

Havens Anchorage
Chart 18640; 12 mi SE of Point Arena; 4 mi NW of Gualala Point
Position: 38°47.95'N, 123°35.08'W

> *Havens Anchorage . . . offers shelter for small vessels from the prevailing NW winds S of Fish Rocks. The cove is constricted by rocks and ledges extending 250 yards SE from the W head. Strangers should approach the anchorage with caution. During the summer the anchorage is used extensively by fishing boats in NW weather. (CP, 33rd Ed.)*

Havens Anchorage is located in the lee of Havens Neck (to the north) and Fish Rocks (to the west). Good shelter can be found east of Fish Rocks in fair weather. Havens Neck (145 feet high and bare), 0.6 mile northwest of Fish Rocks, is connected to the mainland bluff by a low spit. Fish Rocks (150 and 100 feet high,

Baidarka beating to windward

respectively)—the largest of which has a gnarly yellow-topped rock with a single tree—are connected to the coast at low water, making them easily confused with Havens Neck a short distance north.

This section of coastline is a series of undulated cliffs covered with trees. On the plateau above the water, there are several nice homes that comprise the settlement of Fish Rock.

As you enter this uncharted area, keep Fish Rocks on your port hand, avoiding rocks and ledges that extend southeast of the west head. Anchorage can be found in front of the settlement in about 7 fathoms.

North of here there are numerous crabpots out to a depth of 33 fathoms.

Arena Cove
Chart 18640; 2.5 mi SE of Point Arena
Position: 38°54.80'N, 123°43.18'W

Arena Cove . . . is a slight indentation affording shelter to small vessels in NW weather. The S head is a high yellow cliff that under favorable circumstances is visible for a considerable distance. A wharf is at the head of the cove. . . . To enter, make the lighted bell buoy, then bring the end of the wharf to bear 074° and stand in on this course. This leads about 150 feet S of a rock covered 16 feet that lies 300 yards 264° from the end of the wharf. In thick weather during the summer in approaching the cove from N or S, the edge of the kelp may be followed which will lead to within 300 yards of the lighted bell buoy. The town of Point Arena is on the highway 1 mile E of the landing.

A breaker is reported in a heavy SW swell 0.8 mile WSW of the N point of Arena Cove, and scattered kelp extends almost out to that position. (CP, 33rd Ed.)

Arena Cove offers moderate shelter in prevailing summer weather. Anchorage can be found in about 3 to 4 fathoms, following the instructions noted above in the *Coast Pilot.*

Arena Cove, itself, is exposed to southerly weather. However, shelter from southeasters may be found on the north side of Point Arena, close to shore, in 6 fathoms over sand once the northwesterly swell diminishes.

Point Arena
Chart 18640; 68 mi NW of Point Reyes
Position (2.0 mi W): 38°57.36'N, 123°47.11'W

Point Arena . . . consists of a long level plateau, diminishing in height to the end of the 60-foot-high point. It is the first prominent point N of Point Reyes. The point is bare of trees for about a mile from the shore.

Vessels approaching Point Arena from N in thick weather are advised to keep outside the 40-fathom curve because Arena Rock is only 0.8 mile inside the 30-fathom curve and shoaling near it is abrupt. (CP, 33rd Ed.)

North of Point Arena, the coast becomes sandier and more desolate-looking. At this point, vessels that have been keeping "one foot on the beach" to minimize northwest swell and chop, must go out to the 40-fathom curve to round Point Arena.

The bight on the north side of Point Arena has been traditionally used as temporary shelter from southeast storms.

Cuffey Cove and Inlet
Chart 18626; 11 mi N of Point Arena
Entrance: 39°08.21'N, 123°44.55'W
Anchor (cove): 39°08.37'N, 123°43.87'W
Anchor (inlet): 39°08.43'N, 123°44.08'W

Cuffey Cove . . . is a small anchorage affording fair shelter in NW winds. Cuffey Inlet, just W of the cove, is an excellent anchorage for small boats in N and W weather. Caution is necessary to avoid the many covered and visible rocks in the approaches to the cove and inlet. A small kelp-covered rock that uncovers lies near the center of the entrance to the inlet. The cove is covered with patches of kelp during most of the year. (CP, 33rd Ed.)

Ten miles north of Point Arena, the coastline for the next 23 miles—as shown on Chart 18626—has five times the detail of that shown on Chart 18640 for the area south of Point Arena. Chart 18628 has a scale of 1:10,000, from Whitesboro Cove to Caspar. With larger scale charts, this section of coast becomes safer and more accessible for exploration.

Good shelter can be found in Cuffey Cove by tucking in close to the 100-foot cliffs. From the

Caution! Electronic charts in error — track crosses this breakwater into Noyo Mooring Basin

Navarro River
Chart 18626; 14.5 mi S of Noyo River
Position: 39°11.37'N, 123°45.75'W

From Cuffey Cove for 3 miles to Navarro River, the coast consists of cliffs 200 feet high, bordered by outlying rocks. Although the mouth of the river is nearly always closed by a bar with only 1 or 2 feet of water over it, the entrance has fair shelter from NW winds. Navarro Head, 405 feet high, is on the N bank of the river. (CP, 33rd Ed.)

The section of convoluted coastline from Cuffey Cove to Noyo River is one of the most fascinating areas to explore in good weather, and that certainly includes the lee below Navarro Head at the outlet of the Navarro River. Some shelter can be found from northwest winds off the river entrance where there is a sandy bottom. Avoid the rocks south of Navarro Head, as well as a submerged rock that breaks 0.4 mile southwest of the opening of the river.

Albion Cove
Chart 18628; 16.5 mi N of Point Arena
Entrance buoy: 39°13.61'N, 123°47.30'W
Anchor (larger craft): 39°13.73'N, 123°46.65'W
Anchor (small craft): 39°13.69'N, 123°46.36'W

Albion Cove . . . affords good shelter in N weather. The S point at the entrance rises to a knoll 179 feet high; low rocks extend nearly 500 yards W of the point. The N point is a rocky islet 80 feet high lying close to the point which has the same elevation; both are bare. Small visible rocks lie 200 yards W of the islet, and covered rocks, showing breakers in a moderate swell, extend out more than 500 yards WSW from it. The principal danger in the approach is a covered rock, usually showing a breaker, 250 yards S of the islet. Mooring Rock, in the middle of the cove, is 30 feet high, pyramidal in shape, and marked by a light and a seasonal fog signal; small rocks extend from it to the N shore. A lighted whistle buoy marks the entrance to the cove.

Between Albion Cove and Colby Reef, breakers are seen in a heavy swell nearly 0.5 mile from shore; vessels should not approach closer than 1 mile. (CP, 33rd Ed.)

Albion Cove offers good shelter in moderate weather from north through southeast winds. Use large-scale Chart 18628 for entering the

entrance point, head due east 0.5 mile toward a 12-foot rock in the center of the cove. There is adequate swinging room for several boats in Cuffey Cove.

Cuffey Inlet, 250 yards west of Cuffey Cove, offers very good anchorage for one small boat in the center of the tiny inlet with almost complete protection from most weather; swinging room is limited at this site. The cove is surrounded by 100-foot cliffs in all directions, except the south.

Greenwood Cove, 0.5 mile southeast of Cuffey Cove off Greenwood Creek, may offer some protection from southeast winds.

Anchor (Cuffey Cove) in 5 fathoms, 200 yards north of the 12-foot rock, over sand and cobble with some kelp; fair-to-good holding.

Anchor (Cuffey Inlet) in 4 fathoms; room for one boat only.

cove. (How we wish that the entire coast were sounded in such detail!) Larger vessels may want to anchor temporarily west of Mooring Rock in about 7 fathoms, while very small craft may find temporary shelter in a 2-fathom hole east of the rock with limited swinging room. Avoid the kelp beds, some of which hide submerged rocks.

Anchor (larger craft) in 7 fathoms over sand with rock and kelp; fair holding.

Anchor (small craft) in the 2-fathom hole over rock sand, stones and kelp; fair holding.

Little River

Chart 18628; 19 mi N of Point Arena
Entrance buoy: 39°15.95'N, 123°48.04'W
Position: 39°16.31'N, 123°47.62'W

The reefs and rocks surrounding the cove are well marked by kelp, and a heavy undertow is felt in the vicinity of the rocks. The northwest shore of the cove is bluff, rocky, and bare of trees for over 0.5 mile. The entrance is marked by a bell buoy, but the channel narrows to 60 yards by covered rocks N of the inner visible rock. The beach area at Little River is a State Park. (CP, 33rd Ed.)

Little River—a favorite of local fishermen working this coast—offers the best protection for small vessels between Bodega Bay and Fort Bragg. The rocks and reefs that extend 0.4 mile from the south side of the cove protect the cove from south and southeast weather. When entering from the south, head directly for the headland before turning east into the small, protected cove.

The bottom is filled with cobble, reported to be ballast unloaded from sailing ships that took on lumber at Little River.

The rocks and reefs along this section of coast may call to mind those of the Inside Passage so, any time you get close to the coast, be sure to station alert lookouts on the bow. Use a slow approach and sound your way carefully into and behind the kelp beds and off-lying rocks—just as you would do in the Northwest and in Alaska.

Mendocino Bay

Chart 18626; 21 mi N of Point Arena
Entrance buoy RW: 39°17.87'N, 123°48.75'W
Position: 39°18.03'N, 123°48.11'W

Mendocino Bay . . . affords fair shelter in NW weather, but vessels are obliged to leave in S or W weather. In heavy SW gales the sea breaks clear

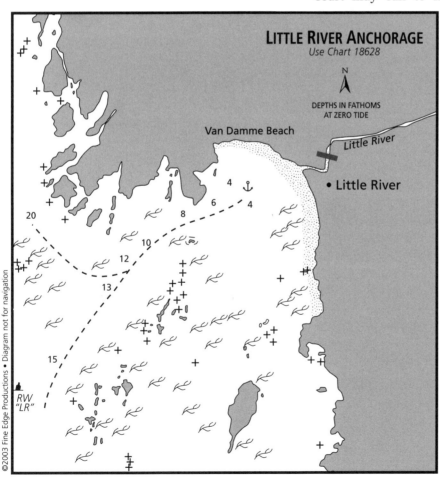

LITTLE RIVER ANCHORAGE
Use Chart 18628

N

DEPTHS IN FATHOMS AT ZERO TIDE

Van Damme Beach

Little River

• Little River

4

4

6

8

10

12

13

20

15

RW "LR"

©2003 Fine Edge Productions • Diagram not for navigation

across the entrance. The S point at the entrance is a rocky, irregular cliff 100 feet high, bordered by numerous rocks extending 150 yards offshore. A knoll 156 feet high is 300 yards inshore from the point. A reef covered 3 1/4 fathoms extends 500 yards NW of the outermost visible rock. This area should be avoided when there is any swell running. The N point is a broken cliff 60 feet high, bordered by numerous rocks close inshore. A whistle buoy marks the entrance to the bay. (CP, 33rd Ed.)

Mendocino Bay is the outlet of Big River below the town of Mendocino. Temporary anchorage can be found off the entrance to the river in about five fathoms.

Russian Gulch
Chart 18628; 2 mi N of Mendocino Bay
Entrance: 39°19.39'N, 123°48.70'W
Anchor: 39°19.69'N, 123°48.46'W

Russian Gulch . . . is a small cove occasionally used as an anchorage by small craft with local knowledge as it affords excellent protection. A State Park is at the head of the cove. The concrete arch highway bridge across Russian Gulch should show well from S to W. An important danger is a rock awash 400 yards NW of the S entrance point. A reef covered 1 1/4 fathoms extends 200 yards SE of the rock. (CP, 33rd Ed.)

Russian Gulch looks like a great kayak haulout place and an anchorage for one small craft with limited swinging room. The reef in the center of the entrance would quite likely break with any swell running. The fairway into the anchor site is narrow, so be cautious to avoid rocks and kelp.

Caspar Anchorage
Chart 18626; 4 mi S of Noyo River
Position: 39°21.82'N, 123°49.37'W

Caspar Anchorage . . . is a small cove at the mouth of Caspar Creek. Fair shelter, except from W, is afforded, but the anchorage is constricted and seldom used. The village of Caspar is on the N bank of the creek near its mouth. (CP, 33rd Ed.)

Caspar Anchorage, which is open to the northwest, is subject to heavy swells. However, it should provide good protection from southerly weather when northwest swells have laid down but, if you've made it this far, Noyo River, 4 miles to the north, provides better shelter.

Noyo Anchorage
Chart 18626; 9.4 mi N of Little River
Position (0.4 mi ESE of buoy R"2"): 39°25.71'N, 123°48.83'W

Noyo Anchorage...affords fair shelter from N or S. The anchorage is limited to an area about 400 yards long and less than 200 yards wide, with depths of 3 1/2 to 6 1/2 fathoms. Buoys mark the entrance to the anchorage. (CP, 33rd Ed.)

Noyo Anchorage, the outer passage to the Noyo River, is seldom used as an anchorage because of the excellent shelter found inside the jetties. The outer area could be used advantageously as a temporary anchorage only if you don't want to enter the river in foul weather, reduced visibility, minus tides, or breaking swells. The Coast Guard rescue station located here can be contacted on VHF 16.

Noyo Anchorage is a picturesque anchorage. When *Baidarka* entered on the leading edge of a northwest gale, we found breakers all about

Aerial view: Fort Bragg

and quickly scooted through the tiny opening into the sheltered river. Temporary anchorage can be found about 150 yards northwest of the north jetty light.

Caution: Many charter sportfishing boats zoom in and out of the river entrance creating large wakes and they may not expect a boat to be anchored in this area.

Anchor in 3 to 4 fathoms over sand and gravel with some rocks and kelp; fair holding if well set.

Fort Bragg (Noyo River)

Chart 18626; 30 mi N of Point Arena
Entrance buoy R"2": (CA424) 39°25.82'N, 123°49.39'W
Breakwater entrance: (CA425, approx 100ft S of G"4") 39°25.67'N, 123°48.61'W
Entrance (Noyo Yacht Basin): 39°25.43'N, 123°48.14'W

Noyo River enters at the head of Noyo Anchorage....

Caution is necessary in entering to avoid the reefs and a rock on the S side of the entrance. Heavy W and SW swells form breakers at the entrance to the river; once inside there is good shelter. With W winds and seas, heavy surge is felt in the river as far as Noyo Basin.

Noyo River . . . above the first sharp bend affords excellent protection for small boats. A dredged channel leads between the jetties to Noyo Basin, about 0.6 mile above the entrance. . . .

The lower section of Noyo River is the principal commercial and sport fishing center of this section of the coast. Many fishing boats are based here. Most of the facilities extend along both banks of the river to about 0.5 mile above the entrance. . . . (CP, 33rd Ed.)

Noyo Harbor is reminiscent of a classic northwest fishing village located on a small river. The entrance, which is open to westerly swells

Looking west out the entrance to Noyo River with Coast Highway overhead

that occasionally break at the jetty entrance, is narrow and shallow (about 7 feet at zero tide) and the first half-mile is chock full of docks and floats of all sizes.

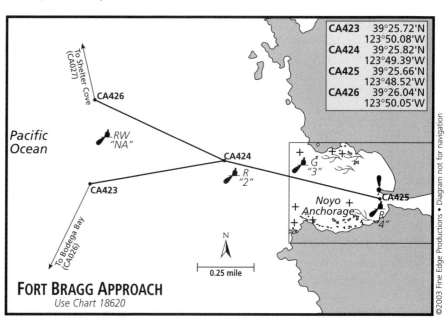

CA423	39°25.72'N 123°50.08'W
CA424	39°25.82'N 123°49.39'W
CA425	39°25.66'N 123°48.52'W
CA426	39°26.04'N 123°50.05'W

Pacific Ocean

To Shelter Cove (CA027)

CA426

RW "NA"

CA424

R "2"

CA423

To Bodega Bay (CA026)

G "3"

Noyo Anchorage

CA425

R "4"

N

0.25 mile

FORT BRAGG APPROACH
Use Chart 18620

©2003 Fine Edge Productions • Diagram not for navigation

Looking up Noyo River into Fort Bragg from the Coast Highway bridge

Breakers south of Noyo Anchorage

Approaching Noyo River and Fort Bragg from the south, identify the whistle buoy "NA," 1.1 mile west northwest of the Noyo River breakwater and steer a course for waypoint CA423; from the north, steer for waypoint CA426. From these waypoints, head for CA425 which is the outer end of the range leading into the very narrow entrance. (East of here you must know your exact position at all times and not attempt to enter Noyo River in poor visibility.)

Next steer for CA424, located 100 feet south of the north jetty light G"5." You should enter the 200-foot-wide channel staying on the range marks and favoring the north breakwater all the way into Noyo River. In the process, you should pass about 120 feet north of buoy R"2" and 120 feet south of buoy G"3." Note that this course takes you through a rock and shoal area where there may be a fair amount of foam on the seas during heavy weather.

Be sure to check the tide tables ahead of time; the entrance bar is quite shallow and large seiners tell us they have hit bottom. At best

The Charms of Fort Bragg
by Michelle Gaylord

We arrived in Fort Bragg on July 12, after 92.7 Nm of rolling seas—about a 4 on the Richter scale. We loved the place. It's a quaint, picturesque, small, fishing harbor. Again, it is a dredged, narrow entrance, but well marked. All along the banks of the river are restaurants, seafood markets, and shops. They all have docks in front with colorful fishing trawlers tied up to them, loaded with fishnets and crab traps. The marina is quite old, with splintered wooden docks, but it has charm. The pine trees come all the way down to the water, and the rest of the terrain is covered with smaller trees and green brush. Just gorgeous. There were gale warnings up for the next four days, but that was okay with us because we found plenty to do. We went upriver one morning, and rode our bikes all around that afternoon. One morning we took off walking and found that the banks of the river were covered with wild boysenberry bushes. We grabbed our buckets and went berry picking for three hours. We had some wonderful, homemade boysenberry ice cream and for days we ate lots and lots of berries. The cruising couple we met in Bodega Bay (on a Willard 40 from Ventura), arrived and we had a wine and cheese get-together. The following day we took the all-day Skunk Train ride through the redwoods. So far on our trip, this has been our favorite port.

Noyo River entrance

you have smooth water to the marina. Favor the north shore until well past the bridge because of a shoal extending two thirds of the way out from the south shore. Do not go beyond the entrance to Noyo Basin unless you have a shallow-draft boat—depths at low water are about 3 feet. *Note and Caution*: be sure to use the inset on Chart 18426 as your guide; *Baidarka* found that the electronic charts were not accurate into Noyo Basin.

there is only about 7 feet at zero tide and, with any swell running and on a spring tide, this number can be cut in half. If necessary you can temporarily drop anchor northwest of the north jetty to wait for favorable tide. Your approach should be slow with alert lookouts. Watch for fast charter fishing boats that may attempt to pass within the entrance at high speed.

Once you pass under the Highway 101 bridge,

Noyo Mooring Basin has slips for 265 boats, but they are usually quite busy. Visiting boats may have to raft along one of the restaurant docks, or the commercial or repair docks along the waterfront. The harbor office (tel: 707.964.4719) will try to make arrangements for you, but large yachts should contact the restaurants or commercial floats ahead of time to assure a vacancy.

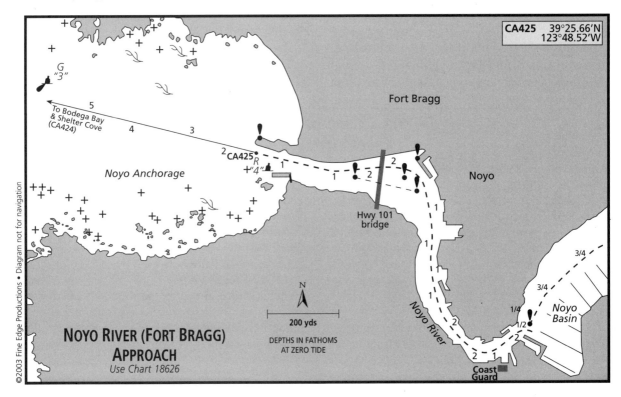

Intimate Noyo River, safe haven for all kinds of vessels

U.S. Coast Guard base in front of Noyo Mooring Basin

Fort Bragg, founded in 1857, is now a tourist destination with its downtown center full of boutiques, restaurants, antique and wine shops. A 20-minute walk from the harbor leads you to a shopping center with Harvest Market, Rite Aid, a couple of pizza parlors and a laundromat (open 0600 to 2100). Dial-a-Ride will take you back to the boat basin with your provisions, but be prepared for a wait and a possible route through town. We found that a hand-held VHF could notify the boat of the shopper's progress. A park on the south side of the boat basin has eight large barbecue pits used, in particular, for an annual salmon bake on the Fourth of July. A memorial dedicated to those lost at sea is inscribed with John Masefield's famous poem, "I must go down to the sea again . . . " (Sea Fever).

Noyo River, with its assortment of commercial

fisherman, sport fishermen, charter operators, delivery skippers, sightseers, coastal cruisers, and various transient boaters, has the flavor of some of the smaller villages and towns of Southeast Alaska—it's a salty place with lots of frontier atmosphere. And, well-moored inside the harbor at night, you can hear sea lions barking outside in Noyo Anchorage.

Soldiers Harbor
Chart 18626; 0.8 mi N of Noyo River
Position: 39°26.49'N, 123°49.28'W

Fort Bragg . . . is the largest coast town between San Francisco and Eureka. It is near the head of a cove formerly known as Soldiers Harbor. . . . The cove is constricted by the rocks and ledges

Noyo Mooring Basin, Fort Bragg

Michelle Gaylord

Charter fishing dock on Noyo River

Baidarka rendezvous with charter skippers in Fort Bragg

extending from both the N and S, leaving only a limited area for small boats to anchor. A rocky reef, partly bare at high water, extends SW from the N head and breaks the force of the swell from NW. In W weather the cove is wide open. Since Noyo River gives better protection, the cove is seldom used. (CP, 33rd Ed.)

Soldiers Harbor is immediately west of the old Fort Bragg city. The bay is full of rocks and offers marginal shelter with limited swinging room. When bound for Fort Bragg, all boats now use Noyo River, 0.8 mile south.

Laguna Point Anchorage
Chart 18626; 4.0 mi N of Noyo River
Position: 39°29.53'N, 123°48.09'W

The cove immediately N of Laguna Point is exposed and only available for small boats. It affords fair protection in S weather and is occasionally used in winter. (CP, 33rd Ed.)

Laguna Point Anchorage is wide open to northwest winds and swells that pound into the sandy beach. However, you can find a well-placed lee that gives protection from southerly winds when northwest swells lay down. Tuck into the cove just off the beach at the north side of the point.

Anchor in about 4 fathoms over an unrecorded bottom.

Cape Vizcaino
Chart 18620; 14 mi N of Laguna Pt

Between Cape Vizcaino and Point Delgada are several small exposed landings available for use only in the summer and in smooth weather. The landings formerly were used to ship ties, tanbark, and shingles which were loaded on vessels by means of wire cables. (CP, 33rd Ed.)

Point Delgada
Chart 18620; 37.5 mi N of Noyo River
Position (1.0 mi W): 40°01.67'N, 124°05.62'W

Point Delgada . . . is a cliff-faced plateau making out about a mile from the general trend of the coast. The seaward face of the plateau is about a mile long and bordered by numerous rocks. A lighted horn buoy is 1.1 miles SW from the point,

Commercial fishing docks on Noyo River

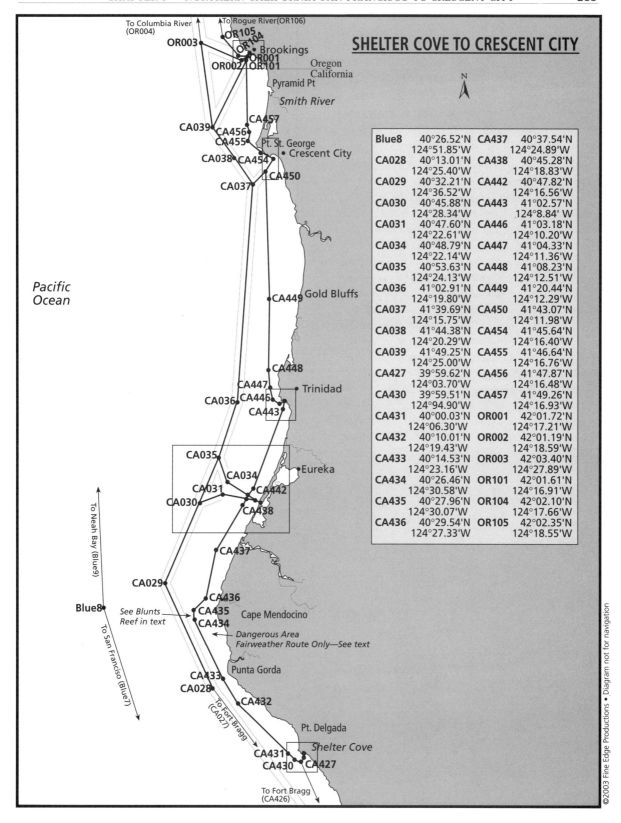

SHELTER COVE TO CRESCENT CITY

Blue8	40°26.52'N 124°51.85'W	**CA437**	40°37.54'N 124°24.89'W
CA028	40°13.01'N 124°25.40'W	**CA438**	40°45.28'N 124°18.83'W
CA029	40°32.21'N 124°36.52'W	**CA442**	40°47.82'N 124°16.56'W
CA030	40°45.88'N 124°28.34'W	**CA443**	41°02.57'N 124°8.84'W
CA031	40°47.60'N 124°22.61'W	**CA446**	41°03.18'N 124°10.20'W
CA034	40°48.79'N 124°22.14'W	**CA447**	41°04.33'N 124°11.36'W
CA035	40°53.63'N 124°24.13'W	**CA448**	41°08.23'N 124°12.51'W
CA036	41°02.91'N 124°19.80'W	**CA449**	41°20.44'N 124°12.29'W
CA037	41°39.69'N 124°15.75'W	**CA450**	41°43.07'N 124°11.98'W
CA038	41°44.38'N 124°20.29'W	**CA454**	41°45.64'N 124°16.40'W
CA039	41°49.25'N 124°25.00'W	**CA455**	41°46.64'N 124°16.76'W
CA427	39°59.62'N 124°03.70'W	**CA456**	41°47.87'N 124°16.48'W
CA430	39°59.51'N 124°94.90'W	**CA457**	41°49.26'N 124°16.93'W
CA431	40°00.03'N 124°06.30'W	**OR001**	42°01.72'N 124°17.21'W
CA432	40°10.01'N 124°19.43'W	**OR002**	42°01.19'N 124°18.59'W
CA433	40°14.53'N 124°23.16'W	**OR003**	42°03.40'N 124°27.89'W
CA434	40°26.46'N 124°30.58'W	**OR101**	42°01.61'N 124°16.91'W
CA435	40°27.96'N 124°30.07'W	**OR104**	42°02.10'N 124°17.66'W
CA436	40°29.54'N 124°27.33'W	**OR105**	42°02.35'N 124°18.55'W

and a bell buoy is 0.8 mile SE from the point. A paved airplane landing strip, about 3,500 feet, is on the point. (CP, 33rd Ed.)

Shelter Cove

Chart 18620; 0.6 mi SE of Pt Delgada
Entrance buoy G"1": 40°00.50'N, 124°03.25'W
Position: (CA429): 40°00.99'N, 124°03.50'W
Anchor: 40°01.16'N, 124°03.52'W

Shelter Cove . . . affords fair shelter in NW weather, but is exposed and dangerous with S or SE winds. Occasionally a swell runs in the cove. There are no wharves in the cove. Water may be obtained ashore, but must be carried down from the plateau. A marine supply store is on the bluff on the W side of the cove. Gasoline, diesel fuel, lubricants, ice, marine supplies, and provisions are available. A launching ramp is at the head of the cove. Shelter Cove is used extensively as an offshore moorage for fishing boats. A pump-out station and dry winter storage are at Shelter Cove. Local boat launch service monitors VHF-FM channel 68. A paved road is maintained to the cove. Telephone service is available.

The rocks covered 1 to 5 fathoms S of Point Delgada can be avoided in approaching Shelter Cove by staying over 200 yards S of the lighted whistle buoy and E of the bell buoy. (CP, 33rd Ed.)

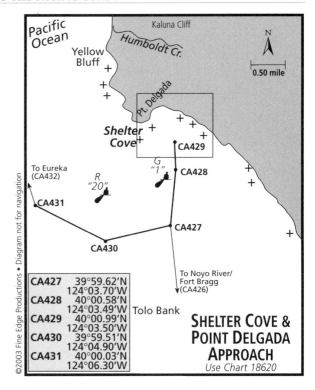

Shelter Cove is the last place to find temporary shelter from prevailing northwest winds on a northbound trip before rounding Punta Gorda and the infamous Cape Mendocino. However, it is fully exposed to the south and to southeast gales. A large kelp bed that extends more than a mile south of Point Delgada breaks the chop and provides a good place to rest before making the 50-mile run to Eureka.

Shelter Cove lies at the base of a long, sloping ridge that ends at Point Delgada. From the south, a cupola and a settlement of houses are visible along the ridge. A black sand beach along the eastern shore is backed by a high bluff. Paragliders sometimes use the area along the ridge for making their take-off.

Approach is made south of buoy R"20" and close east of

Aerial view: Shelter Cove

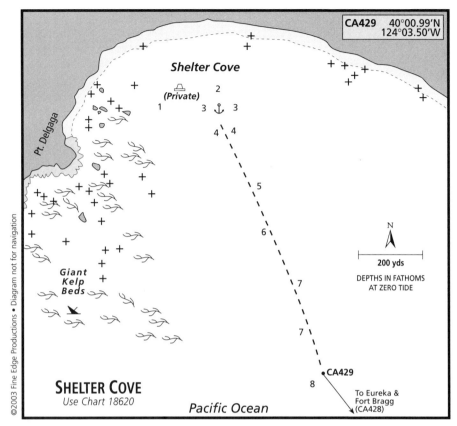

Anchor in about 4 fathoms over sand with some kelp; fair-to-good holding.

Punta Gorda
Chart 18623; 11 mi S of Cape Mendocino
Position (1.25 mi W):
40°15.63'N, 124°23.37'W

Punta Gorda is a high, bold, rounding cape. . . . The seaward face rises to about 900 feet, 400 yards back from the beach, and terminates in a spur, 140 feet high, almost overhanging the sea. . . .

The wind, sea, and currents off Punta Gorda are probably as strong as off any point on the coast; frequent and strong tide rips have been noted. Many times when the weather at Shelter

buoy G"1," then along the eastern edge of the giant kelp bed. Anchorage can be found between 7 and 3 fathoms; avoid the kelp by following a course of True North to Northeast. Swinging room is somewhat limited by the kelp. If you intend to leave in the dark, be sure to plan and write down your exit route beforehand during daylight hours! (Not recommended.)

A few small private buoys used by small sportfishing boats lie close to shore in front of a launch ramp; and a few buildings are behind.

Point Delgada, Baidarka anchored in Shelter Cove

Rockin' and Rollin' at Shelter Cove
by DCD

Baidarka arrived at Shelter Cove late in the afternoon and we dropped our main anchor, intending to remain overnight. It was quite comfortable and I took a nap while the Réanne and our son-in-law, Jeff, worked on dinner. Before dinner was ready, the wind and/or current shifted to a light southerly (perhaps an eddy current?). *Baidarka* now pointed south instead of west as earlier and the boat began to roll heavily as low westerly swells came through the kelp beds. The cook wasn't happy. Even with the guardrails secured tightly around it, the soup pot refused to stay in place, and the gimbaled stove thumped noisily against the stainless-lined bulkhead.

Before I could get a stern anchor down to hold the boat facing west, Réanne said, "This is not fun. I vote we leave now and run all night." Jeff agreed. They wanted to get to Eureka as early as possible the next morning.

So, we raised anchor and set out for Cape Mendocino and Eureka—our only all-night passage at sea on this trip.

Windshift passes Baidarka *northbound at Punta Gorda*

Cove and even at Big Flat is clear and calm and the sea smooth, both the wind and the sea will pick up as Punta Gorda is approached, until just N of this point where strong breezes to moderate gales will be experienced. At other times clear weather S of this point will lead to fog N, or vice versa. . . .

From Punta Gorda to Cape Mendocino the hills back of the coast are lower than those S; *they are bare of trees and bordered by stretches of low, narrow, sandy flats with a narrow, low-water beach. The outlying rocks are not more than 0.7 mile offshore until about 2.5 miles S of Cape Mendocino, where they extend offshore to Blunts Reef, 2.5 miles W of the cape. (CP, 33rd Ed.)*

Punta Gorda is the start of the turbulent and rough water found along this exposed coast.

Cape Mendocino

Chart 18623; 185 mi N of entr to San Francisco Bay
Buoy R "2B" (4.5 mi W of point):
40°26.45'N, 124°30.32'W

Cape Mendocino . . . is a mountainous headland, the famous landmark of the old Spanish navigators and the galleons from the West Indies. The cape is the turning point for nearly all vessels bound N or S. In view of the dangers in the vicinity, it should be approached with considerable caution in thick weather; the bottom and the cur-

---

Baidarka Rounds Cape Mendocino By Night
by DCD

We pulled up anchor in Shelter Cove at 1900 and, by midnight, were 3.4 miles northwest of Punta Gordo in light fog.

By 0200 we were 4 miles off Cape Mendocino Light, alongside the Cape Mendocino buoy. Seas were confused and choppy, winds were northwest at 20 knots, and there was still light fog. Since we were a mile or more west of "The Great Break"—the dangerous part of Blunts Reef—I decided to turn northeast and head inside the 5-fathom shoals, 3 miles north of the buoy. It was getting pretty lumpy and I wanted to slow the boat down to make the ride as comfortable as possible for the crew.

I was confident that the buoy, our electronic chart position, and the bearings of Cape Mendocino Light (visible only erratically in the fog banks) gave us a good fix so I took a departure, set the depth sounder alarm for 15 fathoms and headed in, thinking we might get a little lee effect from the extreme north end of Blunt Reef.

The wind was picking up and whatever lee the reef could have provided was offset by increasing northwest wind-swell and chop. By reducing the rpm to a fast idle (1000 rpm), the speed over the ground dropped to 1.5 knots against the 25-knot wind. Except for an occasional slap to starboard from a breaking crest, the autopilot—coupled to the electronic charting—managed to maintain steerage about 30 degrees off the wind, holding *Baidarka* right on our course line. I used the radar range and bearings to double-check our position and monitor our progress; the depth sounder alarm never went off.

At this slow speed, the ride became much more bearable. I remained on watch until dawn, periodically shining the spotlight to watch for breaking chop. It was hard to say what sea conditions were, but I estimated 12-foot seas, with occasional breaking tops. I was satisfied with the route (about 16 fathoms minimum) and the fact that the autopilot was able to maintain a fixed course. The other three crew members slept through our rounding of Cape Mendocino and I found myself nodding off at times. It was similar to lying ahull, except that we were making good on a course to windward. (Our passage was vastly different from the Gaylords' experience.)

rents are very irregular. It is in the latitude of great climatic change; the winds do not blow home so violently in the bight S of it, and the amount of rainfall increases rapidly to the N. Fog is more prevalent S. The strong NW winds of summer are less violent S of the cape, which forms a parallel lee for vessels working their way N. (CP, 33rd Ed.)

Cape Mendocino is the major navigational challenge of the Pacific Coast south of Alaska. Blunts Reef requires staying offshore 5 miles to give this notorious cape a wide berth. (Read Michelle Gaylord's sidebar.)

Rounding Cape Mendocino on a typical blustery summer day

Blunts Reef
Chart 18623; 2.9 mi W of Cape Mendocino Lt
Position: 40°26.79'N, 124°28.74'W

Blunts Reef . . . is one of the outermost visible dangers off Cape Mendocino. The reef consists of two small black rocks awash about 230 yards apart. Blunts Reef Lighted Horn Buoy 2B . . . replacing Blunts Reef Lightship, is an exposed location buoy (ELB) 1.7 miles WSW of the outer rock. The currents at the buoy are described in the Tidal Current Tables.

The area as far W as Blunts Reef Lighted Buoy B and for about 4 miles N and S of Cape Mendocino includes dangerous rocks and covered ledges. Vessels should not attempt the passage between Blunts Reef Lighted Buoy B and the cape under any circumstances. A heavy W swell breaks even in 9 to 10 fathoms in this locality. (CP, 33rd Ed.)

Blunts Reef, which extends 5 miles off Cape Mendocino Light, creates turbulence where the south- and north-flowing currents meet and fight it out; to a small degree it also creates a lee. In fair weather, once past Blunts Reef light buoy R"2B," *Baidarka* sets a course west of Blunts Reef but east of the shoal that lies 4.4 to 5.4 miles northwest of Cape Mendocino light. This route, which is a shortcut, can be dangerous, is not recommended to all, and should not be used in foul weather or poor visibility.

Eel River
Chart 18620; 7.9 mi S of Humboldt Bay
Exit to ocean position: 40°38.68'N, 124°19.06'W

Eel River . . . is a stream of considerable size and is occasionally entered by light-draft vessels, but the channel over the bar is continually shifting. The depth on the bar varies largely with the amount of water in the river, depending upon the character of the winter, and has been at times as much as 14 feet, but generally the depth is about

South jetty, Humboldt Bay breakwater—caution required on entering

8 or 9 feet. The river is seldom entered except by fishing boats and other very small craft, and then only by those with local knowledge of the bar. (CP, 33rd Ed.)

We have heard of one kayaker who crossed the bar and entered the river for safety reasons; he found good camping along the shore of the lagoon.

Humboldt Bay (Eureka)

Chart 18622; 21 mi N of Cape Mendocino Lt
Outer entrance range: 40°46.29'N, 124°15.90'W
Inner entrance range: 40°46.03'N, 124°14.66'W
Buoy G"5" midchannel: 40°45.38'N, 124°13.96'W

Humboldt Bay . . . is the first important harbor N of San Francisco and is used by vessels drawing up to 35 feet. Humboldt Bay is the second largest natural bay on the coast of California and as such contains many environmentally and economically important wetland habitats. In addition to being a nursery area for many species of commercially and recreationally important fish and invertebrates, Humboldt Bay also produces more than 50 percent of the oysters harvested n California. Due to Humboldt Bay's location on the Pacific Flyway, it is also an important feeding, resting, and nesting area for thousands of migratory shorebirds and waterfowl. . . .

Humboldt Bay can be used as a harbor of refuge in impending bad weather, providing a vessel can get inside before the bar becomes impassable. The bay consists of two shallow

---

Fort Bragg to Eureka via Cape Mendocino
by Michelle Gaylord

A weather window finally opened up on July 16 so we left Fort Bragg bound for Eureka. We had wanted to stop in what we'd read was a neat little anchorage called Shelter Cove. But since the weather looked good we decided we'd better get around Cape Mendocino and continue on to Eureka. What a mistake.

I don't even know how to describe how bad the seas were. Just before Cape Mendocino I had made lunch and we sat down in the pilothouse to eat. On the horizon, we could see a wall of white water rolling toward us. I'm not talking white caps, I am talking a *wall* of white water. Then, all hell broke loose.

Our cushions and canvas on the bow blew out, and one of the lids on the storage units beneath broke free. We were in totally confused seas and being tossed all about, with no way to even turn around and go back. We were fighting 16- to 20-foot seas that were about 5 seconds apart; they literally came from all sides. The only way I can describe it was like being in a washing machine on the fastest agitation cycle.

Jerry insisted on retrieving the hatch cover and the cushions and opened the pilothouse door. Not only could he *not* retrieve the cover because the water was so fierce, but the door jammed open. He tried to fix the door so we could close it, but it was impossible. We now had seas of 20 feet plus, and winds of 20 to 30 knots. I was so frightened that he would be washed over the side, that I said, "To hell with the door—let the water come in!"

He came back inside just drenched and stripped down while I crawled below and got dry clothes. At this point we were in completely confused seas and taking breakers over the fly bridge from every angle. The water was pounding on all the windows so fiercely that we couldn't see out. We just had to have faith in the autopilot and hope for the best.

These conditions lasted for about two hours. The destruction we endured on this boat were unbelievable. When we finally pulled into a slip at Eureka we found that our boarding ladders and steps had torn free from their brackets and had been held tight only by being wedged in the walkway. All the cushions were water logged; the canvas was ripped and torn. Worst of all for Jerry, our satellite dish was damaged so he would have to survive without TV until we could get it replaced!

Once we assessed the outside damage I went down to the v-berth. We knew that the portholes and hatches were leaking in the v-berth, but we thought we had pretty much prepared for that problem: we had stripped all the cushions, curtains, and towels and, other than having to use dry towels to soak up the water, we thought we were okay. *Wrong!*

Everything in every cupboard and closet was soaked; the brand new rug in the guest stateroom was soaked. We spent five days in Eureka just cleaning up and repairing the mess. That was okay, though, because Eureka isn't one of the more charming ports and we didn't feel the pull to go sightseeing! I must say, though, that I now have complete faith in the stability of *Passing Thru.*

Aerial view: Eureka

basins, South Bay in the S and Arcata Bay in the N part, connected by a narrow channel about 5 miles long.

A pilot should be engaged by deep-draft vessels and by strangers if there is any sea on the bar. Because the bar is subject to change, the entrance ranges may not always mark the deepest channel. . . .

In clear weather the high land of Cape Mendocino and Punta Gorda S, and Trinidad Head N of the entrance, are good landmarks. At night, the lights are a good guide. In thick weather soundings should be taken frequently, and upon getting depths of 30 fathoms or less great caution must be exercised until sure of the vessel's position, when the course should be shaped for the lighted whistle buoy.

Sailing craft during the prevailing NW winds of summer should try to make the land in the vicinity of Trinidad Head; this gives a fair slant for the entrance and is an additional precaution against the irregular S set of the current. In thick weather soundings should be taken constantly when inside of 50 fathoms. Making the land N of the entrance avoids the irregular bottom and dangerous currents in the vicinity of Cape Mendocino.

From the Humboldt Bay Entrance Lighted Whistle Buoy HB, make good a course of 105° following the Humboldt Bay Approach Range to the intersection with Humboldt Bay Entrance Range, thence a course of 140° on the entrance range into the

Pacific Ocean

To Crescent City (CA036)

CA035

HUMBOLDT BAY (EUREKA) APPROACH
Use Chart 18010

N

1 mile

DEPTHS IN FATHOMS AT ZERO TIDE

Express Route (Crabpot-Free Tow Lane)

CA034

To Trinidad Harbor (CA443)

Dump Site

CA031

CA442

CA033   North Spit

CA032

CA030

To San Francisco (CA029)

CA438

To Shelter Cove (CA437)

Dump Site

Humboldt Bay

CA030	40°45.88'N 124°28.34'W	**CA034**	40°48.79'N 124°22.14'W
CA031	40°47.60'N 124°22.61'W	**CA035**	40°53.63'N 124°24.13'W
CA032	40°46.28'N 124°16.38'W	**CA438**	40°45.28'N 124°18.83'W
CA033	40°46.54'N 124°16.26'W		

©2003 Fine Edge Productions • Diagram not for navigation

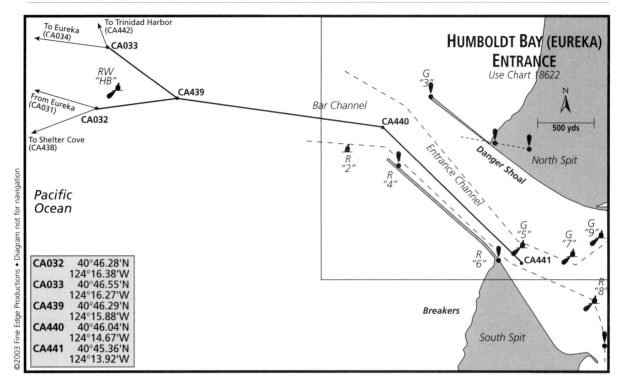

bay. The entrance range parallels the S jetty and is only about 150 yards from it. The turn from the approach to the entrance range, 200 yards off the outer end of the S jetty, is rather abrupt and is difficult under certain conditions of wind, sea, and current. Inside the bay the channels are well marked by navigational aids.

The approach to the bay is marked by a lighted whistle buoy and a bell buoy off the entrance, and approach range lights and a fog signal on the outer end of the North Spit. . . . Range lights and lighted buoys mark the entrance channel inside the bar. . . .

In the past Humboldt Bar was considered treacherous and dangerous, and many disasters have occurred there. Even with present improvements, mariners are still advised to use extreme caution on the bar. The strong currents that may be encountered, and the abrupt turn at the outer end of the S jetty, are apt to be dangerous for strangers. The bar is the smoothest during the last of the flood current, and it is often passable at this time and impassable 2 hours later, when the ebb current has set in. Mariners are advised to contact Coast Guard Station Humboldt Bay on VHF-FM channel 16 or 22A prior to transitting (sic) the bar.

Caution should also be exercised inside the jetties due to the rapid change in the channel conditions. Deep-draft vessels are usually taken in and out of the bay at high tide if there is any swell on the bar because of the shoaling in the entrance channel. . . .

In the summer, vessels are entered on flood and ebb tidal currents; in the winter, vessels usually are entered on the first or last of the flood or first of the ebb. Vessels depart on flood tidal currents only, regardless of the time of year. . . .

Eureka Public Marina—first marina to starboard

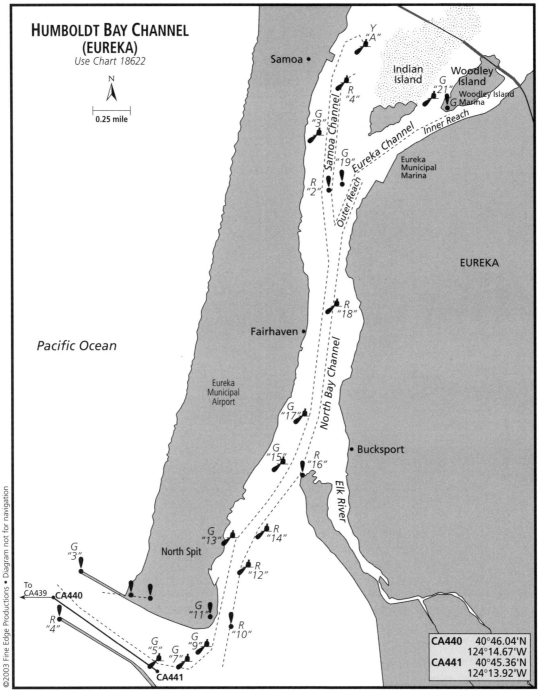

HUMBOLDT BAY CHANNEL
(EUREKA)
Use Chart 18622

N

0.25 mile

Samoa

Indian
Island

Woodley
Island

Woodley Island
Marina

G Marina

Y
"A"

R
"4"

G
"21"

G
"3"

Samoa Channel

Eureka Channel

Inner Reach

G
"19"

Eureka
Municipal
Marina

R
"2"

Outer Reach

EUREKA

Pacific Ocean

R
"18"

Fairhaven

North Bay Channel

Eureka
Municipal
Airport

G
"17"

G
"15"

R
"16"

Bucksport

Elk River

G
"13"

R
"14"

G
"3"

North Spit

R
"12"

To
CA439

CA440

R
"4"

G
"11"

R
"10"

G
"5"

G
"7"

G
"9"

CA441

©2003 Fine Edge Productions • Diagram not for navigation

CA440	40°46.04'N
	124°14.67'W
CA441	40°45.36'N
	124°13.92'W

Pilots report that strong current creates a N set in the Bar Channel from October to April. When vessels enter the jetties, this current has a tendency to twist vessels by setting the stern N and turning the bow S toward the S jetty. During or shortly after SE, S, and SW storms, currents in the Bar Channel and Entrance Channel are reported to attain a velocity of about 4 to 5.5 knots. Heavy swells about 6 to 8 feet high occur well inside the jetties when seas from the SW are deflected, about midway along the N jetty . . . Humboldt Bay Coast Guard Station is on North Spit. (CP, 33rd Ed.)

Entering Humboldt Bay, pass close to whistle buoy RW"HB" and head for our waypoint CA439 to intersect and follow the first range to the entrance bar channel just west of the two breakwater jetties. Next turn about 35° to the south and follow the second ranges along the south jetty to CA441, then to the turning basin and north to Eureka. Note that the northern three-quarters of the entrance channel is filled with sand and used by surfers when the surf is up. Stay to the south side of the channel and keep shoal buoys to port when entering. Use extreme caution when entering or exiting on an ebb current. Do not transit on breaking seas.

Woodley Island Marina office

Use Chart 18622 (edition 2001) as your guide and, for a current bar report, don't hesitate to call Humboldt Bay Coast Guard on channel 16 or 22A for a bar report before entering or exiting.

Eureka
Chart 18622

> *The climate of Eureka is completely maritime, and high humidity prevails the entire year, which is divided into the "rainy" season and the "dry" season. The rainy season begins in October and continues through April. About 90 percent of the year's precipitation falls during this period. The dry season extends from May through September and is marked by considerable fog or low cloudiness. On average, 23 of the 31 days in August will record fog where only 10 of the 31 days in March will note fog. Usually, however, the fog clears in the late forenoon and the early afternoons are generally sunny. . . .*
>
> *Small-craft facilities. Transient berths with*

Sharing the Docks at Woodley
by RHD

First, a 107-foot mega-yacht pulled up to the end dock shortly after we had tied up in our assigned slip. The crew, sporting dark glasses, and shirtless in white pants and shoes, or wearing bikinis, were "pure" So Cal. We watched as they dropped the stern line in the water, pulled it in again and threw it again, *incorrectly*. Several tries later, one of the crew managed to toss a spring line to some visiting boaters who secured the yacht. The yacht was bound for Vancouver, B.C. and we wondered how they had survived their journey with such an inexperienced crew.

Then, at the other extreme, an Outboard—was one of the most amazing boats we met on our entire trip. Docked near *Baidarka*, across from the mega-yacht—was an 18-foot outboard with just a canvas dodger for its "cabin." The little boat had come all the way from Sweden. Its owner, Roy Karlsen, a Dane, along with his Swedish partner, had been traveling in this tiny craft for two years. The boat was filled with jerry cans of fuel, plastic bins of food, a couple of sleeping bags, and there was barely room to turn around. The two men had crossed the Atlantic via Iceland, Greenland, and Labrador, come down the East Coast of the U.S., through the Panama Canal then up the Pacific Coast. They had been holed up in Eureka waiting out the same gales that had been hitting us on the nose as we pushed northward.

"We can afford to wait it out," Roy told me. "When the weather improves and the seas are flat we'll crank it up and go. We'll pass you in a hurry, because we can go 20 knots."

Somewhere on our route to Lituya Bay, Alaska, they did pass us, and they made it all the way to Kodiak Island before the end of the summer.

electricity are available at the marina on the S side of Woodley Island and at Eureka Boat Basin. [Eureka Public Marina] . . . Water, gasoline, diesel fuel, marine supplies, and launching ramps are available at most marinas in Humboldt Bay.

Wet winter storage is at the marina at the S side of Woodley Island. (CP, 33rd Ed.)

Eureka, the largest coastal town between San Francisco and the Oregon border is a Customs Port of Entry. Dating from Gold Rush days, Eureka began as a lumbering town whose red-

A scenic view of the slips at Woodley Island Marina

wood harvest rapidly developed into a world-wide market. In 1855 the town housed nine mills, and hundreds of schooners entered and left the bay loaded with timber. With the limiting of timber harvesting, many of the mills have been closed and much of this industry's history is now viewed in museums.

Woodley Island Marina on the southwest side

of Woodley Island, 4 miles from the entrance, is operated by the Humboldt Bay Harbor District which has jurisdiction over much of Humboldt Bay. The well-maintained marina offers transient berths for visiting vessels from 30 to 70 feet; larger boats are asked to contact the dockmaster at least 24 hours prior to arrival. Marina facilities include laundry and showers, a coffee

Another Eureka Bar Story
by DCD

Later that summer, friends of ours learned a different kind of lesson. They, too, were leaving Humboldt Bay in the early morning. Fog was heavy and they were proceeding slowly. As they made their final turn southwest into the entrance channel, the skipper switched his radar to a very short range to keep a good track of his distance from the south jetty. (The north half of the entrance channel fills with sand.) The first mate headed down to the galley to get a coffee refill.

The skipper checked his radar, then looked out through the windows. To his horror he saw a black shadow closing in at high speed directly in front. He jammed the helm to starboard and yelled to his wife, just as their boat glanced off a steel fishing vessel. He made a quick May Day call on Channel 16, giving his position, as the two boats drifted apart. The damage turned out to be mainly superficial and, with temporary repairs and a lot

of duct tape, they made it down the coast for a serious fiberglass job.

Lessons learned: First, keep crewmembers on an alert watch when navigating in close quarters during limited visibility. Second, keep switching radar ranges to make sure no high-speed vessels are approaching from any direction. (Fixation on short range is false security. A quarter-mile or half-mile range does not give adequate advance warning for fast-closing vessels.) Third, make a Security Announcement on Channel 16 (your position and intentions, as ferry boats do in northwest passes). In tight quarters, with limited visibility, listen for fog signals and sound your own horn frequently.

We can report that our friends have safely navigated from California to Alaska and back and through the Panama Canal for an Atlantic Crossing.

shop and bar, pump-out station, storage yard and work area; the fuel dock is nearby, and Woodley Island Ship Shop (chandlery) is on the north side of the harbor offices. As we go to press a new restaurant is being built on site. The harbor office will permit you to use one of their telephone lines for Internet if you have a laptop and an 800 number to dial. The marina operates on Channels 14 and 16. Vessels that need to have packages sent to Woodley Island by UPS or FEDEX should let the marina know ahead of time. Send care of: The Marina, 601 Sartare Drive, Eureka, CA 95501; include your name, and your vessel's name. The staff are particularly helpful and friendly and they do their best to make visiting boaters comfortable. (This marina was one of our favorites.)

Eureka Public Marina (also known as City Basin), which opened in 2000, although nearer the center of town, has fewer facilities than Woodley Island Marina. In addition, strong northwest or northerly winds can make berthing and leaving uncomfortable.

The NOAA office is located two blocks north of Woodley Island Marina; there you can see a computer-generated model of the compressed isobars bars that indicate increasing northwest winds in the foreseeable future. You can also see the effects of a thermally-induced low-pressure centered in the southwest deserts as it

Crossing the Bar
by DCD

We left Woodley Island Marina at 0550 on 16 June 2000. The weather in the predawn hours looked favorable—negligible wind, patchy light fog, an up-tick on the barometer and a strong ebb tide. I assumed that the swell and chop from the previous day's strong-to-gale-force afternoon winds had calmed and that we would have a quick and easy exit from Eureka. (A miscalculation!)

Because of the still conditions, I didn't bother to call the Coast Guard for a bar check and, when we rounded into the entrance channel at the beginning of the breakwater, it was still fairly dark. However, I could see white foam ahead of us. Concerned, I went into idle to study what was going on and I was amazed how fast the current was carrying us out to sea. The crew could see large breaking swells looming outside. I asked Réanne and our grandson, Josh, if they felt comfortable continuing. Réanne scanned the horizon with the binoculars and said she thought we should give it a try.

Baidarka quickly reached the end of the breakwater but kept hobbyhorsing. "I think we can make it," Réanne kept saying and then, suddenly, we were facing some very large, steep waves and it was too late to turn around—we would have been put on our beam ends. We kept minimum power on to maintain steerage, climbed a nearly vertical wall of water and slammed down with a snap on the other side. We continued this maneuver five times in the next hundred yards as we were carried through the standing waves.

Confused seas and waves, snarling with foam, continued for roughly a mile offshore. We had deployed the stabilization poles but we couldn't put the paravanes in the water until we had passed northwest of the entrance buoy.

In our logbook, I estimated the waves to be in the 10- to 15-foot range. They reminded me of some of the standing waves found in the Grand Canyon, famous for white-water rafting photos. Except for a few loose items that flew around, the boat and crew took it well but, as the sun rose and we looked back at the entrance, we realized how vulnerable we'd been.

Josh had gone to the forepeak to secure the anchor chain. When he returned to the pilothouse, his eyes wide, I said, "Josh, you can't get much more excitement than this in an amusement park, can you?"

"Yeah, but even a roller coaster is a lot safer!" he replied. Impressed by Réanne's "cool," he kept shaking his head. "I can't believe she kept saying 'I think we can make it.' Wow, what a grandmother!"

So what did I learn *again*? Call for a bar check. That moderate chop or swell doubles or triples in height and becomes steep and dangerous when it opposes a strong ebb in the 3- to 5-knot range. I should have turned around while we still could and held our position for a more serious study of the waves outside—a delay of just a few more minutes would have given the sun time to rise over the horizon for better visibility.

By noon the wind had increased to more than 25 knots from the northwest, giving us a bouncy ride; but by 1700 we completed the 60-mile run to Crescent City and tied up at the dock in very windy conditions.

moves toward the coast, pushing the high-pressure farther offshore.

Mariner statue on Woodley Island

Anchorage can be found in 2 fathoms in the channel between Woodley and Indian islands. However, the Humboldt Bay Harbor District authorities have had some problems with boats that anchored here in the past and they are now studying the feasibility of allowing anchoring at this site. Be sure to check with harbor authorities before you drop an anchor here.

Attractions in the area include the popular Samoa Cookhouse and museum on the North Spit; this is the last surviving cookhouse of a former lumber camp. Another treat in Eureka is taking in all the magnificent Victorian homes and mansions, beginning with the spectacular Carson Mansion, built in 1876 by a pioneer lumber magnate; there are literally dozens of these Victorians, and tour maps are widely available. If you carry a bicycle on your boat, you may want to use it—the center of town is a good hearty walk from Woodley Island.

Woodley Island is a bird sanctuary and we have enjoyed watching snowy egrets, great blue herons, and pelicans along the shore. It's also a good place to watch river otters and sea lions.

Be sure to check out the impressive bronze statue at the western end of the island—a memorial to the fishermen lost at sea. A star by the name indicates those whose bodies were never recovered. It's sobering to note that the starred names are in the majority.

National Wildlife Refuge, in South Bay, along with Arcata Marsh and Wildlife Sanctuary, in North Bay, lie along the Pacific Flyway. Fall through spring are the best viewing months and, if you stop here in September or May you may catch a glimpse of the migratory geese, ducks, swans and shorebirds that stop here. Eureka is also the gateway to the redwoods; both national and state parks lie within easy driving distance.

Aerial view: Trinidad Harbor

⚓ **Woodley Island Marina** position: 40°48.41'N, 124°09.96W; tel: 707.443.0801

⚓ **Eureka Public Marina** position: 40°48.20'N, 124°10.76'W

⚓ **U.S. Coast Guard** tel: 707-443-2213

⚓ **U.S. Customs Service** tel: 707.442.4822; cell phone: 707.321.6831; website: www.customs.ustreas.gov

⚓ **National Weather Service** tel: 707.443.6484

⚓ **Fuel Dock** tel: 707.444.9266

⚓ **Anchor** (N of Woodley Is): 40°48.65'N, 124°09.96'W (Please check with Humboldt Harbor authorities before anchoring here.)

Trinidad Head

Chart 18605; about 39 mi NNE of Cape Mendocino; 17.5 mi N of Humboldt Bay entr
Position (0.25 mi S): (CA445) 41°02.85'N, 124°09.14'W

> *Trinidad Head . . . rises to a height of 380 feet. The sides are steep and covered with chaparral. From N or S the head is generally raised as a dark, round-topped island. . . . (CP, 33rd Ed.)*

There is a narrow small craft (kayak) route close west of Trinidad Head and Blank and Flatiron Rocks. Seas break heavily on Trinidad Head when swell is running. Navigation in and around Trindad Head requires careful skill because of many rocks and islets. Trinidad Harbor, immediately east, offers fair shelter in northwest winds.

Close-up of the historic lighthouse south of Battery Point

David J. Shuler

Trinidad Harbor

Chart 18605; E of Trinidad Head
Entrance: (CA444) 41°03.10'N, 124°08.77'W
Anchor: 41°03.17'N, 124°08.76'W

> *Trinidad Harbor, a small cove, . . . affords shelter in NW weather, but is dangerous in W or S weather. The cove is small and is further constricted by several rocks, and, as a rule, there is always a swell even in N weather. It is used by fishing boats to a considerable extent during the summer, even*

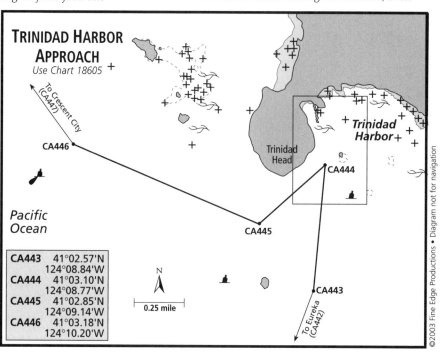

TRINIDAD HARBOR APPROACH
Use Chart 18605

To Crescent City (CA447)

CA446

Pacific Ocean

Trinidad Head

Trinidad Harbor

CA444

CA445

CA443	41°02.57'N 124°08.84'W
CA444	41°03.10'N 124°08.77'W
CA445	41°02.85'N 124°09.14'W
CA446	41°03.18'N 124°10.20'W

N

0.25 mile

CA443

To Eureka (CA442)

©2003 Fine Edge Productions • Diagram not for navigation

This 18-foot outboard carried a pair of Scandinavian men on their quest to circle the world

though the holding ground is only fair. . . . A small marine railway near the foot of the pier is used for launching and retrieving small craft up to 26 feet long and 9 feet wide. . . .

The best anchorage is in 42 feet, muddy bottom, about halfway between Prisoner Rock and Trinidad Head, with Flat Rock, bearing 073°, just

open S of Prisoner Rock. . . . (CP, 33rd Ed.)

Scenic Trinidad Harbor is one of our favorite kayaking spots. We could spend hours paddling within a radius of one to two miles of Trinidad Head and not see everything we wanted to see. Our favorite lunch stop when we're kayaking is in a tiny channel in Double Rock where only occasional surge is felt. Because of its proximity to Eureka, its rocky bottom and limited swinging room, Trinidad Harbor is not the first choice of coastal cruising boats. However, it does make a good temporary rest stop or emergency shelter. (See sidebar below.) The harbor caters mainly to small, trailerable boats.

We have enjoyed watching river otters chasing each other in and out of dinghies moored to the small pier. In good stable weather, you may want to go ashore to stretch your legs on the trails over Trinidad Head, poke around the boutiques in the village or have a meal at one of the restaurants. The pier is reserved for commercial and sportfishing boats; inquire about tying your dinghy there.

Anchor in 6 fathoms over sand, mud and rock; fair-to-good holding. Be sure to use an anchor light if you stay overnight (this site is in the fairway).

Roy Karlsen and crew meet Baidarka *in Eureka on their 'round-the-world attempt*

TRINIDAD HARBOR
Use Chart 18605

CA444 41°03.10'N 124°08.77'W

©2003 Fine Edge Productions • Diagram not for navigation

Trinidad Head to Point St. George
Charts 18605, 18600

From Trinidad Head for 5.5 miles to Rocky Point, the coast is rocky, with numerous outlying islets and ledges extending as much as 1.2 miles offshore and cliffs reaching elevations of over 100 feet. The mountains back of Trinidad Head are good landmarks for vessels approaching from seaward. . . . The coast trends in a general NW direction with a shallow bight known as Pelican Bay immediately N of Point St. George. (CP, 33rd Ed.)

Klamath River
Chart 18600; 16 mi S of Point St. George; 29.8 mi N of Trinidad Head
Entrance position: 41°32.73'N, 124°05.32'W

Klamath River . . . is a large river draining an extensive mountainous area. The entrance is no longer navigable, but there is small-craft traffic on the river. There are several float landings where sport fishing craft berth. Gasoline, water, ice, launching ramps, and marine supplies are available. (CP, 33rd Ed.)

The Klamath River is a well-known sportfishing area; the famous Klamath dory is a popular skiff along the river.

Crescent City Harbor
Chart 18603; 41.4 mi N of Trinidad Head
Entrance buoy R"4": 41°43.57'N, 124°11.43'W
Harbor entrance: (CA452) 41°44.26'N, 124°11.35'W
Inner Basin entrance: 41°44.78'N, 124°11.06'W

Caution. Care should be exercised in approaching Crescent City Harbor because of the many rocks and shoals. Chase Ledge, covered 21 feet, lies 0.9 mile S of Round Rock. Mussel Rock, only a few feet high, is 0.6 mile SE of Round Rock; a rock covered 7 feet, 700 yards to the S, breaks only in a heavy swell. Other covered rocks extend N to Whaler Island. Foul ground with many bare and covered rocks extends nearly a mile offshore along the low but rocky coast NW of Crescent City Harbor for 3.5 miles to Point St. George. This area should be avoided.

The long wharf in the W part of the harbor is used by fishing vessels to offload fish. The remains of two other wharves, just E, were almost completely wiped out by the seismic sea wave which struck the harbor following the March 27, 1964, Alaska earthquake. The seismic wave caused considerable damage and changes to the harbor shoreline. . . .

The W breakwater gives protection from NW

Kimosabe Disabled by "Sci-Fi" Wave
by DCD

Kimosabe—a 67-foot Hatteris, with a professional delivery crew of three—was on its way north from Newport Beach to British Columbia when it was hit by a "sci-fi" (rogue) wave at 0145 west of Trinidad during the night of 15 June 2000. The yacht was about 20 miles offshore at the time it was hit. The wave was reported to be twice the size (35 feet) of other waves (17 feet) during rough sea conditions. The NOAA area weather forecast for June 14 had called for heavy gales with gusts to 60 knots and seas to 30 feet.

The rogue wave broke out the windows, flooding much of the boat, and causing loss of steerage, thereby disabling the vessel. Two Coast Guard helicopters hovered over the vessel until dawn when they instructed the two moderately injured crew to put on their survival suits and jump into the water so they could be picked up and flown to Mad River Hospital. The skipper stayed aboard *Kimosabe* and—because conditions over the bar at Humboldt Bay were too rough to attempt entry—the vessel was towed into Trinidad Harbor and anchored by a USCG motor lifeboat.

Kimosabe had passed *Baidarka* some time previously and, when we caught up with her in Trinidad several days later, the skipper told us by radio what had happened. We had been more fortunate rounding Cape Mendocino two nights before.

Just a day or two can make a big difference in the conditions as well as the choice of route when cruising. Having an alternative place to duck into in an emergency can also make a big difference.

Baidarka had moved each day along the inshore route, and the strongest winds we experienced were 25 knots northwest, with afternoon gusts to 40 knots and occasional 12-foot seas. We frequently marveled at the yachts with big windows and hotel-sized furniture that passed us at high speed, throwing lots of spray. After hearing about *Kimosabe*'s experience, we felt safer than ever on *Baidarka*.

Aerial view: Crescent City

Mermaid sculpture near the harbor-master's office, Crescent City

winds for vessels anchored in the outer harbor, but the harbor is open to the S. The basin N of Whaler Island provides excellent anchorage for small craft.

The harbormaster with an office at the basin N of Whaler Island assigns berths. He monitors VHF-FM channels 9 and 16, Monday through Friday from 0500 to 2100. . . .

The inner small-craft basin just N of Citizens Dock can accommodate about 500 boats. . . . The reported controlling depth was 12 feet in the entrance channel in the basin. (CP, 33rd Ed.)

Midway between San Francisco and the Columbia River, Crescent City Harbor is protected by breakwaters and distinguished by a historic private light on the islet south of Battery Point. Crescent City, a harbor of refuge, can be entered in almost all weather, ex-

cept very strong southerlies. Entering the harbor can be a bit of a problem because the range marks are small and low. Identify whistle buoy R"4"; get on the range heading due north and pass between the entrance narrows, keeping buoy R"6" to starboard and G"7" to port. Leave the range once past the north (inner) jetty, and turn east-north-east into the inner basin. *Baidarka* found that the dredged channel was less than the charted depths of 10 feet.

Crescent City caters to commercial and sport-fishing boats. Crabbing, itself, is a principal industry of the city, which typically has drawn the highest concentration of catch anywhere along the coast of California. Although Del

The rugged coast off Crescent City

David J. Shuler

Norte County used to be a center of logging mills, in recent years most of the mills have been closed. (A bumper sticker we spotted on a pickup truck gives an idea of how locals feel: "Help destroy America. Join an environmental group.")

Anchorage can be taken anywhere in the outer basin *with due regard to the depths*—the basin shoals rapidly around the north shore. Although harbor officials try to warn boats by using spotlights, a hailer or VHF radio, their efforts are sometimes to no avail—about 12 boats a year go aground here. The skippers anchor at night, then hit the sack. "They always wake up *after* the boat starts tipping over," harbor officials told us with a smile.

EXPLORING THE PACIFIC COAST

Historic Private lighthouse south of Battery Point

Fuel, water and ice are available at the pier where fishing boats unload their catch along the outer spurs. The inner basin berths (245 total) have electricity; fuel, launching ramps, and pump-out station are also available. Provisions can be found in the center of town, about a mile from the harbor. Restaurants in the city feature fresh local catch. Englund Marine Supply, headquartered in Astoria, has stores along the coast from Eureka to Westport, Washington; it is a serious outfitter that caters mainly to the commercial and sportfishing trade.

Del Norte coast is known for its tasty Dungeness crab—witness the thousands of crab traps lining the area near the harbormaster's office, but note that you need a crab permit everywhere except at the B Street Pier.

Although its reputation as a working port may discourage some pleasure craft from stopping, Crescent City, itself, has a

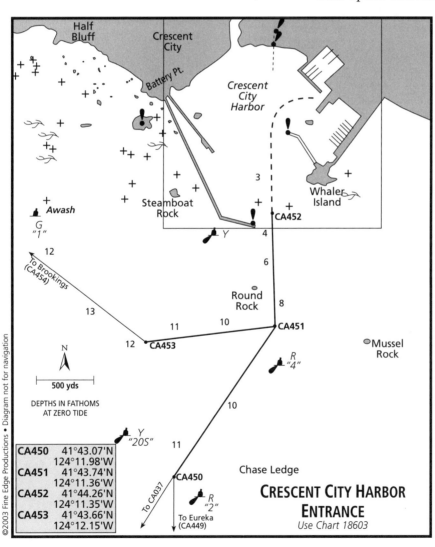

CRESCENT CITY HARBOR ENTRANCE
Use Chart 18603

Marina breakwater at the inner bay, Crescent City

number of attractions worth visiting. Ocean World, just north of the harbor, features a half-million gallon tank with a sandy bottom and reef exhibit, a touch tide-pool and other wonderful exhibits. Battery Point Lighthouse, built in 1856 and now a museum, offers guided tours five days a week. Del Norte County merits a visit by rental car. From here you can drive to the Redwood National and State Parks. Five miles north of Crescent City is

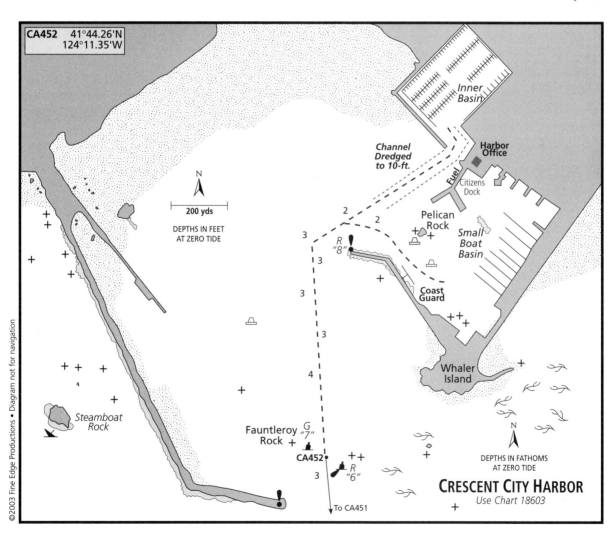

This dragger is part of the commercial fleet at Crescent City

Lake Earl, a 5000-acre wildlife habitat popular for fishing, hiking, small-boating, and waterfowl hunting.

Note: Early in the morning, while *Baidarka* was still moored at the dock in Crescent City, we were able to raise Chetco River Coast Guard on Channel 22A for an update on weather and bar conditions before leaving.

Point St. George
Chart 18603; 3 mi NW of Battery Point

> *Point St. George . . . is low with several irregular and rocky hillocks near the beach. . . .* (CP, 33rd Ed.)

Brown rock and foul ground extend 0.5 mile northwest of Point St. George.

St. George Channel
Chart 18603
Entrance (S): (CA454)
41°45.64'N, 124°16.40'W
Entrance (N): (CA457)
41°49.26'N, 124°16.93'W

> *St. George Channel, over a mile wide, is clear between the visible rocks fringing Point St. George and the E rocks of St. George Reef. It is frequently used in clear weather by coastwise vessels.* (CP, 33rd Ed.)

Baidarka found St. George Channel useful as a shortcut on a northbound route to Chetco River. However, it is filled with crabpots that can be difficult to avoid.

St. George Reef
Chart 18603; 6.5 mi NW & W of Point St. George

> *St. George Reef is composed of rocks and covered ledges. . . . Nine visible rocks are in the group. . . . All the rocks of St. George Reef rise abruptly; soundings made in the vicinity give no warning of their presence. In thick weather, the greatest cau-*

Eureka to Crescent City
by Michelle Gaylord

On July 21 we had recovered enough to leave Eureka and head for Crescent City. The seas were as flat as a duck pond on a calm day. It's really amazing how the sea conditions can change so drastically from day to day. When we arrived in Crescent City, the harbor was loaded with fishing boats and the dock ambiance reflects that. There were only a few pleasure boats here, and next to the workboats they stuck out like a sore thumb. Most of the cruisers we met in Ft. Bragg and Eureka were going to bypass this harbor and head for Brookings. We spent two days here resting; we didn't do much of anything interesting—we were just too pooped.

The commercial fishing fleet in Crescent City

tion should be observed and the reef given a wide berth. (CP, 33rd Ed.)

Pelican Bay
Chart 18600; extends 15 mi N of Point St. George

For about 10 miles N of Point St. George, the shores of Pelican Bay are composed of sand dunes, with a broad beach extending to the mouth of Smith River. Lake Talawa and Lake Earl are surrounded by Low marshy land behind this stretch of dunes. (CP, 33rd Ed.)

Crescent City is home to thousands of crabpots

Pelican Bay is a broad, exposed bight between Point St. George and the Checto River area. Smith River empties into Pelican Bay, 9.4 miles, and Winchuck River, 13.1 miles, north of Cape St. George.

Smith River
Chart 18602; 6.6 mi SE of Brookings
Entrance: 41°56.43'N, 124°12.98'W

From Smith River for 3.2 miles to the California-Oregon boundary, the coast is composed of low rocky cliffs, bordered by numerous rocks and ledges, covered and awash, and back by a low narrow tableland. Several prominent rocky knolls rise from 100 to 200 feet above this tableland.

Pyramid Point, a rocky knoll 22 feet high, marks the N point of Smith River. (CP, 33rd Ed.)

Smith River enters the Pacific 0.5 mile southeast of Prince Island. This island and a series of rocks and kelp beds to the south provide some shelter in fair weather for kayakers or small craft that want to enter the river or land at the beach. Stay north of the 10-foot rock 0.5 mile off the beach and avoid the many isolated rocks along this coast.

This section of coastline looks interesting and is on our "to do" list the next time we're in Brookings.

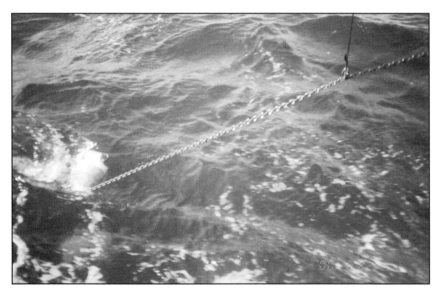

Baidarka snags a crabpot with its paravane stabilizer in St. George Channel

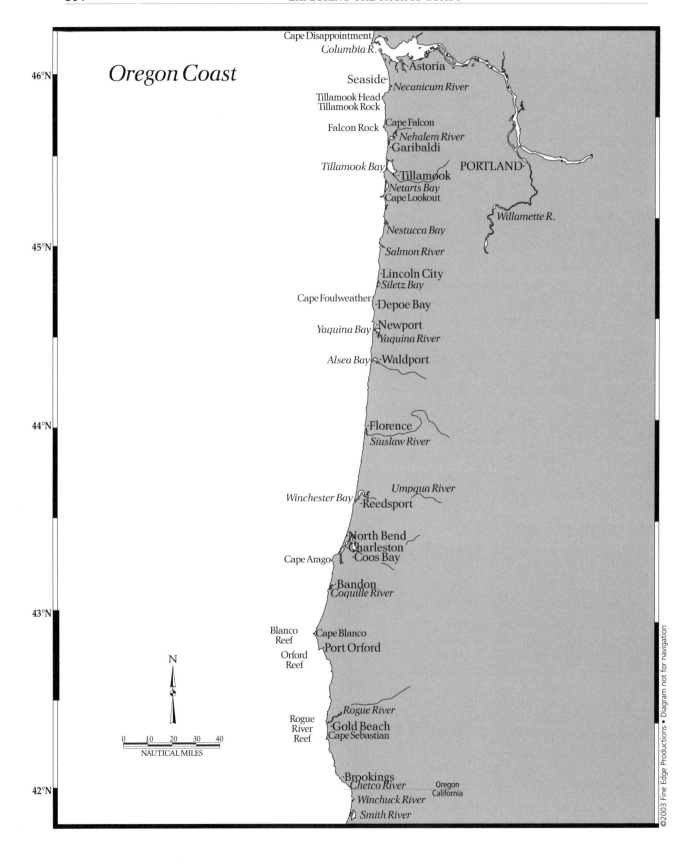

Oregon Coast

6

Oregon Coast:
Chetco River to Tillamook Head

Introduction

The 42nd Parallel, which marks the border between California and Oregon, lies 13 nautical miles northeast of Point St. George, immediately south of Winchuck River. The nearly 400-mile-long coast of Oregon is varied and beautiful: sandy beaches, sand dunes, rugged cliffs and ridges that tower above the water, stunning arches, and numerous flat-topped rocky islets, known as "haystacks." Along this coast, a number of capes and headlands create a natural lee where reasonable temporary shelter can be found. These coves make good rest stops in prevailing northwest winds, but they are exposed in southerly weather and in all gales and storms. The capes frequently create back eddies that can help small vessels go to windward. Many of the freshwater rivers provide excellent protection in lagoons or bights inside the entrance, but they all require crossing a shallow sandbar that can be difficult or closed to traffic by the Coast Guard when conditions warrant it.

Because numerous reefs, rocks and shoals extend from the Oregon shore, it's critical to carry updated charts and to know your precise position at all times. If you like to keep "one foot on the beach" to look for favorable back eddies, enjoy the sights and odors near land, or take advantage of a welcome rest under a lee, be sure to maintain an alert bow lookout; many of the areas along the coast are poorly sounded and lacking in large-scale charts.

Like a good part of the entire Pacific Coast, crabpot floats by the thousands have become hazards to coastal boaters. These pots are usually set between shore and the 30-fathom curve, although they can be found all the way out to 50 fathoms. Maintain a sharp lookout and carry skin diving gear to clear your propeller in case you should snag a float line. Fishermen realize this growing problem and admit that they are losing many of their pots. To minimize this hazard, we suggest you consider using the crabpot-free, tugboat tow-zone (our suggested Express Route).

In heavy weather or strong ebb currents, seas heap up off the entrance bars and develop breaking waves that become dangerous, often restricting entry. Flashing yellow, rough-bar lights are activated by the Coast Guard when seas reach 4 feet in height and, at such times, small sportfishing-boat transits are usually restricted. When seas reach 6 feet and start to break, larger boats are restricted; when seas

Rugged southern Oregon Coast

reach 8 feet, the entry bars are generally closed to all recreational traffic. Actual bar conditions depend on many factors and should be carefully checked by calling the local Coast Guard station on VHF Channel 16 prior to entering or exiting. *The bar lights can be seen only from land (not from sea!).*

It is generally unsafe to cross a river bar on an ebb tide with any sizeable seas running outside. The safest time to cross a bar in either direction is on a flood tide just before high water. Coos Bay is considered the safest harbor to enter because of its greater depths. However, it too is closed to small craft any time a brisk northwest wind creates sizeable breaking waves at its entrance. But it is frequently one of the last to close in southeast gales due to the lee effect provided by nearby Cape Arago.

Yaquina Bay at Newport is also well situated for entering during summer winds, while Coquille and Tillamook are among the first entrances to be closed on rising seas. Always prepare alternative plans should conditions change. Contact the local Coast Guard station on Channel 16 to verify weather and bar conditions. Seven local Coast Guard stations can give you updated reports on any of the regional bars. Some stations have recorded messages which may be reached by cell phone. (See listings within the text or ask the Coast Guard for current numbers.) The Coast Guard is happy to provide an escort when a visiting boat wants assistance to enter their harbor; they will meet you at the entrance buoy with a Coast Guard rescue boat, crewed by friendly experts, and escort you safely inside—at no charge!

All of the Oregon inner harbors offer excellent shelter and have villages or towns where you can wait for conditions to improve before continuing your voyage. The residents are friendly and helpful, and you can usually choose from a number of attractions and good restaurants while you're safely docked at a marina.

Between Rogue River and Cape Blanco, the westernmost tip of Oregon, two major reefs—Rogue River Reef and Cape Blanco Reef—require vessels to remain about 5 miles offshore. Tight, fair-weather routes for small craft can be found behind these reefs, but they require threading through some kelp-infested shoals and "rock piles." Unless you like to keep one foot on the beach and explore some of the tiny gunkholes, it's best to give these obstacles a wide berth.

Port Orford, a popular anchorage for coastal cruisers, is well sheltered from summer northwest gales and one of the few places in Oregon where good anchorage can be found without crossing a river bar. Coos Bay bar is closed the least frequently during rough seas; both Coos Bay and Newport are relatively easy to enter and have many points of interest. Cape Falcon, an open roadstead without a bar, can provide helpful, temporary anchorage for timing an entrance to the Columbia River. The Oregon coast is a great cruising ground, and day-hopping from one end to the other with a calm, snug mooring every night can be great fun.

Note: In this chapter, immediately following the abridged *Coast Pilot* quotations, we

Crabs, fresh for cooking at Newport

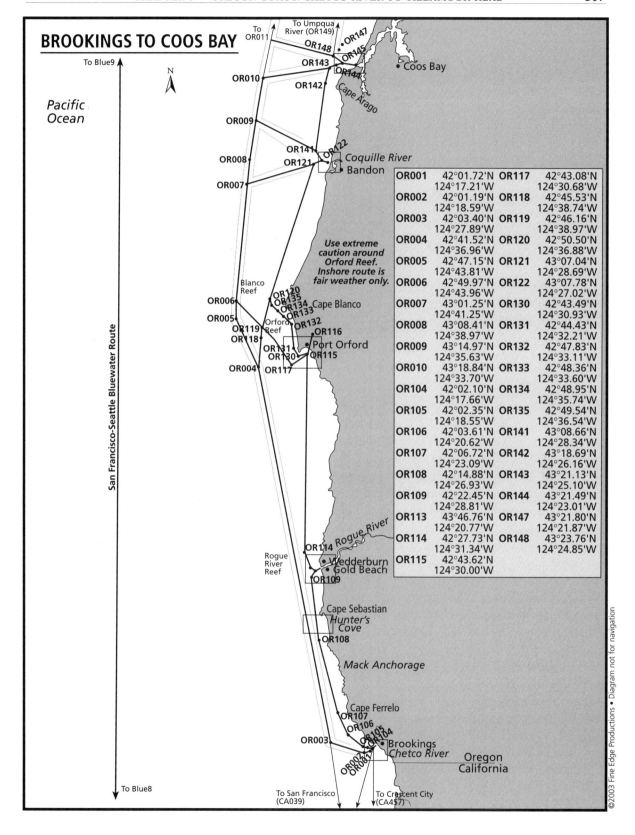

BROOKINGS TO COOS BAY

To Blue9

Pacific
Ocean

N

To OR011
To Umpqua
River (OR149)
OR147
OR148
OR145
OR143
OR144
Coos Bay
OR010
OR142
Cape Arago
OR009
OR141
OR122
OR008   OR121
Coquille River
Bandon
OR007

Use extreme
caution around
Orford Reef.
Inshore route is
fair weather only.

Blanco
Reef
OR120
OR135
OR134   Cape Blanco
OR133
OR006
OR132
OR005
Orford
Reef
OR119   OR116
OR118
OR131   Port Orford
OR130   OR115
OR004   OR117

San Francisco-Seattle Bluewater Route

Rogue River
Rogue
River
Reef
OR114
OR109   Wedderburn
Gold Beach

Cape Sebastian
Hunter's
Cove
OR108

Mack Anchorage

Cape Ferrelo
OR107
OR106
OR105
OR003   OR104
OR002   Brookings
OR001   Chetco River   Oregon
California

To Blue8

To San Francisco
(CA039)
To Crescent City
(CA457)

OR001	42°01.72'N	OR117	42°43.08'N
	124°17.21'W		124°30.68'W
OR002	42°01.19'N	OR118	42°45.53'N
	124°18.59'W		124°38.74'W
OR003	42°03.40'N	OR119	42°46.16'N
	124°27.89'W		124°38.97'W
OR004	42°41.52'N	OR120	42°50.50'N
	124°36.96'W		124°36.88'W
OR005	42°47.15'N	OR121	43°07.04'N
	124°43.81'W		124°28.69'W
OR006	42°49.97'N	OR122	43°07.78'N
	124°43.96'W		124°27.02'W
OR007	43°01.25'N	OR130	42°43.49'N
	124°41.25'W		124°30.93'W
OR008	43°08.41'N	OR131	42°44.43'N
	124°38.97'W		124°32.21'W
OR009	43°14.97'N	OR132	42°47.83'N
	124°35.63'W		124°33.11'W
OR010	43°18.84'N	OR133	42°48.36'N
	124°33.70'W		124°33.60'W
OR104	42°02.10'N	OR134	42°48.95'N
	124°17.66'W		124°35.74'W
OR105	42°02.35'N	OR135	42°49.54'N
	124°18.55'W		124°36.54'W
OR106	42°03.61'N	OR141	43°08.66'N
	124°20.62'W		124°28.34'W
OR107	42°06.72'N	OR142	43°18.69'N
	124°23.09'W		124°26.16'W
OR108	42°14.88'N	OR143	43°21.13'N
	124°26.93'W		124°25.10'W
OR109	42°22.45'N	OR144	43°21.49'N
	124°28.81'W		124°23.01'W
OR113	43°46.76'N	OR147	43°21.80'N
	124°20.77'W		124°21.87'W
OR114	42°27.73'N	OR148	43°23.76'N
	124°31.34'W		124°24.85'W
OR115	42°43.62'N		
	124°30.00'W		

include local hazard information from *Boating in Oregon
Coastal Waters* (BOCW), published by the Oregon State
Marine Board; this is an excellent reference with aerial photos for all entrances. Although
BOCW is designed for small
sportfishing boats leaving the
shelter of the harbors, we feel
that it provides valuable knowledge on local conditions and
potential problems for coastal
cruising boats. (Please see
Bibliography.)

Aerial view: Winchuck River

Winchuck River
Chart 18602; 3.1 mi SE of
Brookings
Position (entr): 42°00.04'N, 124°14.69'W

> *Dangerous—not suitable for crossings.* (BOCW,
> 2001 Ed., p. 45)

Winchuck River is a small, scenic river that
drains the area just north of the California-
Oregon State line. There is no *Coast Pilot* information on Winchuck River. BOCW's terse
warning quoted above indicates that it should
not be considered a cruising destination.

The Winchuck flows through gentle and
rolling, tree-covered hills and out across a wide,
mostly drying, sandy beach, that prevents
motorized craft from entering. However the
beach is somewhat protected by an off-lying
sand and rock bar and thick kelp beds, creating
a possible temporary anchor site. Smooth water
behind the kelp makes the beach a feasible
haulout spot for kayaks in fair weather. The
lagoon behind the drying bar is a good place to
explore by dinghy or kayak.

There appears to be a narrow passage leading
from the ocean to the calmer water behind the
kelp beds close north of Camel Rock. This passage, which carries about 3 fathoms, lies between
Camel Rock (13 feet above high water) and a rock
awash 100 yards to the north. Avoid the dangerous submerged rock cluster, 3 feet high, at the
"entering point" west of Camel Rock, just inside

the 10-fathom curve. This is a fascinating area,
but it is dangerous and not recommended for
larger vessels and is certainly a bad lee shore in
foul weather.

Isolated rocks that lie just below the surface
a mile or more offshore of the Winchuck may
heap up and break without warning. An alert
bow watch and slow-approach speed are
required for boats passing close to shore.

Both Winchuck River, and Smith River in California, can be explored in fair weather by kayak
or a ship's tender from the security of Brookings
Harbor a few miles north.

Chetco Cove (approach to Brookings)
Charts 18602, 18600; 18.5 mi N of Crescent City
Position Entr Buoy R"2": (OR102) 42°02.11'N,
124°16.69'W

> *Chetco Cove . . . affords some protection from NW
> winds, but is exposed in S weather. . . .* (CP, 33rd
> Ed.)

Chetco Cove, the bight east of Chetco Point at
the outlet of the Chetco River, is sometimes
used as an anchorage by fishing boats. The cove
has several shoals and rocky areas, so use caution when approaching 10 fathoms or the area
inside buoy R"2."

To safely enter Chetco Cove, first close the
"CR" entrance buoy and set a course northeast to
pass close to waypoints OR102 and OR103; then

follow the range marks through the dredged channel into the Chetco River. Beware of the areas on either side of the jetties as noted below. Chetco Cove is seldom used as an anchorage by cruising boats because such good shelter can be found inside the Port of Brookings.

Chetco River
(Port of Brookings)
Charts 18602, 18600; 15.5 mi N of Pt. St. George and 43 mi S of Port Orford
Entrance buoy R"2": (OR102) 42°02.11'N, 124°16.69'W
Dredged Channel buoy G"3": 42°02.37'N, 124°16.49'W
Midchannel pos: (OR103) 42°02.65'N, 124°16.27'W
Transient float: 42°02.81'N, 124°16.01'W
USCG Base position: 42°02.78'N, 124°16.03'W
Recreation Basin position: 42°02.96'W, 124°16.15'W
Commercial Basin position: 42°02.76'N, 124°15.99'W

Chetco River . . . is entered through a dredged channel which leads between two stone jetties to the Port of Brookings turning basin, about 0.3 mile above the jetties. The turning basin and a small-craft basin just N of it are protected to the W by a 1,800-foot-long dike. Another small-craft basin is about 250 yards SE of the turning basin. . . . The river entrance channel is marked by a 030° lighted range and other aids; a light and fog signal are off

Aerial view: Port of Brookings

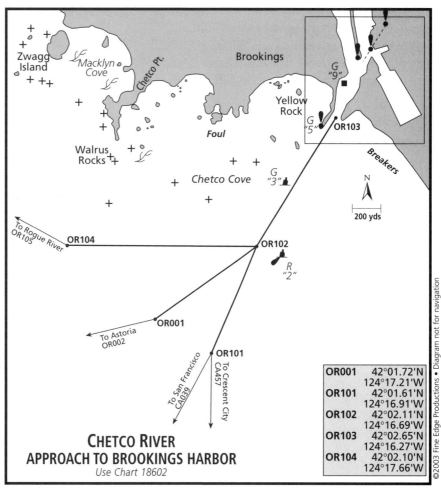

OR001	42°01.72'N
	124°17.21'W
OR101	42°01.61'N
	124°16.91'W
OR102	42°02.11'N
	124°16.69'W
OR103	42°02.65'N
	124°16.27'W
OR104	42°02.10'N
	124°17.66'W

CHETCO RIVER
APPROACH TO BROOKINGS HARBOR
Use Chart 18602

Baidarka *approaching Chetco River with dredge in entrance*

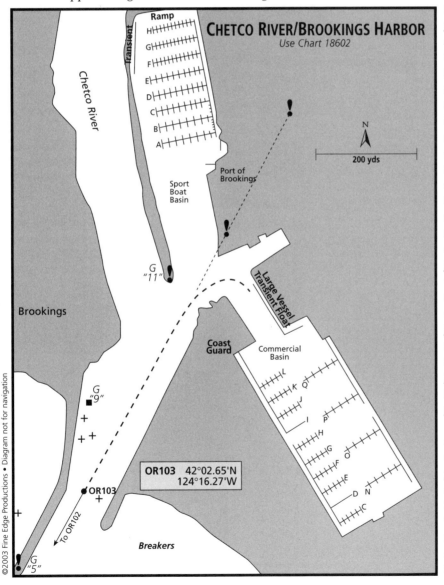

the outer end of the W jetty. In 1999-August 2000, the controlling depths were 9 feet (12 feet in midchannel) in the entrance channel, thence 7 to 14 feet in the barge turning basin; thence 7 to 12 feet to the head of the upper small-craft basin, except for lesser depths along the N and W edges, thence 6 feet (11 at midchannel) in the entrance to the lower small-craft basin to the beginning of the floating slips, thence 5 to 9 feet in the barge slip. An overhead power cable crossing the river about 0.6 mile above the jetties has a clearance of about 46 feet. The highway bridge has a clearance of 59 feet. . . .

Chetco River Coast Guard Station is on the E side of the river 450 yards inside the entrance. A lookout tower atop a building at the station is used to observe the bar during heavy weather. The Coast Guard has established . . . a rough bar advisory sign, 13 feet above the water, visible from the channel looking seaward, on the N end of the Coast Guard moorings, to promote safety for small-boat operators. . . . The sign is equipped with two quick flashing amber lights that will be activated when seas exceed 4 feet in height and are considered hazardous for small boats. Boatmen are cautioned, however, that if the lights are not flashing, it is no guarantee that sea conditions are favorable. . . .

The upper basin has over 500 berths, most with electricity; gasoline, diesel fuel, water, ice, marine supplies, and a launching ramp are available. Berths with electricity and water are reported to be available in the lower basin. . . . (CP, 33rd Ed.)

Dredge Yaquina *at work, Chetco River*

DANGEROUS AREAS

A. West jetty rock area. *This area is dangerous because of many rocks and shoaling. At high tide the rocks are covered by water and the area appears navigable but is extremely dangerous. Avoid this area at all times. Do not pass between the green day board and the North Jetty.*

B. Jetty and shoal areas. *These areas are extremely dangerous at all times because of submerged rocks and breakers. Two rocks in this area may be seen at low tide. Avoid this area at all times.*

Brookings
by Michelle Gaylord

July 22 we left Crescent City for Brookings, just an 18-mile passage. Once again, we had wonderful seas. Brookings, the first harbor in Oregon, is on the Chetco River. The pine trees here are thick and dense and grow all the way down to the water line—it's really pretty.

Once again we decided to dinghy upriver. I wasn't sure how far upriver we could go, or how long we would be gone, so I packed cameras, jackets, drinks, snacks, etc. I had it all stacked on the swim step ready to load into the dinghy when I decided I'd better grab my wallet in case there was something to buy upstream; so I climbed back up on the boat. As I was coming back down the ladder, Jerry was untying the dinghy. At this point I'm not exactly sure what transpired; all I know is that I was trying to stay out of his way. I tripped over one of the swim step dinghy rails, and then saw my camera case in a very precarious position. Afraid I was going to knock both of my cameras in the drink, I sidestepped. Well, it was a step just a little far to the side, and in I went.

It's funny, but when something like that happens there is a split second of time where you think you might just be all right, and then realize "Nope, I'm a goner."

All I could think about was keeping my wallet above water, and I think I did for the most part, but Jerry says I went down like a rock. I do know I swallowed at least a cup of saltwater.

I was in the water longer than I would have liked, but Jerry had a hard time getting the swim ladder down, and I was too out of shape to hoist myself up like a true athlete. The water was pretty darn cold, but I didn't get frostbite, so I guess we haven't gotten into the really frigid waters yet.

We were docked right across from the Coast Guard Station and I don't know if they witnessed this fiasco, but I had no choice but to strip down on the back deck,

because I was damned if I was going to soak any more water onto my new carpet. So there I was, buck-naked on the back deck in front of the whole Chetco River Coast Guard.

I wasn't going to let a minor mishap ruin our day, so I dried off, got dressed, and off we went. The river here is a lot wider than the Noyo River at Ft. Bragg, and it felt more like running down a regular channel, but the scenery with all the pine trees was spectacular, and the water in the river is a beautiful shade of turquoise blue. Not at all the color you would expect to see in either the ocean (except maybe in the Caribbean) or a river.

When we returned from the dinghy ride, we hopped onto our bikes and passed the large parking lot, just above the commercial fishing trawlers, where there were thousands of crab traps—I *mean* thousands. They were full of lines and colorful buoys, and it was quite a sight. We found a great little hole-in-the-wall restaurant that served the best and freshest fish we'd had in a long time, so we ate lunch there both days.

New marina floats at Brookings

Baidarka *tied to transient float at Brookings*

RANGE MARKERS

The range markers consist of a red rectangular shape with a black vertical stripe mounted on a skeleton tower. By steering a course that keeps the two range markers in line, you will remain within the channel.

ROUGH BAR ADVISORY SIGN

Positioned on the Coast Guard fuel dock facing north-northwest.

BAR CONDITION REPORTS

KURY (910 kHz). Hourly or more often if the bar is rough. For weather reports call 541.469.4571.

Michelle Gaylord

Lighthouse at Brookings, Chetco River

Reports updated throughout the day. (BOCW, 2001 Ed., p. 42)

Chetco River's Port of Brookings Harbor provides welcome and friendly shelter along with

Aerial view: Chetco River & Port of Brookings

Crabpot storage, Brookings

convenient facilities in a picturesque setting. When entering Chetco River, be sure to locate entrance buoy RW"CR" and line up on the range lights through the dredged channel between the two jetty breakwaters. It is important to stay on the range marks until you have passed the Coast Guard base because of shoals and rocks along the narrow dredged channel— especially on the north side. (When the government dredge is working inside this channel, passing allowance is restricted, and you may have to wait until it is safe to pass the dredge.)

Chetco River is relatively easy to enter during strong northwest weather because the rocks and kelp beds to the west of the river entrance create a lee. The entrance, however, is open to southwest swells. Call Chetco River Coast Guard on Channel 16 for a current bar report. (We have been able to contact them from as far away as the inner harbor at Crescent City.) The transient dock is located on the long float next to the east sea wall, across from the Coast Guard base, on the north side of the commercial floats. Rafting is encouraged when the float is full. East of this float a large parking lot is filled with thousands of crabpots during the off-season.

The Brookings marina, which monitors VHF Channel 12, has over 500 small- to large-sized berths—most of which are new—with water and electricity. The harbor office is on the north side of the upper sport boat basin. Facilities in the sport boat basin include electricity, water, showers, pump out, fuel dock, and mail/message service. Provisions and marine supplies lie

close-by, or you can head to town for a greater selection of stores. The lower basin, east of the Coast Guard Base used by commercial fishing boats, offers berths with water and electricity for larger craft.

Brookings Harbor boasts the mildest climate on the Oregon coast and is famous for growing nearly 90% of America's Easter lilies. If you arrive in time to take an early summer drive between Brookings and Crescent City you'll be rewarded with a breathtaking view of the lily fields in bloom. The area offers many beautiful hiking trails along the spectacular and scenic coastline. Port of Brookings Harbor hosts an annual Kite Festival that attracts professional as well as amateur kite flyers.

Brookings is a good place to wait for favorable weather before continuing either a north- or southbound voyage. Port Orford, 43 miles north, is the closest anchorage on a northbound voyage; Coos Bay, 80 miles north, is the next all-weather shelter; Crescent City is 18 miles south of Brookings.

Early morning on the Brookings transient dock

⚓ **Port of Brookings Harbor** hrs 0800-1700 weekdays; during fishing season also open Saturdays 0800-1600; tel: 541.469.2218; fax: 541.469.0672; website: www.port-brookings-harbor.org; email: info@port-brookings-harbor.org; monitors VHF Channel 12

⚓ **Chetco River Coast Guard** tel: 541.469.3885; monitors VHF Channel 16

Mack Arch Bight and Mack Arch Cove

Charts 18602; 13.0 mi NW of Brookings
Entrance (cove): 42°13.46'N, 124°24.23'W
Anchor (larger craft): 42°13.46'N, 124°23.90'W
Anchor (small craft): 42°14.22'N, 124°24.45'W

The bight . . . has been used as a temporary anchorage during moderate NW weather. The rocks and reefs break the swell. In approaching the anchorage, pass to the S of Mack Arch about midway between it and Yellow Rock. Anchor in 11 fathoms, sand bottom, with Mack Arch bearing 296° and Yellow Rock bearing 155°. No breakers have been observed, but caution should be exercised as the place has not been closely surveyed. . . . Mack Arch Cove . . . affords fair shelter in NW weather in 6 to 7 fathoms, sandy bottom. In enter-

ing from S, pass E of Mack Arch, giving it a berth of about 150 yards, but taking care to avoid the rock 125 yards S of its E point. Then bring the 125-foot rock, in the N part of the reef, to bear 352° and steer for it on that bearing until up to the area abreast the group of rocks 0.5 mile N of Mack Arch. (CP, 33rd Ed.)

Mack Arch Cove, nestled close east of Mack Reef, offers moderate shelter for small craft from prevailing northwest winds. Mack Reef— a group of above- and underwater rocks and kelp beds—extends 1.5 miles south of Crook Point, creating a good-sized lee in a somewhat exposed and wild-looking environment. Pay attention to the *Coast Pilot* caution noted above that "the place has not been closely surveyed." The reef cuts down the chop but the swells and surge can still be felt here. The cove is exposed to the south and is not a safe anchorage in strong winds with a southerly component.

Mack Arch Cove is entered south of Mack Arch, a 231-foot-high islet at the extreme south end of Mack Reef. Avoid the submerged rock 50 yards south of the arch. Small craft can find fair shelter tucked in close to the kelp, 0.5 mile north of Mack Arch. Larger craft will want to anchor southeast of Mack Arch where there is more swinging room, as indicated on the chart.

Anchor (large craft) 11 fathoms over sand; fair holding.

Anchor (small craft) 6 fathoms over sand and shell with some kelp; good holding.

Hunters Cove

Charts 18602, 18600; under SE face of Cape Sebastian, 5.3 mi N of Mack Arch Cove
Entrance: 42°19.07'N, 124°26.07'W
Anchor: 42°19.02'N, 124°25.46'W

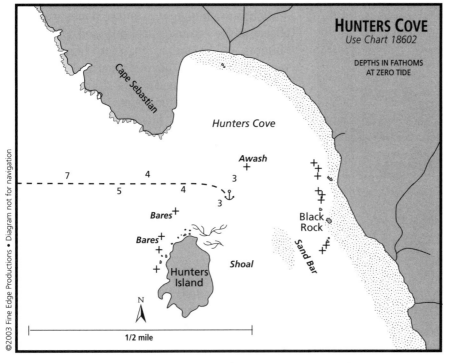

HUNTERS COVE
Use Chart 18602

DEPTHS IN FATHOMS AT ZERO TIDE

©2003 Fine Edge Productions • Diagram not for navigation

Cape Sebastian

Hunters Cove

Awash

7   4   3
5   4   3

Bares
Bares

Black Rock

Shoal

Sand Bar

Hunters Island

N

1/2 mile

Hunters Cove, a small, constricted cove . . . is formed partly by the cape and partly by Hunters Island in the entrance. The island is 0.2 mile in extent, rocky, flat-topped, and 113 feet high. Shoal water extends from it E to the beach. The cove is used occasionally by launches and small craft. During strong NW weather the sea at the entrance is rather lumpy for small boats. With moderate SW weather a heavy sea piles up across the entrance between the cape and Hunters Island. (CP, 33rd Ed.)

Hunters Cove is a snug bight, somewhat hidden behind Cape Sebastian, that offers a good temporary stop for those looking for relief from prevailing northwest winds and chop; it is moderately sheltered from all but westerly winds. The cove is easy to miss unless you are close to shore. The cove has room for only a couple of boats and swinging room is limited; its wide sandy beach makes a very good kayak haulout. It is inadequate in anything but prevailing offshore winds due to swells that break across the shallow entrance, making entering and leaving very dangerous. Hunters Cove is rolly when swells are running.

When entering, study the inset on chart 18602. The entrance waypoint noted above is 0.25 mile southwest of Cape Sebastian. Head east midway between Cape Sebastian and Hunter Island and avoid rocks awash at midtide about 60 yards off the north and west ends of Hunter Island. Anchor short of the rock awash at high water in the east center of the cove surrounded by 2.5 fathoms located at 42°19.67'N, 124°25.38'W.

Deep-draft vessels anchor southwest of the mid-cove rock; shallow-draft vessels can find more shelter and less rolling farther north behind the cape, as depths allow. *Caution:* Avoid the area east of Hunters Island where depths are shallow. Hunters Cove has picturesque surroundings— its shores are typical of the southern Oregon coast, with a rugged headland and offshore rocks.

Anchor in 3 to 4 fathoms over sand with some rocks and kelp. Fair-to-good holding.

Rogue River Approach
(Gold Beach)
Charts 18601, 18589; 6 mi N of Cape Sebastian
Entr buoy RW"R"; 0.25 mi NE of buoy: (OR110)
42°23.74'N, 124°28.31'W
Breakwater entr: (OR112) 42°25.19'N,
124°25.96'W
Gold Beach boat basin: 42°25.32'N, 124°25.20'W

Rogue River . . . is an important sport fishing stream. Several float landings and a hoist for trailer-drawn craft are just above the old lumber dock on the N side of the river near the mouth. Gold Beach, on the opposite side of the river from Wedderburn, is the larger town. The entrance to Rogue River is protected by stone jetties; buoys mark the approach. A seasonal light and fog signal are on the seaward end of the NW jetty. A Federal project provides for a 13-foot channel from the ocean along the N jetty to a point about 0.4 mile above the ends of the jetties. In July 1998, the controlling depths were 5 feet in the NW half and 3 feet in the SE half; much deeper water can be carried in the NW outside quarter of the channel.

. . . a seasonal rough bar advisory sign [is] on the N side of the river, 0.6 mile upstream of the entrance. . . . The sign is equipped with two quick flashing amber lights that will be activated when the seas exceed 4 feet in height and are

Aerial view: Rogue River

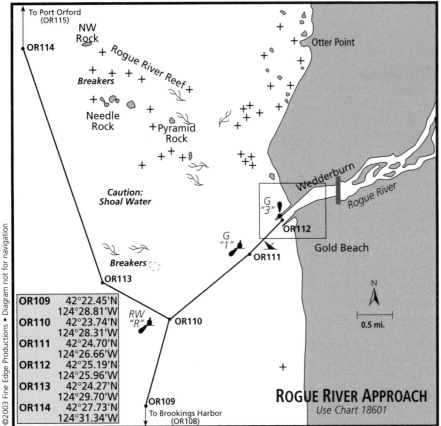

ROGUE RIVER APPROACH
Use Chart 18601

OR109	42°22.45'N 124°28.81'W
OR110	42°23.74'N 124°28.31'W
OR111	42°24.70'N 124°26.66'W
OR112	42°25.19'N 124°25.96'W
OR113	42°24.27'N 124°29.70'W
OR114	42°27.73'N 124°31.34'W

©2003 Fine Edge Productions • Diagram not for navigation

within a matter of min-utes.

B. Outer end, north jetty. *Breakers are almost always present here because of shoal water. When the sea is running from the west or south-west, it is particularly dangerous.*

C. Outer end, south jetty. *Breakers are almost always present. Even when it appears calm, there may be occasional breakers 1,000 feet out-side the south jetty. When the sea is running from the west or southwest, this area is very dangerous.*

CHANNEL

The Rogue River channel lies along the north jetty. Under existing condi-tions, a channel 13 feet deep and 200 feet wide, extending from the ocean to the inner end of the north jetty, is provided. Boaters are urged to use and stay within this channel. The river entrance

considered hazardous for small boats. Boaters are cautioned, however, that if the lights are not flashing, it is no guarantee that sea conditions are favorable.

Caution. The controlling depths in Rogue River channel and basin are usually considerably less than project depth and are subject to contin-ual and pronounced change; vessels are advised not to enter the river without local knowledge.

About 200 berths, some with electricity, gaso-line, diesel fuel, water, ice, launching ramps, wet and dry winter storage, and marine supplies, are available in Gold Beach. (CP, 33rd Ed.)

DANGER AREAS

A. Shoal water, south side. *Along the south side of the Rogue River channel are shoal water and gravel bars. This shoal water breaks to a height of six feet when a swell is running. Many boaters fishing inside the river or trolling between the jet-ties find themselves set into this dangerous area by northwest winds. If a vessel breaks down in the channel and is not anchored, the northwest wind and ebb tide will set it into this dangerous area*

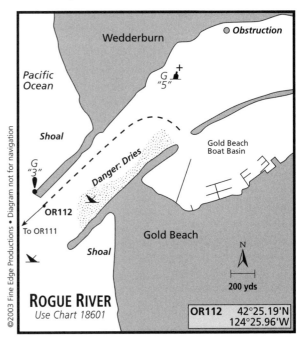

ROGUE RIVER
Use Chart 18601

| OR112 | 42°25.19'N 124°25.96'W |

©2003 Fine Edge Productions • Diagram not for navigation

is subject to frequent shoaling and depth changes. Do not rely on charted depths.

FISHING INSIDE THE CHANNEL

During recent years small boats, which do not usually go out into the ocean, fish just inside the bar and troll in an area between the north and south jetties. Frequently, there are a great number of boats in this area, and they tend to crowd each other. Because trolling is the most frequent fishing method, lines can get caught accidentally in a boat propeller. Should this happen, the disabled boat should anchor immediately and call for aid. A northwest wind or ebb tide could set a boat into a dangerous area in a matter of minutes.

COAST GUARD PRESENCE

Coast Guard mans a seasonal station from approximately Memorial Day through Labor Day. This unit is located on the north jetty. During times when this station is not active, persons should call Coast Guard Station Chetco River for assistance. (BOCW, 2001 Ed., p. 40)

Rogue River, a sportfishing mecca for both fresh and saltwater fishermen with trailerable boats, is not a frequent destination for coastal cruisers. The entrance bar and shoaling channel between the jetties is considered unsafe for boats with a draft of 4 feet or more and, only then, with local knowledge. Locate the entrance buoy "R" (for Rogue River), 2.5 miles off the jetties, before turning northeast into the river entrance. Rogue River Reef to the north of this buoy extends over 2 miles offshore and must be given wide birth. (See Rogue River Reef below.)

The bar may have less than 6 feet of water over it at high water, and the channel inside the jetties and into the marina less than 4 feet. Entrance to Rogue River should not be attempted with outside seas running; the entrance breaks clear across during these conditions. The north jetty light (G"3," flashing 2.5 seconds and horn) are maintained only from June 1 to October 31.

Rogue waves at Rogue River break as far as 0.25 mile off the jetties, especially during times of strong ebb currents where depths of less than 2 fathoms are found. Depending on seasonal river runoff, depths over the bar constantly shift; the southern two-thirds of the width of the channel along the south jetty tends to fill with sand, baring at low water.

The rough bar advisory sign, noted above, can be seen only from land. Before attempting an entry, all boats should make inquiry about bar depths, channel shoaling, and sea conditions by calling either Rogue River or Chetco River Coast Guard on Channel 16.

Réanne at the helm as afternoon gale picks up

Rough water to windward

Breaking seas off Island Rock

The small craft harbor and town of Gold Beach is inside the south jetty. The marina (tel: 541.247.6269) caters to sportfishing boats; facilities include gasoline, water, fishing tackle and limited supplies. This is also the headquarters for Rogue River jet boat trips up-river.

Rogue River Reef and Coast Channel

Charts 18601; extends 4 mi NW from Rogue River entr
Position: 42°26.64'N, 124°27.29'W

Rogue River Reef . . . includes many visible and covered rocks; because of the broken bottom, vessels should stay over 5 miles offshore when passing this area. A 0.5-mile-wide channel separates the reef from the beach, but it is not safe to use without local knowledge. . . .

The channel between Rogue River Reef and the mainland, and North Rock and the mainland, is sometimes used by coastwise freighters in clear weather. This channel should not be attempted by strangers. (CP, 33rd Ed.)

Rogue River Reef is a dangerous mass of rocks and kelp that extends 4 miles off the coast. The reef, which is unmarked and unlighted, should be given a wide birth.

Rogue Rover Reef inner channel, an intriguing shortcut for northbound small craft that leads inside Rogue River Reef appears to be about 100 yards wide between kelp patches, with an average depth of about 7 fathoms. It looks like the kind of route *Baidarka* would try if we were keeping one foot on the beach. However, not having done so, it's on our list for next time. Use Chart 18601, and on a northbound cruise, take your departure from buoy G"1." We would not attempt this route either in a large craft, in foul weather, or with limited visibility.

Port Orford

Chart 18589; 19 mi N of Rogue River, 6.5 mi S of Cape Blanco
Entrance (outer): (OR117) 42°43.08'N, 124°30.68'W
Entrance (middle): (OR115) 42°43.62'N, 124°30.00'W
Inner Hbr pos: (OR116) 42°44.30'N, 124°29.71'W
Anchor (west of Graveyard Pt): 42°44.25'N, 124°30.00'W

Port Orford . . . is a cove that affords good shelter in NW weather, but is exposed and dangerous in S weather. It is easy of access and is probably the best natural NW lee N of Point Reyes.

The town of Port Orford, on the N side of the cove, is the home of the famous yellow cedar. . .

Underwater Eruptions 130 miles off the Oregon Coast

A volcano in the undersea Gorda tectonic ridge, at a point 130 miles off the southern Oregon coast, has been restless lately. Scientists at the National Oceanic and Atmospheric Administration's Vents Program have recorded seismic activity in the area that has oozed molten lava onto the ocean floor and generated over 2,500 earthquakes—although they say it currently poses no threat to ships or coastal communities. Signs of the eruption were first observed on Tuesday, April 2, 2002, and some of the quakes have been powerful enough for land-based instruments to pick up—the largest measuring 4.5 magnitude.

Like the Juan de Fuca Ridge farther north off the Oregon and Washington coasts, the Gorda Ridge is a spreading center where molten lava squeezes out from hot spots on the ocean floor ("like toothpaste," according to one scientist) to form pillow-shaped layers of new oceanic crust. Most underwater volcanoes aren't explosive like their above-ground counterparts, but they are far more common. Scientists monitoring the situation say that more than 90% of the Earth's volcanic activity is underwater, and they estimate that there are thousands of active volcanoes on the ocean floor.

While the lava initially kills everything it contacts, underwater bacteria feed on the chemicals that flow out of the vents to provide an immediate source of food for communities of tube worms, shrimp and snails—helping underwater ecosystems to recover much more quickly than would plant and animal life above ground. At the time of this writing, biologists, chemists and geologists were mobilizing research vessels to the site of the activity, hoping to arrive in time to find and study megaplumes, or gigantic bursts of hot, mineral-rich water released by the eruptions.

Anchorage may be had in about the center of Port Orford in 6 to 10 fathoms, sand bottom, however, it is reported that many anchors have been lost near the rocky 1 3/4-fathom shoal 0.2 mile E of the S end of the breakwater. The cove is marked by a lighted bell buoy and a lighted buoy, 0.5 mile S and 0.8 mile ENE of Tichenor Rock, respectively. Small craft may anchor closer to The Heads where better protection is afforded against the NW winds, which sweep with considerable force through the depression at the head of the cove.

. . . fishing boats to 12 1/2 tons are lifted to cradles on the wharf by a hoist. Marine supplies and ice are available in town. Dry winter boat storage is available on the wharf; minor repairs can be made. (CP, 33rd Ed.)

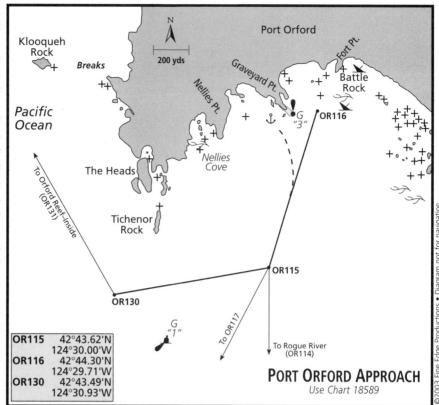

OR115	42°43.62'N 124°30.00'W
OR116	42°44.30'N 124°29.71'W
OR130	42°43.49'N 124°30.93'W

PORT ORFORD APPROACH
Use Chart 18589

©2003 Fine Edge Productions • Diagram not for navigation

There is no bar at Port Orford; departure from and entrance to the harbor are direct with the ocean. The harbor is protected from the northwest winds that prevail during the summer months but is exposed to southerly winds, which can cause unfavorable harbor conditions. (BOCW, 2001 Ed., p. 44)

Port Orford is a nice summer anchorage for coastal cruisers. Its strategic location makes it a convenient place to wait out strong northwesterly winds until conditions are favorable for the 39-mile run north to Coos Bay. In stable summer weather, securely anchored beneath the cliffs of Port Orford, the anchorage is similar to San Simeon or Point Reyes, on the California coast. A gentle rocking and the scent of the land across the water make it a nice, restful anchorage. Without a bar to

Aerial view: Port Orford

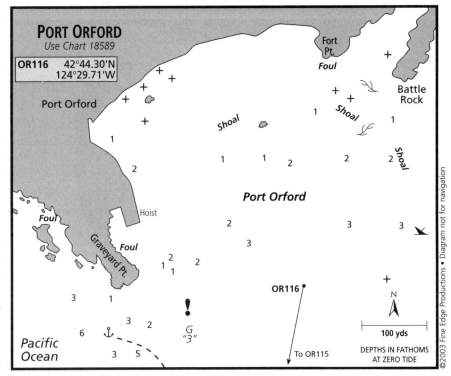

cross, or narrow, dredged channel to navigate, it's easy to enter.

Although Port Orford provides very good shelter from northwest gales, it is exposed to southerly winds and gales with a rocky lee shore. When approaching Orford, use the inset on paper Chart 18589 (which may not be available on some electronic charts) to avoid the numerous rocks and shoals. Seen from the south with our anthropomorphic eyes, Tichenor Rock reminds us of a toppled Easter Island Moai, its protruding belly facing upward toward the sky.

On a southbound course, the reefs off Cape Blanco—the westernmost point of the Oregon coast, 8 miles northwest of Port Orford—must be avoided. Pass west of Fox Rock, where the seas always break, and locate Orford Reef whistle buoy 20R (42°45.60'N, 124°38.80'W) before turning southeast to the Port Orford entrance buoy G"1"; then turn northeast to the anchorage.

Northbound from Rogue River or Chetco River, avoid Rogue River Reef that extends 4 miles off the coast. Once past the reef, you can set a course for waypoint OR115. Pass both Island Rock, (4 miles south of Port Orford) and Redfish Rocks (2 miles south) to starboard. (If you are a small vessel wanting to keep one foot on the beach, you can use these rocks for their lee effect on a windy day, but you may have to wend your way through the kelp east of Redfish Rocks.)

Contrary to the *Coast Pilot* and another source, we do not find the small anchorage near The Heads to be favorable in northwest gales. Most cruising boats find that the area to the west

Anchored east of the Heads, Port Orford

Anchored in the lee of Port Orford

The reefs off Cape Blanco

or southwest of Graveyard Point (see diagram) offers better shelter. (It is *Baidarka*'s preferred site.) The bottom is good mud with occasional rocks or gravel.

In fair weather, boaters wanting to go ashore may prefer to anchor east of the wharf where they can keep their boat in view. However, as prevailing northwesterlies pick up, strong gusts tend to spill over the flat spit to the north, raking the inner bay, so it's always prudent to leave an experienced crew member aboard.

The wharf, used as a dry-dock for boats up to about 10 tons, has two yellow cranes for launching and retrieving commercial and sportfishing boats. A ladder on the wharf below the cranes can be used to make a dinghy landing. Fuel, water and showers are available on the wharf. Groceries and restaurants are within easy walking distance in the small community of Port Orford, 0.5 mile to the northeast.

The community of Port Orford dates to 1859, when it was established as the first townsite on the Oregon Coast. Battle Rock, to the east of the wharf—now a city park—takes its name from a skirmish that occurred between the Natives and the first Whites who were attempting to settle the area.

The area is known for its Port Orford yellow cedar, widely used as a premium boat-building material. (The William Garden ketch in which the authors circumnavigated South America and pitchpoled off Cape Horn was strip-planked with this strong, fine-grained wood.) The areas surrounding Port Orford are known also for stands of Pacific myrtle whose lovely wood yields coveted artisan pieces such as bowls and lamp bases.

Note: The light at the end of Graveyard Point (2.5 second flashing G"3") is maintained only from May 15 to October 15.

⚓ **Port of Port Orford** open 0800-1700, Mon-Fri; tel: 541.332.7121; email: portoffice@harborside.com; website: www.portofportorford.com

⚓ **Port Orford Visitors Center** tel: 541.332.8055; email: pochamb@harborside.com

Anchor in 5 to 7 fathoms over mostly gray mud with good holding.

Beach Condo *of Dana Point anchored off Port Orford*

Orford Reef
Chart 18589; 2 to 5 mi offshore btw The Heads & Cape Blanco
Position: (Fox Rock) 42°46.10'N 124°38.15'W

Orford Reef . . . is composed of a group of irregular rocks up to 149 feet high and ledges, many of which are awash or show a break. Kelp extends from Orford Reef to within 1.3 miles of the shore. A lighted whistle buoy, 6.5 miles SW of Cape Blanco, is the guide for clearing this reef. . . .

Blanco Reef, extending 1.5 miles SW from Cape Blanco, consists of numerous rocks and ledges, some of which are marked by kelp. . . .

In clear weather small vessels with local knowledge sometimes use the passage inside Orford Reef and between Orford Reef and Blanco Reef. (CP, 33rd Ed.)

When transiting Cape Blanco, it is important to stay west of the dangerous 2-foot Fox Rock, 5.7 miles northwest of The Heads, and 1.2 miles almost due west of the south end of Orford Reef. Fox Rock breaks on all tides and is marked with kelp. Fox Rock and various rocks, reefs, islets, and large kelp beds extend all the way to Cape Blanco, 6 miles north. From the south, the rocks of Orford Reef resemble the fins of sharks swimming south.

An interesting smooth-water route northward can be found between Orford Reef and the mainland, then west between Orford Reef and Blanco Reef, but this route should be attempted only in fair weather and good visibility. *Baidarka* followed this short cut, roughly along the 12-fathom curve north of Klooqueh Rock, then made a slow turn to the northwest, exiting southwest of Black Rock.

Along a portion of this course the depths rise to about 7 fathoms, and bull kelp is thick. We sought a lead through the kelp and avoided signs of possible uncharted rocks. This is a fun route and gives a challenge in exchange for outside swells. However, if you're in a hurry, it is faster to go outside Orford Reef, avoiding Fox Rock, and be done with it.

There may be a tiny complex kayak route midway between Pyramid Rock and Cape Blanco, itself, but we have not tried it—it looks like a foul mess of kelp and submerged rocks that should be explored by dinghy first.

Cape Blanco
Chart 18589; 8 mi NW of Port Orford, 19 mi SE of Coquille River
Position: (OR120 2.2mi W) 42°50.50'N, 124°36.88'W

Cape Blanco projects about 1.5 miles from the general trend of the coast. It is a small bare tableland, terminating seaward in a cliff 203 feet high, with low land behind it. . . .

Cape Blanco Light, . . . 245 feet above the water, is shown from a 59-foot white conical tower near the center of the flat part of the cape. . . . (CP, 33rd Ed.)

Cape Blanco is the westernmost part of the Oregon Coast and a turning point for all coastal cruisers. North of Cape Blanco, the yellow sandy beaches and giant sand dunes of Oregon are abundant, the mountains are not as high, and there are fewer off-lying obstructions. Along this section, the coastline trends east of due north all the way to the Columbia River. South of Cape Blanco the coast trends east of south and becomes more mountainous, with numerous rocks, reefs and kelp beds. Give the dangerous Blanco and Orford reefs (noted in the previous entry) a wide birth when transit-

Oregon coastline seen from Cape Blanco Lighthouse

Michelle Gaylord

Cape Blanco Lighthouse

Michelle Gaylord

ing this area in poor visibility. From Waypoint OR120 you can head 17.6 miles directly to OR121—the south approach to Coquille River.

Coquille River

(Bandon)
Chart 18588; 14.8 mi S of Coos Bay, 26 mi N of Port Orford
Entrance buoy R"2": 43°08.13'N, 124°27.85'W
Range entrance: (OR123) 43°07.53'N, 124°26.56'W
Mid-channel: (OR124) 43°07.39'N, 124°25.63'W
Small craft basin entrance: 43°07.29'N, 124°24.68'W

Coquille Point is 0.6 mile S of Coquille River entrance. Several rocky islets extend 0.5 mile off

the point and rocks showing breakers in any swell extend 1.2 miles W and a mile NW of the point.

Coquille Rock, 1.6 miles NW of the point, is covered 28 feet and breaks in heavy weather. . . . The entrance to Coquille River is protected by jetties; a seasonal light and fog signals are on the S jetty. . . . The channel is subject to frequent change, and the deepest water is not always on the entrance range. Local knowledge is essential when the bar is rough. . . . A Coast Guard motor lifeboat is stationed at the mooring basin at Bandon on the S side of the river about 0.8 mile above the entrance.

The Coast Guard has established . . . a seasonal rough bar advisory sign, 29 feet above the water, visible from the channel looking seaward, on the same structure as Coquille River Light 12 on the S shore just N of the Coast Guard station, to promote safety for small-boat operators. . . . The sign is equipped with two quick flashing amber lights that will be activated when the seas exceed 4 feet in height and are considered hazardous for small boats. Boatmen are cautioned, however, that if the lights are not flashing, it is no guarantee that sea conditions are favorable.

A small-craft basin, on the S side of the river about 0.9 mile above the entrance, has about 180 berths and a launching ramp; marine supplies are available. . . . (CP, 33rd Ed.)

DANGER AREAS

A. South jetty. *It is always dangerous to get too close to the end of a jetty. An unexpected breaker could carry a small boat into the end of the*

Aerial view #1: composite photo of Coquille River Entrance conditions

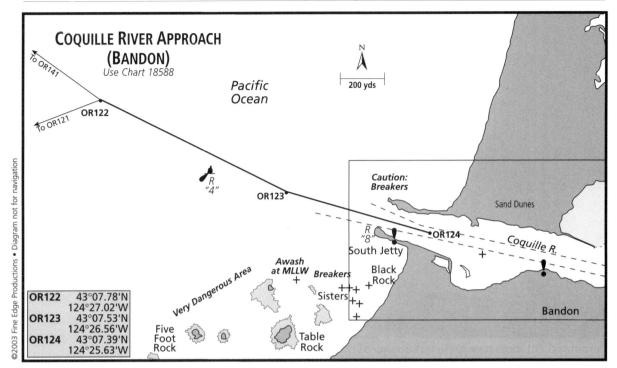

COQUILLE RIVER APPROACH
(BANDON)
Use Chart 18588

Pacific Ocean

N

200 yds

To OR141
To OR121   OR122

R "4"

OR123

Caution: Breakers

Sand Dunes

R "8"
OR124
Coquille R.
South Jetty

Awash at MLLW   Breakers
Black Rock
Very Dangerous Area
Sisters

Five Foot Rock   Table Rock

Bandon

©2003 Fine Edge Productions • Diagram not for navigation

OR122	43°07.78'N
	124°27.02'W
OR123	43°07.53'N
	124°26.56'W
OR124	43°07.39'N
	124°25.63'W

jetty with great force. The inside of the south jetty is a dangerous area, and boaters should remain clear. The prevailing northwest wind could send a powerless boat into the jetty.

B. North jetty. *Stay clear of the end of this jetty, because the sea breaks almost continuously in this area. A shallow area with partially submerged rocks extends from the abandoned lighthouse to the end of the jetty. The large swells that occur in this area could put a boat onto the rocks.*

C. South side of Coquille River entrance. *The area to the south of the entrance can be very dangerous. There are several rocks just below the surface that cannot be seen except during very heavy seas. There is a prevailing northwest wind during the summer months, and the sea currents run to the south. These two conditions could combine to send a powerless boat in this area onto the rocks.*

RANGE MARKERS

Front and area range markers are identical: a rectangular red daymark with a white stripe on a skeleton tower. By steering a course that keeps the two range markers in line, you will remain within the channel. See the latest CG-162 Light List.

ROUGH BAR ADVISORY SIGN

Positioned on shore, 300 yards west of the Port of Bandon boat ramp on the south side of the channel.

Aerial view#2: Coquille River Entrance on a calm day

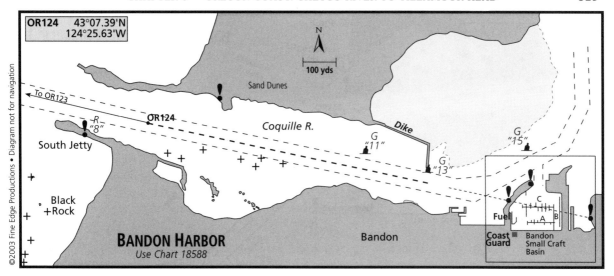

BAR CONDITION REPORTS

Call the Coos Bay Coast Guard station, 541.888-3266, for reports. There is an active Coast Guard Search and Rescue station in Bandon from Memorial Day to Labor Day. (BOCW, 2001 Ed., p. 38)

Authors' note: The diagram in *BOCW*, page 39, is incorrect; please see Chart 18588, corrected to March 25, 2000 or later.

Bandon

by Michelle Gaylord

We had planned to bypass the little harbor of Bandon and go all the way to Coos Bay but changed our minds at the last minute, when I reminded Jerry we were not in the Transpac race. We pulled into Bandon, and am I glad we did. We spent four days there, loving every minute of our stay!

Bandon Harbor is situated at the entrance to the Coquille River, so once again we had to check bar conditions and be sure to follow the channel ranges when entering. Just before entering the harbor there are numerous sea stacks (protruding and odd-shaped rock formations)—one reason this harbor is famous and such a tourist attraction. Bandon, which boasts one of the most beautiful beaches on the coast of Oregon, is also the cranberry capital of the entire west coast.

On the breakwater, at the entrance to the harbor, is a scenic, abandoned lighthouse, now a museum and one of the most photographed lighthouses in Oregon. Along the waterfront are interesting art galleries, gift and book shops, interspersed with tackle and crabpot shops that remind you of stores you would find on the wharves in the New England states. It is such a picturesque little town.

We went upriver one day in the dinghy and found lots of abandoned lumber mills, along with beautiful scenery. We traveled about 25 miles in the dinghy, and

just about a mile before we got back to the boat, we had to pass through an area where the river water meets the ocean water. That was a disaster!

Once again, we were taking water over the bow—but this time in the dinghy, *not Passing Thru*—and we got drenched. About every three minutes we took a big one aboard and, by the time we made it back to the boat, the dinghy was about 3/4 full of water.

Another afternoon we rode our bikes out to the sea stacks. It's quite an impressive sight, and we spent some time just watching the waves crashing and pounding against these rock formations. After careful consideration, I have come to the conclusion that boating is a love/hate relationship!

While in Bandon, we bought a crab trap, and we're having a ball. I haven't got the guts to touch the little suckers yet (that's Jerry's job), but it sure is fun to pull the trap up just loaded with crab! Only problem is that females are illegal, and the males have to be a certain size. So, I figure we get to keep about one out of every 50 caught.

After dark, Bandon reminded us a lot of Catalina Island's Avalon with its restaurants and stores on the main boardwalk lighted up at night. The only difference—Bandon has docks, courteous tourists and no cruise ships.

Michelle Gaylord

The Coquille River Lighthouse is now a museum

Coquille River and Bandon offer cruising boats full shelter from all weather in the Bandon Small Craft Harbor, 0.9 mile inside the jetties. Bandon is a small, quaint town known for its beautiful beach, nearby sea stacks, cranberry farms and boutiques with a New England charm.

The authors have noticed that Coquille River is one of the first entrances along this section of coast to close to small-vessel traffic when northwest winds pick up causing seas to build rapidly to 4 feet. This is due to the fact that the entrance channel faces northwest, the bar is shallow, and a number of dangerous rocks lie along the entire south side of the route. When weather comes from the south, we're not sure if the entrance is more protected. In prevailing northwest conditions, your chances of entering Coquille River are better if you arrive prior to noon. In any case, be sure to call the Coquille River or Coos

Bay Coast Guard on Channel 16 for bar conditions before entering. When entrance to Coquille River is closed, Coos Bay is the alternative deep-water entrance.

The channel across the bar at Coquille River, and the range lights and buoy system, have been changed in the last several years. Please note the new positions; buoy R"6," shown on earlier charts, is no longer there. Be sure to use the latest version of Chart 18588, and be alert when entering.

To enter Coquille River from the north, first pass whistle buoy R"2" (1.5 miles northwest of the south jetty) on your starboard hand, then head toward bell buoy R"4," keeping it to starboard, also.

When entering from the south stay west of Coquille Rock and pass R"2" on your starboard hand. In fair weather only you may take the short cut from CA121 to CA122.

From waypoint OR122, turn southeast to intercept the range lights at OR123. Buoy R"6" no longer exists, and our new waypoint OR123

Michelle Gaylord

Passing Thru in the small boat harbor, Bandon

marks the channel to the point where you pick up the course of the new range marks. Follow the range marks into the river, past OR124—the mid-point of the south jetty—and continue on the range marks to the point where the river turns north. You make a jog to the left (northeast) for 250 yards before turning south at G"15" into the small-craft harbor entrance.

Old Town Bandon

The outside beach to the south of the south jetty is particularly picturesque with several large sea stacks on which the seas break heavily during foul weather. The south side of the entrance bar can be quite spectacular when seas are running—a 12-foot shoal extends 300 yards from the south jetty and you may find yourself with breakers alongside! When a south-flowing current is running, be careful not to be set into the shoal.

Bandon is sometimes called the storm-watching capital of the west coast, so be sure you are safely inside the harbor *before* you take time to watch. *Baidarka*'s crew watched from offshore as the Coast Guard rescue boat responded to a Pan Pan radio call from an 85-foot Army tugboat ahead of us that had a seriously injured crew member. The rescue vessel exited the entrance, which had already been closed to traffic due to 6- to 8-foot breaking seas—it was quite a sight! We followed the rescue boat and tug north into Coos Bay Marina.

The scenic Port of Bandon has space-available slips for cruising vessels up to 90 feet (call ahead) and, soon to be completed, four new large-vessel berths for 90 feet and up. Facilities include electricity, water, restrooms, pump out station and fuel, plus a crabbing pier and excellent fishing. The Bandon Lighthouse, built in 1896, affords a striking view of the Coquille River where it enters the ocean, and there are visitor amenities up and down the shoreline. The Port of Bandon's waterfront along First Street in Old Town Bandon includes a launching ramp, rentals for fishing and crabbing, kayaking, charter fishing and excellent restaurants.

⚓ **Port of Bandon** open 0800-1630; tel: 541.347.3206; fax: 541.347.4645; as we go to press the Port is not set up to monitor VHF; website: www.portofbandon.com

South Cove
Chart 18580; 3.9 mi SW of Coos Bay S jetty
Position: 43°17.89'N, 124°23.85'W

South Cove . . . is used extensively as a summer anchorage by small craft and fishing boats with local knowledge. (CP, 33rd Ed.)

South Cove is a small bight, 10.5 miles north of Coquille River, in a rugged area known as the Seven Devils. The cove is poorly charted and caution is advised. The Cape Arago coast is cut by deep gulches, that descend from the Seven Devils above. We find the shoreline here fascinating, with numerous rocks of varying shapes and sizes that border the beach. Watch for turbulence or surge along this stretch.

Anchorage is reportedly found in 4 to 6 fathoms immediately south of the off-lying rocks.

Cape Arago

Chart 18580; 4 mi SW of Coos
Bay, 29 mi NNE of Cape Blanco
Position: (OR142 1.5 mi W)
43°18.69'N, 124°26.16'W

Passing the tug Daniel Foss *off Coos Bay*

> *Cape Arago . . . is an irregular
> jagged point projecting about a
> mile from the general trend of the
> coast. . . . Immediately off the
> cape are reefs extending NW for
> about a mile. A small cove near
> the N end, inside the reefs, is
> sometimes used by small boats
> with local knowledge.* (CP, 33rd
> Ed.)

Cape Arago and its "rock piles"
extend two miles or more from
the coast. *Baidarka*'s crew
found this an intriguing but
complex and ill-defined coastline with rugged
cliffs and deep gulches with tiny beaches that
offer possible temporary shelter or kayak haul-
out sites for the intrepid in fair weather. If you
follow a 15-fathom contour along the coast from
the south you will find yourself too close to an
interesting, but dangerous, reef area several
miles long. In foul weather, remain at least a
mile offshore in 30 fathoms until west of the
Coos Bay entrance buoy.

Off Cape Arago, we found confused seas and
strong, turbulent currents close-in. The Cape
Arago light is located 2.5 miles north of the
westernmost part of the cape itself. Give this
area a wide berth if you are uncertain of your
exact position, or are in poor visibility or unsettled weather. GPS is very useful to find your
way through this area.

When arriving from the south, avoid cutting
the corner and heading too soon for the Coos
Bay south entrance jetty. Pass buoy Y"2BR" to
starboard to avoid Baltimore Rock and the reefs
off the point, then head for Coos Bay entrance
buoy RW"K" before turning east. The entire
coast from just south of Cape
Arago to the south jetty of
Coos Bay is a truly fascinating place to explore by kayak
or sport craft in fair weather.

Sunset Bay

Chart 18587; 1.7 mi SW of
Coos Bay S jetty
Position: 43°20.10'N,
124°23.02'W

Sunset Bay is a small, almost
landlocked, unsounded bay
just south of the Cape Arago
light and about 1.8 miles
northeast of Cape Arago
itself. It is mentioned, with-

Michelle Gaylord

The rugged coastline off Cape Arago is ill defined with dangerous rocks

out name, in the *Coast Pilot* under Cape Arago (see *CP* quotation above under Cape Arago). It appears to contain a number of rocks in its entrance and, although this is quite a scenic area it looks dangerous except in fair weather; its potential for cruising vessels is unknown. *Caution:* turbulence and surge may be hazardous.

Coos Bay Bar

Charts 18587, 18580; 33 mi N of Cape Blanco
Entr buoy RW"K": 43°22.22'N, 124°23.08'W
Entr range: (OR147) 43°21.80'N, 124°21.87'W
Breakwater midchannel near buoy R"2":
(OR145) 43°21.54'N, 124°21.12'W

Coos Bay. . . is used as a harbor of refuge and can be entered at any time except in extreme weather. . . . [It] is one of the most important harbors between San Francisco and the Columbia River. . . .

Vessels should make sure of the entrance range before standing close in. There is usually a current sweeping either N or S just off the jetties, and this current should be guarded against. The entrance ranges should be watched carefully until clear of all dangers. The S current is often encountered during the summer. With strong S winds during the winter, the current sometimes sets to the N.

Approaching from any direction in thick weather, great caution is essential. The currents are variable and uncertain. Velocities of 3 to 3.5 knots have been observed offshore between Blunts Reef and Swiftsure Bank, and greater velocities have been reported. The most favorable time for crossing the bar is on the last of the flood current, and occasionally it is passable only at this time. . . .

The Coast Guard has established . . . a rough bar advisory sign, on the E end of the breakwater at Charleston Boat Basin in about 43°20'48"N, 124°19'18"W. . . . The sign is equipped with two flashing amber lights that will be activated when the seas exceed 4 feet in height and are considered hazardous for small boats. Boatmen are cautioned, however, that if the lights are not flashing, it is no guarantee that the sea conditions are favorable.

. . . Anchorage for small craft can be had almost anywhere in the bay outside the dredged channels and below the railroad bridge. . . .

A submerged section of the N entrance jetty extends about 300 yards W of the visible jetty; and a submerged section of the S entrance jetty extends about 100 yards W of the visible jetty. Because of the submerged jetties, it is reported

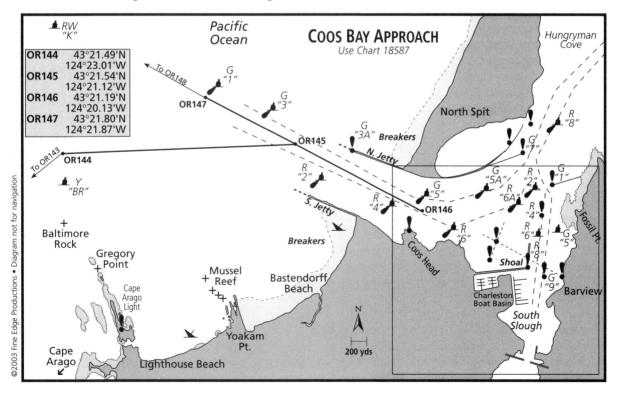

OR144	43°21.49'N 124°23.01'W
OR145	43°21.54'N 124°21.12'W
OR146	43°21.19'N 124°20.13'W
OR147	43°21.80'N 124°21.87'W

©2003 Fine Edge Productions • Diagram not for navigation

Aerial view: Coos Bay

that there are breakers in these areas most of the time. Extreme care must be exercised at all times. . . .

Current observations in the entrance to Coos Bay indicated a velocity of about 2 knots. The greatest observed ebb velocity was a little over 3 knots. . . . (CP, 33rd Ed.)

DANGER AREAS

A. Sand spit, South Slough. As you leave the Charleston Boat Basin, the South Slough sand spit is on your left. It extends north, parallel to the channel from South Slough buoy #4, approximately 450 yards toward South Slough light #2. Presently, nun buoy #2T marks the north end of the sand spit. Do not cross this area.

B. Submerged jetty. When you proceed out from the Charleston Boat Basin in the South Slough channel, and are directly between South Slough light #4 and can buoy #5, directly ahead will be South Slough light #1, marking the end of the submerged jetty. This jetty is visible only at low water. When departing the Charleston Boat Basin, stay to the left of light #1 at all times.

C. Sand spit, north beach. This area is dangerous because of shoal waters and submerged jetties. Occasionally, on a strong

ebb, there will be breakers in this area. Avoid this area because of the possibility of going aground or striking submerged jetties and pilings. Note, too, that inbound and outbound tugs with tows, freighters, and so forth, pass close aboard this area and cannot stop for obstructions in the channel—including small vessels.

D. South jetty, Guano Rock area. This is a very dangerous area because of shoals that extend out from the south jetty to the entrance channel. Breakers are frequently experienced from Guano Rock lighted whistle buoy #4 extending out to just past the end of the south jetty. Exercise care in this area at all times, especially on ebb tides.

E. North jetty, submerged. The north jetty extends approximately 200 yards to the west. The outward end of the jetty is submerged from the visible end of the jetty out toward buoy #3. Never cross this area. There are breakers in this area most of the time. When departing the bar northbound, be sure to pass buoy #3 before turning to the north.

F. Area north of buoy #5. This area can be very dangerous when there are any large swells on the bar or during ebb tide. Freak breakers are common in this area. Many boats do transit this area on occasion, but it is strongly recommended that you never cross here.

Aerial view: Coos Bay

ROUGH BAR ADVISORY SIGN

Positioned eight feet above the water on jetty just north of the Charleston Boat Basin. This is a two-part sign, facing toward the Charleston Boat Basin and toward South Slough light #2.

BAR CONDITION REPORTS

The Charleston Coast Guard station records weather and bar conditions; you may obtain this information by phoning 541.888.3102 or 541.888.3267. KBBR (1340 kHz) broadcasts reports hourly during the summer months and as notified by the Coast Guard. The Charleston Coast Guard station also posts current weather advisories. Weather and wind warning flags are displayed at the Charleston Port office during daylight hours. (BOCW, 2001 Ed., p. 36)

The busy Port of Coos Bay is a harbor of refuge offering good shelter to all boats; it is also a Customs Port of Entry. It is the largest deep-draft coastal harbor between San Francisco Bay and Puget Sound, and Oregon's second-busiest maritime commerce center. Over 120 deep-draft vessels and 120 cargo barges call at the harbor annually, moving an average of 3 million tons of commodities. Coos Bay boasts the safest entrance bar on the Pacific Northwest coast and claims that its bar is closed fewer days than any other bar on the west coast. While these claims are assuring, boaters cannot be complacent when approaching Coos Bay and crossing its bar.

Because Coos Bay lies in the lee of Cape Arago, during southeast weather it is reportedly the safest entrance on the Oregon Coast during gales from that direction; however, we can't answer for storm conditions.

The bar is routinely patrolled by the local Coast Guard rescue vessel and a call to Coos Bay Coast Guard on Channel 16 to request a bar report (Bar Report by telephone 541.888.3102) before entering or exiting is strongly recommended. The Coast Guard will provide an escort if you are a newcomer to the area and feel unsure or uncomfortable about crossing the bar.

An approach to Coos Bay from the north is best made from entrance whistle buoy RW"K," located 1.6 miles northwest of the jetties in 16 fathoms. Make for waypoint OR148 before turning to the southeast and passing the buoy. Proceed to waypoint OR147 which marks the start of the entrance-bar range marks. By the time you pass south of buoy G"1" (waypoint OR147), you should have visually identified the range marks; follow them closely to OR145, mid-channel at the entrance jetties, and to OR146 at the turning basin. Because strong and unpredictable currents sweep the coast off Cape Arago and add to the uncertainty of entering Coos Bay, check your position carefully and remain on the range until well east of Coos Head, inside the bay.

When entering from the south, in fair weather you can head northeast from waypoint OR143 straight to waypoint OR147, the beginning of the range marks, then follow the range course. In good visibility, local boats cross to the entrance channel by staying north of bell buoy Y"BR," 0.4 mile north of Baltimore Rock (waypoint OR144), then heading for waypoint OR145 to intersect the range mark course close off the jetty entrance. In foul weather or poor visibility, it is safer to enter by closing entrance buoy RW"K" noted above.

The dredged channel across the bar favors the north side of the jetty until well in the bay, and remains fairly close to North Spit inside the bay.

On brisk northwest winds, breakers extend seaward 300 yards from both jetties and, on

Coast Guard vessel on its daily bar check

occasion, large breaking waves can be found in the entrance channel, itself—especially on strong ebb currents. Pay close attention to the cautions noted above in the *BOCW*. Inside Coos Bay, use the many lighted buoys and Chart 18587 to avoid the shoals along shore. Once inside the bay, make a jog to the northeast and be sure to pass new buoys R"6" and R"6A" on your starboard hand to find the entrance to South Slough at the waypoint given below under South Slough. *Note:* Charts dating previous to 2001 do not show buoys R"6" and R"6A."

When leaving Coos Bay, study the foam blowing across the entrance opening to make sure it is from the adjacent breakers and *not* from the center of the channel. To minimize encountering heaping seas, time both an entrance and exit for flood waters, with the last of the flood being optimum.

The Coast Guard rescue vessel transits the bar at about 0500 hours to make a check of daily conditions. You can call them for an early spot-report even before they return to base to file their observations.

On *Baidarka*'s first visit to Coos Bay, the Coast Guard was reporting 2- to 4-foot wind waves at 0950 hours, with occasional 6-foot waves on the bar. The bar was closed to boats under 26 feet. (When we had passed Coquille River earlier, their bar was already closed at 6- to 8-foot breaking seas.) When we arrived at the entrance and crossed the Coos Bay Bar, it was 1530 and the bar report gave 4- to 6-foot seas, occasionally breaking. The Coast Guard asked if we wanted an escort. We respectfully declined

and timed the entrance to avoid major wave sets. We had no problems, although it might have been difficult had there been a strong ebb flowing.

The morning we departed Coos Bay at 0600, there was a brisk northwest wind and seas were already 6- to 8-foot high and breaking occasionally. *Baidarka* was tossed around quite a bit at the breakwater entrance—enough to set our vessel on its bow and stern ends. At 0734, Coos Bay Coast Guard announced hazardous bar conditions and closed the bar to vessels 40 feet or less. At 0900 they announced extremely hazardous conditions with 6- to 8-foot breakers and seas to 10 feet and, at that time, they closed the bar to all recreational vessels.

By then, *Baidarka* was north of Coos Bay by several miles and we wondered if we would be able to enter Yaquina Bay that afternoon. However, by the time we arrived, we had no problems entering with a 1.5-knot ebb, and we found excellent shelter in Newport.

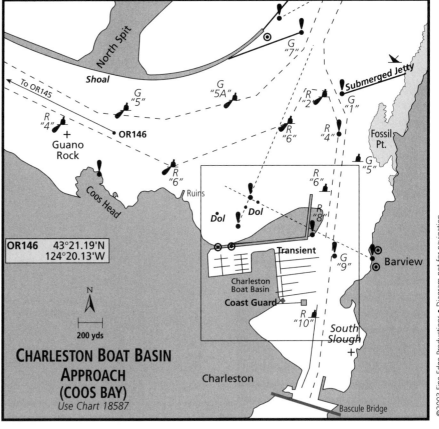

OR146 43°21.19'N
       124°20.13'W

N

200 yds

CHARLESTON BOAT BASIN
APPROACH
(COOS BAY)
Use Chart 18587

⚓ **Coos Bay Coast Guard** tel: 541.888.3267; monitors VHF Channel 16

South Slough (Coos Bay)
Charts 18587, 18580; 0.5 mi S of Charleston Boat Basin
Entrance (South Slough channel): Basin 43°21.30'N, 124°19.16'W
USCG Base position: 43°20.66'N, 124°19.25'W

Approaching Charleston Boat Basin on a windy day

South Slough [is] shoal and navigable only for small boats. . . . The channel, from the junction with Coos Bay to Charleston Boat Basin, is subject to shoaling. Mariners are advised to seek local knowledge when transiting this area. (CP, 33rd Ed.)

South Slough, 1.4 miles inside the Coos Bay jetties, is home to Charleston Boat Basin. Follow the well-marked channels closely or you'll risk going aground in the soft shallow mud.

Most coastal cruising boats use Charleston Boat Basin when visiting Coos Bay, or they anchor in shallow water nearby. The 10-mile trip upriver to the city of Coos Bay is somewhat tedious and less convenient for an early-morning take-off. Anchorage during the summer can be found in the shallow water along the shores of Coos Bay, keeping well clear of the shipping channel. Make local inquiries before anchoring.

Charleston Boat Basin (Coos Bay, South Slough)
Charts 18587, 18580; 0.3 mi N of Charleston
Position: 43°20.79'N, 124°19.20'W
Transient float: 43°20.79'N, 124°19.28W

Charleston Boat Basin [is] operated and maintained by the Port of Coos Bay. . . . In June 1997, the controlling depth was 8 feet (11 feet at midchannel) from the entrance to the basin, thence

---

Coos Bay
by Michelle Gaylord

On July 28 we left Bandon for Coos Bay. The ride up was short and calm, and we docked at the little town of Charleston, which is just inside the breakwater. Coos Bay is okay, but nothing spectacular or scenic. The facilities were certainly nice enough, and it's an easy port to get into, but I think I would only recommend it as a fuel and rest stop.

While there, we rented a car and did some inland touring. One day we went all the way to Crater Lake. It was a long 600-mile round trip, but the rivers, lakes, trees, little towns, and scenery made it well worth the miles. The shades of blue in Crater Lake are just gorgeous. The surrounding areas were still covered with snow, even though it was 90°F when we were there.

In Coos Bay we also spent time doing some re-provisioning, errands, shopping—and, unfortunately, Gaylord was able to get his satellite dish repaired. So my peace and quiet was over. Jerry was so thrilled to have the tube and his channel flipper back in working order that I left him on the boat one day and headed north along the coast in the car. Again, I encountered more spectacular scenery, drove through the Oregon Dunes, and passed lake after lake after lake. Oregon is one beautiful state! I ended up at a little town on the Siuslaw River called Florence, which is about halfway between Coos Bay and Newport. I fell in love again. It reminded me a lot of Bandon. When I got back to the boat I told Jerry we just had to make a stop in Florence on our way to Newport; it can be a tricky harbor to enter but, after checking bar reports and talking to the Coast Guard, we decided to give it a try.

depths of 12 to 14 feet were available in the basin. The basin is used by commercial and sport fishermen. About 500 berths with electricity, gasoline, diesel fuel, water, ice, a launching ramp, and marine supplies are available. (CP, 33rd Ed.)

Charleston Boat Basin Marina is a full-service marina with slips for up to 700 boats. The transient float (B dock), noticeable by its yellow railing, is located on the first finger as you approach from the north. Turn right at the first fairway and tie up along the yellow railing. In order to make an exiting easier, you may want to make a sharp U-turn and put your starboard side along the float, facing eastbound. This way, in the usually brisk summer westerlies, you can use a spring line when you leave the dock.

Note: The public uses this same transient dock for fishing and crabbing. If you see lawn chairs lined up along the dock with crab-trap lines leading into the water, be sure you have the attention of those people sitting in the chairs well in advance of your approach. Otherwise, you may find your boat enmeshed in crab-trap and fishing lines as the westerly wind pushes you toward the dock.

When we arrived in a stiff afternoon westerly, we found *Baidarka* being pushed rapidly downwind toward the dock. Gesturing to the "public" to move wasn't effective; they just smiled and waved back, not understanding that we were about to run over their gear. We finally had to sound our horn several long blasts to help them get the message—and did they scurry!

After you tie up, walk up to the Harbormaster's office to register and receive a slip assign-

ment. (Although they monitor Channels 16 and 12 they don't always respond.) Harbormaster Don Yost and his crew are friendly and helpful. Marina services are complete with electricity, showers, laundry, pump-out, phone hook-ups, fuel, oil dump, boat wash area, and a picnic site. The marina office has mail and message service, as well as a weather fax. Groceries and a restaurant are also available on site. For complete marine services and repairs, Charleston Shipyard, just south of the Coast Guard Base, has a 40-ton travel lift and a 200-ton-marine ways.

The small town of Charleston, within walking distance of the marina, has a wider selection for re-provisioning. And for art galleries, shops and restaurants, take your dinghy up-river or catch a bus to North Bend or Coos Bay. Port Side restaurant in Charleston is popular for its Saturday and Sunday seafood buffet. Englund Chandlery is located across the bridge south of the marina, at the head of the basin.

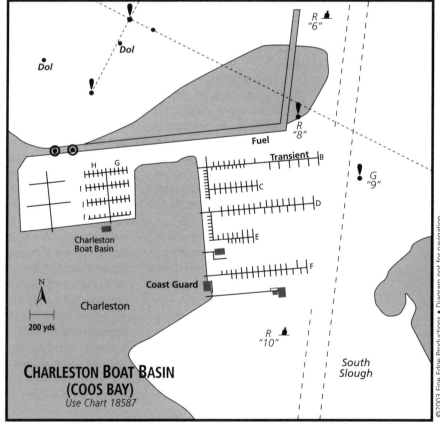

CHARLESTON BOAT BASIN
(COOS BAY)
Use Chart 18587

©2003 Fine Edge Productions • Diagram not for navigation

Charleston mariner statue

Take time to explore the tidal sloughs—North Slough, Haynes Inlet, or the three arms of South Slough by kayak or dinghy. (But be sure to watch the tide levels or you could be caught inconveniently on a mud flat!) South Slough Estuarine Research Reserve, 4.3 miles south of Charleston Basin, has an interpretive center where you can pick up a detailed paddle guide, hike their nature trails, or take a guided tour. If you have a bicycle or are an inveterate hiker, Sunset State Beach and Cape Arago State Park are 3 and 6 miles, respectively, from Charleston. Trails along the ridge at Cape Arago provide good vantage spots from which to view marine animals. (Some of the highest winter winds have been recorded off this cape!) And, of course, if you have access to a vehicle, there are beautiful dunes and lakes within easy driving distance of the marina. If you happen to be in the area the last two weeks of July, you might want to take in the annual Oregon Music Festival which has been running annually since 1978.

⚓ **Charleston Boat Basin** open 0800-1700, Mon-Fri; tel: 541.888.2548; fax: 541.888.6111; website: www.portofcoosbay.com; email: donyost@charlestonmarina.com

⚓ **Charleston Shipyard** tel: 541.888.3703

Hungryman Cove
Chart 18587; 1.3 mi N of Charleston Boat Basin
Entrance: 43°21.96'N, 124°19.06'W

Hungryman Cove, inside Coos Bay, 1.3 miles north of Charleston Boat Basin, is a narrow shallow meandering on the east side of North Spit tucked behind a drying sand bar. It looks like it might be a possible temporary anchor site during stable weather but, with shifting sand and shoals, it may be difficult or impossible to locate the shallow entrance. Make local inquiry.

Umpqua River
(Winchester Bay, Salmon Harbor)
Charts 18584, 18580; 19.3 mi NE of Coos Bay
Entrance buoy RW"U," 0.9 mi W of S jetty: 43°39.98'N, 124°14.44'W
Breakwater midchannel at "2A": 43°40.03'N, 124°13.23'W
Lookout tower midchannel: (OR151) 43°40.07'N, 124°12.49'W
W Basin entr ch: 43°41.01'N, 124°11.29'W
E Basin entr ch: 43°41.20'N, 124°10.90'W

Trawler docked at Coos Bay floats

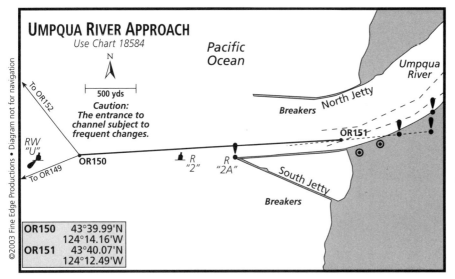

ber. Later in the season the river cuts a deeper channel through the bar. Depths in the channels and basins may vary considerably between dredging operations.

The Coast Guard has established . . . a rough bar advisory sign, visible from the river channel looking seaward, on Winchester Point about 1.5 miles inside the river entrance. . . . The sign is equipped with two flashing yellow lights that will be activated when the seas exceed 4 feet in height and are considered hazardous for small boats. Boatmen are advised, however, that if the lights are not flashing, it is no guarantee that conditions are favorable.

East Basin, a small-boat basin . . . is entered through a dredged channel that leads from the main river channel to a turning basin, about 0.4 mile above the entrance, and continues for an additional 0.23 mile to the head of the project. The channel is marked at the entrance by two lights. A seasonal fog signal is at the W entrance light. In February 1998, the midchannel controlling depth was 15 feet from the main river channel to the turning basin about 0.4 mile southward,

Some lumber, sand, crushed rock, and oil are barged on the river, but commercial traffic is very light . . .

The S point at the entrance to the river is marked by sand dunes, partly covered with trees, that reach elevations of 300 feet. About a mile below the entrance is a bright bare spot in the dunes that shows prominently among the trees. Shifting sand dunes about 100 feet high are on the N side of the entrance.

The entrance to the river is protected by jetties. The S jetty extends 1,200 yards seaward from the shoreline and is marked by a light with a seasonal fog signal and radar reflector. About 160 yards of the outer end of the jetty is submerged. A lighted whistle buoy, about 0.9 mile W of the S jetty light, marks the approach. A 086° lighted range and a lighted gong buoy mark the entrance channel which is subject to frequent changes. The middle jetty extends from the shoreline and connects with the outer section of the S jetty. The N jetty extends 1,100 yards seaward from the shoreline. . . . it was reported that dangerous shoals exist in the N side of the entrance. The river channels are marked by lighted ranges, lights, buoys, and daybeacons. A Coast Guard lookout tower is about midway out on the middle jetty.

The channel over the bar is reported shoalest usually during Septem-

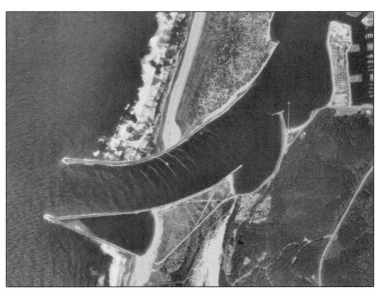

Aerial view: Umpqua River

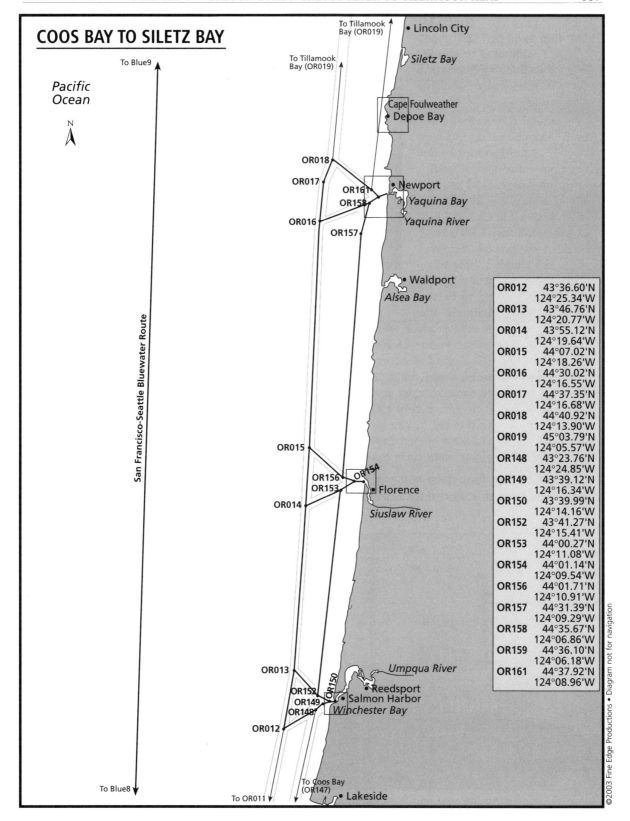

COOS BAY TO SILETZ BAY

To Blue9

Pacific Ocean

N

To Tillamook Bay (OR019)

To Tillamook Bay (OR019)

• Lincoln City

Siletz Bay

Cape Foulweather

• Depoe Bay

OR018

OR017

OR161

• Newport

OR158

Yaquina Bay

OR016

Yaquina River

OR157

• Waldport

Alsea Bay

San Francisco-Seattle Bluewater Route

OR015

OR154

OR156

OR153

• Florence

OR014

Siuslaw River

Umpqua River

OR013

OR152

OR150

• Reedsport

OR149

• Salmon Harbor

OR148

Winchester Bay

OR012

To Blue8

To OR011

To Coos Bay (OR147)

• Lakeside

OR012	43°36.60'N 124°25.34'W
OR013	43°46.76'N 124°20.77'W
OR014	43°55.12'N 124°19.64'W
OR015	44°07.02'N 124°18.26'W
OR016	44°30.02'N 124°16.55'W
OR017	44°37.35'N 124°16.68'W
OR018	44°40.92'N 124°13.90'W
OR019	45°03.79'N 124°05.57'W
OR148	43°23.76'N 124°24.85'W
OR149	43°39.12'N 124°16.34'W
OR150	43°39.99'N 124°14.16'W
OR152	43°41.27'N 124°15.41'W
OR153	44°00.27'N 124°11.08'W
OR154	44°01.14'N 124°09.54'W
OR156	44°01.71'N 124°10.91'W
OR157	44°31.39'N 124°09.29'W
OR158	44°35.67'N 124°06.86'W
OR159	44°36.10'N 124°06.18'W
OR161	44°37.92'N 124°08.96'W

thence depths of 10 to 16 feet were in the basin, thence 12 feet at midchannel to just within 450 feet of the head of the project, thence gradual shoaling to the southernmost 450-foot end. Berths with electricity, gasoline, diesel fuel, water, ice, launching ramps, marine supplies, and an 8-ton crane are available in the basin; hull, engine, and electronic repairs can be made. A fish wharf with a cold storage and ice plant on its outer end is on the W side of the basin. . . .

The village of Winchester Bay is a fishing resort on the E side of the East Basin. . . .

Reedsport, on the SW bank of the river . . . is a station on the railroad and the principal town on the river. . . .

A machine shop is at Reedsport; a maritime railway here can handle craft to 150 feet. . . .

At high tide Umpqua River is navigable by vessels of 6-foot draft to Scottsburg, 14.8 miles above Reedsport. (CP, 33rd Ed.)

Middle ground and north spit. *The north spit is to the right when proceeding down the Umpqua River, starting from the first rock spar jetty and the long pier on the east side of the channel. The north spit has small breakers when a swell is running and gets rougher toward the north jetty. The middle ground area extends from the north jetty about 1,000 yards seaward. This area is dangerous because a little swell can create large breakers that may capsize a vessel. Boaters should not linger near the mouth of the river during ebb tide, because if their power fails, their boats could be carried out to sea before an anchor would be effective or oars could be put to work.*

A. North and south jetty. *The areas north of the north jetty and south of the south jetty can be very dangerous. Whenever breakers are observed, boaters should avoid this area.*

B. Training jetty. *On the ebb tide, the current will pull boats into the jetty. Refraction waves are often encountered in this area, creating extremely choppy conditions.*

C. Buoy 6A, old Coast Guard docks. *Current on ebb or flood will often set boats into this area.*

RANGE MARKERS

The range marker consists of a red rectangular shape with a black vertical stripe mounted on a skeleton tower. By steering a course that keeps the two range markers in line, boaters will remain within the channel. In hazardous conditions, boaters should stay close to the training jetty rather than on the range line until well clear of the surf zone.

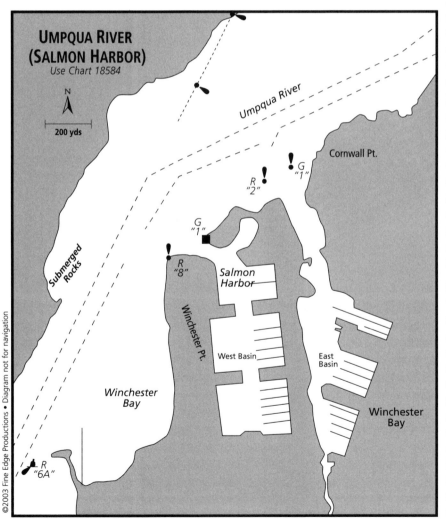

UMPQUA RIVER
(SALMON HARBOR)
Use Chart 18584

N

200 yds

Umpqua River

Cornwall Pt.

G "1"

R "2"

G "1"

Submerged Rocks

R "8"

Salmon Harbor

Winchester Pt.

West Basin

East Basin

Winchester Bay

Winchester Bay

R "6A"

ROUGH BAR ADVISORY SIGN

Storm warning display has been moved to the lookout tower. Rough bar warning light is located at Aid "6."

BAR CONDITION REPORTS

Recorded weather and bar condition reports are available by calling 541.271.4244.

Note: *Breaking waves can be encountered on the Umpqua River at any time.* (BOCW, 2001 Ed., p. 34)

The Umpqua River is a sportfishing and sightseeing center. While not often visited by cruising boats, its entrance is straight-forward without difficulty in fair weather —unless the bar is silted up with river sand and breaking, as noted above. Coos Bay, 19.3 miles south, is considered safer to enter under most, if not all, conditions.

Aerial view: Umpqua River Entrance

The entrance whistle buoy (red and white "U"), 0.9 mile west of the south jetty, should be identified before heading east. Waypoint OR150, 0.2 mile east of the entrance buoy, lines up with the range marks on a course that favors the south jetty of the channel. Pass buoy R"2" close along its north side and follow the first range mark across the bar to a turning basin where you jog to port (northeast), and pick up a second range mark; follow the second range mark until the turnoff to either the West Basin or East Basin of Salmon Harbor in Winchester Bay. *Caution:* Chart 18584 states that the entrance channel is subject to frequent changes.

Shoaling during the summer can be pronounced, especially on the north side of the channel. The dredged channel across the bar favors the south jetty; the northern half can be very shallow with breakers until you cross over to the North Spit in the river north of buoy "6A." Due to the possibility of hazardous conditions, as noted in *Coast Pilot* and *BOCW,* you should contact Umpqua River Coast Guard on Channel 16 for a current bar status and/or to request an escort before entering or exiting.

Moorage is available on the south shore, 2 miles northeast of the breakwaters in Winchester Bay village in one of the two basins of Salmon Harbor. Salmon Harbor Marina is one of the largest on the Oregon coast. Guest slips are available by the day or week, with a range of services that include

Courtesy Salmon Harbor Marina

Aerial view: Salmon Harbor Marina looking northwest

fuel dock, electricity, water, restrooms, showers, mail/message service, boat wash, and security. Restaurants and groceries are within walking distance. The fuel dock and pump out station are located at the north end of the West Basin. Transient dock is A dock, the northernmost dock in the East Basin. There is no convenient anchorage on the Umpqua River except temporarily along the shore adjacent to the dredged channel.

Visitor attractions in the area include the Umpqua Discovery Center and the jetboat dock next door. Specialty shops and restaurants line Winchester Bay, along with oyster farms, sand dunes, campgrounds and a 100-year-old light-house.

The traditional lumber town of Reedsport is located 9 miles up-river on the Umpqua's south bank. The dredged channel is marked with ranges and numerous buoys to serve the ply-wood and lumber plants and paper mill. Umpqua River is navigable by small craft for a distance of 24 miles.

Siuslaw River (Florence)

Charts 18583, 18580; 21.2 mi N of Umpqua River
Entr buoy RW"S": (OR154) 44°01.14'N,
124°09.54'W
Breakwater entr: (OR155) 44°01.11'N,
124°08.87'W
USCG base: 44°00.13'N, 124°07.40'W

Siuslaw River . . . is entered through a dredged channel between two jetties and leads S to a turn-

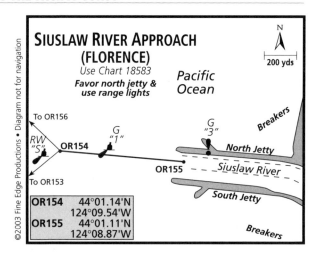

ing basin off the town of Florence, 4.4 miles above the entrance, thence E for about 2 miles to Cushman. A light, seasonal fog signal, and a Coast Guard tower are on the N jetty. The channel is marked by a 094° lighted entrance range that favors the N side of the channel, and by other ranges and navigational aids to 1 mile above Florence. The uncharted buoys at the mouth of the river are frequently shifted to mark the best water. The bar at the entrance is narrow, and the depths vary greatly because of storms and freshets. The entrance and south jetty shoals tend to build during late winter and spring. Mariners are advised to contact Siuslaw River Coast Guard Station on VHF-FM channel 16 before attempting to cross the bar. A Federal project provides for an 18- to 16-foot depth in the entrance channel to the highway bridge at Florence; thence 16 feet in the turning basin; thence 12 feet to Cushman.*

The Coast Guard has established . . . a rough bar advisory sign, 37 feet above the water, visible from the channel looking seaward, on the Coast Guard lookout tower on the N jetty, to promote safety for small-boat operators. . . . The sign is equipped with two flashing amber lights that are activated when the seas exceed 4 feet in height and are considered hazardous for small boats. Boatmen are cautioned, however, that if the lights are not flashing, it is no guarantee that sea conditions are favorable. (CP, 33rd Ed.)

Aerial view: Siuslaw River Entrance

Passing Thru *entering Siuslaw River, Florence, OR*

DANGER AREAS

A. Shoal water, *on the northeast side of the channel, has a depth of two to three feet at high tide, which extends from G"7" to G"9."*

B. Shoal water, *on the south side of the channel, extends from buoy #6 to buoy #4 and approximately 50 yards out toward the south jetty tips.*

C. Outer end of south jetty. *Breakers are almost always present. When the seas are from the southwest or west, breakers may extend to the entrance buoy.*

D. Outer end of north jetty. *Breakers are almost always present. When the seas are from the west, the breakers may extend to the entrance buoy.*

CHANNEL

Siuslaw River channel lies along the northern half of the river entrance. Water depth ranges from 6 to 20 feet. When swells are running from the northwest, boaters should stay in the channel. When the swells run from the west or southwest, stay closer to the south jetty until clear of rough water.

When conditions are questionable, contact the Coast Guard station for advise on VHF channel 16 or 22A, or CB channel 9. Once inside the bar, head for the channel. Ranges mark the preferred depth channel, but depending on conditions they do not mark the best route to follow.

BAR

The Siuslaw River bar has a very narrow channel extending out past the jetties. Unlike larger bars on the Oregon coast, the Siuslaw River bar may be rendered impassable for small boats by a moderate swell, particularly at ebb tide. Boaters should use extreme caution when operating near this bar. Due to shoaling and jetty extensions, bar conditions are unpredictable. When the bar is rough, expect continuous breakers 50 to 100 yards off the jetty tips.

BRIDGE

Clearance beneath the Siuslaw River bridge is low. Use caution when crossing under the bridge on the flood tide to avoid damaging superstructure such as antennas and troll poles.

Rough bar advisory sign is positioned on the Coast Guard tower facing 150 degrees true.

WEATHER AND BAR CONDITION REPORTS

Call the Coast Guard station, 541.997.8303 for recorded weather and bar conditions. (BOCW, 2001 Ed., p. 32)

Siuslaw River, although a straight-forward entrance, is infrequently entered by cruising boats because of its narrow, somewhat daunting bar and the necessity to travel 5 miles upriver to Florence. As noted in *Coast Pilot* and *BOCW,* the bar can be hazardous due to changing shoals and breaking waves. Contact Siuslaw River Coast Guard Station on Channel 16 for current bar status, water depth, or to request an escort before entering or exiting the bar. As we go to press, depths in the entrance channel are reported to be 18 feet; depths in the waterway to the turning basis are 16 feet.

If you have the time and want to make an exceptional stop, follow the Suislaw River for 5 miles to Florence or 7 miles to Cushman and experience the excitement and thrill of "passing under" the Highway 101 drawbridge. To reach the public marina in Florence, if your boat's mast or fly bridge is over 17 feet, you must call the bridge-keeper in Coos Bay and wait for two hours or more for the drawbridge to open (tel: 541.271.4515 or 541.888.4340).

Coast Highway 101 bridge opens for Passing Thru

marks south, hence a winding course following a series of lighted buoys and day marks until buoy R"28"—the Port of Siuslaw sportboat basin in Florence. *Caution:* Note B on Chart 18583 mentions that buoys R"4" and R"6" are not charted because they are frequently shifted in position as the bar shoal changes.

On the river, chop can build at any time the wind opposes the current. Temporary anchorage is reported between buoys R"14" and R"18" in about 25 feet. The Siuslaw River is navigable by small craft for 24 miles.

The Siuslaw River Coast Guard Station (tel: 541.997.2486) which monitors VHF Channel 16 is located 2 miles inside the entrance bar on the south side of Cannery Hill on the east bank of the river opposite daymark R12.

Florence (Siuslaw River)
Charts 18583, 18580; River Mile 5
Port of Siuslaw Marina (E of bridge):
43°58.04'N, 124°06.09'W

Florence is a small town on the N bank of the Siuslaw River 4.4 miles above the entrance. A

The Port of Siuslaw, Florence's public marina at River Mile 5, has one basin limited to commercial fishing vessels and a second for small pleasure craft up to about 50 feet. The village of Cushman is 2 miles east of Florence at River Mile 8.5.

The entrance whistle buoy RW"S" for Siuslaw River is barely 0.5 mile off the breakwaters. Waypoint OR154, 150 yards east of the entrance buoy, can be used for either in- or outbound travel. Follow the course defined by the range marks east to waypoint OR155, which is mid-channel at the entrance close south of the north jetty. Between the jetties, the entrance channel is only 200 yards wide. The south half is unusable because of shallow water that breaks on strong ebbs or during conditions of moderate swells. The dredged channel across the bar favors the north shore until it turns due south. Pass buoys R"4" and R"6" close on your starboard hand, then follow the second range

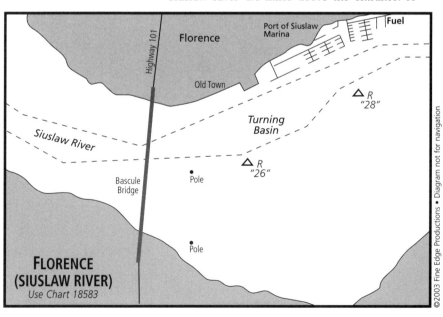

bascule highway bridge with a clearance of 17 feet crosses the river from Florence to Glenada, a small settlement on the S bank of the river opposite Florence. . . .

A cannery wharf, and a small port-operated boat basin, and marina are at Florence; fish are shipped by truck. Another marina, about 0.15 mile W of the bridge, has about 80 berths, dockside electricity, gasoline, water, ice, launching ramp, and marine supplies; minor engine repairs can be made. The Port of Siuslaw Marina, about 0.3 mile E of the bridge, has over 250 berths, gasoline, diesel fuel, water, ice, some marine supplies, and launching ramps. Wet and dry winter storage is also available. (CP, 33rd Ed.)

Passing Thru *at transient dock, Florence*

To reach the Port of Siuslaw Marina in Florence, if your boat's mast or fly bridge is over 17 feet, you must call the bridgekeeper in Coos Bay at *least* an hour before you wish to transit and wait for the keeper to open the Highway 101 drawbridge. The bridge has a vertical clearance of 17 feet and a horizontal clearance of 110 feet (tel: 541.271.4515 or 541-888.4340).

Port of Siuslaw Marina, on the east side of the Highway 101 bridge, has 400 feet of transient moorage (side tie) for boats up to about 50 feet. The Gaylord's vessel, *Passing Thru* (a 50-foot Ocean Alexander power trawler) had no difficulty entering the river in fair weather and

Florence
by Michelle Gaylord

On August 2, we set out for Florence from Coos Bay. Entering the Siuslaw River was a piece of cake, with the Coast Guard even offering to give us an escort if we felt we needed it. We declined, but it's nice to know that they are so willing and cooperative up here. A drawbridge here that spans the Siuslaw River is part of Highway 101. It has only a 17-foot clearance so they had to open it for us. You call about two hours ahead, and they send a bridge-keeper up from Coos Bay. They tell us the bridge gets opened only about 10 times a year because very few large pleasure craft ever visit this harbor. It seems most cruising boats have a limited time schedule and bypass all these little harbors in their race to get to the San Juan Islands and/or Alaska. What a shame—they don't know what they are missing!

As we were plowing up-river, we suddenly heard horns and an ear-piercing siren. When we rounded the bend we saw the bridge. All traffic on Highway 101 had come to a complete halt in both directions, and the bridge was beginning to open. Boy, did we feel important and special! The entire town ran down to the waterfront to see what was coming under the bridge. We spent the next seven days enjoying the harbor and the people—fishermen and shopkeepers—who live there. We found out that Florence was actually closer than Newport for all Jerry's Oregon relatives to travel to, so we had a big reunion here. Just imagine, being surrounded by 22 Gaylords!

En route to Newport the seas were about 4 feet and a little confused, the sky overcast, but the ride was not too bad. While in Florence we finally got our portholes resealed and the rest of the damage cleaned up from the rough water we had encountered off Cape Mendocino. So, once again we were shipshape and dry!

cruising up to Florence. The marina has guest slips for vessels from 20 to about 50 feet; it's a good idea to call them for status on moorage (tel: 541.997.3040) before you cross the entrance bar; in September, in particular, there's often a waiting list and the marina does take reservations up to a year in advance! The marina has electricity, showers and restrooms. Fuel is available at the fuel dock at the east end of the marina.

Florence—once a mill town—has become a popular tourist destination with its Old Town of antique stores, galleries, gift and clothing shops, and restaurants along the waterfront, immediately above the Port of Siuslaw Marina. Coastal cruising boats have recently become aware of its attributes, as well of those of the surrounding area that features one of Oregon's most dramatic coastlines and the spectacular Oregon Dunes National Recreation Area. You can explore the upper reaches of Siuslaw River by boat, dinghy or kayak, take a ride in a sea-plane, rent an ORV at Sand Dunes Frontier Park, or take a hike across some of the most beautiful sand dunes on the coast.

While some guidebooks recommend bypassing Siuslaw River, we agree with the Gaylords that, in fair conditions, a coastal cruiser with experienced crew can enjoy a pleasant, well-sheltered stay in Florence!

⚓ **Port of Siuslaw Marina** open 0900-1700 daily; tel: 541.997.3040; fax: 541.997.9407

⚓ **Highway 101 drawbridge** call 1 to 2 hrs in advance of transit if your mast or flybridge is over 17 feet; tel: 541.271.4515 or 541.888.4340

Cushman (Siuslaw River)
Charts 18583, 18580; River Mile 8.52 mi
Position: 43°58.68'N, 124°03.48'W

Cushman . . . has lumber and shingle mills. The products from these mills are shipped by rail and barge. A small-craft repair facility here has a marine railway that can handle craft to 60 feet long, for engine and hull repairs. A 50-ton hoist is also available for handling small craft. About 50 berths with electricity, water, and a launching ramp are available. Wet and dry winter storage is also available at this facility. A large marine supply firm is at Cushman. An overhead power cable with a clearance of 75 feet crosses the river at Cushman.

Light-draft vessels can go to Mapleton, 17 miles above the mouth. . . . (CP, 33rd Ed.)

Cushman is a small town on the north side of the Siuslaw with two private sportfishing marinas. The town is a good launching place for an exploration of the upper 17 miles of the Siuslaw by small boat. There is a swinging railroad bridge one mile east of town. Up-river the channel becomes narrow and winding. Wood products are barged down the river from a facility 14 miles above the river's entrance.

Cape Cove (Heceta Head)
Chart 18580; 7.1 mi N of Siuslaw R
Position: 44°08.04'N, 124°07.76'W

Heceta Head . . . has a seaward face 2.5 miles long with nearly vertical cliffs 100 to 200 feet high. . . . A sharp black conical rock, 180 feet high, marks the extreme W and N part of the head, and is easily made out from either N or S. Cox Rock, 1.5 miles S of the S part of the head, is conical and usually white on top with bird droppings. . . .

Heceta Head Light . . . 205 feet above the water, is shown from a 56-foot white conical tower on a bench cut in the high bluff near the W extremity. (CP, 33rd Ed.)

Cape Cove is a small, uncharted area on the south side of Heceta Head that offers somewhat exposed temporary anchorage in northwest winds and chop in the lee of the high cliffs. Florence, 7 miles south, or Newport, 36 miles north, are the nearest recommended shelters. The southwest swells tend to deflect off Heceta Head and crabpots are strung all along this coast.

Yachats River
Chart 18580; 7 mi S of Alsea Bay (Waldport)
Position: 44°18.55'N, 124°06.52'W

Yachats River, navigable only for canoes, breaks through the coast hills immediately N from Cape Perpetua. (CP, 33rd Ed.)

The cove and entrance to Yachats River are uncharted. The small village of Yachats looks out over a tiny narrow cove full of rocks and kelp with reefs extending well off-shore. Its potential for cruising boats is unknown at this time.

Alsea Bay (Alsea River)
Chart 18561; 24.6 mi N of Suislaw River
River position: 44°25.39'N,
124°05.85'W

Aerial view: Alsea Bay

> *The entrance has a shifting bar with a depth of about 6 feet. With a rising tide, the bar fills in with sand and the full effect of the tide cannot be counted on. There are considerable fishing and crabbing in the bay and river, but boats rarely cross the bar.* (CP, 33rd Ed.)

> *There are no jetties at Alsea Bay. With the bar shifting frequently, the entrance is unstable.*
>
> *Fishing or crabbing near the mouth of the bay can be dangerous if the boat motor fails on an ebb tide. Boaters should have an anchor ready when operating near the entrance.* (BOCW, 2001 Ed., p. 27)

Alsea Bay is unsurveyed and is of little use to cruising boats, but it has potential for kayakers, jet skis or small craft that can navigate the occasionally breaking surf. It reminds the *Baidarka* crew of our experience following whales into uncharted lagoons in Baja. Without the special forward-looking sonar of whales, navigation could be a tough call. Newport, 11.2 miles north, is the recommended shelter.

Waldport (Alsea Bay)
Chart 18561; 1 mi inside entr

> *Waldorf [sic] . . . is the principal settlement. A marina with about 100 berths, gasoline, and a launching ramp is on the NE side of the town. The river, marked by seasonal private buoys, is navigable by small craft to about 10 miles above the mouth. There are several marinas along the river above Waldorf; most have berths and gasoline. Outboard engine repairs can be made at a marina about 3 miles above the mouth.* (CP, 33rd Ed.)

The Highway 101 bridge across Alsea Bay has plenty of clearance for cruising boats, but until the entrance is dredged and charted, Alsea Bay is essentially for trailerable sportfishing boats only. The 2001 *Coast Pilot* refers to the town as Waldorf—a rather amusing, typo!

Yaquina Bay (Newport)
Charts 18581, 18561; 4 mi S of Yaquina Head
Entr buoy RW"Y": (OR158) 44°35.67'N,
124°06.86'W
Entr buoy G"1": (OR159) 44°36.10'N,
124°06.18'W
Brkwtr mid-channel entr: (OR160) 44°36.75'N,
124°04.53'W

Aerial view: Yaquina Bay Entrance

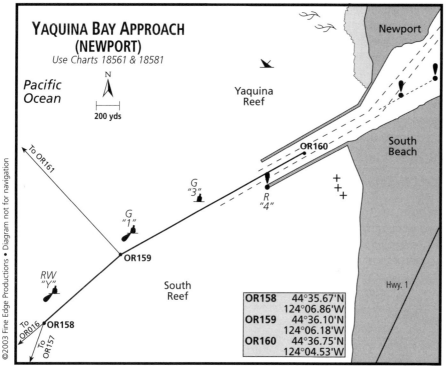

At the entrance to Yaquina Bay and River, the buoys cannot be relied upon to indicate the best water, and in the river, depths are subject to frequent change. Recreational boaters unfamiliar with the area are advised to contact the Coast Guard on VHF-FM channel 16 or telephone 541-265-5381 for the latest bar conditions. Professional mariners desiring to enter Yaquina Bay should employ a pilot or someone with local knowledge. (CP, 33rd Ed.)

DANGER AREAS

A. South jetty. There are submerged rocks along the length of the jetty; do not hug the jetty on either side. Boaters should remain in the channel entering and leaving the river so that if their engines fail, they will have time to anchor before the current or wind sweeps them into the rocks.

B. North jetty. This jetty affords excellent protection from northerly winds. However, the same caution should be exercised in running close to it as with the south jetty. Be especially cautious of submerged rocks near the tip of the north jetty. On an ebb tide, stay well clear, up to the end of the north jetty, as there is danger of being swept into the breakers at the extreme end. Remain in the channel outbound until you pass buoy #1 at the south end of Yaquina reef. This applies to entering the river as well as leaving.

C. South reef. This reef can be considered an extension of Yaquina reef and is equally dangerous because it has the same surf conditions. When going south, continue out the channel to the entrance buoy before turning south.

D. Yaquina reef. This reef is extremely dangerous, even when the winds are light and few breakers can be seen. A large swell coming from seaward can cause a tremendous breaker on this reef with little or no warning, even when the sea is otherwise calm. Never fish close to the reef and

The bay is a tidal estuary, the harbor itself being merely the widening of Yaquina River just inside the entrance. . . .

During the summer, when the swell is approximately parallel with the coast, the bar is comparatively smooth, being particularly sheltered by Yaquina Head. In winter, however, the heavy W swell makes the bar very rough. A smooth bar and a favorable tide are necessary for large vessels leaving Yaquina Bay.

The Coast Guard has established . . . a rough bar advisory sign, 25 feet above the water, visible from the channel looking toward seaward, on the Coast Guard station, to promote safety. . . . The sign is equipped with two quick flashing amber lights that will be activated when seas exceed 4 feet in height and are considered hazardous for small boats. Boatmen are cautioned, however, that if the lights are not flashing, it is no guarantee that sea conditions are favorable.

A Federal project provides for a 40-foot entrance channel, thence 30 feet from the first turn in the channel to and in the turning basin at McLean Point, thence 18 feet to Yaquina, thence 10 feet to Toledo at the head of the project. Controlling depths may be considerably less than these project depths. . . .

do not turn north between the end of the north jetty and buoy #1.

ROUGH BAR ADVISORY SIGNS
Positioned on the shore, east end of Coast Guard pier.

BAR CONDITION REPORTS
KNPT, Newport (1310 AM); twice daily winter and summer, and at Coast Guard request. Recorded weather and bar condition reports: 541.265.5511. When the Coast Guard restricts the bar, the restriction applies to the area from the bridge west to the entrance buoy. (BOCW, 2001 Ed., p. 30)

Entrance to the small-boat basin at Newport

Yaquina Bay is the wide spot inside the entrance to the Yaquina River. The town of Newport lies on the north bank of the river, just east of the Highway 101 bridge. Port of Newport Marina at South Beach is a large recreational marina with excellent shelter and very good facilities. The deep entrance channel to Yaquina Bay opens to the southwest and is fairly easy to enter in strong prevailing northwesterlies. We were able to use the lee of the jetty in 5 to 7 fathoms to raise *Baidarka*'s stabilizer gear and had no problems with swells, even on a 1.5-knot ebb current.

The entrance is reported to be uncomfortable-to-dangerous in strong west-to-southwest winds, especially on a strong ebb tide with large seas from that same direction. Prior to entering or exiting, call Yaquina Coast Guard on Channel 16 (or tel: 541.265.5381) for a bar report.

When entering the bay, identify entrance whistle buoy RW"Y," 1.6 mile southwest of the jetties. On a southbound coastal transit, turn southeast at OR161 and head to OR159, 0.5 mile northeast of the entrance buoy, and closely follow the range marks heading for midchannel waypoint OR160. Northbound, turn northeast at OR158 and head for OR159, then follow the range marks to OR160. Upon entering, be sure to pass buoys G"1" and G"3" close on your port hand. (The last 100 yards of the north jetty has been demolished by severe wave action over the years.)

Dangerous Yaquina Reef—which extends from just outside the end of the north jetty for a full 4 miles north to Yaquina Head—has 1 to 3 fathoms over it and breaks heavily; the reef lies 0.5 to 1.0 mile offshore.

South Reef, a second dangerous reef, extends southwest from the end of the south jetty for a distance of 1.5 miles. The safe route for entering Yaquina Bay leads between these natural hazards

Aerial view: Yaquina Bay Entrance

Floats at the Newport small-boat basin

where seas have a history of heaping up and breaking without warning. *Baidarka's* crew finds Yaquina Bay one of the easier coastal river bars to cross during northwest winds, but it does require careful and accurate monitoring of position at all times. (As along much of the Oregon coast, you must watch for and avoid crabpot floats between shore and out to depths of 30 fathoms or more.)

Once inside Yaquina Bay, jog to the left (north) and pass under the

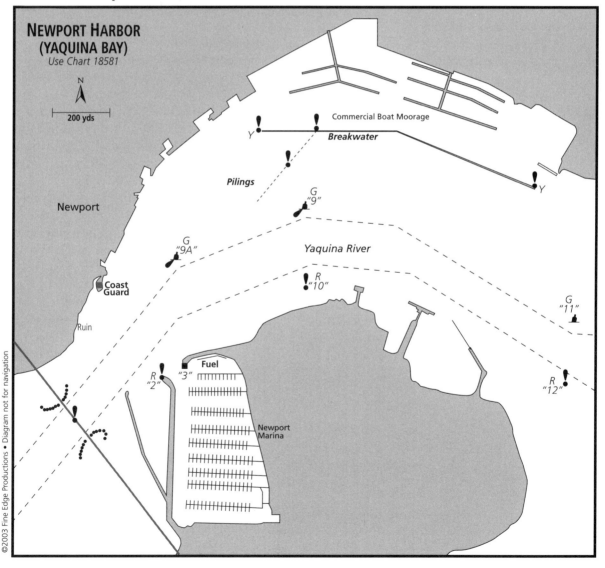

classic Highway 101 bridge (vertical clearance 129 feet). Recreational vessels turn right, within 300 yards, to the Port of Newport Marina. The City of Newport lies on the hillside to your left; the Coast Guard Station is 300 yards east of the bridge on the north shore; the commercial basin is also on the north shore, 0.7 mile east of the bridge.

Newport
(Yaquina Bay)
Chart 18581; 1.5 mi from entr buoy
Port of Newport Marina entr: 44°37.45'N, 124°03.23'W
Marina fuel dock: 44°37.46'N, 124°03.14'W
Commercial boat basin pos: 44°37.84'N, 124°02.76'W
USCG Base pos: 44°37.54'N, 124°03.37'W

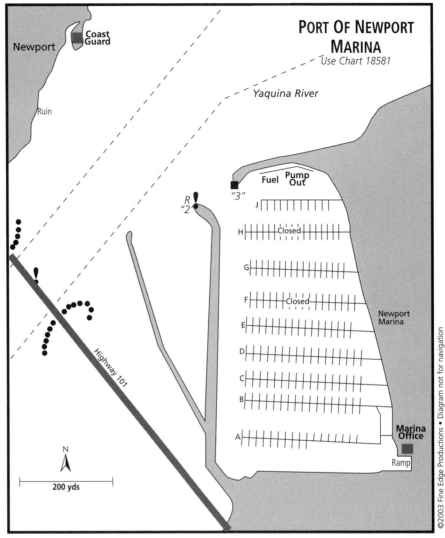

Newport . . . is the principal town on the bay and river. The town has a considerable fishing industry with several small fish-processing plants. . . .

The current velocity is about 2.4 knots, on the flood, and 2.3 knots, on the ebb, in Yaquina Bay entrance. . . .

Small-craft facilities. The Port of Newport operates a small-boat basin that can handle small craft up to 80 feet on the S side of the bay about 350 yards E of the bridge. The basin is protected to the N and W by jetties marked on the outer ends by a daybeacon and a light, respectively. A dredged entrance channel leads through the jetties, thence S along the W jetty turning E at the foot and terminating at a boat ramp at the head of the boat basin. In August 2000, the controlling depth was 6 feet. Gasoline, berths, diesel fuel, electricity, water, ice, and a pump out station

facility are available. Hull, engine, and shaft repairs can be made. Facilities can be contacted on VHF-FM channel 12 by hailing the Port of Newport South. The Port of Newport Internet address is www.portofnewport.com.

The Port of Newport operates a commercial moorage on the N shore about 0.7 mile above the highway bridge; a marina is also in this area. . . . There are several marine repair facilities on the river above Newport. Just N of Oneatta Point, 3.8 miles above the highway bridge at the entrance to the bay, full marine services and repairs are available. The facility has two travel lifts, one 15-ton and one 70-ton, and two 60-ton cranes. (CP, 33rd Ed.)

Newport, which calls itself the friendliest city on the Oregon Coast, has long catered to tourists, and its welcoming reputation certainly extends

Small-craft floats

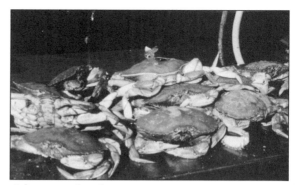

A harvest of crabs

to cruising boats. (See Sidebar below.) The Port of Newport Marina—one of the largest full-service marinas on the Oregon coast—lies just 1.5 miles upriver from the entrance buoy and east of the Highway 101 bridge. The modern marina, with its well-protected slips for cruising boats, can accommodate about 500 boats from 24 feet and up. Looking west from the marina, there is an impressive view of the historic bridge built in 1936. On-site facilities include electricity, showers, laundry, small store, pump-out, fuel dock, picnic area, fish-cleaning and crab-cooking station, and a pub. At the southeastern end of the marina there is a substantial RV park. The marina monitors and responds on Channel 12.

Although a supermarket and the center of Newport are a bit of a walk from the marina, shuttle bus service and water taxis are available to deposit you closer to your desired destination. However, we recommend that you do take time to walk across the Highway 101 bridge, from where you have spectacular views in clear weather; plan also to visit the restored Yaquina Bay Lighthouse at the north end of the bridge.

Embarcadero Resort and Marina—a privately run facility with 237 slips located on the north shore, east of the bridge, has transient moorage for boats up to 60 feet. Both the Port of Newport Marina and Embarcadero recommend that boaters phone ahead for slip availability.

Newport does not lack diversions for boaters who are able to spend a few days here. Oregon State University's Mark O. Hatfield Marine

Newport fuel dock

Crab cookers at the marina prepare the day's catch

Passing Thru *docked at South Beach, Newport Marina*

Science Center, which attracts over a half-million visitors a year and is just a short walk from the marina, includes a touch tank of tidal creatures and other informative displays. The acclaimed Oregon State Aquarium, ranked among the nation's top ten, is also a mandatory stop. Newport's Historic Bayfront, along the north shore east of the bridge, has elegant boutiques, galleries and restaurants. Thanks to the

considerable fishing industry, this city offers wonderful possibilities for seafood—particularly local crab, shrimp, clams and oysters, as well as halibut and rock fish and—depending on the year—fresh tuna.

Yaquina Head, with its lighthouse built in 1878, is worth at least a half-day's visit. Features include an interpretive center, hiking trails, a lovely beach and rocky outcroppings where you can sight thousands of common murres and perhaps a whale or two. Boaters not planning to attempt the entry at Depoe Bay might want to visit the charming little town by car or bicycle—it's only about 13 miles north of Newport.

Anchorage can be found along the north side of the river, just south of the commercial basin. However, you should check depths carefully; some silting has occurred on the south side of

Newport
by Michelle Gaylord

We arrived in Newport, Oregon on August 9 and spent four nights there. The first person we encountered after checking in with the port office was a lady working in the little grocery store next door. We asked her about public transportation to get us into town, and she insisted that we simply use her car! We accepted her offer and did a little exploring and ran some errands. We were surprised daily by the utter generosity of the people up here.

The town of Newport, divided in half by the Yaquina River, is connected by a long bridge. It was quite overcast

and rainy in Newport, but we did get one break in the weather so we were able to hike over the bridge, see some beautiful views of the harbor, and get some exercise. They have an outstanding aquarium there that took up the better part of one day; this is the aquarium that nursed Keiko the orca (Free Willy) back to health.

We did a lot of crabbing here, and took them up to shore where, all day long, they keep a big black cauldron full of boiling water. For $5 a dozen they will cook, clean, and crack the crabs for you.

the commercial basin breakwater and it now dries at low water.

⚓ **Port of Newport Marina** open 0700-2200 (summer), 0800-1700 (winter) tel: 541.867.3321; fax: 541.867.3352; email: Vickie@portofnewport.com; monitors VHF Channel 12

⚓ **Embarcadero Resort & Marina** tel: 541.265.8521; fax: 541.265.7844; email: Paul@actionnet.com

⚓ **Yaquina Bay Coast Guard Station** tel: 541.265.5381; 541.265.5511 for automated weather and bar reports; monitors VHF Channel 16

Cape Foulweather
Chart 18561; 10.5 mi N of Yaquina Bay
Position (1.0 mi W): 44°46.35'N, 124°05.93'W

Cape Foulweather is a prominent headland with about 6 miles of seaward face consisting of rocky cliffs over 60 feet high. The cape is formed by several grass-covered headlands, separated by densely wooded gulches. (CP, 33rd Ed.)

The coast along either side of Cape Foulweather has rocks and reefs that extend a mile or more from shore. Depoe Bay is 2 miles north of Cape Foulweather.

Two Boats on Autopilot Equals a Near Miss
by DCD

To get a good start to windward before the brisk north-westerlies picked up, *Baidarka* left Newport Marina at 0450 hours and headed out the entrance channel as the pre-dawn glow crept over the mountains to the east.

We continued on a southwesterly course until we were clear of any shoals off Yaquina Reef and could safely turn northwest. The channel to Yaquina Bay was quiet and there were no boats entering or exiting. It looked like a good cruising day.

Within a few minutes of our northward turn, we noticed a large commercial fishing boat rapidly approaching off our starboard quarter. We had already settled on the first leg of our day's route (OR161) with the autopilot engaged.

"That fishing boat isn't slowing down!" Réanne's voice had raised an octave.

She was right. The fishing boat was overtaking us *fast* and we appeared to be on a collision course.

I hailed it on Channel 16. There was no response. I turned our spotlight on it. No response. I held down our horn. The vessel just kept coming without a let-up in speed.

At that point, I immediately took power off *Baidarka* and let the vessel cross just ahead of us, with about 100 feet to spare.

As it went by, with the binoculars, Réanne could see a guy just entering the pilothouse with a cup of coffee in his hands—a major missile headed on a preset course. He glanced at us through his port side window as if to say,

Near-collision with Newport fishing boat at dawn

"What's the big flap about?" and continued at full speed.

It was too close a call and could have led to disaster if we hadn't been watching and had continued obliviously on autopilot, as apparently he had done.

In retrospect, the fishing boat skipper may have seen us heading west in the pre-dawn light as we exited the channel and assumed we were heading south. He turned northwest, apparently dialed in his autopilot course to the offshore fishing grounds, and went below to get a cup of coffee.

The lesson from this experience is that *nothing* replaces constant visual watch. Autopilots are a great help in short-handed cruising, but they can be agents for nasty collisions!

Depoe Bay

Chart 18561; 12 mi N of
Yaquina Bay
Entrance buoy RW"DB":
44°48.51'N, 124°05.32'W
Buoy R"2": 44°48.54'N,
124°04.45'W
Channel entrance: (approx.)
44°48.56N, 124°03.80'W
USCG Base position: 44°48.59'N,
124°03.61'W

Aerial view: tiny Depoe Bay

Depoe Bay . . . has one of the best small-boat shelters along this part of the coast. The bay proper has foul ground on both the N and S sides, but the channel leading to the narrow dredged channel to the inner basin is deep and well marked. The foul areas break in moderate seas and are marked by kelp. Prominent from seaward is the concrete arch bridge over the entrance to the basin. A lighted whistle buoy is 1.1 miles W of the entrance to the bay, and a bell buoy, seasonally lighted, is closer inshore. . . .

In September 1986, the reported controlling depth in the dredged channel to the fixed arched bridge was 8 feet; thence in June 1999, 6 to 8 feet in the basin, except for lesser depths along the edges of the basin and in 1994, shoaling to 4 feet was reported near the W edge of the channel under the bridge.

The fixed concrete arched bridge is unusual in that its width of 30 feet is less than the clearance of 42 feet. A lighted whistle buoy marks the en-trance to the bay and a direction light (44°48'33.6"N, 124°03'42.9"W) and a lighted bell buoy mark the entrance to the bay and the approach to the dredged channel to the basin; a fog signal is about 50 yards SW of the direction light. The navigator is cautioned against the dangerous surge in the narrow entrance to the basin. Boats over 50 feet long cannot enter the basin without a special waiver from the harbormaster, and then only at highwater. The entrance should not be attempted at night or in rough weather without local knowledge. Depoe Bay Coast Guard Station, at the inner basin, monitors VHF-FM channel 16 or may be contacted at 541-765-2123.

The Coast Guard has established . . . a rough bar advisory sign, 25 feet above the water, visible from the channel looking seaward, on a building on the N side of the basin entrance channel. . . . The sign is equipped with two quick flashing yellow lights that will be activated when the seas exceed 4 feet in height and are considered hazardous for small boats. Boatmen are cautioned, however, that if the lights are not flashing, it

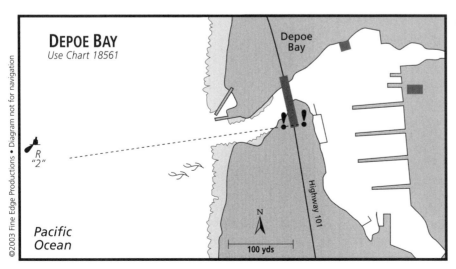

DEPOE BAY
Use Chart 18561

Depoe
Bay

R
"2"

Pacific
Ocean

N

Highway 101

100 yds

©2003 Fine Edge Productions • Diagram not for navigation

is no guarantee that sea conditions are favorable.

The town of Depoe Bay is on the N side of the basin. The basin has a concrete bulkhead, mooring floats, and a tidal grid for minor hull repair work. Also available are berths with electricity, gasoline, diesel fuel, water, ice, launching ramp, and marine supplies. Hull and engine repairs can be made. (CP, 33rd Ed.)

DANGER AREAS
A. North reef. *Once a boat has cleared the entrance, waters to the north are hazardous until the red bell buoy is reached. The seas break from the northwest and southwest at the same time, so this area must be avoided at all times.*

B. South reef. *Better known as Flat Rock, this area lies just south of the channel. Breakers are almost always present. Boaters coming from the south should never use this area as a shortcut to the channel. Avoid this area at all times.*

C. Channel from the red bell buoy in. *The passage into and out of Depoe Bay is unusually short and difficult. The Coast Guard recommends studying it before attempting to operate a boat in it. Because the north and south reefs are so close*

Another Way to Cruise the Coast

A friend of ours bought an old 34-foot fishing boat in Seattle for $7,500 with an antiquated Chrysler marine gas engine. He took his boat, *Flamingo,* down to Santa Barbara and back, gunkholing up and down the coast in just over a year. His book, *The Flights of the Flamingo: (29 days before the mast),* illustrates what is possible and is yet another side to coastal cruising. Jeff's descriptions of *Flamingo*'s Depoe Bay experiences are quite interesting. On the way south, his fuel pump gave out and he spent an afternoon and evening bobbing around off Depoe Bay and, at midnight, was finally led into Depoe Bay by the Coast Guard rescue boat.

On his way north, not to be intimidated by these new-fangled navigational gadgets (GPS), he cut the corner inside entrance buoy RW"DB" and channel buoy R"2" and nearly got caught in breaking waves on Flat Rock Reef. He was warned off by Coast Guard radio, and when he finally entered Depoe Bay and docked inside he received a written warning for steering inside (S) buoy R"2."

To read "another way to see the coast," don't miss this unending thriller!

to the channel, this area sometimes becomes very hazardous. During adverse conditions, breakers from the north reef will cross the channel and run into the entrance. When this condition exists, it is better to stand by at the entrance buoy until the Coast Guard advises it is safe to enter or is there to escort boats in. An important rule at Depoe Bay: **Never fish between the entrance and the red bell buoy.**

ENTRANCE
The entrance should not be attempted at night or in rough weather without consulting local fishers. Boats over 50 feet should not enter the bay without checking with the harbormaster and the Coast Guard.

All vessels are required to sound one prolonged (four to six second) blast when departing or entering Depoe Bay. Local protocol gives the right-of-way to any inbound vessel.

Mariners should check Local Notice to Mariners (LNM) for #2 marker; it may be off station due to winter weather.

On a building north of the entrance channel, a Rough Bar Warning Light is positioned 25 feet above the water displaying two flashing yellow lights. When lights are flashing, check with Depoe Bay Coast Guard on VHF Channel 16 for crossing restrictions. When visibility is less than one nautical mile, the Coast Guard activates its fog signal. The horn then sounds for 2 seconds, once every 30 seconds.

BAR CONDITIONS REPORT
Recorded weather and bar condition reports: 514.765.2112. (BOCW, 2001 Ed., p. 28)

Depoe Bay is reputed to be the smallest harbor in the world and we haven't heard of any challengers. It is a thriving port in a bay of only 6 acres in area. The bay is completely hidden by a high rock wall and a tiny entrance—a true hole-in-the-wall—that passes under a Highway 101 bridge with 42 feet of clearance. There is considerable surge inside the bay when swells are running outside.

During a howling gale, the authors once watched the Depoe Bay Coast Guard rescue boat surf into the bay between the extremely narrow rock walls, then pass underneath the highway bridge and into the safety of the tiny bay. This is not a place for large boats, faint hearted boaters or—in foul weather—any human being who loves life. The Coast Guard Station has a giant scrapbook of newspaper clippings and photos of disasters that have occurred off Depoe Bay. Some people might describe Depoe Bay as a nautical disaster waiting to happen—these disasters repeat themselves over and over.

For cruising vessels interested in entering Depoe Bay in fair weather, first give Depoe Bay Coast Guard a call on Channel 16 (tel: 541.765. 2124) to check on bar conditions. *Caution:* Once you start into the tiny entrance, you are committed to continuing into the basin itself—it is impossible to turn around. Be sure you have paper Chart 18561 so you can use the inset, which—as we go to press—is not yet available on the Maptech electronic chart Edition 3.2.

The key to the approach is to locate and pass close to the entrance whistle buoy RW"DB," 1.1 miles almost due west of the tiny entrance. From here, line up with the range marks at the south side of the bridge (following a course of about 085 degrees True) and pass buoy R"2" close on your starboard hand. The arch bridge and a 3-sector light at the foot of the bridge are the best visual clues to locating the opening. (If you see green from the 3-sector light you are too far north; if you see red, you are too far south.)

At buoy R"2" you have dangerous reefs 150 yards ahead both to the northeast (North Reef) and southeast (Flat Rock). Seas frequently heap up and break heavily over these reefs on moderate swells. Because there is frequently foam on the water as you approach the entrance, you need to determine whether the foam is blowing in from the rocks on either side or if it is caused by breakers. It is extremely dangerous to try to surf even small waves into Depoe Bay; you can quickly lose steerage and be dashed upon the south rock face. Just before you pass under the bridge, you must execute a small left turn and then turn sharp right as you come out from under the bridge. The Coast Guard base is a few yards directly east. Public floats are at south end of the bay.

On *Baidarka*'s northbound shakedown cruise, there was much regret from the bridge deck when the second mate decided that Tillamook would be our stop for the night. So, with the wind freshening, we scooted right on by Depoe Bay.

Along the north wall of this tiny harbor (only six square acres), natural rock tubes that are flooded by the incoming tide spout geyser-like sprays that sometimes arch over Highway 101 and drench passing cars. The area features five scenic state park or wayside areas along 101, all offering spectacular coastal views. Depoe calls itself the whale-watching capital of the Oregon Coast. Taking one of their commercial boats may be the best way to experience the smallest harbor.

Siletz Bay

Chart 18520; 15 mi N of Yaquina Head
Position (entrance): 44°55.58'N, 124°02.12'W

The entrance channel is subject to frequent change, and drafts of 4 or 5 feet are considered the deepest that can be safely taken in at high water. . . .

Taft and Cutler City are communities on the bay; both are parts of Lincoln City, which is 1.8 miles north. There are several marinas on the bay. . . . (CP, 33rd Ed.)

Aerial view: Siletz Bay

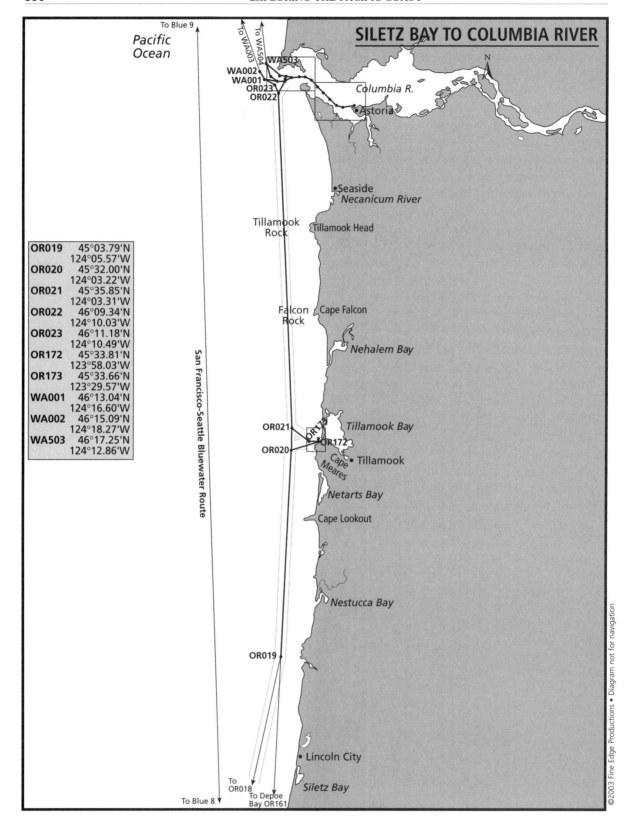

SILETZ BAY TO COLUMBIA RIVER

Pacific Ocean

To Blue 9

To WA503
To WA003

WA503

WA002
WA001
OR023
OR022

To WA504

Columbia R.

•Astoria

•Seaside
Necanicum River

Tillamook Rock

Tillamook Head

Falcon Rock

Cape Falcon

Nehalem Bay

OR021
OR172
OR020

Tillamook Bay

Cape Meares

• Tillamook

Netarts Bay

Cape Lookout

Nestucca Bay

OR019•

San Francisco-Seattle Bluewater Route

•Lincoln City

To OR018

To Depoe Bay OR161

Siletz Bay

To Blue 8

OR019	45°03.79'N 124°05.57'W
OR020	45°32.00'N 124°03.22'W
OR021	45°35.85'N 124°03.31'W
OR022	46°09.34'N 124°10.03'W
OR023	46°11.18'N 124°10.49'W
OR172	45°33.81'N 123°58.03'W
OR173	45°33.66'N 123°29.57'W
WA001	46°13.04'N 124°16.60'W
WA002	46°15.09'N 124°18.27'W
WA503	46°17.25'N 124°12.86'W

Do not attempt to cross the bar at any time. The entrance is unimproved and not intended for navigation.

Most boat traffic is concentrated on the river or in the bay channels. Because there are no jetties and the channel is shallow, surf is usually present. On the strong ebb tide, the current reaches five to seven knots at the entrance, enough force to pull an underpowered vessel or one having engine failure over the bar into the surf. (BOCW, 2001 Ed., p. 26)

Aerial view: Salmon River

Siletz Bay is a lagoon behind a long, low sandspit through which the Siletz River has punched an outlet. Sport boats ply the lagoon but the entrance bar breaks clear across on ebb tides with any swell running and is suitable only for surf runners and experienced sea kayakers.

Salmon River

Chart 18520; 14.1 mi N of Depoe Bay
Position: 45°02.42'N, 124°01.00'W

Salmon River empties at the S extremity of Cascade Head; the entrance is nearly closed by sandbars. . . .

Cascade Head . . . is very jagged and heavily wooded. The face of the cliff is 3 miles long, is over 700 feet high in places, and is cut by several deep gorges through which the waters of three creeks are discharged in cascades 60 to 80 feet high. Several rocks are about 0.1 mile offshore.

Two Arches, 30 feet high . . . . are visible from N; the inner is the larger. (CP, 3rd Ed.)

Dangerous—*not suitable for crossings.* (BOCW, 2001 Ed., p. 24)

Salmon River is a small, scenic river that winds down a wooded canyon along the south side of Cascade Head. The sand bar is located behind several rocks, the largest of which is 56 feet high. These rocks create a small lee just outside the river's entrance; in northwest weather it would be an interesting area to explore by sea kayak. Two Arches is an unusual rock formation 30 feet high, 0.9 mile north of the south

point of Cascade Head. Cascade Head is a beautiful 700-foot-high grassy and heavily wooded headland.

South of Salmon River by 2.5 miles you cross the 45th parallel, the halfway point between the Equator and the North Pole. Welcome to the high latitudes of the northern hemisphere!

Nestucca River and Bay

Chart 18520; 5.5 miles N of Cascade Head
Position (entr): 45°09.64'N, 123°59.01'W

Nestucca River empties into Nestucca Bay 5.5 miles N of Cascade head. The channel over the bar changes frequently in position and depth, and only light-draft vessels having local knowledge are able to cross. . . . The river has many snags that change the depths and shift the channel. Even in a moderate sea, the bar is extremely dangerous. . . .

Pacific City is a summer resort about 3 miles above the entrance to Nestucca Bay. Gasoline and supplies are available in the community. (CP, 33rd Ed.)

Continual shoaling and shifting of sandbars makes the entrance to Nestucca Bay difficult or impossible to enter, and so it is rarely used. To the north of the entrance, Cape Kiwanda gives protection from northwesterly winds that predominate during the summer months. (BOCW, 2001 Ed., p. 25)

Aerial view: Nestucca River and Bay

The Nestucca River has punched out of its lagoon at its south end across a low sandy peninsula, 3.3 mi south of Cape Kiwanda. Since there is no developed entrance and the bar shifts with each season, Nestucca Bay is another one of those entrances for explorers in surf-capable vessels only.

Cape Kiwanda and Haystack Rock

Chart 18520; (cape) 33 mi N or Yaquina Head;
(Haystack) 0.5 mi SW of Cape Kiwanda,
0.5 mi offshore
Buoy R"2" position: 45°12.93'N, 123°59.56'W

Cape Kiwanda, 33 miles N of Yaquina Head, is a low yellow rocky point, much broken and eroded, that projects about 0.5 mile from the general trend of the coast. Behind the cape are bright sand dunes, 500 feet high, which are prominent from seaward. Just S of Cape Kiwanda is a beach resort area; a public launching ramp is here. A seasonal whistle buoy is about 0.6 mile W of the cape.

Haystack Rock, 327 feet high, . . . is a prominent landmark. The rock is conical and dark for about half its height, and in summer the top is whitened by bird droppings. A lighted seasonal whistle buoy is just NW of the rock. (CP, 33rd Ed.)

Cape Kiwanda, like several capes along the Pacific Coast, creates a lee effect opposite its windward side during the prevailing summer weather pattern. This has helped develop a fleet of dories that launch and return through the surf on the south side of the Cape. The dories fish until the wind picks up, then quickly surf back onto the beach. Cape Kiwanda like its lagoon opening, 3.3 miles south, is another uncharted area with potential for temporary cruising stops. *Baidarka* passed inside Haystack Rock and buoy R"2" and found a minimum of 6 fathoms, suggesting that a stopping place could be found in this area.

Cape Lookout

Chart 18520; 40 mi N of Yaquina Head
Anchor: 45°20.04'N, 123°59.12'W

Cape Lookout . . . projects W for 1.5 miles, forming a narrow rocky promontory 432 feet in height at its seaward extremity. The S face is nearly straight, and its precipitous cliffs have numerous caves. . . . Fair shelter in NW winds may be had under the S side of the cape in 6 to 8 fathoms, sandy bottom. (CP, 33rd Ed.)

Cape Lookout is an unusually shaped ridge that

Aerial view: Cape Kiwanda

extends 1.5 miles from the coast like a very tall breakwater. While Cape Lookout is not well charted, good temporary anchorage, with fair shelter from northwest winds, can be found deep against the shore off a cave. Avoid kelp patches and watch for a few isolated rocks near shore. Locals use the scar on Cape Lookout, 200 feet up at the north end of the sandy beach, as a landmark to head for from the south; they then anchor off a sea cave, halfway between the scar and Lookout Point.

The south side is exposed to southeast gales, but it appears that you may find emergency relief on the north side in such conditions.

Anchor in 6 fathoms over sand and shells; fair-to-good holding.

Netarts Bay
Chart 18520; 7.7 mi S of Tillamook Bay
Position: 45°26.50'N, 123°58.27'W

Netarts Bay is a shallow lagoon most of which is bare at low water. The village of Netarts is on the N shore a mile inside the entrance. Only light-draft boats with local knowledge can enter. A small-boat basin with two floating piers and a launching ramp are at Netarts. . . . (CP, 33rd Ed.)

NETARTS BAY
Netarts Bay is shallow with numerous sandbars that are exposed at low water. There are no jetties

at this entrance. Very few boats cross the bar, and they cross only when the most favorable conditions exist. There is considerable sportfishing and crabbing inside the bay. Boats fishing inside the bay should exercise caution on the ebb tide when near the bar, since the strong current can pull a small boat out over the bar and into the surf. (BOCW, 2001 Ed., p. 22)

Netarts Bay has a shallow entrance more appropriate for sea kayaks and surf riders than for cruising boats.

Cape Meares
Chart 18558; 48 mi N of Yaquina Head
Position (Three Arch Rocks): 45°27.66'N, 123°59.86'W

Cape Meares . . . is high and rocky, with a 2-mile-long seaward face. The N part is the higher, with nearly vertical cliffs 640 feet high. The W point is narrow, covered with fern and brush, and terminates seaward in a cliff 200 feet high. (CP, 33rd Ed.)

Cape Meares has some interesting offshore rock piles which could offer some temporary shelter on their lee sides, however the area is uncharted and its cruising potential is unknown. Three Arch Rocks could offer a lee effect on either side of its mile-long projection into the ocean. The water on either side of the rocks is relatively shallow, but nothing is known about its bottom or holding; it is the same with the rocks off Cape Meares. Three Arch Rocks extend a mile from the coast and are prominent when cruising close to shore. The middle rock has the most impressive arch.

Tillamook Bay
Chart 18558; 45.8 mi N of Depoe Bay, 42 mi S of Columbia River Entrance buoy RW"T": 45°34.29'N, 123°59.62'W
Mid-channel on range at brkwtr: (OR171) 45°34.13'N, 123°58.03'W
Rough water route: (OR173) 45°33.66'N, 123°59.57'W
(OR172) 45°33.81'N, 123°58.03'W

Tillamook Bay . . . has a tidal area of about 13 square miles, most of which,

Aerial view: Netarts Bay

Aerial view: Tillamook Bay

. . . *Tillamook Bay Coast Guard Station is on the N shore W of Garibaldi. A lookout tower is near the intersection of the N entrance jetty and the shore. . . .*

The current velocity is 3 knots in the entrance to Tillamook Bay.

The Coast Guard has established . . . a rough bar advisory sign, on the N side of the channel near the beginning of Garibaldi Channel, visible from the channel . . . . The sign is equipped with two quick flashing yellow lights that will be activated when seas exceed 4 feet in height and are considered hazardous for small boats. Boatmen are cautioned, however, that if the lights are not flashing, it is no guarantee that sea conditions are favorable. (CP, 33rd Ed.)

at low tide, presents a succession of sand and mud flats. There is no commercial traffic in the bay except for fishing boats and pleasure craft.

. . . The entrance to Tillamook Bay is protected by jetties. The N jetty extends about 800 yards offshore. The westernmost 80 yards of the jetty is submerged. A lighted whistle buoy is 1.1 miles W of the N jetty. The channel to Garibaldi is marked by a directional light, buoys, and daybeacons. The area from the whistle buoy to the bay entrance frequently shoals which causes heavy breakers when on the range. [Authors' Note: The range lights have been replaced by a 3-sector directional light.]

DANGER AREAS

A. Bar area. *The entire area between the beach and the 20-foot curve is bar area and breaks on the ebbing tide. The water runs out from four to six knots on the average and is very strong. Boaters proceeding out should stop in the channel east of the seaward end of the breakwater and carefully evaluate the bar. If you decide to cross, proceed out—but do not attempt to turn around if the bar is breaking.*

B. North jetty. *About 100 yards of the outer end of the north jetty is submerged. This area and the portion of the channel just south of it are extremely dangerous. Avoid the sunken jetty and use caution in the channel south of it.*

C. Middle grounds. *Shoaling makes this area unpredictable and hazardous; it should be avoided.*

D. South jetty. *About 100 yards of the outer end of the south jetty is submerged. Use caution and avoid the sunken jetty when entering or exiting.*

CHANNEL

Tillamook Bay channel lies just south of the

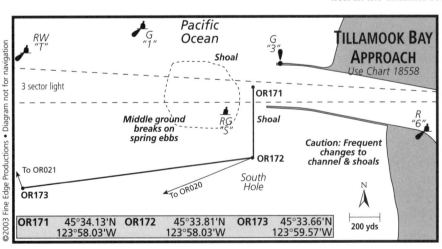

north jetty. Navigate with extreme caution. This channel changes constantly because of continuous natural silting and scouring. Obtain up-to-date information on channel conditions from the Coast Guard or other authoritative local sources. Do not rely on the sector light without first inquiring whether they mark the present channel location.

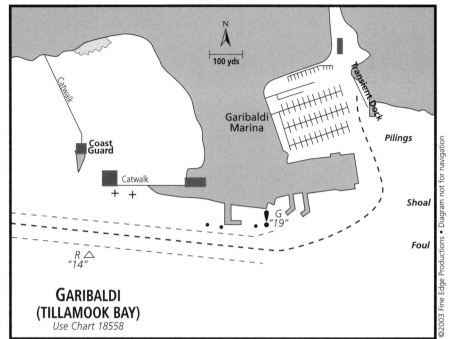

GARIBALDI
(TILLAMOOK BAY)
Use Chart 18558

©2003 Fine Edge Productions • Diagram not for navigation

ROUGH BAR ADVISORY SIGNS

One sign is located on the Coast Guard lookout tower on the north jetty. Both signs are lighted when the bar is restricted.

BAR CONDITION REPORTS

KTIL, Tillamook (104.1 FM); seasonally; daily in the early morning. Call the Coast Guard 503.322.3234, 24-hours a day for weather and bar conditions. For emergencies, call the Coast Guard 24 hours a day at 503.322.3246. The Coast Guard also broadcasts bar conditions on VHF channels 16 and 22. (BOCW, 2001 Ed., p. 20)

Authors' Note: Buoy G"1," on p. 21 *BOCW,* is shown north of its present position.

Tillamook Bay—the last major harbor before the entrance to the Columbia River—is used as an overnight stop to help time a Columbia River Bar crossing when headed for Ilwaco or Astoria. The bar at Tillamook Bay has the reputation of being one of the more difficult to cross—which is understandable when you try to gather definitive information from the two government publications noted above. However, if the weather is moderate and settled, there is no reason you can't enter Tillamook Bay. The transient dock in Garibaldi offers good shelter and is quiet and restful.

When entering or exiting Tillamook Bay we stress the importance of calling the Coast Guard Station on VHF Channel 16 or by cell phone at 503.322.3531 (voice) or 503.322.3234 (taped weather report) for the latest bar status. *Ask specifically* whether they recommend following the 3-sector entrance light across the bar, or the south entrance channel ("South Hole") between gong buoy RG"S" and the south jetty. *Caution:* It is important to use the latest version of Chart 18588, corrected by Notices to Mariners, before you attempt to enter Tillamook Bay.

If you are uncomfortable for any reason, tell the Coast Guard you are new to the area. They may offer you an escort, even if you do not request one. Do not hesitate to accept their offer. We accepted, and the crew told us afterwards they would much rather escort a cruising boat into Tillamook Bay than have to look for (or recover) a vessel in distress.

We were told to put on our life vests and meet them at the entrance whistle buoy RW"T," 1.15 miles west of the jetties. Since the bar conditions were just moderate that day, and seas were not breaking, they asked us to proceed first, following the middle ground route; they followed us. (Be sure to pull up any passive stabilizer gear before reaching buoy G"1" and the shoals!)

U.S. Coast Guard escorts Baidarka *into Tillamook Bay*

the channel before dying out. The USCG lifeboats are tested only to 20-foot breakers, so they are unable to train in worst conditions and, certainly, cruising boats should not venture near Tillamook under such conditions. The Coast Guard normally mans the lookout tower on the north jetty seven days a week from 45 minutes before sunrise to 1600 hours.

The two entrance range lights mentioned in *Coast Pilot* have recently been replaced by a single 3-sector directional light.

In general, if a boat is too far north of the range track, the 3-sector light will indicate a green range light; red if too far south; and white, or a combination of both if it is on track. Our diagram and

Except for momentarily losing sight of the Coast Guard rescue boat in growing swells on the 3-fathom shoal just outside the entrance, we had an uneventful bar crossing. They then led the way to the Garibaldi transient dock where the crew came aboard *Baidarka* to discuss their experiences and to receive our expressions of appreciation.

The Tillamook rescue boat crew considers "South Hole" (the south entrance route) the primary escort route in marginal conditions— especially near the last of an ebb when swells heap up and break across the "middle ground" as far south as gong buoy RG"S." Avoid the west end of the south jetty where rocks have broken off during past storms. South Hole is generally a slightly deeper route and the one indicated on our approach diagram.

The worst part of the bar, called the "middle ground," is from buoy G"1" to the north jetty as far south as buoy RG"S." A strong ebb current (as much as 6 knots on spring tides) is known to create breaking seas as far out as the 20-fathom contour! The best time to cross the bar is generally on the last of a flood tide.

The shoals outside the breakwaters and along the entrance channel change from season to season and, on occasions (during winter storms), Tillamook gets 20- to 40-foot breaking seas at the entrance that travel a good way up

Coast Guard cutter follows Baidarka *across the bar*

route information for Tillamook entrance are for the deepwater area between buoy "S" and the south jetty. When the direct route across the middle ground is approved by the Coast Guard as the safer route, follow the 3-sector light from entrance buoy RW"T."

Once inside the jetties, follow the buoys and daymarks to the dredged channel that leads south past Sow and Pigs rocks then turns east, passing the Coast Guard station and entering the marina at Garibaldi. The 300-foot-long transient dock is located on

Following the USCG into Garibaldi

the east side of the Garibaldi Marina. When rounding up into the marina, favor the west dock; the east shore is a shallow mud flat. Very few boats go south of Garibaldi due to the changing channels and shoals, and the opaque water.

⚓ **Tillamook Coast Guard Station**
503.322.3531 (voice) or 503.322.3234 (taped weather report); monitors VHF Channel 16

Anchorage can be found at the north end of South Channel on a flat that carries 8 feet of water at zero tide, or in 22 to 28 feet west of light R12. You may also find anchorage south of Kincheloe Point in Crab Harbor in about 10 feet mud and sand with good holding.

Tillamook Bay
by Michelle Gaylord

On August 13 we took off for Garibaldi in Tillamook Bay. It's a tiny, cute little harbor, but doesn't have a whole lot to offer, other than friendly people. The economy in the area is rather depressed and many of the shops, stores, and processing plants were closed and up for sale. The sportfishing boats here are quite unique. If you want to go bottom fishing on one of the boats, you also get your own personal crab traps. So, these guys not only come back with a boat full of cod, but they also get their limit in crab!

Caution: Once again, when leaving Tillamook, ask for a bar status. If you are northbound, do not turn north until you are beyond buoy G"1" due to shoaling west of the north jetty and its submerged section.

Garibaldi (Tillamook Bay)
Chart 18558; 2 mi inside Tillamook Bay
Transient float pos: 45°33.36'N, 123°54.70'W
Tillamook USCG Base pos: 45°33.27'N, 123°55.19'W

> *Garibaldi [is] a lumber and fishing town. . . . A black concrete stack and a silver elevated tank are conspicuous. There are several small fish companies at Garibaldi.*
>
> *The town has a boat basin for commercial and sport fishing vessels. Berths for about 200 craft, electricity, gasoline, diesel fuel, water, ice, a launching ramp, and marine supplies are available at the basin. . . .* (CP, 33rd Ed.)

Garibaldi is a friendly, but rough and tumble, small town currently finding its way after having been a commercial fishing and lumber town for so long. Sportfishing is still active, but commercial fishing—as in so many of the coastal ports—has decreased. (As we went to press, fish processing was limited to one company.) The marina has one transient dock at the east side of the harbor across from the commercial docks. Facilities for cruising boats are limited, as is the possibility for re-provisioning. Activities in the area are geared to the outdoors—crabbing, clamming, bird-watching, windsurfing, kayaking and canoeing. Although we arrived in *Baidarka* around 1600 hours, most of the stores in town were already closed. There was no harbormaster available and the showers and restrooms were locked.

Local lore has it that when the sun shines inside Tillamook Bay, the winds are blowing outside.

Tillamook and Trask Rivers
Chart 18558; S of Garibaldi
Tillamook and Trask Rivers intersection pos:
45°28.04'N, 123°52.85'W

Tillamook River empties into the S part of Tillamook Bay just W of the entrance to Hoquarten Slough. A fixed highway bridge with a clearance of 15 feet crosses the river about 0.7 mile above the mouth. A small marina is just S of the bridge on the W bank of Trask River, just inside the mouth; berths with electricity, water, ice, gasoline, a launching ramp, and marine supplies are available. Outboard engine repairs can be made. This marina is only open during the summer. Depths of about 2 feet can be carried in Tillamook River to the highway bridge. Wet and dry winter boat storage is available at the marina. (CP, 33rd Ed.)

Transient float at Garibaldi

Tillamook River enters the southern part of Tillamook Bay, just west of the entrance to Hoquarten Slough. The Tillamook and Trask Rivers are part of a complex series of channels and shoals at the south end of Tillamook Bay. This area is best explored by shallow-draft boat and kayaks with local knowledge. The opaque waters make transiting risky since the channels are poorly marked. Very few boats go south of Garibaldi due to these conditions.

Nehalem River
Chart 18556, 5.3 mi N of
Tillamook Bay
Entrance buoy RW"NR":
45°39.29'N, 123°57.54'W
Nehalem Bay jetty entrance:
45°39.38'N, 123°56.69'W

Aerial view: Nehalem River

Nehalem River . . . is tidal for about 10 miles from the entrance. . . .

The entrance is protected by jetties extending 600 yards from the shoreline, though there are a number of breaks in the jetties. A whistle buoy is nearly 1 mile W of the entrance, and a private buoy marks the submerged W end of the S jetty. A private range marks the entrance channel. Mariners are advised to seek local knowledge before using the entrance channel because of seasonal changes.

The depths on the bar and within the bay are not sufficient for coastwise shipping. The controlling depth is about 4 feet on the bar, and 3 to 8 feet to Wheeler. The channel is changeable. (CP, 33rd Ed.)

DANGER AREAS

A. Crab Rock. *Crab Rock is located about 150 yards southeast of Jetty Fisheries Resort docks and is a hazard to small boats when it is covered by water. The hazard is sometimes marked by a privately maintained red buoy just westward of the rock. If the buoy is present, stay to the right of it when outbound and to the left when inbound.*

B. Bar area. *The entire area between the beach and the 30-foot curve is bar area and breaks on the ebbing current. The safest channel across the bar is subject to frequent change. Boaters proceeding out should stop just inside the entrance and carefully evaluate the bar. If the bar is breaking, do not cross. If you decide to cross, pick the calmest area and proceed, but do not attempt to turn around if the bar is breaking.*

ENTRANCE

The best weather is close to the south jetty. The channel seaward of the jetties is continually shifting and familiarity is needed to cross it safely. The range markers, therefore, do not necessarily show the exact channel and are also obstructed by trees.

BAR CONDITION REPORTS

During the summer, the Coast Guard broadcasts bar conditions on VHF channels 16 and 22 only when a Coast Guard boat is patrolling the area. (BOCW, 2001 Ed., p. 18)

Nehalem River is a sportfishing river with little coastal traffic passing across its bar. The entrance is marked with whistle buoy RW"NR"

about 0.7 mile offshore in 10 fathoms. Nehalem River should be entered only in calm weather, on a rising flood tide, and with local knowledge. The entrance channel favors the south jetty (see waypoint above); shoals and breakers fill the northern half of the inside channel. There is a privately maintained set of range marks but we understand they are not clearly visible and cannot be depended upon to correctly mark the changing channel. Shoals that break extend 0.25 mile west of both poorly maintained jetties to a depth of little more than one fathom.

Because of its poorly charted and poorly maintained entrance, Nehalem River is largely the domain of local boats willing to risk the uncertainties of its entrance bar.

Jetty (Nehalem River)
Chart 18556; E side of the river, inside entr
Marina position: 45°39.66'N, 123°55.82'W

A marina is at Jetty on the E side of the river just inside the entrance. Berths with electricity, gasoline, water, ice, launching ramp, and marine supplies are available. Engine repairs can be made; wet winter boat storage is also available. (CP, 33rd Ed.)

Jetty is a sportfishing center for Nehalem River.

Brighton (Nehalem River)
Chart 18556; 1 mi inside entr of Nehalem Riv
Marina position: 45°40.17'N, 123°55.53'W

Brighton is a small settlement on the E shore. . . . A marina is at Brighton. Berths with electricity, gasoline, water, ice, and a launching ramp is [sic] *at the marina.* (CP, 33rd Ed.)

Brighton is primarily a sportfishing center that caters to trailerable boats.

Cape Falcon
Charts 18520, 18003; 11.5 mi N of Tillamook Bay
Position (Cape Falcon Rock):
45°45.90'N, 123°59.91'W

Cape Falcon . . . projects about 2 miles from the general trend of the coast. The seaward face, less than 0.5 mile in extent, is very jagged with numerous rocks under the cliffs. The SW point of

Bow watch on approach to Cape Falcon

the cape is composed of nearly vertical cliffs, 200 feet high, and is partially timbered. Falcon Rock . . . is small and not very conspicuous. (CP, 33rd Ed.)

Falcon Rock is a dangerous, small 15-foot-high rock located 0.6 mile west of Cape Falcon. It can be confused with a similar rock, close in, just off the Cape. Caution should be used in poor visibility when approaching this area. *Baidarka* found the route inside Falcon Rock to be clear, with depths of 23 fathoms. However it's necessary to avoid the charted rocks and reef awash 0.2 mile northeast of Falcon Rock.

The south side of Cape Falcon benefits from a substantial lee effect that offers a good temporary anchor site, known locally as Smuggler Cove. Notice the small arch that cuts clear through the rock face of the cape at water level; it appears that a dinghy or kayak could pass through this arch in calm weather.

Smuggler Cove
Charts 18520; S side of Cape Falcon
Entrance: 45°45.26'N, 123°59.18'W
Anchor: 45°45.70'N, 123°58.31'W

Smuggler Cove . . . is an excellent anchorage for small boats. The best anchorage is close to the N shore in 4 to 5 fathoms, protected from all except SW winds. Care should be taken to avoid two rocks, bare at extreme low water, that are about

150 yards from the N shore of the cove and rise abruptly from deep water.

In July 1983, a sunken crane barge with 30 feet over it was reported about 0.8 mile S of Cape Falcon in about 45°44.9'N, 123°58.6'W. (CP, 33rd Ed.)

Smuggler Cove is a pleasant temporary rest stop or a place to await proper timing to cross the Columbia River bar, 28 miles to the north. It is poorly charted and caution is advised. Good temporary anchorage can be found tucked close-in to the small beach in the northeast corner of the cove, avoiding occasional small kelp patches. We anchored south of the bluffs where there are a number of blowholes—about halfway from Cape Falcon—and a small waterfall at the north end of the beach. There is a small landing beach in the cove and lots of swinging room. Avoid two submerged rocks 150 yards off the north shore, as noted above in *Coast Pilot.* (We did not notice them.) While we found no chop here in northwest winds we did feel some swell. Smuggler Cove is exposed to southwest chop and swell and we would wonder, contrary to the *Coast Pilot*, how good a site this is in a southeast gale. Cape Falcon has a small natural arch near its west end seen when close to shore—a good place to explore by dinghy.

Baidarka crossed over the site of the sunken barge mentioned in *Coast Pilot,* with 30 feet of water below our keel and without a change in depth. We did not see either of the charted wrecks or the two reported rocks 150 yards off the north shore; so keep your eyes open. The route inside Falcon Rock is clear; however, avoid the rocks awash 0.2 mile to the northeast.

Local fishing boats say they prefer to anchor mid-cove in 5 to 6 fathoms over a gravel bottom.

Anchor in about 5 fathoms over sand, mud and gravel with fair-to-good holding.

Tillamook Rock

Chart 185201; 2 mi W of Tillamook Head
Position: 45°56.25'N, 124°01.13'W

Tillamook Rock . . . has an abandoned lighthouse and buildings on it. (CP, 33rd Ed.)

Tillamook Rock is a striking, vertical-sided rock with an abandoned lighthouse. From the south, well offshore Tillamook Head, the rock resembles a giant tugboat. We have found the route inside Tillamook Rock to be clear outside the 10-fathom contour; some kelp patches surround the rock itself. The rock is quite a sight. We did not see any sign of a charted submerged rock northeast of the lighthouse, but beware—this area is poorly charted.

The entrance to the Columbia River lies 18 miles northwest of Tillamook Rock. The coast is low and indefinite. Keep a sharp eye on your echo sounder as you approach the Columbia River; flat, shallow water extends 1 to 2 miles from shore near the south jetty.

Passing inside Tillamook Rock

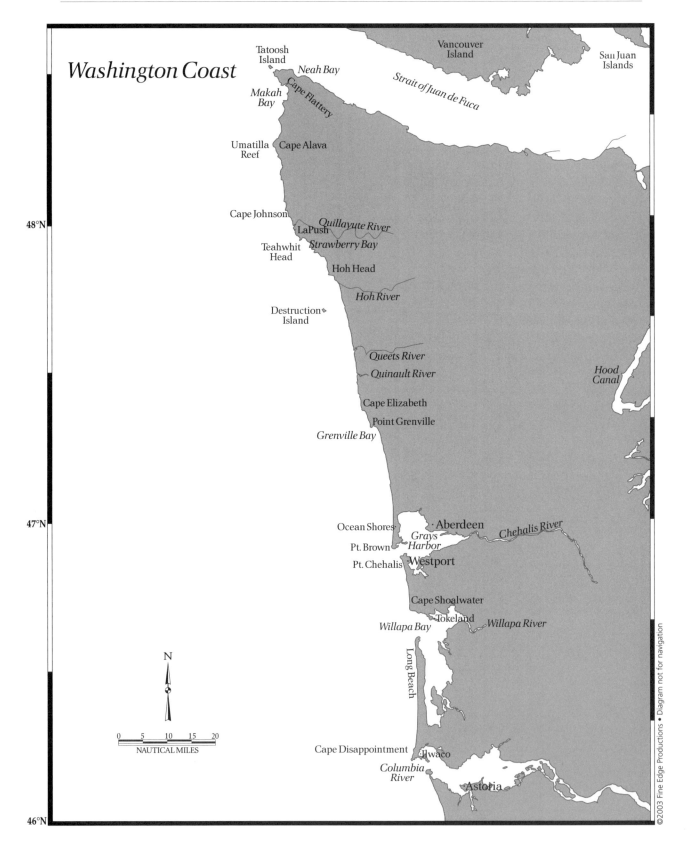

Washington Coast

7

Columbia River to Cape Flattery

Introduction

Between the big, freshwater Columbia River and the reversing saltwater "river" of the Strait of Juan de Fuca, the coastline is formed mainly of a long stretch of low, sandy beaches backed by small hills; depths for 2 to 4 miles offshore do not exceed 10 fathoms. The coastal features are not remarkable until the northern reaches where the Olympic Mountains come into view and the shore regains its rugged appearance— similar to southern Oregon and northern California.

Baidarka *with paravanes up for bar crossing*

The 1000-mile-long Columbia—a major marine feature of the Pacific Coast—is navigable to Pasco and Kennewick, Washington, nearly 300 miles above its entrance, where pleasure craft and ships can then navigate the Snake River all the way to Lewiston, Idaho. Several locks located on the Columbia allow boats to travel on a series of "lakes."

The Columbia River is a frequent cruising stop, with the nearest marinas found either in Ilwaco, on the Washington shore, or Astoria on the Oregon side. A number of sailboats and trawlers berth in Portland or in up-river marinas along the way. In fair weather during fishing season, sportfishing boats by the hundreds line the entrance to the Columbia. For the many Oregonians and Washingtonians who live along the Columbia, it's all "local boating."

The "Great River of the West," as the Columbia River was once called, has earned the reputation of being one of the most treacherous river bars in the world. Before jetties were constructed to control its moving sandbar, the mouth of the Columbia was referred to as the "Graveyard of the Pacific." According to local history, more than 2,000 vessels and 700 lives have been lost over this bar. The area is so challenging, the U.S. Coast Guard's only rescue training station is located at Cape Disappointment.

Thousands of ships, tugs with barges, commercial fishing boats and sportfishing boats enter and exit the Columbia River safely every year. Today, only a handful of vessels run aground or are caught in breaking seas. You can minimize the risks of crossing the bar by carefully studying the *Coast Pilot* and large-scale charts, tide tables, weather forecasts, and by contacting the Cape Disappointment Coast Guard station on VHF Channel 16 for a bar status report—*before* the day of your transit!

Avoid entering the Columbia River during strong ebb tides, with large swells running outside, with contrary winds, or in poor visibility.

Don't hesitate to call the Coast Guard to discuss any concerns you might have about weather, bar conditions, your progress, traffic in the channels, or to ask them for assistance. Our experience shows they are more than willing to help if you let them know you are new to the area. However, do not ask for advice on whether to cross the bar or not. The Coast Guard doesn't advise—they just report the bar conditions! Gather the information you need, then make your own judgment call prior to attempting a transit.

Grays Harbor, 40 miles north of the Columbia and 93 miles south of Cape Flattery, is a popular place to await favorable conditions before continuing either a south- or northbound voyage. Once the home of an active and large fishing fleet, the harbor now welcomes pleasure craft as never before.

Crabpot floats between the Columbia River and the area north of Grays Harbor remain a navigational hazard to small craft, so always maintain a sharp lookout along this shore. To avoid these hazards, you may want to follow the crabpot-free express route, remaining farther offshore. (The crabpot-free route into and out of Grays Harbor simplifies making a stop here.)

From north of Grays Harbor to the Strait of Juan de Fuca, just a handful of marginal anchor sites offer temporary shelter. (Neah Bay, east of Cape Flattery, is the first all-weather anchorage inside the strait.) Umatilla Reef, north of La Push, is a major navigational hazard and, at that point—if you have been following an inshore route—you must head farther offshore until you pass the westernmost part of the coast at Cape Alava.

North of Destruction Island, coastal features

Haystacks and off-lying rocks are prominent north of Destruction Island

include picturesque haystacks and off-lying rocks. If you have the time and favorable weather and tide, stop at picturesque La Push to experience a Northwest Native village and enjoy a stunningly scenic beach. Once you make the turn east into the Strait of Juan de Fuca, Vancouver Island provides a lee where sheltered coves and harbors abound.

Cape Disappointment
Chart 18521; N pt of Columbia River entr, 43 mi N of Tillamook Bay
Position: (Cape Disappointment Light)
46°16.56'N, 124°03.14'W

Cape Disappointment . . . is the first major headland along the 20 miles of sand beach north from Tillamook Head. It comprises a group of rounding hills covering an area 2.5 miles long and 1 mile wide, divided by a narrow valley extending NNW. The seaward faces of these hills are precipitous cliffs with jagged, rocky points and small strips of sand beach. Cape Disappointment Light . . . 220 feet above the water, is shown from a 53-foot white conical tower with white horizontal band at top and bottom, and black horizontal band in the middle, on the S point of the cape. Cape Disappointment Coast Guard Station is at Fort Canby on the E side of the cape. (CP, 33rd Ed.)

The coast from Tillamook Head to Cape Shoalwater, nearly 50 miles north, is composed almost entirely of a sand beach with few dis-

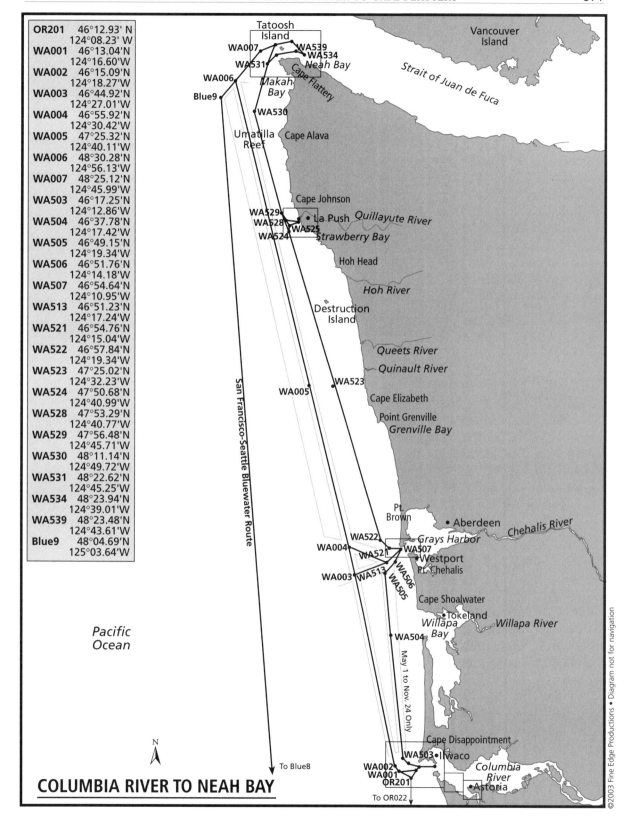

OR201	46°12.93' N
	124°08.23' W
WA001	46°13.04'N
	124°16.60'W
WA002	46°15.09'N
	124°18.27'W
WA003	46°44.92'N
	124°27.01'W
WA004	46°55.92'N
	124°30.42'W
WA005	47°25.32'N
	124°40.11'W
WA006	48°30.28'N
	124°56.13'W
WA007	48°25.12'N
	124°45.99'W
WA503	46°17.25'N
	124°12.86'W
WA504	46°37.78'N
	124°17.42'W
WA505	46°49.15'N
	124°19.34'W
WA506	46°51.76'N
	124°14.18'W
WA507	46°54.64'N
	124°10.95'W
WA513	46°51.23'N
	124°17.24'W
WA521	46°54.76'N
	124°15.04'W
WA522	46°57.84'N
	124°19.34'W
WA523	47°25.02'N
	124°32.23'W
WA524	47°50.68'N
	124°40.99'W
WA528	47°53.29'N
	124°40.77'W
WA529	47°56.48'N
	124°45.71'W
WA530	48°11.14'N
	124°49.72'W
WA531	48°22.62'N
	124°45.25'W
WA534	48°23.94'N
	124°39.01'W
WA539	48°23.48'N
	124°43.61'W
Blue9	48°04.69'N
	125°03.64'W

Pacific
Ocean

N

COLUMBIA RIVER TO NEAH BAY

San Francisco-Seattle Bluewater Route

To Blue8

To OR022

Tatoosh
Island

Vancouver
Island

Strait of Juan de Fuca

WA007   WA539
         WA534
WA531   Neah Bay
WA006   Cape Flattery
Makah
Bay
Blue9

WA530

Umatilla
Reef   Cape Alava

Cape Johnson
WA529   La Push   Quillayute River
WA528   WA525
WA524   Strawberry Bay

Hoh Head

Hoh River

Destruction
Island

Queets River

Quinault River
WA523
WA005   Cape Elizabeth
               Point Grenville
               Grenville Bay

Pt.
Brown   • Aberdeen   Chehalis River
WA522   Grays Harbor
WA004   WA521 WA507
        WA52   Westport
WA003 WA513   Pt. Chehalis
        WA506
        WA505
               Cape Shoalwater

                • Tokeland
        Willapa   Willapa River
WA504   Bay

May 1 to Nov. 24 Only

Cape Disappointment
WA503 • Ilwaco
WA002   Columbia
WA001   River
OR201   • Astoria

©2003 Fine Edge Productions • Diagram not for navigation

cernable land features. Upon approaching the Columbia River from the south, the first visible signs are the low hills of Cape Disappointment along the north shore.

Cape Disappointment is marked by North Head light, visible for 36 miles, and an 18-mile light on the east end of the Cape adjacent to the range lights that mark the dredged channel. It is important to identify the channel over the bar before closing the coast south of Cape Disappointment.

Because this part of the coast is so low and flat, distance and bearings are difficult to determine. GPS and electronic charting, along with positive identification of the entrance and channel buoys, are helpful in fixing position and in tracking progress. Cruising boats should avoid crossing the Columbia River bar at night; the numerous lights along shore can make it difficult to distinguish the closer nav-aids.

Approach to the Columbia River Bar

A transit of the Columbia River Bar requires careful planning and execution, but anyone capable of coastal navigation should have no reason to fear it. Planning an approach for proper weather and bar conditions should be done securely moored in a safe haven within a reasonable distance. The first thing to do when you are nearing the vicinity is to call Cape Disappointment Coast Guard Station on Channel 16 for a bar-condition report, paying close attention to the time of maximum ebb current. As skipper you must decide *if* and *when* conditions are acceptable for proceeding across the bar.

The entrance channel to the Columbia River starts well offshore, like that of San Francisco, and the preferred, deep-water route is well-marked. The bar entrance channel is marked by a RACON buoy RW"CR," 6.2 mi SW of the North Jetty. Buoy G"1,"

Cape Disappointment as seen from the beginning of the Columbia Bar Channel

a port hand mark, and buoy R"2," a starboard hand whistle buoy, are the first of a series of numbered buoys that mark the edges of the deep-water channel.

Our Columbia River Bar Approach diagram indicates the waypoints *Baidarka* uses inbound to stay close to the right side of the channel. Once abeam waypoint OR201, you should be able to use the range lights on Cape Disappointment as

Cape Disappointment Coast Guard Station

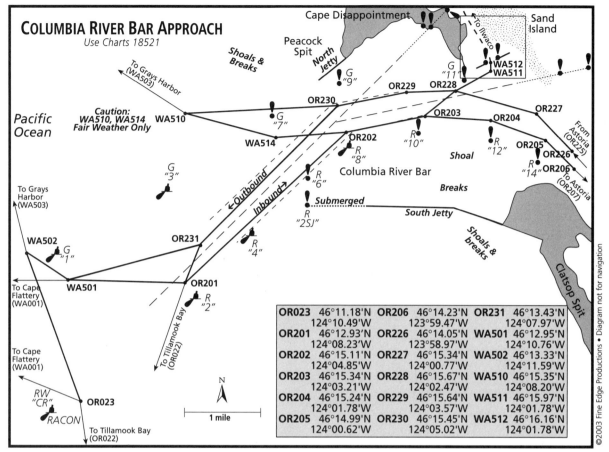

COLUMBIA RIVER BAR APPROACH
Use Charts 18521

OR023	46°11.18'N	OR206	46°14.23'N	OR231	46°13.43'N
	124°10.49'W		123°59.47'W		124°07.97'W
OR201	46°12.93'N	OR226	46°14.05'N	WA501	46°12.95'N
	124°08.23'W		123°58.97'W		124°10.76'W
OR202	46°15.11'N	OR227	46°15.34'N	WA502	46°13.33'N
	124°04.85'W		124°00.77'W		124°11.59'W
OR203	46°15.34'N	OR228	46°15.67'N	WA510	46°15.35'N
	124°03.21'W		124°02.47'W		124°08.20'W
OR204	46°15.24'N	OR229	46°15.64'N	WA511	46°15.97'N
	124°01.78'W		124°03.57'W		124°01.78'W
OR205	46°14.99'N	OR230	46°15.45'N	WA512	46°16.16'N
	124°00.62'W		124°05.02'W		124°01.78'W

©2003 Fine Edge Productions • Diagram not for navigation

guides for the first leg, and the range lights on the south end of Sand Island for the second leg. As you cross the bar, ocean swells diminish and you enter the freshwater river.

Northbound vessels navigating close to the Oregon shore will have to head well offshore several miles to intersect the entrance buoy or the dredged channel. In fair weather, the channel can be intersected at buoy R"4," but in all cases you want to avoid the submerged South Jetty by giving buoy R"2SJ" a wide birth on your starboard hand. Shortcuts to the dredged channel should be considered *only* in fair weather, favorable tidal conditions, and in good visibility.

Study large-scale Chart 18521 carefully to avoid the extensive shoals; breaking waves occur occasionally off either jetty and close abeam the marked route. It is a good idea to visually identify each numbered buoy and daymark, and check them off on the chart as you pass them to avoid inadvertently cutting a cor-

ner and finding your boat suddenly grounded. [See Michelle Gaylord's Sidebar "The Columbia River" later in the chapter.]

Large ships move through the channel at 20 knots or more, leaving a heavy wake, so it's essential to keep a sharp lookout and move aside; head into their wake to minimize severe rolling.

Entrance Channels

The entrance to Columbia River is marked by two jetties. The S jetty extends 2.7 miles seaward from the NW end of Clatsop Spit; the westernmost mile of the jetty is submerged. The N jetty extends 800 yards seaward from the shoreline on the N side of the entrance. Lighted ranges, lights, buoys, and daybeacons mark the channels.

Federal project depths in the Columbia River are 48 feet over the bar, thence 40 feet to the Broadway Bridge at Portland, Oreg.; 40 feet from the confluence of the Willamette and Columbia

Tug and tow exiting the Columbia River Bar

This is the barge the tug is towing

Rivers through the lower turning basin at Vancouver; and thence 35 feet through the upper turning basin at Vancouver. . . . (CP, 33rd Ed.)

The natural sandbar that builds up where freshwater meets the ocean occurs several miles offshore and does not differ greatly from the bar off San Francisco. A dredged channel, 48 feet deep, is well marked with aids to navigation, including several entrance and turning ranges. The currents of the Columbia River are frequently stronger than those of the entrance to San Francisco Bay. Along with stronger winds and larger swells, it's critical that a vessel time a crossing of the bar when conditions are least hazardous.

Entrance Currents

Caution. The Columbia River bar is reported to be very dangerous because of sudden and unpredictable changes in the currents often accompanied by breakers. It is reported that ebb currents on the N side of the bar attain velocities of 6 to 8 knots, and that strong NW winds sometimes cause currents that set N or against the wind in the area outside the jetties.

In the entrance the currents are variable, and at times reach a velocity of over 5 knots on the ebb; on the flood they seldom exceed a velocity of 4 knots. The current velocity is 3.5 knots, but this tidal current is always modified both as to velocity and time of slack water by the river discharge.

On the flood there is a dangerous set toward Clatsop Spit, its direction being approximately ESE; on the ebb the current sets along the line of buoys. Heavy breakers have been reported as far inside the entrance as Buoy 20, N of Clatsop Spit. (CP, 33rd Ed.)

Columbia River

Chart 18521; 548 mi N of San Francisco; 145 mi S of Str of Juan de Fuca Channel entrance buoy: R"4": 46°13.58'N, 124°06.81'W

Columbia River rises in British Columbia, Canada, through which it flows for

Aerial view: Columbia River Entrance from the north; South Jetty in the distance (note the turbulent water)

some 370 miles before entering the continental United States in NE Washington. Thence it flows S to its junction with Snake River, from which it curves W and forms the boundary between the States of Washington and Oregon for the remainder of its course to the Pacific Ocean. . . . The length of the river is 647 miles in the United States. Between the Cascade Mountains, the river flows through a canyon averaging about 5 miles wide between high cliffs on each side; of this width, the river occupies about 1 mile, the rest being marsh, low islands, and lowlands. Near the mouth, the river becomes wider, and in some places is 5 miles across.

Columbia and Willamette Rivers are navigable by deep-draft vessels to Vancouver, Wash., and Portland, Oreg. Barges navigate the Columbia River to Pasco and Kennewick, Wash., 286 miles above the mouth.

Navigation on the tributary Snake River, which joins the Columbia at Pasco, is possible to Lewiston, Idaho. . . .

The volcanic eruptions of Mount Saint Helens in mid-1980 caused extensive flooding with resulting heavy siltation in the lower Columbia River . . . just east of Longview at Mile 59. In late 1980, dredging was done in the aforementioned area, however, mariners are advised to use caution in the Columbia River and its tributaries.

In clear weather, vessels should have no difficulty in entering the river as the aids to navigation

Northwest Tidal Ranges and Currents
by DCD

In general, the higher the latitude, the more the tidal range increases. What varies just a few feet near the Equator increases to over 20 feet at higher latitudes and in remote inlets, and these increasing tides cause stronger currents and turbulence.

Current that flows in smooth channels is called laminar flow and, while it can be fast, the water is fairly smooth, without whirlpools or strong turbulence. Laminar flow is generally not a threat to cruising boats.

When the channels are irregular and have obstacles such as submerged rocks, reefs or ledges, the water quickly becomes confused, rough, and potentially hazardous. Sharp-faced, breaking waves become a common occurrence, threatening the stability of a vessel. Turbulent water and whirlpools can make steering difficult or, in extreme cases, impossible.

The power of the waves grows as the square of the height of the waves, so it pays to gauge the surface ahead and be ready to take evasive action when necessary.

Smaller vessels are threatened by smaller waves and must therefore pay more attention to current, determining whether the flow is laminar or irregular. Currents caused by tidal effects decrease during neap tides (first and third quarters of the lunar cycle); during spring tides (full and new moons) the velocity of the currents increases by two to three times that of neap tides. A prudent navigator should check both Tide and Current Tables whenever planning a passage in the Northwest.

Any current of about 3 knots or more can create serious turbulence and should be avoided by small craft. A current of 2 to 3 knots against opposing swells can cause the swell to double in size and become hazardous. Currents of 5 knots or more require special attention, as standing waves can grow to alarming heights. The safest time to cross any shallow bar is during the last of the flood when water is the deepest and currents are approaching slack. Above all, avoid periods of dangerous maximum flow at spring ebbs.

The Coast Guard issues the time and velocity of maximum ebb current for some areas such as the Columbia River bar; this is usually the time that breaking waves occur on the bar—the time to avoid! With experience you can judge how much time to leave on either side of the time of maximum ebb current. As a general rule, you should avoid crossing a bar that is exposed to ocean swells within a couple of hours of maximum ebb; in extreme cases, transit at slack water only.

Baidarka regularly travels through passages where the laminar flow is running up to 5 knots. In passages of non-laminar flow, where rocks and ledges lie beneath the flowing water, currents of more than 3 knots can cause hazardous turbulence. As the current increases to over 3 knots, your heading will change abruptly when you meet large upwellings, whirlpools or still water. In narrow passages, or when other vessels are present, reduced steerage of your vessel can be dangerous.

Before entering turbulent waters, batten down the hatches, stow any loose items including trailing dinghies, put on your life jackets and hang on!

are numerous. In thick weather, however, when aids cannot be seen, strangers should not attempt to enter without a pilot.

Local vessels entering in thick weather and with a rising tide, as a rule, do not attempt to pass beyond Desdemona Sands Light, because of the difficulty under such circumstances of avoiding vessels anchored in the narrow channel above the light. Strangers should not attempt to navigate the river at night.

Dredges will usually be found at work in the channels; these dredges should be passed with caution and reduced speed. . . .

Aids to navigation. During the seasonal high-water conditions, aids to navigation may be destroyed or rendered unreliable. Mariners are warned to exercise caution in navigating the river and to obtain the latest information regarding aids to navigation by local inquiry and through local Notice to Mariners, available upon request to the Commander, 13th Coast Guard District, Seattle. . . . (CP, 33rd Ed.)

DANGER AREAS

Chinook Spur and upper, lower, and middle Sand Island *spurs are built on two rows of staggered pilings. Currents flowing through these pilings attain a velocity of five knots or more. A boat that becomes disabled or is maneuvered in such a way that it comes in contact with any of these spurs is almost sure to suffer damage. Even large boats have capsized in these areas. Give these spurs a wide berth and never get close to them on the up-current side.*

Clatsop Spit *is an unpredictable area of the river entrance. During flood currents and slacks, it may be relatively calm, with only a gentle swell breaking far in on the spit. Yet 5 or 10 minutes later, when the current has started to ebb, it can become extremely treacherous, with breakers extending far out toward the channel. Boaters should remain north of the red buoys in this area, particularly just before or during the ebb.*

Breakers extend out past buoy #8. On a flood tide, you can be carried into Clatsop Spit. Be prepared to anchor.

The south jetty has a section broken away on the outer end. The broken section is under water, close to the surface. If you are relatively close and your engine fails, the flood or ebb current will take you across the submerged jetty. Boaters should use extra caution in the area from the visible tip of the jetty to buoy #2SJ, which marks the western end of the submerged portion of the south jetty. On the flood, a dangerous rip can occur over the sunken jetty. Do not cross the submerged jetty.

Jetty A, *which is southeast of Cape Disappointment, presents a particularly strong danger when the current is ebbing. Water flowing out of the river is deflected by the jetty, and frequently the current reaches eight knots. Boats proceeding into Baker Bay west channel make very little speed against the swift current and are exposed to the rough water (or surf on rough days) for long periods of time. Small craft should avoid the shallow, sandy area when heavy seas are running because of the surf that breaks on the beach. Look for the entrance marked by daymarks one and two and with green and red lights, respectively.*

Peacock Spit. *Waves in Peacock Spit break from three different directions. If you lose power on the bar during an ebb current, your vessel will be carried into Peacock Spit and is in danger of capsizing. Breakers may be heavy in any type of current. Sports craft leaving the river should never be on the north side of the green*

Watch for salmon seekers at North Jetty

Discovery of the "Great River of the West" *by DCD*

The Columbia River was discovered in the late 1700s by the American Captain Robert Gray aboard the 83-foot, 212-ton, 10-gun sailing ship *Columbia Rediviva*. Gray was an entrepreneur financed by a group of Bostonians who put $50,000 into a risky venture to sell northwest sea otter skins to China. His ship was the first to circumnavigate the world under the U.S. flag.

In the spring of 1792, after having wintered in Nootka Sound, Gray sailed south to map North America's then poorly-known coastline. At latitude 46°10'N, he came across the outlet of what appeared to be a mighty river. He and his crew spent a week hove-to just outside the breakers, but because he didn't want to risk crossing the surf line, he turned *Columbia* around again and headed north.

On April 29, he chanced upon Capt. George Vancouver aboard *Discovery,* accompanied by its small brig, the *Chatham,* under command of Lt. Broughton. These vessels were on an official British mission to map the North American coast from 30° to 60°N. Gray spoke openly and at length to Vancouver about the coast he had mapped. Vancouver was quite interested in the report about a possible "Great River of the West" but did not believe that Gray had truly seen such evidence.

Vancouver had already carefully explored and mapped the entire coast north of San Diego and had passed the 46th parallel without detecting any evidence that would compel him to close the breaking surf. He continued northward and became the first to document and map the Strait of Juan de Fuca.

Rebuffed, Gray turned around and headed south to re-explore the coast—this time, with heightened determination to find the Great River of the West. On May 7, the *Columbia* sailed into what is now called Grays Harbor to rest before continuing south. Four days later, they found themselves once again off what appeared to be the entrance to the Great River. They sailed back and forth for four hours just outside the line of breakers, charting the depths and, finally turning east in a possible deep-water route, they crossed the bar in about 5 to 7 fathoms. Once behind the breakers, they realized they were in fresh water in what, indeed, was a giant river.

Shortly thereafter, *Columbia* was surrounded by local Indians in canoes who indicated "great astonishment and no doubt that we were the first civilized people that they ever saw." Gray and his men traded with the Natives for several days and occupied themselves with ship's maintenance in conditions they found favorable.

Gray instructed his crew to empty the ship's drinking water casks that were filled with semi-salty water and refill them with fresh water from the river. The *Columbia* sailed up-river for several miles and, on May 15, took possession of the land in the name of America, naming the river after his trusty sailing vessel. This event later gave major importance to the U.S. claim to the Pacific Northwest.

Upon leaving the Great River on May 20, they were becalmed just east of the entrance bar on a strong ebb. Not wanting to be carried out into the breakers without steerage, they managed to bring the boat to a stop in the 5-knot current by carefully anchoring in 3.5 fathoms. That evening the wind picked up and they were able to sail across the bar into 20 fathoms. To have bested George Vancouver—one of the most methodical explorers and chart-makers of the day, and an expedition financed by the British Crown—was a great joy to Gray and his crew.

Word spread quickly up-coast about the new Columbia River that Robert Gray had finally documented and, on hearing this, Vancouver commanded his two ships to proceed to investigate this great river on their southbound trip in October 1792.

Both *Discovery* and *Chatham* arrived off the entrance of the Columbia River October 19. Two days later Vancouver sent the *Chatham* ahead to scout a possible route across the bar. After cheering their successful transit of the bar the *Chatham* signaled to the *Discovery,* which had been following them, that there were, in fact, depths of 4 to 6 fathoms across the bar. Vancouver followed the route of the *Chatham*. But—perhaps concerned about maintaining ample steerage—he quickly changed his mind at the last minute and gave orders to turn around and anchor outside the bar in 13 fathoms, intending to try again in the morning. But fate was such that, with a falling barometer and a rising fresh southeaster the next morning, he gave up the pursuit and sailed south to California, never personally entering the Columbia River.

Following Vancouver's standing orders, Broughton sailed the *Chatham* as far as he felt safe and anchored. Then he and several crew members rowed the ship's boat up-river for another week until they had only three days' rations left. At this point, under the towering Mt. Hood (which he named), he took possession of the Great River and all its drainage area in the name of the British Crown. He rowed back to the *Chatham*, hauled his long boat aboard and sailed across the bar without incident, later rendezvousing with *Discovery* in Monterey Bay where he gave Vancouver the details of his findings.

The United States prevailed in its land claims, and written history now attributes the discovery of the great river to a Boston merchant trader ship, the *Columbia*. George Vancouver's oversight proved to be one of his toughest setbacks in an otherwise spectacular career.

Columbia River on a calm day

buoys. When rounding Peacock Spit, even on a calm summer day, give the breakers at least a half-mile clearance. On these same summer days, "sneakers"—unusually large swells coming in from the sea—can suddenly begin breaking 1/4 to 1/2 mile outside the usual break on the end of the north jetty.

Middle ground. This is a shallower area between the north jetty and the main ship channel that is subject to breaking seas when swells as small as four feet are present. Breakers are much wider and have more velocity than in other areas. Conditions can change in minutes with tide current changes.

BAR CONDITIONS REPORTS

KAST, Astoria (1370 KHz): periodically throughout the day, 7 days a week.

WEATHER CONDITIONS

KPD485 (1610 kHz) (BOCW, 2001 Ed., pg. 16)

On the Columbia River bar, carefully monitor the currents and turbulence discussed in the quotations from *Coast Pilot* and *Boating in Oregon Coastal Waters* (BOCW) cited above. *Remember:* Also keep a sharp lookout for large fast-moving ships that can sneak up on you from behind and create large wakes adding to your discomfort. It is best to keep well to the side of the channel if possible, decrease your speed, and take any large wake on your bow quarter.

On an approach from the south, if you have been following an inbound course, you will have to head out to intersect the entrance channel no farther east than lighted buoy R"4." Avoid the westernmost mile of the south jetty which is submerged and marked on its west end by buoy R"2SJ." The submerged section of the South Jetty is apparent from the north only; the shoal area south of the jetty can break when swells are as low as 4 feet.

When entering from the north, avoid the temptation to cut the corner off the north jetty; the area is shallow and subject to breaking waves when ebb cur-

Aerial view: Entrance to Ilwaco Channel; Cape Disappointment to the west

rents spill out around Cape Disappointment. *Baidarka* found that, during favorable conditions, we could enter the Columbia River by staying south of buoy G"7," before making a turn to the east at waypoint WA514.

During marginal conditions, it is imperative to use the deeper main channel and pass south of buoy G"1" at WA501 before making a turn to the northeast.

It is important to know your precise position when entering the Columbia River and heading up-river. It also helps to identify each nav-aid by number, marking each one off on your large-scale chart as you pass. The ranges are useful for marking the center of the channel, but prepare to move aside when large ships or barges approach from astern or ahead. By noting your progress on large-scale Chart 18521, you have less chance of becoming confused when large vessels pass at high speed and you're forced to move out of the way.

Try to identify each nav-aid *in sequence* so that you know what to anticipate, and avoid cutting corners on turns between nav-aids. Remember that shoals lurk nearby! (See the sidebar below about *Passing Thru's* experience on the bar.)

Once you are safely behind either the Ilwaco jetties at Sand Island or in the lee east of Clatsop Spit, you are out of potential breakers from the ocean caused by heaping seas during strong ebb currents.

Port of Ilwaco (Baker Bay)
Chart 18521; 9 mi NE of Columbia Riv entr buoy RW"CR"
Ilwaco channel entr buoy G"1": (WA512)
46°16.16'N, 124°01.78'W
Position (USCG Sta): 46°16.88'N, 124°02.78'W
Entr (Boat Basin): 46°18.07'N, 124°02.47'W
Boat Basin transient floats: 46°18.32'N, 124°02.35'W

A dredged channel leads N from the Columbia River along the W side of Sand Island thence to the Port of Ilwaco mooring basin about 3 miles above the entrance. The entrance is between two detached jetties marked at the channel ends by lights. The channel is marked by lights and daybeacons.

In October-December 1999, the controlling depth was 8 feet (9 feet at midchannel) from the entrance to the Port of Ilwaco mooring basin. In 1980, depths in the mooring basin varied considerably, ranging from 7 to 16 feet in the W part to 4 to 1 foot in the E part. The entrance is subject to continual change. As there is usually a swell here, the channel

ILWACO CHANNEL ENTRANCE
Use Chart 18521

Cape Disappointment
Sand Island
Dries
N
100 yds
Pilings
Shoal
G "9"
R "8"
Shoal Water
G "7"
Shoal
R "6"
Jetty A
Shoal
R "2"
Jetty
Pilings
Shoal
G "1" WA512
Jetty
Breakers
Pilings
Shoal
WA511 46°15.97'N 124°01.78'W
WA512 46°16.16'N 124°01.78'W
Pilings
Shoal
WA511
To OR228
Shoal

©2003 Fine Edge Productions • Diagram not for navigation

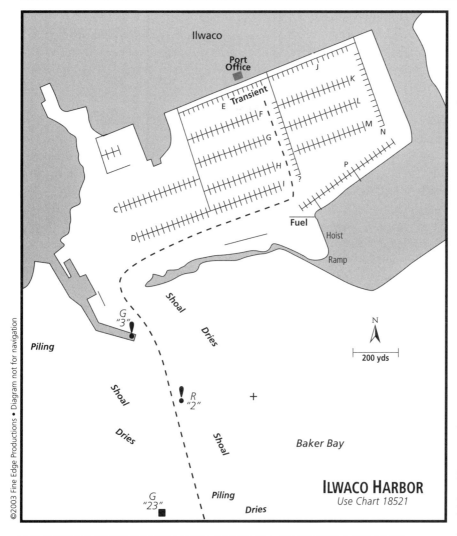

should be navigated only at high water with local knowledge. The rest of Baker Bay is covered with shoals and abandoned fish traps.

Ilwaco is the base for a large commercial and sport fishing fleet. Berths with electricity, gasoline, diesel fuel, ice, water, and other supplies are available. The largest marine railway can handle vessels up to 75 feet long for all types of repairs. Lifts up to 50 tons are also available. Wet winter boat storage is available at this port. (CP, 33rd Ed.)

The Port of Ilwaco, on the north shore of the Columbia River, is the first small-craft mooring basin inside the river's entrance. It provides good shelter for cruising boats of all sizes. A narrow, dredged channel between Cape Disappointment and Sand Island leads north 3 miles to the Port of Ilwaco. Baker Bay, the large bight east of Cape Disappointment, is filled with drying mud flats and provides little useful shelter.

Approach: From Waypoint OR203 safely cross the river channel, heading for waypoint WA511 and passing close to Columbia River buoy G"11." WA511 is a quarter-mile south of the break in two rather strange looking wooden jetties that define the entrance to the Ilwaco Channel. Turn toward

Entrance to Ilwaco Channel: G"1" at west jetty

waypoint WA512, the center of the opening in the jetties and the beginning of the Ilwaco Channel; then proceed north up the channel on a curvilinear route, watching for opposing traffic. Use the inset on Chart 18521, following the channel markers, monitoring your depth sounder and posting an alert bow watch.

Along the way, one mile from the entrance, the channel passes the Cape Disappointment USCG station, 3.75 miles southeast of Ilwaco. This station is the home of one of the largest search-and-rescue facilities in the nation. It also houses the Coast Guard's only heavy-weather Motor Lifeboat School. As you enter, you can see its many rescue boats close on your port side. Slow to a 3-knot speed (or even less) and be sure you leave no wake.

Cape Disappointment Coast Guard Station

Ilwaco
by Michelle Gaylord

While we were in Florence one of our trim tabs was damaged and our bilge pumps had been working overtime after that. Jerry found a boat yard in Ilwaco that would haul, block, launch, and power wash for $265. It would have cost about four times that much in our home port, Channel Islands. So he decided to have the boat pulled to assess the damage and find out where all the water was coming from.

So, we sat on stilts in the Ilwaco boat yard while the damage was being repaired. We also had the trim tabs removed because we never found a need for them!

We hopped a bus and headed 5 miles north to Long Beach—26 miles long and billed as the longest beach in the world—for the 18th Annual, Long Beach World Kite Competition and Festival. There were thousands of people there from all over the world with their kites of every size, shape and color. It was quite a spectacular sight. Another treat were the blackberries growing wild everywhere we looked, so I kept an empty baggie in my purse at all times, and we had fresh blackberry ice cream almost every night!

Life on the high seas is never dull. Just when you think all necessary repairs have been completed, all hell breaks loose. One night, after *Passing Thru* was back in the water, Jerry was down in the engine room at mid-night doing whatever guys do in the engine room at that hour, and I was playing on the computer. I heard some pounding but didn't think much of it.

Suddenly, in the dead silence of the night, Jerry bellowed, "We've got a major problem down here." I bolted down the stairs, and saw a geyser of water flooding the engine room. Jerry was on his knees stuffing various sizes of wooden dowels into a through-hull fitting that had broken off. (I had an instant flash of the little Dutch boy who stuck his finger in the dike to prevent a flood.) He finally got the hole plugged and the geyser under control. The following day was a Sunday and all the marine stores were closed, so we had to wait until Monday to get the needed parts and find a diver who would do the in-water portion of the repair job.

Our new dinghy was finally delivered to Ilwaco; however, the boat dealer forgot to bring the bridle that allows us to hoist the dinghy up to the fly bridge. So . . . our departure from Ilwaco was delayed *another* two days while we waited for the bridle to arrive via UPS.

Ilwaco is a friendly little harbor, but there wasn't much of anything there. After 10 days we were starting to get antsy. Although the weather forecast was not the best, we left the day after the bridle arrived.

Baidarka *at Ilwaco transient slip*

fully—the channel is filling in at certain turns.

Ilwaco is a sleepy fishing village that has seen more prosperous days. The marina is well-maintained and quiet and personnel are helpful and courteous. Boats up to 125 feet can be accommodated and, although moorage is available on a first-come, first-served basis, you will rarely be turned away. A nice feature at the harbormaster's office is the use of free bicycles for port visitors.

The Port has repair services, a boat hoist for smaller vessels, and a boat ramp. The town has one small market close to the marina, but it does not keep supermarket hours.

The entire channel is narrow and you should always slow when nearing opposing traffic. Continue to monitor your depth sounder care-

---

Desdemona Sands Incident
by Michelle Gaylord

About 2 miles off the mouth of the Columbia River, where the fresh water meets saltwater, the waters got weird on us, churning in the various tidal and current actions.

Just as we cleared the south jetty, we saw 500 to 600 boats, all shapes and sizes, heading out of the river toward our boat. It was as if an evacuation order had been issued and everyone was leaving but us! We were truly the only boat seemingly going in the wrong direction. As we got closer we saw that every one of these hundreds of boats were trolling with a salmon line! All we could figure was that this must have been opening day for salmon, and everyone and his grandmother were out there to get in on the action. It was a real feat trying to dodge all those boats, take pictures, and still locate all the channel markers. We found out later that it was *not* opening day, but simply the typical weekend crowd!

The Columbia River is one of the most dangerous bars in the world to navigate, and we had to time our entrance just right with tides and currents. About 5 miles up-river, Jerry was watching the instruments and noticed that the fathometer indicated we were getting into shallower and shallower water. He immediately

pulled back on the throttle, and *boom*, we were aground.

After trying unsuccessfully to back *Passing Thru* off the bar we gave up and called the Coast Guard to send a tow boat. As we waited, the tides and currents would temporarily lift us off the bar and then set us right back down again. Each time, the boat listed to one side or the other and all I could envision was *Passing Thru* lying on her side in the mud! Every time a wake lifted us off the ground, Jerry would ease the throttles back and forth in an effort to find deeper water.

When a large freighter passed about 1/8-mile away in water deep enough to handle it, we suddenly noticed the channel marker we had missed! We were outside the marked shipping channel and had gone astray and aground on the Desdemona Sandbar.

After about 10 minutes (it seemed like hours), he was able to guide us slowly into deeper and deeper water. Whew, we were finally okay!

Just as I got on the radio to advise the Coast Guard, I could see a rescue boat screaming toward us down the channel. But they must have received the word, because suddenly they slowed down, turned around, and went back.

Passing Thru *at the Ilwaco boatyard for power wash*

To stretch your legs, you might see if one of the free bicycles could handle a trip out to Fort Canby State Park at Cape Disappointment or to the Willapa National Wildlife Refuge. Ilwaco

Long Beach International Kite Festival

Heritage Museum has interesting displays that depict frontier life of the area.

Anchorage may be found in the basin south of the fuel dock. Inquire first at the harbormaster's office.

Desdemona Sands
Chart 18521; bwt River Mi 5 & 13, N side of channel

Desdemona Sands, marked by a light near the W end, is a shoal area extending SE for about 8 miles from just inside the entrance to Columbia River. Desdemona Sands has the main river channel to the S and a secondary channel to the N. (CP, 33rd Ed.)

Hammond, Oregon
Chart 18521; River Mi 8.5; OR side of the Columbia
Entrance boat basin: 46°12.30'N, 123°56.91'W

A boat basin is in Hammond, 0.2 mile SE of the wharf. Its entrance is marked by a light and a day-beacon on the east and west jetties, respectively. In August 1997, the controlling depth was 6 feet in the basin channel, with gradual shoaling to lesser depths at the S end. Berths with electricity, for about 140 craft, gasoline, diesel fuel, water, ice, marine supplies, and a launching ramp are available at the basin. . . . (CP, 33rd Ed.)

Hammond is the first Oregon town inside the entrance to the Columbia with a boat basin. Hammond Marina, operated by the City of Warrenton, has 175 slips, mainly for smaller sportfishing and commercial fishing vessels. Although it has full services including fuel, large cruising vessels will find more convenient moorage in Astoria. If you want to give it try, it's best to phone ahead to see if they have space and can accommodate the length of your vessel.

To approach Hammond boat basin, head up-river to waypoint OR208 then proceed directly to the entrance waypoint shown for the boat basin.

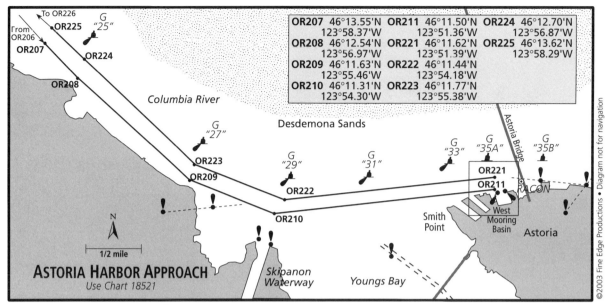

OR207	46°13.55'N	OR211	46°11.50'N	OR224	46°12.70'N
	123°58.37'W		123°51.36'W		123°56.87'W
OR208	46°12.54'N	OR221	46°11.62'N	OR225	46°13.62'N
	123°56.97'W		123°51.39'W		123°58.29'W
OR209	46°11.63'N	OR222	46°11.44'N		
	123°55.46'W		123°54.18'W		
OR210	46°11.31'N	OR223	46°11.77'N		
	123°54.30'W		123°55.38'W		

ASTORIA HARBOR APPROACH
Use Chart 18521

From Hammond, you can drive or cycle to 700-acre Fort Stevens State Park which served as a military fort from the Civil War to shortly after World War II. The fort carries the distinction of having been the only military installation in the continental U.S. to have been fired on during World War II. The park has a military museum, interpretive displays, and miles of beaches along which you can view the remains of the iron-hulled *Peter Iredale,* a three-master that went aground off the Columbia in 1906 during a storm.

⚓ **Hammond Marina** open 0800-1700; tel: 503.861.3197 (or 503.861.3822 Warrenton); fax: 503-861.2351; monitors Channel 16

Warrenton (Skipanon Waterway)
Chart 18521; River Mi 9.5, OR side of the Columbia
Entrance (Skipanon Waterway): 46°11.08'N, 123°54.39'W
Position (Warrenton Marina): 46°10.07'N, 123°55.12'W

Warrenton . . . is the base of a large sport fishing fleet. About 1 mile above the entrance to the waterway is a basin with a marina on the S side. Berths with electricity, gasoline, diesel fuel, water, ice, marine supplies, and a launching ramp are available. A marine railway that can handle boats up to 80 feet long is at the marina for hull repairs.

In August 1999, the controlling depths were 7 feet (10 feet at midchannel) in the entrance channel to the basin, thence 5 to 10 feet in the N half and 10 to 13 feet in the S half of the basin, and thence 5 feet at midchannel to the head of the project at the railroad bridge. There are general depths of about 5 feet above the railroad bridge . . . The channel to the turning basin is marked by

Kites of every size, shape, and color

Michelle Gaylord

©2003 Fine Edge Productions • Diagram not for navigation

West Mooring Basin and Astoria Bridge

Astoria

Chart 18521; at River mile 14, OR side of Columbia Entrance (W Boat Basin): 46°11.46′N, 123°51.34′W

Astoria . . . extends from Youngs Bay to Tongue Point. It is the principal city on the Columbia River below Longview, Wash. . . .

Two mooring basins for small craft and fishing vessels are maintained by the Port of Astoria. The West Basin, 0.3 (0.3) mile W of the S end of the Astoria Bridge, has 15 feet reported through the entrance and depths of about 5 feet at the floats. The entrance to the basin is marked by private lights. Berths with electricity, gasoline, diesel fuel, water, ice, and some marine supplies are available. All types of repairs can be made at several firms on the basin. . . . The East Basin, 2 (2.3) miles E of the Astoria Bridge, has berths and a launching ramp; however, no services are available. Reported depths of 15 feet through the entrance and 10 feet at the floats are available. West Basin has wet winter storage, and East Basin has wet and dry winter storage. (CP, 33rd Ed.)

a 198°30′ lighted range; lights mark the channel entrance. (CP, 33rd Ed.)

Warrenton Marina, at the east side of the end of Skipanon Waterway, can accommodate pleasure craft up to 55 feet. Facilities include restrooms, showers, pump-out station, water and electricity. As with Hammond, its slips are frequently filled with commercial and sport-fishing vessels, so be sure to call ahead before you make the mile detour down the waterway. To approach Warrenton, continue up-river to waypoint OR210, then turn southwest into Skipanon Waterway.

Warrenton sits mainly on tidal flats protected by dikes that were constructed by Chinese laborers in the early 1900s. If you happen to carry a windsurfing board with you, Youngs Bay, to the east of Warrenton, is popular with windsurfers because of its shallow waters and good winds.

⚓ **Warrenton Marina** open 0800-1700; tel: 503.861.3822; fax: 503.861.2351; monitors Channel 16

Astoria, the first deep-draft port on the Columbia and a vibrant historical town, has two moor-

Retired Lightship Columbia *and high seas entrance buoy, Columbia River Maritime Museum*

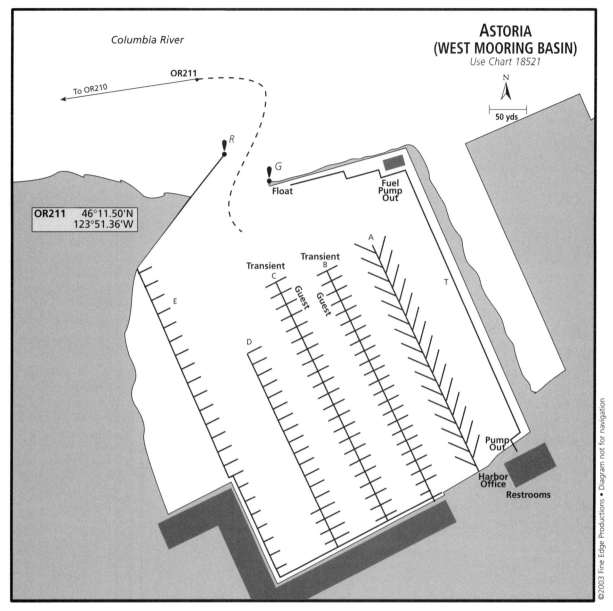

ASTORIA (WEST MOORING BASIN)
Use Chart 18521

Columbia River

To OR210 — OR211

R

G
Float

Fuel
Pump
Out

OR211   46°11.50'N
        123°51.36'W

N

50 yds

Transient
A

Transient
B

Transient
C

Guest

Guest

D

E

T

Pump
Out

Harbor
Office
Restrooms

©2003 Fine Edge Productions • Diagram not for navigation

ing basins for pleasure craft—West Basin and East Basin. To make your approach to Astoria, continue up-river to waypoint OR211 then turn southwest to the entrance. The West Basin has full transient facilities that include restrooms, showers, laundry facilities, fish-cleaning station, pump-out station, launch ramp, fuel and a restaurant. The East Basin caters to small sportfishing craft. A trolley runs between the two marinas. Both basins are within walking distance of shops, galleries, and all supplies. The marina sits just below the Astoria-Megler

Bridge that connects Oregon and Washington; this bridge has the longest continuous truss span in North America.

As the oldest American settlement west of the Rockies, Astoria is steeped in history. The area was first visited by Captain Robert Gray in 1792, then by the Lewis & Clark Corps of Discovery in 1805. The Fort Clatsop National Memorial, 5 miles from Astoria, features a replica of the log fort built by the Lewis and Clark expedition.

First built on pilings above the Columbia

River, the downtown area burned to the ground in 1922 and was rebuilt on filled land. Architectural buffs may want to take a trek on the hill above the center of town to view the many Victorian houses that date from late 1800s or early 1900s. (Local literature relates that 25% of Astoria's homes are eligible for Historic Landmark status.) While you're walking around the upper part of the city, take time to visit Astoria Column on Coxcomb Hill. In this 125-foot column, 164 steps lead up to a spectacular view of the Columbia, the Pacific, and the surrounding hills. The Columbia River Maritime Museum is home to one of the nation's finest displays of model ships and nautical artifacts.

Astoria waterfront trolley for sightseeing

⚓ **Astoria Mooring Basins** open 0830-1700; tel: 503.325.8279: fax: 503.325.4525; website: <u>port-of-astoria.com</u>

Astoria
by Michelle Gaylord

Still hyperventilating from the Desdemona Sands episode, we found and entered Astoria's tightly-packed yacht basin. The space assigned to us lay along a 600-foot transient dock, sandwiched between a powerboat and a sailboat. Not only did the space look too small, but we had to go down a narrow fairway, turn around, then try to maneuver our way between the two boats. I swear—and I am not exaggerating—the width of the fairway Jerry had to turn the boat around in was no more than 55 feet.

I told him, "No way—back out. Let's find something else." I was convinced that not only would we tear out the stern of our boat, but we'd take the sterns of about six other boats with us. He insisted that he could make it, so I thought, "Oh, what the hell, this is as good a place to sink as anywhere."

I wasn't able to give him much help watching our stern because I was too busy changing the lines and fenders from the port to the starboard side at the last minute. He completed the turn just as I finished with the last line.

I couldn't believe it. He had literally turned our big monster on a dime. Now all he had to do was get all 53 feet of us into a 60-foot space, dealing with tides, currents, and winds—and no bow thruster. Fortunately, a guy on the dock was waiting to give us a hand. I really don't think we would have made it without him.

We spent four days in Astoria. The marina we were in was right under the Astoria bridge and, all afternoon, freighters were coming down-river, their cargo holds loaded, heading for places unknown. It was really fascinating to see all these huge ships from all over the world at such close range.

Another day we visited the Columbia River Maritime Museum. What a wonderful place! They had a conning tower from a submarine where we could look out at the river, an entire helm station from a destroyer (which was so large the museum was built around it), many light beacons from various periods of time, all sorts of artifacts from ships destroyed right here at the Columbia Bar, displays about the shipwrecks, lighthouses, fishing, navigation, and naval history. They also had on display in the water the old Lightship *Columbia*, which was anchored at the mouth of the harbor until it was taken out of commission in the late 1950s. This museum alone made our trip to Astoria worth it.

Hail Columbia *by Roderick Frazier Nash*

Once across the rightfully dreaded Columbia River Bar, it's possible to cruise for weeks on the largest river of the west coast of North America. Think about that. From Alaska to Cape Horn at the tip of South America, only the Fraser River in British Columbia and the combined Sacramento-San Joaquin, flowing out San Francisco's Golden Gate, come close in size.

Portland, Oregon lies inland on the Columbia, 100 miles from Astoria and the ocean. And from Portland, the Columbia rambles along at a low gradient through lightly developed country with lots of backwaters for secluded anchorages. Lewis and Clark sites are a major feature of this trip all the way up-river to the confluence with the Snake River and then on the Snake to Lewiston, Idaho. The Columbia was truly a highway of discovery— and it still is. Take a month and go explore the interior of the American west in an ocean-going boat!

Control of the river begins 45 miles upstream from Portland at the Bonneville Dam—a serious obstacle to navigation for both salmon and boaters. The first thing to remember is to forget everything you thought you knew about locks. The Columbia River locks are not like those of Seattle or the French canals.

The Chittenden Locks (commonly known as the Ballard Locks), which connect Seattle's Shilshole Bay with Lake Union, raise and lower the water about 30 feet. Boaters need to have mooring lines ready to toss to attendants on top of the concrete rims. There are always tourists around and friendly boating conversation. The scale is not overwhelming, particularly in the smaller lock used for most recreational vessels.

The same friendliness is even more apparent on the legendary Canal du Midi in France, which my wife and I traveled a few years ago with the Douglasses on a rented canal boat. Constructed in the 1680s, a series of more than 60 locks allow boats to pass over a 600-foot rise of land between the Atlantic and Mediterranean. Negotiating them is pretty straightforward. The locks raise or lower boats only an average of 10 feet each. There are vegetables, flowers and wine for sale by the lock keepers. If you have some cowboy instincts, you can learn to flip your mooring line on and off the bollards that secure boats during the locking process.

The French locking experience is fun, but it's no preparation at all for what the Corps of Engineers has in store for you on the Columbia. Cruising upstream, you enter a 120-foot-deep canyon of steel and wet concrete. Forget the flowers and friendly lockkeepers. This is new millennium boating; post-September 11 boating. As you enter the lock, a loudspeaker instructs you to tie to a set of cleats on the wall. Surveillance cameras focus on your every move. It's spooky, and you may well be the only boat in the eighth-mile-long lock. The federal government is spending thousands of dollars and using millions of gallons of water to move *your* boat.

Of course your GPS starts beeping "no coverage" because you are in a nautical coffin! And just when you think it might be a good idea to turn around and cruise on the lower Columbia, the massive 100-foot hydraulic doors close behind you with a thud. Soon, enough water is released into the lock. It's not the Panama Canal (we've all read those horror stories of yachts being crushed under freighters), but the force of the water does rile the surface as it slowly begins to rise. The cleats you tie to rise, also, on metal tracks. You ascend 100 feet. The GPS comes back. The front lock doors open and you face a placid reservoir some 50 miles long.

Returning downstream it's the reverse. You cruise off the lake and into a long, low box. The water level falls a hundred feet and it's a good feeling to see the downstream lock doors open.

There are four dams, locks, and upstream reservoirs on the Columbia below the confluence with the Snake. One of them—the Dalles Dam—inundates some of the most fearsome stretches of whitewater in American western history, including Celilo Falls where Native peoples fished salmon for millennia. The salmon are mostly gone now and the Natives are drawing food stamps. The Columbia is emasculated and so is the Snake with four more big dams below Lewiston, Idaho. There is talk of removing, or "breaching," some of these dams that were built when our nation believed paradise came from controlling the wildness in nature. Almost too late, we began to understand that what really needed controlling was our population, itself, and its inclination to excessive growth.

Today, you can cruise the 465 river miles to Lewiston and even a little further up into the end of Hells Canyon on the Snake River where whitewater rapids roar again. The geological and ecological variety on the trip is remarkable. From the rainforests of the Columbia River Gorge (with snow-capped Mt. Hood looming above), boaters travel east into an arid region resembling the Great Plains. A lot of the cruising is on reservoirs. The wind can howl, drawing board-sailors to Hood River, Oregon, making it their stronghold, but from the cruising standpoint this is powerboat country. You anchor in backwaters and navigable river mouths under lava buttes and, finally, when you get to Lewiston, Idaho—the easternmost west coast port of the United States—you feel a long way from the Pacific Ocean. And, in fact, you are. Hail Columbia!

Greater Portland Area: St. Helens to North Portland Harbor

Chart 18524; 75 to 107 mi above Columbia River Bar

Afternoon chop kicking up

Berths with electricity, gasoline, water, ice, and some marine supplies are available at the marina at Saint Helens. Engine repairs can be made.

A dredged channel with a reported controlling depth of 6 feet in September 1986 leads to a marina in Scappoose Bay, SW of Saint Helens. This marina, owned by the Port of Saint Helens, has berths with gasoline, water, and ice available.

Most of the small-craft facilities [in Portland], including practically all of the moorage, is in North Portland Harbor and along the S bank of the Columbia River between Interstate 5 highway bridge and the W end of Government Island. Complete facilities are available. Berths with electricity, gasoline, diesel fuel, water, ice, marine supplies, launching ramps, pumpout stations, and wet and dry winter boat storage can be obtained at many marinas. Hull, engine, and electronic repairs can be made. Drydocks to 70 tons, 55 feet long, and 16 feet wide are available in North Portland Harbor. (CP, 33rd Ed.)

The Greater Portland area may appeal to cruising boaters that want moorage near a metropolitan area and/or full repair facilities. The area makes a good base from which to explore downtown Portland and the nearby Willamette River, or to mount an expedition up the Columbia River and the Snake River to Idaho. Necessary for any cruise to the upper reaches of the Columbia are sources of local knowledge, large-scale charts, and a complete study of the numerous locks and bridges.

Although there are numerous small and medium-sized marinas along the route to Portland, most have limited services; many cannot accommodate lengths over 40 feet or do not have fuel available. For more complete information and a full list of marinas, we suggest that you visit the Oregon State Marine Board website: www.boatoregon.com

⚓ **St. Helen's Marina** open 0800-1700; tel: 503.397.4162; restrooms, fuel, electricity & water; no showers for transients; boats up to 50 ft.

⚓ **Rocky Pointe Marina** (located on Multnomah Channel) open 0700-1900; tel & fax: 503.543.7003; full services include fuel; boats up to 65 ft.; phone ahead 24 hours

⚓ **Fred's Marina** (N. Portland) tel: 503.286.5537; fax: 503.286.9317; slips to 100 ft.; website: www.fredsmarina.com

⚓ **McCuddy's Marina** (N. Portland) open 0900-1700; tel: 503.289.7879; fax 503.283.1308; boats up to 60 ft.

Cape Disappointment to Willapa Bay

From Cape Disappointment, the coast extends N for 22 miles to Willapa Bay as a low sandy beach, with sandy ridges about 20 feet high parallel with the shore. Back of the beach, the country is heavily wooded. Numerous summer resorts and cottages are along the beach. Landmarks along this

section of the coast are few. The 10-fathom curve averages a distance of about 2.5 miles from the shore. There are no known offlying dangers S of the Willapa Bay entrance bar.

The weather along this coast is usually mild, windy and rainy in winter, cool and pleasant in summer, with some periods of fog. Close to shore, and particularly in Willapa Bay and Grays Harbor, wind and fog conditions are often local and different from conditions offshore. . . .

Summer is the true fog season along these shores. In general, advection fog reduces visibilities [sic] to below 0.5 mile on 3 to 10 days per month; up to 16 days per month at Tatoosh Island. Fog signals blow 15 to 30 percent of the time. Conditions are worst in Grays harbor and near the entrance to the Strait of Juan de Fuca. . . .

Fog remains a problem in autumn, although it is less frequent. (CP, 33rd Ed.)

Willapa Bay

Chart 18504; 24 mi N of Columbia River entr; 8 mi S of Grays Hbr
Entrance buoy RW"W": 46°44.02'N, 124°10.95'W

Willapa Bay . . . is used primarily by fishing and oyster boats. No deep-draft vessels have entered Willapa Bay since 1976. . . .

Willapa Bar extends about 3 miles outside of a line joining Willapa Bay Light and Leadbetter Point. The bar channel is continually shifting, and depths over it vary from season to season. Because of the frequent changes in the position of the bar and difficulty in dredging the bar to project depth, depths have consistently been less that the 26-foot project depth. The buoys marking the channel over the bar are non lateral and moved from time to time because of the shifting sands and changing channel. . . . The entrance buoys and the dredging range lights do not necessarily mark the best

water. The major channels in the bay are marked by aids to navigation. . . .

The channel over the bar into Willapa Bay is subject to frequent change. . . .

Approaching from any direction in any weather, great caution is essential. The currents are variable and uncertain. Velocities of 3 to 3.5 knots have been observed between Blunts Reef and the Swiftsure Bank, and velocities considerably in excess of these amounts have been reported. Under such conditions, vessels should not shoal the water to less than 20 fathoms until the lighted whistle buoy off the entrance has been made. . . .

In the entrance the current velocity is about 2.5 knots. Currents of 4 to 6 knots occur at times; the velocity is greatest on the ebb, particularly with S wind.

Navigators of deep-draft vessels should bear in mind the changeable nature of the bar. Strangers should not navigate the bay in thick weather.

South Bend is on the S bank of Willapa River, 8 miles above Toke Point. . . . Raymond, the principal town, is on the S bank of Willapa River at the junction of the South Fork, 3 miles above South Bend. . . .

Both South Bend and Raymond have small-craft moorages operated by the respective towns. (CP, 33rd Ed.)

Willapa Bay is seldom visited by cruising boats; almost all bay traffic consists of trailerable boats launched from inside the bay proper. Located at

Kites flying at 26-mile-long Long Beach

Michelle Gaylord

the north end of 26-mile-Long Beach, the bay is an interesting estuary of mud flats laced with rivers and shallow channels.

While Willapa Bay has an entrance buoy and a crabpot-free tow zone approach from the southwest, entry is not recommended for cruising boats due to its shallow, shifting bar. Breakers extend most of the way if not entirely across the entrance a good part of the time. Good local knowledge and favorable weather and sea conditions are required for any vessel that wishes to enter. Grays Harbor, 8 miles north, is the preferred shelter for cruising vessels.

Chart 18504 does not show the positions for buoys A, B, C, D, 8 and 9 because the bar changes so rapidly from season to season. Compare the 1993, 1996, and 1998 editions of this chart to see how much depths have changed over the bar and how the bar moves north and south along the opening of Willapa Bay.

For trailerable, sportfishing vessels, Tokeland is the easiest, most convenient place to find moorage.

Tokeland (Willapa Bay)
Chart 18504; 9 mi E of entr buoy "W"
Entrance (small-boat basin): 46°42.46'N, 123°57.97'W

Anchorage with good holding ground may be had at almost any point inside the bay. The anchorage generally used is off Toke Point in 30 to 40 feet, about 4.5 miles SE of Willapa Bay Light. . . .

Tokeland . . . is a summer resort. There is a dredged channel and small-craft basin on the N side of the point. A light is on the outer end of a jetty of the S side and a daybeacon is the N side of the entrance. In February 1993, the controlling depth was 11 feet in the entrance channel and basin except for shoaling to bare in the W 150 feet of the basin. Berths, gasoline, diesel fuel, water and ice are available either at the basin or nearby. A launching ramp is at the basin. (CP, 3rd Ed.)

Tokeland Marina, which caters to trailerable and sportfishing boats, offers limited transient moorage during fishing season. Facilities include a fuel dock, restrooms, and a launch ramp. (See the dangers of entering Willapa Bay mentioned in *Coast Pilot* under Willapa Bay.)

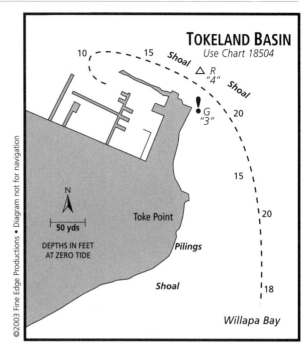

©2003 Fine Edge Productions • Diagram not for navigation

TOKELAND BASIN
Use Chart 18504

Crabbing, fishing, and clam digging are popular activities in Willapa Bay. The Tokeland Hotel, built in 1886, is the oldest resort hotel in Washington and operates the only full-service restaurant in the area. The surrounding communities of North Pacific County feature many examples of beautiful public art, from murals and steel sculptures to carved cedar memorials. Exhibits and displays at the Pacific Coast Historical Society Museum in South Bend and the Willapa Seaport Museum in Raymond relate the history of the region.

⚓ **Tokeland Marina** tel: 360-267.2888

South Bend (Willapa Bay)
Chart 18504; 7.5 mi SE of Tokeland
Position (Willapa River): 46°39.91'N, 123°48.40'W

South bend is on the S bank of Willapa River, 8 miles above Toke Point. The principal industries are lumbering, oystering, and fishing . . . (CP, 33rd Ed.)

Bay Center (Willapa Bay)
Chart 18504; just S of Goose Pt
Position (Palix River): 46°37.78'N, 123°57.02'W

The S part of Willapa Bay is used by light-draft vessels. Bay Center . . . is one of the many oyster places in this bay; there is also some fishing and crabbing. There are floats here for mooring fishing vessels; gasoline is available. (CP, 33rd Ed.)

Naselle River (Willapa Bay)
Chart 18504; E side of the bay

Naselle River . . . is navigable by boats of 5 feet or less draft, at half tide or higher water, as far as the bridge at the village of Naselle, 10 miles above the mouth. . . . passage should not be attempted without local knowledge. (CP, 33rd Ed.)

Grays Harbor
Chart 18502; 40 mi N of Cape Disappointment; 93 mi S of Cape Flattery
Entrance buoy RW"GH": 46°51.89'N, 124°14.37'W
Westport turnoff buoy RG"A": 46°55.03'N, 124°06.84'W
Breakwater buoy R"8" (0.15 mi NW): 46°54.62'N, 124°11.00'W

Aerial view: Entrance into Grays Harbor and Westport Marina

Grays Harbor . . . and its tributaries furnish an outlet to an extensive timber area. . . .

The bay at the entrance is about 2 miles wide, but shoals extending S from Point Brown contract the navigable channel to a width of 0.7 mile. From its entrance the bay extends E for 15 miles to the mouth of Chehalis River. The bay is filled by shoals and flats; these bare at low water and are cut by numerous channels. . . .

Grays Harbor Light . . . 123 feet above the water, is shown from a 107-foot white truncated octagonal pyramidal tower on the seaward side of Point Chehalis. . . .

The best anchorage is N of Westport and SE of Damon Point in 30 to 60 feet. The holding ground is good, and there is more swinging room here than elsewhere in the harbor. . . .

In the entrance, the average current velocity is about 1.9 knots on the flood and 2.8 knots on the ebb, but velocities may reach 5 knots. In the channels through the bay, the velocities seldom exceed 3 knots. It was reported that currents in the vicinity of the bar are very erratic, setting N close inshore and S offshore. . . .

Approaching from any direction in thick weather, great caution is essential. The currents are variable and uncertain. . . . Because of the possibility of a strong onshore set, especially in SW weather, vessels should not shoal the depths to less than 20 fathoms unless sure of the position. . . .

Information concerning conditions on the bar can be obtained from the Grays Harbor Pilots Association or from the Coast Guard on VHF-FM channel 16. The bar channel and harbor should not be attempted in thick weather. (CP, 33rd Ed.)

Grays Harbor has the only all-weather shelter for cruising boats between the Columbia River and Neah Bay. The Westport Marina in Westhaven Cove accommodates one of the biggest commercial fishing fleets in the Northwest and offers ample transient space to cruising boats.

Approach: Grays Harbor lighted entrance whistle buoy RW"GH" marks the beginning of the dredged entrance channel. Approaching from the south, use waypoint WA506 then head for waypoint WA507, keeping the series of red buoys on your starboard hand.

Approaching from the north, you can follow the directions above or, in fair weather, take a

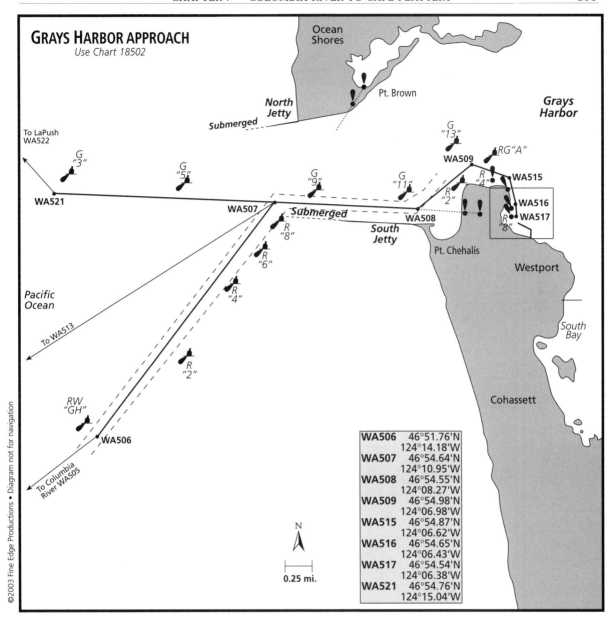

GRAYS HARBOR APPROACH
Use Chart 18502

Ocean Shores

Pt. Brown

North Jetty

Submerged

Grays Harbor

To LaPush WA522

G "3"

G "5"

WA521

G "9"

WA507

Submerged

G "11"

G "13"

WA509

RG "A"

WA515

R "4"

R "2"

WA516

WA517

R "8"

WA508

South Jetty

R "8"

R "6"

Pt. Chehalis

Pacific Ocean

Westport

R "4"

To WA513

R "2"

South Bay

RW "GH"

WA506

Cohassett

To Columbia River WA505

©2003 Fine Edge Productions • Diagram not for navigation

WA506	46°51.76'N 124°14.18'W
WA507	46°54.64'N 124°10.95'W
WA508	46°54.55'N 124°08.27'W
WA509	46°54.98'N 124°06.98'W
WA515	46°54.87'N 124°06.62'W
WA516	46°54.65'N 124°06.43'W
WA517	46°54.54'N 124°06.38'W
WA521	46°54.76'N 124°15.04'W

N

0.25 mi.

shortcut by heading for WA521 located just south of buoy G"3," then turn east to WA507. From here, follow the south jetty to WA508. When exiting to the north in fair weather, this shortcut can save several miles.

We have noticed that in stable weather, many commercial fishing boats use the center of the entrance between the two jetties as their preferred route, both on entering or leaving, because the dredged channel is frequently full of barges or slow vessels.

Westport Marina (Port of Grays Harbor)
Chart 18502; inner side N tip of Point Chehalis
Entrance (Marina): 46°54.52'N, 124°06.39'W
Marina transient float: 46°54.62'N, 124°06.69'W

[Westport Marina] *is protected by breakwaters marked by lights. The harbor is a large sport and commercial fishing center operated by the Port of Grays Harbor. . . .*

Grays Harbor Coast Guard Station is on the S side of Westhaven Cove. . . .

A boatyard at the S end of the harbor has a mobile lift that can handle craft to 60 tons for hull or engine repairs; the yard includes a ship chandlery. Electronic repair service is available at the harbor . . .

The Coast Guard has established . . . a rough bar advisory sign, 20 feet above the water, visible from the channel looking seaward, on the N side of Westhaven Cove. . . . The sign is equipped with a seasonal alternating quick flashing yellow light. The light will be activated when seas exceed 4 feet in height and are considered hazardous for small boats. Boatmen are cautioned, however, that if the light is not flashing, it is no guarantee that sea conditions are favorable. (CP, 33rd Ed.)

Westport Marina, which is the largest coastal marina in the Pacific Northwest, has moorage for up to 650 commercial and pleasure craft. About 20 transient berths are available to

Dealing with the Unexpected
by Mark Bunzel

Recently a professional delivery skipper told us the tale of an unexpected incident that almost ruined his day. The vessel he was contracted to deliver—a 20-ton trawler—had already been to Alaska when he picked it up for its return passage to Southern California. Before the skipper and his two crew departed Anacortes, he carefully checked the weather. The forecast appeared ideal for an offshore cruise—beautiful late-September weather.

A pre-dawn departure, with calm seas, bode well for their trip. They rounded Cape Flattery and started south along the coast, following a course that took them about 6 miles offshore.

Toward morning, as they were off Grays Harbor in stiff prevailing northwesterlies, the skipper lay down for a rest, letting the crew take watch. Suddenly, before dozing off, he noticed the motion becoming violent. He ran to the bridge and saw a large wave moving toward the boat. Turning quickly west, he powered directly into the wave. The trawler lifted, came out the other side and took a free fall—hard, but straight. The impact hurled the crew to the floor, and the skipper sprained his shoulder.

Seeing that they were too close to shore, he continued west and, as they approached deeper water, the high water alarm sounded. A quick survey showed a flooding engine room—the water had exceeded the ability of the automatic bilge pump. The skipper directed one crew-member to man the manual bilge pump while he called the Coast Guard to report their position and the fact they were taking on water.

He ran below and immediately began checking the through-hulls. He found the source under a stateroom bunk where a stream of water was gushing up through the hole for the speed log paddle wheel that had popped out of its through-hull fitting. He managed to jam the tube back in place, this time inserting the safety pin and keeper back in place, and stopping the leak.

He reported to the Coast Guard that they appeared to have things under control. Since he and the crew were tired and a bit shaken, he decided they should head in to Grays Harbor for the night and asked for a bar report. Twelve-foot waves and "straight up" was the answer.

"We're not a commercial vessel," the skipper told the Coast Guard.

"Then stand by, Sir. We'll come out to escort you into the harbor once the flood tide knocks down the swells."

They stood off waiting for the right time, then followed the Coast Guard into Grays Harbor where they spent a quiet night at dock.

This trawler had made its voyage to Alaska and back without problems; the incident could have occurred at any time. But the problem proved to be that the speed log was held in place by only its O-ring seal. Knowing the skipper's credentials we surmise that a previous crew had removed the sensor to clean it and forgotten to secure it properly with the O-ring.) The jolt of the wave popped it out. This experienced delivery skipper admitted he had not thoroughly checked all the through-hulls before the southbound trip.

While this incident could have been life-threatening, it proved otherwise. However, it illustrates how serious the unexpected can be.

What saved the day? A sturdy vessel with a high-water alarm; an alert and responsible skipper who sensed they were in shallow water; a quick call to the Coast Guard to report the vessel's position and problem; a crew that worked efficiently at the helm and on the manual bilge pump while the skipper found the leak and stopped it.

The skipper commented, "While that was a tough day, many times the Pacific can be like a mill pond." A good boat, a crew that didn't panic, and a little luck and skill dealing with the unexpected allowed the trawler to continue on the following day for an uneventful trip down the Pacific Coast.

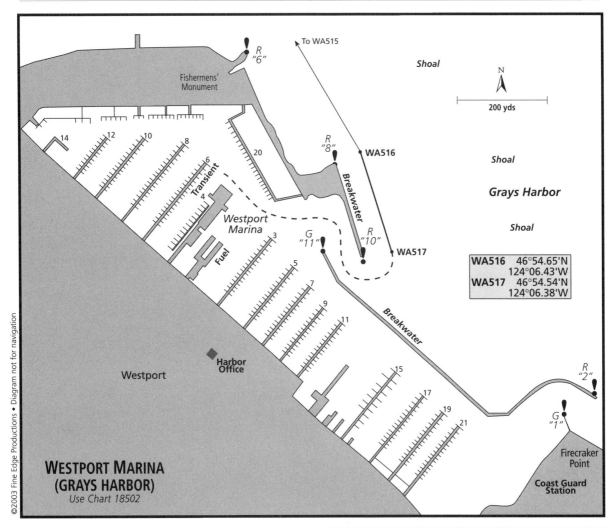

To WA515

Shoal

N

200 yds

Shoal

Grays Harbor

Shoal

WA516	46°54.65'N
	124°06.43'W
WA517	46°54.54'N
	124°06.38'W

Fishermens' Monument

R "6"

R "8"   WA516

Breakwater

14   12   10   8   20

Transient

6

4

Westport Marina

Fuel   3

G "11"   R "10"   WA517

5

7   Breakwater

9

11

Harbor Office

Westport

15

R "2"

17

19   G "1"

21

Firecraker Point

Coast Guard Station

WESTPORT MARINA (GRAYS HARBOR)
Use Chart 18502

©2003 Fine Edge Productions • Diagram not for navigation

accommodate cruising vessels. While the harbor caters mostly to charter and commercial fishing boat, they welcome cruising vessels and offer facilities that include wide, well-maintained floats, pump-out station, fuel dock, launching ramp, marine supplies and full repairs. The harbor office is located at 326 East Lamb Street, one block off Westhaven Avenue; showers are available at the harbor office. There are two city-owned toilets above the float area; a laundromat is just a block from Float 6, the usual transient dock. Chevron & Texaco fuel docks lie south of the transient docks (Chevron on south side of dock; Texaco on north side). The pump-out station is at Float 20 as you enter the harbor. The harbor office monitors Channel 71.

Grays Harbor transient dock

A three-story observation tower is located at the northwest end of the harbor; near the inside end of the jetty, there is a viewing platform. The harbor area has gift shops, a few restaurants, and a convenience store inside one of the gift shops; there is no trash deposit immediately above the dock. The center of Westport is about 2 miles south of the marina—a good hike if you're not planning to haul groceries; but if you are, bus transportation is available.

The Coast Guard Museum, a half-block from the transient docks and housed in a 1930s lifeboat station, is worth a visit to view the display of Minke and gray whale skeletons. The 6-ton, 17-foot high Fresnel lens that was formerly housed in the Destruction Island lighthouse can also be viewed here.

The historic Westport Lighthouse on the south point of the entrance to Grays Harbor, dedicated in 1898, still stands as a beacon for mariners. The area is a small-but-busy center for fishing, shellfishing, seafood processing, and tourism.

⚓ **Westport Marina** tel: 360.268.9665; monitors Channel 71; website: www.portofgraysharbor.com

Ocean Shores (Grays Harbor)
Chart 18502; N side Grays Hbr
Entrance (outer): 46°56.94'N, 124°06.36'W
Entrance to canals: 46°56.95'N, 124°07.62'W

Ocean Shores is a real estate development in North Bay with a series of water canals north of Damon Point. It is reachable by water taxi from Westport Marina, or by sportfishing boats that follow the daymarks into the canals.

Grays Harbor
by Michelle Gaylord

The problem with timing the tides correctly for one harbor is that invariably you will enter the destination harbor on a low ebb tide. This is what happened when we arrived at the entrance to Grays Harbor on August 25. The swells were rolling into the harbor at 10 feet, with an occasional 12-footer, complete with white water at their crests. I thought for sure we were going to take a big one over the stern and be swamped. And at that point, I couldn't take refuge in my little cubbyhole because I had to help the skipper locate channel markers.

We saw a charter fishing boat returning to the harbor and decided to follow him. We were riding the swells like a surfboard, and it was all Jerry could do to keep the boat relatively on course. We were only about 150 yards behind the charter boat, but every 60 seconds or so we would lose sight of him when he was swallowed by one of the rollers.

When we finally tied up in the marina it was sunny, calm, and beautiful. Grays Harbor has quite a large bay, and they have ferryboats that run you from one side to the other. It's a cute little place with shops and restaurants; their major source of income here is from charter fishing boats. The weather was so gorgeous that we ran around in our new dinghy and rode our bikes everywhere.

We visited the Maritime Museum, which was worth the entry fee, but lacking in comparison to the Astoria Maritime Museum. We tried out our new "bigger" crab trap in Grays Harbor and started catching bigger crabs! In fact, these crabs were so big they couldn't have possibly entered our little trap. No wonder everyone else was getting the big guys but us!

They were having a county fair while we were there, and when I found out they were having a pygmy goat show I really thought we should go. But somehow I couldn't convince Jerry. One afternoon we took the ferry across the bay but didn't find anything of much interest on the other side. One thing we did a lot of in Gray's Harbor was eat crab—I fixed it every way I could imagine!

We left Grays Harbor at ebb tide because we needed to time our arrival at La Push for high flood tide. We had talked previously to several commercial fishing boats skippers who said the bar had been okay at low tide and not to worry. They lied; it was *rough* and swells were running 12 to 15 feet. I wanted to turn around, but Jerry informed me we couldn't turn around safely without the possibility of broaching. Then, over the radio, we heard some of the fishermen talking: "I think this is the roughest we've seen it." . . . "I second that." . . . "I don't know why they didn't close the bar." We fought those seas for 30 minutes until we were out of the harbor, and they were still a confused 6 to 8 feet. I think confused seas are the norm for this area; I don't recall the swell having any pattern at all since we left Florence, Oregon.

Chehalis River (Grays Harbor)
Chart 18502; E end of Grays Harbor

Chehalis River . . . is marked by lights to Cosmopolis. It is navigable by small boats to Elma, 24 miles above the mouth. The upper portion of the river, for a distance of about 45 miles above Elma, is used for floating logs. (CP, 33rd Ed.)

Hoquiam and Aberdeen are located on the north shore of the Chehalis River which is navigable by shallow-draft vessels via a dredged channel.

Hoquiam River (Grays Harbor)
Chart 18502; about 2 mi E of the mouth of Chehalis River
Entrance: 46°58.12'N, 123°52.71'W

Hoquiam River . . . is practically a tidal slough 11 miles long. In November 1980, the midchannel controlling depth was 6 feet from the mouth of Hoquiam River to the junction of the Hoquiam River and the East Fork of the Hoquiam River, a distance of about 2.5 miles. Traffic on the river consists of log tows, tugs, and other small craft. . . . (CP, 33rd Ed.)

Hoquiam and Little Hoquiam River have boat building facilities where a good percentage of the Alaska commercial fishing vessels have been built. Call ahead for current information.

Point Grenville
Chart 18500; 10 m N of Copalis Head, 4 mi S of Cape Elizabeth
Anchor: 47°17.83'N, 124°15.80'W

Point Grenville . . . is a broken rocky promontory with nearly vertical whitish cliffs over 100 feet high. Numerous rocks extend for some distance off the point. Grenville Arch, dark in color, 83 feet high, is the outer and more prominent of two rocks lying W of the point; it is over 0.5 mile SW of the inner extremity of the point. . . .

An indifferent anchorage in NW weather may be had under Point Grenville by vessels of moderate draft, but the depths compel anchoring at such a distance from the beach that little shelter is afforded. The anchorage is in 4 fathoms, sandy bottom, with the inner extremity of the point bearing 338°, and Grenville Arch bearing 239°. This anchorage is not recommended for ordinary use. (CP, 33rd Ed.)

Michelle Gaylord

Lady Washington *tied up at transient dock Grays Harbor*

Although Point Grenville appears to offer temporary anchorage as a rest stop only in fair weather, we have no local knowledge to share. Rocks and reefs extend over a mile from shore for the next 8 miles north to Split Rock. On a northbound passage, we would use Destruction Island as a temporary rest stop.

Destruction Island
Chart 18500; 3 miles offshore, 20 mi NW of Cape Elizabeth
Position (Destruction I. Light): 47°40.48'N, 124°29.22'W
Anchor: (approx) 47°40.21'N, 124°29.07'W

Destruction Island, 90 feet high . . . is flat-topped and covered with brush, with a few clumps of trees. The island is 0.5 mile long and 300 yards wide at its S part. From the N end rocks and

Approaching Destruction Island from the south

ledges extend about a mile from the cliffs; these are bordered by a line of kelp on the inshore side.

Destruction Island Light . . . 147 feet above the water, is shown from a 94-foot white conical tower with black gallery on the SW part of the island; a fog signal is at the light.

An indifferent anchorage, affording shelter from NW winds, may be had off the SE face of the island in 10 fathoms, sandy bottom, with the light bearing between 293° and 315°. Vessels must leave if the wind hauls W or S. During the fishing season many small fishing boats anchor for the night under Destruction Island; it is the only shelter from offshore winds between Grays Harbor and Cape Flattery. (CP, 33rd Ed.)

During stable northwesterly winds, temporary anchorage that could provide moderate overnight protection can be found in the lee of Destruction Island, 47 miles northwest of Grays Harbor. The island is only about a half-mile long, but adjacent rocks piles and kelp patches extend out about 2 miles overall, making a sizeable lee 3 miles offshore.

Baidarka found a good lee under Destruction Island during prevailing northwest winds but the area is not well charted and the bottom is not as simple as the *Coast Pilot* suggests. If you decide to anchor here, use *caution*. We found irregular depths, suggesting a very rocky bottom close to the island itself. There appears to be a large ledge that extends about 150 yards south of the steep southeastern shore where depths

are about 5 fathoms; a fair amount of bull kelp exists in this area so you may want to stay farther out in about 9 to 11 fathoms where there's ample room for a number of vessels. In fair weather, we would stay at Destruction Island if we wanted a rest-break or a good meal.

When approaching the island avoid all kelp beds which may hide submerged rocks. The sandy bottom mentioned in the *Coast Pilot* occurs, apparently, in small patches between gravel, rocks and kelp close to the island. Farther out, the bottom is nearly flat, but the sand may be hard and holding fair only with a well-set anchor.

We found many above-water and submerged rocks up to a half-mile southwest of the south

Fresnel lens from old Destruction Island lighthouse, Maritime Museum, Grays Harbor

tip of the island; seas heap up in this area and break without warning. The north side of the island is worse—breaking rocks extend over a mile off-shore. On a northbound route, we would exit around the southwest side of the island, giving the tip a wide berth.

Although Destruction Island can provide moderate shelter from pre-vailing northwest swells and chop, a boat can roll here if the wind swings around to the west. While the north side of the island might provide some emergency shelter from southeast storms, we wouldn't recommend using it; the island has not been surveyed. In marginal conditions, when approaching the island from any direction, use *extreme* caution.

The windswept island has only about three stunted trees, about 15 feet high, and a few bushes on its north end. The faded red roofs of the former lighthouse crew quarters on the south side of Destruction Island are still visible, as well as an old tram and steps.

To approach Destruction Island from the south, head for the center of the island, favor-ing the area to the right of the light tower. When the steps are visible, begin looking for a flat spot in 10 fathoms or less to anchor.

Anchor out from the old tram and stairs in 5 to 10 fathoms over a mixed bottom of sand and rocks; poor-to-fair holding. Check your anchor set and avoid kelp.

Baidarka *anchored at Destruction Island*

Hoh River
Chart 18480; 2 mi SE of Hoh Head
Entrance Position: 47°44.81'N, 124°26.93'W

At the mouth of Hoh River . . . is a broad sand beach; the absence of cliffs for 0.5 mile is notice-able for a considerable distance offshore. In smooth weather the river can be entered by canoes, but the channel shifts. An Indian village is on the S bank at its mouth. (CP, 33rd Ed.)

The Hoh River takes its source in the peaks of the Olympic Range that tower above to the east. The entrance to the river has several visible and submerged rocks and shoals. It is poorly chart-ed and should be approached only in calm weather and with local knowledge.

James Island Light
Chart 18480; immediately W of La Push jetty
Position (James Island Light): 47°54.29'N,
124°38.85'W

James Island Light, . . . 150 feet above the water, is shown from a white house on the S part of the Island. A fog signal is at the light. (CP, 33rd Ed.)

James Island, which obscures the entrance to the Quillayute River and the La Push Marina, is one of the many small, steep-sided islands and islets that have a thick growth of trees or "haystacks" on their summit. The entrance to Quillayute River, which lies east of James Island, is approached from the south. It is not unusual to see white foam extending all the

Destruction Island as seen from the northwest

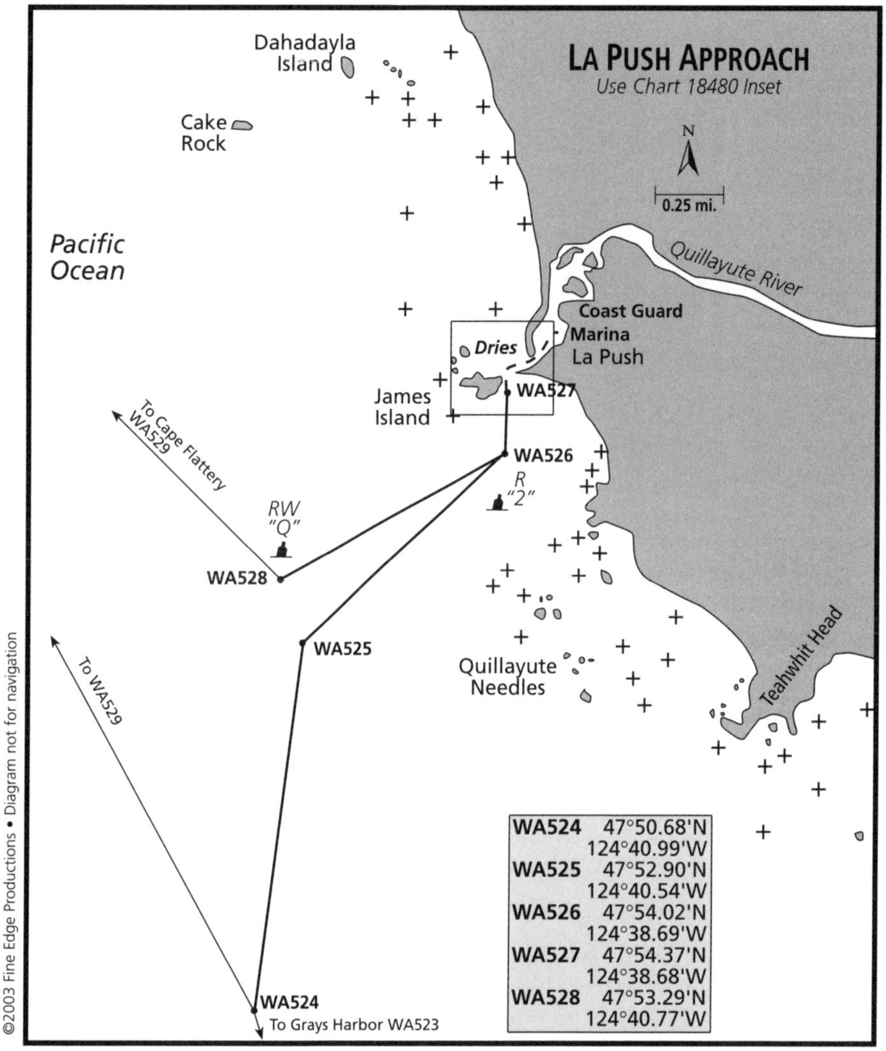
LA PUSH APPROACH
Use Chart 18480 Inset
N
0.25 mi.
Dahadayla Island
Cake Rock
Pacific Ocean
Quillayute River
Coast Guard
Marina
La Push
Dries
James Island
WA527
WA526
R "2"
RW "Q"
To Cape Flattery WA529
WA528
WA525
Quillayute Needles
Teahwhit Head
To WA529
WA524
To Grays Harbor WA523
WA524 47°50.68'N 124°40.99'W
WA525 47°52.90'N 124°40.54'W
WA526 47°54.02'N 124°38.69'W
WA527 47°54.37'N 124°38.68'W
WA528 47°53.29'N 124°40.77'W
©2003 Fine Edge Productions • Diagram not for navigation

way from the island across to the La Push beach.

La Push (Quillayute River)

Chart 18480; about 0.4 mile above entr to Quillayute Riv
Entrance buoy RW"Q": 47°53.14'N, 124°40.54'W
River Entrance (inside breakwater): (WA527) 47°54.36'N, 124°38.69'W
Marina Entrance: 47°54.63'N, 124°38.29'W
USCG dock: 47°54.91'N, 124°38.18'W

La Push, an Indian village, . . . is an important sport fishing center.

The river channel is protected by a jetty on the SE side and a dike on the NW side; a lighted whistle buoy is about 1.8 miles SW from the outer end of the jetty. About 250 feet of the outer end of the jetty is awash at high water. . . .

The river channel leads from the sea to a small-craft basin at La Push. The entrance channel is marked by a directional light. The channel to the basin is marked by a light and seasonal buoys. In August 2000, the controlling depth was 4.8 feet to the basin; thence in 1996, depths of 1 to 3 feet were in the basin with much lesser depths along the sides. The N and S sides of the entrance to the basin are marked by lights. A power cable with a clearance of about 100 feet crosses the river near its mouth.

The channel, which passes close to the SE shore of James Island, is sometimes dangerous, especially in heavy S weather.

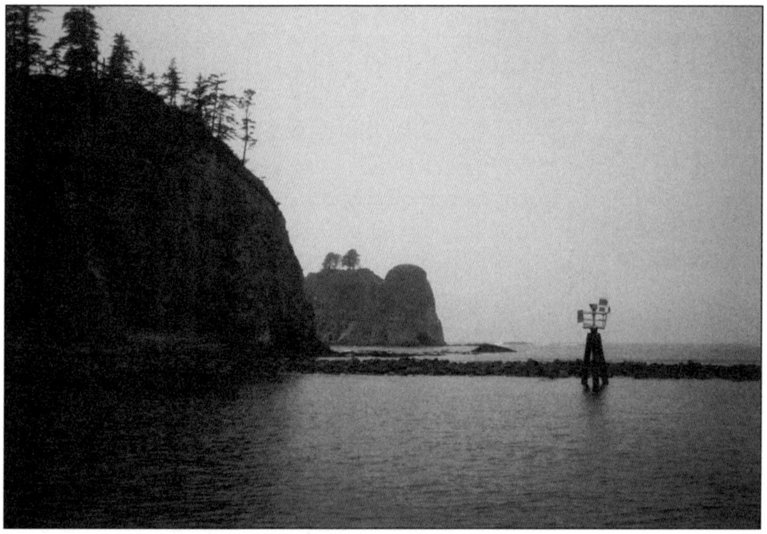

The dike and sector light on the Quillayute

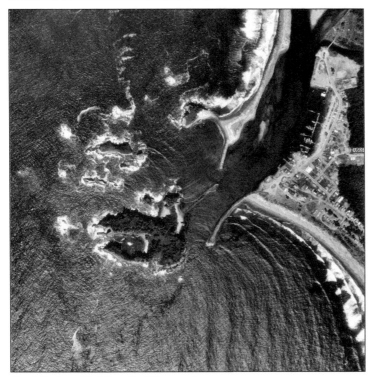

Aerial view: Quillayute River entrance

Weather conditions which make the entrance hazardous normally occur only in the winters, usually in December and January. When there are breakers of any size making across the entrance, it should not be attempted except at better than half tide and with a well-powered boat. Strangers may request assistance from the Quillayute River Coast Guard Station at La Push by radio or signals; a Coast Guard boat will lead the vessel in if practicable. The tank at the Coast Guard station is prominent.

In late summer and fall mariners are advised to use caution when transiting the channel because fish nets may be present. . . .

The Coast Guard has established Quillayute River Entrance Small Boat Warning Sign, a rough bar advisory sign, 34 feet above the water, visible from the channel looking seaward, on the NW corner of the old Coast Guard boathouse to promote safety for small-boat operators. The sign is diamond shaped, painted white with an international orange border, and with the words "Rough Bar" in black letters. The sign is equipped with two alternating flashing amber lights. The lights will be activated when seas exceed 4 feet in height and are considered hazardous for small boats. Boatmen are cautioned, however, that if the lights are not flashing, it is no guarantee that sea conditions are favorable. (CP, 33rd Ed.)

La Push, in the authors' judgment, has the most dramatic and scenic entrance along the entire west coast of the U.S.

Dugout canoes at Tribal Community Center, La Push

The south side of the bay is guarded by the striking Quillayute Needles—rocks of solid granite that look, from the center of the bay, like a pod of

orcas; they are wild-looking, especially in fog.

James Island is a "fortress" that hides the Quillayute River. Across from the island, a beautiful, dark sand beach curves around the bay; bleached and polished drift logs on shore give evidence of violent winter storms. Farther south lie rocky outcroppings. Large Native canoes beached on the sand were once used by the tribe for whaling; for the hunt, they were filled with harpoon lines and sealskin floats and manned by a harpooner, a helmsman, and six paddlers.

The La Push beach and the campground to the south are popular with kayakers and tourists who sometimes drive from the Seattle area for just a day or two.

Approach: The entrance to Quillayute River is hidden from view by James Island. From outside La Push Bay call Quillayute Coast Guard Station on VHF channel 16 for a bar report. Their rescue boat will escort you into the harbor if you request help.

On *Baidarka*'s approach, the Coast Guard asked us to stand by outside while they called the local chief for permission for us to stay in the tribal marina. As it happened, the harbormaster was away that day and, while we rolled about in the outside swells, it took about 30 minutes for them to find someone who could

Totem Pole in front of Tribal Community Center, La Push

Michelle Gaylord

La Push
by Michelle Gaylord

We arrived at La Push on the afternoon of August 30, and it was rather difficult to find the entrance to the harbor due to all the exposed rocks, seastacks, and little islands that surround it. We managed to find our way in with a little help from the Coast Guard and were met on the dock by a large group of Natives. What wonderful, warm, friendly people they were. We spent the next couple of days just visiting with them and wandering around the settlement. There were no stores or restaurants, just tribal community buildings and schools.

say, "Sure; go in and pick up an empty slip."

We were told later that they have about 8 to 10 boat visitors a month during the busy summer season. (We were the only cruising boat in the marina for two days, and the USCG boat making their bar check the following day was the only other boat that entered or exited.)

Study the inset on Chart 18480 before entering the narrow, shallow river. From entrance buoy RW"Q" (near WA525 and WA528), head for the center of the bay, passing north of buoy R"2" to waypoint WA526. From this point, line up with the sector light that leads you across the narrow bar just west of the small jetty on your starboard hand. Avoid two small rocks about 50 yards off the south side of James Island and a large shoal alongside the jetty. North of this shoal, favor the east shore.

The bar appears to be at its shallowest abeam the end of the jetty. *Baidarka* found about 1.8 fathoms under the keel here near low water. In the river, depths are slightly deeper until inside the marina. The marina facilities are 0.4 mile up the shallow Quillayute River.

While the marina advertises electricity and laundry with showers at the store, we didn't find anything open during the two days we were there the last week in June, nor did we see many Natives, contrary to the Gaylords' experience. There was no trash pick up when we were there, so please pack it out with you.

The village is composed of a few houses and native community buildings. Don't miss a stroll on the beach just south of the village to inspect the whaling canoes and to view the impressive Quillayute Needles. We found fledgling puffins paddling along James Island and had our first sightings of adult puffins at nearby Cake Rock—the 116-foot rock gets its name from its similarity to a cake with green frosting. We advise staying outside all offshore rocks north of La Push; the area is poorly charted.

Heading for the tiny entrance between James Island and the breakwater

James Island to Cape Alava

Between James Island and Umatilla Reef, on an inshore route northbound of La Push, avoid the many interesting, but hazardous, islets and rocks.

Cape Alava
Chart 18480; 16.4 mi NNW of James Island
WA530 (0.2 mi W of buoy R"2UR"): 48°11.14'N, 124°49.72'W

> *From James Island . . . to Cape Alava, the rugged coast continues, with rocks and foul ground extending as much as 2 miles offshore. . . .* (CP, 33rd Ed.)

Cape Alava extends well west of the coast just south of the Ozette River; a complex rock pile

La Push Marina fuel dock; Baidarka *at transient dock*

Michelle Gaylord

Quillayute Needles from La Push beach

composed of Ozette, Tskawahyah and Bodelteh Islands, Flattery Rocks and Umatilla Reef lies 2.4 miles farther offshore.

Cape Alava has the potential to provide moderate protection from southeast gales on its north side. Just looking at the chart, it appears that temporary protection could be found about 0.8 mile northwest of the outlet of the Ozette River, 1.9 miles south of Father and Son Rock in about 7 to 10 fathoms over a hard sand and shell bottom with scattered rocks. We have not explored this potential anchor site, an area that was once a traditional village and hunting site of Native peoples.

Coast Guard checking La Push Bar

Umatilla Reef
Charts 18485, 18460; 2.3 mi NW of Cape Alava
Buoy R"2UR": 48°11.16'N, 124°49.32'W

Umatilla Reef . . . [is] the greatest danger to navigation off this section of the coast. . . . It extends for 200 yards in a W direction and is about 75 yards wide. The reef consists of small, low, black rocks and some breakers. There is a reported breaker 1.1 miles NNE of this reef, and a rock covered 3 feet, 0.3 mile E of the reef, which endangers the passage inside Umatilla Reef, sometimes used by small boats. *Umatilla Reef is difficult to make out, especially in thick weather. . . .* (CP, 33rd Ed.)

Umatilla Reef is the westernmost point of the coast between San Diego and Cape Flattery. Cape Alava is slightly west of Cape Mendocino, California and in general does not present the difficulty incurred in rounding the more southerly cape. While at Cape Mendocino there is usually an abrupt shift in weather and wind, at Umatilla Reef in summer weather, Vancouver Island already provides a lee, and there is not such a noticeable shift in weather

Umatilla Reef has a 4-foot-high rock that is somewhat ill-defined and makes a poor radar target. The western extremity of the reef is marked by whistle buoy R"2UR." To clear the reef and its buoy, set a course well offshore. We recommend using waypoint WA530 unless calm weather prevails. There may be a fair-weather, small-boat passage a quarter-mile-wide northwest of the westernmost of the Bodelteh Islands; however, a submerged 3-foot-high rock, 1.85 miles east of the whistle buoy, represents a hazard.

Makah Bay (Waatch River)

Chart 18485; 4 mi SE of Tatoosh Island
Entrance: 48°19.48′N, 124°42.03′W
Anchor (N): (Waatch River) 48°20.08′N, 124°40.62′W
Anchor (S): (Flat N of Anderson Pt) 48°18.54′N, 124°40.51′W

Makah Bay is a shallow bight included between Portage Head and Waatch Point. It affords indifferent shelter in N and E weather and a smooth sea, but is little used. The shores are low and sandy.

Waatch River enters in the N part of the bight immediately E of Waatch Point. It is a tidal slough, and the valley through which it runs extends about 2 miles to Neah Bay on the Strait of Juan de Fuca. (CP, 33rd Ed.)

Makah Bay has surprisingly smooth water in fair weather, and we find it a good place to take a temporary break or to time the currents and determine conditions at Cape Flattery. In good weather, it can also be a good place to explore the rocks, reefs and tidepools along the coast by kayak or high-speed dinghy, paying careful attention to tide levels and local currents.

Anchorage can be found in a small bight 0.4 mile southeast of Waatch Point, south of the outlet of the Wastch River. Anchor in about 5 fathoms over a sandy bottom.

There is also a small 7-fathom flat, 0.8 mile north-northeast of Anderson Point and 1.7 miles south-southeast of Waatch Point, where temporary shelter from southeast winds can be found. This flat is protected by rocks and kelp-

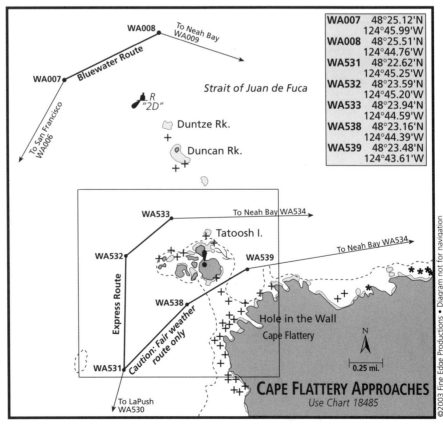

WA007	48°25.12′N 124°45.99′W
WA008	48°25.51′N 124°44.76′W
WA531	48°22.62′N 124°45.25′W
WA532	48°23.59′N 124°45.20′W
WA533	48°23.94′N 124°44.59′W
WA538	48°23.16′N 124°44.39′W
WA539	48°23.48′N 124°43.61′W

©2003 Fine Edge Productions • Diagram not for navigation

CAPE FLATTERY APPROACHES
Use Chart 18485

covered reefs that lie to the west and near shore; avoid both areas when entering. The approach is about 0.3-mile-wide between charted hazards. Do not approach without first plotting your route on Chart 18485. Enter this south portion of Makah Bay carefully, north and east of 6-foot-high Strawberry Rock. There appears to be swinging room for several boats 1.0 mile east-southeast of Strawberry Rock. Anchor about 0.2 mile northeast of the 45-foot-high rock, 0.5 mile northeast of Anderson Point. The bottom is reported to be hard sand with scattered rocks and kelp.

Cape Flattery

Charts 18485, 18460; 6 mi W of Neah Bay; 91 mi N of Grays Harbor
Position (Cape Flattery Light; on W end of main Tatoosh I): 48°23.48′N, 124°44.21′W

Cape Flattery, a bold, rocky head with cliffs 120 feet high, rises to nearly 1,500 feet about 2 miles back from the beach. From S it looks like an island because of the low land in the valley of Waatch River. Numerous rocks and reefs border the cliffs E and S of the cape. Tide rips are particularly heavy off Cape Flattery.

A large radar dome, highest and most prominent structure in the area, is on Bahokus Peak, the part of Cape Flattery about 2 miles back from the beach that rises to nearly 1,500 feet. This inflated plastic dome, about 50 feet in diameter, is on top of a tower, and was reported to be a very good landmark over low dense fog for vessels coming from the S. (CP, 33rd Ed.)

Cape Flattery, at the northwest corner of Washington State, is the southern entrance to the Strait of Juan de Fuca. The cape is 13 miles south of Carmanah Point on Vancouver Island, 32 miles south of the village of Bamfield, 54 miles west of Victoria, B.C., and 105 miles northwest of Seattle.

Tatoosh Island

Charts 18485, 18460; 0.4 mi NW of Cape Flattery
Bluewater Route: (WA007) 48°25.12′N, 124°45.99′W; (WA008) 48°25.51′N, 124°44.76′W
Express Route (close W of Tatoosh I & inside Duncan Rock): (WA 531) 48°22.62′N, 124°45.25′W; (WA532) 48°23.59′N, 124°45.20′W; (WA533) 48°23.94′N, 124°44.59′W
Fair-weather Route (inside Tatoosh I, W of Jones Rock): (WA 531) 48°22.62′N, 124°45.25′W; (WA538) 48°23.16′N, 124°44.39′W; (WA539) 48°23.48′N, 124°43.61′W
Whistle buoy R"2D": (1.6 mi NW of Cape Flattery light) 48°25.02′N, 124°45.02′W

Tatoosh Island . . . is about 0.2 mile in diameter, 108 feet high, flat-topped, and bare. It is the largest of the group of rocks and reefs making out about 0.9 mile NW from the cape. The

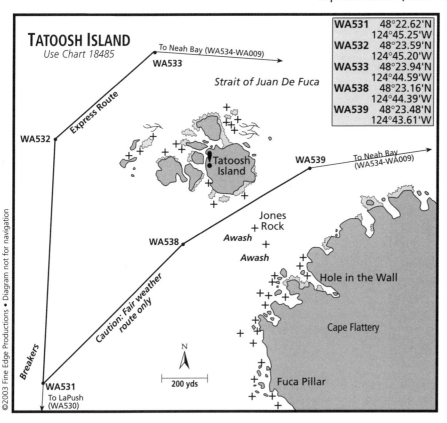

WA531	48°22.62′N 124°45.25′W
WA532	48°23.59′N 124°45.20′W
WA533	48°23.94′N 124°44.59′W
WA538	48°23.16′N 124°44.39′W
WA539	48°23.48′N 124°43.61′W

TATOOSH ISLAND
Use Chart 18485

To Neah Bay (WA534-WA009)
WA533
Strait of Juan De Fuca
WA532
Express Route
WA539
To Neah Bay (WA534-WA009)
Tatoosh Island
Jones Rock
Awash
Awash
WA538
Caution: Fair weather route only
Hole in the Wall
Cape Flattery
N
Breakers
200 yds
WA531
To LaPush (WA530)
Fuca Pillar

©2003 Fine Edge Productions • Diagram not for navigation

passage between Tatoosh Island and the cape is dangerous and constricted by two rocks awash near its center. Although sometimes used by local small craft, it cannot be recommended. The currents are strong and treacherous. Breakers may be in the area, especially during maximum currents.

Cape Flattery Light . . . 165 feet above the water, is shown from a 65-foot white conical tower on a sandstone dwelling on the W end of Tatoosh Island. A fog signal is at the light. (CP, 33rd Ed.)

Aerial view of the fair-weather route inside Tatoosh Island

Baidarka's Suggested Routes for Rounding Tatoosh Island
by DCD

Tatoosh Island is composed of a round main island, with Cape Flattery light on its west end, and many fractured islets off its west side that extend 0.4 mile offshore. There can be strong turbulent currents in the vicinity in foul weather or during spring tides.

There are three possible routes around Tatoosh, depending on the weather and sea conditions:

1. *The Bluewater Route* is the safest all-weather route to use when rounding Cape Flattery and entering the Strait of Juan de Fuca. Pass west and north of whistle buoy R"2D" using waypoints WA007 and WA008 to clear Tatoosh Island and pass north of the rocks and shoals around Duntze and Duncan rocks. On both their north and southbound trips in *Passing Thru,* the Gaylords rounded Cape Flattery using the Blue Water Route. Jerry Gaylord felt they did not have the benefit of local knowledge, so they chose the conservative route and had no problems either time.

2. *The Express Route.* In fair conditions and good visibility, you can pass close west of Tatoosh Island but south of Duncan Rock using waypoints WA532 and WA533. This route saves about 3 miles over the Bluewater Route.

3. *The Fair-Weather Route.* During stable weather, *Baidarka* and small-craft delivery skippers we know usually use the shortcut inside Tatoosh Island because it is much shorter; it is also generally smoother and avoids uncomfortable beam seas. This route passes close east of Tatoosh Island through a narrow, shallow fairway west of Jones Rock which bares at mid-tide. (Do not confuse Jones Rock with another rock, 400 feet southeast, that is awash at high water.) For this fair-weather shortcut (shown on Cape Flattery Approach diagram), plot waypoints WA538 and WA539 on Chart 18485. The route, which leads through depths of about 7 fathoms minimum, lies midway 150 yards from both Tatoosh Island and Jones Rock. Do not attempt to go this way unless you have plotted your position first on Chart 18485 and are confident of your abilities.

This route inside Tatoosh Island can be particularly pleasant in nearly calm seas, with current of only a couple of knots. On the other hand, it can be hazardous during spring tides and when the wind opposes the currents. It is no place to be caught in foul weather or limited visibility and with inadequate power, or if you are unsure of your position.

At night and times of limited visibility, or during any period of uncertain weather, use the safer Bluewater Route for its greater clearance from the hazards of Cape Flattery. Neah Bay, 6 miles east of Cape Flattery, offers good all-weather shelter and marine facilities.

Using the inside route, you can view numerous sea caves along the steep bluffs of Cape Flattery. Tatoosh Island is also full of deep sea caves. Sea lions haul out on the islets, nesting gulls circle constantly overhead, screaming at the top of their lungs, and murres feed in the nearly flat-water passage.

Along the inside route, south of Tatoosh Island, *Baidarka* encountered a substantial north-flowing back eddy of 2 knots that carried us through the passage at a time when the Strait of Juan de Fuca was ebbing west.

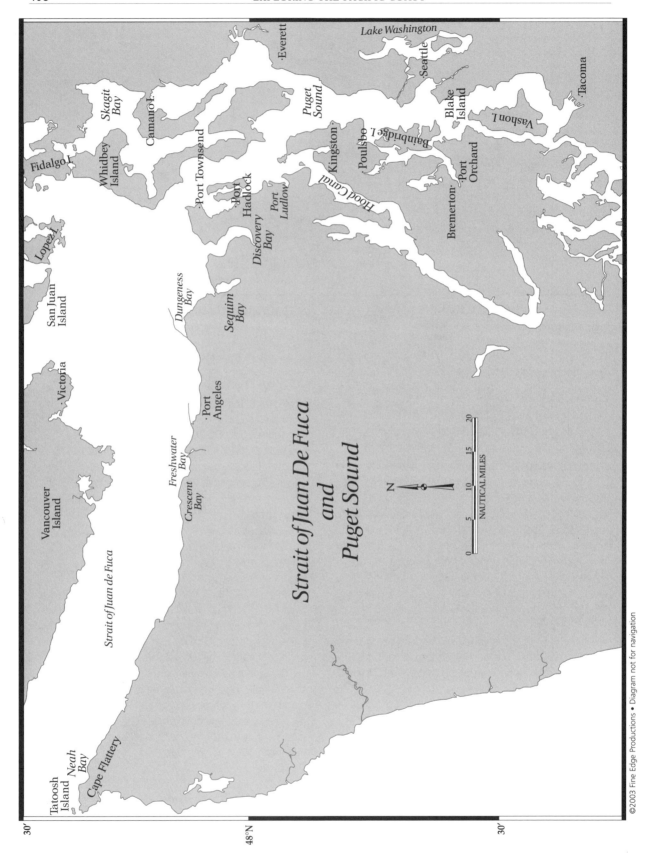

Strait of Juan De Fuca and Puget Sound

NAUTICAL MILES

8

Strait of Juan de Fuca & Greater Puget Sound

Introduction

Cape Flattery marks the transition from the open-ocean challenge of the Pacific to a smooth-water route. As you enter the Strait of Juan de Fuca, a waterway of over a thousand square miles opens up innumerable opportunities for cruising. Seattle and Victoria now lie within easy reach and, to the north lies the fabled Inside Passage—a 1000-mile-long archipelago of tree-covered islands and well-protected channels—that stretches all the way to Southeast Alaska.

The open swells of the Pacific decrease rapidly as you head east in the Strait of Juan de Fuca. With Vancouver Island providing a lee in northerly winds and the Olympic Peninsula in southerlies.

However, this geographic phenomenon doesn't always guarantee a smooth ride because, on these inside waters, the combination of swell and chop depends on the interaction of wind and current at any given moment. Occasional southeast or northwest gales funnel in or out of the Strait of Juan de Fuca, influenced by climatic conditions in Puget Sound and the Strait of Georgia. During spring tides, when strong winds oppose strong currents, chop heaps up, quickly becoming hazardous. Currents in the Strait of Juan de Fuca are fed by inland waters from as far north as Desolation Sound and as far south as the channels of Admiralty Inlet and Hood Canal.

To further complicate matters, strong river runoffs—especially from the mighty Frazer River—enhance the ebb currents. Because of these conditions, tide or current tables are particularly important for pleasure craft. Don't be surprised to find turbulent waters or steep "square" waves occurring in narrow passages, near headlands, and over submerged rocks. These conditions are exaggerated and frequent-

ly dangerous at Race Rocks, Point Wilson, Boundary Pass, Cattle Pass, Rosario Strait, Deception Pass, and other similar passages. A prudent skipper always plans ahead to avoid difficulties and, in marginal conditions, chooses a safe anchorage or harbor.

Despite these cautions about the vagaries of sea conditions in the Northwest, be assured that most boaters find the ride smoother as they proceed east or north on inside waters. Now out of the rolling seas, weary coastal crew come alive and appetites improve dramatically. Puget Sound and the San Juan and Gulf Islands offer unlimited opportunities for spectacular cruising and, as a general rule, the waters on a summer night are as flat as a pond.

In Chapter 8 we give just an introduction to the highlights of Puget Sound. To do justice to the entire area requires studying several of the excellent guidebooks available on the market. (Please refer to the Bibliography for a list of titles that give detailed information on the many places to explore in Puget Sound and British Columbia.)

Upon entering the Strait of Juan de Fuca, you have three choices for continuing your cruise:

1) To turn north toward Victoria, entering British Columbia and clearing Customs in either Victoria, Sidney, Nanaimo or Vancouver. 2) To continue east or northeast, remaining in U.S. waters and enjoying the beauty of the San Juan Islands and the conveniences of Anacortes or Bellingham as transportation, supply and repair centers. 3) To turn south at Point Wilson, entering Admiralty Inlet and exploring Puget Sound or Hood Canal. An alternative to the Admiralty Inlet route leads south from Anacortes through Swinomish Channel—a smooth-water, less crowded route that allows a stop at the quaint town of La Conner.

The convoluted Seattle area, Hood Canal, and South Sound are just a few of the interesting destinations. Within a 75-mile radius of Port Townsend there exists a lifetime of cruising possibilities. From Cape Flattery to Bellingham and Anacortes on the east, to Olympia on the south, and to Vancouver and Nanaimo on the north, there are hundreds of wonderful marinas, state and provincial marine parks and intimate coves where you can anchor largely by yourself. In addition, many of these places are beautiful during the fall and winter months. If you don't mind cool or drizzly weather, it can be particularly restful to anchor in a quiet bay and go ashore to explore the beaches and hike the trails of these areas. (We once spent a lovely snowy Thanksgiving holiday anchored at Sucia Island—one of the San Juans—along with just two other boats.) And, if you feel the call of Alaska, you can continue north along the Inside Passage, always knowing you are seldom more than 60 minutes or so from a place you can drop the hook and find temporary shelter.

In addition to checking our Bibliography, we suggest that you study the FineEdge.com planning maps for 5,000 waypoints of all the places to tie up or anchor from San Diego to Glacier Bay. And please visit our website www.FineEdge.com for updates and news on the areas covered in this book, as well as for a list of FineEdge guidebooks that cover the Northwest from the San Juan and Gulf Islands to Alaska.

Strait of Juan de Fuca
Chart 18400; Cape Flattery to Admiralty Inlet (83 mi)

Strait of Juan de Fuca . . . is the connecting channel between the ocean and the inter-island passages extending S to Puget Sound and N to the inland waters of British Columbia and southeastern Alaska.

The Strait of Juan de Fuca Traffic Separation Scheme has been established in the Strait of Juan de Fuca. . . . Vessels so desiring, may while transiting the Strait, contact the Puget Sound Vessel Traffic Service by calling SEATTLE TRAFFIC on VHF-FM [Channel 5A; see Note below] to receive

desired information on known traffic, aids to navigation discrepancies, and locally hazardous weather conditions. . . .

In few parts of the world is the vigilance of the mariner more called upon than when entering the Strait of Juan de Fuca from the Pacific in fog. Sea fog is the most common type, and it is at its worst from about July through October. . . .

The currents may attain velocities of 2 to 4 knots, varying with the range of tide, and are influenced by strong winds. E of Race Rocks, in the wider portion of the strait, the velocity is considerably less. At Race Rocks and Discovery Island the velocity may be 6 knots or more. . . .

Tide rips occur off the prominent points and in the vicinity of the banks. These are particularly off Cape Flattery, Race Rocks, Dungeness Spit, and Point Wilson, at times becoming dangerous to small vessels. (CP, 33rd Ed.)

The Strait of Juan de Fuca, which separates the State of Washington and Canada, is the entrance to the waterways of Puget Sound, British Columbia, and the Inside Passage to Alaska. The Strait is large enough to develop its own particular local weather patterns; weather fronts frequently meet here and break up into small complex cells. It is somewhat difficult to forecast the exact weather patterns, so don't be surprised to find the wind blowing from different directions or at varying force at the west and east ends of the Strait, or at Haro Strait, Rosario Strait, and Admiralty Inlet.

The same complexity seems to hold for pockets of fog. There are times when you simply have to poke your bow out into the Strait and make your own judgment call. A good part of the time during the summer months, the Strait of Juan de Fuca is often nearly flat-calm forcing sailboats to motor. But one thing you can count on is that when spring tides and their associated strong currents meet with heavy winds from the opposite direction, steep and hazardous seas occur. At such times, or in times of thick weather, it's good strategy to stay put in a safe anchorage or, if you're underway, to seek temporary shelter until conditions improve. Be sure to listen to the Canadian weather channels for their "take" on this area, as well as to U.S.

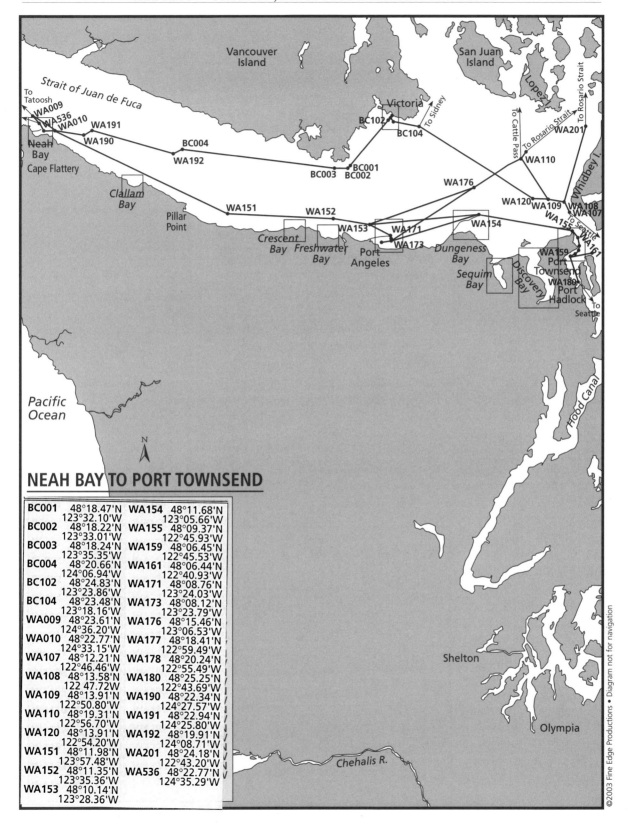

NEAH BAY TO PORT TOWNSEND

BC001	48°18.47'N 123°32.10'W	WA154	48°11.68'N 123°05.66'W
BC002	48°18.22'N 123°33.01'W	WA155	48°09.37'N 122°45.93'W
BC003	48°18.24'N 123°35.35'W	WA159	48°06.45'N 122°45.53'W
BC004	48°20.66'N 124°06.94'W	WA161	48°06.44'N 122°40.93'W
BC102	48°24.83'N 123°23.86'W	WA171	48°08.76'N 123°24.03'W
BC104	48°23.48'N 123°18.16'W	WA173	48°08.12'N 123°23.79'W
WA009	48°23.61'N 124°36.20'W	WA176	48°15.46'N 123°06.53'W
WA010	48°22.77'N 124°33.15'W	WA177	48°18.41'N 122°59.49'W
WA107	48°12.21'N 122°46.46'W	WA178	48°20.24'N 122°55.49'W
WA108	48°13.58'N 122 47.72'W	WA180	48°25.25'N 122°43.69'W
WA109	48°13.91'N 122°50.80'W	WA190	48°22.34'N 124°27.57'W
WA110	48°19.31'N 122°56.70'W	WA191	48°22.94'N 124°25.80'W
WA120	48°13.91'N 122°54.20'W	WA192	48°19.91'N 124°08.71'W
WA151	48°11.98'N 123°57.48'W	WA201	48°24.18'N 122°43.20'W
WA152	48°11.35'N 123°35.36'W	WA536	48°22.77'N 124°35.29'W
WA153	48°10.14'N 123°28.36'W		

Cruise ship entering the Strait of Juan de Fuca

stations.

On average, tides reverse every six hours and, unless there is exceptional runoff, currents reverse shortly after high or low water. It generally does not pay to drive against square waves or turbulent seas; it is as hard on your crew as it is on your boat. Poor visibility with strong currents can be a formula to put your vessel on the rocks or carry you into the dangerous shipping lanes. You don't have to go into a port or a marina for temporary shelter; many times all it takes on these inside waters is to carefully approach the shore and look for a lee where you can anchor and "hide out" for a while. For your convenience, *Baidarka* has researched a number of such places from Neah Bay to Port Townsend.

Call Port Angeles Coast Guard on VHF Channel 16 if you are concerned about weather; call Seattle Vessel Traffic Service (VTS), Channel 5A, to discuss large vessels in the vicinity or to voluntari-

ly announce that you are crossing the busy shipping lanes. If you're concerned about the course of a particular vessel, call that ship by name on bridge-to-bridge VHF Channel 13 to give them your position and let them know your intentions.

Note: VTS monitors Channel 5A in the Strait of Juan de Fuca and the San Juan Islands; within Admiralty Inlet (everything south of Point Wilson), they monitor Channel 14. Remember VTS cannot see small craft or track them on their radar. If you are concerned about commercial traffic in your vicinity, or the potential for collision, be sure to call VTS and let them know your position and intentions. To aid your safety, be sure that you have a good radar reflector deployed and that you monitor VTS channels so you are aware of traffic.

Neah Bay

Charts 18484; 5 mi E of Cape Flattery.
Entrance: (WA536) 48°22.77'N, 124°35.29' W
Entrance (Makah Marina): 48°22.11'N, 124°36.87' W

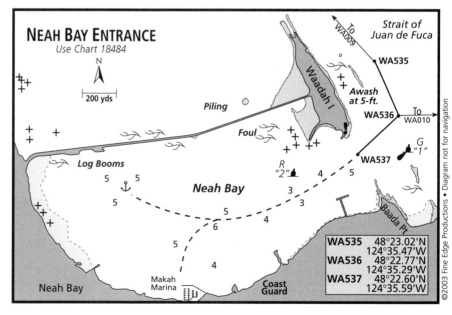

NEAH BAY ENTRANCE
Use Chart 18484
N
200 yds

Strait of Juan de Fuca
To WA009
WA535
Waadah I
Piling
Awash at 5-ft.
To WA010
WA536
Foul
G "1"
WA537
R "2"
Log Booms
Neah Bay
Baada Pt
Makah Marina
Coast Guard
Neah Bay

WA535	48°23.02'N 124°35.47'W
WA536	48°22.77'N 124°35.29'W
WA537	48°22.60'N 124°35.59'W

©2003 Fine Edge Productions • Diagram not for navigation

Anchor: 48°22.50'N, 124°37.98' W

Neah Bay . . . is used extensively by small vessels as a harbor of refuge in foul weather. Its proximity to Cape Flattery and ease of access at any time make the anchorage very useful. It is protected from all but E weather. . . .

The buildings of Neah Bay Coast Guard Station, 0.4 mile SW of Baada Point, are prominent from the entrance.

The buoyed entrance to the bay is between Waadah Island and Baada Point. Depths of 14 to 16 feet can be carried into the bay. The careful navigator can carry 16 feet through the entrance by use of the chart and by favoring the S side of the entrance, passing close aboard the end of the Makah Indian T-head pier about 375 yards W of Baada Point. After passing the pier let the chart be the guide to the best water. Anchorage is in 20 to 40 feet, sandy bottom. . . .

There are many small-craft floats extending along the S shore of the bay. Neah Bay has no public haulout or repair facilities. (CP, 33rd Ed.)

Large and well-protected, Neah Bay is frequently the first or last port used by cruising boats in the Strait of Juan de Fuca; it is a U.S. Customs Port of Entry. The land around the bay belongs to the Makah Indian Reserve. Makah Marina, run by the tribe, has upgraded and expanded its floats in recent years. The northwest corner of the bay—an area extensively used by cruising boats—has ample space for a number of boats, with good swinging room.

With one important exception, the approach to Neah Bay is well marked with lights and buoys; the exception is a dangerous reef that lies 0.15 mile (300 yards) off the northeast side of Waadah Island. The reef, a quarter-mile-long and parallel to the shore of Waadah Island, is awash on a 5-foot tide. Waypoint WA535 is placed 200 yards east of the reef to keep your approach from the west sufficiently off. After turning south, any longitude greater than 124°35.47'W will put a vessel in danger. There is no entrance buoy as such for Neah Bay, so use waypoint WA536 before turning back west. The only buoy near the entrance to Neah Bay is G"1" that marks a reef off the south shore; it is useless as a clearing mark for vessels coming from Cape Flattery. If you are 0.25 mile north of Waadah Island and should happen to head for buoy G"1," mistakenly thinking it's is an entrance buoy, you will run aground on the unnamed reef.

Makah Marina has 1,100 feet of transient moorage, with space almost always available except during sport-fishing season. From May to September it's best to call ahead. There are two fuel docks in the harbor; one at Makah Fuel Sales, another at Big Salmon Marina; the latter primarily serves large commercial fishing vessels. Provisions are within walking distance.

Charter outfits in Neah Bay offer salt-water fishing and wildlife viewing. Although it is permitted to walk the beach-

Aerial view: Makah Marina

Makah Marina entrance

es in the tribal reserve, shellfish gathering is not permitted for other than tribal members. Well worth visiting, here, is the Makah Museum and Cultural Center that exhibits some of the finest artifacts and Indian art in the Northwest. Built in 1979, the museum houses the Ozette Archaeological collection—the largest pre-contact collection in the U.S. Buried centuries ago in mud slides, the artifacts were uncovered in 1970 near the village of Ozette, 15 miles south of Neah Bay on the coast near Cape Alava. The museum also features replicas of longhouses and Native canoes. (The museum is open in summer months only.)

To stand on the northwesternmost point of the continental U.S., and for spectacular views of Tatoosh Island and the entrance to the Strait of Juan de Fuca, bicycle or drive through the town of Neah Bay toward the ocean from where a path leads to a lookout.

In July, during the weeks preceding the Fourth, you may think you're in a war zone. Every evening until midnight, you'll hear and see fireworks exploding. (Fire-

work stands are big business on Native reserves.) And if you happen to visit the bay at the end of August, the tribe hosts an annual Makah Days celebration.

The 1.3-mile-causeway on the north side of the bay that connects the mainland to Waadah Island creates a large and excellent anchorage. In winter, it is exposed to northeast winds and chop that blow in through the entrance and, during such conditions, you may want to avoid anchoring here. In years past, the west side of the bay held a large logboom-storage area; be aware that the bottom in this area may have decaying slash. *Baidarka* found very good holding at the spot indicated on the accompanying diagram. Be aware that the area just west of Waadah Island dries and is foul for about 0.3 mile. As long as you anchor in 4 to 5 fathoms (at zero tide), you shouldn't have a problem. Notice that the entrance channel to Neah Bay is narrower than it may seem at high water, and there are isolated shallow patches between 2 and 3 fathoms.

Fishing boats in Makah Marina

Aerial view: Tatoosh Island looking east across the fair weather route in background

Washington State Department of Ecology

Anchor in 5 fathoms over sand and mud with very good holding.

⚓ **Makah Marina** tel: 360.645.3015; fax: 360.645.3016; email: mtcport@olypen.com; monitors Channels 16, 66

Crossing the Strait of Juan de Fuca to Canada

Boats heading north into British Columbia may want to cross directly over into Canadian waters just east of Neah Bay and clear Customs in either Victoria (48 miles east) or points north. To enter at Victoria, you can use waypoints WA010, WA190 to WA191, heading east for 12

La Push to Neah Bay
by Michelle Gaylord

Although the seas were a little lumpy and confused, our 40-mile run from La Push to Neah Bay on August 31 was pleasant, compared to our previous couple of runs. The shoreline along this stretch of the Olympic Peninsula is rather rugged and a maze of sea stacks, exposed rocks, and little islands. Neah Bay, the first harbor after entering the Straight of Juan de Fuca, is another Indian settlement, but larger than La Push. We anchored out and spent only one night there, since we were anxious to get into the Puget Sound area.

---

miles across the inbound shipping lane and the 2-mile-wide separation zone to WA192; from there crossing the outbound shipping lane to BC004, thence to BC003, transiting Race Passage using waypoints BC002, BC001 to BC 102 at the entrance to Victoria. Be sure to monitor Vessel Traffic Sevices, VHF Channel 5A and call them with any traffic concerns you may have, or contact any large ship on Channel 13, Bridge-to-Bridge.

Be sure to consult Canadian *Sailing Directions, British Columbia Coast (South Portion), 16th Edition,* before entering Victoria harbour.

From Victoria, 34 different routes that lead to Alaska are given in *Proven Cruising Routes* by Monahan and Douglass published by FineEdge.com.

For information on Border Crossing Issues, please see the Appendix.

Victoria, British Columbia

Victoria, British Columbia's capital, sometimes called the "City of Gardens," is historic and lovely with an old-world charm. First settled in 1843, the original Hudson's Bay fort has become a sophisticated city, home to the Provincial Legislature, the famous Empress Hotel, and the Maritime and Royal British Columbia museums. With its Thunderbird Park totems, Chinatown, rose gardens and horse-drawn buggies, Victoria captivates all her visitors.

Approaches to Victoria Outer Harbour (Vancouver Island)

Charts 3415, 3440, 3313
Entrance (200 yds W of breakwtr lt.):
48°24.81' N, 123°23.78' W
Entrance (100 yds W of Shoal Pt. Lt.):
48°25.41' N, 123°23.41' W

Victoria Harbour is entered between Macaulay Point and the Ogden Point breakwater. East of a

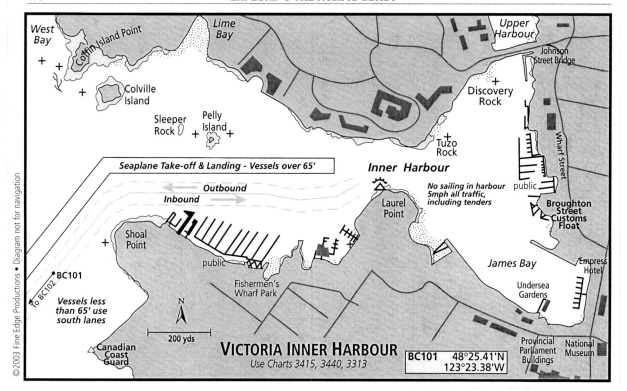

line joining Colville Island and Shoal Point up to the Johnson Street Bridge is known as Inner Harbour.

The harbour entrance is easily recognized by the breakwater and a long, low grey building close north on the east side of the entrance. McLoughlin Point, on the west side of the entrance, has conspicuous white buildings and oil storage tanks on it. . . .

The Harbour Master's office and the harbour patrol craft are equipped with VHF radios and monitor Channel 73.

"Speed limit 5 knots" signs are posted and proceeding under sail is prohibited north of a line drawn between Shoal Point and Berens Island lights.

Anchoring in the approach to Victoria Harbour is prohibited. Vessels wishing to anchor must obtain permission from the Harbour Master . . . (Sailing Directions, Vol. 1, 16th Ed.)

Erie Street Government Wharf

Known locally as Fishermen's Wharf (Victoria Harbour), Erie Street Government Wharf, on the south side of the Victoria Harbour, is 0.1 mile east of Shoal Point.

Charts 3415, 3440, 3313
Fuel dock: 48°25.44' N, 123°23.11' W
Wharf Street public floats: 48°25.43' N, 123°23.06' W

Victoria, James Bay floats

The fisherman's floats with ten finger floats, close east of Shoal Point, are generally used by the fishing fleet. Between May 30 and August 31, when the fishing fleet is at sea, they are used by pleasure craft. (Small Craft Guide, Vol. 1)

Fishermen's Wharf—the public floats just east of the fuel dock—may offer transient moorage for pleasure craft, depending on commercial fishing activities. The floats are usually quite crowded and rafting may be required. Power, water, and shower facilities are available. Call on VHF Channel 73 for space availability. A second fuel dock is at the east end of the floats at Raymur Point.

Victoria Inner Harbour
Charts 3415, 3440, 3313; btwn. Shoal Point and Johnson Street Bridge
Entrance (btwn. Laurel and Songhees pts.):
48°25.50' N, 123°22.61' W

Victoria Harbour is a water aerodrome. The normal landing and taking off area is between Shoal and Laurel Points. A seaplane taxiing area has been established for that portion of Victoria Harbour bounded on the west by a line between Laurel and Songhees Points and on the north by Johnson Street Bridge.

Large freighters and cruise ships use the outer part of the harbour and berth at Ogden Point wharves. The Inner Harbour is used by large ferries, tugs towing logbooms or barges, fishing vessels and, during summer months, by numerous pleasure craft.

Tidal streams of 2 kn can be encountered flowing across the entrance to the harbour, between Macaulay Point and Brotchie Ledge; the flood sets SE and the ebb NW. In the Inner Harbour tidal streams do not present any difficulties. (Small Craft Guide, Vol. 1)

James Bay (Victoria Inner Harbour)
Charts 3415, 3440, 3313; 1.2 mi. NE of harbour entr.
Entrance: 48°25.40' N, 123°22.36' W
Public docks (Empress Hotel): 48°25.31' N, 123°22.17' W

Victoria is a Port of Entry. A telephone reporting system is available in Victoria for pleasure boaters entering Canada from the United States. A Customs Officer may issue verbal clearance or if documentation is required an Officer will go to the Customs Dock, on the east side of Inner Harbour close SW of the foot of Fort Street. The Customs office is nearby at the corner of Government and Wharf Streets. (Small Craft Guide, Vol. 1)

The public dock just below the Empress Hotel in James Bay is our favorite urban port of call. Moorage is usually limited to two days and a nominal fee is charged. Water and power (15 amp) are available; restrooms, showers, and laundry facilities are located below the InfoCentre on the lower quay.

For further information, please refer to The Fine Edge publications: *Exploring the San Juan and Gulf Islands* and *Exploring the South Coast of British Columbia*.

⚓ **Victoria Harbour Master** tel: 250.363.3578; monitors Channel 73

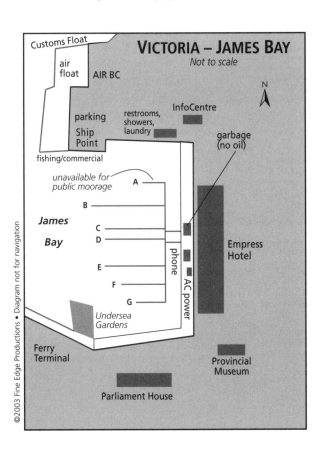

Sail and Seal Rock

Chart 18460; 2 mi E of Neah Bay
Position (Sail Rock): 48°21.48′N, 124 °32.69′W

> *A marina is along the shore near Sail Rock . . . Mariners are advised to exercise caution in approaching the marinas because of the numerous rocks and ledges. The floats at the marina bare at low water.* (CP, 33rd Ed.)

Sail Rock and nearby Seal Rock are a quarter-mile offshore and about 30 feet high. Sail Rock is the more pointed of the two rocks. The rocks are connected to each other and to the shore on their east side by a series of submerged rocks. The coast here is very poorly charted and local knowledge is required. Avoid the rocks and ledges noted above. Sportfishing facilities lie on shore west of Sail Rock. The Sail River outlet is 0.5 mile west of Sail Rock.

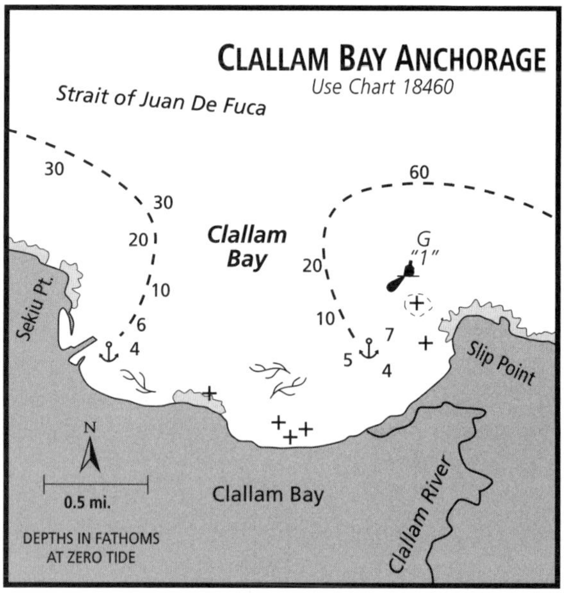

Clallam Bay (Sekiu)

Chart 18460; 15 mi SE of Neah Bay.
Entrance: 48°16.10′N, 124°16.73′W
Anchor (W): 48°15.69′N, 124°17.66′W
Anchor (E): 48°15.74′N, 124°15.74′W

> *Clallam Bay . . . is a broad open bight about 2 miles long and 1 mile wide. It affords anchorage in 6 to 10 fathoms, sandy bottom, and is used to some extent in S or thick weather.* (CP, 33rd Ed.) *Sekiu is a resort and sport fishing town. . . . The town has berths, gasoline, water, ice, launching ramps and limited marine supplies. . . .* (CP, 33rd Ed.)

Olson's Marina

The Marina at Sekiu

Clallam Bay is a convenient place to seek temporary shelter when fog rolls in, chop picks up, or when strong southeasterlies threaten. This small bight offers moderate shelter from both northwest and southeast winds and chop. A broad gravel beach backed by white buildings curves around the bight. Olson's Resort, a rural sportfishing center with a few slips, can handle boats to 39 feet. They have fuel but no pump-out station and they monitor CB but not VHF. In summer 2002, to the surprise of the locals, a cruise ship anchored offshore and sent in shore taxies so its passengers could see a rain forest up close.

Approaching from the west, round up once you've passed Sekiu Point and head for the jetty that protects the small sportfishing boat facilities. You can find temporary anchorage to the east of the jetty in about 4 fathoms. Approaching from the east, avoid the reef off Slip Point by passing north and west of bell buoy G"1." Good temporary anchorage in strong southeasterlies can be found in the lee of Slip Point and the reef 0.4 mile southwest of the bell buoy; this site has good swinging room.

Fuel, showers, and laundromat are

available at Sekiu, the village at the west end of the bay. Pillar Point, 7.5 miles southeast, is the next temporary shelter from northwest chop.

Anchor (W) in about 4 fathoms over sand and kelp with fair holding.

Anchor (E) in 5 to 7 fathoms over sand; fair-to-good holding.

Pillar Point

Chart 18460; 7.5 miles SE of Clallam Bay
Anchor: 48°12.26'N, 124°05.51' W

Container ship in the traffic lanes off Crescent Bay

> *Pillar Point . . . is bold, 700 feet high, wooded up to its summit, with a dark pillar-shaped rock more than 100 feet high lying close under its E face. The rock shows prominently from W. Good anchorage may be had in 9 to 12 fathoms, sticky bottom, about 0.8 mile SE of Pillar Point. This anchorage offers good shelter from the heavy W swell, but gives no protection from the brisk E and NW winds that prevail in winter. (CP, 33rd Ed.)*

Pillar Point is the high headland along the shore east of Clallam Bay. This area, although an open roadstead, offers a modicum of shelter from northwest swells and winds about a mile southeast of the point; it can be used as a temporary stop to wait for fog to lift. The shore is steep-to off Psyht River, so continue east until you find the sand flat then anchor in depths of 6 to 8 fathoms.

Anchor (temporarily) in 6 to 8 fathoms over sand and mud with good holding.

Crescent Bay

Chart 18465 16 mi E of Pillar Pt.; 4 mi NW of Freshwater Bay
Entrance: 48°10.36'N, 123°43.02'W
Anchor (W): 48°09.71'N, 123°43.47'W
Anchor (E): 48°09.75'N, 123°42.78

> *Crescent Bay . . . is a small semi-circular bight 1 mile in diameter. The E part is shoal and near the W shore the remains of a wharf should be avoided. This is not a good landing place in N weather. The anchorage is of limited extent and suitable only for small vessels. . . . (CP, 33rd Ed.)*

Crescent Bay is a favorite temporary stop of *Baidarka*'s crew for its fair-to-good shelter from westerlies and southeasterlies. Use caution in an approach due to the narrow entrance and strong currents. Entering in poor visibility is not recommended.

With a moderately strong westerly breeze, white caps blow by on the north side of Crescent Rock, while inside the bay there is no chop or surf along the west beach.

The entrance buoy to Crescent Bay is less than two miles south of the inbound (eastbound) shipping channel. If you are following close to the coast to avoid large ships, entrance

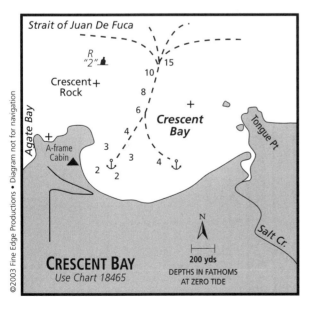

©2003 Fine Edge Productions • Diagram not for navigation

Strait of Juan De Fuca

R "2"

15
10
8
6
Crescent Rock
Crescent Bay
4
3
3
4
2
2
A-frame Cabin
Agate Bay
Tongue Pt.
Salt Cr.

N

200 yds

CRESCENT BAY
Use Chart 18465

DEPTHS IN FATHOMS
AT ZERO TIDE

buoy R"2" will appear to be positioned off Tongue Point further east. *Do not be fooled;* the buoy is on the north end of a reef that extends from the west end of the bight. If you try to pass inside the buoy you may ground on Crescent Rock or its adjacent kelp-covered reef. On a flood, you will find a several-knot east-flowing current between Crescent Rock and the entrance buoy, while just a little south inside the bay, a back eddy flows west along shore. Harbor porpoises frequently play along here in the nearby current swirls.

Buoy at entrance to Crescent Bay

Caution: Crescent Bay is shallow; be careful to avoid the shoal and rock that extend for 0.3 mile west of Tongue Point. The islet off Salt Creek outlet has trees growing on it and ashore, there are two or three houses.

In westerlies, you can find anchorage in about 2 fathoms off the beach in front of an A-Frame cabin on the west side of the bay. Swinging room is somewhat limited by the shoal water and eddy currents.

In heavy southeast weather, we would seek temporary anchorage against the south shore, west of Salt Creek outlet. To keep your vessel from swinging too much, use lots of scope and perhaps a stern anchor. During spring tides turbulent current occurs off Tongue Point.

Anchor (W) in 2 fathoms over a hard bottom of brown sand, gray mud, scattered kelp, and eel grass; poor-to-fair holding unless you set your anchor well; limited swinging room.

Anchor (E) in about 3 fathoms or less, taking care to set your anchor well in the eel grass.

Freshwater Bay

Chart 18465; 4 mi E of Crescent Bay
Entrance (W-bound): 48°09.11'N, 123°38.00'W
Entrance (E-bound): 48°09.07'N, 123°34.88'W
Anchor (W): 48°08.89'N, 123°38.20'W
Anchor (E): 48°08.55'N, 123°34.80'W

> *Freshwater Bay . . . is a broad open bight, affording anchorage in 6 to 10 fathoms. . . . A park with a launching ramp is along the SW shore of Freshwater Bay.* (CP, 33rd Ed.)

Freshwater Bay, the open bight between Observatory Point (west) and Angeles Point

Crescent Bay anchor check with brown sand, gray mud and scattered kelp

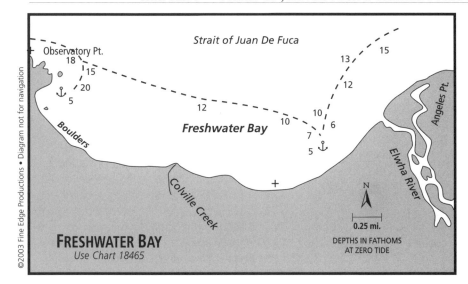

Strait of Juan De Fuca

Observatory Pt.
18
15
20
5

Boulders

12

Freshwater Bay

13
15
12
10
10
10
6
7
5

Angeles Pt.

Elwha River

Colville Creek

0.25 mi.

FRESHWATER BAY
Use Chart 18465

DEPTHS IN FATHOMS
AT ZERO TIDE

©2003 Fine Edge Productions • Diagram not for navigation

ered pillar on it. The passage inside the pillar islet is foul. Pass 100 yards east of the islet before making a turn to the southwest and rounding up into the wind in the anchorage area south of the islet. (See photo of the anchor site between the islet and the shore.)

The eastern anchor site, useful in strong southeast winds, is approached by heading for a point 0.5 mile west of the low flats at the outlet of Elwha River, just east of the beginning of the low bluffs.

Baidarka finds good temporary anchorage from westerlies between the small islet off Observatory Point, as noted above, and the paved launch ramp on the beach; there is little chop or surf along shore in westerly winds. The bay is shallow, so pay attention to depths as you close the shore. Do not attempt to pass between the islet and shore; the bottom is foul and awash near high water.

In southeast gales, moderate protection can be found in the lee of Angeles Point along the 5-fathom curve where there is unlimited swinging room over a generally flat bottom. The outlet of the Elwha River which has its source in the Olympic mountains, lies on the west side of Angeles Point. (The oldest commercial ferryboat in service in the U.S., which plies the San Juan Island waters, is named *Elwha*.)

For full shelter from all weather conditions, head to the marina inside Port Angeles, 7 miles east.

(east), offers temporary anchorage from westerly winds and chop in the lee of its west point. The far eastern end of the bay, 0.5 mile southwest of the outlet of Elwha River, offers shelter in southeast gales. The bay is easy to enter in foul weather; it has a long sand and gravel beach but it is exposed to all northerly winds. Freshwater Bay is a designated Alternate Explosive Anchorage for commercial vessels.

Approaching Freshwater Bay from the west during northwest winds, pass east of both Observatory Point bluff and a small islet 100 yards due east before turning south. The islet is poorly charted and has a 20-foot-high bush-cov-

Entering Freshwater Bay; the launch ramp in the background

Freshwater Bay entrance rock looking north from anchor site

Anchor (W) in 2 fathoms over light brown sand and mud with sea lettuce; poor-to-fair holding unless you set your anchor well in the sea lettuce.

Anchor (E) in 5 fathoms over a bottom of gray sand and mud; good holding.

Port Angeles

Chart 18468; 7 mi E of Freshwater Bay; 51 mi E Neah Bay
Entrance (Port Angeles Boat Haven):
48°07.67'N, 123°27.23'W
Anchor (Hollywood Beach): 48°07.27'N, 123°25.40'W

Port Angeles . . . is entered between Ediz Hook, a low, narrow, and bare sandspit 3 miles long, and the main shore to the S. The harbor, about 2.5 miles long, is easy of access by the largest vessels, which frequently use it when refueling, making topside repairs, waiting for orders or a tug, and when weatherbound.

The harbor is protected from all except E winds, which occasionally blow during the winter. During SE winter gales, the wind is not usually felt but some swells roll in. The depths are greatest on the N shore and decrease from 30 to 15 fathoms in the middle of the harbor. . . .

Extra caution in navigating the waters inside Ediz Hook should be exercised because of the large number of submerged deadheads or sinkers in the area. Deadheads or sinkers are logs that have become adrift from rafts or booms, have become waterlogged, and float in a vertical position with one end just awash, rising and falling with the tide.

The best anchorage is off the wharves, in 7 to 12 fathoms, sticky bottom. . . .

Port Angeles Boat Haven, operated by the port, is a large, well-equipped small-craft basin in the SW part of the harbor that can accommodate a large fleet of fishing boats and some pleasure craft. The basin is marked by lights. . . . The harbormaster controls the moorings in the basin. (CP, 33rd Ed.)

Port Angeles—the first major industrial port inside the Strait of Juan de Fuca—is used by large ships, as well as pleasure craft. The harbor is well protected from prevailing northwest winds, swell, and chop by Ediz Hook—a natural sand spit that extends eastward from shore for 3 miles, creating Port Angeles. The small

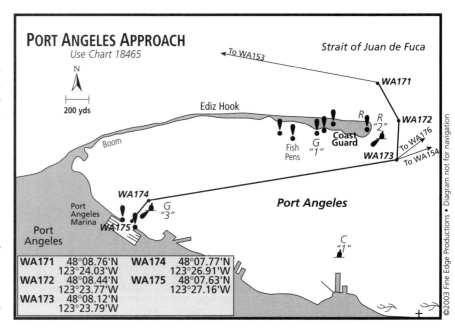

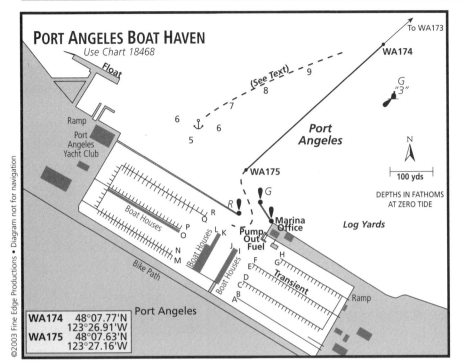

PORT ANGELES BOAT HAVEN
Use Chart 18468

To WA173

WA174

(See Text) 9
8

7

6   6

5

Port Angeles

G
"3"

N

100 yds

DEPTHS IN FATHOMS
AT ZERO TIDE

Float

Ramp

Port
Angeles
Yacht Club

WA175

Boat Houses
P
O
N
M

Boat Houses
Q
R
L K
J
I
F
E
D
C
B
A

Boat Houses

G
R

Pump
Out
Fuel

Marina
Office

Log Yards

H
G

Transient

Ramp

Bike Path

Port Angeles

WA174	48°07.77'N
	123°26.91'W
WA175	48°07.63'N
	123°27.16'W

©2003 Fine Edge Productions • Diagram not for navigation

WA171, WA172 and WA173 on our diagram are placed to give you about a quarter-mile clearance rounding the point. Trans-Pacific ships frequently pick up or drop off their escort tugs and pilots just outside the entrance. Inside the bay, watch for anchored ships, barges or other commercial vessels and head to Port Angeles Boat Haven for moorage or to Hollywood Beach for anchoring.

In 1791, the Spaniard Captain Francisco Eliza named this deep natural harbor *Puerto de Nuestra Senora de Los Angeles*, "Port of Our Lady of Angels," from which the name is derived.

Port Angeles Boat Haven Marina has transient slips with power and water, showers, pump-out, and fuel dock. Repair facilities are available. Ediz Hook, the four-mile sandbar that forms the harbor, houses a Coast Guard station and airport at its outer end. A hike along the

boat basin is located at the far west end of the bay, beyond the ferry dock.

The busy harbor is crowded with traffic, cranes, mills, and logbooms—all related to the timber industry. You'll see great piles of logs almost everywhere you look, and you can't miss the odor of sawdust wafting from the nearby paper mill. Port Angeles is also a Customs Port of entry, and a terminus for the car ferry to Victoria. After a cruise along the pristine and sparsely-populated coast, the noise, smells, and bustle of Port Angeles can be a bit overpowering.

Approaching Port Angeles from the west, be careful not to head for the town and industrial complex before you run the full distance to the end of the Ediz Hook. At night, or during times of poor visibility, the spit can be indistinguishable due to background lights, buildings, and smoke. Be sure to identify the red beacon and horn on the tip of the spit and pass buoy R"2" on your starboard hand. Waypoints

Paper plant in Port Angeles

Michelle Gaylord

Logging operation in Port Angeles

spit offers a panoramic view of the city and mountains to the south. The Port Angeles Yacht Club on the west side of the Boat Haven, provides reciprocal slips to yacht club members only. Phone the club for advance reservations.

Port Angeles calls itself the "Gateway to the Olympic National Park." If you're new to the area, it's worth renting a car to make an excursion into the park; if you can spare only a day, drive up to nearby Hurricane Ridge, remarkable for its spectacular overlook of the Olympics.

Anchorage may be found 100 yards outside the Boat Haven's western breakwater, east of

Port Angeles Yacht Club entrance; this area, which is known locally as Hollywood Beach, is convenient to downtown.

Anchor in about 3 fathoms over sand and soft mud with fair-to-good holding.

⚓ **Port Angeles Boat Haven Marina** open 0800-1700; tel: 360.457.4505; fax: 360.457.4921; website: www.portofpa.com

⚓ **Port Angeles Yacht Club** tel: 360.457.4132

Dungeness Bay

Chart 18471; 14 mi E of Port Angeles
Entrance: (WA154) 48°11.68′N, 123°05.66′W
Anchor (W): 48°10.24′N, 123°07.36′W
Anchor (SE): 48°10.24′N, 123°07.30′W

Dungeness Bay . . . affords shelter in W winds, but is open E; in N weather, the protection afforded is only fair. It is a dangerous place in winter gales, especially from the SE. The bay is formed by a sandspit extending NE 4 miles and forming, in addition to Dungeness Bay, a small lagoon at the head of the harbor that can be entered by light-draft vessels with local knowledge. . . .

From the end of the spit a shoal extends NE for 0.8 mile from the light. This has been reported as extending farther N, and it should be passed with caution. A lighted bell buoy marks the shoal but it may be submerging during periods of strong current; vessels should not pass between the buoy and the light. A shoal makes out about 1 mile from the S side of the bay.

The best anchorage is in 5 to 9 fathoms, sticky bottom, about 1 mile SE of the light, clear of the cable area. (CP, 33rd Ed.)

Dungeness Bay is protected by a long, natural sandspit that offers some shelter and recreation. The lagoon at the far west end of the

Aerial view: Port Angeles Boat Haven

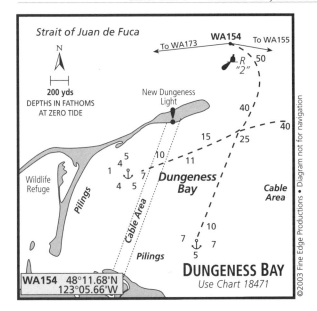

bay, designated as a wildlife refuge, is marked by private buoys.

Anchorage can be found on either side of the cable area that services the New Dungeness

Light. For less fetch in strong westerlies, anchor to the west of the cable area, being careful not to get too close; depths here are 4 to 5 fathoms over a sizeable area with adequate swinging room.

As indicated on the diagram, anchorage can also be found about 1.3 miles south of the light in a large flat area of 7 fathoms, sand and shell bottom.

Approach Dungeness Bay being careful not to turn south until the tip of the spit has been positively identified. Use waypoint WA154, and pass buoy R"2" on the starboard hand.

While Dungeness Bay is well sheltered from westerlies, it is exposed to easterlies and is dangerous in southeasterlies. Small boats caught in southeast gales have been lost while crabbing in this area. Sequim Bay, immediately south of Dungeness Bay, is more secure and the recommended shelter in foul weather.

Anchor (W) in 4 to 5 fathoms over sand and shell; fair holding; adequate swinging room.

Anchor (SE) in 7 fathoms over sand and shell; fair holding; ample swinging room.

Neah Bay to Port Angeles
by Michelle Gaylord

From Neah Bay to Port Angeles the water was flat as glass! We sighted our first orca on this leg of the trip; he was right next to the boat and surfaced two or three times. (I guess they are a familiar sight up here.) Surrounded by industrial plants, a lumber mill, and a paper mill, Port Angeles is definitely not a tourist area. However, there is a nice little town with good shopping and provisioning just a short bike ride away. We stayed in Port Angeles long enough to get our dinghy cradle reworked to better fit our new dinghy, and then we were off to a more scenic harbor.

Passing Thru *in the Port Angeles Harbor*

Aerial view: Caution around the shoals of Travis Spit

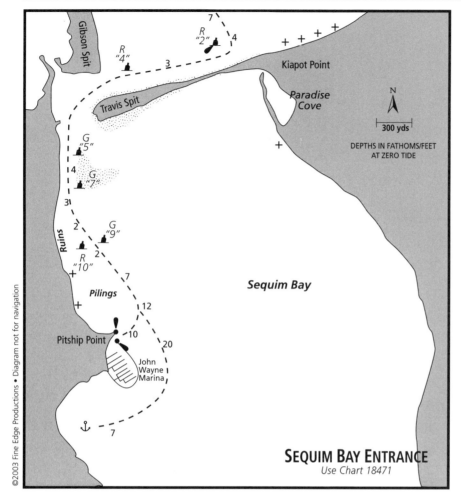

Gibson Spit

7

R "2"

4

R "4"

3

Kiapot Point

Travis Spit

Paradise Cove

N

300 yds

DEPTHS IN FATHOMS/FEET
AT ZERO TIDE

G "5"

4

G "7"

3

2

G "9"

Ruins

2

R "10"

7

Sequim Bay

Pilings

12

10

20

Pitship Point

John Wayne Marina

7

SEQUIM BAY ENTRANCE
Use Chart 18471

©2003 Fine Edge Productions • Diagram not for navigation

ed. Inside is a good anchorage anywhere in 6 to 21 fathoms, muddy bottom. A marina with lights at the NE ends of the entrance breakwaters is in the small cove just N of Pitship Point on the W side of the bay. Berths with electricity, gasoline, diesel fuel, water, ice, marine supplies, provisions, a launching ramp and a pump-out station. . . . (CP, 33rd Ed.)

Sequim Bay is a completely landlocked, 4 mile-long inlet, protected from ocean swell. The John Wayne Marina, on the west shore is a cruising boater's delight. Anchorage with very good shelter from northwest winds can be found anywhere along the eastern shore of the bay south of the bar. During southeast storms, chop can be felt inside the bay due to the sizeable fetch, but protection can be found at its southern end off the drying mud flats.

Approach: Entering Sequim Bay requires following a curvilinear route carefully through

Sequim Bay

Chart 18471; 6 mi SE of Dungeness Bay
Entrance (near buoy R"2"): 48°05.07'N, 123°01.65'W
Anchor (0.3 mi S of marina): 48°03.45'N, 123°02.40'W

Sequim Bay . . . is a landlocked bay 3.8 miles long. The bay is separated from the Straits by Travis Spit, a sandspit that extends W from the NE corner of the bay almost to the W shore. A long, narrow channel marked by lighted and unlighted buoys leads around Travis Spit and W of a shoal area called The Middle Ground into the bay. Depths of about 9 feet are available with local knowledge in the marked channel. The area between the lighted buoy at the entrance and Gibson Spit on the W shore reportedly bares at minus tide and several groundings are known to occur. Caution is advised. Strong currents that tend to follow the channel have also been report-

Michelle Gaylord

Yachts moored and at anchor in Sequim Bay

two very narrow channels—first to the north of Travis Spit, east of Gibson Spit, then over the bar to the south— with depths that rise to as little as one foot, alongside, at low water. *Caution:* Currents can contribute a significant grounding hazard. (See Chart 18471.)

Entrance and transient dock at John Wayne Marina

After safely passing Dungeness Spit, head for buoy R"2," 0.5 mile east of Gibson Spit and close northwest of Kiapot Point; then, pass close east and south of R"2" to enter the first channel. Turn westerly, along Travis Spit, favoring the west shore as you turn south for about 0.5 mile. Take buoys G"5" and G"7" on your port hand (passing close to the "Middle Ground Sand Bar"), then turn southeast, taking buoy G"9" also on your port hand. After you cross the bar into deeper waters, you can head for the marina or find an anchor site.

Sequim Bay, which lies in the rain shadow of the Olympic Mountains, receives only about 17 to 19 inches of rain a year, making it the driest spot in Puget Sound—popular for real estate development! The 90-acre Sequim Bay State Park, north of Schoolhouse Point, has a seasonal float. Sequim Bay is a lovely, quiet anchorage that was a favorite of actor John Wayne, who came here often in his *Wild Goose.* Wayne donated 22 acres of waterfront property to the Port of Port Angeles with the stipulation that the port build a marina here.

Anchor (0.3 mi S of marina) in about 7 fathoms over sand and mud; good holding.

John Wayne Marina
Chart 18471; 7 mi SE of Dungeness Bay
John Wayne Marina is a pleasant place to unwind. Attractive facilities include electricity, water, showers, laundry, pump-out, and fuel dock; a restaurant and marine supply store with limited grocery items are on-site. Benches and picnic tables are attractively placed along

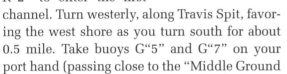

Hallelujah—Inside Waters!
by Michelle Gaylord

Now that we were in the Strait, surrounded by so many landmasses and islands, the water was calm and beautiful. I untied all my bungies, took off the tape, pulled out the nails, and put everything back in its place on the boat. Hallelujah—no more crash, bang, boom, smash. On September 4, we pulled into Sequim Bay, a huge horseshoe-shaped bay almost completely closed in by a natural sand spit. One side of the bay is a State Park with campgrounds and hiking trails through the woods. There is only one marina here, John Wayne Marina. It seems this was a favorite spot of his, and he spent quite a lot of time here on the *Wild Goose.* We found a beautiful spot just off the park and anchored for the night. If ever there is a place for peace, quiet, solitude, and tranquility, Sequim Bay is it! While there, we studied charts and read books about Puget Sound, San Juan Islands, Gulf Islands, Queen Charlotte Islands, etc. We decided we wouldn't be able to see it all if we stayed in the Northwest for 10 years. So, as nice as Sequim Bay was, we decided to leave the following day for Port Townsend.

the walkway south of the clubhouse. Although most of the marina's slips are permanently rented, transient slips are usually available. Guests can tie up at the first float inside the breakwater and check with the office. After hours, see the list of open slips posted at the marina office. John Wayne Marina does not monitor VHF. For more extensive supplies, the town of Sequim is 3 miles from the marina.

⚓ **John Wayne Marina** tel: 360.417.3440; fax: 360.417.3442; website: www.portofpa.com

⚓ **Sequim Bay Marine State Park** tel: 360.417.3440; fax: 360.417.3442

Discovery Bay
Chart18471; 2 mi SSE of Protection Island
Entrance 48°06.07'N, 122°54.13'W
Entrance (Cape George Club): 48°06.08'N, 122°53.10'W
Anchor (South Bay): 47°60.00'N, 122°51.76'W

George Vancouver, the English explorer, anchored and refitted his ships here for his exploration of these regions in 1792. The bay trends in a SE direction for about 8 miles. The entrance is masked from seaward by Protection Island, which protects it from NW winds. There are no outlying dangers, and the depths are great. A marina, located at Cape George, the E entrance point of Discovery Bay, has water, electricity, and a boat launching ramp. The entrance has a reported main depth of 3 1/2 feet.

A dangerous sunken wreck is on the W side of the bay about 300 yards S of Mill Point. . . . (CP, 33rd Ed.)

Discovery Bay is 8 miles long with good shelter and lots of maneuvering and swinging room. Both Protection Island above its entrance and its hook shape make it almost landlocked and keep

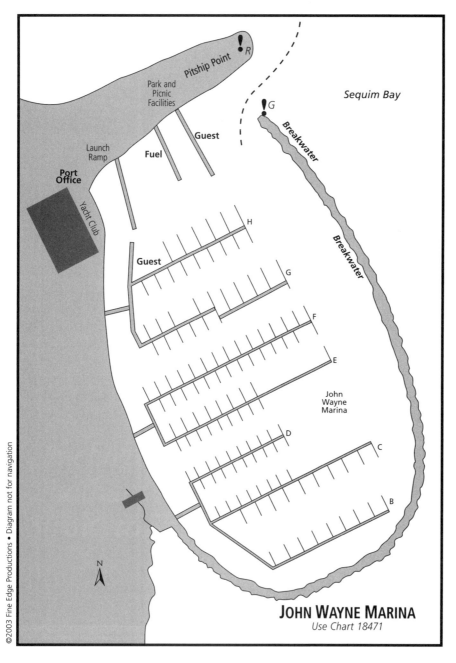

JOHN WAYNE MARINA
Use Chart 18471

©2003 Fine Edge Productions • Diagram not for navigation

out any serious chop with a northerly component. Deeper into the bay, the more prevailing winds die off. The bay is largely undeveloped and is a quiet place to anchor before heading to the urban areas. Although large enough to develop its own afternoon weather pattern and chop, most nights within the bay are calm unless a front is moving through.

Approach Discovery Bay by using either channel around Protection Island, avoiding the shoals on its north side. For the most part, the bay is too deep for convenient anchoring except near shore (avoiding cable areas, old wrecks and pilings). The head of the bay off the large drying mud flat has almost unlimited swinging room and is a good place to ride out gales and storms; however, it takes about an hour or more to reach the head, so it may be inconvenient for boaters that are pressed for time. The area near Mill Point on the west shore known locally as Port Discovery, was probably the site of Vancouver's original camp.

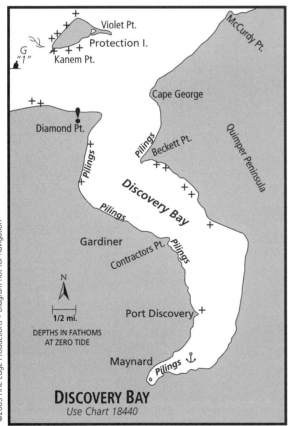

N

1/2 mi.

DEPTHS IN FATHOMS
AT ZERO TIDE

DISCOVERY BAY
Use Chart 18440

Cape George Marina, at the far northeast tip, is operated by the Cape George Colony Club and is private. Its slips are for members only, and the marina does not monitor VHF. The entrance to the marina is narrow and shallow with little inside turning room. The mooring buoys outside the entrance are for members only who must wait outside on low tide for adequate water before entering.

Anchor (off the mud flat) in 8 fathoms over sand and gravel; fair-to-good holding.

Puget Sound (from Point Wilson south) and Admiralty Inlet
Chart 18440; extends about 90 mi S from Str of Juan de Fuca to Olympia

From McCurdy Point, the shore trends east . . . to Point Wilson, the W point at the entrance to Admiralty Inlet, and consists of high, bare, clay bluffs, sparsely wooded on top, decreasing in height near McCurdy Point, and ending abruptly close W to Point Wilson. . . .

Point Wilson Light, . . . 51 feet above the water, is shown from a white octagonal tower on a building on the E extremity of the low point. A fog signal is at the light. . . .

Puget Sound [is] a bay with numerous channels and branches. . . .

Navigation of the area is comparatively easy in clear weather; the outlying dangers are few and marked by aids. The currents follow the general direction of the channels and have considerable velocity. In thick weather, because of the uncertainty of the currents and the great depths which render soundings useless in many places, strangers are advised to take a pilot.

Vessel Traffic Service Puget Sound, operated by the U.S. Coast Guard, has been established in the Strait of Juan de Fuca, E of Port Angeles, and in the waters of Rosario Strait, Admiralty Inlet, Puget Sound, and the navigable waters adjacent to these areas. . . . (CP, 33rd Ed.)

Point Wilson
Chart 18440; 2 mi N of Port Townsend
Position (0.3 mi E of Pt. Wilson): (WA156)
48°08.72'N, 122°44.72'W

Point Wilson is the "choke point" for all traffic entering or leaving Admiralty Inlet and Puget

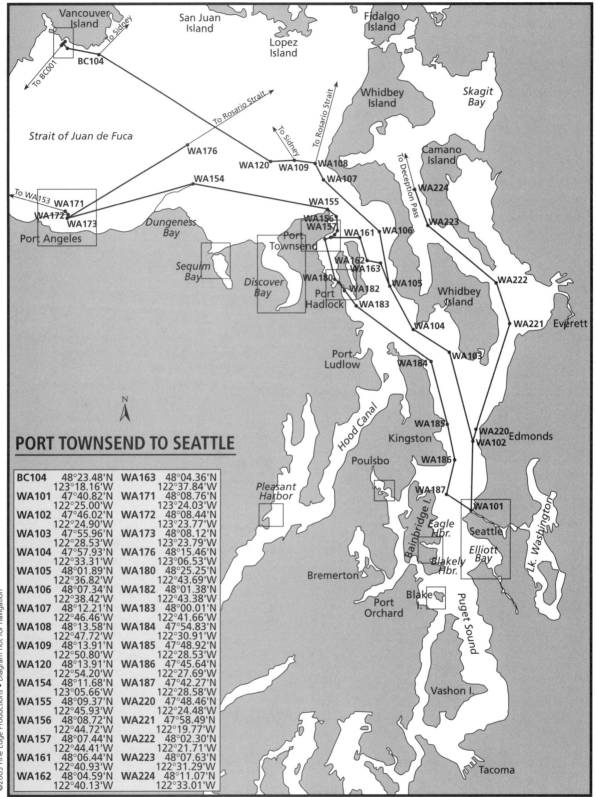

PORT TOWNSEND TO SEATTLE

BC104	48°23.48'N	**WA163**	48°04.36'N
	123°18.16'W		122°37.84'W
WA101	47°40.82'N	**WA171**	48°08.76'N
	122°25.00'W		123°24.03'W
WA102	47°46.02'N	**WA172**	48°08.44'N
	122°24.90'W		123°23.77'W
WA103	47°55.96'N	**WA173**	48°08.12'N
	122°28.53'W		123°23.79'W
WA104	47°57.93'N	**WA176**	48°15.46'N
	122°33.31'W		123°06.53'W
WA105	48°01.89'N	**WA180**	48°25.25'N
	122°36.82'W		122°43.69'W
WA106	48°07.34'N	**WA182**	48°01.38'N
	122°38.42'W		122°43.38'W
WA107	48°12.21'N	**WA183**	48°00.01'N
	122°46.46'W		122°41.66'W
WA108	48°13.58'N	**WA184**	47°54.83'N
	122°47.72'W		122°30.91'W
WA109	48°13.91'N	**WA185**	47°48.92'N
	122°50.80'W		122°28.53'W
WA120	48°13.91'N	**WA186**	47°45.64'N
	122°54.20'W		122°27.69'W
WA154	48°11.68'N	**WA187**	47°42.27'N
	123°05.66'W		122°28.58'W
WA155	48°09.37'N	**WA220**	47°48.46'N
	122°45.93'W		122°24.48'W
WA156	48°08.72'N	**WA221**	47°58.49'N
	122°44.72'W		122°19.77'W
WA157	48°07.44'N	**WA222**	48°02.30'N
	122°44.41'W		122°21.71'W
WA161	48°06.44'N	**WA223**	48°07.63'N
	122°40.93'W		122°31.29'W
WA162	48°04.59'N	**WA224**	48°11.07'N
	122°40.13'W		122°33.01'W

Sound. Because the shipping lanes lead into Admiralty Inlet at this point, crossing the area is a high-performance endeavor, and you and your crew need to be prepared and alert.

Traffic congestion can be severe on either side of Point Wilson and strong turbulence and rip tides on spring tides can cause rough water. In heavy weather, the convergence of freighters, military and commercial vessels, ferries, cruise ships, pleasure craft, and sport-fishing boats adds to congestion and anxiety.

Strait of Juan de Fuca from Baidarka's *pilothouse*

Try to time your approach for Point Wilson and the eastern Strait of Juan de Fuca during a period of good visibility and near slack water. *Baidarka* has made several radar approaches at Point Wilson in near-zero visibility, but it's not much fun. Foghorns blow from all directions and you can easily be as confused as the seas that bounce you around in all directions.

As always, any time you near shipping lanes or need to cross them, check with Vessel Traffic Services for a traffic update. *Note:* South of Point Wilson, use Channel 14; in the Strait of Juan de Fuca, use Channel 5A.

Due to the converging shipping lanes, and with commercial ships having complete priority in their lanes, pleasure craft must know their exact position at all times. Avoid crossing shipping lanes, as much as possi-

ble, and yield to all larger craft (see Rule 10). *Caution:* Large ships have the right-of-way from

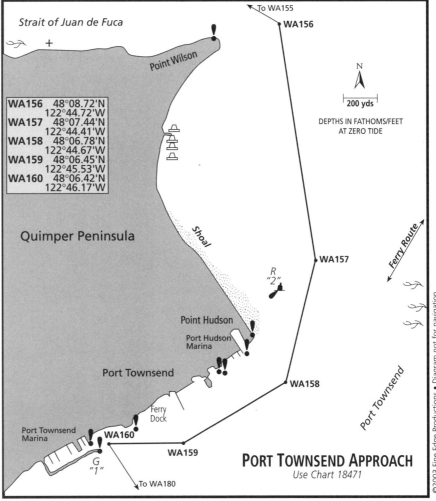

WA156	48°08.72'N 122°44.72'W
WA157	48°07.44'N 122°44.41'W
WA158	48°06.78'N 122°44.67'W
WA159	48°06.45'N 122°45.53'W
WA160	48°06.42'N 122°46.17'W

PORT TOWNSEND APPROACH
Use Chart 18471

©2003 Fine Edge Productions • Diagram not for navigation

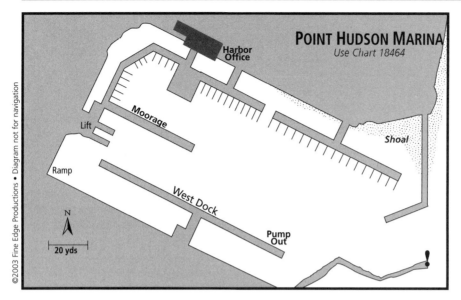

©2003 Fine Edge Productions • Diagram not for navigation

POINT HUDSON MARINA
Use Chart 18464

Harbor Office

Lift

Moorage

Ramp

West Dock

Shoal

Pump Out

N

20 yds

Townsend Bay, is a private marina convenient for boaters seeking sailboat rigging, sail-loft and specialized services. It is also a major kayak and canoe center and home to the Wooden Boat Festival, a popular annual event that completely fills the marinas and motels the first weekend after Labor Day in September.

The Wooden Boat Foundation, located in the harbor, is a great resource for all aspects of boat-building, seamanship and small-boat handling; here, you can watch vessels-in-progress, browse their library or make purchases at their chandlery and maritime bookstore. The harbor, with its surrounding buildings, is reminiscent of a tiny seafaring village with white clapboard houses and a quiet, relaxed ambience. As we go to press, major plans that include additional RV and camping sites, and expansion of motel facilities are in store for Point Hudson Harbor.

The entrance to the harbor is very narrow, with little if any passing room; once you enter, you're committed!

a quarter-mile off Point Wilson all the way east to a mile off Admiralty Head at the Keystone Ferry dock. (Skippers may find *Proven Cruising Routes,* published by FineEdge.com and the companion waypoints disk for Nobeltec systems, a help in minimizing exposure to shipping lanes and in transiting the urban areas between Victoria, Seattle, Vancouver and points north.)

Port Townsend, 2 miles south of Point Wilson, and a major cruising destination, is an excellent place to wait for optimal conditions when cruising in the vicinity.

Point Hudson Harbor (Port Townsend)
Chart 18464; 1.8 mi S of Point Wilson
Entrance (harbor): 48°06.96'N, 122°44.98'W

Point Hudson Harbor, just W of Point Hudson, is leased by the Port of Port Townsend to a private company. The entrance, protected by jetties, is marked by a private light on the end of the S jetty. Over 100 small-craft berths, electricity, water, ice and marine supplies are available. Hull and engine repairs for small craft can be made. In 1973, reported depths of 15 feet were available through the entrance of the harbor and to the hoist at the NW end of the basin.

The terminus of the Port Townsend-Keystone ferry is 0.7 mile WSW of Point Hudson harbor. (CP, 33rd Ed.)

Point Hudson Harbor, immediately west of Point Hudson at the northern end of Port

Washington State Department of Ecology

Aerial view: Port Hudson and Port Townsend waterfront

Port Hudson Harbor, Port Townsend

Port Townsend offers well-sheltered waters, a large busy marina, and several anchor sites at both the north and south ends of the bay. Every conceivable pleasure craft repair and outfitting service can be found in Port Townsend; this is a serious cruiser's destination.

The Port of Port Townsend maintains guest slips for vessels, along with complete services and facilities; Port Townsend Yacht Club is active and very friendly.

Groceries, restaurants, and picnicking spots are nearby. The harbor hosts over 6,000 visiting boats each year.

The city boasts a National Landmark Historic District along its waterfront (Old Town), and an abundance of outstanding Victorian-era homes. A healthy, small-town atmosphere is coupled with a thriving cultural and entertainment scene, year-round, that includes a Blues Festival, Jazz Festival, Wooden Boat Festival, Rhododendron Festival, Port Townsend Film Festival, and the Port Townsend Art Festival.

The approach to Port Townsend is made favoring the north shore, avoiding the shoal

While some temporary anchorage in fair weather can be found north of Point Hudson and south of Point Wilson, you must avoid the drying shoal that extends 300 yards from shore north of Point Hudson. Anchorage in the vicinity can also be found off the center of Port Townsend, as noted below.

Port Townsend

Chart 18464; 2 mi S of Point Wilson
Entrance (Boat Haven Marina): (WA160)
48°06.42'N, 122°46.17'W
Anchor (NE of public pier): 48°06.68'N,
122°45.42'W

> *Port Townsend . . . is entered between Point Hudson and Marrowstone Point. It extends in a general SSW direction for 2.5 miles, and then turns SSE for 3 miles, with a reduced width to its head. Inside Point Hudson, depths generally range from 5 to 20 fathoms. It is an excellent harbor and is easily entered. The prevailing winds in summer are from W to SW, and in winter are generally in the SE quadrant. . . .*
>
> *Port Townsend, the principal town, is on the W shore immediately W of Point Hudson. . . .*
>
> *The usual anchorage is about 0.5 to 0.7 mile S of the railroad ferry landing in 8 to 10 fathoms, muddy bottom. In S gales better anchorage is afforded closer inshore off the N end of Marrowstone Island or near the head of the bay in moderate depths, muddy bottom. (CP, 33rd Ed.)*

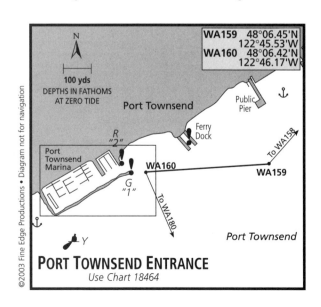

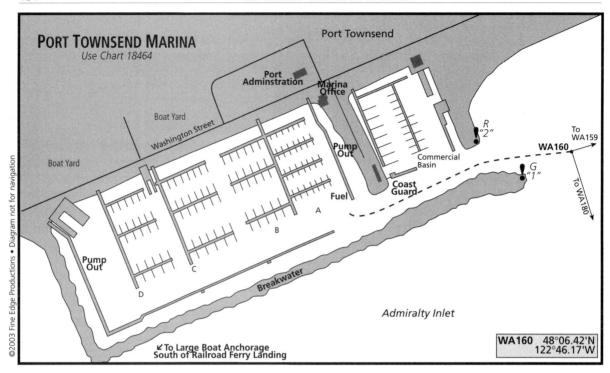

and kelp patches north of Marrowstone Point. Visiting yachts can find anchorage south of the old railroad pier (immediately southwest of the Port Townsend Marina); we also see boats anchoring just outside—but clear of—the marina entrance where access and landing are easier. Some pleasure craft anchor between Port Townsend and Point Wilson; while the northwest corner of this small bight is good in westerlies, it does receive more wake from freighters and is even more exposed to southeast winds than Port Townsend Bay.

Baidarka's favorite temporary anchorage lies off Old Town; at this site there's good access to the public dinghy dock and downtown businesses. Most of the several anchor sites are useful only during prevailing northwesterlies and are not satisfactory in southerly weather. In fact, the bay can occasionally be dangerous in strong southerlies. Every year or two we hear of a boat being blown onto the beach during a southeast gale. If you are well anchored and don't mind an occasional ferry wake, you may like it in pleasant weather, but you should *not* leave your boat here for any extended time or overnight without a responsible person aboard.

For more protection from southeast weather and for a quieter site, Port Hadlock can be used as an alternative to Port Townsend.

Anchor (NE of public pier) in 8 to 9 fathoms over sand and mud; fair-to-good holding.

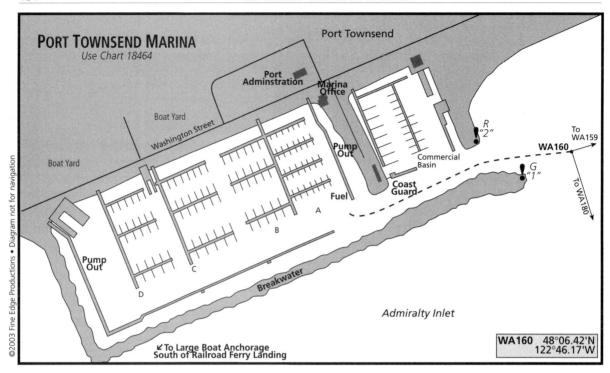

Aerial view: Port Townsend Boat Haven

City anchor site on Port Townsend waterfront

Busy entrance to Port Townsend Boat Haven

Endeavor at Port Townsend waterfront

Port Hadlock
Chart 18464; 5 mi S of Port Townsend
Anchor: 48°01.90'N, 122°44.89'W

Port Hadlock, a village at the head of the harbor, has landings with depths of 10 feet and 12 feet. The Port of Port Townsend maintains a mooring float during the summer. Submerged pilings are in the vicinity of the mooring float, and local knowledge is necessary to avoid them. A marina, 0.4 mile SW of the N entrance to the Port Townsend Canal has berths for over 155 craft; water and electricity are available. (CP, 33rd Ed.)

Port Hadlock, located at the far end of Port Townsend Bay just west of the north entrance to Port Townsend Canal, is an alternative when Port Townsend is too busy or crowded. Good shelter in a quiet, protected setting can be found here. The Canal (called "The Cut") is a smooth-water alternative to Admiralty Inlet for boats en route to Hood Canal. *Caution*: A Navy Ammunition Depot is located on Indian Island near Crane Point; boaters are advised to stay clear of the north end of the island by 1,000 feet to avoid the restricted area; since 11 September 2001, this area is being patrolled.

The marina lies 100 yards east of Skunk Island and somewhat offshore due to the shallow mud flats that fill this end of the bay. You can enter the marina at the end of the breakwater; however, the water is shallow so approach extremely slowly.

The channel has a fairway of 25 yards and carries about 12 feet minimum. To transit, we recommend lining up with the channel at waypoint WA181 when heading south, or WA182 when heading north. GPS and electronic charts

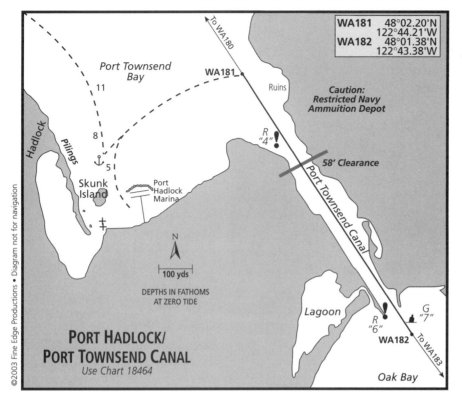

WA181   48°02.20'N
        122°44.21'W
WA182   48°01.38'N
        122°43.38'W

Port Townsend Bay

11

Hadlock

pilings

8

5

Skunk Island

Port Hadlock Marina

Ruins

Caution:
Restricted Navy
Ammuition Depot

R "4"

58' Clearance

Port Townsend Canal

To WA180

To WA181

N

100 yds

DEPTHS IN FATHOMS
AT ZERO TIDE

Lagoon

R "6"

WA182

G "7"

To WA183

Oak Bay

**PORT HADLOCK/
PORT TOWNSEND CANAL**
Use Chart 18464

©2003 Fine Edge Productions • Diagram not for navigation

round marina located at the old Alcohol Plant, consists mainly of permanent moorage; it can accommodate guest boaters on a limited, space-available basis only. Provisions are nearby within walking distance; the closest fuel dock is at Port Townsend. If you're arriving late at night, just tie up at one of the empty docks until the marina staff arrives in the morning.

Anchorage can be found outside the marina, 100 yards or so north of Skunk Island, avoiding private buoys and the shoals.

do a good job of positioning in this area. (We have observed an interesting peculiarity of The Cut: the current flows north (ebb current) for about two-thirds of a tidal cycle.)

The Port Hadlock Inn and Marina, a year-

Anchor in 8 fathoms over mud and shells with good holding.

⚓ **Port Hadlock Inn & Marina** tel: 360-385-6368; monitors Channel 16.

Washington State Department of Ecology

Aerial view: North end of Port Townsend Canal with Port Hadlock Marina in background

Port Ludlow

Chart 18477; 12 mi S of Port Townsend
Entrance (NE of Colvos Rock):
47°57.32'N, 122°40.36'W
Position (Marina): 47°55.30'N,
122°41.17'W
Anchor (The Twins): 47°54.93'N,
122°41.76'W
Anchor (outer bay): 47°55.02'N,
122°41.18'W

The entrance to Port Ludlow, in the W part of Admiralty Inlet, is just W of Colvos Rocks on the W side at the entrance to Hood Canal. From the broad entrance the bay extends in the general S direction 2.5 miles, terminating in a basin 0.5 mile in diameter. The basin affords good anchorage in 40-50 feet, soft bottom; the shores are fairly steep. (CP, 33rd Ed.)

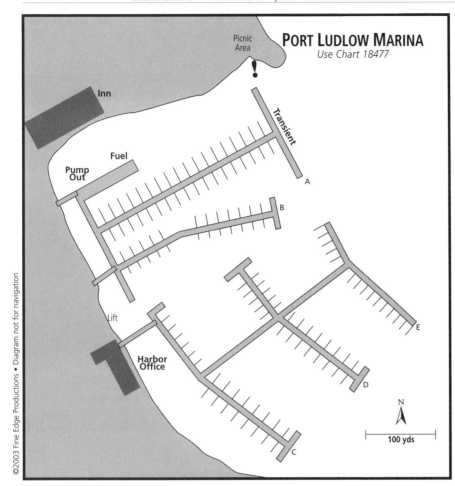

Picnic Area

PORT LUDLOW MARINA
Use Chart 18477

Inn

Transient

Fuel

Pump Out

A

B

Lift

E

Harbor Office

D

N

100 yds

C

©2003 Fine Edge Productions • Diagram not for navigation

oms minimum) lies west of Colvos Rocks, avoiding Snake Rocks, 0.35 mile southwest of Colvos Rocks Light and Klas Rocks, 0.6 mile north. Turn west and round Burner Point; the marina, which is hidden by Burner Point, is on the starboard hand.

On a northbound transit from Hood Canal, small vessels should remain at least 0.5 mile north of Tala Point, taking nun buoy R"2" to starboard and avoiding all kelp patches; the channel carries 3 fathoms.

Anchorage with unlimited swinging room can be found in suitable depths almost anywhere around the outer bay. At the bitter southwest end of the inner

Port Ludlow has developed into a cruising and resort destination from a once-proud lumber town. Well sheltered from all weather, it is a quiet, beautiful place, as Michelle Gaylord's sidebar confirms. While it is somewhat remote and without repair and outfitting facilities, it is a great place to unwind and stretch unused muscles by kayaking, swimming, biking, hiking, or playing tennis; there is also a golf course here.

The Resort at Ludlow Bay Marina has over 300 slips for permanent and guest boaters and side ties for vessels up to 180 feet; facilities include water and power, showers, fuel, pumpout, kayak and sea cycle rental, and limited supplies. Reservations are advised.

Approaching Port Ludlow from the north, pay close attention to Chart 18477 and to Colvos Rocks, a reef with a number of submerged rocks. The deep-water route (12 fath-

Port Townsend
by Michelle Gaylord

After another peaceful ride, we tied up in Port Townsend's Boat Haven Marina and were surrounded by every conceivable type of boat repair, fabrication, yard, and maintenance facility imaginable. This is definitely the place to stop for repairs or maintenance. One afternoon we caught a shuttle into Old Town. The Victorian architecture here is abundant, and the city is recognized as one of only three Victorian seaports on the National Historic Register. It's a lovely, quaint little town with many unique and quality galleries and boutiques. While we were there, the town was getting ready for the famous Wooden Boat Show held every year and the *Endeavor* arrived in port just for the boat show. We decided not to fight the crowds and left before the big event, but we heard it's quite a production.

Aerial view: Port Ludlow Harbor

ty along the east shore. Since this area has now become popular, you may find The Twins more desirable off-season.

Anchor (The Twins) in 2 fathoms over mud with good holding; limited swinging room.

Anchor (outer bay) in about 8 fathoms over mud with good holding.

⚓ **The Resort at Ludlow Bay Marina** open 0800-1700; summer weekends 0700-2100; tel: 360.437.0513; fax: 360.437.2428; email: marina@ludlow-baymarina.com; website: www.ludlow-bayresort.com; monitors Channels 16 and 68

bay, between the two islets known as The Twins, there is a particularly scenic anchor site that offers bombproof shelter. Enter through a narrow, shallow channel between The Twins that leads to a 2-fathom hole on their south side; avoid a rock south of the smaller island. This intimate, landlocked site resembles a pond. Anchor in 2 fathoms avoiding the Meydenbauer Bay Yacht Club outstation facili-

---

Ludlow Bay
by Michelle Gaylord

Our run from Port Townsend to Port Ludlow was only 16 miles, and we opted to take the route inside Indian Island, through a very narrow, shallow canal. The weather was perfect—warm, sunny, no wind, and clear visibility. After we'd been anchored for about an hour, Jerry said, "I think we've found Shangri-la." I wish I could have put into words the beauty of the area. There wasn't much other than recreational activities—golf courses, tennis courts, swimming pools, squash courts, boat and kayak rentals. It's pretty much a 'yuppie' bedroom community, with beautiful houses and condos built along the shores.

We were still getting a grasp on the fact that we were in the Strait of Juan de Fuca, at the entrance to Puget Sound just across the channel from Canada, and within an hour's travel time to the San Juan and Gulf Islands—*so* much to see and do! We could hardly see each other over the pile of books and charts we'd accumulated. The most frustrating part of the trip was trying to decide where to go next!

Hood Canal
Charts 18445, 18476, 18458

The entrance to Hood Canal is at the lower end of Admiralty Inlet between Foulweather Bluff and Tala Point, about 10 miles S of Marrowstone Point. It extends in a general S direction for about 44 miles and then bends sharply NE for 11 miles, terminating in flats bare at low water. The head of Case Inlet, in the S part of Puget Sound, is less than 2 miles from the head of Hood Canal. The shores are high, bold, and wooded, and the water is deep, except at the heads of the bays and at the mouth of the streams. Many small craft ply these waters. There are mostly small float-landings and private docks in the canal. Gasoline is available at numerous resorts and marinas. (CP, 33rd Ed.)

Hood Canal, a restful introduction to the

Port Ludlow Marina as seen from the outer anchor site

Aerial view: Port Ludlow Twins anchor site

Pleasant Harbor
Chart 18458; 18 mi S of Hood Canal
Bridge
Entrance: 47°39.96'N, 122°54.37'W
Anchor: 47°39.65'N, 122°55.11'W

Pleasant Harbor is a small cove on the W shore of Hood Canal about 3 miles W of Misery Point. It is about 300 yards wide, and has a narrow shallow entrance. Owing to the narrowness of the entrance, boats should keep in midchannel until clear of the 6-foot shoal. Two marinas inside the harbor have berths for about 250 craft, electricity, gasoline, water, ice, and limited supplies. Anchorage in about 36 feet, mud bottom is available inside the harbor. A state park pier is in the harbor. (CP, 33rd Ed.)

Pleasant Harbor's name is well-deserved. Surrounded by trees, it is an all-weather harbor, pleasant and quiet, with a marina at its head. There is also good anchorage nearby.

The entrance to Pleasant Harbor is narrow and shallow. Enter north of Black Point through a narrow fairway that lies mid-channel with drying mud flats on either side. The channel carries only about 6 feet at low water, and deep-draft vessels could have problems on a minus tide; local inquiry is advised. The bay itself has between 3 and 6 fathoms.

Pleasant Harbor Marina, open year-round seven days a week, is a destination resort with

Northwest, is mostly rural and quiet. An atomic submarine base is located on the east shore at Bangor and, occasionally, you may pass one of these ships escorted by one or more USCG frigates. Do not approach closely—the subs can produce a large wake when traveling on the surface. The west shore of Hood Canal, which sits in the rain shadow of the Olympics, is an important viniculture area. Pleasant Harbor, 18 miles south of the Hood Canal Bridge, is one of the most secure and easy-going destinations in this area.

full services (water, electricity, showers, laundry, fuel, pump-out) and a well-stocked store with groceries and deli. Reservations are encouraged for the high-traffic summer months and in May during shrimping season. Outside of the busy season, this harbor is a quiet, peaceful stop on a cruise through Hood Canal. As we go to press, expansion plans

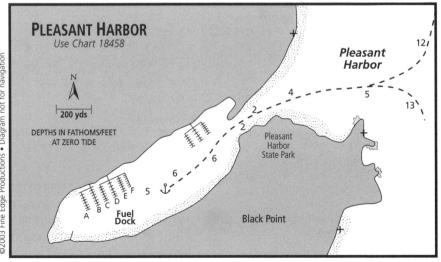

Washington State Department of Ecology

Aerial view: Pleasant Harbor

that include a conference center and an 18-hole golf course are underway.

Pleasant Harbor Marine State Park, the small cove on your starboard hand upon entering, has limited moorage without facilities other than pump-out.

Michelle Gaylord

Pleasant Harbor Marina in Hood Canal

Anchor in 3 fathoms, over sand and mud; fair-to-good holding; limited swinging room.

⚓ **Pleasant Harbor Marina** open year round 0800-1900; tel: 360.796.4611; 800.547.3479; fax: 360.796.4898; website; www.pleasantharbormarina.com; monitors channels 16 and 09

⚓ **Pleasant Harbor Marine State Park** tel: 360.902.8844

GREATER SEATTLE AREA
Port of Seattle
Charts 18450, 18449 and 18474; 98 mi SE of Neah Bay

The outer saltwater harbor (of Seattle) *includes Elliott Bay; East, West, and Duwamish Waterways; Shilshole Bay, and the portions of Puget Sound adjacent to Ballard on the N and West Seattle to the S of the entrance of Elliott Bay. Seattle's freshwater inner harbor consists of Lakes Union and Washington, which are connected with each other and with Puget Sound by the Lake Washington Ship Canal.*

Elliott Bay indents the E shore of Puget Sound just N of Duwamish Head. The entrance is between West Point of the N and Alki Point 5 miles S. The bay proper, lying E of a line between Magnolia Bluff and Duwamish Head has a width of about 2 miles and extends SE for nearly the same distance. The bay is deep through most of its area. (CP, 33rd Ed.)

The Port of Seattle is the center of Seattle's considerable shipping industry and one of the busiest ports in the world. As such, it attracts commercial shipping from all over the world, especially the Pacific Rim. Traffic in the bay includes ferry traffic, tugboats—often with tows—and commercial vessels of all shapes and sizes. Most commercial activity in the bay takes place at piers 89, 90, and 91, and in the Harbor Island area to the south.

Busy Elliott Bay Marina in Seattle

Seattle's waterfront extends 6.5 miles from Shilshole Marina south to Alki Point. The major cruising marinas—north to south—are Shilshole, Elliott Bay and Bell Harbor. The landmark Space Needle is located in a low pass, 1.5 miles east of Elliott Bay Marina.

There are four federally designated anchorage areas off the Seattle waterfront.

"Lake Tahoe" in Hood Canal
by Michelle Gaylord

Just when we thought it couldn't possibly get any better, well it did. We left Port Ludlow for Pleasant Harbor in the Hood Canal and the first thing that went through my mind when we got there was, "We've arrived at Lake Tahoe." The entrance to the harbor leads through a tiny, narrow inlet and, of course, we arrived at low tide with only 3 feet of water under our keel. Once we were inside, the harbor opened up into a beautiful emerald-green "lake," surrounded by evergreen trees. The harbor itself is only about 300 yards wide and a quarter-mile long.

As we cruised down the Hood Canal, the snow-capped Olympic Mountains were visible for our entire trip. For some reason, very few pleasure craft take advantage of the Hood Canal, I guess because there are so few good anchorages and even fewer facilities for boaters. It's a dead-end canal and you must retrace your course to exit. Due to the lack of boats, and the fact that most of the canal is isolated and undeveloped, we felt like Lewis and Clark traversing uncharted territory. En route, we passed the Bangor nuclear submarine station, which was quite awesome. We were told that unscheduled maneuvers are carried out, so there was always a chance we'd come face to face with one of those leviathans, but we had no such luck.

Unlike Port Ludlow, Pleasant Harbor has very few houses along the shoreline. A handful of private docks and ramps appear to grow right out of the woods, with no sign of life at the other end. The woods and trees are so dense there I assumed there were houses hidden behind and that we just weren't able to see them. The minute we stepped off the dock we were in the forest. There are narrow, gravel-lined paths that cut through the trees; no roads, no parking lots or cars. At the top of the main ramp there was a little Cape Cod-type shack that served nothing but clam chowder in a sourdough bowl, espresso, and root beer floats! Just after we tied up, a seaplane arrived, floated up to the fuel dock, filled up, and then took off again. So, not only did we have to dodge deadheads, freighters, other boats, wildlife, and submarines, we also had to keep an eye out for floating aircraft! (*Editor's Note:* Michelle and Jerry's experience in 1999 pre-dates the present facilities!)

Passing Thru at the Pleasant Harbor Marina

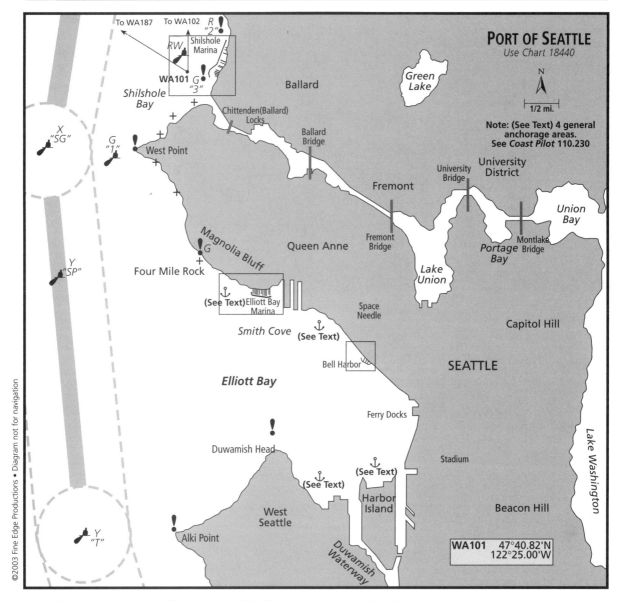

Vessels under Vessel Traffic Services (VTS) have priority. The most northerly site—Smith Cove West—due west and adjacent to Elliott Bay Marina off Magnolia Bluff—is useful only as a temporary site in calm weather. Anchorage can be found inside the 10-fathom curve about 150 yards off the beach; this site is open and exposed to all weather and chop from west through southeast, as well as to wake from all sizes of vessels. This site can be useful in emergencies or when temporary anchorage is needed.

The second site—Smith Cove East—east of the Elliott Bay Marina and Pier 89, although somewhat less exposed, is subject to large-vessel traffic.

The third—East Waterway—is a deep-water site in the south end of Elliott Bay, north of Harbor Island; this site has protection from southeast gales.

The fourth (West Waterway), between Duwamish Head and West Waterway is protected from both southwest and southeast gales.

Most of these four sites require anchoring in deep water, but you may find temporary anchorage in 10 fathoms close to shore, as long as you don't impede traffic. See Note A on Chart

18474 or consult paragraph 110.230 (Puget Sound Area, Washington) in *Coast Pilot*. These general anchorage areas are under the control of VTS. *All four anchor sites are exposed and are not for long-term anchorage. It is not advised to leave your boat unattended. And again, we remind you, you must anchor so as not to impede traffic. At night you must display proper lights.* For further information, call VTS on Channel 14 and ask for the Watch Supervisor, or call 206.217.6152 direct.

Pier 36, south of the ferry dock, houses the U.S. Coast Guard Seattle Headquarters, the Coast Guard Museum, and Vessel Traffic Services. The piers along the central waterfront have been renovated and "upgraded" for tourist activities, with Myrtle Edwards Park bordering the water at the north end of this strip. Bell Harbor is centrally located at Pier 66.

Shilshole Bay and Marina
Chart 18447; 29 mi SE of Port Townsend
Approach waypoint (WA101): 47°40.82'N, 122°25.00'W
Entrance (S): 47°40.61'N, 122°24.67'W
Entrance (N): 47°41.29'N, 122°24.27'W
Position (marina transient dock): 47°40.87'N, 122°24.46'W

Shilshole Bay Marina, the small-craft basin just N of the canal entrance, is administered by the Port of Seattle. A 4,400-foot breakwater, market at each end by a light, protects the basin on its W side. The basin has two entrances. . . .

In June 1998, the reported controlling depths were 15 feet in the N and S entrances, depths alongside the floats in the basin were about 10 feet. (CP, 33rd Ed.)

Shilshole Bay, the large open bight between Meadow Point and West Point, has Shilshole Marina and the Lake Washington Ship Canal at

---

Seattle
by Michelle Gaylord

We *loved* Seattle. Although one or both of us has previously visited many of these cities, we got an entirely new perspective arriving by sea. With the Space Needle dominating the skyline, it was almost as exciting as entering San Francisco Bay, except we didn't have to go under a big red bridge. We got a slip at the Bell Harbor Marina, which is right downtown and within easy walking distance to everything.

While in Seattle we took a city tour, walked along the wharves, had dinner at the top of the Space Needle where there's a breathtaking view of the city at night,

and spent lots of time at the Pike Place open-air market. We had never experienced any place like this. It was an extravaganza featuring a little bit of everything, including produce fresh from the farm, fresh seafood, baked goods, arts, crafts and antiques. Pike Place is an indoor-outdoor market that encompasses more than seven acres, three floors and over 300 stalls, 100 farmers, and more than 200 artists and craftspeople. They say it serves more than nine million shoppers per year and is the oldest continuously operating farmers' market in the U.S.

Passing Thru *moored at the Bell Harbor Marina in downtown Seatle*

Fresh crab at Seattle's Pike Street Market

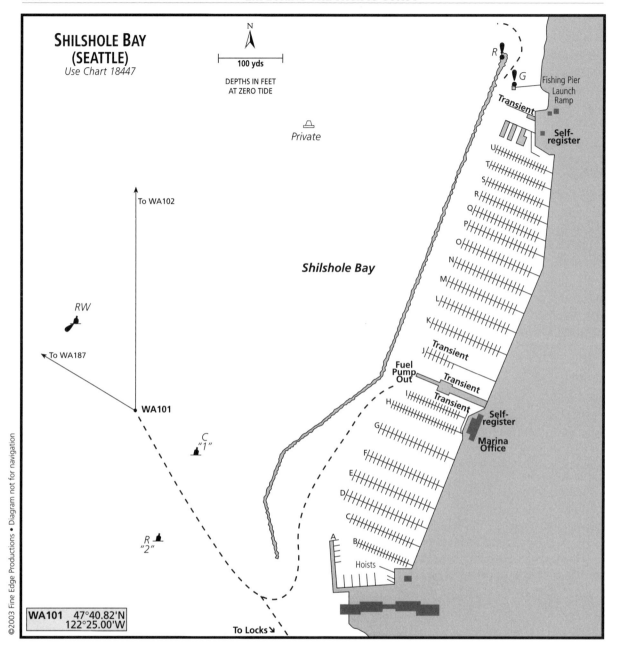

SHILSHOLE BAY
(SEATTLE)
Use Chart 18447

N

100 yds

DEPTHS IN FEET
AT ZERO TIDE

Private

To WA102

Shilshole Bay

RW

To WA187

WA101

C
"1"

R
"2"

WA101   47°40.82'N
122°25.00'W

To Locks ↘

©2003 Fine Edge Productions • Diagram not for navigation

Fishing Pier
Launch
Ramp

R

G

Transient

Self-register

U
T
S
R
Q
P
O
N
M
L
K
J
Transient
Fuel
Pump
Out
Transient
Transient
I
H
Self-register
G
Marina
Office
F
E
D
C
B
A
Hoists

its mid-point. Shilshole Marina, the largest marina in the Seattle area, is well protected by a 4,400-foot breakwater that can be entered at either end. The Hiram M. Chittenden Locks 0.75 mile southeast of Shilshole Bay—known as the Ballard Locks—separate the fresh- and saltwater boating areas, giving access to Lakes Union and Washington. (See below.) During the busy summer months the locks are a buzz of activity.

Facilities include water and power, showers, laundry, fuel dock with pump-out, and hazardous waste and oil disposal. Also on-site or nearby are a boatyard for structural or engine repair, restaurants, marine supply stores, and chandleries. The marina prides itself for its reputation as one of Washington State's most environmentally conscious marinas. Reservations are advised but taken only 3 days in advance.

Speed inside the breakwater is limited to 4

Hiram M. Chittenden Locks (Ballard Locks)
Charts 18447; 0.75 mi SE of Shilshole Bay

Lake Washington Ship Canal extends from Puget Sound through Shilshole Bay, Salmon Bay, Lake Union, Portage Bay, and Union Bay to deep water in Lake Washington. Federal project depth through the canal is 30 feet, which is generally maintained. (See Notice to Mariners and latest editions of charts for controlling depths.) The entrance to Lake Washington Ship Canal is market by a lighted range, lights and buoys. A speed limit of 4 knots is enforced within the guided piers of the Hiram M. Chittenden Locks. A speed limit of 7 knots is enforced elsewhere in the Lake Washington Ship Canal except in an area market by four private buoys in the N part of Lake Union. (CP, 33rd Ed.)

If you're heading to Lake Union or farther east to Lake Washington, you're in for an encounter with the Hiram M. Chittendon Locks, known locally as the Ballard Locks or simply "The Locks." Over 100,000 commercial and pleasure craft make this passage each year, rising or lowering anywhere from 6 to 26 feet—depending on the tide and lake level—to connect with Ship Canal, the freshwater channel that leads to Lake Union. The two parallel locks fill and drain by gravity using underwater culverts, and each carries traffic in both directions.

To enter the Ship Canal, make for the dredged channel entrance marked by the red-and-white-striped ("RW") Ballard buoy. Pass under the Burlington Northern bascule bridge, which is kept open unless a train is due. The opening signal is one long and one short blast. Pay close attention to the stop signals for the small and large locks, as indicated on Chart 18447.

Aerial view: Shilshole Marina South entrance

knots (no wake) and no sailing is permitted. The marina is home to *Northwest Yachting* and *Sea Kayaker* magazines. Just north of the marina, past the public boat ramp, is the beautiful Golden Gardens Park.

⚓ **Shilshole Marina Office** open year round 0800-1630 M-F; 0800-1300 Sat; tel: 206.728.3006; fax: 206.728.3391; website: www.portseattle.org; email: sbm@portseattle.org; monitors Channel 17

Aerial view: Shilshole Marina; entrance to Chittenden Locks lies to the south (right)

Aerial view: Chittenden Locks in Ballard

Boats are admitted to the locks on a strict priority basis, which means that vessels arriving after you have may go through before you (pleasure craft are near the last on the priority list). The priority is as follows: 1) government ves- sels; 2) commercial vessels carrying passengers on scheduled runs; 3) commercial vessels of all types; 4) pleasure boats; 5) log tows.

Preparation is the key to a successful lock passage. The Locks personnel note that they generally see two types of boaters: those who are very knowledgeable and experienced; and those who don't know the first thing about boating. *Locking-Through* programs are offered from April to September and January to March each year. Problems arise when boats don't have the necessary equipment, such as enough lines or fenders on both sides, or when boats don't have enough crew to handle the lines. (Safety also depends upon which vessels squeeze in with you and how skilled they are in boat handling.)

For a safe, even enjoyable transit, have your

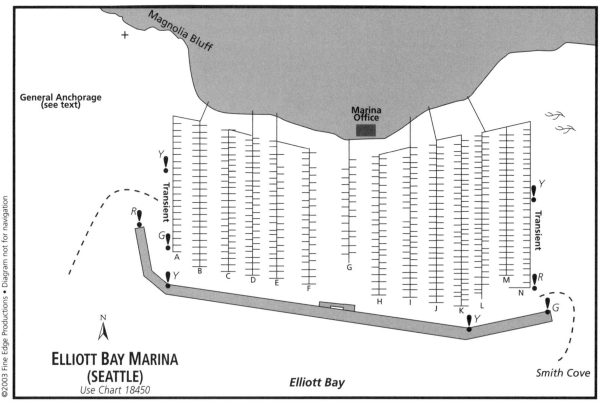

fenders and line in place (and know how to use them!); be prepared to have other boats tie up against you; don't be in a hurry; relax and enjoy the experience. *Baidarka*'s crew has found each of our many transits different and interesting. We have transited the locks several times in our tandem sea kayak and found it exciting to say the least!

Note: To inquire about *Locking-Through* classes or to request the brochure *Guideline for Boaters*, telephone the Lockmaster at 206.789.2622 or visit the website: www.nws.usac.army.mil/opdiv/wsc

Salty trawler plying Puget Sound

Elliott Bay Marina

Chart 18450; 3.25 mi S of Shilshole Marina
Entrance (marina W): 47°37.74'N, 122°23.83'W
Entrance (marina E): 47°37.66, 122°23.21'W
Anchor: 47°37.85'N, 122°23.94'W

Perfectly maintained and tastefully appointed Elliott Bay Marina, located off Magnolia Bluff just north of downtown Seattle, is open year-round. The marina features 1,200 slips ranging in size from 32 to 63 feet, as well as end-ties that can accommodate virtually any size yacht. Not least among its attractions is a panoramic view encompassing the Olympic Peninsula, Mt. Rainier, and downtown Seattle.

In addition to full amenities at Elliott Bay Marina, fuel, pump-out, hazardous waste disposal, and 24-hour security are provided. There are three restaurants above the floats, including one of our favorite Japanese restaurants. By car it's five minutes to downtown Seattle, and there's a scenic bike and walking path that runs along the Myrtle Edwards Park. Reservations are preferred, so it's a good idea to call ahead.

Temporary anchorage is available in Seattle General Anchorage area as noted above under Port of Seattle. The nearest sheltered anchorage is Blakely Harbor, 6 miles to the west.

⚓ **Elliott Bay Marina** open year-round 0800-sunset; tel: 206.285.4817; fax: 206.282.0626; monitors Channel 78A

Bell Harbor Marina

Chart 18450; 2 mi SE of Elliott Bay Marina
Entrance: 47°36.60'N, 122°20.91'W

For easy access to downtown Seattle there's no more convenient place to tie up than lovely new Bell Harbor Marina at the Bell Street Pier. Guest moorage is available for up to 70 vessels in slips ranging from 30 to 120 feet; reservations are accepted for stays exceeding 24 hours. Behind the breakwater are wide concrete docks with

---

Bell Street Pier

BELL HARBOR MARINA
Use Chart 18450
(not shown on chart)

C
B
A

Harbor Office

N

200 yds

DEPTHS IN FATHOMS
AT ZERO TIDE

Elliott Bay

©2003 Fine Edge Productions • Diagram not for navigation

security, water, showers, electricity, garbage and recycling, restrooms, and pump-out.

There's no fuel available here; the nearest is at Elliott Bay Marina to the north. Bell Harbor accepts reservations either by phone or online, and it's smart to check ahead for space availability. Marina staff advise against tying up at night on weekends, as empty slips may be reserved. This 24/7 operation is a great place to stay when you want to visit Seattle's downtown area.

It's only a short walk or bus ride to the shopping district, restaurants, the Seattle Center (home of the Space Needle), Pike Place Public Market, Benaroya Symphony Hall, the Odyssey Maritime Discovery Center, the Seattle Art Museum and the Seattle Aquarium. You can visit historic Pioneer Square, take a tour of underground Seattle, or catch a bus out to Safeco Field for a Mariners' game. The pier

itself offers restaurants and scenic plazas with breathtaking views, and there are nearby jogging paths, and public parks.

⚓ **Bell Harbor Marina** tel: 206.615.3952; fax: 206.615.3965; website: www.portseattle.org; email: bhm@portseattle.org; monitors Channel 66A

PUGET SOUND WEST (North to South)

For boaters who prefer alternatives to Seattle, we offer just a few selections among numerous possibilities. (Please refer to the Bibliography for a list of helpful references on the entire Puget Sound area.)

Kingston (Appletree Cove)
Charts 18446, 18445; 22 mi SE of Port Townsend
Entrance (Marina): 47°47.57'N, 122°29.94'W

Appletree Cove is the open bight on the W side of

Kingston—A Convenient Stop
by Michelle Gaylord

Kingston was really nothing more than a ferry landing, but it was a convenient stop on our way into South Puget Sound. We stayed at the Kingston Cove Yacht Club guest dock, which was only about 75 yards from the ferry dock, so we saw a lot of pedestrian and automobile activity. The small commercial area around the ferry dock was limited to a few small shops and lots of ice cream stands. It seemed everyone on the bay-front had an ice cream cone and was wandering around licking up a storm.

We laid over in Kingston for a few days waiting for mail delivery and had a chance to talk to various locals. We asked them for recommendations on a dry spot to hole up for the winter, and they either looked at us like we were making some smart aleck remark or they laughed hysterically. So, we had to base our decision on the proximity of stores. If we were going to have to fight the elements on foot for a carton of milk or a bottle of gin, we wanted it to be close.

Since entering the Strait of Juan de Fuca, the weather had been gorgeous—sunny with flat seas. (We began to think it was a bad day if we got a one-foot wind chop.) I didn't realize how rough the waters had been coming up the coast until we encountered these waters that are protected by so many islands and landmasses. My bruises and the lumps on my head disappeared, and

I was able to prepare gourmet meals underway when the mood hit.

One of the greatest marital-aid gadgets I bought along the way was a pair of cordless earphones for the TV. Those earphones alone made *Passing Thru* a happy home. Jerry could sit endlessly in the evenings flipping channels to his heart's content, and I could listen to my classical music while I played on the computer or read. Had it not been for this marvelous piece of technology, one of us would probably have done some physical harm to the other.

Passing Thru *enjoys Kingston Marina*

the sound about 1.5 miles S of Apple Cove Point. It affords anchorage in 30 to 60 feet inside the line of the entrance points with some shelter from winds drawing in or out of the sound, but not from N and SE. Shoaling to 18 feet exists about 0.2 mile S to SE of the end of Kingston breakwater. (CP, 33rd Ed.)

Kingston, across the Sound from Edmonds at the north side of Appletree Cove, is the western terminus of the Edmonds-Kingston ferry route. Just 7.5 miles northeast of Shilshoe Marina on the Kitsap Peninsula (called Great Peninsula on charts), Kingston is a convenient stop for pleasure craft transiting Puget Sound.

The ferry dock lies east of the breakwater at the foot of the town. The Port of Kingston Marina in Appletree Cove lies west of the breakwater; the approach leads through a narrow entrance with shoal-water; favor the south end of the breakwater marked by a light R"2."

Although most of the Kingston Marina's slips are for permanent moorage, transient vessels up to 50 feet can be accommodated on a first-come, first-served basis. (Reservations for larger vessels with side-tie are accepted.) Facilities include water and electricity, showers, laundry, and a fuel dock (gasoline, diesel, and propane) and pump-out station. A marine store, restaurants and other provisions lie a short distance away.

On summer Saturdays there's a popular farmer's market in the adjacent Mike Wallace Marina Park, and the area features good fishing off Point Jefferson, especially when the salmon are running.

Somewhat exposed anchorage can be found in 3 to 5 fathoms about 300 yards southeast of the marina entrance in 3 to 5 fathoms over a bottom of gray sand with fair holding.

⚓ **Port of Kingston Marina** tel: 360.297.3545; fax: 360. 297.2945; website: www.kingston-wa.com; email: ptkingston@aol.com

Poulsbo (Liberty Bay)

Chart 18446; 10 mi W of Shilshole Bay
Entrance (Liberty Bay at Keyport Narrows): 47°41.52'N, 122°36.44'W
Entrance (Port of Poulsbo Marina): 47°43.94, 122°39.02'W
Entrance (Poulsbo YC): 47°43.55'N, 122°38.72'W
Anchor: 47°43.90'N, 122°39.15'W

Poulsbo, a fishing and pleasure resort on the E shore at the head of Liberty Bay, is the principal town of the area. The small-craft harbor at Poulsbo, protected on the S and W sides by an angled timbered breakwater, can accommodate about 400 fishing boats and pleasure craft. The breakwater is well marked by private lights. Piers and floats are in the harbor, depths are about 12 feet at the outer floats. The NE float, parallel to the shore, is used by seaplanes. Electricity, water, ice, a launching ramp, pump-out facility, a marine railway to 30 tons, a 50-foot tidal grid, and hull and engine repairs are available at the basin.

. . . Oysters are cultivated on the flats at the head of the bay. . . . A covered rock is about 175 yards SE of the oyster wharf. A marina immediately S of the oyster company plant offer berths with electricity for about 140 small craft; a 30-ton marine railway and engine repairs are available. (CP, 33rd Ed.)

Poulsbo, tucked into the Great Peninsula west of Port Madison, is well sheltered from outside weather. The approach, via Agate Passage and the narrows north of

Aerial view: Shoals and bridge at Agate Pass

Aerial view: Port of Poulsbo Marina

Washington State Department of Ecology

Keyport is an underwater warfare station; during operations red flashing lights indicate that the passage is temporarily closed. Shallow water is found off Jefferson Point, through Agate Pass, and along the narrows into and along the shore of Liberty Bay. The shoal 0.5 mile northeast of Point Bolin is marked with kelp patches and light R"6."

Poulsbo is a major attraction for cruising boaters—not only because it's close to major population centers and facilities, but because the town has succeeded in maintaining a distinctive Scandinavian charm. The waterfront is beautifully maintained and the town features lovely

Keyport, is without difficulty as long as you stay in the fairway and avoid the shoals.

Poulsbo–Little Norway
by Michelle Gaylord

We left for Poulsbo on the Kitsap Peninsula September 14 and tied up at the Poulsbo Yacht Club. Although the Club wasn't open, they have a kiosk with all the visitor information, including envelopes in which to leave your $3 per night! Also in the kiosk was a regular dial-out phone. Their only request is that you make only local calls! Once again we were astounded at the honor system in the Northwest.

Poulsbo is at the end of Liberty Bay. The entrance to the bay is dominated by the Naval Undersea Warfare Engineering Station at Keyport which began operation in 1910 as a torpedo testing station, and still continues today. If the flashing red lights are illuminated at the entrance to the bay, you are supposed to stay out. Fortunately, the lights were dark when we arrived.

After we got situated, we walked into Old Town, which has been renovated to preserve the heritage of its Scandinavian settlers. It is now known as "Little Norway." It's a great little town with some unusual shops. We were able to find a few gifts for people who are always a challenge when it comes to gift-buying. A wonderful wooden boardwalk along the harbor side of town runs for about a mile. You weave in and out of forests and parks, and there are sections where you are elevated right above the water.

Shopping in downtown Poulsbo

Michelle Gaylord

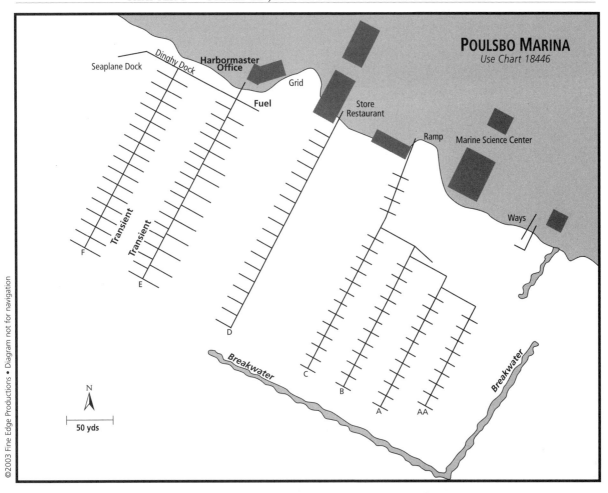

POULSBO MARINA
Use Chart 18446

Seaplane Dock

Dinghy Dock

Harbormaster Office

Grid

Fuel

Store
Restaurant

Ramp

Marine Science Center

Ways

Transient

Transient

F

E

D

C

B

A

AA

Breakwater

Breakwater

N

50 yds

Underway on a sunny day in Puget Sound

restored Victorian homes and gardens. Be sure to check out the famous Poulsbo Bakery, too—it's been a favorite of locals for decades.

The Poulsbo Marina, open seven days a week year-round, features 126 slips for guest moorage. The marina takes reservations only for groups of 15 or larger. You'll find a full range of facilities including water and power, showers, restrooms,

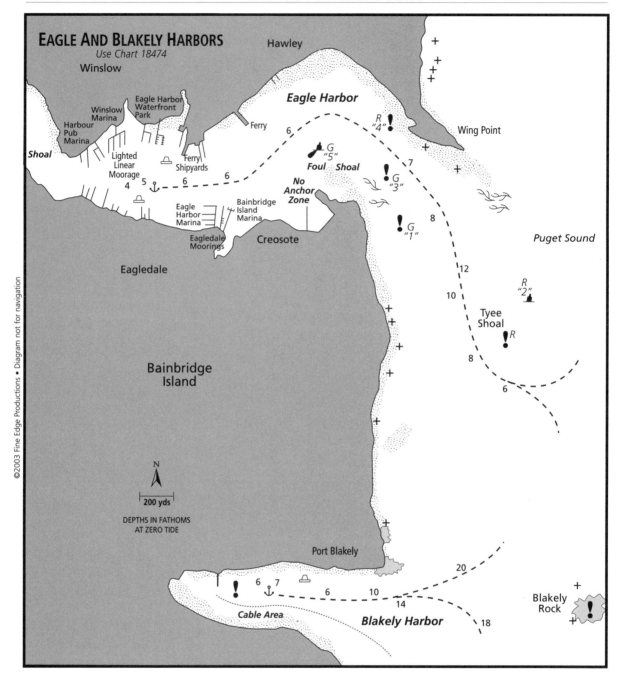

EAGLE AND BLAKELY HARBORS
Use Chart 18474

Winslow

Hawley

Eagle Harbor

Winslow Marina

Eagle Harbor Waterfront Park

Harbour Pub Marina

Ferry

Shoal

Lighted Linear Moorage

Ferry Shipyards

Eagle Harbor Marina

Bainbridge Island Marina

Eagledale Moorings

Eagledale

Creosote

No Anchor Zone

Foul Shoal

Wing Point

Puget Sound

Tyee Shoal

Bainbridge Island

N

200 yds

DEPTHS IN FATHOMS
AT ZERO TIDE

Port Blakely

Cable Area

Blakely Harbor

Blakely Rock

©2003 Fine Edge Productions • Diagram not for navigation

power, pump-out, laundry, fuel, power hook-ups, a launch ramp, and picnic area. There's no shortage of good restaurants and gift shops, and the Marine Science Center is a popular family destination. The authors have spent many weekends here and enjoy its friendly, warm atmosphere; Poulsbo Yacht Club is no exception (see the Gaylord sidebar below).

Poulsbo is the home of the annual Trawler Fest and numerous cruising rendezvous—all delightful experiences.

Anchorage is available for about 50 boats in the bay off the Marina. Use the dinghy dock on the inside of the Poulsbo Marina for access to the downtown area. Although southeast winds can pick up in the 1.2-mile-long bay, chop is minimal.

Anchor in 8 to 12 feet of water over sticky mud with good holding.

⚓ **Poulsbo Marina** tel: 360.779.9905; website: www.poulsbo.net; email: port@poulsbo.net; does not monitor VHF

⚓ **Poulsbo Yacht Club** reciprocal yacht club members only; tel: 360.779.3116

Eagle Harbor (Bainbridge Island)

Charts: 18449,18445; 4 mi W of Elliott Bay Marina
Position (Winslow Wharf Marina): 47°37.23'N, 122°31.26'W
Position (Waterfront Park): 47°37.24'N, 122°31.10'W
Position (Bainbridge Is Marina): 47°37.04'N, 122°30.65'W
Position (Eagle Hbr Marina): 47°37.06'N, 122°30.78'W
Anchor: 47°37.16'N, 122°31.10'W

Eagle Harbor indents the E shore of Bainbridge Island opposite Elliott Bay. It is 2 miles long and affords excellent anchorage in 30 to 39 feet, muddy bottom. It narrows at the head to 300 yards. The entrance is deep, but caution is necessary in entering because the natural channel is only 200 yards wide between the reef S of Wing Point and the spit on the W side of the channel entrance. The channel is marked by lights and bouys. (CP, 33rd Ed.)

Eagle Harbor, 5 miles west of downtown Seattle and almost directly across the Sound, is a well-sheltered bay and popular boating center. It has several marinas, open anchoring and convenient ferry transportation to Seattle. There are no fuel docks; the closest fuel is across the sound at Elliott Bay Marina.

The approach to Eagle Harbor is via a channel entered south of Tyee Shoal which extends 0.75 mile south-southeast of Wing Point. The safe channel keeps the two red buoys on the starboard hand. After turning north, keep buoys G"1," G"3," and G"5" on the port hand, and avoid shortcuts between these nav-aids since shoals extend 200 yards or more from shore to well inside the harbor. The harbor has established a 5-knot No-Wake Zone inside buoy G"5" and enforces it. The area south of

buoy G"5" and into the cove is a no-anchor zone.

The ferry terminal and the ferry shipyards lie on the north shore of the harbor. Anchorage can be found in the center of the harbor west of the ferry landing and ferry shipyards in 5 fathoms.

Eagle Harbor Waterfront, located west of the ferry shipyards, in front of the Waterfront Park area, is run by the city with space available on a first-come, first-served basis.

Winslow Wharf Marina, also on the north shore, is open all year, with guest moorage for boats up to 50 feet in empty slips when they come available. There's a well-stocked marine store at the marina, and a boat repair yard closer to the harbor's entrance. Electricity, restrooms, showers, laundry, and pump-out, are available here. A Lighted Linear Moorage maintained by the city is available and is located off the Winslow Wharf Marina. In addition, four mooring buoys maintained by the city are available on a first-come, first-served basis near the Linear Moorage.

Unless you are a member, avoid the designated dock spaces reserved for the Seattle Yacht Club and the Meydenbauer Bay Yacht Club. A two-block walk takes you to downtown Winslow with its post office, galleries, shops, and restaurants; there's also a Saturday farmers' market.

Harbour Pub Marina (tel: 206.842.4003), a "condo marina," maintains no guest slips or transient facilities, although you can sometimes secure a berth if one happens to become available. They do not accept reservations.

South of the ferry shipyards, along the south shore, there are three public marinas. East to west they are: Bainbridge Island Marina (tel: 206.842.9292); Eagledale Moorings; Eagle Harbor Marina (tel: 206.842.4003). The docks along the south shore to the west of these marinas are all private.

Anchor in about 5 fathoms over mud with fair-to-good holding.

⚓ **Winslow Wharf Marina** open year-round;
  tel: 206.842.4202; monitors Channel 09

Blakely Harbor

Chart 18449; 5 mi SW
of Elliott Bay Marina
Anchor: 47°35.76'N,
122°30.35'W

Blakely Harbor, across the Sound from Seattle, is as quiet as Eagle Harbor is busy. The harbor can be used for temporary anchorage with shelter from prevailing northwest winds, and evenings are generally calm.

Approaching Blakely Harbor, avoid Blakely Rock — a 10-foot-high rock with an adjacent reef marked with a flashing light — and kelp patches. Although there are no boating facilities in the harbor, just anchoring overnight is worth it for the view of downtown when the city is an oasis of lights in the darkness. You can still see the pilings and remnants of a lumber mill that operated here in the mid-1800s and a concrete structure that enclosed a holding pond at the head of the bay.

Good depths exists throughout the middle of the harbor, and anchoring is possible in 5 to 8 fathoms, north of the cable area. The south shore, which is a designated cable area, is shoal and exposed at low tide for about 150 yards. Blakely Rock, a half-mile offshore, is a popular spot for scuba diving and a home for seals; on a summer minus tide all kinds of boaters stop by the rock for a picnic or a close look.

Anchor (mid-channel north of cable area) in about 6 fathoms over mud with good holding.

Aerial view: Float docks at North end of Blake Island

BLAKE ISLAND
Use Chart 18449

Blake
Island

N

200 yds

R "2"
R "4"
R "6"
G "1"
G "3"
"5"

W OR
SP "A"
(Private)

Tillicum Tribal Village on Blake Island

Blake Island

Chart 18449; 6 mi SW of Elliott Bay Marina
Entrance (Marina): 47°32.67'N, 122°28.95'W
Anchor (W): 47°32.41'N, 122°30.21'W
Anchor (E): 47°32.31'N, 122°28.89'W

> [Blake Island is] *about 1 mile long, 249 feet high, and covered with trees, is off the N entrance to Colvos Passage. Heavy tide rips, strongest with a flood current, and strong S winds are encountered at the N entrance to Colvos Passage S of Blake Island. Shallow irregular bottom extends about 0.5 mile off the N shore of the island. A light is on the NE point of the Island. Just S of the NW point of the island are the ruins of a wharf. A State-run marine park small-craft basin, protected by a breakwater, is at the NE end of the island. The entrance to the basin is marked by a private light and day beacon. A pumpout station is available.* (CP, 33rd Ed.)

Blake Island—a Washington State Marine Park encompassing 475 acres—has become a tradition for visiting cruisers, for its excellent introduction to Northwest Native culture. Just over 2 miles south of Bainbridge Island and 6 miles west of downtown Seattle, it's a convenient destination for thousands of visitors each year who seek temporary refuge from the stress and noise of every-

day life. There are no ferries to the island, so the only access is via private or tour boat.

The tiny small-craft basin in the northeast corner can be entered carefully through a narrow channel marked with both port and starboard hand day-marks. There are a number of mooring buoys around the periphery of Blake Island: west of the breakwater; on the east and west sides; and at the south end. The buoys on the west side use the Linear Mooring System. Temporary anchorage can be found adjacent to the mooring buoys on narrow flats with limited swinging room. Set your anchor well or it may drag. These mooring and anchor sites are open roadsteads and subject to chop and wake, depending on wind and traffic.

The float docks at the northeast corner are entered off the western end of the breakwater. Follow the well-marked channel to avoid the shallows on either side. The first float you come

Salmon bake at Tillicum Village longhouse on Blake Island

A carving in process at Tillicum Village, Blake Island

beach strolling, swimming, clamming, bird watching, and marine life observation. An underwater park for scuba divers offers opportunities for spear fishing or underwater photography. In summer, the Indian salmon barbecue is a big attraction. Park rangers advise that moorage for private boats gets tight on summer weekends; the best time to come, if possible, is from Sunday evening through Tuesday.

to is designated for tour boats, the next for State Park boats; the next four floats are for visiting boaters. The Park campground has water and restrooms with one shower. There is no fuel available here, and no trash pickup—so be prepared to pack out your own garbage.

Blake Island is an excellent place to enjoy picnicking, camping, water skiing, fishing, hiking,

Anchor (W) in 5 to 10 fathoms over hard sand and mud; fair holding with limited swinging room. Avoid the mooring buoys.

Anchor (E) in 5 to 10 fathoms over hard sand and mud; fair holding with limited swinging room. Avoid the mooring buoys.

⚓ **Blake Island Marine State Park** open year-round; tel: 360.731.8330, 360.902.8844

Narrow entrance to the small marina on Blake Island

Wonderful Blake Island

by Michelle Gaylord

What a *wonderful* place little Blake Island is! The entire island is a State Park and mostly undeveloped, with miles of beautiful hiking trails. The island is accessible only by boat, and there is a small settlement called Tillicum Village where the Natives put on a real honest-to-goodness salmon bake prepared in a longhouse, with a traditional Indian dance and stage show following dinner.

The marina entrance is surrounded by shoals, and its very narrow dredged channel must be followed to avoid going aground. The marina is small, and we arrived just in time to get a space at the dock (no power or water). Right in front of the marina is a huge grassy park with volleyball courts, horseshoe pits, picnic tables with barbecues, a kiddie playground, bathrooms, showers, and numerous colorful totem poles. In addition to the outside picnic tables and barbecues there are two enclosed shelters, each with a huge rock fire pit in the middle, surrounded by picnic tables.

We enjoyed a terrific evening in the Tillicum longhouse. The dinner was fabulous, and I'm not even a salmon fan. They had four big round pits right in the floor of the longhouse where they built a teepee-style fire out of logs. Then they took the salmon, spread them open flat and staked them to wooden posts which they pounded into the ground surrounding the fire.

While we waited for dinner to cook we wandered around the longhouse which included a small gift shop, museum, and a workshop where Indian carvers were working on masks and totems out of alder wood. When we wandered outside, the yard was full of tiny deer. One came right up to me, sniffed my camera, stuck her nose in my purse, and completely looked me over to see if I was a possible source of a handout.

Before dinner began, we were served bowls of steamed clams outside with the deer watching. The salmon was the best we'd ever tasted, and the sweet black Indian bread they served complemented it perfectly. The bread was so good I bought a couple of loaves to take back to the boat. The show after dinner was very entertaining, although the musical accompaniment could have used a little variety—I guess musical isn't the right word, a more fitting term would be "beat." The costumes and masks were all authentic and handmade, and the designs on the blankets were beautiful.

We took the four-mile hike around the entire island. Oh my, what a walk that was. We had planned on a nice flat road around the circumference of the island. *Not.* It was more like a rocky goat trail, weaving up into the interior of the island and then down again to the water. Once we were about half-way around the island, we were ready to quit, but we didn't have an option—we had to keep going. That night we decided to have dinner in one of the barbecue huts ashore. We built a roaring fire in the pit, and while Jerry put the meat on to cook, I walked up to the longhouse to buy another loaf of bread. When I came out there were two deer standing right outside the front door. As I went back to the barbecue area, I'll be darned if they didn't follow me and bring a few of their friends. They were a little skittish, so we ignored them and went on making dinner. They got braver and braver, and came closer and closer. We watched them and played with them so long that our meat got overdone. Then, while we ate our dinner, we had 12 of the most beautiful brown eyes you have ever seen watching us.

Authors' note: We hope you have enjoyed Michelle and Jerry Gaylord's perspectives of their cruise on *Passing Thru.* The Gaylords left their home port—Channel Islands, California—in May 1999. What they had originally planned as a 12-month cruise to the Northwest and Alaska extended to nearly four years. (They left Anacortes, Washington in September 2002 to head south again.) Their 15-day southbound itinerary included calls at Port Angeles, Neah Bay; Newport, Brookings; Eureka, Bodega Bay, San Francisco, Monterey and Oxnard Channel Islands. They encountered no problems or bar closures. As we go to press, Michelle writes: *Although we feel we could spend a lifetime up north and never get tired of the scenery or run out of places to explore, we have decided to venture south into Mexican waters . . . Perhaps we will continue south into Central American and the Caribbean, or perhaps we will long for the lush greenery of the Pacific Northwest and decide to make an about-face. . . .*

Appendices and References

APPENDIX A
Favorite Itineraries: San Diego to Seattle

I. Bluewater Route:

The Bluewater Route—the direct north or south offshore route, and the route with the least traffic—is favored by power boats and sailboats that want the shortest distance, with few or no stops.

The Bluewater Route begins north of San Diego and ends off Cape Flattery where it joins the Inshore Route to Seattle or Victoria. This route, which includes GPS waypoints for each turn, is described and illustrated in the Introduction to this book.

Total Distance: 1150 miles

Duration: 6 to 10 days

Advantages: The fastest route, weather permitting, for crews willing to make around-the-clock passages

Feasibility: With reasonable weather, this route is feasible for a capable ocean-going boat with crew experienced in offshore passages

Best Time: Spring through fall, avoiding storms or storm fronts

Challenges: Crew stamina and adequate fuel for a non-stop trip

II. Express Route (Fast Itinerary)

The Express Route is a favorite of delivery skippers and others who want a fast route with the option of several overnight stops. The Express Route takes advantage of the Crabpot Free Tow Lanes to minimize chances of snagging a float. For boaters wishing daylight passages only, an alternative Express Route (Harbor Hopping) is given below.

The various legs of the Express Route are indicated on the regional Route Diagrams; the GPS waypoints of each leg are given on each diagram.

Delivery skippers willing to run up to 36 hours per leg find they can follow the itinerary given below in about 7 legs, averaging approximately 170 miles per day (plus distance to and from harbor).

Total Distance: 1190 miles

Duration: 7 to 10 days

Advantages: Best for faster boats with professional crew capable of longer daily runs or overnight passages; gives the option of stopping for weather conditions or crew changes

Feasibility: With reasonable weather, highly feasible for a capable boat and experienced crew.

Best Time: Spring through fall avoiding, storms or storm fronts

Challenges: Planning around unforeseen harbor bar closings

Leg 1 San Diego to Coho	200 mi.		Day 10 to Newport	77 mi.
Leg 2 to Pillar Point Harbor	207 mi.		Day 11 to Ilawaco	101 mi.
Leg 3 to Fort Bragg	135 mi.		Day 12 to Grays Harbor	48 mi.
Leg 4 to Crescent City	139 mi.		Day 13 to Neah Bay	96 mi.
Leg 5 to Newport	158 mi.		Day 14 to Port Townsend	82 mi.
Leg 6 to Grays Harbor	139 mi.		Day 15 to Seattle	38 mi.
Leg 7 to Seattle	213 mi.			

Total mileage   1190 nautical miles

Total mileage   1244 nautical miles

Express Route (Harbor Hopping Itinerary)

The Express Route is also used by coastal cruisers as a series of daylight passages only. The Harbor Hopping Itinerary requires a minimum of 15 days, plus layover for weather or crew. Because of weather changes or the uncertainty of entrance-bar closures, vessels following this itinerary should be prepared for an overnight passage if necessary.

Total Distance: 1244 miles, plus distance in and out of harbors

Duration: 6 to 10 days

Advantages: Crabpot-free (in Tow Lanes or in deeper water); remains closer to shore than Bluewater Route, reducing travel time to harbors or alternative shelter

Feasibility: Feasible for boats that can maintain about 5.5 knots to windward and can take time to remain in port during unstable weather

Best Time: Spring through fall, avoiding storms or storm fronts

Challenges: Requires a careful watch of the weather and pre-planning for harbor entrance-bar conditions

Day 1 San Diego to Marina del Rey	100 mi.
Day 2 to Coho	108 mi.
Day 3 to San Simeon	81 mi.
Day 4 to Monterey	72 mi.
Day 5 to Bodega Bay	117 mi.
Day 6 to Fort Bragg	78 mi.
Day 7 to Eureka	88 mi.
Day 8 to Brookings	77 mi.
Day 9 to Coos Bay	81 mi.

III. Inshore Route

A moderately-paced coastal itinerary for powered vessels capable of averaging 5.5 knots to windward. The Inshore Routes are shown on the regional Route Diagrams, along with the actual GPS waypoints.

Duration: Typically 30 to 75 days to allow for weather or tourism

Average daily run: 44 miles; 60 to 80 miles on long days

Total Distance: 1309 miles (plus approaches and internal harbor mileage)

Duration: Minumum of 15 days of daylight travel (must allow additional days for weather or lay-over days)

Average daily run: 44 miles

Advantages: Daylight travel only (Bodega Bay to Fort Bragg, 78 miles, is longest run); visits many small and scenic fishing villages; remains close to shore, taking advantage of lees and back eddies; minimizes exposure to weather; maximizes cell phone coverage.

Feasibility: Suitable for well-found, small-to-moderate-sized power and sailboats (with diesel auxiliary) able to maintain an average speed of about 5.5 knots to windward for a average of 8 hours per day; requires 6 days or more of motoring in excess of 12 hours per day. Skippers must be experienced with coastal passage-making.

Best Time: May through September for maximum daylight and more stable weather

Anchoring required: Requires anchoring in open roadsteads 4 nights (Coho Anchorage, San Simeon, Shelter Cove, Port Orford); many harbors allow anchoring but some do not.

Challenges: The trip is weather dependent. Harbors from Fort Bragg northward lie mostly on rivers behind shallow bars that are subject to closure in heavy seas; requires close monitoring of weather forecasts and confirming of bar-crossing conditions with USCG; must allow time to remain inside harbors in times of heavy weather or be prepared to spend a night at sea if conditions prevent entering a harbor. This route crosses an area with a high concentration of crabpots. Avoiding snagging a crabpot float requires sharp helmsmanship at all times.

Day 1	San Diego to Dana Point	47 mi.
Day 2	to Marina del Rey	50 mi.
Day 3	to Ventura	45 mi.
Day 4	to Santa Barbara	22 mi.
Day 5	to Coho Anchorage	38 mi.
Day 6	to Port San Luis	46 mi.
Day 7	to Morro Bay	14 mi.
Day 8	to San Simeon	22 mi.
Day 9	to Carmel	67 mi.*
Day 10	to Santa Cruz	25 mi.
Day 11	to Pillar Pt. Harbor (Half Moon Bay)	41 mi.
Day 12	to San Francisco Bay	22 mi.
Day 13	to Bodega Bay	44 mi.
Day 14	to Fort Bragg (Noyo River)	78 mi.*
Day 15	to Shelter Cove	37 mi.
Day 16	to Eureka (via Cape Mendocino)	63 mi.*
Day 17	to Crescent City	61 mi.*
Day 18	to Brookings (Chetco River inshore)	27 mi.
Day 19	to Port Orford	45 mi.
Day 20	to Coos Bay	46 mi.
Day 21	to Florence (Siuslaw River)	41 mi.
Day 22	to Newport (Yaquina Bay)	37 mi.
Day 23	to Tillamook	59 mi.
Day 24	to Ilwaco (via Columbia River Bar)	50 mi.
Day 25	to Grays Harbor (Westport, WA)	58 mi.
Day 26	to La Push (Quiyalute River)	69 mi.*
Day 27	to Neah Bay	41 mi.
Day 28	to Port Angeles	51 mi.
Day 29	to Port Townsend (via Point Wilson)	31 mi.
Day 30	to Shilshole Marina Seattle	32 mi.

Total mileage	1,309 nautical miles

Alternative Routes:

Neah Bay to Victoria B.C.	52 mi.
Port Townsend to Anacortes	30 mi.

(*) Extra long days—may require 12 to 15 hours; schedule does not allow for weather or layover days

Note: Smaller vessels unable to maintain 5.5 knots to windward will require additional time for the Inshore Routes Itinerary. Skippers of such vessels may want to leave pre-dawn to reach the next port before afternoon northerlies pick up. This itinerary may also require an occasional overnight run or the need to seek temporary anchorage in one of the tiny sites used by local fishing boats.

Larger vessels able to maintain a faster speed to windward may easily bypass one or more harbors per day, reducing elapsed time accordingly.

APPENDIX B
"Dream" Itinerary

Introducing the Inside Passage to Alaska

The Strait of Juan de Fuca is just the beginning of the smooth water route to Alaska, the fabled Inside Passage. Ocean swells seldom penetrate the over 1,000-mile-long archipelago northbound from Seattle or Victoria to Glacier Bay and Lynn Canal. This is prime wilderness cruising at or near the top of the list for any world cruiser. Cavorting whales and bears, lush rain forests with stunning waterfalls, tidewater glaciers with calving icebergs, world-class salmon and halibut fishing are all there in a breathtaking natural environment.

We have included what we call the *Dream Itinerary*, a prototype 100-day schedule, which covers many of the highlights of the Inside Passage. After the Itinerary are the maps showing various routes frequently used by boaters. The diagrams will give you an idea of where the destinations of the Dream Itinerary are located, what different routes you can use to connect them, and why the routes are so well protected from ocean swells. Please see our six *Exploring Series* guidebooks for full descriptions on 4,000 places to anchor or tie up whenever the fog rolls in, the chop picks up, or the wind begins to howl. When cruising to Alaska, you are seldom more than an hour from a place to drop the hook and wait for the tide to reverse, the visibility to improve, or to just take a rest.

Off-the-beaten-path round-trip with exposure to full Outer Passage
Three months (97 days or more) minimum

Features:
Ultra-scenic route includes Nakwakto Rapids, the top hot springs, Fjordland, Misty Fjords, Tracy Arm and Glacier Bay, Lynn Canal and Skagway; full West Coast Outer Passage, including Vancouver Island's West Coast

Total distance:
3,006 miles

Average daily run:
31 miles

Advantages: Self-paced immersion trip for those who want to do the Inside Passage to Alaska "right" with time to explore the West Coast Outer Passage and to visit the Northwest's secluded spots and major scenic and historical places; this can be undertaken by most well-equipped cruising boats.

Feasibility: Suitable for boats equipped for extended travel with a cruising speed of 5 knots or more; radar and GPS recommended.

Best time: Mid-May to early September
Anchoring required:
80 percent or more of the time in secluded coves, off the beaten path; balance as desired at public mooring buoys, or public floats

Day 1	Anacortes to Stuart Island	32 mi.
Day 2	to Princess Bay, Wallace Island	25 mi.
Day 3	to Nanaimo	28 mi.
Day 4	to Scottie Bay	33 mi.
Day 5	to Copeland Islands	35 mi.
Day 6	to Thurston Bay via Yuculta Rapids	43 mi.
Day 7	to Port Neville	34 mi.
Day 8	to Mamalilaculla	37 mi.
Day 9	to Cypress Harbour	25 mi.
Day 10	to Blunden Harbour	30 mi.
Day 11	to Goose Point Cove (Nakwakto Rapids)	18 mi.
Day 12	to Miles Inlet via Seymour Inlet	13 mi.
Day 13	to Millbrook Cove via Indian Island Cove	29 mi.
Day 14	to Joe's Bay, Fish Egg Inlet	26 mi.
Day 15	to Codville Lagoon	33 mi.
Day 16	to Ocean Falls via McKenzie Rock	46 mi.
Day 17	to Troup Narrows (Deer Passage)	24 mi.
Day 18	to Rescue Bay	38 mi.
Day 19	to Windy Bay via waterfall and Fjordland	40 mi.
Day 20	to Swanson Bay	23 mi.
Day 21	to Bishop Hot Springs	36 mi.
Day 22	to Sue Channel via Weewanie Hot Springs	25 mi.
Day 23	to Coghlan Anchorage	28 mi.

Day 24 to East Inlet	33 mi.
Day 25 to Lawson Harbour	33 mi.
Day 26 to Prince Rupert	19 mi.
Day 27 to Tongass Island Cove	43 mi.
Day 28 to Foggy Bay via Very Inlet	28 mi.
Day 29 to Ketchikan	37 mi.
Day 30 to Carp Island	32 mi.
Day 31 to Manzanita Bay via Rudyard Bay	40 mi.
Day 32 to Yes Bay	48 mi.
Day 33 to Meyers Chuck	48 mi.
Day 34 to Frosty Bay	25 mi.
Day 35 to Wrangell	30 mi.
Day 36 to Petersburg	40 mi.
Day 37 to Fanshaw	38 mi.
Day 38 to Tracy Arm Cove	40 mi.
Day 39 to Tracy Arm Cove via Sawyer Glacier	40 mi.
Day 40 to Taku Harbor	25 mi.
Day 41 to Juneau	20 mi.
Day 42 to Auke Bay	19 mi.
Day 43 to Rescue Harbor	43 mi.
Day 44 to Skagway	32 mi.
Day 45 to Boat Harbor or St. James Bay	48 mi.
Day 46 to Swanson Harbor	29 mi.
Day 47 to Pleasant Island	19 mi.
Day 48 to N. Sandy Cove	40 mi.
Day 49 to N. Sandy Cove via Muir Glacier	45 mi.
Day 50 to Russell Island Cove via Grand Pacific Glacier and Margerie Glacier	52 mi.
Day 51 to Blue Mouse Cove via Hopkins Glacier	37 mi.
Day 52 to North Inian Island	46 mi.
Day 53 to Lost Cove, Lisianski Strait	33 mi.
Day 54 to Mirror Harbor, White Sulphur Springs	12 mi.
Day 55 to Double Cove	20 mi.
Day 56 to Whitestone Cove	28 mi.
Day 57 to Sitka	15 mi.
Day 58 to "Annie's Pocket"	34 mi.
Day 59 to Ell Cove	46 mi.
Day 60 to Baranof Warm Springs	13 mi.
Day 61 to "Honeydew Cove"	22 mi.
Day 62 to "Baidarka Anchorage" via Kake	34 mi.
Day 63 to Hole in the Wall (Prince of Wales Island)	28 mi.
Day 64 to Devilfish Bay	28 mi.
Day 65 to Bob's Place	38 mi.
Day 66 to Craig via Klawock	24 mi.
Day 67 to South Pass Cove	33 mi.
Day 68 to Charlies Cove	37 mi.
Day 69 to Nichols Bay	20 mi.
Day 70 to Prince Rupert via Duke Island and Foggy Bay if necessary	68 mi.
Day 71 to Captains Cove	38 mi.
Day 72 to Patterson Inlet	33 mi.
Day 73 to Weinberg Inlet	27 mi.
Day 74 to Helmcken Island Cove	30 mi.
Day 75 to Oliver Cove	45 mi.
Day 76 to Rock Inlet Cove	42 mi.
Day 77 to Millbrook Cove (Return to San Juans Islands via east or west coast of Vancouver Island. We suggest West Coast of Vancouver Island.)	40 mi.
Day 78 to Bull Harbour	33 mi.
Day 79 to Sea Otter Cove	32 mi.
Day 80 to Winter Harbour	26 mi.
Day 81 to Klaskino Inlet	19 mi.
Day 82 to Klaskish Inlet	12 mi.
Day 83 to Baidarka Cove	23 mi.
Day 84 to Gay Passage	10 mi.
Day 85 to Petroglyph Cove	17 mi.
Day 86 to Queen Cove	23 mi.
Day 87 to Friendly Cove (Yuquot)	30 mi.
Day 88 to Hot Springs Cove	30 mi.
Day 89 to Little White Pine Cove	19 mi.
Day 90 to Adventure Cove via Tofino	20 mi.
Day 91 to Ucluelet	32 mi.
Day 92 to Broken Group	12 mi.
Day 93 to Dodger Pass via Broken Group	15 mi.
Day 94 to Port San Juan	42 mi.
Day 95 to Victoria	53 mi.
Day 96 layover	
Day 97 to Anacortes	40 mi.

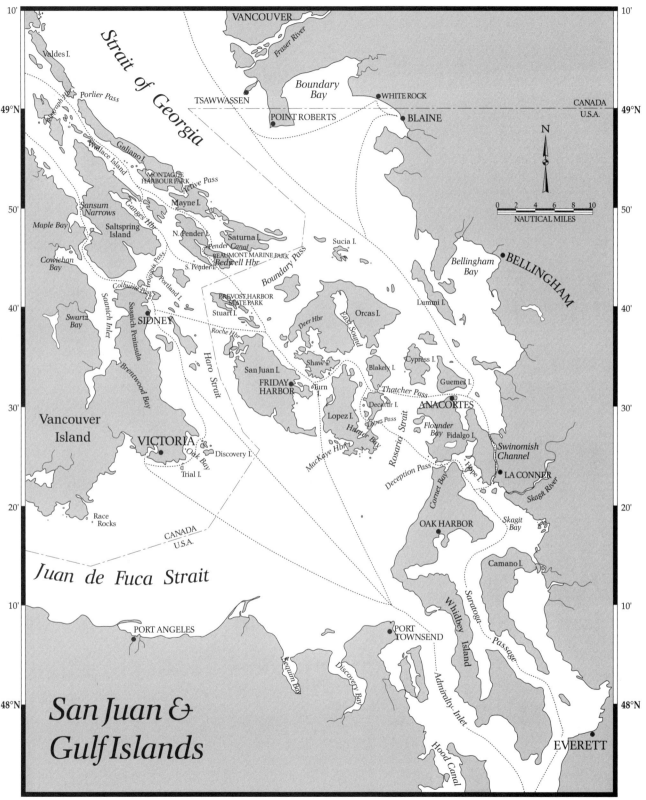

San Juan & Gulf Islands

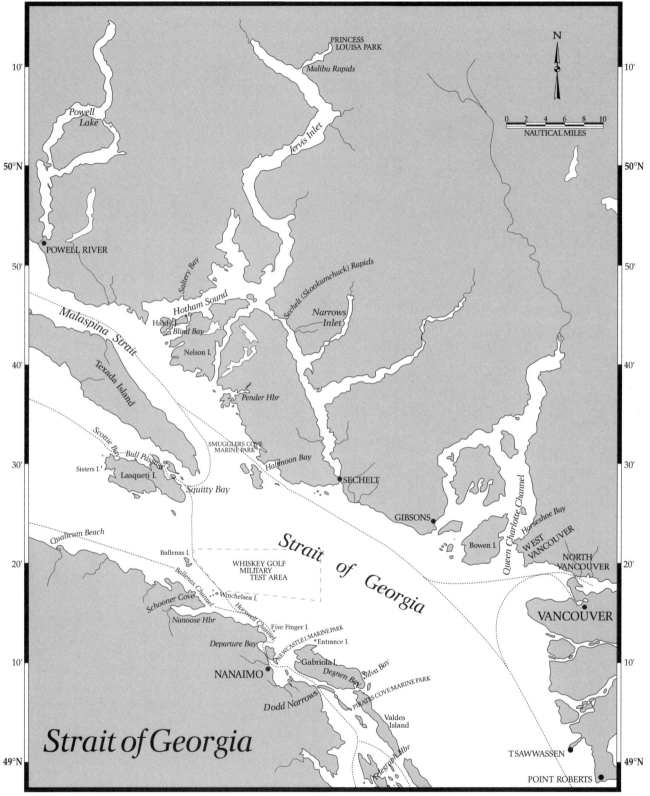

PRINCESS
LOUISA PARK

Malibu Rapids

Jervis Inlet

Powell
Lake

N

0 2 4 6 8 10
NAUTICAL MILES

10'

50°N

50'

POWELL RIVER

Saltery Bay

Sechelt (Skookumchuck) Rapids

Hotham Sound

*Narrows
Inlet*

Malaspina Strait

Handy I.
Blind Bay

Nelson I.

Texada Island

Pender Hbr

Scottie Bay

Bull Passage

SMUGGLERS COVE
MARINE PARK

Sisters I.

Lasqueti I.

Halfmoon Bay

SECHELT

Squitty Bay

GIBSONS

Qualicum Beach

Bowen I.

Strait of Georgia

Queen Charlotte Channel

Horseshoe Bay

WEST
VANCOUVER

NORTH
VANCOUVER

Ballenas I.

WHISKEY GOLF
MILITARY
TEST AREA

VANCOUVER

Ballenas Channel

Winchelsea I.

Schooner Cove

Horswell Channel

Nanoose Hbr

Five Finger I.

NEWCASTLE I. MARINE PARK

Departure Bay

Entrance I.

Gabriola I.

NANAIMO

Degnen Bay

Silva Bay

PIRATES COVE MARINE PARK

Dodd Narrows

Valdes
Island

TSAWWASSEN

Strait of Georgia

Telegraph Hbr

49°N

POINT ROBERTS

©2003 Fine Edge Productions • Diagram not for navigation

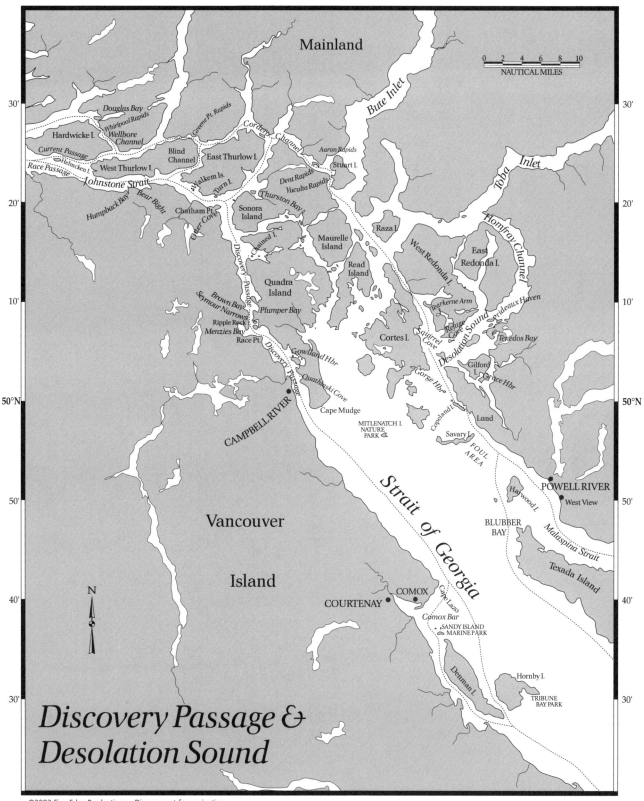

Discovery Passage & Desolation Sound

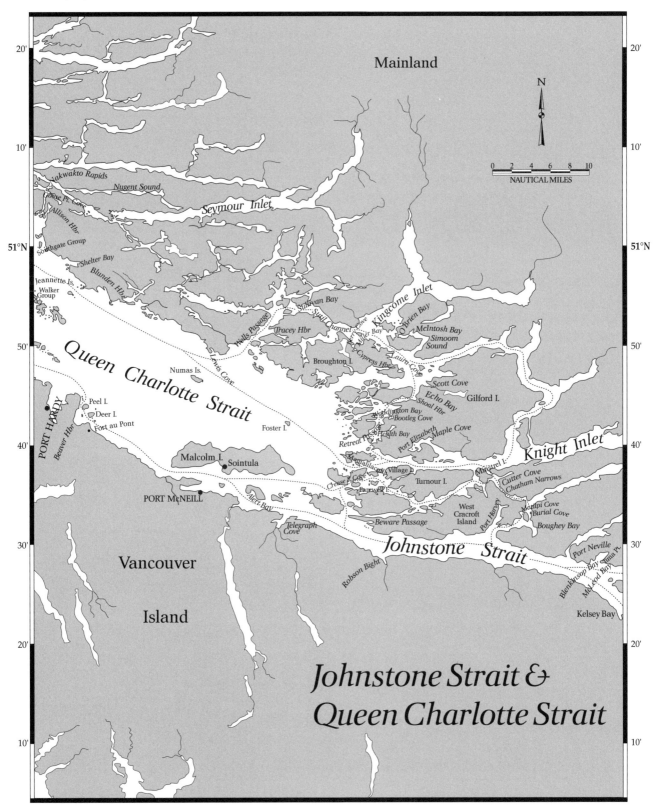

Johnstone Strait &
Queen Charlotte Strait

Queen Charlotte Sound—
Outer Passage

To
Queen
Charlotte
Islands

©2003 Fine Edge Productions • Diagram not for navigation

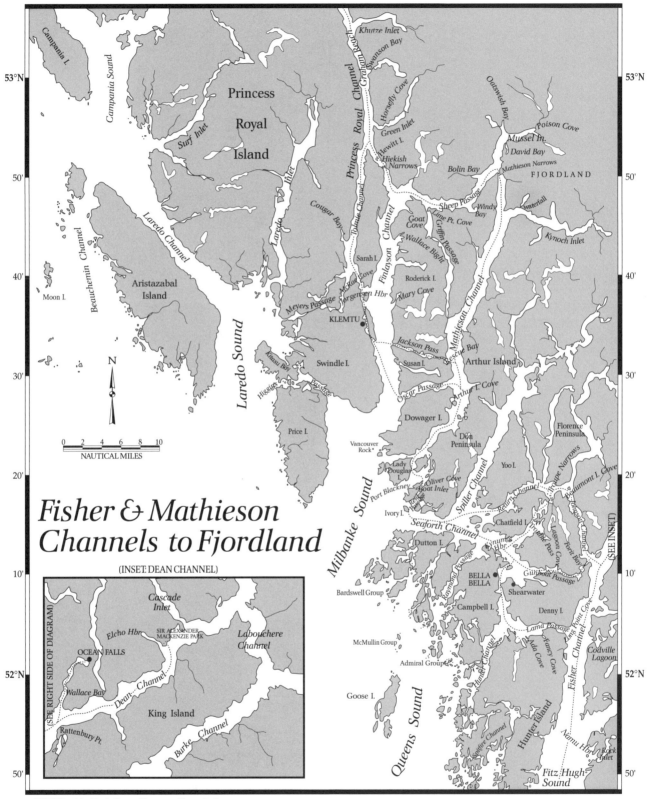

Fisher & Mathieson Channels to Fjordland

(INSET: DEAN CHANNEL)

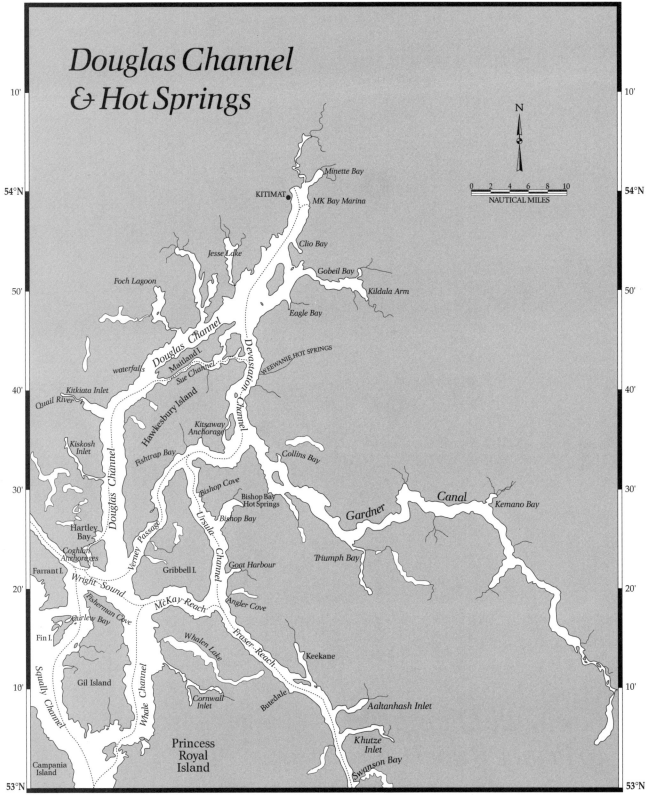

Douglas Channel
& Hot Springs

N

0 2 4 6 8 10
NAUTICAL MILES

Minette Bay

KITIMAT ●

MK Bay Marina

Clio Bay

Jesse Lake

Gobeil Bay

Foch Lagoon

Kildala Arm

Eagle Bay

Douglas Channel

Maitland I.

Sue Channel

Devastation Channel

WEEWANIE HOT SPRINGS

waterfalls

Kitkiata Inlet

Quail River

Hawkesbury Island

Kitsaway
Anchorage

Kiskosh
Inlet

Collins Bay

Fishtrap Bay

Canal

Bishop Cove

Bishop Bay
Hot Springs

Gardner

Kemano Bay

Douglas Channel

Bishop Bay

Hartley
Bay

Coghlan
Anchorages

Ursula Channel

Verney Passage

Gribbell I.

Goat Harbour

Triumph Bay

Farrant I.

Wright Sound

Fisherman Cove

McKay Reach

Angler Cove

Curlew Bay

Fin I.

Whalen Lake

Fraser Reach

Keekane

Squally Channel

Whale Channel

Gil Island

Cornwall
Inlet

Butedale

Aaltanhash Inlet

Campania
Island

Princess
Royal
Island

Khutze
Inlet

Swanson Bay

©2003 Fine Edge Productions • Diagram not for navigation

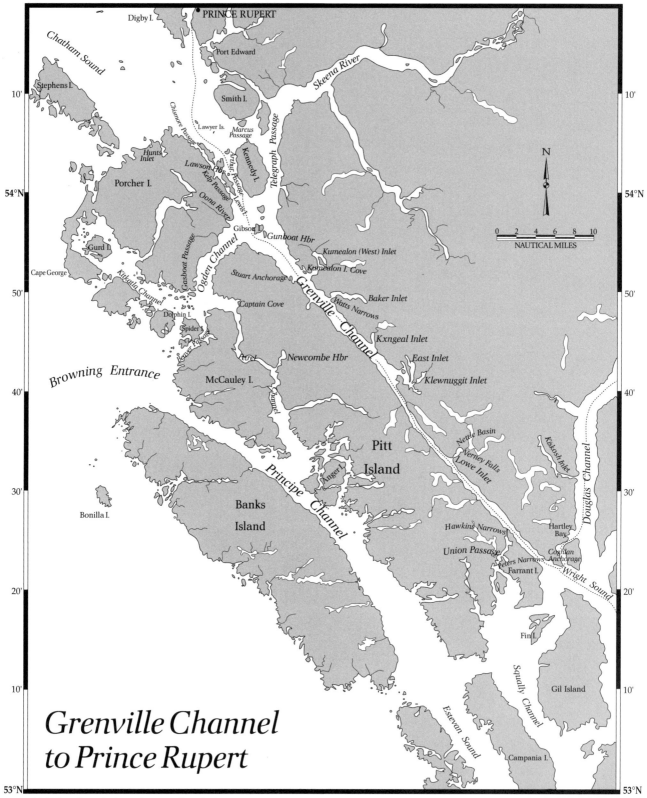

Grenville Channel
to Prince Rupert

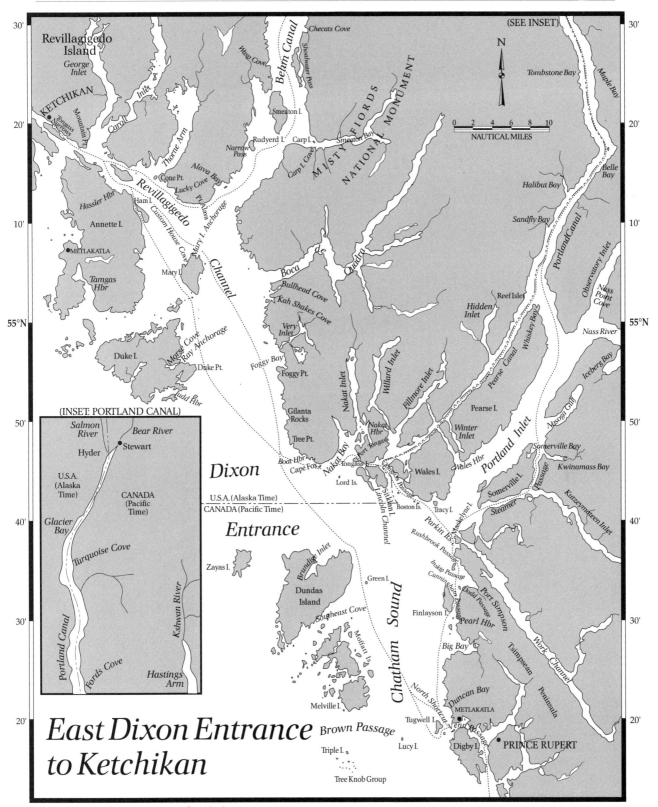

East Dixon Entrance to Ketchikan

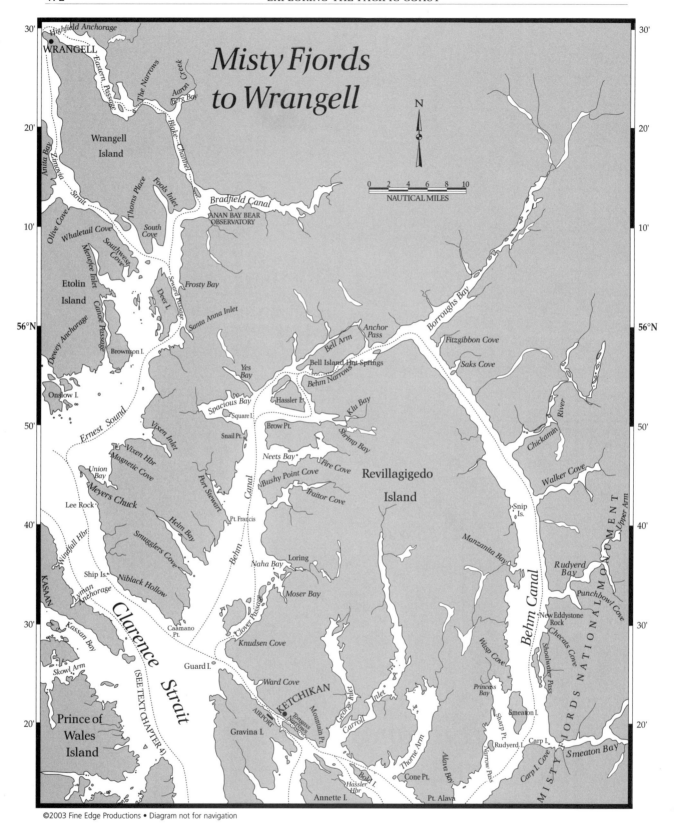

Misty Fjords to Wrangell

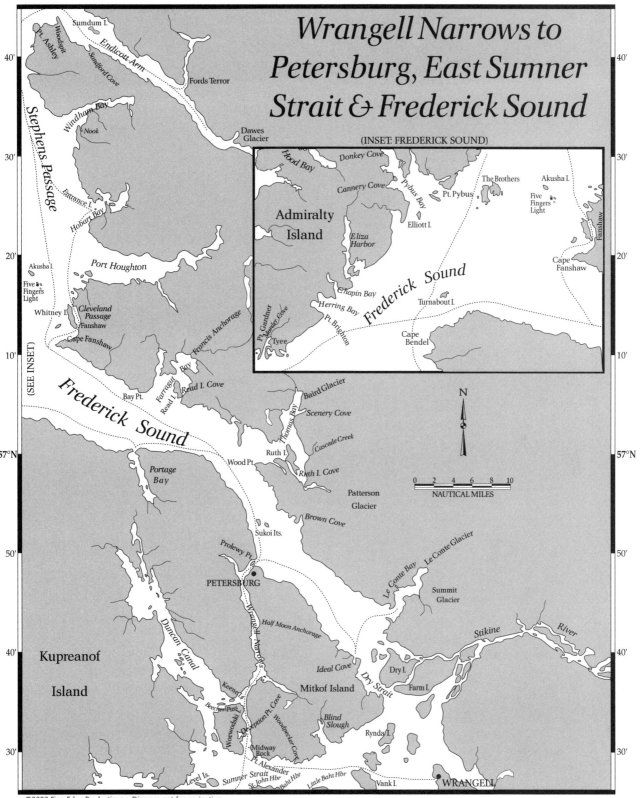

Wrangell Narrows to Petersburg, East Sumner Strait & Frederick Sound

(INSET: FREDERICK SOUND)

Sumdum I.
Pt. Ashley
Woodspit
Endicott Arm
Sandford Cove
Windham Bay
Nook
Fords Terror
Dawes Glacier
Stephens Passage
Entrance I.
Hobart Bay
Port Houghton
Akusha I.
Five Fingers Light
Whitney I.
Cleveland Passage
Fanshaw
Cape Fanshaw
Francis Anchorage
Bay
Farragut Bay
Read I.
Read I. Cove
Bay Pt.
Frederick Sound

Hood Bay
Donkey Cove
Cannery Cove
Pybus Bay
Pt. Pybus
The Brothers
Akusha I.
Five Fingers Light
Admiralty Island
Eliza Harbor
Elliott I.
Frederick Sound
Fanshaw
Chapin Bay
Herring Bay
Turnabout I.
Cape Fanshaw
Pt. Gardner
Surdier Cove
Pt. Brighton
Tyee
Cape Bendel

N

Baird Glacier
Scenery Cove
Thomas Bay
Cascade Creek
Ruth I.
Wood Pt.
Ruth I. Cove
57°N

0 2 4 6 8 10
NAUTICAL MILES

Patterson Glacier

Portage Bay
Brown Cove
Sukoi Its.
Prolewy Pt.
PETERSBURG
Le Conte Bay
Le Conte Glacier
Summit Glacier
Half Moon Anchorage
Duncan Canal
Stikine
River
Kupreanof Island
Wrangell Narrows
Ideal Cove
Dry I.
Farm I.
Keene
Mitkof Island
Dry Strait
Beecher Pass
Deception Pt. Cove
Woewodski
Woodpecker Cove
Blind Slough
Rynda I.
Midway Rock
Pt. Alexander
Level Is.
Sumner Strait
St. John Hbr
Baht Hbr
Little Baht Hbr
Vank I.
WRANGELL

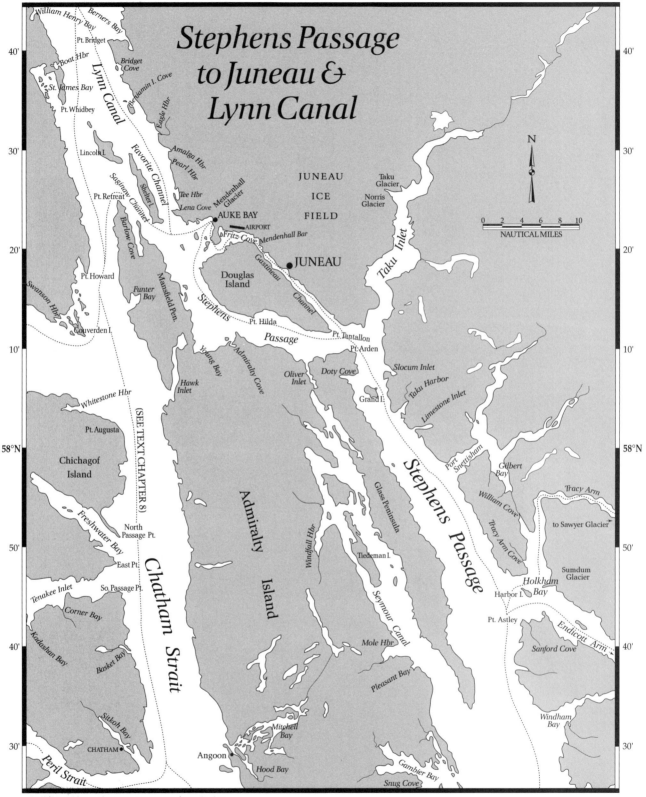

Stephens Passage to Juneau & Lynn Canal

©2003 Fine Edge Productions • Diagram not for navigation

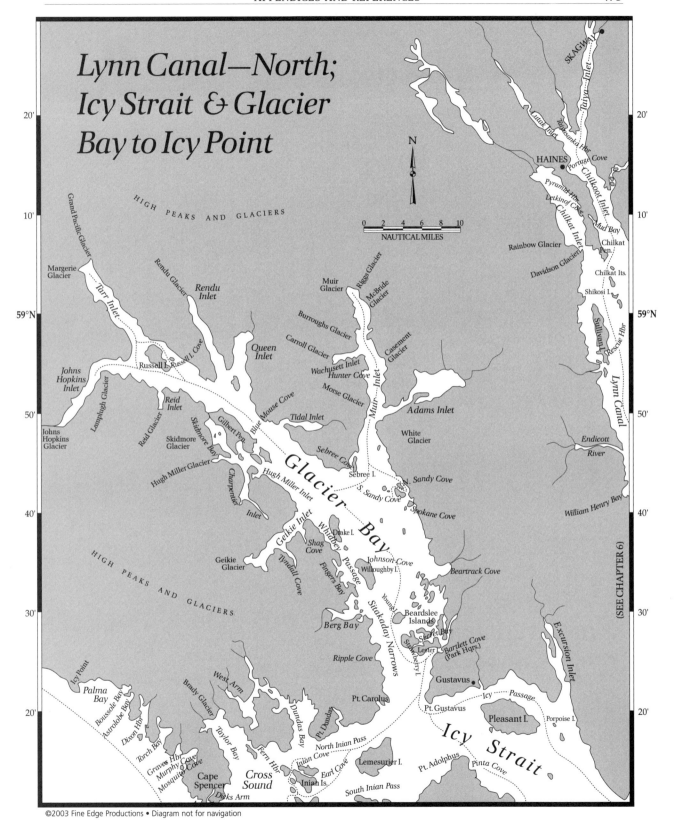

Lynn Canal—North;
Icy Strait & Glacier
Bay to Icy Point

HIGH PEAKS AND GLACIERS

N

0 2 4 6 8 10
NAUTICAL MILES

SKAGWAY

Taiya Inlet

Lutak Inlet

Talsanka Hbr

HAINES

Portage Cove

Chilkoot Inlet

Pyramid Hbr

Letnikof Cove

Mud Bay

Chilkat Pen.

Chilkat Inlet

Rainbow Glacier

Davidson Glacier

Chilkat Its.

Shikosi I.

Sullivan I.

Rescue Hbr

Lynn Canal

59°N

Grand Pacific Glacier

Margerie Glacier

Rendu Glacier

Rendu Inlet

Muir Glacier

Riggs Glacier

McBride Glacier

Turr Inlet

Burroughs Glacier

Casement Glacier

Carroll Glacier

Queen Inlet

Wachusett Inlet

Hunter Cove

Johns Hopkins Inlet

Russell I. Russell I. Cove

Morse Glacier

Muir Inlet

Adams Inlet

Lamplugh Glacier

Reid Inlet

Blue Mouse Cove

Tidal Inlet

White Glacier

Red Glacier

Skidmore Bay

Gilbert Pen.

Sebree Cove

Endicott River

Johns Hopkins Glacier

Skidmore Glacier

Sebree I.

N. Sandy Cove

Hugh Miller Glacier

Charpentier Inlet

Hugh Miller Inlet

Glacier Bay

S. Sandy Cove

Spokane Cove

William Henry Bay

Geikie Inlet

Drake I.

Whidbey Passage

Johnson Cove

Willoughby I.

Beartrack Cove

Shag Cove

Geikie Glacier

Tyndall Cove

Fingers Bay

Sitakaday Narrows

Young I.

Beardslee Islands

HIGH PEAKS AND GLACIERS

Berg Bay

Secret Bay

Bartlett Cove (Park Hqrs.)

Lester I.

Strawberry I.

Excursion Inlet

Ripple Cove

Icy Point

Palma Bay

Boussole Bay

West Arm

Brady Glacier

Gustavus

Pt. Carolus

Pt. Gustavus

Icy Passage

Pleasant I.

Porpoise I.

Astrolabe Bay

Dixon Hbr

Taylor Bay

Dundas Bay

Pt. Dundas

North Inian Pass

Icy Strait

Torch Bay

Graves Hbr

Murphy Cove

Mosquito Cove

Cape Spencer

Cross Sound

Fern Hbr

Inian Cove

Earl Cove

Lemesurier I.

Pt. Adolphus

Pinta Cove

Dicks Arm

Iniah Is.

South Inian Pass

(SEE CHAPTER 6)

©2003 Fine Edge Productions • Diagram not for navigation

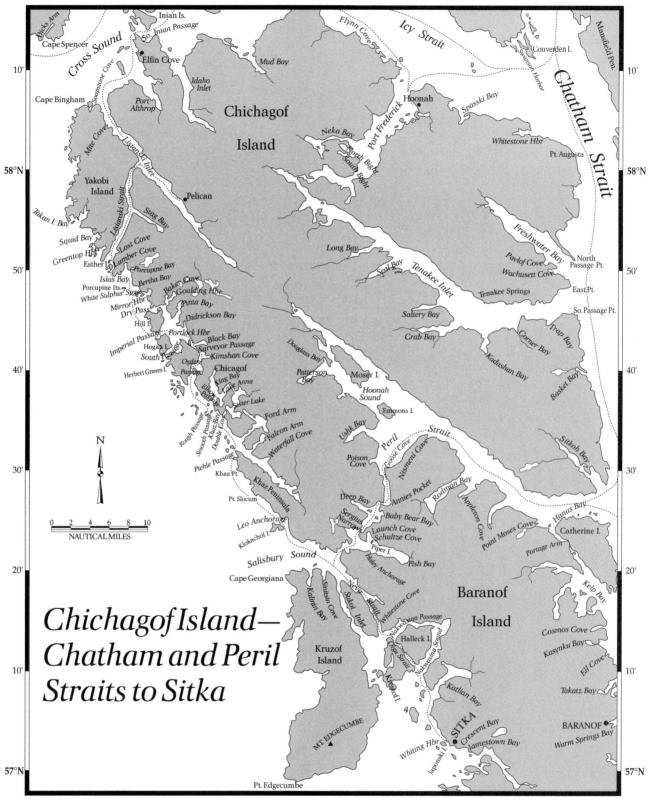

Chichagof Island—Chatham and Peril Straits to Sitka

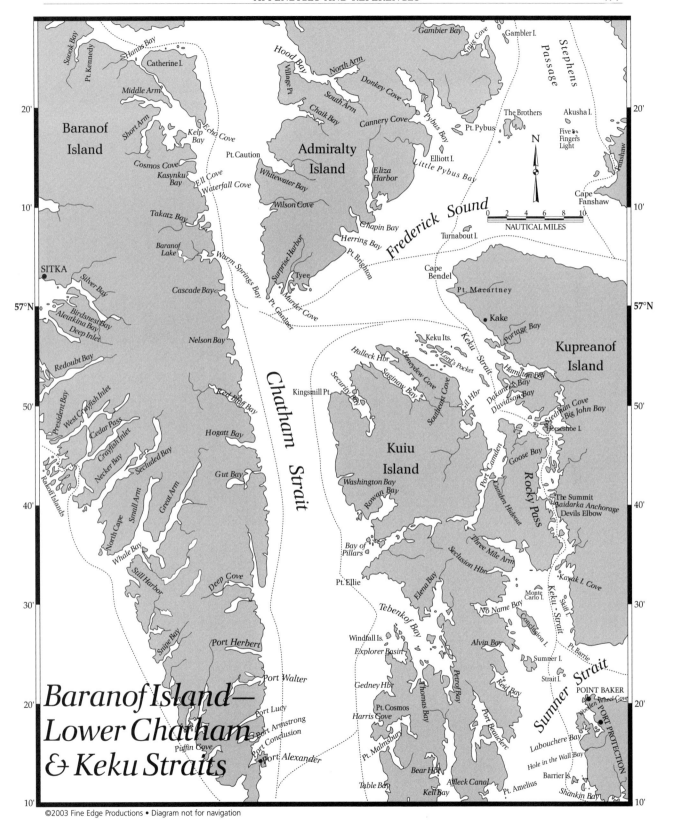

Baranof Island—
Lower Chatham
& Keku Straits

APPENDIX C
Mileage Charts

PACIFIC COAST DISTANCES
SAN DIEGO, CALIFORNIA, TO CAPE FLATTERY, WASHINGTON
(Nautical Miles)

From \ To	San Diego, CA	Newport Beach, CA	Long Beach, CA	Los Angeles, CA	Port Hueneme, CA	Santa Barbara, CA	Port San Luis, CA	Monterey, CA	San Francisco, CA	Oakland, CA	Stockton, CA	Sacramento, CA	Eureka, CA	Crescent City, CA	Coos Bay, OR	Gardiner, OR	Florence, OR	Newport, OR	Depoe Bay, OR	Garibaldi, OR	Astoria, OR	Longview, WA	Vancouver, WA	Portland, OR	South Bend, WA	Aberdeen, WA
SAN DIEGO, CA 32°43.0'N, 117°10.5'W																										
Newport Beach, CA 33°37.1'N, 117°55.5'W	78																									
Long Beach, CA 33°46.2'N, 118°13.3'W	94	25																								
Los Angeles, CA 33°45.0'N, 118°16.2'W	95	27	3																							
Port Hueneme, CA 34°09.0'N, 119°12.4'W	147	81	66	62																						
Santa Barbara, CA 34°24.5'N, 119°41.1'W	174	108	94	90	29																					
Port San Luis, CA 35°10.4'N, 120°44.8'W	259	193	179	175	116	91																				
Monterey, CA 36°36.5'N, 121°53.0'W	370	304	290	286	228	203	121																			
San Francisco, CA 37°48.5'N, 122°24.0'W	455	389	374	371	312	287	205	96																		
Oakland, CA 37°48.2'N, 122°19.5'W	458	392	377	374	315	290	208	100	3																	
Stockton, CA 37°57.7'N, 121°18.8'W	526	460	445	442	383	358	276	167	75	78																
Sacramento, CA 38°33.8'N, 121°33.0'W	530	464	449	446	387	362	280	171	79	82	75															
Eureka, CA 40°47.8'N, 124°11.2'W	653	587	572	569	510	485	403	294	232	235	303	307														
Crescent City, CA 41°44.5'N, 124°11.6'W	704	638	624	620	561	537	455	346	283	287	354	358	64													
Coos Bay, OR 43°22.4'N, 124°12.5'W	817	751	736	733	674	649	567	459	396	399	467	471	180	125												
Gardiner, OR 43°43.5'N, 124°06.8'W	832	766	751	748	689	664	582	474	411	414	482	486	195	140	42											
Florence, OR 43°58.0'N, 124°06.3'W	848	782	768	764	706	681	599	490	427	430	498	502	212	156	59	36										
Newport, OR 44°37.8'N, 124°03.1'W	881	815	800	797	737	713	631	522	459	463	531	534	244	188	92	69	43									
Depoe Bay, OR 44°48.6'N, 124°03.6'W	891	825	810	807	748	723	641	532	469	473	541	544	254	199	101	78	54	16								
Garibaldi, OR 45°33.3'N, 123°55.1'W	937	871	857	853	794	770	687	579	516	520	588	591	301	245	150	127	102	63	50							
Astoria, OR 46°11.7'N, 123°50.0'W	989	922	908	904	845	821	739	630	567	570	639	642	352	296	201	178	153	115	101	58						
Longview, WA 46°06.3'N, 122°57.7'W	1034	967	953	949	890	866	783	675	612	615	684	687	397	341	246	223	198	160	146	103	45					
Vancouver, WA 45°37.6'N, 122°41.1'W	1070	1003	988	985	925	901	819	710	647	651	719	722	432	377	281	258	234	196	182	138	80	34				
Portland, OR 45°33.0'N, 122°41.7'W	1074	1007	992	989	930	905	823	714	652	655	723	727	436	381	285	262	238	200	186	142	85	39	13			
South Bend, WA 46°40.1'N, 123°47.5'W	1019	953	939	935	876	852	769	661	598	601	670	673	383	327	232	209	184	146	133	90	63	108	143	147		
Aberdeen, WA 46°58.4'N, 123°48.5'W	1031	965	951	947	888	864	781	673	610	613	682	685	395	339	244	221	196	158	144	102	75	119	155	159	53	
CAPE FLATTERY, WA 48°26.0'N, 124°47.0'W	1104	1038	1024	1020	961	937	854	746	683	686	755	758	468	411	321	298	273	235	222	179	153	198	234	238	131	117

APPENDIX C
Mileage Charts

SAN FRANCISCO BAY AREA DISTANCES
(Nautical Miles)

	San Francisco Bay							San Pablo Bay			Suisun Bay			San Joaquin R.		Sacramento River				
	San Francisco	Hunters Point	Redwood City	Oakland	Richmond	Sausalito	San Rafael	Petaluma	Vallejo	Napa	Benicia	Pittsburg	Antioch	Stockton	Hills Ferry	Rio Vista	Sacramento	Knights Landing	Colusa	Chico Landing
Chico Landing	197	203	219	200	194	196	192	204	178	193	171	159	163	174	246	146	119	89	42	-
Colusa	155	161	177	158	152	154	150	162	136	151	129	117	121	132	204	104	77	47	-	
Knights Landing	107	113	129	110	104	106	102	114	88	103	81	69	73	84	156	56	29	-		
Sacramento	78	84	100	81	75	77	73	85	59	74	52	40	44	75	127	27	-			
Rio Vista	52	58	73	55	49	51	47	58	33	48	26	14	17	48	100	-				
Hills Ferry	147	153	168	149	143	145	141	153	127	142	120	107	103	74	-					
Stockton	75	81	96	78	71	73	69	81	55	70	48	35	31	-						
Antioch	44	50	65	47	40	42	38	50	24	39	17	3	-							
Pittsburg	40	46	62	43	37	39	35	46	21	36	14	-								
Benicia	27	33	49	30	24	25	21	33	8	22	-									
Napa	37	43	58	40	34	36	32	43	15	-										
Vallejo	23	29	44	26	19	21	17	28	-											
Petaluma	33	39	54	36	29	31	27	-												
San Rafael	13	19	35	16	9	11	-													
Sausalito	5	11	27	8	7	-														
Richmond	11	17	32	14	-															
Oakland	3	7	22	-																
Redwood City	22	16	-																	
Hunters Point	6	-																		
San Francisco	-																			

APPENDIX C
Mileage Charts

DISTANCES ON COLUMBIA RIVER SYSTEM
(Nautical and Statute Miles)

Nautical miles on top (upright text)
Statute miles on the bottom (shaded, slant text)

River	From \ To	Johnson Bar Landing, ID	Lewiston, ID	Central Ferry, WA	Ice Harbor Dam, WA	Harrisburg, OR	Corvallis, OR	Albany, OR	Salem, OR	Oregon City, OR	Portland, OR	Richland, WA	Pasco, WA	Port of Walla Walla, WA	McNary Lock & Dam	Umatilla, OR	Arlington, OR	John Day Lock & Dam	The Dalles Lock & Dam	Hood River (town), OR	Bonneville Lock & Dam	Vancouver, WA	St. Helens, OR	Longview, WA	Astoria, OR	Warrenton, OR	Ilwaco, WA	Columbia River Mouth
Columbia River	Columbia River Mouth 46°14.8'N, 124°05.5'W	483	404	354	291	230	203	192	162	110	97	293	285	276	254	251	210	188	166	148	126	92	75	58	12	11	6	–
	Ilwaco, WA	484	404	355	292	230	203	193	163	111	98	294	286	276	254	252	211	189	167	149	127	93	76	59	13	12	–	7
	Warrenton, OR	475	396	346	283	222	195	184	154	103	89	285	277	268	246	244	202	180	159	140	118	84	67	50	4	–	14	13
	Astoria, OR	470	391	342	278	217	190	180	149	98	85	281	273	263	241	239	198	175	154	136	114	80	62	45	–	5	15	14
	Longview, WA	425	345	296	233	171	144	134	104	52	39	235	227	217	195	193	152	130	108	90	68	34	17	–	20	52	68	67
	St. Helens, OR	411	332	282	219	158	131	121	90	39	25	222	214	204	182	180	138	117	95	76	55	20	–	23	39	77	87	86
	Vancouver, WA	391	312	262	199	145	118	108	77	26	13	202	193	184	162	160	118	96	75	56	35	–	20	39	92	97	107	106
	Bonneville Lock & Dam	356	277	228	164	180	153	142	112	61	47	167	159	149	127	125	84	62	40	22	–	40	63	78	131	136	146	145
	Hood River (town), OR	335	256	206	143	201	174	164	134	82	69	145	137	128	106	103	62	40	18	–	25	64	87	104	157	161	171	170
	The Dalles Lock & Dam	316	237	188	124	220	193	183	152	101	87	127	119	109	87	85	44	22	–	21	46	86	109	124	177	183	192	191
	John Day Lock & Dam	294	215	166	102	242	215	204	174	123	109	105	97	87	65	63	22	–	25	46	71	110	135	150	203	207	217	216
	Arlington, OR	273	194	144	81	263	236	226	195	144	130	83	75	66	44	42	–	25	51	71	97	136	159	175	228	232	243	242
	Umatilla, OR	231	152	103	39	305	278	268	237	186	172	42	34	24	2	–	48	72	98	119	144	184	207	222	275	281	290	289
	McNary Lock & Dam	229	150	101	37	307	280	270	239	188	174	40	32	22	–	2	51	75	100	122	146	186	209	224	277	283	292	292
	Port of Walla Walla, WA	207	128	79	15	329	302	292	261	210	196	18	10	–	25	28	76	100	125	147	171	212	235	250	303	308	318	318
	Pasco, WA	204	125	75	12	339	312	301	271	220	206	8	–	12	37	39	86	112	137	158	183	222	246	261	314	319	329	328
Willamette River	Richland, WA	212	133	83	20	347	320	309	279	228	214	–	9	21	46	48	96	121	146	167	192	232	255	270	323	328	338	337
	Portland, OR	403	324	275	211	133	106	96	65	14	–	246	237	226	200	198	150	125	100	79	54	15	29	45	98	102	113	112
	Oregon City, OR	417	338	288	225	119	92	82	51	–	16	262	253	242	216	214	166	142	116	94	70	30	45	60	113	119	128	127
	Salem, OR	468	389	340	276	68	41	31	–	59	75	321	312	300	275	273	224	200	175	154	129	89	104	120	171	177	188	186
	Albany, OR	499	420	370	307	37	10	–	36	94	110	356	346	336	311	308	260	235	211	189	163	124	139	154	207	212	222	221
	Corvallis, OR	509	430	380	317	27	–	12	47	106	122	368	359	348	322	320	272	247	222	200	176	136	151	166	219	224	234	234
	Harrisburg, OR	536	457	407	344	–	31	43	78	137	153	399	390	379	353	351	303	278	253	231	207	167	182	197	250	255	265	265
Snake River	Ice Harbor Dam, WA	192	113	63	–	396	365	353	318	259	243	23	14	17	43	45	93	117	143	165	189	229	252	268	320	326	336	335
	Central Ferry, WA	129	50	–	72	468	437	426	391	331	316	96	86	91	116	119	166	191	216	237	262	302	325	341	394	398	409	407
	Lewiston, ID	79	–	58	130	526	495	483	448	389	373	153	144	147	173	175	223	247	273	295	319	359	382	397	450	456	465	465
	Johnson Bar Landing, ID	–	91	148	221	617	586	574	539	480	464	244	235	238	264	266	314	338	364	386	410	450	473	489	541	547	557	556

APPENDIX D
Determination of Wind Speed by Sea Condition

Miles Per Hour	Knots	Descriptive	Sea Conditions	Wind Force (Beaufort)	Probable Wave Height (ft.)
0-1	0-1	Calm	Sea smooth and mirror-like.	0	-
1-3	1-3	Light air	Scale-like ripples without foam crests	1	¼
4-7	4-6	Light breeze	Small, short wavelets; crests have a glassy appearance and do not break.	2	½
8-12	7-10	Gentle breeze	Large wavelets; some crests begin to break; foam has glassy appearance. Occasional white foam crests.	3	2
13-18	11-16	Moderate breeze	Small waves, become longer; fairly frequent white foam crests.	4	4
19-24	17-21	Fresh breeze	Moderate waves, taking a more pronounced long form; many white foam crests; there may be some spray.	5	6
25-31	22-27	Strong breeze	Large waves begin to form; white foam crests are more extensive everywhere; there may be some spray.	6	10
32-38	28-33	Near gale	Sea heaps up and white foam from breaking waves begin to be blown in streaks along the direction of the wind; spindrift begins.	7	14
39-46	34-40	Gale	Moderately high waves of greater length; edges of crests break into spindrift; foam is blown in well-marked streaks along the direction of the wind.	8	18
47-54	41-47	Strong gale	High waves; dense streaks of foam along the direction of the wind; crests of waves begin to topple, tumble and roll over; spray may reduce visibility.	9	23
55-63	48-55	Storm	Very high waves with long overhanging crests. The resulting foam in great patches is blown in dense white streaks along the direction of the wind. On the whole, the surface of the sea is white in appearance. The tumbling of the sea becomes heavy and shock-like. Visibility is reduced.	10	29
64-72	56-63	Violent storm	Exceptionally high waves that may obscure small and medium-sized ships. The sea is completely covered with long white patches of foam lying along the direction of the wind. Everywhere the edges of the wave crests are blown into froth. Visibility is reduced.	11	37
73+	64+	Hurricane	The air is filled with foam and spray. Sea completely white with driving spray; visibility is very much reduced.	12	45

ATMOSPHERIC PRESSURE CONVERSION TABLE

Inches	Millibars	Inches	Millibars	Inches	Millibars
28.44	963	29.32	993	30.21	1023
28.53	966	29.41	996	30.30	1026
28.62	969	29.50	999	30.39	1029
28.70	972	29.59	1002	30.48	1032
28.79	975	29.68	1005	30.56	1035
28.88	978	29.77	1008	30.65	1038
28.97	981	29.86	1011	30.74	1041
29.06	984	29.94	1014	30.83	1044
29.15	987	30.03	1017	30.92	1047
29.24	990	30.12	1020	31.01	1050

APPENDIX E
Procedures Used in Documenting Local Knowledge

1. Coves, bays or bights that seem to offer full or limited protection from different weather situations are identified and visited by the authors.
2. Routes are sketched and photographed.
3. Perusal of a possible anchor site is made with a dual-frequency recording echo sounder; major underwater obstacles are identified; depth and flatness of the bottom over the expected swinging area are checked; depths are then recorded on the sketches.
4. A sample test of the bottom is made by using a small "lunch hook" attached to light line and six feet of chain for maximum responsiveness and feel of the bottom.
5. The response of the anchor to the bottom is noted (i.e. soft or hard mud, sand, gravel, rocky, etc.; digging power, bounce, fouling with kelp, pull-out, etc.).
6. Additional line is let out to fully set the anchor.
7. A pull-down, with the engine in reverse, is made against the anchor to test holding power of the bottom.
8. Upon retrieving the anchor, we inspect the residue on its flukes to verify bottom material, as well as the type of grass, kelp, etc.
9. Discussions are held with local residents and fishermen about anchorages, names, etc., and their comments are noted on the sketches. In some cases rough drafts of the manuscript are sent to experts for review.
10. The information gathered from our tests, or that submitted by local experts, is consolidated and edited and becomes the "Local Knowledge" we have presented in our diagrams and text.

APPENDIX F
New Homeland Security Procedures

New security regulations have been imposed by the U.S. government to provide a protective zone around certain ships, facilities and ports. A security zone has been established around all U.S. Navy vessels whether they are docked or underway: boats must stay at least 100 yards away and reduce speed to a minimum within 500 yards. In areas of narrow passage, skippers need to contact the naval vessel on Channel 16 with a request to pass within 100 yards.

In addition, the Coast Guard Captain of the Port is authorized to create local security zones as needed. For updated information on security zones boaters are encouraged to consult the Coast Guard's web site at: www.uscg.mil/hq/gm/gifs/msoMap_files/slide0001.htm or the local Coast Guard marine safety officer listed for each area on the web site. The penalties and fines for an infraction can be severe. Gone are the days of passing closely by military vessels to wave at the crew.

APPENDIX G
Border Crossing Issues

CANPASS
The popular CANPASS program allows previously approved U.S. boats meeting certain criteria to clear customs and immigration into Canada by calling 1.888.CANPASS up to 4 hours before arrival. This speedy system was suspended for seven months after the 9/11 attacks. As we go to press, the CANPASS program has been re-instated. However, boaters must report to a designated Customs site and may be subject to random boarding. Current details can be obtained by calling 604.535.9346 or checking the web at www.ccra.adrc.gc.ca.

Certification Requirements for Canada
On September 15, 2002, mandatory certification requirements came into effect for operators of pleasure craft less than 4 meters in length. These requirements will be initiated over a period of several years for all vessels. For more information call 1.800.267. 6687 or see the website: www. pacific.ccggcc.gc.ca/obs.

Bibliography & References

Bailey, Jo & Carl Nyberg, *Gunkholing in South Puget Sound.* Seattle: San Juan Enterprises, Inc., 1997.

California Boater's Guide to the Harbors & Marinas of the San Francisco Bay, Delta, Outer Coast & Hawaii (updated biannually and published by Bald Eagle Enterprises).

Douthewaite, Jeff, *Flights of the Flamingo—Seattle to Santa Barbara and Return.* Seattle: Jeff Douthewaite, 2000.

Fagan, Brian. *Cruising Guide to Central and Southern California.* Camden, Maine: International Marine, 2002.

Fagan, Brian. *Boating Guide—San Francisco Bay.* Santa Barbara: Caractacus Corp, 1998.

Gamble, Fred et al. *Mariner's Guide to Santa Anas.* Santa Barbara: Channel Crossings Press, 1999. *[Ed. Note:* chart of Santa Ana Gale Representative Wind Pattern available from Channel Crossings; also other annotated charts for the Southern California coast.]

Gates, Margy, Don & Réanne Douglass, Ed., *Exploring California's Channel Islands—an Artist's View.* Bishop, CA: Fine Edge Productions, 1986

Heizer, Robert F. & Albert B. Elsasser, Eds. *Original Accounts of the Lone Woman of San Nicolas Island.* Ramona, California: Ballena Press, 1976 (reprinted from University of California Archaeological Survey, No. 55, Berkeley).

Hinz, Earl R. *Complete Book of Anchoring and Mooring.* Centreville, Maryland: Cornell Maritime Press, 1994.

Hoar, David & Noreen Rudd. *Cooks Afloat!* Madeira Park, B.C.: Harbour Publishing, 2001.

Katz, David. *The Burgee—Premier Marina Guidebook.* Kingston, WA: Pierside Publishing, 2000.

Kozloff, Eugene N. *Plants and Animals of the Pacific Northwest.* Seattle: University of Washington Press, 1976.

W. Kaye Lamb, Ed. *The Voyage of George Vancouver, 1791–1795.* 4 vols. London: Hakluyt Society, 1984.

Mehaffy, Carolyn & Bob. *Cruising Guide to San Francisco Bay.* Arcata, California: Paradise Cay Publications, 1999.

Northwest Boat Travel. Anacortes, WA: Anderson Publishing Co., published annually.

Oregon State Marine Board, *Oregon Marina Guide,* Salem, Oregon: Oregon State Marine Board, 2001.

Oregon State Marine Board, *Boating in Oregon Coastal Waters,* Salem, Oregon: Oregon State Marine Board, 2001.

Renner, Jeff. *Northwest Marine Weather.* Seattle: The Mountaineers, 1993.

Scherer, Migael. *Cruising Guide to Puget Sound.* Camden, Maine: International Marine, 1995.

Southern California Boater's Guide. Santa Monica: Santa Monica Bay Restoration Project, 1999.

Steber, Rick & Jerry Gildlemeister. *Where Rolls the Oregon.* Union, Oregon: Bear Wallow Publishing, 1985.

United States Coast Pilot 7, Pacific Coast: California, Oregon, Washington, and Hawaii. Washington, D.C.: NOAA, 33rd Ed., 2001.

Vassilopoulos, Peter. *Docks and Destinations.* Vancouver: Seagraphic Publications, 2000.

Waggoner Cruising Guide, Ed. Robert Hale. Seattle: Waverly Press, published annually.

Western Explorer, Vol. V, nos. 2 & 3. *Cabrillo's Log.* San Diego: Cabrillo Historical Assn, 1968.

Wood, Charles & Margo. *Charlie's Charts of the U.S. Pacific Coast.* Surrey, B.C.: Charlie's Charts, 2001.

About the Authors & Contributors

Authors Don Douglass and Réanne Hemingway-Douglass have sailed from 60°N to 56°S latitude—Alaska to Cape Horn—logging more than 160,000 miles of offshore cruising over the past 30 years. They spend their summers cruising on their trawler, *Baidarka*, gathering data for new titles and updating their acclaimed *Exploring* series of nautical guidebooks. Together they have documented 5,000 anchor sites between San Diego and the Gulf of Alaska.

Don began exploring Northwest waters in 1949 as a youth. He has sailed the Inside Passage on everything from a 26-foot pleasure craft and commercial fishing boat to a Coast Guard icebreaker. Don holds a BSEE degree from California State University, Pomona, and a Masters in Business

Economics from Claremont Graduate University. He and Réanne have co-authored: *Exploring Vancouver Island's West Coast; Exploring Southeast Alaska; Exploring the South Coast of British Columbia; Exploring the North Coast of British Columbia;* and *Exploring the San Juan and Gulf Islands*. Don holds honorary membership in the International Association of Cape Horners. He has written several mountain biking guidebooks and, as a father of the sport, was elected to the Mountain Biking Hall of Fame.

Réanne holds a BA degree in French from Pomona College. She attended Claremont Graduate University and the University of Grenoble, France. Sailor, writer, cyclist and language teacher, Réanne's articles have appeared in numerous outdoor magazines. Her classic, *Cape Horn: One Man's Dream, One Woman's Nightmare* has been published in French and Italian. Réanne led the first women's bicycling team to cross Tierra del Fuego at the tip of South America. Réanne is the chief editor of Fine Edge.com.

Kevin Monahan

Kevin Monahan is a Canadian Coast Guard officer with over 20 years experience navigating the British Columbia coast as a small-vessel captain. Born in London, England in 1951, Monahan emigrated to Canada in 1957 with his family, later attending the University of B.C. Kevin spent over 12 years working in almost every commercial fishery on the B.C. Coast. In the 1980s he and his wife, Nancy, owned and operated one of the most successful prawn freezer boats in B.C. He received his nautical certification from Transport Canada before joining the Department of Fisheries and Oceans (now the Coast Guard). As a Patrol Vessel captain, he often testified as an expert witness in navigation, especially in the navigational uses of GPS. Kevin is the principal author of *GPS Instant Navigation* and *Proven Cruising Routes, Vol I, Seattle to Kechikan*. He and Nancy, live in Sidney, B.C.

Réanne enjoying a sunny day on Baidarka

Bob and Carol Mehaffy

Freelance writers Carolyn and Bob Mehaffy lived and sailed in the San Francisco Bay Area for over 25 years. Since their retirement they have been full-time sailors on their Hardin 45 ketch, *Carricklee,* devoting over three years to cruising the waters of Mexico and Hawaii. They are the authors of three books: *Destination Mexico; Cruising Guide to San Francisco Bay;* and *Cruising Guide to the Hawaiian Islands.* Their boating articles have appeared in *Cruising World, Northwest Yachting, Ocean Navigator, Sail, Sailing,* and *Sea.*

Ann Kinner

Ann Kinner is a USCG licensed charter and delivery captain and certified Tow Vessel operator. She has been a Master Instructor for Coast Guard Auxiliary Search and Rescue training and licensing programs. When she is not at sea, she serves as assistant manager for Seabreeze Limited, a nautical book and chart store in San Diego. Ann lives aboard her Newport Trawler, *Ocean's Child.*

Michelle and Jerry Gaylord

Michelle and Jerry Gaylord took early retirement, sold their house, bought a 53' DeFever Trawler on the East Coast and brought her through the Panama Canal to their home port, Channel Islands, California in 59 days. Five years ago they said goodbye to their families, and headed to the Pacific Northwest, British Columbia and Alaska where they lived and cruised for four years. Although they feel they could spend a lifetime in the Northwest and never run out of new places to explore, they have decided to venture south into Mexican waters. Together, the Gaylords have a combined boating experience of 70 years.

Exploring the Marquesas Islands
Joe Russell
Russell, who has lived and sailed in the Marquesas, documents the first cruising guide to this beautiful, little-known place. Includes history, language guide, chart diagrams, mileages and heading tables and archaeology. "A must reference for those wanting to thoroughly enjoy their first landfall on the famous Coconut Milk Run."—Earl Hinz, author, *Landfalls of Paradise—Cruising Guide to the Pacific Islands*

Pacific Coast Route Planning Maps
South Portion—San Diego to Fort Bragg

North Portion—Cape Mendocino to Seattle/Victoria

The perfect complement for the *Exploring the Pacific Coast—San Diego to Seattle* book. In beautiful color and full topographic detail, each 24' x 60" map includes the GPS waypoints for the three popular routes for cruising the coast, the Bluewater Route, the Express Route and the Inshore Route. Also included are over 500 places to tie up or anchor. Inset maps are included to show harbor approaches with local waypoints for the entrances to major harbors and coves. Plan your own custom itinerary and prepare for the trip of a lifetime. Both maps are available folded, rolled, or laminated rolled.

Inside Passage Maps *North and South portions*
The Inside Passage to British Columbia and Alaska is one of the most sheltered and scenic waterways in the world. Now, for the first time, our maps include an index to all harbors and coves in this superb wilderness allowing you to customize your own routes.

GPS Instant Navigation
A Practical Guide from Basics to Advanced Techniques
Kevin Monahan and Don Douglass
In this clear, well-illustrated manual, mariners will find simple solutions to navigational challenges. Includes 150 detailed diagrams, which illustrate the many ways you can use GPS to solve classic piloting and navigation problems.

Cape Horn
One Man's Dream, One Woman's Nightmare—2nd Ed.
Réanne Hemingway-Douglass
His dream: To round Cape Horn and circumnavigate the Southern Hemisphere. Her nightmare: Coping with a driven captain and the frightening seas of the Great Southern Ocean. "This is the sea story to read if you read only one."—McGraw Hill, *International Marine Catalog* "Easily the hairy-chested adventure yarn of the decade, if not the half-century."—Peter H. Spectre, *Wooden Boat*

Trekka Round the World
John Guzzwell
Long out-of-print, this international classic is the story of Guzzwell's circumnavigation on his 20-foot yawl, *Trekka*. Includes previously unpublished photos and a foreword by America's renowned bluewater sailor-author Hal Roth.

Sea Stories of the Inside Passage
Iain Lawrence
A collection of first-person experiences about cruising the North Coast; entertaining and insightful writing by the author of *Far-Away Places*.

Enjoy these other publications from FineEdge.com

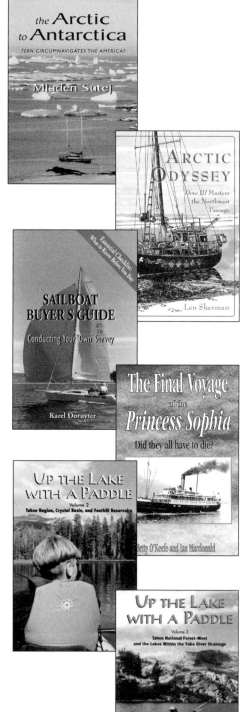

The Arctic to Antarctica *Cigra Circumnavigates the Americas*
Mladen Sutej
The dramatic account of the first circumnavigation of the North and South American continents, continuing around Cape Horn via Easter Island and then to Antarctica before returning to Europe. Told through the words of a notable circumnavigator with beautiful photographs throughout.

Arctic Odyssey
Dove III *Masters the Northwest Passage*
Len Sherman
Len Sherman was the third crew member on the epic Northwest Passage voyage of the *Dove III*, one of the first west-to-east single-year passages on record.

Sailboat Buyer's Guide *Conducting Your Own Survey*
Karel Doruyter
This book guides you and provides you with an essential checklist of what to know and look for *before* you buy a sailboat!
"Armed with this book a buyer can confidently inspect a new or used boat."—John Guzzwell, custom boat builder

Destination Cortez Island
A sailor's life along the BC Coast
June Cameron
A nostalgic memoir of the lives of coastal pioneers—the old timers and their boats, that were essential in the days when the ocean was the only highway.

The Final Voyage of the *Princess Sophia*
Did they all have to die?
Betty O'Keefe and Ian Macdonald
This story explores the heroic efforts of those who answered the SOS at first to save, then later to recover, the bodies of those lost.

Up the Lake with a Paddle
Volume 1: Sierra Foothills and Sacramento Region
Volume 2: Lake Tahoe & Sierra Lakes
Volume 3: Tahoe National Forest–West, Lakes within the Yuba River Drainage
William Van der Ven
The essential paddling books on all the great places to paddle in the foothills and mountains of California's Sierra Nevada.

For all nautical titles, visit our website: www.fineedge.com

Index

Please Note: Names in italics refer to sidebars

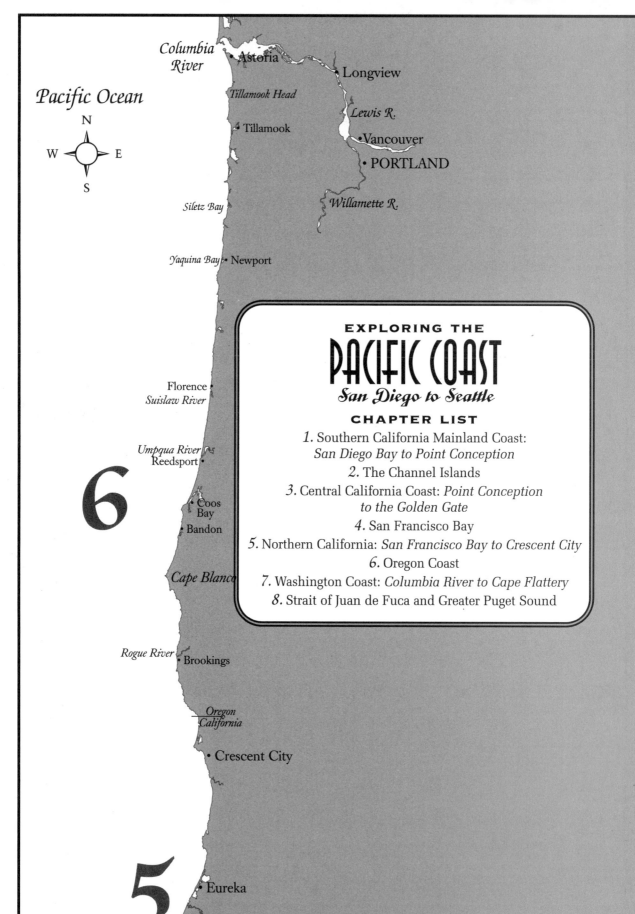

Columbia River

Pacific Ocean

N
W   E
S

Astoria

Longview

Tillamook Head

Lewis R.

Tillamook

Vancouver

PORTLAND

Siletz Bay

Willamette R.

Yaquina Bay • Newport

EXPLORING THE

PACIFIC COAST

San Diego to Seattle

CHAPTER LIST

1. Southern California Mainland Coast:
San Diego Bay to Point Conception

2. The Channel Islands

3. Central California Coast: *Point Conception
to the Golden Gate*

4. San Francisco Bay

5. Northern California: *San Francisco Bay to Crescent City*

6. Oregon Coast

7. Washington Coast: *Columbia River to Cape Flattery*

8. Strait of Juan de Fuca and Greater Puget Sound

Florence
Suislaw River

Umpqua River
Reedsport

6

Coos
Bay

Bandon

Cape Blanco

Rogue River • Brookings

Oregon
California

• Crescent City

5

• Eureka

Cape Mendocino